organizational behavior
essentials for improving performance and commitment

Jason A. Colquitt
University of Florida

Jeffery A. LePine
University of Florida

Michael J. Wesson
Texas A&M University

McGraw-Hill Irwin

Boston   Burr Ridge, IL   Dubuque, IA   New York   San Francisco   St. Louis
Bangkok   Bogotá   Caracas   Kuala Lumpur   Lisbon   London   Madrid   Mexico City
Milan   Montreal   New Delhi   Santiago   Seoul   Singapore   Sydney   Taipei   Toronto

ORGANIZATIONAL BEHAVIOR: ESSENTIALS FOR IMPROVING
PERFORMANCE AND COMMITMENT

Published by McGraw-Hill/Irwin, a business unit of The McGraw-Hill Companies, Inc., 1221
Avenue of the Americas, New York, NY, 10020.

Some ancillaries, including electronic and print components, may not be available to customers
outside the United States.

This book is printed on acid-free paper.

1 2 3 4 5 6 7 8 9 0 VNH/VNH 0 9

ISBN 978-0-07-811255-3
MHID 0-07-811255-9

Vice president and editor-in-chief: *Brent Gordon*
Publisher: *Paul Ducham*
Executive editor: *John Weimeister*
Developmental editor: *Donielle Xu*
Editorial assistant: *Heather Darr*
Marketing manager: *Natalie Zook*
Marketing coordinator: *Michael Gedatus*
Senior project manager: *Bruce Gin*
Lead production supervisor: *Michael R. McCormick*
Lead designer: *Matthew Baldwin*
Senior photo research coordinator: *Jeremy Cheshareck*
Photo researcher: *Keri Johnson*
Senior media project manager: *Susan Lombardi*
Cover design: *Laurie Entringer*
Cover image: © Getty Images
Typeface: *10/12 Minon Pro Regular*
Compositor: *Laserwords Private Limited*
Printer: *R. R. Donnelley*

Library of Congress Cataloging-in-Publication Data

Colquitt, Jason.
    Organizational behavior : essentials for improving performance and commitment / Jason A.
Colquitt, Jeffery A. LePine, Michael J. Wesson.
        p. cm.
    Includes index.
    ISBN-13: 978-0-07-811255-3 (alk. paper)
    ISBN-10: 0-07-811255-9 (alk. paper)
    1. Organizational behavior. 2. Organizational culture. 3. Personnel management. 4. Job
satisfaction. I. LePine, Jeffery A. II. Wesson, Michael J. III. Title.
HD58.7.C6254 2010
658.3—dc22

                                                                                    2008050331

To Catherine, Cameron, Riley, and Connor, and also to Mom, Dad, Alan, and Shawn. The most wonderful family I could imagine, two times over.

-J.A.C.

To my parents who made me, and to Marcie, Izzy, and Eli, who made my life complete.

-J.A.L.

To Liesl and Dylan: Their support in all I do is incomparable. They are my life and I love them both. To my parents: They provide a foundation that never wavers.

-M.J.W.

Jason A. Colquitt

Is a professor in the Management Department at the University of Florida's Warrington College of Business. He received his Ph.D. from Michigan State University's Eli Broad Graduate School of Management and earned his B.S. in Psychology from Indiana University. He teaches organizational behavior and human resource management at the undergraduate, master's, and executive levels and also teaches research methods at the doctoral level. He was recognized as one of the Warrington College's Teachers of the Year due to his high marks in the classroom.

Jason's research interests include organizational justice, trust, team effectiveness, and personality influences on task and learning performance. He has published more than 20 articles on these and other topics in *Academy of Management Journal, Academy of Management Review, Journal of Applied Psychology, Organizational Behavior and Human Decision Processes,* and *Personnel Psychology.* He is currently serving as an Associate Editor for *Academy of Management Journal* and has served (or is serving) on a number of editorial boards, including *Academy of Management Journal, Journal of Applied Psychology, Organizational Behavior and Human Decision Processes, Personnel Psychology, Journal of Management,* and *International Journal of Conflict Management.* He is a recipient of the Society for Industrial and Organizational Psychology's Distinguished Early Career Contributions Award and the Cummings Scholar Award for early to mid-career achievement, sponsored by the Organizational Behavior division of the Academy of Management. He also was elected to be a representative-at-large for the Organizational Behavior division.

Jason enjoys spending time with his wife, Catherine, and three sons, Cameron, Riley, and Connor. His hobbies include playing basketball, playing the trumpet, watching movies, and rooting on (in no particular order) the Pacers, Colts, Cubs, Hoosiers, Spartans, and Gators.

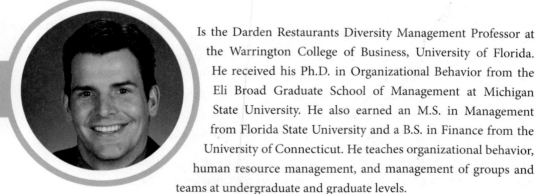

Jeffery A. LePine

Is the Darden Restaurants Diversity Management Professor at the Warrington College of Business, University of Florida. He received his Ph.D. in Organizational Behavior from the Eli Broad Graduate School of Management at Michigan State University. He also earned an M.S. in Management from Florida State University and a B.S. in Finance from the University of Connecticut. He teaches organizational behavior, human resource management, and management of groups and teams at undergraduate and graduate levels.

Jeff's research interests include team functioning and effectiveness, individual and team adaptation, citizenship behavior, voice, and occupational stress. He has published more than 20 articles on these and other topics in *Academy of Management Journal, Academy of Management Review, Journal of Applied Psychology, Organizational Behavior and Human*

Decision Processes, and *Personnel Psychology*. He is currently serving as an associate editor for *Academy of Management Review* and is currently serving or has served on the editorial boards of *Academy of Management Journal*, *Journal of Applied Psychology*, *Organizational Behavior and Human Decision Processes*, *Personnel Psychology*, *Journal of Management*, *Journal of Organizational Behavior*, and *Journal of Occupational and Organizational Psychology*. He is a recipient of the Society for Industrial and Organizational Psychology's Distinguished Early Career Contributions Award and the Cummings Scholar Award for early to mid-career achievement, sponsored by the Organizational Behavior division of the Academy of Management. He also was elected to the Executive Committee of the Human Resource Division of the Academy of Management. Prior to earning his Ph.D., Jeff was an officer in the U.S. Air Force.

Jeff spends most of his free time with his wife Marcie, his daughter Izzy, and his son Eli. He also enjoys playing guitar, avoiding sharks, devising ways to keep mole crickets off his lawn, and watching NCAA championship games.

Is an associate professor in the Management Department at Texas A&M University's Mays Business School. He received his Ph.D. from Michigan State University's Eli Broad Graduate School of Management. He also holds an M.S. in human resource management from Texas A&M University and a B.B.A. from Baylor University. He has taught organizational behavior and human resource management–based classes at all levels but currently spends most of his time teaching Mays MBAs, EMBAs, and executive development at Texas A&M. He was awarded Texas A&M's Montague Center for Teaching Excellence Award.

Michael J. Wesson

Michael's research interests include organizational justice, goal-setting, organizational entry (employee recruitment, selection, and socialization), person–organization fit, and compensation and benefits. His articles have been published in journals such as *Journal of Applied Psychology*, *Personnel Psychology*, *Academy of Management Review*, and *Organizational Behavior and Human Decision Processes*. He currently serves on the editorial boards of the *Journal of Applied Psychology* and the *Journal of Organizational Behavior* and is an ad hoc reviewer for many others. He is active in the Academy of Management and the Society for Industrial and Organizational Psychology. Prior to returning to school, Michael worked as a human resources manager for a Fortune 500 firm. He has served as a consultant to the automotive supplier, health care, oil and gas, and technology industries in areas dealing with recruiting, selection, onboarding, compensation, and turnover.

Michael spends most of his time trying to keep up with his wife Liesl and son Dylan. He is a self-admitted food and wine snob, home theater aficionado, and college sports addict (Gig 'em Aggies!).

Organizational Behavior: Essentials for Improving Performance and Commitment

The Complete Package

Online Quizzing • Self-Assessments • iPod Content • Narrated Lectures • Manager's Hot Seat • Company Videos • Online Learning Center • Chapter Review • Application Exercises • Concept Testing • Comprehensive Cases • OB in Sports • OB on Screen • OB for Students • OB Internationally • End-of-Chapter Material • eBooks • Management in the Movies

FEATURES

OB on Screen

This feature uses movie quotes and scenes from recent and classic films to illustrate OB concepts. From *Office Space* to *300*, *Talladega Nights* to *The Queen*, Hollywood continues to offer rich, vivid examples of OB in action.

Organizational Behavior remains a fascinating topic that everyone can relate to because everyone either has worked or is going to work in the future.

● ● instructor OBJECTIVES

IO1 Engage students in the classroom.

IO2 Utilize technology and visual resources effectively.

IO3 Incorporate timely examples from the real world into class lectures.

IO4 Use models in each chapter to tie content together.

OB in Sports

The sports world gives us a wide variety of applications for Organizational Behavior. Flipping through the text, you'll see that these examples include famous and infamous players, young and old, male and female. Each of them ties directly into the learning objectives for the chapter.

"Organizational Behavior might be the most relevant class any student ever takes."

OB Internationally

Changes in technology, communications, and economic forces have made business more global than ever. This feature spotlights the impact of globalization on the organizational behavior concepts described in this book. It describes cross-cultural differences in OB theories, how to apply them in international corporations, and how to use OB to manage cultural diversity in the workplace.

● ● student OBJECTIVES

SO1 Stimulate an intrinsic interest in OB through textbook features.

SO2 Learn from company examples that are familiar and compelling.

SO3 Recognize the importance of OB in the real world.

SO4 Review, apply, and test concepts from the text on the Online Learning Center.

> **"Research on motivation to learn shows that students learn more when they have an intrinsic interest in the topic."**

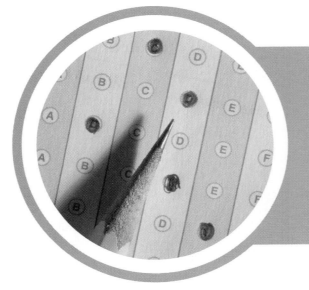

OB for Students

Whether undergraduates, master's, or executives, everyone enrolled in an OB class has one thing in common: They're students. This feature applies OB theories and concepts to student life. It examines questions like "What makes students satisfied with their university?" "What personality traits improve performance in student groups?" and "How does absenteeism impact student learning and performance?"

APPLICATION

OB Video DVD

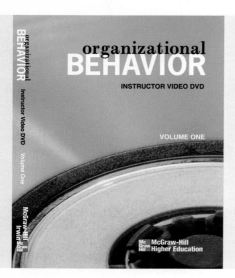

The OB Video DVD contains 43 short clips highlighting small and large companies such as One Smooth Stone and Best Buy. It is organized by topic and covers each of the chapters in the text. Video cases, quizzes, and instructor support materials are available via the Online Learning Center.

Assessments

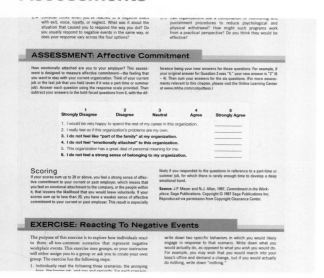

This feature helps students see where they stand on key OB concepts in each chapter. Students gain insights into their personality, their emotional intelligence, their style of leadership, and their ability to cope with stress, which can help them understand their reactions to the working world.

Management in the Movies DVD

(ISBN: 0073317713, 13-digit ISBN: 9780073317717)
Looking for another way to engage your students in the classroom? The Management in the Movies DVD is available exclusively to adopters of McGraw-Hill textbooks and contains a collection of "Big Screen" Hollywood films that students will recognize. Each movie has been clipped to highlight a specific scene (each is less than two and a half minutes) and linked to specific topics. Along with the DVD, McGraw-Hill provides instructor notes with suggestions for using the clip, clip summaries, and discussion questions to accompany each segment! Material for both you and your students can be found on the OLC.

Cases

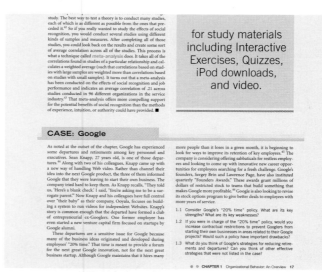

To help bring students full circle, a case appears at the end of every chapter that provides a follow-up to the company highlighted in the Opening Vignette.

Manager's Hot Seat

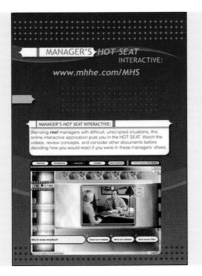

www.mhhe.com/mhs
EXPANDED 6 NEW CLIPS! This interactive, video-based application puts students in the manager's hot seat and builds critical-thinking and decision-making skills. It allows students to apply concepts to real managerial challenges. Students watch as 21 real managers apply their years of experience when confronting unscripted issues such as ethical dilemmas, bullying in the workplace, cyber loafing, globalization, intergenerational work conflict, and office romance.

Exercises

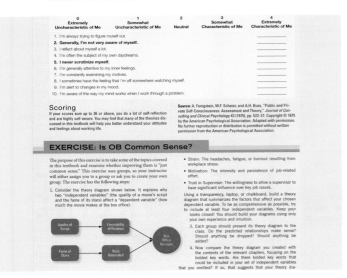

Included at the end of each chapter is a topic-appropriate Exercise. Some of them have been created by the author team over the years, and some are "classics" that are tried and true and that nearly every OB instructor uses in class. These exercises help students apply what they have learned in the chapter.

OB on Screen

Throughout the text, popular movies are used to represent applicable OB concepts in the OB on Screen box. While these videos are not available on the OB Video DVD, full instructor notes are provided in the Instructor's Manual for specific scenes and where they can be located on the film's DVD, either rented or purchased by the instructor.

Asset Gallery

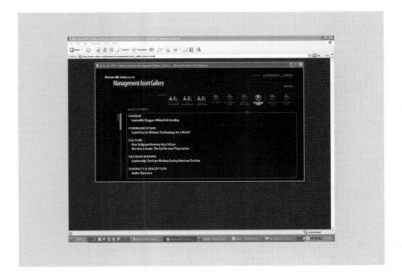

This all-new, one-stop-shop for our wealth of assets makes it quick and easy for instructors to locate specific materials to enhance their courses. The Asset Gallery contains our comprehensive package of management resources (Self-Assessments, Test Your Knowledge exercises, videos, group exercises), along with supporting Power-Point and instructor materials. To help incorporate the assets in the classroom, a text-specific guide is provided specific to this text on the Instructor OLC. Ask your sales rep for more info!

Instructor Resources

PowerPoint Presentations

Based on instructor feedback, the PowerPoint Presentation slides, prepared by Liesl Wesson, Texas A&M University, give instructors the flexibility to tailor their presentations to their class needs. Utilizing figures, tables, and art from the text, these lively slides provide a detailed outline for instructors to use in their classroom lectures.

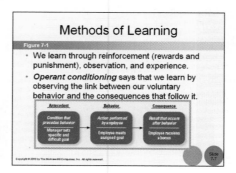

Instructor's Manual

Prepared by Carol Moore of California State–East Bay, this manual was developed to help you organize your classroom presentation. It contains an extensive "chapter roadmap" with an outline of each chapter, Teaching Tips, suggestions on using the assessments and exercises in the text, suggestions about the self-assessments and group exercises found in the Asset Gallery, and ideas and suggestions about where to use the clips from Management in the Movies, the OB Video DVD, the Manager's Hot Seat, and the OB on Screen box feature.

Test Bank and EZTest Online

Our test bank contains a variety of true/false, multiple choice, and essay questions, as well as scenario-based application questions. We've aligned the test bank questions in accordance with Bloom's Taxonomy, AACSB guidelines, the chapter learning objectives, and difficulty level. Test bank files can be delivered through McGraw-Hill's EZTest Online, which enables instructors to create, manage, and edit tests. For more information, visit www.eztestonline.com.

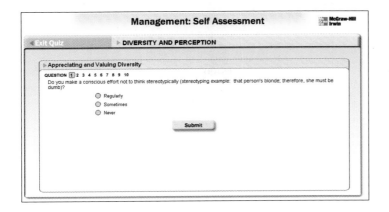

Self-Assessment Gallery

Students who are looking to personally apply the chapter content to their own lives and careers will find these Self-Assessments to be an invaluable tool. Upon completion of every assessment, students will receive detailed, printable feedback on topics such as leadership styles, diversity, and ethics. Every self-assessment is supported with instructor teaching notes and PowerPoint slides to help facilitate an engaging classroom discussion.

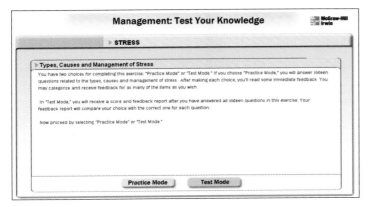

Test Your Knowledge

Similar to the style of our online Self-Assessments, these Test Your Knowledge quizzes help students reinforce their own understanding of key management concepts. They provide a review of topics covered in the text, followed by application-based questions. Students can choose to take these quizzes in Practice Mode, in which they receive detailed feedback immediately after each question, or Test Mode, which provides summary feedback after the entire test has been completed. Every exercise is supported with instructor teaching notes and PowerPoint slides, making this tool another easy way for instructors to create an engaging classroom discussion surrounding the material.

iPod Content

With purchase of McGraw-Hill's premium content, students have access to videos, narrated lecture slides, and quizzes, all ready to be downloaded to an iPod or MP3 player for study on the go!

Management History Timeline

This Web application allows instructors to present, and students to learn, the history of management in an engaging and interactive way. Management history is presented along an intuitive timeline that can be traveled through sequentially or by selected decade. With the click of a mouse, students learn the important dates, see the people who influenced the field, and understand the general management theories that have molded and shaped management as we know it today.

Assurance of Learning Ready

Educational institutions are often focused on the notion of assurance of learning, an important element of many accreditation standards. *Organizational Behavior: Essentials for Improving Performance and Commitment* is designed specifically to support your assurance of learning initiatives with a simple, yet powerful, solution.

Each test bank question for this textbook maps to a specific chapter learning outcome/objective listed in the text. You can use our test bank software, EZTest, to easily query and find learning objectives that directly relate to the learning outcomes for your course. You also can use the reporting features of EZTest to aggregate student results in a similar fashion, making the collection and presentation of assurance of learning data quick and easy.

ORGANIZATIONAL BEHAVIOR: an OVERVIEW

learning OBJECTIVES

After reading this chapter, you should be able to:

1.1 Define "organizational behavior" (OB).
1.2 Describe the two primary outcomes in studies of OB.
1.3 Identify the factors that influence the two primary OB outcomes.
1.4 Understand why firms that are good at OB tend to be more profitable.
1.5 Define "theory" and explain its role in the scientific method.
1.6 Describe what a "correlation" represents, and what "big," "moderate," and "small" sized correlations are.

1. Read learning objectives at the start of each chapter.

ORGANIZATIONAL BEHAVIOR

Before we define exactly what the field of organizational behavior represents, take a moment to ponder the following question: Who was the single *worst* coworker you've ever had? Picture fellow students with whom you've worked on class projects; colleagues from part-time or summer jobs; or peers, subordinates, or supervisors working in your current organization. What did this coworker do that earned him or her "worst coworker" status? Was it some of the behaviors shown in the right column of Table 1-1 (or perhaps all of them)? Now take a moment to consider the single *best* coworker you've ever had. Again, what did this coworker do to earn "best coworker" status—some or most of the behaviors shown in the left column of Table 1-1?

Who would receive the first prize for coworkers with whom you have worked? What made him or her a great coworker?

If you ever found yourself working alongside the two people profiled in the table, two questions probably would be foremost on your mind: "*Why* does the worst coworker act that way?" and "*Why* does the best coworker act that way?" Once you understand

why the two coworkers act so differently, you might be able to figure out ways to interact with the worst coworker more effectively (thereby making your working life a bit more pleasant). If you happen to be a manager, you could formulate plans for how to improve attitudes and behaviors in the unit. Such plans might include how to screen applicants, train and socialize new organizational members, manage evaluations and rewards for performance, and deal with conflicts that arise between employees. Without understanding why employees act the way they do, it's very difficult to find a way to change their attitudes and behaviors at work.

● ● **L01**
Define "organizational behavior" (OB).

Organizational behavior (OB) is a field of study devoted to understanding, explaining, and ultimately improving the attitudes and behaviors of individuals and groups in

> **ORGANIZATIONAL BEHAVIOR** A field of study devoted to understanding, explaining, and ultimately improving the attitudes and behaviors of individuals and groups in organizations.

TABLE 1-1	The Best of Coworkers, the Worst of Coworkers
The Best	**The Worst**
Have you ever had a coworker who usually acted this way?	Have you ever had a coworker who usually acted this way?
√ Got the job done, without having to be managed or reminded.	√ Did not get the job done, even with a great deal of hand-holding.

2. Recall objectives as they are discussed in the text.

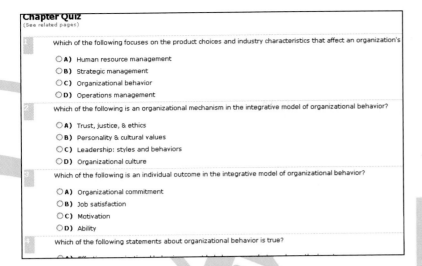

Chapter Quiz
(See related pages)

1. Which of the following focuses on the product choices and industry characteristics that affect an organization's

   ○ **A)** Human resource management
   ○ **B)** Strategic management
   ○ **C)** Organizational behavior
   ○ **D)** Operations management

2. Which of the following is an organizational mechanism in the integrative model of organizational behavior?

   ○ **A)** Trust, justice, & ethics
   ○ **B)** Personality & cultural values
   ○ **C)** Leadership: styles and behaviors
   ○ **D)** Organizational culture

3. Which of the following is an individual outcome in the integrative model of organizational behavior?

   ○ **A)** Organizational commitment
   ○ **B)** Job satisfaction
   ○ **C)** Motivation
   ○ **D)** Ability

4. Which of the following statements about organizational behavior is true?

4. Take practice quizzes testing knowledge across all learning objectives. Reread any sections of the text that require more practice.

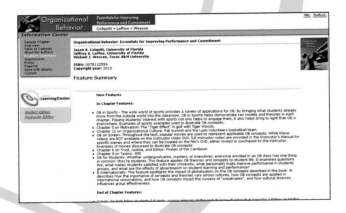

3. Review objectives at the textbook OLC.

• AACSB Statement

McGraw-Hill Companies is a proud corporate member of AACSB International. Understanding the importance and value of AACSB accreditation, the authors of *Organizational Behavior: Essentials for Improving Performance and Commitment* have sought to recognize the curriculum guidelines detailed in the AACSB standards for business accreditation by connecting selected questions in *Organizational Behavior: Essentials for Improving Performance and Commitment* to the general knowledge and skill guidelines found in the AACSB standards.

The statements contained in *Organizational Behavior: Essentials for Improving Performance and Commitment* are provided only as a guide for the users of this text. The AACSB leaves content coverage and assessment clearly within the realm and control of individual schools, the mission of the school, and the faculty. The AACSB also charges schools with the obligation of performing assessments against their own content and learning goals. While *Organizational Behavior: Essentials for Improving Performance and Commitment* and the teaching package make no claim of any specific AACSB qualification or evaluation, we have, within the test bank, labeled selected questions according to the six general knowledge and skills areas. The AACSB labels or tags within the test bank of *Organizational Behavior: Essentials for Improving Performance and Commitment* include communication abilities, ethical understanding and reasoning abilities, analytic skills, use of information technology, multicultural and diversity understanding, and reflective thinking skills. There are, of course, many more benchmarks within the test bank, the text, and the teaching package that may be used as a standard for your course.

Acknowledgements

An enormous number of persons played a role in helping us put the first edition of this textbook together. Truth be told, we had no idea that we would have to rely on and put our success in the hands of so many different people! Each of them had unique and useful contributions to make toward the publication of this book, and they deserve and thus receive our sincere gratitude.

A special thanks goes out to Carol Moore (California State University–East Bay) for her outstanding work on our Instructor's Manual and for helping us develop some of the end-of-chapter exercises and to Liesl Wesson (Texas A&M University) for her development of the PowerPoint presentations.

We are overly indebted to John Weimeister, our sponsoring editor, for his encouragement to write the textbook and his steadfast belief in our doing things in a more "unorthodox" way at times. John has been taking good care of us all the way back to our graduate school days. Thanks also go out to Donielle Xu, our Development Editor, who did her best to keep us on track in terms of actually getting things done and provided valuable feedback throughout the process. We also owe much gratitude to our Marketing Manager, Natalie Zook, who is behind this endeavor 100 percent. We also would like to thank Bruce Gin, Gina Hangos, Matthew Baldwin, Jeremy Cheshareck, Keri Johnson, and Susan Lombardi at McGraw-Hill/Irwin, as they are the masterminds of much of how the book actually looks as it sits in students' hands; their work and effort were spectacular.

We also have had the great fortune of having had contact with more than 50 faculty members from colleges and universities around the country. They provided us with feedback on various aspects of the content of this textbook. Whether by providing feedback on chapters or attending focus groups, their input made our writing substantially better:

Grace Auyang, University of Cincinnati
Joy Beatty, University of Michigan–Dearborn
Carrie Blair, College of Charleston
Fred Blass, Florida State University
Bryan Bonner, University of Utah
James H. Browne, Colorado State University–Pueblo
Judy Bullock, Keller Graduate School of Management
Deborah Butler, Georgia State University
Diane Caggiano, Fitchburg State College
Jerry Carbo, Fairmont State University
Macgorine Cassell, Fairmont State University
Jeewon Cho, Montclair State University
Beth Chung-Herrera, San Diego State University
Vince Daviero, Pasco-Hermando Community College
Fred Dorn, University of Mississippi
Lon Doty, San Jose State University
John A. Drexler Jr., Oregon State University
Ken Dunegan, Cleveland State University
Kathy Edwards, University of Texas–Austin
Susan Eisner, Ramapo College of New Jersey
Leslie Elrod, University of Cincinnati
Berrin Erdogan, Portland State University
Matthew Eriksen, Providence College
Linda Evans, University of Dayton
David Fearon, Central Connecticut State University
Mark Fichman, Carnegie Mellon University
Laura Fuller, Wilmington College
Megan Gerhardt, Miami University of Ohio
Treena Gillespie, California State University–Fullerton
Melissa Gruys, Wright State University
Jonathon Halbesleben, Univ. of Wisconsin–Eau Claire
Wayne Hochwarter, Florida State University
Kristin Holmberg-Wright, Univ. of Wisconsin–Parkside
Ron Humphrey, Virginia Commonwealth University
Christine Jackson, Purdue University
Paul H. Jacques, Western Carolina University
Sheryl Joshua, University of North Carolina, Greensboro
Dong Jung, San Diego State University
Jason Kanov, Western Washington University
Christian Kiewitz, University of Dayton
Patricia Laidler, Massasoit Community College

Robin Lightner, University of Cincinnati
Mary Sue Love, Southern Illinois Univ.-Edwardsville
Carolyn Mann, Sinclair Community College
Catherine Marsh, North Park University
John Michel, Towson University
Donna Mickens, Southern Illinois Univ.–Edwardsville
Stephen Miller, California State University, East Bay
Nathan Moates, Valdosta State University
Karthik Namasivayam, Pennsylvania State University
Muhammad Obeidat, Southern Polytechnic State Univ.
Rhonda Palladi, Georgia State University
Laura Poms, George Mason University
Patrizia Porrini, Long Island University
Elizabeth Ravlin, University of South Carolina
Clint Relyea, Arkansas State University
Barbara Ritter, Coastal Carolina University
Benson Rosen, University of North Carolina
Joe Santora, Essex County College
James Schmidtke, California State University–Fresno
Don Schreiber, Baylor University
Holly Schroth, University of California, Berkeley
John Shaw, Mississippi State University
Bret Simmons, University of Nevada–Reno
Randi Sims, Nova Southeastern University
Ronald Sims, College of William and Mary
Dennis Slevin, University of Pittsburgh
Karen J. Smith, Columbia Southern University
Dan Spencer, University of Kansas–Lawrence
Shane Spiller, Western Kentucky University
Lynda St. Clair, Bryant University
Don Strickland, Southern Illinois Univ.-Edwardsville
David Tansik, University of Arizona
Ed Tomlinson, John Carroll University
Joy Turnheim Smith, IUPUI–Fort Wayne
William Turnley, Kansas State University
Sean Valentine, University of Wyoming
Jim Whitney, Champlain College
Les Wiletzky, Pierce College
Paige Wolf, George Mason University
Joana Young, Baylor University

We also would like to thank our students at the undergraduate, master's, and executive levels who were taught with early versions of these chapters for their constructive feedback toward making them more effective in the classroom. Thanks also to our Ph.D. students for allowing us to take time out from research projects to focus on this book. Finally, we thank our families, who gave up substantial amounts of time with us and put up with the stress that necessarily comes at times during an endeavor such as this.

Jason A. Colquitt   Jeffery A. LePine   Michael J. Wesson

brief table of contents

contents

part 3

Individual Characteristics

part 4

Group Mechanisms

part 5

Organizational Mechanisms

Index 294

organizational behavior

ORGANIZATIONAL BEHAVIOR: an OVERVIEW

● ● learning OBJECTIVES

After reading this chapter, you should be able to:

1.1 Define "organizational behavior" (OB).

1.2 Describe the two primary outcomes in studies of OB.

1.3 Identify the factors that influence the two primary OB outcomes.

1.4 Understand why firms that are good at OB tend to be more profitable.

1.5 Define "theory" and explain its role in the scientific method.

1.6 Describe what a "correlation" represents, and what "big," "moderate," and "small" sized correlations are.

GOOGLE

If you're near a computer as you read this, do a Web search on this phrase: "best company to work for 2008." Did you see Google at the top of the lists that came up in your search? Did you also instinctively use Google to do it? Probably so, because the company based in Mountain View, California, has become a fixture in many of our daily lives. From Web searches to Google Maps, from Gmail to Google Earth, it's difficult to go very long without using a Google product. Since its 2004 initial public offering, the company has grown from approximately 2,000 employees to almost 17,000, and its financial performance often outpaces competitors such as Yahoo and Microsoft.[1] The company came up on your Web search because it headed *Fortune* magazine's "100 Best Companies to Work For" list in both 2007 and 2008.[2]

So what makes Google such a great place to work? One of the most oft-cited reasons is Google's "20% time," a policy that mandates employees spend 20 percent of their workweek on projects that they dream up that might help the company.[3] Many of Google's innovations, including Gmail, originated as "20% time" products. Providing that kind of autonomy allows employees to work on what they're most passionate about. When asked about the long hours that Google employees put in, Dennis Hwang, a Google webmaster, remarked that so-called Googlers are "here because there's no place they'd rather be."[4] Google

also provides a number of enticing perks that make those long hours more comfortable, including free gourmet food, free laundry services, onsite doctors and car washes, and a number of gaming and exercise facilities. If roasted black bass with parsley pesto and bread crumbs sounds good tonight, then the Google cafeterias are the place for you!

Despite its successes—and perhaps even because of them—Google is currently facing some unique challenges. For one, some Googlers have left to start their own businesses, starting firms with creative names like FriendFeed, Mogad, and Mechanical Zoo, to name a few, while others have "retired" after selling their stock.[5] Some key executives have also left to take positions at Facebook, Twitter, and EMI Music.[6] Although Google's corporate turnover rate remains among the lowest in its industry—5 percent—the departures have come at a time when Google's stock price is increasingly volatile.[7] The bulk of Google's revenue comes from the ads it places next to its search results, but a research firm has found that clicks on those ads have remained flat in recent months.[8] Certainly Google has other products to turn to if ad revenues decline, but the markets for those other products are crowded and competitive.[9] Google executives have therefore focused on new initiatives aimed at reducing employee departures.[10]

ORGANIZATIONAL BEHAVIOR

Before we define exactly what the field of organizational behavior represents, take a moment to ponder the following question: Who was the single *worst* coworker you've ever had? Picture fellow students with whom you've worked on class projects; colleagues from part-time or summer jobs; or peers, subordinates, or supervisors working in your current organization. What did this coworker do that earned him or her "worst coworker" status? Was it some of the behaviors shown in the right column of Table 1-1 (or perhaps all of them)? Now take a moment to consider the single *best* coworker you've ever had. Again, what did this coworker do to earn "best coworker" status—some or most of the behaviors shown in the left column of Table 1-1?

Who would receive the first prize for coworkers with whom you have worked? What made him or her a great coworker?

If you ever found yourself working alongside the two people profiled in the table, two questions probably would be foremost on your mind: "*Why* does the worst coworker act that way?" and "*Why* does the best coworker act that way?" Once you understand why the two coworkers act so differently, you might be able to figure out ways to interact with the worst coworker more effectively (thereby making your working life a bit more pleasant). If you happen to be a manager, you could formulate plans for how to improve attitudes and behaviors in the unit. Such plans might include how to screen applicants, train and socialize new organizational members, manage evaluations and rewards for performance, and deal with conflicts that arise between employees. Without understanding why employees act the way they do, it's very difficult to find a way to change their attitudes and behaviors at work.

● ● ● **1.1**

Define "organizational behavior" (OB).

Organizational behavior (OB) is a field of study devoted to understanding, explaining, and ultimately improving the attitudes and behaviors of individuals and groups in

● **ORGANIZATIONAL BEHAVIOR** A field of study devoted to understanding, explaining, and ultimately improving the attitudes and behaviors of individuals and groups in organizations.

TABLE 1-1	The Best of Coworkers, the Worst of Coworkers
The Best	**The Worst**
Have you ever had a coworker who usually acted this way?	Have you ever had a coworker who usually acted this way?
√ Got the job done, without having to be managed or reminded	√ Did not get the job done, even with a great deal of hand-holding
√ Adapted when something needed to be changed or done differently	√ Was resistant to any and every form of change, even when changes were beneficial
√ Was always a "good sport," even when bad things happened at work	√ Whined and complained, no matter what was happening
√ Attended optional meetings or functions to support colleagues	√ Optional meetings? Was too lazy to make it to some required meetings and functions!
√ Helped new coworkers or people who seemed to need a hand	√ Made fun of new coworkers or people who seemed to need a hand
√ Followed key rules, even when the reasons for them were not apparent	√ Broke virtually any rule that somehow made his or her work more difficult
√ Felt an attachment and obligation to the employer for the long haul	√ Seemed to always be looking for something else, even if it wasn't better
√ Was first to arrive, last to leave	√ Was first to leave for lunch, last to return

The Million Dollar Question:

Why do these two employees act so differently?

"MOST EMPLOYEES HAVE TWO PRIMARY GOALS FOR THEIR WORKING LIVES: TO PERFORM THEIR JOBS WELL AND TO REMAIN A MEMBER OF AN ORGANIZATION THAT THEY RESPECT."

organizations. Scholars in management departments of universities and scientists in business organizations conduct research on OB. The findings from those research studies are then applied by managers or consultants to see whether they help meet "real-world" challenges. The theories and concepts found in OB are drawn from a wide variety of disciplines. For example, research on job performance and individual characteristics draws primarily from studies in industrial and organizational psychology. Research on satisfaction, emotions, and team processes draws heavily from social psychology. Sociology research is vital to research on team characteristics and organizational structure, and anthropology research helps inform the study of organizational culture. Finally, models from economics are used to understand motivation, learning, and decision making. This diversity brings a unique quality to the study of OB, as most students will be able to find a particular topic that is intrinsically interesting and thought provoking to them.

An Integrative Model of Organizational Behavior

Because of the diversity in its topics and disciplinary roots, it's common for students in an organizational behavior class to wonder "How does all this stuff fit together?" How does what gets covered in Chapter 3 relate to what gets covered in Chapter 12? To clarify such issues, this textbook is structured around an integrative model of OB, shown in Figure 1-1, that is designed to provide a roadmap for the field of organizational behavior. The model shows how the topics in the next 11 chapters—represented by the ovals in the model—all fit together. We should stress that there are other potential ways of combining the 11 topics, and Figure 1-1 certainly oversimplifies the connections among the topics. Still, we believe the model provides a helpful guide as you move through this course. Figure 1-1 includes five different kinds of topics.

●● 1.2

Describe the two primary outcomes in studies of OB.

Attitudes and behaviors of individuals and groups within organizations are the focus of OB.

Individual Outcomes. The right-most portion of the model contains the two primary outcomes of interest to organizational behavior researchers (and employees and managers in organizations): *Job Performance* and *Organizational Commitment*. Most employees have two primary goals for their working lives: to perform their jobs well and to remain a member of an organization that they respect. Likewise, most managers have two primary goals for their employees: to maximize their job performance and to ensure that they stay with the firm for a significant length of time. As described in Chapter 2, there are several specific behaviors that, when taken together, constitute good job performance. There are also a number of beliefs, attitudes, and emotions that cause an employee to remain committed to an employer.[11]

This book starts by covering job performance and organizational commitment so that you can better understand the two primary organizational behavior goals. Our hope is that by using performance and commitment as starting points, we can highlight the practical importance of OB topics. After all, what could be more important than having employees who perform well and want to stay with the company? This structure also enables us to conclude the other chapters in the book with sections that describe the relationships between each chapter's topic and performance and commitment. For example, the chapter on motivation concludes by describing the relationships between motivation and performance and motivation and commitment. In this way, you'll learn which of the topics in the model are most useful for understanding your own job performance and your own desires to stay with (or leave) your company.

FIGURE 1-1 Integrative Model of Organizational Behavior

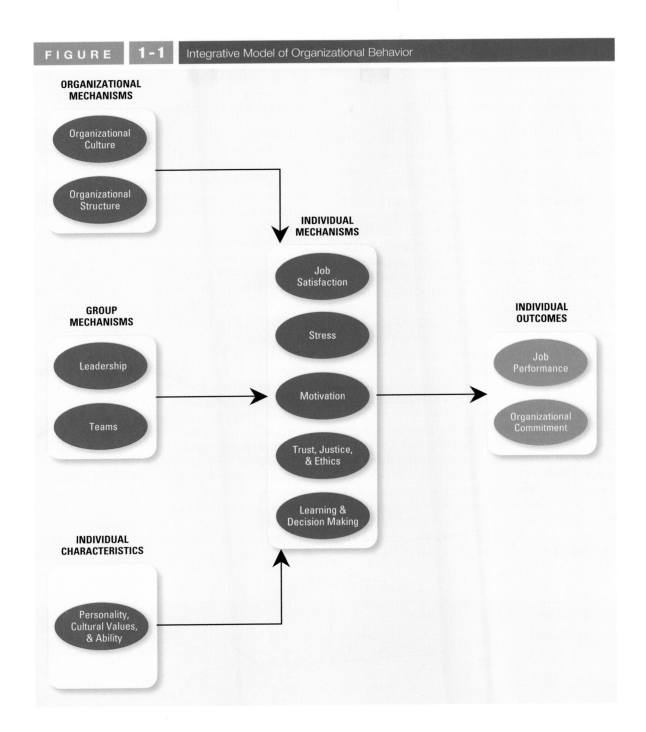

1.3

Identify the factors that influence the two primary OB outcomes.

Individual Mechanisms.

Our integrative model also illustrates a number of individual mechanisms that directly affect job performance and organizational commitment. These include *Job Satisfaction*, which captures what employees feel when thinking about their jobs and doing their day-to-day work (Chapter 3). Another individual mechanism is *Stress*, which reflects employees' psychological responses to job demands that tax or exceed their capacities (Chapter 4). The model also includes *Motivation*, which captures the energetic forces that drive employees' work effort (Chapter 5). *Trust, Justice, and Ethics* reflect the degree to which employees feel that their company does business with fairness, honesty, and integrity (Chapter 6). The final individual mechanism shown in the model is *Learning and Decision Making*, which deals with how employees gain job knowledge and how they use that knowledge to make accurate judgments on the job (Chapter 7).

Individual Characteristics.
Of course, if satisfaction, stress, motivation, and so forth are key drivers of job performance and organizational commitment, it becomes important to understand what factors improve these individual mechanisms. Three such factors, all covered in Chapter 8, reflect the characteristics of individual employees. *Personality* reflects the various traits that explain a person's typical patterns of thought, emotion, and behavior, with commonly studied traits including extraversion, conscientiousness, and agreeableness. *Cultural Values* reflect the shared beliefs about desirable modes of conduct that exist in certain cultures. Finally, *Ability* describes the cognitive abilities (verbal, quantitative, etc.), emotional skills (other awareness, emotion regulation, etc.), and physical abilities (strength, endurance, etc.) that employees bring to a job. Taken together, these individual characteristics help summarize what employees are like and what employees can do.

Group Mechanisms.
The integrative model in Figure 1-1 also acknowledges that employees do not work alone. Instead, they typically work in one or more work teams led by some formal (or sometimes informal) leader. Like the individual characteristics, these group mechanisms shape satisfaction, stress, motivation, trust, and learning. Chapter 9 on *Teams* describes the qualities that work groups possess, such as their norms, their roles, and the way members depend on one another. The chapter also describes the *processes* that summarize how groups behave, including topics like cooperation, conflict, and communication. Chapter 10 focuses on the leaders of those teams. We begin by describing how individuals become leaders in the first place by considering the power and influence dynamics within organizational groups. We then describe how leaders behave in their leadership roles as they use specific actions to influence others at work.

Organizational Mechanisms.
Finally, our integrative model acknowledges that the teams described in the prior section are grouped into larger organizations that themselves affect satisfaction, stress, motivation, and so forth. For example, every company has an *Organizational Structure* that dictates how the units within the firm link to (and communicate with) other units (Chapter 11). Sometimes structures are centralized around a decision-making authority, whereas other times, structures are decentralized, affording each unit some autonomy. Every company also has an *Organizational Culture* that captures "the way things are" in the organization—shared knowledge about the rules, norms, and values that shape employee attitudes and behaviors (Chapter 12).

Summary

We hope that this integrative model will serve as a guide for where you are in this book, as well as where you've been and where you're going. Some of you will be able to apply the topics in the chapters to your current working life, whether you're working full-time or part-time and whether you occupy a managerial or nonmanagerial role. Of course, some of you are full-time students or between jobs at the moment. Regardless of your work status, one thing all of you have in common is that you're students. As it turns out, many of the same concepts that predict success in an organization also predict success in a classroom. We will explore some of those commonalities in our **OB for Students** feature, which appears in each chapter and illustrates how OB concepts can be applied to improve academic success.

OB for Students

This feature is designed to demonstrate the generalizability of many OB principles by applying them to another area of life: life as a student. Each chapter will explore how a particular topic applies in the classroom. This inaugural edition highlights some of the things you can expect in the chapters to come:

Job Satisfaction (Chapter 3). How do students judge how satisfied they are with their university life? How do they weigh things like where they live, how much they like their classmates, and how much they enjoy what they're studying?

Stress (Chapter 4). The working world doesn't corner the market on stress; juggling several classes along with life's other responsibilities can be quite stressful in its own right. We'll explore how various kinds of stressful demands affect student learning and class performance.

Trust, Justice, and Ethics (Chapter 6). Why do students cheat? Do most students view cheating as unethical, or are some forms of cheating viewed as normal and acceptable behaviors in today's instructional environment?

Personality, Cultural Values, and Ability (Chapter 8). Most students have first-hand experience with one of the most widely used cognitive ability tests: the SAT. Does the SAT really help predict who will excel in college?

How does its predictive value compare to other kinds of screening information?

Organizational Structure (Chapter 11). What kinds of organizational structures do most students find attractive when they're applying for jobs? Do some students have different structural preferences than others?

Organizational Culture (Chapter 12). How do new students learn about the culture of a university? Are there benefits to socializing new students in the same way that organizations socialize new employees? What would such socialization efforts look like? ❖

DOES ORGANIZATIONAL BEHAVIOR MATTER?

Having described exactly what OB is, it's time to discuss another fundamental question: Does it really matter? After all, if a firm has a good-enough product, won't people buy it regardless of how happy, motivated, or committed its workforce is? Perhaps for a time, but effective OB can help keep a product good over the long term. This same argument can be made in reverse: If a firm has a bad-enough product, isn't it true that people won't buy it, regardless of how happy, motivated, or committed its workforce is? Again, perhaps for a time, but the effective management of OB can help make a product get better, incrementally, over the long term.

Consider this pop quiz about the automotive industry: Name the four best-selling foreign nameplates in the United States from 2002 to 2005. You earn a B if you knew that Toyota was #1 (1.67 million) and Honda was #2 (1.2 million). You earn an A if you knew that Nissan was #3 (855,002). But who is #4? Mazda? Volkswagen? Mercedes? Nope—the answer is Hyundai (418,615).[12] Hyundai's offerings were once criticized as being "cheap," with Jay Leno famously comparing a Hyundai to a bobsled ("It has no room, you have to push it to get going, and it only goes downhill!").[13] More recent models—including those built in a new manufacturing plant in Montgomery, Alabama—are regarded as good looking and well made, and the Sonata was labeled the most reliable car in America by *Consumer Reports* in 2004.[14] This shift represents Hyundai's increased emphasis on quality; work teams devoted to quality have been expanded eightfold, and almost all employees have enrolled in special training programs devoted to quality issues.[15] Hyundai also represents a case in which OB principles are being applied to multiple cultures. Our **OB Internationally** feature spotlights such international and cross-cultural applications of OB topics in each chapter.

Building a Conceptual Argument

Of course, we shouldn't just accept it on faith that OB matters, nor should we merely look for specific companies that appear to support the premise. What we need instead is a logical conceptual argument that captures exactly why OB might affect the bottom-line profitability of an organization. One such argument is based on the **resource-based view** of organizations. This perspective describes what exactly makes resources valuable—that is, what makes them capable of creating long-term profits for the firm.[16] A firm's resources include financial (revenue, equity, etc.) and physical (buildings, machines, technology) resources, but they also include resources related to organizational behavior such as the knowledge, decision making, ability, and wisdom of the workforce, as well as the image, culture, and goodwill of the organization.

> ● **RESOURCE-BASED VIEW** A perspective that describes what exactly makes resources valuable, and therefore capable of creating long-term profits for the firm.

After it enrolled its employees in quality training programs and dramatically increased its reliance on work teams, Hyundai produced Consumer Reports' *"most reliable car of the year" for 2004—the Sonata.*

OB Internationally

Changes in technology, communications, and economic forces have made business more global and international than ever. To use Thomas Friedman's line, "the world is flat." The playing field has been leveled between the United States and the rest of the world.[17] This feature spotlights the impact of globalization on the organizational behavior concepts described in this book. More specifically, this feature will cover a variety of topics:

Cross-Cultural Differences. Research in cross-cultural organizational behavior has illustrated that national cultures affect many of the relationships in our integrative model. Put differently, there is little that we know about OB that is "universal" or "culture free."[18]

International Corporations. An increasing number of organizations are international in scope, with both foreign and domestic operations. Applying organizational behavior concepts in these firms represents a special challenge—should policies and practices be consistent across locations or tailored to meet the needs of the culture?

Expatriation. Working as an expatriate—an employee who lives outside his or her native country—can be particularly challenging. What factors influence expatriates' job performance and organizational commitment levels?

Managing Diversity. More and more work groups are composed of members of different cultural backgrounds. What are the special challenges involved in leading and working in such groups? ❖

●● 1.4

Understand why firms that are good at OB tend to be more profitable.

The resource-based view suggests that the value of resources depends on several factors, shown in Figure 1-2. For example, a resource is more valuable when it is *rare*. Diamonds, oil, Babe Ruth baseball cards, and Action Comics #1 (the debut of Superman) are all expensive precisely because they are rare. Good people are also rare—witness the adage "good people are hard to find." Ask yourself what percentage of the people you have worked with have been talented, motivated, satisfied, and good team players. In some organizations, cities, or job markets, such employees are the exception rather than the rule. If good people really are rare, then the effective management of OB should prove to be a valuable resource.

The resource-based view also suggests that a resource is more valuable when it is **inimitable,** meaning that it cannot be imitated. A new form of technology can help a firm gain an advantage for a short time, but what happens when a competing firm adopts the same technology? Many of a firm's resources can be imitated, though it is sometimes expensive. Manufacturing practices can be copied, building layouts can be mimicked, equipment and tools can be approximated. Good people, in contrast, are much more difficult to imitate. As shown in Figure 1-2, there are three reasons why people are inimitable.

Diamonds, and good people in organizations, are both rare and valuable commodities.

History. People create a *history*—a collective pool of experience, wisdom, and knowledge that benefits the organization. History cannot be bought. Consider an example from the discount airline industry. Southwest and JetBlue are the market leaders in this industry, profiting from more frequent point-to-point daily schedules routed into less expensive airports. Delta launched its own discount brand—Song—to compete in this market, though the brand was ultimately abandoned and folded back into Delta's regular operations.[19] One challenge facing Song was that it was competing, for the first time, in a market in which Southwest had existed for decades. Their respective positions on the "industry learning curve" were quite different.

Numerous Small Decisions. The concept of *numerous small decisions* captures the idea that people make many small decisions day in and day out, week in and week out. "So what?" you might say, "Why worry about small decisions?" Ask yourself how much time elapsed between the arrival of *Diet Coke With Lime* on grocery store shelves and the arrival of *Diet Pepsi Lime.* Answer? About two months.[20] Big decisions can be copied; they are visible to competitors and observable by industry experts and analysts. In the case of Song, the company was able to copy one of Jet-Blue's signatures—a television for every seat—so that Song passengers were able to watch pay-per-view movies or play video games.[21] However, it would be more difficult to copy one of Southwest's signatures—the playful, whimsical style displayed by flight attendants and service personnel.[22] Officials from Song may not have the opportunity to observe a Southwest flight attendant turning the seatbelt instructions into a comedy routine on a given day or finding a way to make an anxious toddler laugh on a particular flight. Those decisions are invisible to competitors but not to the travelers who make mental notes about their next trip.

Socially Complex Resources. People also create **socially complex resources**, like culture, trust, and reputation. These resources are termed "socially complex" because it's not always clear how they came to develop, though it is clear which organizations do (and do not) possess them. An upper manager at Song could have exited a Southwest flight convinced that the company would benefit from adopting the competitor's playful and fun culture. But how exactly would that be done? A new culture cannot just be implemented like a change in software systems. It springs from the social dynamics within a given firm at a given point in time.

FIGURE 1-2 What Makes a Resource Valuable?

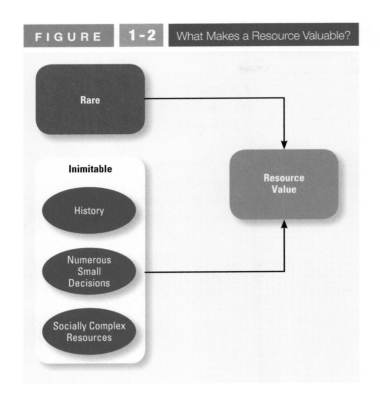

The authors coded each prospectus for information that might suggest OB issues were valued. Examples of valuing OB issues included describing employees as a source of competitive advantage in strategy and mission statements, emphasizing training and continuing education, having a human resources management officer, and emphasizing full-time rather than temporary or contract employees. By 1993, 81 of the 136 firms included in the study had survived (60 percent). The key question is whether the value placed on OB predicted which firms did (and did not) survive. The results revealed that firms that valued OB had a 19 percent higher survival rate than firms that did not value OB.

Another study focused on *Fortune*'s "100 Best Companies to Work For" list, which has appeared annually since 1998.[24] Table 1-2 provides the 2007 version of the list. If the 100 firms on the list really do have good OB practices, and if good OB practices really do influence firm profitability, then it follows that the 100 firms should be more profitable. To explore this premise, the study went back to the original 1998 list and found a "matching firm" for the companies that were included.[25] The matching firm consisted of the most similar company with respect to industry and size in that particular year, with the added requirement that the company had not appeared on the "100 Best" list. This process essentially created two groups of

> ❝ **"The results revealed that firms that valued OB had a 19 percent higher survival rate than firms that did not value OB."** ❞

Research Evidence

In sum, we can build a conceptual argument for why OB might affect an organization's profitability: Good people are both rare and inimitable and therefore serve as a resource that is valuable for creating competitive advantage. Conceptual arguments are helpful, of course, but it would be even better if there were hard data to back them up. Fortunately, it turns out that there is a great deal of research evidence supporting the importance of OB for company performance. Several research studies have been conducted on the topic, each employing a somewhat different approach.

One study focused on 136 nonfinancial companies who made initial public offerings (IPOs) in 1988.[23] Firms that undergo an IPO typically have shorter histories and need an infusion of cash to grow or introduce some new technology. The authors of this study examined the prospectus filed by each firm (the Securities and Exchange Commission requires that prospectuses contain honest information, and firms can be liable for any inaccuracies that might mislead investors).

companies that differ only in terms of their inclusion in the "100 Best." The study then compared the profitability of those two groups of companies. The results revealed that the "100 Best" firms were more profitable than their peers. Indeed, the study's authors noted that an investment portfolio based on the 1998 "100 Best" list would have earned an 82 percent cumulative investment return from 1998–2000 compared with only 37 percent for the broader market.

So What's So Hard?

Clearly this research evidence seems to support the conceptual argument that good people constitute a valuable resource for companies. Good OB does seem to matter in terms of company profitability. You may wonder then, "What's so hard?" Why doesn't every company prioritize the effective management of OB, devoting as much attention to it as they do accounting, finance, marketing, technology, physical assets, and so on? Certainly some companies do a very poor job of managing their people. Why is that?

TABLE 1-2	The "100 Best Companies to Work For" in 2007

1. Google	35. Children's Healthcare Atl.	69. Nike
2. Genentech	36. Goldman Sachs	70. Paychex
3. Wegman's Food Markets	37. Northwest Comm. Hosp.	71. AstraZeneca
4. The Container Store	38. Robert W. Baird	72. Medtronic
5. Whole Foods Market	39. J. M. Smucker	73. Aflac
6. Network Appliance	40. Amgen	74. American Express
7. S.C. Johnson & Son	41. JM Family Enterprises	75. Quad/Graphics
8. Boston Consulting	42. PCL Construction	76. Deloitte & Touche USA
9. Methodist Hospital	43. Genzyme	77. Principal Financial Grp.
10. W.L. Gore	44. Yahoo	78. Timberland
11. Cisco Systems	45. Bain & Co.	79. TDIndustries
12. David Weekley Homes	46. First Horizon National	80. Lehigh Valley Hospital
13. Nugget Market	47. American Fidelity Assur.	81. Baptist Health S. Florida
14. Qualcomm	48. SAS Institute	82. CDW
15. American Century Invest.	49. Nixon Peabody	83. EOG Resources
16. Starbucks	50. Microsoft	84. Capital One Financial
17. Quicken Loans	51. Stew Leonard's	85. Standard Pacific
18. Station Casinos	52. OhioHealth	86. National Instruments
19. Alston & Bird	53. Four Seasons Hotels	87. Texas Instruments
20. QuikTrip	54. Baptist Health Care	88. CarMax
21. Griffin Hospital	55. Dow Corning	89. Marriott International
22. Valero Energy	56. Granite Construction	90. Men's Wearhouse
23. Vision Service Plan	57. Publix Supermarkets	91. Memorial Health
24. Nordstrom	58. PricewaterhouseCoopers	92. Bright Horizons
25. Ernst & Young	59. Pella	93. Milliken
26. Arnold & Porter	60. MITRE	94. Bingham McCutchen
27. Recreational Equip. (REI)	61. SRA International	95. Vanguard
28. Kimley-Horn & Assoc.	62. Mayo Clinic	96. IKEA North America
29. Edward Jones	63. Booz Allen Hamilton	97. KPMG
30. Russell Investment Grp.	64. Perkins Coie	98. Synovus
31. Adobe Systems	65. Alcon Laboratories	99. A.G. Edwards
32. Plante & Moran	66. Jones Lang LaSalle	100. Stanley
33. Intuit	67. HomeBanc Mortgage	
34. Umpqua Bank	68. Procter & Gamble	

● **RULE OF ONE-EIGHTH** A rule that explains why so few organizations are truly effective at how they manage their people.

Work by Jeffrey Pfeffer provides one potential answer. Pfeffer has written extensively about the OB practices that tend to be used by successful organizations. He also has described why more organizations do not use seemingly "commonsense" practices. One reason is that there is no "magic bullet" OB practice—one thing that, in and of itself, can increase profitability. Instead, the effective management of OB requires a belief that several different practices are important, along with a long-term commitment to improving those practices. This premise can be summarized with what might be called the **rule of one-eighth**:

One must bear in mind that one-half of organizations won't believe the connection between how they manage their people and the profits they earn. One-half of those who do see the connection will do what many organizations have done—try to make a single change to solve their problems, not realizing that the effective management of people requires a more comprehensive and systematic approach. Of the firms that make comprehensive changes, probably only about one-half will persist with their practices long enough to actually derive economic benefits. Since one-half times one-half times one-half equals one-eighth, at best 12 percent of organizations will actually do what is required to build profits by putting people first.[26]

The integrative model of OB used to structure this book was designed with this rule of one-eighth in mind.

Good OB matters in terms of company profitability, so why is it so hard to implement?

Figure 1-1 suggests that high job performance depends not just on employee motivation but also on fostering high levels of satisfaction, effectively managing stress, creating a trusting climate, and committing to employee learning. Failing to do any one of those things could hinder the effectiveness of the other concepts in the model. Of course, that systemic nature reveals another reality of organizational behavior: It is often difficult to "fix" companies that struggle with OB issues. Such companies often struggle in a number of different areas and on a number of different levels. One such (fictitious) company is spotlighted in our **OB on Screen** feature, which appears in each chapter and uses well-known movies to demonstrate OB concepts.

OB on Screen

Office Space

This feature is designed to allow you to imagine OB in action on the silver screen. Once you've read about an OB topic, you'll find that you see it play out all around you, especially in movies. This inaugural edition spotlights (what else?) *Office Space* (Dir: Mike Judge. 20th Century Fox, 1999).

> Since I started working, every single day has been worse than the day before, so that every day you see me is the worst day of my life.

With these words, Peter Gibbons summarizes what it's like to work at Initech, the computer programming firm where he updates bank software. Peter doesn't exhibit particularly good job performance, nor is he very committed to the organization.

Why does Peter act that way? From the perspective of our integrative model of OB,

the problem starts at the top and flows down. The culture of the organization is rigid and emotionless, with management seeming to delight in pointing out mistakes (like Peter's failure to use a cover sheet on his reports). The structure of the organization somehow assigns eight different bosses to Peter (providing eight opportunities to relive the cover sheet conversation). From a leadership perspective, the evil Bill Lumbergh seems to relish the power that comes with his title but does little to improve the functioning of his unit. The result is a workforce that feels little to no motivation because performance has no impact on the money they earn. All this is worsened by the arrival of "the two Bobs," consultants whose job it is to choose which employees to fire and which to retain.

Clearly it would take a lot of time and effort to turn Initech around. The effort would require several changes to several different

practices to address several different components of our OB model. And those changes would need to be in place for a long period of time before the company could turn the corner. An uphill climb, to be sure, but Initech has one thing going for it: The Bobs are on the job! ❖

HOW DO WE "KNOW" WHAT WE KNOW ABOUT ORGANIZATIONAL BEHAVIOR?

Now that we've described what OB is and why it's an important topic of study, we now turn to how we "know" what we know about the topic. In other words, where does the knowledge in this textbook come from? To answer this question, we must first explore how people "know" about anything. Philosophers have argued that there are several different ways of knowing things:[27]

- **Method of Experience:** People hold firmly to some belief because it is consistent with their own experience and observations.

- **Method of Intuition:** People hold firmly to some belief because it "just stands to reason"—it seems obvious or self-evident.

out by your boss. Or it may seem logical that social recognition will be viewed as "cheap talk," with employees longing for financial incentives rather than verbal compliments. Or perhaps the best boss you ever worked for never offered a single piece of social recognition in her life, yet her employees always worked their hardest on her behalf.

1.5

Define "theory" and explain its role in the scientific method.

From a scientist's point of view, it doesn't really matter what a person's experience, intuition, or authority suggests; the prediction must be tested with data. In other words, scientists don't simply assume that their beliefs are accurate; they acknowledge that their beliefs must be tested scientifically. Scientific studies are based on the scientific method, originated by Sir Francis Bacon in the 1600s and adapted in Figure 1-3.[28] The scientific method begins with **theory**, defined as a collection of assertions—both verbal and symbolic—that specify how and why variables are related, as well as the conditions in which they should (and should not) be related.[29] More simply, a theory tells a story and supplies the familiar who, what, where, when, and why elements found in any newspaper or magazine article.[30] Theories are often summarized with theory diagrams, the "boxes and arrows" that graphically depict relationships between variables.

> **"From a scientist's point of view, it doesn't really matter what a person's experience, intuition, or authority suggests; the prediction must be tested with data."**

- **Method of Authority:** People hold firmly to some belief because some respected official, agency, or source has said it is so.

- **Method of Science:** People accept some belief because scientific studies have tended to replicate that result using a series of samples, settings, and methods.

Consider the following prediction: Providing social recognition, in the form of public praise and appreciation for good behavior, will increase the performance and commitment of work units. Perhaps you feel that you "know" this claim to be true because you yourself have always responded well to praise and recognition. Or perhaps you feel that you "know" it to be true because it seems like common sense—who wouldn't work harder after a few public pats on the back? Maybe you feel that you "know" it to be true because a respected boss from your past always extolled the virtue of public praise and recognition.

However, the methods of experience, intuition, and authority also might have led you to the opposite belief—that providing social recognition has no impact on the performance and commitment of work units. It may be that public praise has always made you uncomfortable or embarrassed, to the point that you tried to hide especially effective behaviors to avoid being singled

A scientist could build a theory explaining why social recognition might influence the performance and commitment of work units. From what sources would that theory be built? Theories may be built from interviews with employees in a work setting, employees who provide insights into their views about the strengths and weaknesses of social recognition. They also may be built from observations of people at work, in which case scientists take notes, keep diaries, and pore over company documents to find all the elements of a theory story.[31] Alternatively, theories may be built from research reviews, which examine findings of previous studies to look for general patterns or themes.[32]

Although many theories are interesting, logical, or thought provoking, many also wind up being completely wrong. After all, scientific theories once predicted that the earth was flat and the sun revolved around it. Closer to home, OB theories once argued that money was not an effective motivator and that the best way to structure jobs was to make them as simple and mundane as possible.[33] Theories must therefore be tested to verify that their predictions are accurate. As shown in Figure 1-3, the scientific method requires that theories be used to inspire **hypotheses**. Hypotheses are written predictions that specify relationships between variables. For example, a theory of social recognition

| FIGURE | 1-3 | The Scientific Method |

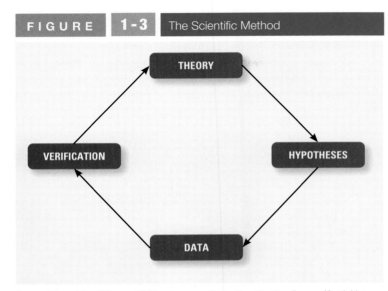

Source: Adapted from F. Bacon, M. Silverthorne, and L. Jardine, *The New Organon* (Cambridge: Cambridge University Press, 2000).

could be used to inspire this hypothesis: "Social recognition behaviors on the part of managers will be positively related to the job performance and organizational commitment of their units." This hypothesis states, in black and white, the expected relationship between social recognition and unit effectiveness.

Assume a family member owned a chain of 21 fast-food restaurants and allowed you to test this hypothesis using the restaurants. Specifically, you decided to train the managers in a subset of the restaurants about how to use social recognition as a tool to reinforce behaviors. Meanwhile, you left another subset of restaurants unchanged to represent a control group. You then tracked the total number of social recognition behaviors exhibited by managers over the next nine months by observing the managers at specific time intervals. You measured job performance by tracking drive-through times for the next nine months and used those times to reflect the minutes it takes for a customer to approach the restaurant, order food, pay, and leave. You also measured the commitment of the work unit by tracking employee retention rates over the next nine months.

●● 1.6

Describe what a "correlation" represents, and what "big," "moderate," and "small" sized correlations are.

So how can you tell whether your hypothesis was supported? You could analyze the data by examining the correlation between social recognition behaviors and drive-through times, as well as the correlation between social recognition behaviors and employee turnover. A correlation, abbreviated *r*, describes the statistical relationship between two variables. Correlations can be positive or negative and range from 0 (no statistical relationship) to ±1 (a perfect statistical relationship). Picture a spreadsheet with two columns of numbers. One column contains

the total numbers of social recognition behaviors for all 21 restaurants, and the other contains the average drive-through times for those same 21 restaurants. The best way to get a feel for the correlation is to look at a scatterplot—a graph made from those two columns of numbers. Figure 1-4 presents three scatterplots, each depicting differently sized correlations. The strength of the correlation can be inferred from the "compactness" of its scatterplot. Panel (a) shows a perfect 1.0 correlation; knowing the score for social recognition allows you to predict the score for drive-through times perfectly. Panel (b) shows a correlation of .50, so the trend in the data is less obvious than in Panel (a) but still easy to see with the naked eye. Finally, Panel (c) shows a correlation of .00—no statistical relationship. Understanding the correlation is important because OB questions are not "yes or no" in nature. That is, the question is not "*Does* social recognition lead to higher job performance?" but rather "*How often* does social recognition lead to higher job performance?" The correlation provides a number that expresses an answer to the "how often" question. For more discussion of the value of correlations, see our **OB in Sports** feature, which describes how OB concepts can be observed and applied in men's and women's athletics.

| FIGURE | 1-4 | Three Different Correlation Sizes |

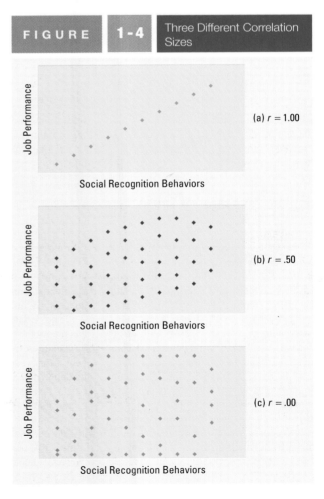

So what is the correlation between social recognition and job performance (and between social recognition and organizational commitment)? It turns out that a study very similar to the one described was actually conducted, using a sample of 21 Burger King restaurants with 525 total employees.[34] The correlation between social recognition and job performance was .28. The restaurants that received training in social recognition averaged 44 seconds of drive-through time nine months later versus 62 seconds for the control group locations. The correlation between social recognition and retention rates was .20. The restaurants that received training in social recognition had a 16 percent better retention rate than the control group locations nine months later. The study also instituted a financial "pay-for-performance" system in a subset of the locations and found that the social recognition effects were actually just as strong as the financial effects.

Of course, you might wonder whether correlations of .28 or .20 are impressive or unimpressive. To put those numbers in context, consider that one estimate puts the correlation between height and weight at .44.[35] If the correlation between height and weight is only .44, then a correlation of .28 between social recognition and job performance doesn't sound too bad! In fact, a correlation of .50 is considered "strong" in organizational behavior research, given the sheer number of things that can affect how employees feel and act.[36] A .30 correlation is considered "moderate," and many studies discussed in this book will have results in this range. Finally, a .10 correlation is considered "weak" in organizational behavior research. It should be noted, however, that even "weak" correlations can be important if they predict costly behaviors such as theft or ethical violations.

Does this one study settle the debate about the value of social recognition for job performance and organizational commitment? Not really, for a variety of reasons. First, it included

A study of Burger King restaurants revealed a correlation between social recognition—praise and appreciation by managers—and employees' performance and commitment. Such studies contribute to the growing body of organizational behavior knowledge.

OB in Sports

This feature is designed to illustrate how OB concepts play out in the sports world. Consider this scenario: you're at a ballgame, enjoying a hot dog and a beverage as the home team bats with no outs in the fourth inning. The lead-off batter gets a double, and you notice that the next batter has squared to bunt the ball. Sure enough, he lays down a bunt, moving his teammate from second to third. "Good move," you think, as now the good guys have a player on third with only one out in the inning.

It turns out you're wrong—it's not a good move. How do we know? Because Bill James has studied it. James, 59, grew up in Kansas, learning about baseball from newspaper writers and radio broadcasters. Even as a child, James was skeptical of what he was learning from these baseball authorities.[37] In his twenties, while working at the Stokely Van Camp pork-and-beans plant, James began collecting data to test his own theories about baseball. He brought his *Baseball Encyclopedia* and a set of box scores from the newspaper to work each day, building his own baseball database. In a nod to the Society for American Baseball Research (SABR), James came to call his work "sabermetrics," defined as the search for objective knowledge about baseball. Using these scientific methods, James began debunking the conventional baseball wisdom that he'd heard growing up—wisdom that he calls "baseball's Kilimanjaro of repeated legends and legerdemain."[38] Among those legends was the value of bunting—it turns out to be negatively correlated with runs scored because it sacrifices a precious out, reducing the odds of a big inning. James's work also illustrated the value of walks, the dangers of stolen base attempts, and the impact of differences in baseball park design.

James's methods and conclusions made him an outsider to the baseball establishment for decades. However, as described in the book *Moneyball*, the general manager of the Oakland Athletics began applying sabermetrics in the late 1990s in an attempt to win with a low team payroll.[39] When the Boston Red Sox assembled their new management team in 2003, one member suggested getting a "Bill James" type. Another suggested hiring James himself.[40] James once said that "the value of a statistic is whether it's tied to winning."[41]

Bill James has said, "the value of a statistic is whether it's tied to winning."

With two World Series titles in the past four years, it would seem that James's statistics have been pretty valuable to the Red Sox! ❖

only 21 restaurants with 525 employees. Maybe the results would have turned out differently if the study had included more locations. Second, maybe there is something unique about fast-food employees or restaurant employees in general that makes them particularly responsive to public praise and recognition. Third, it may be that social recognition affects drive-through times but not other forms of job performance, like customer service ratings or the accuracy of completed food orders.

The important point is that little can be learned from a single study. The best way to test a theory is to conduct many studies, each of which is as different as possible from the ones that preceded it.[42] So if you really wanted to study the effects of social recognition, you would conduct several studies using different kinds of samples and measures. After completing all of those studies, you could look back on the results and create some sort of average correlation across all of the studies. This process is what a technique called meta-analysis does. It takes all of the correlations found in studies of a particular relationship and calculates a weighted average (such that correlations based on studies with large samples are weighted more than correlations based on studies with small samples). It turns out that a meta-analysis has been conducted on the effects of social recognition and job performance and indicates an average correlation of .21 across studies conducted in 96 different organizations in the service industry.[43] That meta-analysis offers more compelling support for the potential benefits of social recognition than the methods of experience, intuition, or authority could have provided. ■

CHECK OUT

www.mhhe.com/ColquittEss

for study materials including Interactive Exercises, Quizzes, iPod downloads, and video.

CASE: Google

As noted at the outset of the chapter, Google has experienced some departures and retirements among key personnel and executives. Sean Knapp, 27 years old, is one of those departures.[44] Along with two of his colleagues, Knapp came up with a new way of handling Web video. Rather than channel their idea into the next Google product, the three of them informed Google that they were leaving to start their own business. The company tried hard to keep them. As Knapp recalls, "They told us, 'Here's a blank check.' I said, 'You're asking me to be a surrogate parent.'" Now Knapp and his colleagues have full control over "their baby" as their company, Ooyala, focuses on building a system to run videos for independent Web sites. Knapp's story is common enough that the departed have formed a club of entrepreneurial ex-Googlers. One former employee has even started a new venture capital firm focused on startups by Google alumni.

These departures are a sensitive issue for Google because many of the business ideas originated and developed during employees' "20% time." That time is meant to provide a forum for the next great Google innovation, not for the next great business startup. Although Google maintains that it hires many

more people than it loses in a given month, it is beginning to look for ways to improve its retention of key employees.[45] The company is considering offering sabbaticals for restless employees and looking to come up with innovative new career opportunities for employees searching for a fresh challenge. Google's founders, Sergey Brin and Lawrence Page, have also instituted quarterly "Founders Awards." These awards grant millions of dollars of restricted stock to teams that build something that makes Google more profitable.[46] Google is also looking to revise its stock options program to give better deals to employees with more years of service.

1.1 Consider Google's "20% time" policy. What are its key strengths? What are its key weaknesses?

1.2 If you were in charge of the "20% time" policy, would you increase contractual restrictions to prevent Googlers from starting their own businesses in areas related to their Google projects? Would such a policy have important drawbacks?

1.3 What do you think of Google's strategies for reducing retirements and departures? Can you think of other effective strategies that were not listed in the case?

TAKEAWAYS

1.1 Organizational behavior is a field of study devoted to understanding and explaining the attitudes and behaviors of individuals and groups in organizations. More simply, it focuses on *why* individuals and groups in organizations act the way they do.

1.2 The two primary outcomes in organizational behavior are job performance and organizational commitment.

1.3 A number of factors affect performance and commitment, including individual mechanisms (job satisfaction; stress; motivation; trust, justice, and ethics; learning and decision making), individual characteristics (personality, cultural values, and ability), group mechanisms (teams, leadership), and organizational mechanisms (organizational structure, organizational culture).

1.4 The effective management of organizational behavior can help a company become more profitable because good people are a valuable resource. Not only are good people rare, but they are also hard to imitate. They create a history that cannot be bought or copied, they make numerous small decisions that cannot be observed by competitors, and they create socially complex resources such as culture, teamwork, trust, and reputation. Many scientific studies support the relationship between effective organizational behavior and company performance.

1.5 A theory is a collection of assertions, both verbal and symbolic, that specifies how and why variables are related, as well as the conditions in which they should (and should not) be related. Theories about organizational behavior are built from a combination of interviews, observation, research reviews, and reflection. Theories form the beginning point for the scientific method and inspire hypotheses that can be tested with data.

1.6 A correlation is a statistic that expresses the strength of a relationship between two variables (ranging from 0 to ± 1). In OB research, a .50 correlation is considered "strong," a .30 correlation is considered "moderate," and a .10 correlation is considered "weak." A meta-analysis summarizes the results of several research studies. It takes the correlations from those research studies and calculates a weighted average to give more weight to studies with larger samples.

DISCUSSION QUESTIONS

1.1 Think again about the worst coworker you've ever had—the one who did some of the things listed in Table 1-1. Think about what that coworker's boss did (or didn't do) to try to improve his or her behavior. What did the boss do well or poorly? What would you have done differently, and which organizational behavior topics would have been most relevant?

1.2 Which of the individual mechanisms in Figure 1-1 (job satisfaction; stress; motivation; trust, justice, and ethics; learning and decision making) seems to drive your performance and commitment the most? Do you think you're unique in that regard, or do you think most people would answer that way?

1.3 Create a list of the most successful companies that you can think of. What do these companies have that others don't? Are the things that those companies possess rare and inimitable (see Figure 1-2)? What makes those things difficult to copy?

1.4 Think of something that you "know" to be true based on the method of experience, the method of intuition, or the method of authority. Could you test your knowledge using the method of science? How would you do it?

ASSESSMENT: Private Self-Consciousness

Many of the theories and concepts in this book can help you understand more about your working life by explaining why you sometimes feel or act a certain way. Those theories and concepts may be particularly informative if you are a self-reflective or introspective person. This assessment is designed to measure private self-consciousness—the tendency to direct attention inward to better understand your attitudes and behaviors. Answer each question using the response scale provided. Then subtract your answers to the bold-faced questions from 4, with the difference being your new answers for those questions. For example, if your original answer for question 5 was "3," your new answer is 1 (4 − 3). Then sum your answers for the ten questions. (For more assessments relevant to this chapter, please visit the Online Learning Center at www.mhhe.com/ColquittEss).

0	1	2	3	4
Extremely Uncharacteristic of Me	**Somewhat Uncharacteristic of Me**	**Neutral**	**Somewhat Characteristic of Me**	**Extremely Characteristic of Me**

1. I'm always trying to figure myself out. _____

2. **Generally, I'm not very aware of myself.** _____

3. I reflect about myself a lot. _____

4. I'm often the subject of my own daydreams. _____

5. **I never scrutinize myself.** _____

6. I'm generally attentive to my inner feelings. _____

7. I'm constantly examining my motives. _____

8. I sometimes have the feeling that I'm off somewhere watching myself. _____

9. I'm alert to changes in my mood. _____

10. I'm aware of the way my mind works when I work through a problem. _____

Scoring

If your scores sum up to 26 or above, you do a lot of self-reflection and are highly self-aware. You may find that many of the theories discussed in this textbook will help you better understand your attitudes and feelings about working life.

Source: A. Fenigstein, M.F. Scheier, and A.H. Buss, "Public and Private Self-Consciousness: Assessment and Theory," *Journal of Consulting and Clinical Psychology* 43 (1975), pp. 522–27. Copyright © 1975 by the American Psychological Association. Adapted with permission. No further reproduction or distribution is permitted without written permission from the American Psychological Association.

EXERCISE: Is OB Common Sense?

The purpose of this exercise is to take some of the topics covered in this textbook and examine whether improving them is "just common sense." This exercise uses groups, so your instructor will either assign you to a group or ask you to create your own group. The exercise has the following steps:

1. Consider the theory diagram shown below. It explains why two "independent variables" (the quality of a movie's script and the fame of its stars) affect a "dependent variable" (how much the movie makes at the box office).

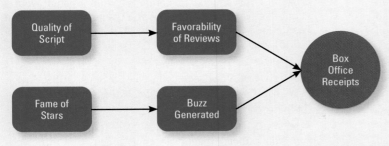

2. Now build your own theory diagram about organizational behavior. In groups, choose one of the following four topics to use as your dependent variable:

   • Job Satisfaction: The pleasurable emotions felt when performing job tasks.

   • Strain: The headaches, fatigue, or burnout resulting from workplace stress.

   • Motivation: The intensity and persistence of job-related effort.

   • Trust in Supervisor: The willingness to allow a supervisor to have significant influence over key job issues.

Using a transparency, laptop, or chalkboard, build a theory diagram that summarizes the factors that affect your chosen dependent variable. To be as comprehensive as possible, try to include at least four independent variables. Keep your books closed! You should build your diagrams using only your own experience and intuition.

3. Each group should present its theory diagram to the class. Do the predicted relationships make sense? Should anything be dropped? Should anything be added?

4. Now compare the theory diagram you created with the contents of the relevant chapters, focusing on the bolded key words. Are there bolded key words that you omitted that could be included in your set of independent variables? If so, that suggests that your theory diagram was incomplete. Are their concepts that you included in your set of independent variables that you don't see discussed in the chapter? If so, that suggests that your theory diagram includes concepts whose importance has not been supported by academic research. In either event, such differences show that OB is more than just common sense.

END NOTES

1. Lashinsky, A. "Where Does Google Go Next?" *Fortune,* May 26, 2008, pp. 104–110.

2. Levering, R., and M. Moskowitz. "In Good Company." *Fortune,* January 22, 2007, pp. 94–114; Levering, R., and M. Moskowitz. "The Rankings." *Fortune,* February 4, 2008, pp. 75–94.

3. Baker, S. "Google and the Wisdom of Clouds." *BusinessWeek,* December 24, 2007, pp. 48–55.

4. Lashinsky, A. "Search and Enjoy." Fortune, January 22, 2007, pp. 70–82.

5. Lashinsky, "Where Does Google Go Next?"

6. Hof, R. D. "Google: What Goes Up . . . ." *BusinessWeek,* April 14, 2008, pp. 21–22.

7. Lashinsky, "Search and Enjoy."

8. Holahan, C. "Google: The Hollow Echo of a Click." *BusinessWeek,* March 10, 2008, p. 36; Hof, "Google: What Goes Up. . . ."

9. Lashinsky, "Where Does Google Go Next?"

10. Lashinsky, "Search and Enjoy."

11. Meyer, J. P., and N. J. Allen. *Commitment in the Workplace.* Thousand Oaks, CA: Sage, 1997.

12. Hart, R. "Born in the USA: Think You Know What Hyundai Is About? Think Again." *Autoweek,* May 23, 2005, p. 20. Retrieved August 19, 2005, from the LexisNexis database.

13. Ihlwan, M., and C. Dawson. "Building a 'Camry Fighter': Can Hyundai Transform Itself into One of the World's Top Auto Makers?" *BusinessWeek,* September 6, 2004, p. 62. Retrieved August 19, 2005, from the LexisNexis database.

14. "A Better Drive: Hyundai Motor." *The Economist,* May 21, 2005. Retrieved August 19, 2005, from the LexisNexis database.

15. Ihlwan, M.; L. Armstrong; and M. Eldam. "Kissing Clunkers Goodbye." *BusinessWeek,* May 17, 2004, p. 45. Retrieved August 19, 2005, from the LexisNexis database.

16. Barney, J. B. "Looking Inside for Competitive Advantage." In *Strategic Human Resource Management,* ed. R. S. Schuler and S. E. Jackson. Malden, MA: Blackwell, 1999, pp. 128–41.

17. Friedman, T. L. *The World Is Flat: A Brief History of the Twenty-First Century.* New York: Farrar, Straus, & Giroux, 2005.

18. Aguinis, H., and C.A. Henle. "The Search for Universals in Cross-Cultural Organizational Behavior." In *Organizational Behavior: The State of the Science,* ed. J. Greenberg. Mahwah, NJ: Lawrence Erlbaum Associates, 2003, pp. 373–411.

19. Mokoto, R. "Designing an Identity to Make a Brand Fly." *New York Times,* November 6, 2003, p. 10. Retrieved August 20, 2005, from the LexisNexis database.

20. "Lime Coke Dashes to Launch." *The Grocer,* March 5, 2005, p. 76. Retrieved August 20, 2005, from the Lexis-Nexis database.

21. Mokoto, "Designing an Identity."

22. Serwer, A. "Southwest Airlines: The Hottest Thing in the Sky." *Fortune,* March 8, 2004, http://www.mutualofamerica.com/articles/Fortune/March04/fortune.asp (accessed August 20, 2005).

23. Welbourne, T. M., and A. O. Andrews. "Predicting the Performance of Initial Public Offerings: Should Human Resource Management Be in the Equation?" *Academy of Management Journal* 39 (1996), pp. 891–919.

24. Levering and Moskowitz, "In Good Company."

25. Fulmer, I. S.; B. Gerhart; and K. S. Scott. "Are the 100 Best Better? An Empirical Investigation of the Relationship between Being a 'Great Place to Work' and Firm Performance." *Personnel Psychology* 56 (2003), pp. 965–93.

26. Pfeffer, J., and J. F. Veiga. "Putting People First for Organizational Success." *Academy of Management Executive* 13 (1999), pp. 37–48.

27. Kerlinger, F. N., and H. B. Lee. *Foundations of Behavioral Research.* Fort Worth, TX: Harcourt, 2000.

28. Bacon, F.; M. Silverthorne; and L. Jardine. *The New Organon.* Cambridge: Cambridge University Press, 2000.

29. Campbell, J. P. "The Role of Theory in Industrial and Organizational Psychology." In *Handbook of Industrial and Organizational Psychology,* Vol. 1, ed. M. D. Dunnette and L. M. Hough. Palo Alto, CA: Consulting Psychologists Press, 1990, pp. 39–74.

30. Whetten, D. A. "What Constitutes a Theoretical Contribution?" *Academy of Management Review* 14 (1989), pp. 490–95.

31. Locke, K. "The Grounded Theory Approach to Qualitative Research." In *Measuring and Analyzing Behavior in Organizations,* ed. F. Drasgow and N. Schmitt. San Francisco, CA: Jossey-Bass, 2002, pp. 17–43.

32. Locke, E. A., and G. P. Latham. "What Should We Do About Motivation Theory? Six Recommendations for the Twenty-First Century." *Academy of Management Review* 29 (2004), pp. 388–403.

33. Herzberg, F.; B. Mausner; and B. B. Snyderman. *The Motivation to Work.* New York: John Wiley & Sons, 1959; Taylor, F. W. *The Principles of Scientific Management.* New York: Harper & Row, 1911.

34. Peterson, S. J., and F. Luthans. "The Impact of Financial and Nonfinancial Incentives on Business-Unit Outcomes over Time." *Journal of Applied Psychology* 91 (2006), pp. 156–65.

35. Hogan, R. "In Defense of Personality Measurement: New Wine for Old Whiners." *Human Performance* 18 (2005), pp. 331–41.

36. Cohen, J.; P. Cohen; S. G. West; and L. S. Aiken. *Applied Multiple Regression/Correlation Analysis for the Behavioral Sciences.* Mahwah, NJ: Lawrence Erlbaum Associates, 2003.

37. McGrath, B. "The Professor of Baseball." *The New Yorker,* July 14, 2003, http://www.newyorker.com/archive/2003/07/14/030714fa_fact1 (accessed June 9, 2008).

38. Ibid.

39. Lewis, M. *Moneyball.* New York: W. W. Norton, 2003.

40. Miliard, M. "Stat Man." *The Boston Phoenix,* April 2, 2008, http://thephoenix.com/Boston/Life/59029-Stat-man/ (accessed June 9, 2008).

41. Lederer, R. "Breakfast with Bill James." *Baseball Beat,* February 28, 2005, http://baseballanalysts.com/archives/2005/02/breakfast_with.php (accessed June 9, 2008).

42. Shadish, W. R.; T. D. Cook; and D. T. Campbell. *Experimental and Quasi-Experimental Designs for Generalized Causal Inference.* Boston, MA: Houghton-Mifflin, 2002.

43. Stajkovic, A. D., and F. Luthans. "A Meta-Analysis of the Effects of Organizational Behavior Modification on Task Performance, 1975–1995." *Academy of Management Journal* 40 (1997), pp. 1122–49.

44. Lashinsky, "Where Does Google Go Next?"

45. Lashinsky, "Search and Enjoy."

46. Hamel, G. "Break Free!" *Fortune,* October 1, 2007, pp. 119–26.

PERFORMANCE and COMMITMENT

● ● learning **OBJECTIVES**

After reading this chapter, you should be able to:

2.1 Define job performance and organizational commitment.

2.2 Define task performance and explain how organizations identify key task behaviors.

2.3 Understand citizenship behavior, and describe some specific examples of it.

2.4 Understand counterproductive behavior, and describe some specific examples of it.

2.5 Describe the three types of organizational commitment.

2.6 Understand the four primary responses to negative events at work.

2.7 Describe examples of psychological withdrawal and physical withdrawal, and explain how they relate to one another.

HOME DEPOT

It's a difficult time to be a home improvement retailer. Midway through 2008, more than a million homes were in foreclosure in the United States.[1] Concerns over gas prices and more general inflation have caused some people to put off their home buying, selling, and improvement plans, creating the weakest housing market in 25 years. In May 2008, Home Depot, the Georgia-based retailer, reported a 66 percent drop in first-quarter profits, with sales at most of its stores falling by 6.5 percent.[2] The economic downturn hit at an already difficult time for Home Depot. The company was still dealing with the end of Bob Nardelli's controversial six-year tenure as CEO.[3] Nardelli, a former executive at General Electric, replaced a folksy, friendly, and entrepreneurial culture with one focused on centralized operations and hard data. Although Nardelli's reign included significant growth in sales, his reduction of store personnel, his reliance on part-timers, and his focus on professional contractor customers were credited with a decline in the company's morale and reputation. Indeed, the retailer dropped from first to last among major retailers in the American Customer Satisfaction Index in 2005.[4]

This situation presents quite a challenge for new CEO Frank Blake and his head of human resources, Tim Crow.[5] Crow, who had worked for Sears and Kmart before coming to Home Depot, had served as Nardelli's senior vice president of organization, talent, and performance systems. Now he's trying to find ways to bolster the job performance and organizational commitment of Home Depot's workforce as the company tries to navigate its way through the economic downturn. One initiative is Crow's "Aprons on the Floor" program, which encourages employees to find ways to cut costs in operations so that more money can be funneled into putting employees on the sales floor.[6] Such efforts could improve service by making Home Depot's huge aisles a little less lonely for wandering customers. Crow also has revamped the company's training programs to bolster employee skill and performance. The new approach deemphasizes "e-learning," relying instead on more self-directed, hands-on learning; more collaboration; and helping among the rank-and-file. Employees also earn financial incentives for being certified as experts in areas that could impact their job performance.

With respect to organizational commitment, Crow notes that Home Depot's "attrition rate" is better than that of most retailers, meaning that it loses fewer employees than the typical store-based business.[7] Still, the new management team is focusing on ways to boost morale, given the state of the economy and the fallout from Nardelli's tenure. One new program awards "Homer Badges" to employees who are recognized for "living the company's core values." Employees who earn three badges receive a cash bonus. Another new program is "Success Sharing," in which stores that achieve certain sales goals receive cash bonuses for all employees. Such initiatives are meant to increase the degree to which employees identify with the organization so that they see its successes (and its mistakes) as their own. Crow believes these programs are working, as Home Depot's rate of voluntary attrition is down 14 percent since 2007.[8] Of course, Crow acknowledges that these sorts of programs can be expensive, given the economy. "A lot of the things we are doing with our associates cost money," he notes, "but we are betting that it's the right thing to do."

PERFORMANCE AND COMMITMENT

We begin our journey through the integrative model of organizational behavior with the two primary outcomes in OB: job performance and organizational commitment. Most managers have two primary goals for their employees: that they perform their jobs well and that they remain a member of their current organization. Similarly, most employees have two kinds of questions about their working lives: what does it take to be a good performer and what factors make them want to stay in their current position? Given the importance of these two outcomes, it's critical to understand what performance and commitment represent, and what concepts affect them. This chapter will provide a detailed overview of performance and commitment. In the remainder of this book, you'll work your way through our integrative model to understand the concepts that drive those two important outcomes.

● ● **2.1**

Define job performance and organizational commitment.

Job performance is defined as the value of the set of employee behaviors that contribute, either positively or negatively, to organizational goal accomplishment.[9] Employees who are "good performers" engage in specific behaviors that create positive value for the firm. Employees who are "bad performers" engage in specific behaviors that hinder organizational goal accomplishment. Organizational commitment is defined as the desire on the part of an employee to remain a member of the organization.[10] Employees who are committed to their organization improve the organization's "retention" because they stay around for the long term. Employees who are not committed are more likely to "turn over"— voluntarily quitting their job and ending their membership with the organization. The first half of this chapter will describe the various behaviors that capture an employee's job performance. The second half will then explore the psychological dynamics of commitment, while also describing what happens when employees aren't committed.

JOB PERFORMANCE

Our definition of job performance raises a number of important questions. Specifically, you might be wondering which employee behaviors fall under the umbrella heading of "job performance." In other words, from an employee's perspective, what exactly does it mean to be a "good performer"? We could probably spend an entire chapter just listing various behaviors that are relevant to job performance. However, those behaviors generally fit into three broad categories.[11] Two categories are task performance and citizenship behavior, both of which contribute positively to the organization. The third category is counterproductive behavior, which contributes negatively to the organization. In our **OB on Screen** feature, you'll find an example of employees who demonstrate various levels of all three aspects of job performance. The sections that follow describe these broad categories of job performance in greater detail.

Task Performance

Task performance includes employee behaviors that are directly involved in the transformation of organizational resources into the goods or services that the organization produces. If you read a description of a job in an employment ad online, that description will focus on task performance behaviors— the tasks, duties, and responsibilities that are a core part of the job. Put differently, task performance is the set of explicit obligations that an employee must fulfill to receive compensation and continued

Managers have two primary goals for their employees: that they perform their jobs well and that they remain committed to the company. This chapter will focus on the details behind why some employees perform well and stay with a company, and why others do not.

employment. For a flight attendant, task performance includes announcing and demonstrating safety and emergency procedures and distributing food and beverages to passengers. For a firefighter, task performance includes searching burning buildings to locate fire victims and operating equipment to put out fires. For an accountant, task performance involves preparing, examining, and analyzing accounting records for accuracy and completeness. Finally, for an advertising executive, task performance includes developing advertising campaigns and preparing and delivering presentations to clients.[12]

●● 2.2

Define task performance and explain how organizations identify key task behaviors.

Although the specific activities that constitute task performance differ widely from one job to another, task performance also can be understood in terms of more general categories. One way of categorizing task performance is to consider the extent to which the context of the job is routine or changing. Routine task performance involves well-known responses to demands that occur in a normal, routine, or otherwise predictable way. In these cases, employees tend to act in habitual or programmed ways that vary little from one instance to another. As an example of a routine task activity, you may recall watching an expressionless flight attendant robotically demonstrate how to insert the seatbelt tongue into the seatbelt buckle before your flight takes off. Seatbelts haven't really changed since . . . oh . . . 1920, so the instructions to passengers tend to be conveyed the same way, over and over again.

In contrast, adaptive task performance, or more commonly "adaptability," involves employee responses to task demands that are novel, unusual, or, at the very least, unpredictable.[13] For example, on August 2, 2005, Air France Flight 358, carrying 297 passengers and 12 crew members from Paris, France, to Toronto, Canada, skidded off the runway during its landing and into a ravine. Amid smoke and flames, the flight attendants quickly responded to the emergency and assisted three-quarters of the 297 passengers safely off the plane within 52 seconds, before the emergency response team arrived. One minute later, the remaining passengers and 12 crew members were out safely.[14] From this example, you can see that flight attendants' task performance shifted from activities such as providing safety demonstrations and handing out beverages to performing emergency

OB on Screen

Monsters, Inc.

> I'm in the zone today, Sullivan. I'm gonna do some serious scaring, putting up some big numbers.

With these words, Randall (the evil-looking purple monster) challenges Sulley (the big, blue, furry lug) to match his task performance in *Monsters, Inc.* (Pixar, 2001, released by Disney).[15] You see, the source of electricity in the monster world is the screams triggered by monster "scarers" who enter the closet doors of unsuspecting human children at night.

Sulley and Randall are both good when it comes to core task performance. They are the two best scarers at Monsters, Inc., and compete with each other throughout the film for the all-time "scare" record. The similarity between Sulley and Randall ends there, however. Sulley has a positive attitude about his job and is more than willing to go above and beyond to help his coworkers and the organization. For example, in one scene, Sulley offers to stay late to do some paperwork for his coworker Mike (the green, pear-shaped guy) so that Mike can keep his date with Celia, his demanding, serpent-haired girlfriend.

Randall would never consider engaging in these sorts of citizenship behaviors.

In terms of counterproductive behavior, much of the film centers on Sulley's covert attempt to return a two-year-old girl named Boo to her bedroom after she finds her way into the monster world. Direct contact with human children is strictly forbidden at Monsters, Inc., because the monsters believe that even the slightest touch from a child can be lethal. Sulley is therefore breaking company rules, though Randall's indiscretions put Sulley's to shame. Randall assaults and kidnaps others to test an illegal (and potentially deadly) new method for extracting energy from children. Fortunately, Sulley (and Mike) are around to try to save the day. Do they return Boo safely to her bedroom? You'll have to watch to find out. ❖

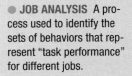
● **JOB ANALYSIS** A process used to identify the sets of behaviors that represent "task performance" for different jobs.

organizations identify the sets of behaviors that represent "task performance" for different jobs. Many organizations identify task performance behaviors by conducting a job analysis. Although there are many different ways to conduct a job analysis, most boil down to the following three steps. First, a list of all the activities involved in a job is generated. This list generally results from data from several sources, including observations, surveys, and interviews of employees. Second, each activity on this list is rated by "subject matter experts" according to things like the importance and frequency of the activity. Subject matter experts generally have experience performing the job or managing people who perform the job and therefore are in a position to judge the degree to which specific activities contribute to the organization. Third, activities that are rated highly in terms of their importance and frequency are retained and used to define task performance.

Those retained behaviors often find their way into the measures that managers use to evaluate the task performance of employees. Men's Wearhouse provides a good example of an organization that uses task performance information in this way.[17] The company first gathers information about the

Flight attendants are required to share safety knowledge with passengers on every flight. This is an example of routine task performance. On the few occasions that they are expected to respond to an emergency and follow through with that knowledge, they would be exhibiting adaptive task performance.

procedures to save passengers' lives. As shown in Table 2-1,[16] the behaviors involved in adaptability are diverse and have become increasingly important in today's economy.

Now that we've given you a general understanding of task performance behaviors, you might be wondering how

TABLE 2-1	Behaviors Involved in Adaptability

Behavior	Example of Activities
Handling emergencies or crisis situations	Quickly analyzing options for dealing with danger or crises and their implications; making split-second decisions based on clear and focused thinking
Handling work stress	Remaining composed and cool when faced with difficult circumstances or a highly demanding workload or schedule; acting as a calming and settling influence to whom others can look for guidance
Solving problems creatively	Turning problems upside-down and inside-out to find fresh new approaches; integrating seemingly unrelated information and developing creative solutions
Dealing with uncertain and unpredictable work situations	Readily and easily changing gears in response to unpredictable or unexpected events and circumstances; effectively adjusting plans, goals, actions, or priorities to deal with changing situations
Learning work tasks, technologies, and work situations	Quickly and proficiently learning new methods or how to perform previously unlearned tasks; anticipating changes in work demands and searching for and participating in assignments or training to prepare for these changes
Demonstrating interpersonal adaptability	Being flexible and open-minded when dealing with others; listening to and considering others' viewpoints and opinions and altering own opinion when it is appropriate to do so
Demonstrating cultural adaptability	Willingly adjusting behavior or appearance as necessary to comply with or show respect for others' values and customs; understanding the implications of one's actions and adjusting one's approach to maintain positive relationships with other groups, organizations, or cultures

Source: E. D. Pulakos, S. Arad, M. A. Donovan, and K. E. Plamondon, "Adaptability in the Workplace: Development of a Taxonomy of Adaptive Performance," *Journal of Applied Psychology* 85 (2000), pp. 612–24. Copyright © 2000 by the American Psychological Association. Adapted with permission. No further reproduction or distribution is permitted without permission from the American Psychological Association.

Performance evaluations at Men's Wearhouse are based on a number of task performance behaviors rather than sales goals. Would you prefer to be evaluated this way if you worked as a wardrobe consultant for the company?

● OCCUPATIONAL INFOR-
MATION NETWORK An
online database that
includes the characteristics
of most jobs in terms of
tasks, behaviors, and the
required knowledge, skills,
and abilities.

course, O*NET represents only a first step in figuring out the important tasks for a given job. Many organizations ask their employees to perform tasks that their competitors do not, ensuring that their workforce performs jobs in a unique and valuable way. O*NET cannot capture those sorts of unique task requirements—the "numerous small decisions" that separate the most effective organizations from their competitors.

For example, the authors of a book entitled *Nuts* identify "fun" as one of the dominant values of Southwest Airlines.[19] Southwest believes that people are willing to work more productively and creatively in an environment that includes humor and laughter. Consistent with this belief, flight attendant task performance at Southwest includes not only generic flight attendant activities such as those identified by O*NET, but also activities that reflect a sense of humor and playfulness. As an example, effective flight attendants tell jokes over the intercom such as, "We'll be dimming the lights in the cabin . . . pushing the light-bulb button will turn your reading light on. However, pushing the flight attendant button will not turn your flight attendant on."[20] Thus, though O*NET may be a good place to start, the task information from the database should be supplemented with information regarding behaviors that support the organization's values and strategy.

employee's on-the-job behavior. Table 2-2 lists some of the factors included in the performance evaluation for wardrobe consultants at Men's Wearhouse. After the behavior information is gathered, senior managers provide feedback and coaching to the employee about which types of behaviors he or she needs to change to improve. The feedback is framed as constructive criticism meant to improve an employee's behavior. Put yourself in the place of a Men's Wearhouse wardrobe consultant for a moment. Wouldn't you rather have your performance evaluated on the basis of the behaviors in Table 2-2 rather than some overall index of sales? After all, those behaviors are completely within your control, and the feedback you receive from your boss will be more informative than the simple directive to "sell more suits next year than you did this year."

When organizations find it impractical to use job analysis to identify the set of behaviors needed to define task performance, they can turn to a database the government has created to help with that important activity. The Occupational Information Network (or O*NET) is an online database that includes, among other things, the characteristics of most jobs in terms of tasks, behaviors, and the required knowledge, skills, and abilities (http://online. onetcenter.org).[18] Figure 2-1 shows the O*NET output for a flight attendant's position, including many of the tasks discussed previously in this chapter. Of

TABLE	2-2	Performance Review Form for a Wardrobe Consultant at Men's Wearhouse

Important Task Behaviors

Greets, interviews, and tapes all customers properly.

Participates in team selling.

Is familiar with merchandise carried at local competitors.

Ensures proper alteration revenue collection.

Treats customers in a warm and caring manner.

Utilizes tailoring staff for fittings whenever possible.

Involves management in all customer problems.

Waits on all customers, without prejudging based on attire, age, or gender.

Contributes to store maintenance and stock work.

Arrives at work at the appointed time and is ready to begin immediately.

Dresses and grooms to the standards set by TMW.

Citizenship Behavior

Citizenship behavior is defined as voluntary employee activities that may or may not be rewarded but that contribute to the organization by improving the overall quality of the setting in which work takes place.[21] Have you ever had a coworker or fellow student who was always willing to help someone who was struggling? Who always attended optional meetings or social functions to support his or her colleagues? Who always maintained a good attitude, even in trying times? We tend to call those people "good citizens" or "good soldiers."[22] High levels of citizenship behavior earn them such titles. Although there are many different types of behaviors that might seem to fit the definition of citizenship behavior, research suggests two main categories that differ according to who benefits from the activity: coworkers or the organization (see Figure 2-2).[23]

● ● **2.3**

Understand citizenship behavior, and describe some specific examples of it.

The first category of citizenship behavior is the one with which you're most likely to be familiar: **interpersonal citizenship behavior.** Such behaviors benefit coworkers and colleagues and involve assisting, supporting, and developing other organizational members in a way that goes beyond normal job expectations.[24] For example, *helping* involves assisting coworkers who have heavy workloads, aiding them with personal matters, and showing new employees the ropes when they first arrive on the job. *Courtesy* refers to keeping coworkers informed about matters that are relevant to them. Some employees have a tendency to keep relevant facts and events secret. Good citizens do the opposite; they keep others in the loop because they never know what information might be useful to someone else. *Sportsmanship* involves maintaining a good attitude with coworkers, even when they've done something annoying or when the unit is going through tough times. Whining and complaining are contagious; good citizens avoid being the squeaky wheel who frequently makes mountains out of molehills.

The second category of citizenship behavior is **organizational citizenship behavior.** These behaviors benefit the larger organization by supporting and defending the company, working to improve its operations, and being especially loyal to it.[25] For example, *voice* involves speaking up and offering constructive suggestions for change. Good citizens react to bad rules or policies by constructively trying to change them as opposed to passively complaining about them.[26] *Civic virtue* refers to participating in the company's operations at a deeper-than-normal level by attending voluntary meetings and functions, reading and keeping up with organizational announcements, and keeping abreast of business news that affects the company. *Boosterism* means representing the organization in a positive way when out in public, away from the office, and away from work. Think of friends you've had who worked for a restaurant. Did they always say good things about the restaurant when talking to you and keep any "kitchen horror stories" to themselves? If so, they were being good citizens by engaging in high levels of boosterism.

As you've probably realized, citizenship behaviors are relevant in virtually any job, regardless of the particular nature

● **CITIZENSHIP BEHAVIOR** Voluntary employee activities that may or may not be rewarded but that contribute to the organization by improving the overall quality of the setting in which work takes place.

● **INTERPERSONAL CITIZENSHIP BEHAVIOR** Voluntary behaviors that benefit coworkers and colleagues such as helping, courtesy, and sportsmanship.

● **ORGANIZATIONAL CITIZENSHIP BEHAVIOR** Voluntary behaviors that benefit the larger organization such as voice, civic virtue, and boosterism.

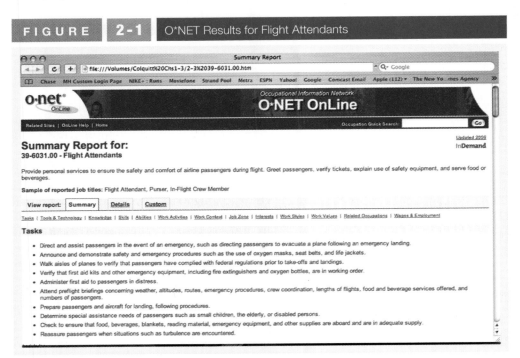

FIGURE 2-1 O*NET Results for Flight Attendants

O*NET, or Occupational Information Network, is an online government database that lists the characteristics of most jobs and the knowledge required for each. This sample is for the job of flight attendant.

The rapid rise in the number of service jobs such as retail sales and customer service means that managers more than ever need to maintain a positive work environment. High levels of citizenship behavior can create that sort of work environment.

FIGURE 2-2 Types of Citizenship Behaviors

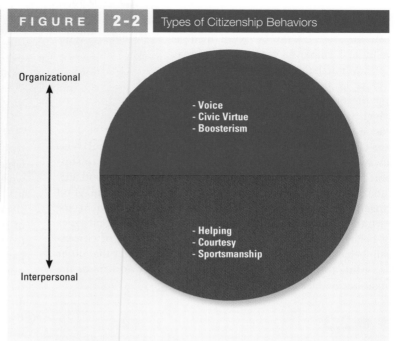

Organizational

- Voice
- Civic Virtue
- Boosterism

- Helping
- Courtesy
- Sportsmanship

Interpersonal

"**Citizenship behaviors are relevant in virtually any job, regardless of the particular nature of its tasks, and these behaviors have clear benefits in terms of the effectiveness of work units and organizations.**"

of its tasks,[27] and these behaviors have clear benefits in terms of the effectiveness of work units and organizations.[28] As an example, research conducted in a paper mill found that the quantity and quality of crew output was higher in crews that included more good citizens.[29] Research on 30 restaurants also showed that higher levels of citizenship behavior promoted higher revenue, better operating efficiency, higher customer satisfaction, higher performance quality, less food waste, and fewer customer complaints.[30] Thus, it seems clear that citizenship behaviors have a significant influence on the bottom line.

From an employee's perspective, it may be tempting to discount the importance of citizenship behaviors—to just focus on your own job tasks and leave aside any "extra" stuff. After all, citizenship behaviors appear to be voluntary and optional, whereas task duties are not. However, discounting citizenship behaviors is a bad idea because supervisors do not always view

such actions as optional. In fact, research on computer salespeople, insurance agents, petrochemical salespeople, pharmaceutical sales managers, office furniture makers, sewing machine operators, U.S. Air Force mechanics, and first-tour U.S. Army soldiers has shown that citizenship behaviors relate strongly to supervisor evaluations of job performance, even when differences in task performance are also considered.[31] As we discuss in our **OB Internationally** feature, the tendency for supervisors to consider citizenship behaviors in evaluating overall job performance appears to hold even across countries with vastly different cultures.[32] Of course, this issue has a lot of relevance to you, given that in most organizations, supervisors' evaluations of job performance play significant roles in determining pay and promotions. Indeed, employee citizenship behavior has been found to influence the salary and promotion recommendations people receive, over and above their task performance.[33] Put simply, it pays to be a good citizen.

Counterproductive Behavior

Now we move from the "good soldiers" to the "bad apples." Whereas task performance and citizenship behavior refer to employee activities that help the organization achieve its goals and objectives, other activities in which employees engage do just the opposite. The third broad category of job performance is **counterproductive behavior**, defined as employee behaviors that intentionally hinder organizational goal accomplishment. The word "intentionally" is a key aspect of this definition; these are things that employees mean to do, not things they accidentally do. Although there are many different kinds of counterproductive behaviors, research suggests that—like task performance and citizenship behavior—they can be grouped into more specific categories (see Figure 2-3).[34]

●● 2.4

Understand counterproductive behavior, and describe some specific examples of it.

Property deviance refers to behaviors that harm the organization's assets and possessions. For example, *sabotage* represents the purposeful destruction of physical equipment, organizational processes, or company products. Do you know what a laser disc is? Probably not—and the reason you don't is because of sabotage. A company called DiscoVision (a subsidiary of MCA) manufactured laser discs in the late 1970s, with popular movie titles like *Smokey and the Bandit* and *Jaws* retailing for $15.95. Although this level matches the price of DVDs today, it was far less than the $50–$100 needed to buy videocassettes (which were of inferior quality) at the time. Unfortunately, laser discs had to be manufactured in "clean rooms" because specks of dust or debris could cause the image on the TV to freeze, repeat, skip, or drop out. When MCA merged with IBM in 1979, the morale of the employees fell, and counterproductive behaviors began to occur. Specifically, employees sabotaged the devices that measured the cleanliness of the rooms and began eating

● **COUNTERPRODUCTIVE BEHAVIOR** Behaviors that intentionally hinder organizational goal accomplishment.

● **PROPERTY DEVIANCE** Behaviors that intentionally harm the organization's assets and possessions, such as sabotage and theft.

Counterproductive behavior by employees can be destructive to the organization's goals. In some settings, such as a restaurant, it can even be a problem for customers.

OB Internationally

As we have already explained, citizenship behavior tends to be viewed as relatively voluntary because it is not often explicitly outlined in job descriptions or directly rewarded. However, people in organizations may vary in their beliefs regarding the degree to which citizenship behavior is truly voluntary, and such differences could have important implications.[35] One might expect that different cultures would weigh citizenship sorts of actions differently, making citizenship more mandatory in some cultures and more voluntary in others. After all, it is widely believed that the culture in countries like the United States, Canada, and the Netherlands encourages behaviors that support competition and individual achievement. In contrast, the culture in countries like China, Colombia, and Portugal encourages behaviors that promote cooperation and group interests over self-interests.[36] On the basis of these cultural differences, it is only natural to expect that people from the former set of countries would consider citizenship performance relatively unimportant compared with people from the latter set of countries.

In reality, however, the findings from one recent study comparing Canadian and Chinese managers found that this cultural stereotype was simply not true.[37] Managers in both countries not only took citizenship behavior into account when evaluating overall job performance, but the weight they gave to citizenship behavior in their overall evaluation of employees was the same. One explanation for this result is that the realities of running effective business organizations in a global economy have a significantly stronger impact

on managerial practices than do cultural norms. So what is the lesson here? Although employees may view citizenship behavior as voluntary because it is not spelled out in job descriptions or explicitly rewarded, managers take these behaviors into account, and this evaluation appears to be true across countries with vastly different cultural traditions. ❖

PRODUCTION DEVIANCE Behaviors that intentionally reduce the efficiency of work output, such as wasting resources and substance abuse.

POLITICAL DEVIANCE Behaviors that intentionally disadvantage other employees, such as gossiping and incivility.

PERSONAL AGGRESSION Hostile verbal and physical actions directed toward other employees, such as harassment and abuse.

in the rooms—even "popping" their potato chip bags to send food particles into the air. This sabotage eventually created a 90 percent disc failure rate that completely alienated customers. As a result, despite its much lower production costs and higher quality picture, the laser disc disappeared, and the organizations that supported the technology suffered incredible losses.[38]

Theft represents another form of property deviance and can be just as expensive as sabotage (if not more). Research has shown that up to three-quarters of all employees have engaged in counterproductive behaviors such as theft, and the cost of these behaviors is staggering.[39] For example, one study estimated that 47 percent of store inventory shrinkage was due to employee theft and that this type of theft costs organizations approximately $14.6 billion per year.[40] Maybe you've had friends who worked at a restaurant or bar and been lucky enough to get discounted (or even free) food and drinks whenever you wanted. Clearly that circumstance is productive for you, but it's quite counterproductive from the perspective of the organization.

Production deviance is also directed against the organization but focuses specifically on reducing the efficiency of work output. *Wasting resources* is the most common form of production deviance, when employees use too many materials or too much time to do too little work. Manufacturing employees who use too much wood or metal are wasting resources, as are restaurant employees who use too many ingredients when preparing the food. *Substance abuse* represents another form of production deviance. If employees abuse drugs or alcohol while on the job or shortly before coming to work, then the efficiency of their production will be compromised because their work will be done more slowly and less accurately.

In contrast to property and production deviance, **political deviance** refers to behaviors that intentionally disadvantage other individuals rather than the larger organization. *Gossiping*—casual conversations about other people in which the facts are not confirmed as true—is one form of political deviance. Everyone has experienced gossip at some point in time and knows the emotions people feel when they discover that other people have been talking about them. Such

FIGURE 2-3 Types of Counterproductive Behaviors

Source: Adapted from S. L. Robinson and R. J. Bennett, "A Typology of Deviant Workplace Behaviors: A Multidimensional Scaling Study," *Academy of Management Journal* 38 (1995), pp. 555–72.

behaviors undermine the morale of both friendship groups and work groups. *Incivility* represents communication that is rude, impolite, discourteous, and lacking in good manners.[41]

Taken one by one, these political forms of counterproductive behavior may not seem particularly serious to most organizations. However, in the aggregate, acts of political deviance can create an organizational climate characterized by distrust and unhealthy competitiveness. Beyond the productivity losses that result from a lack of cooperation among employees, organizations with this type of climate likely cannot retain good employees. Moreover, there is some evidence that gossip and incivility can "spiral"—meaning that they gradually get worse and worse until some tipping point—after which more serious forms of interpersonal actions can occur.[42]

> **"…there is some evidence that gossip and incivility can 'spiral'— meaning that they gradually get worse and worse until some tipping point…"**

Those more serious interpersonal actions may involve **personal aggression**, defined as hostile verbal and physical actions directed toward other employees. *Harassment* falls under this heading and occurs when employees are subjected to unwanted physical contact or verbal remarks from a colleague. *Abuse* also falls under this heading; it occurs when an employee is assaulted or endangered in such a way that physical and psychological injuries may occur. You might be surprised to know that even the most extreme forms of personal aggression are actually quite prevalent in organizations; one employee

● WITHDRAWAL
BEHAVIOR A set of actions
that employees perform to
avoid the work situation.

is killed by a current or former employee on average each week in the United States.[43] Acts of personal aggression also can be quite costly to organizations. For example, Mitsubishi Motor Manufacturing of America settled a class action sexual harassment lawsuit in 1998 for $34 million after women at a plant in Normal, Illinois, complained of widespread and routine groping, fondling, lewd jokes, lewd behavior, and pornographic graffiti.[44]

Three points should be noted about counterproductive behavior. First, there is evidence that people who engage in one form of counterproductive behavior also engage in others.[45] In other words, such behaviors tend to represent a pattern of behavior rather than isolated incidents. In this sense, there really are "bad apples." Second, like citizenship behavior, counterproductive behavior is relevant to any job. It doesn't matter what the job entails; there are going to be things to steal, resources to waste, and people to be uncivil toward. Third, it is often surprising which employees engage in counterproductive behavior. You might be tempted to guess that poor task performers will be the ones who do these sorts of things, but there is only a weak negative correlation between task performance and counterproductive behavior.[46] Sometimes the best task performers are the ones who can best get away with counterproductive actions because they are less likely to be suspected or blamed.

ORGANIZATIONAL COMMITMENT

As a manager or an employee, you'll probably agree that it's nice to work with a coworker who engages in high levels of task performance, frequent instances of citizenship behavior, and little or no counterproductive behaviors. Clearly that's the best-case scenario, and only one thing could disrupt that rosy picture: losing that coworker to a competitor. Unfortunately, such a scenario is not far-fetched. One recent survey by the Society for Human Resource Management showed that 75 percent of employees were looking for a new job.[47] Of those job seekers, 43 percent were looking for more money, and 35 percent were reacting to a sense of dissatisfaction with their cur-

rent employer. Organizations should be worried about these sorts of numbers because the cost of turnover can be very high. Estimates suggest that it costs about 0.5 times the annual salary + benefits to replace an hourly worker, 1.5 times the annual salary + benefits to replace a salaried employee, and as much as 5 times the annual salary + benefits to replace an executive.[48] Why so expensive? Those estimates include various costs, including the administrative costs involved in the separation, recruitment expenses, screening costs, and training and orientation expenses for the new hire.[49] They also include "hidden costs" due to decreased morale, lost organizational knowledge, and lost productivity.

Organizational commitment influences whether an employee stays a member of the organization (is retained) or leaves to pursue another job (turns over). Employees who are not committed to their organizations engage in withdrawal behavior, defined as a set of actions that employees perform to avoid the work situation—behaviors that may eventually culminate in quitting the organization.[50] The relationship between commitment and withdrawal is illustrated in Figure 2-4. Some employees may exhibit much more commitment than withdrawal, finding themselves on the green end of the continuum. Leaving aside personal or family issues, these employees are not "retention risks" for the moment. Other employees exhibit much more withdrawal than commitment, finding themselves on the red end of the continuum. These employees are retention risks—teetering on the edge of quitting their jobs. The sections that follow review both commitment and withdrawal in more detail.

One key to understanding organizational commitment is to understand where it comes from. In other words, what creates a desire to remain a member of an organization? To explore this question, consider the following scenario: You've been working full-time for your employer for around five years. The company gave you your start in the business, and you've enjoyed your time there. Your salary is competitive enough that you were able to purchase a home in a good school system, which is important because you have one young child and another on the way. Now assume that a competing firm contacted you

Employees who are committed to an organization often feel an emotional attachment to it, as well as a sense of obligation to remain loyal.

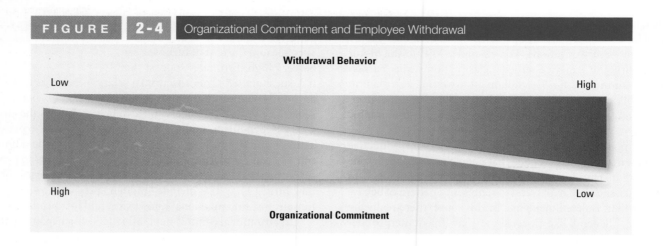

FIGURE 2-4 Organizational Commitment and Employee Withdrawal

Withdrawal Behavior

Low   High

High   Low

Organizational Commitment

while you were attending a conference and offered you a similar position in its company. What kinds of things might you think about? If you created a list to organize your thoughts, what kinds of issues would appear on that list?

One potential list is shown in Table 2-3. The left-hand column

● ● **2.5**

Describe the three types of organizational commitment.

reflects some emotional reasons for staying with the current organization, including feelings about friendships, the atmo-

sphere or culture of the company, and a sense of enjoyment when completing job duties. These sorts of emotional reasons create **affective commitment**, defined as a desire to remain a member of an organization due to an emotional attachment to, and involvement with, that organization.[51] Put simply, you stay because you *want* to. The middle column reflects some cost-based reasons for staying, including issues of salary, benefits, and promotions, as well as concerns about uprooting a family. These sorts of reasons create **continuance commitment**, defined as a desire to remain a member of an organization because of an awareness of the costs associated with leaving it.[52] In other words, you stay because you *need* to. The right-hand column reflects some obligation-based reasons for staying with the current organization, including a sense that a debt is owed to a boss, a colleague, or the larger company. These sorts of reasons create **normative commitment**, defined as a desire to remain a member of an organization due to a feeling of obliga-

TABLE 2-3 The Three Types of Organizational Commitment

What Makes Someone Want to Stay with Their Current Organization?		
Affective Commitment	*Continuance Commitment*	*Normative Commitment*
Emotion-Based Reasons	*Cost-Based Reasons*	*Obligation-Based Reasons*
Some of my best friends work in my office . . . I'd miss them if I left.	I'm due for a promotion soon . . . will I advance as quickly at the new company?	My boss has invested so much time in me, mentoring me, training me, showing me "the ropes."
I really like the atmosphere at my current job . . . it's fun and relaxed.	My salary and benefits get us a nice house in our town . . . the cost of living is higher in this new area.	My organization gave me my start . . . they hired me when others thought I wasn't qualified.
My current job duties are very rewarding . . . I enjoy coming to work each morning.	The school system is good here, my spouse has a good job . . . we've really "put down roots" where we are.	My employer has helped me out of a jam on a number of occasions . . . how could I leave now?
Staying because you want to.	*Staying because you need to.*	*Staying because you ought to.*

tion.[53] In this case, you stay because you *ought* to.

As shown in Figure 2-5, the three types of organizational commitment combine to create an overall sense of psychological attachment to the company. Of course, different people may weight the three types differently. One person may be very rational and cautious by nature, focusing primarily on continuance commitment when evaluating his or her overall desire to stay. Another person may be more emotional and intuitive by nature, going more on "feel" than on a calculated assessment of costs and benefits. The importance of the three commitment types also may vary over the course of a career. For example, you might prioritize affective reasons early in your work life before shifting your attention to continuance reasons as you start a family or become more established in a community. Regardless of how the three types are prioritized, however, they offer an important insight into *why* someone might be committed and what an organization can do to make employees feel more committed.

Figure 2-5 also shows that organizational commitment depends on more than just "the organization." That is, people aren't always committed to companies; they're also committed to the top management that leads the firm at a given time, the

● **CONTINUANCE COMMITMENT** A desire to remain a member of an organization because of an awareness of the costs associated with leaving it.

● **NORMATIVE COMMITMENT** A desire to remain a member of an organization due to a feeling of obligation.

● **FOCUS OF COMMITMENT** The various people, places, and things that can inspire a desire to remain a member of an organization.

department in which they work, the manager who directly supervises them, or the specific team or coworkers with whom they work most closely.[54] We use the term focus of commitment to refer to the various people, places, and things that can inspire a desire to remain a member of an organization. For example, you might choose to stay with your current employer because you are emotionally attached to your work team, worry about the costs associated with losing your company's salary and benefits package, and feel a sense of obligation to your current manager. If so, your desire to remain cuts across multiple types of commitment (affective, continuance, and normative) and multiple foci (or focuses) of commitment (work team, company, manager). Now that you're familiar with the drivers of commitment in a general sense, let's go into more depth about each type.

Affective Commitment

One way to understand the differences among the three types of commitment is to ask yourself what you would feel if you left the organization. Consider the reasons listed in the left-hand

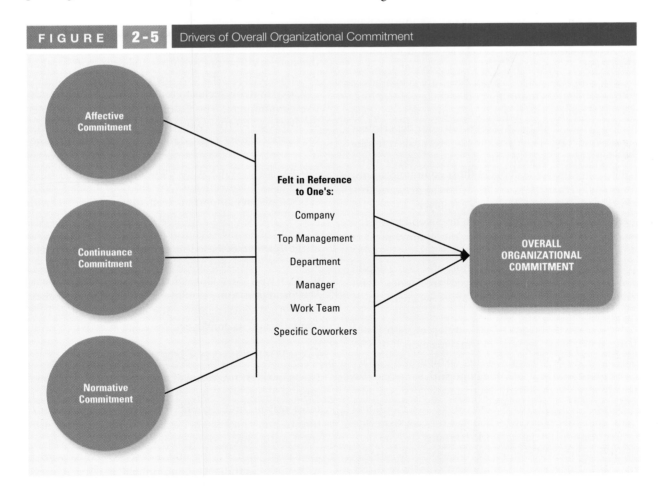

FIGURE 2-5 Drivers of Overall Organizational Commitment

Affective Commitment

Continuance Commitment

Normative Commitment

Felt in Reference to One's:

Company

Top Management

Department

Manager

Work Team

Specific Coworkers

OVERALL ORGANIZATIONAL COMMITMENT

● **EROSION MODEL** A theory that suggests that employees with fewer bonds will be most likely to quit the organization.

● **SOCIAL INFLUENCE MODEL** A theory that suggests that employees who have direct linkages with "leavers" will themselves become more likely to leave.

column of Table 2-3. What would you feel if, even after taking all those reasons into account, you decided to leave your organization to join another one? Answer: You'd feel a sense of *sadness*. Employees who feel a sense of affective commitment identify with the organization, accept that organization's goals and values, and are more willing to exert extra effort on behalf of the organization.[55]

It's safe to say that if managers could choose which type of commitment they'd like to instill in their employees, they would choose affective commitment. Moreover, when a manager looks at an employee and says, "She's committed" or "He's loyal," that manager usually is referring to a behavioral expression of affective commitment.[56] For example, employees who are affectively committed to their employer tend to engage in more interpersonal and organizational citizenship behaviors such as helping, sportsmanship, and boosterism. One meta-analysis of 22 studies with more than 6,000 participants revealed a moderately strong correlation between affective commitment and citizenship behavior.[57] (Recall that a meta-analysis averages together results from multiple studies investigating the same relationship.) Such results suggest that emotionally committed employees express that commitment by "going the extra mile" whenever they can.

Because affective commitment reflects an emotional bond to the organization, it's only natural that the emotional bonds among coworkers influence it.[58] We can therefore gain a better understanding of affective commitment if we take a closer look at the bonds that tie employees together. Assume you were given a sheet with the names of all the employees in your department or members of your class. Then assume you were asked to rate the frequency with which you communicated with each of those people, as well as the emotional depth of those communications. Those ratings could be used to create a "social network diagram" that summarizes the bonds among employees. Figure 2-6 provides a sample of such a diagram. The lines connecting the 10 members of the work unit represent the communication bonds that connect each of them, with thicker lines representing more frequent communication with more emotional depth. The diagram illustrates that some employees are "nodes," with several direct connections to other employees, whereas others remain at the fringes of the network.

The erosion model suggests that employees with fewer bonds will be most likely to quit the organization.[59] If you look at Figure 2-6, who's most at risk for turning over? That's right—the employee who only has one bond with someone else (and a relatively weak bond at that). From an affective commitment perspective, that employee is likely to feel less emotional attachment to work colleagues, which makes it easier to decide to leave the organization. Social network diagrams also can help us understand another explanation for turnover. The social influence model suggests that employees who have direct

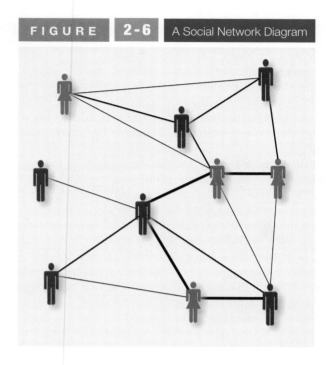

FIGURE 2-6 A Social Network Diagram

linkages with "leavers" will themselves become more likely to leave.[60] In this way, reductions in affective commitment become contagious, spreading like a disease across the work unit. Think about the damage that would be caused if the central figure in the network (the one who has linkages to five other people) became unhappy with the organization.

Cisco Systems seems to understand the importance of affective commitment. The California-based leader in networking hardware and software enjoys one of the lowest voluntary turnover rates among organizations surveyed by *Fortune* in 2004 (3 percent).[61] Cisco employees point to the fun workplace culture as a key factor, with company cafes offering movie-themed menus at Academy Awards time or "nerd lunches" during which experts discuss important tech topics. Harley-Davidson also appears to understand the importance of fostering an emotional attachment to the organization. The voluntary turnover rate at the Milwaukee-based motorcycle manufacturer is less than 2 percent, and employee surveys reveal that workers strongly identify with the culture of motorcycle riding. In fact, Harley-Davidson pays some employees to work at biker rallies.[62] These sorts of activities reinforce the emotional bonds between the company and its employees, fostering affective commitment.

Continuance Commitment

Now consider the reasons for staying listed in the middle column of Table 2-3. What would you feel if, even after taking all those reasons into account, you decided to leave your organization to join another one? Answer: You'd feel a sense of *anxiety*. Continuance commitment exists when there is a profit associated with staying and a cost associated with leaving,[63] with high continuance commitment making it very difficult to change organizations because of the steep penalties associated with the switch.[64] One factor that increases continuance commitment is the total amount of investment (in terms of time, effort, energy, etc.) an employee has made in mastering his or her work role or fulfilling his or her organizational duties.[65] Picture a scenario in which you've worked extremely hard for a number of years to finally master the "ins and outs" of working at a particular organization, and now you're beginning to enjoy the fruits of that labor in terms of financial rewards and better work assignments. That effort might be wasted if you moved to another organization (and had to start over on the learning curve).

Another factor that increases continuance commitment is a lack of employment alternatives.[66] If an employee has nowhere else to go, the need to stay will be higher. Employment alternatives themselves depend on several factors, including economic conditions, the unemployment rate, and the marketability of a person's skills and abilities.[67] Of course, no one likes to feel "stuck" in a situation, so it may not be surprising that the behavioral benefits associated with affective commitment do not really occur with continuance commitment. There is no statistical relationship between continuance commitment and citizenship behavior, for example, or any other aspects of job performance.[68] Continuance commitment therefore tends to create more of a passive (as opposed to active) form of loyalty.[69]

Alcon Labs seems to understand the value of continuance commitment. The Texas-based leader in eye care products enjoys a voluntary turnover rate of less than 2 percent.[70] One likely reason for that low rate is the benefits package Alcon offers its employees. For example, Alcon offers a 401(k) retirement plan in which it matches 240 percent of what employees contribute, up to a total of 5 percent of total compensation. So, for example, if an employee invests $500 toward retirement in a given month, Alcon contributes $1,200. That policy more than doubles the most generous rates of other companies, allowing employees to build a comfortable "nest egg" for retirement more quickly. Clearly employees would feel a bit anxious about giving up that benefit if a competitor came calling.

Normative Commitment

Now consider the reasons for staying listed in the right-hand column of Table 2-3. What would you feel if, even after taking all those reasons into account, you decided to leave your organization to join another one? Answer: You'd feel a sense of

Not only are Harley riders loyal to their bikes, but employees are dedicated to the company and identify with the culture of motorcycle riding. Some even get to work at biker rallies like this one.

guilt. Normative commitment exists when there is a sense that staying is the "right" or "moral" thing to do.[71] The sense that people *should* stay with their current employers may result from personal work philosophies or more general codes of right and wrong developed over the course of their lives. They also may be dictated by early experiences within the company, if employees are socialized to believe that long-term loyalty is the norm rather than the exception.[72]

In addition to personal work philosophies or organizational socialization, there seem to be two ways to build a sense of obligation-based commitment among employees. One way is to create a feeling that the employee is in the organization's debt— that he or she owes something to the organization. For example, an organization may spend a great deal of money training and developing an employee. In recognition of that investment, the employee may feel obligated to "repay" the organization with several more years of loyal service.[73] Picture a scenario in which your employer paid your tuition, allowing you to further your education, while also providing you with training and developmental job assignments that increased your skills. Wouldn't you feel a little guilty if you took the first job opportunity that came your way?

Another possible way to build an obligation-based sense of commitment is by becoming a particularly charitable organization. Did you ever wonder why organizations spend time and money on charitable things—for example, building playgrounds in the local community? Don't those kinds of projects take away from research and development, product improvements, or profits for shareholders? Well, charitable efforts have several potential advantages. First, they can provide good public relations for the organization, potentially generating goodwill for its products and services and help-ing attract new recruits.[74] Second, they can help existing employees feel better about the organization, creating a deeper sense of normative commitment.

Qualcomm recognizes the value of normative commitment. The California-based firm, specializing in wireless technolo-gies, has a voluntary turnover rate of just over 3 percent. After six Qualcomm employees lost their homes in a forest fire, other Qualcomm employees collected donations and contributed $60,000 to the Red Cross disaster relief fund.[75] Qualcomm matched that contribution and gives 1–2 percent of its pretax profits to charitable causes each year.[76] Charitable actions are also an important element of Microsoft's culture. Not only does Bill Gates, the founder of the Washington-based software giant, donate a large percentage of his wealth to philanthropic efforts,[77] but his organization matches any charitable contribution made by its employees.[78] These sorts of activities create a sense that employees ought to remain in their current positions.

Bill Gates donates time and money toward philanthropic efforts, and charitable actions are an important element of the Microsoft culture.

Withdrawal Behavior

What happens when an employee doesn't feel particularly high levels of affective, continuance, or normative commitment? One likely outcome is that the employee will begin withdraw-ing from the organization. Such withdrawal might be especially likely when some negative workplace event occurs because orga-nizational commitment can be especially vital in tough times. To paraphrase the old saying, "When the going gets tough, the organization doesn't want you to get going." In tough times, organizations need their employees to demonstrate loyalty, not "get going" right out the door.[79] Of course, it's those same tough times that put an employee's loyalty and allegiance to the test.

Consider the following scenario: You've been working at your company for three years and served on a key product development team for the past several months. Unfortunately, the team has been struggling of late. In an effort to enhance the team's performance, the organization has added a new member to the group. This member has a solid history of product devel-opment but is, by all accounts, a horrible person with whom to work. You can easily see the employee's talent but find yourself hating every moment spent in the employee's presence. This sit-uation is particularly distressing because the team won't finish its work for another nine months, at the earliest. What would you do in this situation?

● ● **2.6**

Understand the four primary responses to negative events at work.

Research on reactions to negative work events suggests that you might respond in one of four general ways.[80] First, you might attempt to remove yourself from the situation, either by being absent from work more frequently or by voluntarily leaving the organization. This removal is termed *exit*, defined as an active, destructive response by which an individual either ends or restricts organizational membership.[81] Second, you might attempt to change the circumstances by meeting with the new team member to attempt to work out the situation. This action is termed *voice*, which was already covered in our dis-cussion of interpersonal citizenship behavior. Voice represents an active, constructive response in which individuals attempt to improve the situation.[82] Third, you might just "grin and bear it," maintaining your effort level despite your unhappiness. This response is termed *loyalty*, defined as a passive, constructive response that maintains public support for the situation while the individual privately hopes for improvement.[83] Fourth, you might just go through the motions, allowing your performance to deteriorate slowly as you mentally "check out." This reaction is termed *neglect*, defined as a passive, destructive response in which interest and effort in the job decline.[84] Sometimes neglect can be even more costly than exit because it is not as readily noticed. Employees may neglect their duties for months (or even years) before their bosses catch on to their poor behaviors.

Taken together, the exit–voice–loyalty–neglect frame-work captures most of the possible responses to a negative work event,[85] like the addition of a new colleague who makes work more difficult. Where does organizational commitment fit in? Organizational commitment should decrease the likeli-hood that an individual will respond to a negative work event with exit or neglect (the two destructive responses). At the same time, organizational commitment should increase the likelihood that the negative work event will prompt voice or loyalty (the two constructive responses). Research suggests

TABLE 2-4	Four Types of Employees		
		Task Performance	
		HIGH	**LOW**
Organizational Commitment	**HIGH**	Stars	Citizens
	LOW	Lone wolves	Apathetics

Source: Adapted from R. W. Griffeth, S. Gaertner, and J. K. Sager, "Taxonomic Model of Withdrawal Behaviors: The Adaptive Response Model," *Human Resource Management Review* 9 (1999), pp. 577–90.

● **STARS** Employees who possess high levels of both organizational commitment and task performance.

● **CITIZENS** Employees who possess high levels of organizational commitment but low levels of task performance.

● **LONE WOLVES** Employees who possess high levels of task performance but low levels of organizational commitment.

● **APATHETICS** Employees who possess low levels of both organizational commitment and task performance.

that factors that promote affective and normative commitment indeed increase the likelihood of voice and loyalty while decreasing the likelihood of exit and neglect.[86]

If we consider employees' task performance levels, together with their organizational commitment levels, we can gain an even clearer picture of how people might respond to negative work events. Consider Table 2-4, which depicts combinations of high and low levels of organizational commitment and task performance. Stars possess high commitment and high performance and are held up as role models for other employees. Stars likely respond to negative events with voice because they have the desire to improve the status quo and the credibility needed to inspire change.[87] It's pretty easy to spot the stars in a given unit, and you can probably think about your current or past job experiences and identify the employees who would fit that description. For an example of stars in the world of women's tennis, see our **OB in Sports** feature. Citizens possess high commitment and low task performance but perform many of the voluntary "extra-role" activities that are needed to make the organization function smoothly.[88] Citizens are likely to respond to negative events with loyalty because they may not have the credibility needed to inspire change but possess the desire to remain a member of the organization. You can spot citizens by looking for the people who do the little things—showing around new employees, picking up birthday cakes, ordering new supplies when needed, and so forth.

Lone wolves possess low levels of organizational commitment but high levels of task performance and are motivated to achieve work goals for themselves, not necessarily for their company.[89] They are likely to respond to negative events with exit. Although their performance would give them the credibility needed to inspire change, their lack of attachment prevents them from using that credibility constructively. Instead, they rely on their performance levels to make them marketable to their next employer. To spot lone wolves, look for the talented employees who never seem to want to get involved in the conflicts or squabbles within a unit. Finally, apathetics possess low levels of both organizational commitment and task performance and merely exert the minimum level of effort needed to keep their jobs. Apathetics

OB in Sports

When a men's tennis player wins Wimbledon, he hoists a silver gilt cup. When a women's tennis player wins Wimbledon, she hoists a sterling silver plate. Beginning in 2007, however, the two champions had one thing in common: the prize money. That year, for the first time, the All-England Lawn Tennis and Croquet Club offered the same prize money—around $1.4 million—to the men's and women's winners of perhaps the most prestigious tournament in professional tennis. Some of the credit for that decision goes to Venus Williams, who was one of the loudest voices in the debate about prize money equality. The year before the change, Williams wrote an opinion piece for England's *The Times,* asking: "How can it be that Wimbledon finds itself on the wrong side of history? How can the words Wimbledon and inequality be allowed to coexist?"[90]

Opponents to equal prize money often pointed out that men's players compete in "best of five" matches, whereas women's players compete in "best of three" matches.[91] On the other hand, there have been many points in tennis history when the women's side generated more buzz and fan interest than the men's players. Regardless, Williams's efforts represent voice in its truest sense—an active, constructive attempt to improve her sport, to the benefit of her contemporaries and women's players in the future. As a three-time Wimbledon champion when she wrote her article, she had the star-like credibility needed to call for change to a longstanding status quo. If she hadn't possessed that credibility, it's doubtful that her voice would have been heard. As it turns out, Williams has personally benefited from the change in Wimbledon's policy, winning her fourth and fifth

Venus Williams challenged the inequality between men's and women's prize money at Wimbledon and has now reaped the benefits twice as winner of the 2007 and 2008 championships.

championships in 2007 and 2008.[92] Sometimes it definitely does pay to be a good citizen! ❖

should respond to negative events with neglect because they lack the performance needed to be marketable and the commitment needed to engage in acts of citizenship.

It's clear from this discussion that exit and neglect represent withdrawal behavior, which we've described as the flipside of organizational commitment. How common is withdrawal behavior within organizations? Quite common, as it turns out. One study clocked employees' on-the-job behaviors over a two-year period and found that only about 51 percent of their time was actually spent working! The other 49 percent was lost to late starts, early departures, long coffee breaks, personal matters, and other forms of withdrawal.[93] As a manager, wouldn't you like to feel like there was more than a coin-flip's chance that your employees were actually working during the course of a given day?

●●● 2.7

Describe examples of psychological withdrawal and physical withdrawal, and explain how they relate to one another.

As shown in Figure 2-7, withdrawal comes in two forms: psychological (or neglect) and physical (or exit). **Psychological withdrawal** consists of actions that provide a mental escape from the work environment.[94] When an employee is engaging in psychological withdrawal, "the lights are on, but nobody's home." Some business articles refer to psychological withdrawal as "warm-chair attrition," meaning that employees have essentially been lost even though their chairs remain occupied.[95] How big of a problem is psychological withdrawal? A recent Gallup poll revealed that more than 70 percent of employees feel

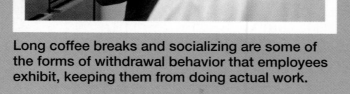

Long coffee breaks and socializing are some of the forms of withdrawal behavior that employees exhibit, keeping them from doing actual work.

about nonwork topics that goes on in cubicles and offices or at the mailbox or vending machines. *Looking busy* indicates an intentional desire on the part of the employee to look like he or she is working, even when not performing work tasks.[97] Sometimes employees decide to reorganize their desks or go for a stroll around the building, even though they have nowhere to go. (Those who are very good at managing impressions do such things very briskly and with a focused look on their faces!) When employees engage in *moonlighting,* they use work time and resources to complete something other than their job duties, such as assignments for another job.[98]

Perhaps the most widespread form of psychological withdrawal among white collar employees is *cyberloafing*—using Internet, e-mail, and instant messaging access for their personal enjoyment rather than work duties.[99] One recent survey of more than 3,000 employees from 750 different organizations revealed that employees spend around 40 percent of their workday responding to personal e-mails or surfing the Web.[100] Ninety-seven percent of those surveyed admitted to using the Internet primarily for personal rather than work use. To see for yourself, go for a stroll around any office and count how many screens you see set to ESPN.com, Amazon.com, eBay, the iTunes store, travel sites, stock-watch sites, and (when the boss is clearly not looking) job hunting sites. At the end of 2003, one estimate suggested that cyberloafing had cost the U.S. economy $250 billion in lost productivity.[101] Some employees view cyberloafing as a way of "balancing the scales" when it comes to personal versus work time. For example, one participant in a cyberloafing study noted, "It is alright for me to use the Internet for personal reasons at work. After all, I do work overtime without receiving extra pay from my employer."[102] Although such views are quite reasonable, other employees view cyberloafing as a means of retaliating against negative work events. One participant in the same study noted, "My boss is not the appreciative kind; I take what I can whenever I can. Surfing the net is my way of hitting back."

Physical withdrawal consists of actions that provide a physical escape, whether short term or long term, from the work environment. Physical withdrawal also comes in a number of shapes and sizes. *Tardiness* reflects the tendency to arrive at work late (or leave work early).[103] Of course, tardiness can

"disengaged" from their work (suggesting that the 51 percent work time result discussed previously may be optimistic!).[96]

Psychological withdrawal comes in a number of shapes and sizes. The least serious is *daydreaming,* when an employee appears to be working but is actually distracted by random thoughts or concerns. *Socializing* refers to the verbal chatting

FIGURE 2-7 Psychological and Physical Withdrawal

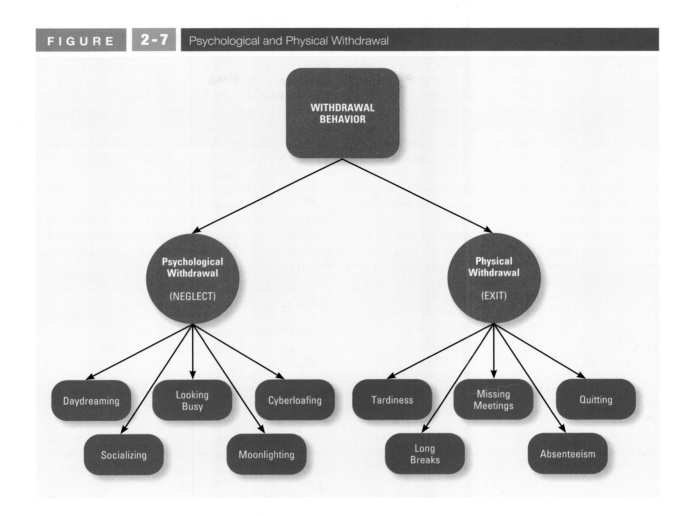

sometimes be unavoidable, as when employees have car trouble or must fight through bad weather, but it often represents a calculated desire to spend less time at work.[104] *Long breaks* involve longer-than-normal lunches, soda breaks, coffee breaks, and so forth that provide a physical escape from work. Ben Hamper's classic book *Rivethead: Tales of the Assembly Line*[105] is filled with examples of General Motors manufacturing employees taking excessively long breaks. For example, employees would routinely take turns covering for one another on the assembly line for half a shift so that they could spend several hours sleeping in their cars or at home, running errands, or even drinking beer at local bars. Sometimes such breaks stretch into *missing meetings*, which means employees neglect important work functions while away from the office. As a manager, you'd like to be sure that employees

who leave for lunch are actually going to come back, but sometimes, that's not a safe bet!

Absenteeism occurs when employees miss

Employees give different reasons for why they view cyberloafing, or spending personal time on the Internet during work hours, as acceptable. Whether it is acceptable or not, it is one clear form of psychological withdrawal from work.

an entire day of work.[106] Of course, people stay home from work for a variety of reasons, including illness and family emergencies. There is also a rhythm to absenteeism. For example, employees are more likely to be absent on Mondays or Fridays.[107] Moreover, streaks of good attendance create a sort of pressure to be absent, as personal responsibilities build until a day at home becomes irresistible.[108] That type of absence can sometimes be functional because people return to work with their "batteries recharged."[109] Group and departmental norms also affect absenteeism by signaling whether an employee can get away with missing a day here or there without being noticed.[110] These issues aside, a consistent pattern of absenteeism, month in and month out, is a symptom of the kind of low commitment that concerns most managers. Should absenteeism (in the form of missed classes) concern instructors as well? See our **OB for Students** feature to find out.

Finally, the most serious form of physical withdrawal is *quitting*—voluntarily leaving the organization. As with the other forms of withdrawal, employees can choose to "turn over" for a variety of reasons. The most frequent reasons include leaving for more money or a better career opportunity; dissatisfaction with supervision, working conditions, or working schedule; family factors; and health.[111] Note that many of those reasons reflect avoidable turnover, meaning that the organization could have done something to keep the employee, perhaps by offering more money, more frequent promotions, or a better work situation. Family factors and health, in contrast, usually reflect unavoidable turnover that doesn't necessarily signal a lack of commitment on the part of employees.

Regardless of their reasons, some employees choose to quit after engaging in a very thorough, careful, and reasoned analysis. Typically some sort of "shock," whether it be a critical job change or a negative work experience, jars employees enough that it triggers the thought of quitting in them.[112] Once the idea of quitting has occurred to them, employees begin searching for other places to work, compare those alternatives to their current job, and—if the comparisons seem favorable—quit.[113] This process may take days, weeks, or even months as employees grapple with the decision. In other cases, though, a shock may result in an impulsive, knee-jerk decision to quit, with little or no thought given to alternative jobs (or how those jobs compare to the current one).[114] Of course, sometimes a shock never occurs. Instead, an employee decides to quit as a result of a slow but steady decrease in happiness until a "straw breaks the camel's back" and voluntary turnover results.

Figure 2-7 shows 10 different behaviors that employees can perform to psychologically or physically escape from a negative work environment. A key question becomes: "How do all those behaviors relate to one another?" Consider the following testimonials from uncommitted (and admittedly fictional) employees:

- "I can't stand my job, so I do what I can to get by. Sometimes I'm absent, sometimes I socialize, sometimes I come in late. There's no real rhyme or reason to it; I just do whatever seems practical at the time."

- "I can't handle being around my boss. I hate to miss work, so I do what's needed to avoid being absent. I figure if I socialize a bit and spend some time surfing the Web, I don't need to ever be absent. But if I couldn't do those things, I'd definitely have to stay home . . . a lot."

- "I just don't have any respect for my employer anymore. In the beginning, I'd daydream a bit during work or socialize with my colleagues. As time went on, I began coming in late or taking a long lunch. Lately I've been staying home altogether, and I'm starting to think I should just quit my job and go somewhere else."

OB for Students

What does withdrawal mean for you as a student? The most obvious form of withdrawal for students is missed classes—the academic version of absenteeism. Why do students choose to stay home from class on a given day? One study identified the top six reasons for missing class, ranked as follows:[115]

1. Needing to complete work for another class.
2. The class is boring.
3. Severe illness (e.g., flu).
4. Minor illness (e.g., cold, sore throat).
5. Tired from social activities.
6. Oversleeping.

These reasons illustrate that there are a number of factors that cause people to be absent. Some are avoidable, some are unavoidable; some are related to the class, some are unrelated. Of the factors listed, the "class is boring" reason most clearly captures absenteeism as a response to a negative class-related event. Students don't like the class, so they engage in exit behaviors. There's also a rhythm and seasonality to absenteeism, as students are most likely to miss Friday classes or classes near the end of the semester (when project deadlines become most pressing).

Here's the million-dollar question for any student: Does absenteeism harm course grades? The clear answer is "yes." One study examined the correlation between class attendance and course grades across 17 different class sections and identified correlations ranging from .29 to .73.[116] Another study found that students who attend all classes average a 0.45-point higher GPA in the course than students who only attend half the classes.[117] This result appears even when taking into account a student's prior cumulative GPA and his or her motivation levels.

These sorts of results explain why some instructors build an attendance requirement into their classes, causing students to sign in each day to reduce absences. The benefits of this policy were tested in two sections of a psychology course.[118] One section required students to sign in to record attendance; the other section didn't. Absenteeism was one-third lower in the section that required sign-ins, and the students in that section performed significantly better on seven of the eight quizzes in the class. The bottom line is clear for you as a student—come to class, and you'll get a better grade. ❖

● **INDEPENDENT FORMS MODEL** A model that argues that the various withdrawal behaviors are uncorrelated with one another.

● **COMPENSATORY FORMS MODEL** A model that argues that the various withdrawal behaviors are negatively correlated with one another.

● **PROGRESSION MODEL** A model that argues that the various withdrawal behaviors are positively correlated with one another.

Each of these statements sounds like something that an uncommitted employee might say. However, each statement makes a different prediction about the relationship between the withdrawal behaviors in Figure 2-7. The first statement summarizes the independent forms model of withdrawal, which argues that the various withdrawal behaviors are uncorrelated with one another, occur for different reasons, and fulfill different needs on the part of employees.[119] From this perspective, knowing that an employee cyberloafs tells you nothing about whether that employee is likely to be absent. The second statement summarizes the compensatory forms model of withdrawal, which argues that the various withdrawal behaviors negatively correlate with one another—that doing one means you're less likely to do another.[120] The idea is that any form of withdrawal can compensate for, or neutralize, a sense of dissatisfaction, which makes the other forms unnecessary. From this perspective, knowing that an employee cyberloafs tells you that the same employee probably isn't going to be absent. The third statement summarizes the progression model of withdrawal, which argues that the various withdrawal behaviors are positively correlated: The tendency to daydream or socialize leads to the tendency to come in late or take long breaks, which leads to the tendency to be absent or quit.[121] From this perspective, knowing that an employee cyberloafs tells you that the same employee is probably going to be absent in the near future.

Which of the three models seems most logical to you? Although all three make some sense, the progression model has received the most scientific support.[122] Studies tend to show that the withdrawal behaviors in Figure 2-7 are positively correlated with one another.[123] Moreover, if you view the behaviors as a causal sequence moving from left (daydreaming) to right (quitting), the behaviors that are closest to each other in the sequence tend to be more highly correlated.[124] For example, quitting is more closely related to absenteeism than to tardiness because absenteeism is right next to it in the withdrawal progression.[125] These results illustrate that withdrawal behaviors may begin with very minor actions but eventually can escalate to more serious actions that may harm the organization. ∎

CHECK OUT

www.mhhe.com/ColquittEss

for study materials including Interactive Exercises, Quizzes, iPod downloads, and video.

CASE: Home Depot

Programs like "Aprons on the Floor," which seeks to cut costs in an effort to boost the number of employees on the sales floor, are designed to improve the performance and commitment of Home Depot's employees at a rough time in the company's history. Although the "Aprons on the Floor" initiative seems promising, some of the cost-cutting actions taken by new CEO Frank Blake and new head of human resources Tim Crow are controversial. For example, the company has cut its 2,200-person human resources (HR) field staff by half, laying off over 1,000 staff members.[126] Under Bob Nardelli,

the company had at least one human resources manager in each store. Under the new structure, a team of one HR district manager and three HR managers will oversee 6 to 10 stores.[127] Stores will still have an administrative person on site to handle scheduling, and a call center has been launched to handle HR-related calls from employees and managers. Home Depot will hire 200 representatives to staff that call center.

Crow argues that many of the responsibilities of the old store-based HR personnel have, over time, become part of the leadership training for store managers.[128] That is, the store managers themselves have gotten more involved in recruiting and screening talent, finding ways to improve career development, and maximizing retention. Crow also maintains that stores will see a member of their "HR team" four to five days a week. He also points out that the call center will be staffed by Home Depot employees, as opposed to outsourcing its function. Still, such massive downscaling sends some signal about how important "people management" is to a company like Home Depot. Clearly tough times demand tough choices. It will be interesting to see how this reorganization ultimately impacts the performance and commitment of Home Depot's employees.

2.1 Do you agree with Home Depot's decision to downsize its HR staff in an effort to boost the number of employees on the sales floor?

2.2 Consider the typical HR functions that occur at a company like Home Depot: recruitment, selection, training, compensation, retention. Can those functions be standardized across stores, or should different stores be allowed to handle them in different ways?

2.3 Downsizing represents a common strategy for reducing costs, particularly during economic downturns. What are the drawbacks to downsizing as a strategy for improving company performance? If you were one of the approximately 1,000 HR managers who kept their job, how would your performance and commitment be affected by the layoffs?

TAKEAWAYS

2.1 Job performance is the set of employee behaviors that contribute to organizational goal accomplishment. Organizational commitment is the desire on the part of an employee to remain a member of the organization.

2.2 Task performance includes employee behaviors that are directly involved in the transformation of organizational resources into the goods or services that the organization produces. Organizations gather information about relevant task behaviors using job analysis.

2.3 Citizenship behaviors are voluntary employee activities that may or may not be rewarded but that contribute to the organization by improving the overall quality of the setting in which work takes place. Examples of citizenship behavior include helping, courtesy, sportsmanship, voice, civic virtue, and boosterism.

2.4 Counterproductive behaviors are employee behaviors that intentionally hinder organizational goal accomplishment. Examples of counterproductive behavior include sabotage, theft, wasting resources, substance abuse, gossiping, incivility, harassment, and abuse.

2.5 There are three types of organizational commitment. Affective commitment occurs when an employee *wants* to stay and is influenced by the emotional bonds between employees. Continuance commitment occurs when an employee *needs* to stay and is influenced by salary, benefits, and other economic factors. Normative commitment occurs when an employee feels that he or she *ought* to stay and is influenced by an organization investing in its employees or engaging in charitable efforts.

2.6 Employees can respond to negative work events in four ways: exit, voice, loyalty, and neglect. Exit is a form of physical withdrawal in which the employee either ends or restricts organizational membership. Voice is an active and constructive response by which employees attempt to improve the situation. Loyalty is passive and constructive; employees remain supportive while hoping the situation improves on its own. Neglect is a form of psychological withdrawal in which interest and effort in the job decrease.

2.7 Examples of psychological withdrawal include daydreaming, socializing, looking busy, moonlighting, and cyberloafing. Examples of physical withdrawal include tardiness, long breaks, missing meetings, absenteeism, and quitting. Consistent with the progression model, withdrawal behaviors tend to start with minor psychological forms before escalating to more major physical varieties.

DISCUSSION QUESTIONS

2.1 Describe a job in which citizenship behaviors would be especially critical to an organization's functioning and one in which citizenship behaviors would be less critical. What is it about a job that makes citizenship more important?

2.2 Figure 2-3 classifies productive deviance and political deviance as more minor in nature than property deviance and personal aggression. When might those types of counterproductive behavior prove especially costly?

2.3 Which type of organizational commitment (affective, continuance, or normative) do you think is most important to the majority of employees? Which do you think is most important to you?

2.4 Consider times when you've reacted to a negative event with exit, voice, loyalty, or neglect. What was it about the situation that caused you to respond the way you did? Do you usually respond to negative events in the same way, or does your response vary across the four options?

2.5 Can organizations use a combination of monitoring and punishment procedures to reduce psychological and physical withdrawal? How might such programs work from a practical perspective? Do you think they would be effective?

ASSESSMENT: Affective Commitment

How emotionally attached are you to your employer? This assessment is designed to measure affective commitment—the feeling that you *want* to stay with your current organization. Think of your current job or the last job that you held (even if it was a part-time or summer job). Answer each question using the response scale provided. Then subtract your answers to the bold-faced questions from 6, with the difference being your new answers for those questions. For example, if your original answer for Question 3 was "4," your new answer is "2" (6 − 4). Then sum your answers for the six questions. (For more assessments relevant to this chapter, please visit the Online Learning Center at www.mhhe.com/ColquittEss.)

1	2	3	4	5
Strongly Disagree	Disagree	Neutral	Agree	Strongly Agree

1. I would be very happy to spend the rest of my career in this organization.   _____
2. I really feel as if this organization's problems are my own.   _____
3. **I do not feel like "part of the family" at my organization.**   _____
4. **I do not feel "emotionally attached" to this organization.**   _____
5. This organization has a great deal of personal meaning for me.   _____
6. **I do not feel a strong sense of belonging to my organization.**   _____

Scoring

If your scores sum up to 20 or above, you feel a strong sense of affective commitment to your current or past employer, which means that you feel an emotional attachment to the company, or the people within it, that lessens the likelihood that you would leave voluntarily. If your scores sum up to less than 20, you have a weaker sense of affective commitment to your current or past employer. This result is especially likely if you responded to the questions in reference to a part-time or summer job, for which there is rarely enough time to develop a deep emotional bond.

Source: J. P. Meyer and N. J. Allen, 1997, *Commitment in the Workplace,* Sage Publications. Copyright © 1997 Sage Publications Inc. Reproduced via permission from Copyright Clearance Center.

EXERCISE: Reacting to Negative Events

The purpose of this exercise is to explore how individuals react to three all-too-common scenarios that represent negative workplace events. This exercise uses groups, so your instructor will either assign you to a group or ask you to create your own group. The exercise has the following steps:

1. Individually read the following three scenarios: the annoying boss, the boring job, and pay and seniority. For each scenario, write down two specific behaviors in which you would likely engage in response to that scenario. Write down what you would actually do, as opposed to what you wish you would do. For example, you may wish that you would march into your boss's office and demand a change, but if you would actually do nothing, write down "nothing."

Annoying Boss	You've been working at your current company for about a year. Over time, your boss has become more and more annoying to you. It's not that your boss is a bad person, or even necessarily a bad boss. It's more a personality conflict—the way your boss talks, the way your boss manages every little thing, even the facial expressions your boss uses. The more time passes, the more you just can't stand to be around your boss.	Two likely behaviors:
Boring Job	You've been working at your current company for about a year. You've come to realize that your job is pretty boring. It's the first real job you've ever had, and at first it was nice to have some money and something to do every day. But the "new job" excitement has worn off, and things are actually quite monotonous. Same thing every day. It's to the point that you check your watch every hour, and Wednesdays feel like they should be Fridays.	Two likely behaviors:
Pay and Seniority	You've been working at your current company for about a year. The consensus is that you're doing a great job—you've gotten excellent performance evaluations and have emerged as a leader on many projects. As you've achieved this high status, however, you've come to feel that you are underpaid. Your company's pay procedures emphasize seniority much more than job performance. As a result, you look at other members of your project teams and see poor performers making much more than you, just because they've been with the company longer.	Two likely behaviors:

2. In groups, compare and contrast your likely responses to the three scenarios. Come to a consensus on the two most likely responses for the group as a whole. Elect one group member to write the two likely responses to each of the three scenarios on the board.

3. Class discussion (whether in groups or as a class) should center on where the likely responses fit into the Exit–Voice–

Loyalty–Neglect framework. What personal and situational factors would lead someone to one category of responses over another? Are there any responses that do not fit into the Exit–Voice–Loyalty–Neglect framework?

END NOTES

1. Marquez, J. "Home Remodel." *Workforce,* July 14, 2008, pp. 1, 24–28.

2. Ibid.

3. Grow, B. "Out at Home Depot." *BusinessWeek,* January 15, 2007, http://www.businessweek.com/magazine/content/07_03/b4017001.htm (accessed July 21, 2008).

4. Hindo, B. "Six Sigma: So Yesterday?" *BusinessWeek,* June 11, 2007, http://www.businessweek.com/magazine/content/07_24/b4038409.htm (accessed June 11, 2007).

5. Marquez, "Home Remodel."

6. Ibid.

7. Ibid.

8. Ibid.

9. Campbell, J. P. "Modeling the Performance Prediction Problem in Industrial and Organizational Psychology." In *Handbook of Industrial and Organizational Psychology,* Vol. 1, 2nd ed., ed. M. D. Dunnette and L. M. Hough. Palo Alto, CA: Consulting Psychologists Press, 1990, pp. 687–732; Motowidlo, S. J.; W. C. Borman; and M. J. Schmit. "A Theory of Individual Differences in Task and Contextual Performance." *Human Performance* 10 (1997), pp. 71–83.

10. Mowday, R. T.; R. M. Steers; and L. W. Porter. "The Measurement of Organizational Commitment." *Journal of Vocational Behavior* 14 (1979), pp. 224–47.

11. Borman, W. C., and S. J. Motowidlo. "Expanding the Criterion Domain to Include Elements of Contextual Performance." In *Personnel Selection in Organizations,* ed. N. Schmitt and W. C. Borman. San Francisco: Jossey-Bass, 1993, pp. 71–98.

12. Occupational Information Network (O*Net) Online. http://online.onetcenter.org/ (accessed August 17, 2005).

13. LePine, J. A.; J. A. Colquitt; and A. Erez. "Adaptability to Changing Task Contexts: Effects of General Cognitive Ability, Conscientiousness, and Openness to Experience." *Personnel Psychology* 53 (2000), pp. 563–93.

14. CBC News. "Plane Fire at Pearson Airport. Flight 358." *Indepth,* August 8, 2005, http://www.cbc.ca/news/background/plane_fire/ (accessed August 17, 2005).

15. Anderson, D. K. (Producer); P. Docter; L. Unkrich; and D. Silverman (Directors). *Monsters, Inc.* Emeryville, CA: Disney Pixar Studios, 2001.

16. Pulakos, E. D.; S. Arad; M. A. Donovan; and K. E. Plamondon. "Adaptability in the Workplace: Development of a Taxonomy of Adaptive Performance." *Journal of Applied Psychology* 85 (2000), pp. 612–24.

17. O'Reilly, C. A., III, and J. Pfeffer. *Hidden Value: How Great Companies Achieve Extraordinary Results with Ordinary People.* Boston: Harvard Business School Press, 2000.

18. Occupational Information Network (O*Net) Online.

19. Freidberg, K., and J. Freidberg. *Nuts! Southwest Airlines' Crazy Recipe for Business and Personal Success.* Austin, TX: Bard Press, 1996.

20. Kaplan, M. D. G. "What Are You, a Comedian?" *USA Weekend.com,* July 13, 2003, http://www.usaweekend.com/03_issues/030713/030713southwest.html (accessed September 15, 2005).

21. Borman and Motowidlo, "Expanding the Criterion Domain."

22. Organ, D. W. *Organizational Citizenship Behavior: The Good Soldier Syndrome.* Lexington, MA: Lexington Books, 1988.

23. Coleman, V. I., and W. C. Borman. "Investigating the Underlying Structure of the Citizenship Performance Domain." *Human Resource Management Review* 10 (2000), pp. 25–44.

24. Ibid.

25. Ibid.

26. Van Dyne, L., and J. A. LePine. "Helping and Voice Extra-Role Behavior: Evidence of Construct and Predictive Validity." *Academy of Management Journal* 41 (1998), pp. 108–19.

27. Motowidlo, S. J. "Some Basic Issues Related to Contextual Performance and Organizational Citizenship Behavior in Human Resource Management." *Human Resource Management Review* 10 (2000), pp. 115–26.

28. Podsakoff, P. M.; S. B. MacKenzie; J. B. Paine; and D. G. Bachrach. "Organizational Citizenship Behaviors: A Critical Review of the Theoretical and Empirical Literature and Suggestions for Future Research." *Journal of Management* 26 (2000), pp. 513–63.

29. Podsakoff, P. M.; M. Ahearne; and S. B. MacKenzie. "Organizational Citizenship Behavior and the Quantity and Quality of Work Group Performance." *Journal of Applied Psychology* 82 (1997), pp. 262–70.

30. Walz, S. M., and B. P. Neihoff. "Organizational Citizenship Behaviors and Their Effect on Organizational Effectiveness in Limited-Menu Restaurants." In *Academy of Management Best Papers Proceedings,* ed. J. B. Keys and L. N. Dosier. Statesboro, GA: College of Business Administration at Georgia Southern University (1996), pp. 307–11.

31. Allen, T. D., and M. C. Rush. "The Effects of Organizational Citizenship Behavior on Performance Judgments: A Field Study and a Laboratory Experiment." *Journal of Applied Psychology* 83 (1998), pp. 247–60; Avila, R. A.; E. F. Fern; and O. K. Mann. "Unraveling Criteria for Assessing the Performance of Sales People: A Causal Analysis." *Journal of Personal Selling and Sales Management* 8 (1988), pp. 45–54; Lowery, C. M., and T. J. Krilowicz. "Relationships Among Nontask Behaviors, Rated Performance, and Objective Performance Measures." *Psychological Reports* 74 (1994), pp. 571–78; MacKenzie, S. B.; P. M. Podsakoff; and R. Fetter. "Organizational Citizenship Behavior and Objective Productivity as Determinants of Managerial Evaluations of Salespersons' Performance." *Organizational Behavior and Human Decision Processes* 50 (1991), pp. 123–50; MacKenzie, S. B.; P. M. Podsakoff; and R. Fetter. "The Impact of Organizational Citizenship Behavior on Evaluation of Sales Performance." *Journal of Marketing* 57 (1993), pp. 70–80; MacKenzie, S. B.; P. M. Podsakoff; and J. B. Paine. "Effects of Organizational Citizenship Behaviors and Productivity on Evaluation of Performance at Different Hierarchical Levels in Sales Organizations." *Journal of the Academy of Marketing Science* 27 (1999), pp. 396–410; Motowidlo, S. J., and J. R. Van Scotter. "Evidence That Task Performance Should Be Distinguished from Contextual Performance." *Journal of Applied Psychology* 79 (1994), pp. 475–80; Podsakoff, P. M., and S. B. MacKenzie. "Organizational Citizenship Behaviors and Sales Unit Effectiveness." *Journal of Marketing Research* 3 (February 1994), pp. 351–63; Van Scotter, J. R., and S. J. Motowidlo. "Interpersonal Facilitation and Job Dedication as Separate Facets of Contextual Performance." *Journal of Applied Psychology* 81 (1996), pp. 525–31.

32. Rotundo, M., and P. R. Sackett. "The Relative Importance of Task, Citizenship, and Counterproductive Performance to Global Ratings of Job Performance: A Policy Capturing Approach." *Journal of Applied Psychology* 87 (2002), pp. 66–80.

33. Allen and Rush, "The Effects of Organizational Citizenship Behavior on Performance Judgments"; Kiker, D. S., and S. J. Motowidlo. "Main and Interaction Effects of Task and Contextual Performance on Supervisory Reward Decisions." *Journal of Applied Psychology* 84 (1999), pp. 602–609; Park, O. S., and H. P Sims Jr. "Beyond Cognition in Leadership: Prosocial Behavior and Affect in Managerial Judgment." Working paper, Seoul National University and Pennsylvania State University, 1989.

34. Robinson, S. L., and R. J. Bennett. "A Typology of Deviant Workplace Behaviors: A Multidimensional Scaling Study." *Academy of Management Journal* 38 (1995), pp. 555–72.

35. Morrison, E. W. "Role Definitions and Organizational Citizenship Behavior: The Importance of the Employee's Perspective." *Academy of Management Journal* 37 (1994), pp. 1543–67.

36. Hofstede, G. *Cultures and Organizations: Software of the Mind.* New York: McGraw-Hill, 1991.

37. Rotundo, M., and J. L. Xie. "Understanding the Domain of Counterproductive Work Behavior in China." Working Paper, University of Toronto, 2007.

38. Cellitti, D. R. "MCA DiscoVision: The Record That Plays Pictures." June 25, 2002, http://www.oz.net/blam/DiscoVision/RecordPlaysPictures.htm (accessed August 16, 2005).

39. Harper, D. "Spotlight Abuse—Save Profits." *Industrial Distribution* 79 (1990), pp. 47–51.

40. Hollinger, R. C., and L. Langton. *2004 National Retail Security Survey.* Gainesville, FL: University of Florida, Security Research Project, Department of Criminology, Law and Society, 2005.

41. Andersson, L. M., and C. M. Pearson. "Tit for Tat? The Spiraling Effect of Incivility in the Workplace." *Academy of Management Review* 24 (1999), pp. 452–71.

42. Ibid.

43. Armour, S. "Managers Not Prepared for Workplace Violence." *USA Today,* July 19, 2004, http://www.usatoday.com/money/workplace/2004-07-15-workplace-violence2_x.htm (accessed September 11, 2005).

44. PBS. "Isolated Incidents?" *Online Newshour,* April 26, 1996, http://www.pbs.org/newshour/bb/business/april96/mitsubishi_4-26.html (accessed September 11, 2005).

45. Sackett, P. R. "The Structure of Counterproductive Work Behaviors: Dimensionality and Performance with Facets of Job Performance." *International Journal of Selection and Assessment* 10 (2002), pp. 5–11.

46. Sackett, P. R., and C. J. DeVore. "Counterproductive Behaviors at Work." In *Handbook of Industrial, Work, and Organizational Psychology,* Vol. 1, ed. N. Anderson, D. S. Ones, H. K. Sinangil, and C. Viswesvaran. Thousand Oaks, CA: Sage, 2001, pp. 145–51.

47. "By the Numbers." *Fortune,* December 27, 2005, p. 32.

48. "Estimating Turnover Costs." http://www.keepemployees.com/turnovercost.htm (accessed October 20, 2005).

49. Ahlrichs, N. S. *Manager of Choice.* Mountain View, CA: Davies-Black Publishing, 2003.

50. Hulin, C. L. "Adaptation, Persistence, and Commitment in Organizations." In *Handbook of Industrial and Organizational Psychology,* Vol. 2, ed. M. D. Dunnette and L. M. Hough. Palo Alto, CA: Consulting Psychologists Press, Inc., 1991, pp. 445–506.

51. Meyer, J. P., and N. J. Allen. "A Three-Component Conceptualization of Organizational Commitment." *Human Resource Management Review* 1 (1991), pp. 61–89.

52. Ibid.

53. Ibid.

54. Meyer, J. P., and N. J. Allen. *Commitment in the Workplace.* Thousand Oaks, CA: Sage, 1997.

55. Mowday, Steers, and Porter, "The Measurement of Organizational Commitment."

56. Ibid.

57. Meyer, J. P.; D. J. Stanley; L. Herscovitch, and L. Topolnytsky. "Affective, Continuance, and Normative Commitment to the Organization: A Meta-Analysis of Antecedents, Correlates, and Consequences." *Journal of Vocational Behavior* 61 (2002), pp. 20–52.

58. Mathieu, J. E., and D. M. Zajac. "A Review and Meta-Analysis of the Antecedents, Correlates, and Consequences of Organizational Commitment." *Psychological Bulletin* 108 (1990), pp. 171–94.

59. Johns, G. "The Psychology of Lateness, Absenteeism, and Turnover." In *Handbook of Industrial, Work, and Organizational Psychology,* ed. N. Anderson, D. S. Ones, H. K. Sinangil, and C. Viswesvaran. Thousand Oaks, CA: Sage, 2001, pp. 232–52.

60. Ibid.

61. Levering, R., and Moskowitz, M. "The 100 Best Companies to Work For." *Fortune,* January 24, 2005, pp. 64–94.

62. Ibid.

63. Meyer and Allen, "A Three-Component Conceptualization."

64. Becker, H. S. "Notes on the Concept of Commitment." *American Journal of Sociology* 66 (1960), pp. 32–42.

65. Meyer and Allen, *Commitment in the Workplace.*

66. Ibid.

67. Ibid.

68. Meyer, Stanley, Herscovitch, and Topolnytsky, "Affective, Continuance, and Normative Commitment."

69. Meyer and Allen, *Commitment in the Workplace.*

70. Levering and Moskowitz, "The 100 Best Companies to Work For."

71. Meyer, J. P.; N. J. Allen; and C. A. Smith. "Commitment to Organizations and Occupations: Extension and Test of a Three-Component Conceptualization." *Journal of Applied Psychology* 78 (1993), pp. 538–51.

72. Meyer and Allen, "A Three-Component Conceptualization."

73. Grow, B. "The Debate over Doing Good." *BusinessWeek,* August 15, 2005, pp. 76–78.

74. Ibid.

75. "Qualcomm Community Involvement–Corporate Giving." 2005, http://www.qualcomm.com/community/corporate_giving.html (accessed October 23, 2005).

76. Levering and Moskowitz, "In Good Company."

77. Roth, D. "The $91 Billion Conversation." *Fortune,* October 31, 2005. Retrieved from http://money.cnn.com/magazines/fortune/fortune_archive/2005/10/31/8359156/ (accessed May 18, 2007).

78. Levering and Moskowitz, "In Good Company."

79. Kiger, P. J. "Retention on the Brink." *Workforce,* November 2000, pp. 59–65.

80. Farrell, D. "Exit, Voice, Loyalty, and Neglect as Responses to Job Dissatisfaction: A Multidimensional Scaling Study." *Academy of Management Journal* 26 (1983), pp. 596–607; Rusbult, C. E., D. Farrell; C. Rogers; and A. G. Mainous III. "Impact of Exchange Variables on Exit, Voice, Loyalty, and Neglect: An Integrating Model of Responses to Declining Job Satisfaction." *Academy of Management Journal* 31 (1988), pp. 599–627.

81. Hirschman, A. O. *Exit, Voice, and Loyalty: Responses to Decline in Firms, Organizations, and States.* Cambridge, MA: Harvard University Press, 1970.

82. Ibid.

83. Farrell, "Exit, Voice, Loyalty, and Neglect."

84. Rusbult, Farrell, Rogers, and Mainous, "Impact of Exchange Variables."

85. Ibid.

86. Griffeth, R. W.; S. Gaertner; and J. K. Sager. "Taxonomic Model of Withdrawal Behaviors: The Adaptive Response Model." *Human Resource Management Review* 9 (1999), pp. 577–90.

87. Ibid.

88. Ibid.

89. Griffeth, Gaertner, and Sager, "Taxonomic Model of Withdrawal Behaviors."

90. Williams, V. "Wimbledon Has Sent Me a Message: I'm Only a Second-Class Champion." *The Times*, June 26, 2006, http://www.timesonline.co.uk/tol/sport/tennis/article679416.ece (accessed July 20, 2008).

91. "Wimbledon Agrees to Equal Prize Money." *USA Today*, February 22, 2007, http://www.usatoday.com/sports/tennis/wimb/2007-02-22-wimbledon-pay_x.htm (accessed July 20, 2008).

92. Clarke, L. "Venus Williams Wins Wimbledon." *Washington Post*, July 6, 2008, http://www.washingtonpost.com/wp-dyn/content/story/2008/07/05/ST2008070501410.html (accessed July 20, 2008).

93. Cherrington, D. *The Work Ethic.* New York: AMACOM, 1980.

94. Hulin, C. L.; M. Roznowski; and D. Hachiya. "Alternative Opportunities and Withdrawal Decisions: Empirical and Theoretical Discrepancies and an Integration." *Psychological Bulletin* 97 (1985), pp. 233–50.

95. Fisher, A. "Turning Clock-Watchers into Stars." *Fortune,* March 22, 2004, p. 60.

96. Ibid.

97. Hulin, "Adaptation, Persistence, and Commitment."

98. Ibid.

99. Lim, V. K. G. "The IT Way of Loafing on the Job: Cyberloafing, Neutralizing, and Organizational Justice." *Journal of Organizational Behavior* 23 (2002), pp. 675–94.

100. "Does Cyberloafing Undermine Productivity?" *Management Issues News,* 2005, http://www.management-issues.com/display_page.asp?section=research&id=1417 (accessed October 24, 2005).

101. "Cyberslacking." *MacMillan English Dictionary,* 2005, http://www.macmillandictionary.com/New-Words/040604-cyberslacking.htm (accessed October 25, 2005).

102. Lim, "The IT Way."

103. Koslowsky, M.; A. Sagie; M. Krausz; and A. D. Singer. "Correlates of Employee Lateness: Some Theoretical Considerations." *Journal of Applied Psychology* 82 (1997), pp. 79–88.

104. Blau, G. "Developing and Testing a Taxonomy of Lateness Behavior." *Journal of Applied Psychology* 79 (1994), pp. 959–70.

105. Hamper, B. *Rivethead: Tales from the Assembly Line.* New York: Warner Books, 1991.

106. Muchinsky, P. M. "Employee Absenteeism: A Review of the Literature." *Journal of Vocational Behavior* 10 (1977), pp. 316–40.

107. Ibid.

108. Fichman, M. "Motivational Consequences of Absence and Attendance: Proportional Hazard Estimation of a Dynamic Motivation Model." *Journal of Applied Psychology* 73 (1988), pp. 119–34.

109. Martocchio, J. J., and D. I. Jimeno. "Employee Absenteeism as an Affective Event." *Human Resource Management Review* 13 (2003), pp. 227–41.

110. Nicholson, N., and G. Johns. "The Absence Climate and the Psychological Contract: Who's in Control of Absence?" *Academy of Management Review* 10 (1985), pp. 397–407.

111. Campion, M. A. "Meaning and Measurement of Turnover: Comparison of Alternative Measures and Recommendations for Research." *Journal of Applied Psychology* 76 (1991), pp. 199–212.

112. Lee, T. W., and T. R. Mitchell. "An Alternative Approach: The Unfolding Model of Voluntary Employee Turnover." *Academy of Management Review* 19 (1984), pp. 51–89.

113. "Mobley, W. "Intermediate Linkages in the Relationship between Job Satisfaction and Employee Turnover." *Journal of Applied Psychology* 62 (1977), pp. 237–40; Hom, P. W.; R. Griffeth; and C. L. Sellaro. "The Validity of Mobley's (1977) Model of Employee Turnover." *Organizational Behavior and Human Performance* 34 (1984), pp. 141–74.

114. Lee and Mitchell, "An Alternative Approach."

115. Van Blerkom, M. L. "Class Attendance in Undergraduate Courses." *Journal of Psychology* 126 (1992), pp. 487–94.

116. Ibid.

117. Devadoss, S., and J. Foltz. "Evaluation of Factors Influencing Student Class Attendance and Performance." *American Journal of Agricultural Economics* 78 (1996), pp. 499–507.

118. Shimoff, E., and A. Catania. "Effects of Recording Attendance on Grades in Introductory Psychology." *Teaching of Psychology* 28 (2001), pp. 192–95.

119. Porter, L. W., and R. M. Steers. "Organizational, Work, and Personal Factors in Employee Turnover and Absenteeism." *Psychological Bulletin* 80 (1973), pp. 151–76.

120. Hill, J. M., and E. L. Trist. "Changes in Accidents and Other Absences with Length of Service: A Further Study of Their Incidence and Relation to Each Other in an Iron and Steel Works." *Human Relations* 8 (1955), pp. 121–52.

121. Rosse, J. G., and H. E. Miller. "Relationship between Absenteeism and Other Employee Behaviors." In *Absenteeism: New Approaches to Understanding, Measuring, and Managing Employee Absence,* ed. P. S. Goodman and R. S. Atkin. San Francisco: Jossey-Bass, 1984, pp. 194–228.

122. Hulin, "Adaptation, Persistence, and Commitment."

123. Griffeth, R. W.; P. W. Hom; and S. Gaertner. "A Meta-Analysis of Antecedents and Correlates of Employee Turnover: Update, Moderator Tests, and Research Implications for the Next Millennium." *Journal of Management* 26 (2000), pp. 463–88.

124. Rosse, J. G. "Relations among Lateness, Absence, and Turnover: Is There a Progression of Withdrawal?" *Human Relations* 41 (1988), pp. 517–31.

125. Koslowsky, Sagie, Krausz, and Singer, "Correlates of Employee Lateness.

126. Marquez, J. "Home Depot Slashes HR Staff by Half; 1000 Will Go." *Workforce*, April 7, 2008, http://www.workforce.com/section/00/article/25/46/42.html

127. Marquez, "Home Remodel."

128. Ibid.

JOB SATISFACTION

PATAGONIA

Picture this scenario: You're 26 years old, with an undergraduate degree and two master's degrees, fresh off internships at two respected European companies (Nestlé and Unilever). You've just been offered a job at an apparel company that specializes in sweaters, jackets, and other outdoor gear. Would you take it? Well, working for an apparel company may not be the most exciting prospect in the world, but if it's a good job with a good salary, you'd probably consider it. What if the job was "stock handler"? "No chance," you're probably thinking. But that's exactly the choice that Scott Robinson of Southern California made—in fact, he begged for the job.[1] Why? Because the company was Patagonia, the California-based seller of outdoor clothing and equipment, and it isn't just any apparel company. As Robinson explains, "I wanted to work for a company that's driven by values." Founded by long-time surfer and mountain climber Yvon Chouinard, the company is dedicated to producing the highest-quality products in the most environmentally sustainable manner possible.

Robinson is not the only twenty-something drawn to a job at Patagonia. The company, with 1,275 employees and 39 stores in seven countries, receives an average of 900 applications for every job opening.[2] With such stiff competition, Patagonia is able to hire passionate individuals while demanding hard work, creativity, and results. Those employees remain satisfied with their jobs because of Patagonia's unique approach to management. Chouinard believes in a "let my people surf" philosophy, meaning that his employees are encouraged to be out surfing, skiing, climbing, or fishing when the conditions are good, rather than stuck at their desk.[3] This attitude gives employees a sense of autonomy about how they structure their work, as well as ample opportunity to test Patagonia's products. The company also offers onsite day care, maternity and paternity leave, and flextime. Compensation is just above the market rate, and everyone receives an annual bonus based on profits.[4]

Aside from the innovative way that it treats its employees, Patagonia is known as a company that is committed to environmental causes. The company began reusing materials decades before recycling became common practice.[5] Its signature fleece jacket is made from polyester that uses discarded soda bottles as an input. It also partnered with a Japanese firm to perfect polyester recycling, encouraging customers to send back worn-out clothing so that it could be turned into new products. Patagonia was also the first California company to use renewable energy, such as solar or wind, to power all of its buildings. Chouinard organized an alliance of businesses called "One Percent for the Planet" that donates 1 percent of gross revenues to environmental causes each year. Patagonia also encourages its employees to get involved, allowing them to take two months off at full pay to work for environmental groups. All these practices give employees a sense of significance to their work—the sense that they're doing something more than selling jackets or sweaters. As one employee puts it, "It's easy to go to work when you get paid to do what you love to do."[6]

JOB SATISFACTION

This chapter takes us to a new portion of our integrative model of organizational behavior. Job satisfaction is one of several individual mechanisms that directly affects job performance and organizational commitment. As shown in the Patagonia example, if employees are very satisfied with their jobs and experience positive emotions while working, they may perform their jobs better and choose to remain with the company for a longer period of time. Think about the worst job that you've held in your life, even if it was just a summer job or a short-term work assignment. What did you feel during the course of the day? How did those feelings influence the way you behaved, in terms of your time spent on task and citizenship behaviors rather than counterproductive or withdrawal behaviors?

about this question for a few moments: What do you want to attain from your job; that is, what things do you want your job to give you? A good wage? A sense of achievement? Colleagues who are fun to be around? If you had to make a list of the things you value with respect to your job, most or all of them would likely be shown in Table 3-1. This table summarizes the values assessed in the five most popular surveys of work values, broken down into more general categories.[10] Many of those values deal with the things that your work can give you, such as good pay or the chance for frequent promotions. Other values

> ## "Unfortunately, workplace surveys suggest that satisfied employees are becoming more and more rare."

● ● **3.1**

Define job satisfaction.

Job satisfaction is defined as a pleasurable emotional state resulting from the appraisal of one's job or job experiences.[7] In other words, it represents how you *feel* about your job and what you *think* about your job. Employees with high job satisfaction experience positive feelings when they think about their duties or take part in task activities. Employees with low job satisfaction experience negative feelings when they think about their duties or take part in their task activities. Unfortunately, workplace surveys suggest that satisfied employees are becoming more and more rare. For example, a recent survey showed that just 49 percent of Americans are satisfied with their jobs, down from 58 percent a decade ago.[8] The survey also revealed that only 20 percent are satisfied with their employer's promotion and reward policies and 33 percent with their pay. Reversing such trends requires a deeper understanding of exactly what drives job satisfaction levels.

So what explains why some employees are more satisfied than others? At a general level, employees are satisfied when their job provides the things that they value. **Values** are those things that people consciously or subconsciously want to seek or attain.[9] Think

pertain to the context that surrounds your work, including whether you have a good boss or good coworkers. Still other values deal with the work itself, like whether your job tasks provide you with freedom or a sense of achievement.

● ● **3.2**

Describe values and how they affect job satisfaction.

Value-Percept Theory

Values play a key role in explaining job satisfaction. **Value-percept theory** argues that job satisfaction depends on whether you *perceive* that your job

49

Percentage of Americans who say they are satisfied with their jobs.

supplies the things that you *value*.[11] This theory can be summarized with the following equation:

$$\text{Dissatisfaction} = (V_{\text{want}} - V_{\text{have}}) \times (V_{\text{importance}})$$

In this equation, V_{want} reflects how much of a value an employee wants, V_{have} indicates how much of that value the

TABLE 3-1	Commonly Assessed Work Values
Categories	**Specific Values**
Pay	High salary Secure salary
Promotions	Frequent promotions Promotions based on ability
Supervision	Good supervisory relations Praise for good work
Coworkers	Enjoyable coworkers Responsible coworkers
Work Itself	Utilization of ability Freedom and independence Intellectual stimulation Creative expression Sense of achievement
Altruism	Helping others Moral causes
Status	Prestige Power over others Fame
Environment	Comfort Safety

Key Question: Which of these things are *most important* to you?

Source: Adapted from R. V. Dawis, "Vocational Interests, Values, and Preferences," in *Handbook of Industrial and Organizational Psychology,* Vol. 2, ed. M. D. Dunnette and L. M. Hough (Palo Alto, CA: Consulting Psychologists Press, 1991), pp. 834–71.

job supplies, and $V_{importance}$ reflects how important the value is to the employee. Big differences between wants and haves create a sense of dissatisfaction, especially when the value in question is important. Note that the difference between V_{want}

pay satisfaction. You want to be earning around $70,000 a year but are currently earning $50,000 a year, so there's a $20,000 discrepancy. Does that mean you feel a great deal of pay dissatisfaction? Only if pay is one of the most important values to you from Table 3-1. If pay isn't that important, you likely don't feel much dissatisfaction.

Value-percept theory also suggests that people evaluate job satisfaction according to specific "facets" of the job.[12] After all, a "job" isn't one thing—it's a collection of tasks, relationships, and rewards.[13] The most common facets that employees consider in judging their job satisfaction appear in Figure 3-1. The figure includes the "want vs. have" calculations that drive satisfaction with pay, promotions, supervision, coworkers, and the work itself. The figure also shows how satisfaction with those five facets adds together to create "overall job satisfaction." Figure 3-1 shows that employees might be satisfied for all kinds of reasons. One person may be satisfied because she's in a high-paying job and working for a good boss. Another person may be satisfied because he has good coworkers and enjoyable work tasks. You may have noticed that a few of the values in Table 3-1—such as working for moral causes and gaining fame and prestige—are not represented in Figure 3-1. This omission is because those values are not relevant in all jobs, unlike pay, promotions, and so forth. For a discussion of values and satisfaction in the world of sports, see our **OB in Sports** feature.

● ● **3.3**

List the specific facets that individuals often use to evaluate their job satisfaction.

The first facet in Figure 3-1, *pay satisfaction*, refers to employees' feelings about their pay, including whether it is as much as they deserve, secure, and adequate for both normal expenses and luxury items.[14] Similar to the other facets, pay satisfaction is based on a comparison of the pay that employees want and the pay they receive.[15] Although more money is almost always better, most employees base their desired pay on a careful examination of their job duties and the pay given

> **"Although more money is almost always better, most employees base their desired pay on a careful examination of their job duties and the pay given to comparable colleagues."**

and V_{have} gets multiplied by importance, so existing discrepancies get magnified for important values and minimized for trivial values. As an example, say that you were evaluating your

to comparable colleagues.[16] As a result, even nonmillionaires can be quite satisfied with their pay (thankfully for most of us!). Take the employees at Bright Horizons, for example. The

FIGURE 3-1 The Value-Percept Theory of Job Satisfaction

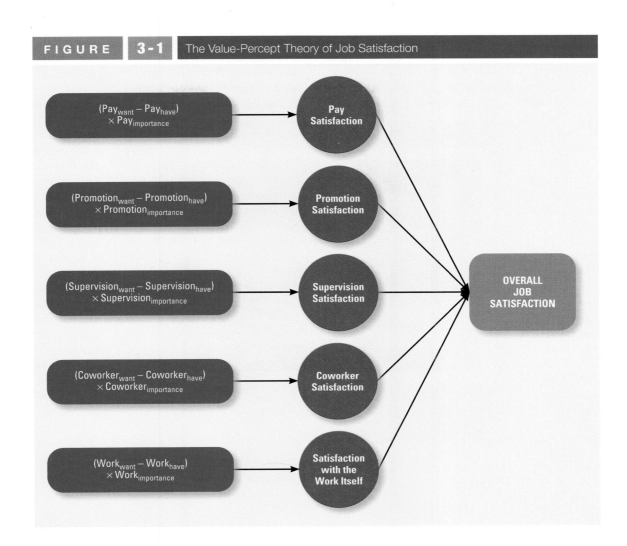

Massachusetts-based provider of child care and early education programs provides its employees with an average salary of around $50,000 in an industry known for significantly lower wages.[17] Bright Horizons employees experience high pay satisfaction because they make more than comparable colleagues working in the child care area.

The next facet in Figure 3-1, *promotion satisfaction*, refers to employees' feelings about the company's promotion policies and their execution, including whether promotions are frequent, fair, and based on ability.[18] Unlike pay, some employees may not want frequent promotions because promotions bring more responsibility and increased work hours.[19] However, many employees value promotions because they provide opportunities for more personal growth, a better wage, and more prestige. QuikTrip, the Oklahoma-based chain of gas and convenience stores, does a good job fostering promotion satisfaction on the part of its employees. "Promote from within" is a key motto in the company, and all 400-plus of its managers worked their way up from entry-level positions.[20]

Supervision satisfaction reflects employees' feelings about their boss, including whether the boss is competent, polite, and a good communicator (rather than lazy, annoying, and too distant).[21] Most employees ask two questions about their supervisors: (1) "Can they help me attain the things that I value?" and (2) "Are they generally likable?"[22] The first question depends on whether supervisors provide rewards for good performance, help employees obtain necessary resources, and protect employees from unnecessary distractions. The second question depends on whether supervisors have good personalities, as well as values and beliefs similar to the employees' philosophies. Valero Energy, the Texas-based oil refiner and gas retailer, works hard to foster a sense of supervision satisfaction. When it comes to receiving bonuses, executives only get theirs when everyone else in the organization has received one.[23] As a result, supervisors work harder to make sure that employees can get their jobs done.

Coworker satisfaction refers to employees' feelings about their fellow employees, including whether coworkers are smart, responsible, helpful, fun, and interesting as opposed to lazy, gossipy, unpleasant, and boring.[24] Employees ask the same kinds of questions about their coworkers that they do about their supervisors: (1) "Can they help me do my job?" and (2) "Do I enjoy being around them?" The first question is critical because most of us rely, to some extent, on our coworkers when performing job tasks. The second question also is important because we spend just as much time with coworkers as we do members of our own family. Coworkers who are pleasant and fun can make the workweek go much faster, whereas coworkers who are disrespectful and annoying can make even one day seem like an eternity. Arbitron, the New York–based radio market research firm, takes an unusual step to increase coworker satisfaction. Employees can

choose to recognize their coworkers' achievements with a $100 American Express gift card, with no restrictions on how many they can give out.[25] Last year, 300 of its 1,400-plus employees received rewards totaling $50,000.

The last facet in Figure 3-1, *satisfaction with the work itself*,

Pay satisfaction is based on a comparison of the pay that employees want and the pay they receive.

reflects employees' feelings about their actual work tasks, including whether those tasks are challenging, interesting, and respected, and make use of key skills rather than being dull, repetitive, and uncomfortable.[26] Whereas the previous four facets described the outcomes that result from work (pay, promotions) and the people who surround work (supervisors, coworkers), this facet focuses on what employees actually *do*. After all, even the best boss or most interesting coworkers can't compensate for 40 or 50 hours of complete

OB in Sports

How would you feel if you found something that you liked and that you were good at, but you couldn't make a living at it in the United States? That's the situation that women's college basketball players found themselves in before the Women's National Basketball Association (WNBA) was formed in 1996. Lisa Leslie, a 6-foot-5 member of the Los Angeles Sparks, was a member of the inaugural WNBA season. More than a decade later, she's a three-time league MVP and perhaps the signature figure of the league.

As Leslie reports for training camp to begin the 2008 season, she's bursting with enthusiasm.[27] The season to come promises to fulfill many different work values. For example, Michael Cooper, who coached the Sparks to 2001 and 2002 titles, has returned, supplying the good supervisory relations so critical to job satisfaction. In addition, Leslie is now joined by Candace Parker, the 6-foot-4 graduate of the University of Tennessee, to form one of the league's premier frontcourts. Parker's addition has supplied the positive

coworker relationships that can foster job satisfaction. Leslie and Parker have already spent time showing each other effective basketball moves, promising to flash an "L" (for Lisa) or "C" (for Candace) with their fingers each time they score with a borrowed move. The WNBA also offers a secure salary, paying an average of $47,000 for the season, with a maximum salary of $91,000.[28]

In addition, Leslie's WNBA career has given her the opportunity to pursue altruistic endeavors. For example, she has used her fame to bring awareness to breast cancer issues, as her mother once had a breast cancer scare.[29] She has also represented her country as a member of gold medal–winning teams at the 1996, 2000, 2004, and 2008 Olympics. All these opportunities bring a significance to Leslie's job that transcends the "Xs and Os" of basketball. When asked how long she intends to keep playing, Leslie responded: "As long as I'm enjoying the game, I intend to keep playing; when it's not fun, I'll quit."[30] ❖

Lisa Leslie has said, "As long as I'm enjoying the game, I intend to keep playing; when it's not fun, I'll quit."

boredom each week! How can employers instill a sense of satisfaction with the work itself? Valassis, a Michigan-based publisher of newspaper inserts and coupons, gives employees annual skill assessments to get a better feel for what they're good at.[31] It then provides employees with growth opportunities, sometimes even creating new positions to employ special talents.

Actual work tasks that make use of key skills rather than those that can be dull and repetitive or are mindless contribute to overall job satisfaction.

In summary, value-percept theory suggests that employees will be satisfied when they perceive that their job offers the pay, promotions, supervision, coworkers, and work tasks that they value. Of course, this theory begs the question: Which of those ingredients is most important? In other words, which of the five facets in Figure 3-1 has the strongest influence on overall job satisfaction? Several research studies have examined these issues and come up with the results shown in Figure 3-2. The figure depicts the correlation between each of the five satisfaction facets and an overall index of job satisfaction. (Recall that correlations of .10, .30, and .50 indicate weak, moderate, and strong relationships, respectively.)

Figure 3-2 suggests that satisfaction with the work itself is the single strongest driver of overall job satisfaction.[32] Supervision and coworker satisfaction are also strong drivers, and promotion and pay satisfaction have moderately strong effects. Why is satisfaction with the work itself so critical? Well, consider that a typical workweek contains around 2,400 minutes. How much of that time is spent thinking about how much money you make? 10 minutes? Maybe 20? The same is true for promotions—we may want them, but we don't necessarily spend hours a day thinking about them. We do spend a significant chunk of that time with other people though. Between lunches, meetings, hallway chats, and other conversations, we might easily spend 600 minutes a week with supervisors and coworkers. That leaves almost 1,800 minutes for just us and our work. As a result, it is difficult to be satisfied with your job if you don't like what you actually do. Of course, those of you who are full-time students might wonder what satisfaction means to you. See our **OB for Students** feature for some facets of student satisfaction.

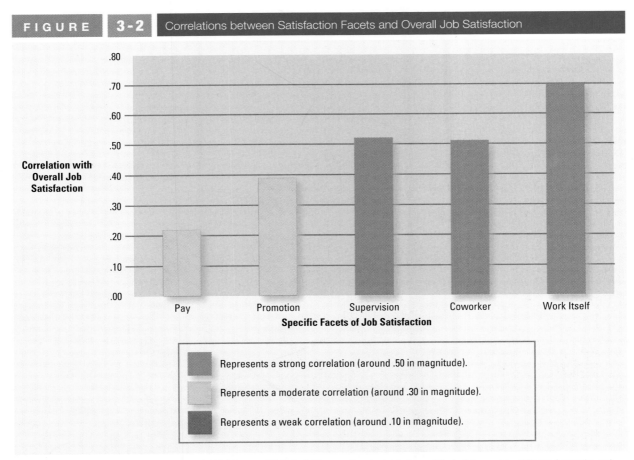

FIGURE 3-2 Correlations between Satisfaction Facets and Overall Job Satisfaction

Represents a strong correlation (around .50 in magnitude).

Represents a moderate correlation (around .30 in magnitude).

Represents a weak correlation (around .10 in magnitude).

Sources: G. H. Ironson, P. C. Smith, M. T. Brannick, W. M. Gibson, and K. B. Paul, "Construction of a Job in General Scale: A Comparison of Global, Composite, and Specific Measures," *Journal of Applied Psychology* 74 (1989), pp. 193–200; S. S. Russell, C. Spitzmuller, L. F. Lin, J. M. Stanton, P. C. Smith, and G. H. Ironson, "Shorter Can Also Be Better: The Abridged Job in General Scale," *Educational and Psychological Measurement* 64 (2004), pp. 878–93.

Job Characteristics Theory

Given how important enjoyable work tasks are to overall job satisfaction, it's worth spending more time describing the kinds of tasks that most people find enjoyable. Researchers began focusing on this question in the 1950s and 1960s, partly in reaction to practices based in the "scientific management" perspective. Scientific management focuses on increasing the efficiency of job tasks by making them more simplified and specialized and using time and motion studies to plan task movements and sequences carefully.[33] The hope was that such steps would increase worker productivity and reduce the breadth of skills required to complete a job, ultimately improving organizational profitability. Instead, the simplified and routine jobs tended to lower job satisfaction while increasing absenteeism and turnover.[34] Put simply: Boring jobs may be easier, but they're not necessarily better.

So what kinds of work tasks are especially satisfying? Research suggests that three "critical psychological states" make work satisfying. The first psychological state is believing in the *meaningfulness of work*, which reflects the degree to which work tasks are viewed as something that "counts" in the employee's system of philosophies and beliefs.[35] Trivial tasks tend to be less satisfying than tasks that make employees feel like they're aiding the organization or society in some meaningful way. The second psychological state is perceiving *responsibility for outcomes*, which captures the degree to which employees feel that they are key drivers of the quality of the unit's work.[36] Sometimes employees feel like their efforts don't really matter because work outcomes are dictated by effective procedures, efficient technologies, or more influential colleagues. Finally, the third psychological state is *knowledge of results*, which reflects the extent to which employees know how well (or how poorly) they are doing.[37] Many employees work in jobs in which they never find out about their mistakes or never fully realize that they've performed well.

  3.4

Understand the job characteristics that can create a sense of satisfaction with the work itself.

Think about times when you felt especially proud of a job well done. At that moment, you were probably experiencing all three psychological states. You were aware of the result

OB for Students

What does satisfaction mean for you as a student? After all, pay, promotions, and supervision are less relevant for full-time students than for full-time employees. One recent study examined the facets of satisfaction for students,[38] including:

- **University satisfaction.** Do students feel good about their university choice and experience, and would they recommend their university to others?

- **Housing satisfaction.** Do students feel good about where they live and the surrounding neighborhood?

- **Leisure satisfaction.** Do students feel good about their social life, their leisure activities, and their friendships?

The results of the study showed that all three facets had moderately strong positive correlations with an index of overall student satisfaction. So students were more satisfied when they liked the university, liked where they lived, and felt that they were having a good time. In addition, the more satisfied the students were, the better they performed in terms of their grade point average (GPA). In other words, happy students tended to be better students.

One word of caution, however. Notice the negative path from leisure satisfaction to student GPA. That path indicates that those two variables actually correlate negatively. In other words, having a lot of fun made students more satisfied, but it also made them perform less well in their classes. Moral of the story: You *can* have too much of a good thing! ❖

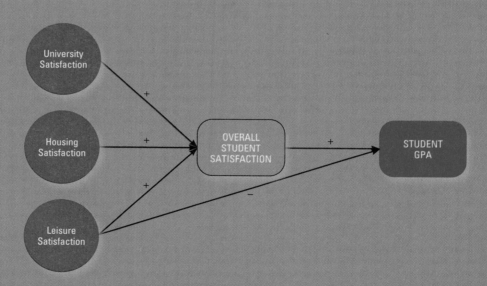

● **JOB CHARACTERISTICS THEORY** A theory that describes the central characteristics of intrinsically satisfying jobs.

● **VARIETY** The degree to which the job requires a number of different activities that involve a number of different skills and talents.

● **IDENTITY** The degree to which the job requires completing a whole, identifiable piece of work from beginning to end with a visible outcome.

● **SIGNIFICANCE** The degree to which the job has a substantial impact on the lives of other people, particularly people in the world at large.

● **AUTONOMY** The degree to which the job provides freedom, independence, and discretion to the individual performing the work.

(after all, some job had been done well). You felt you were somehow responsible for that result (otherwise, why would you feel proud?). Finally, you felt that the result of the work was somehow meaningful (otherwise, why would you have remembered it just now?). The next obvious question then becomes, "What kinds of tasks create these psychological states?" **Job characteristics theory**, which describes the central characteristics of intrinsically satisfying jobs, attempts to answer this question. As shown in Figure 3-3, job characteristics theory argues that five core job characteristics (variety, identity, significance, autonomy, and feedback, which you can remember with the acronym "VISAF") result in high levels of the three psychological states, making work tasks more satisfying.[39]

Three core characteristics are especially relevant to the perceived meaningfulness of work. **Variety** is the degree to which the job requires a number of different activities that involve a number of different skills and talents.[40] When variety is high, almost every workday is different in some way, and job holders rarely feel a sense of monotony or repetition.[41] Of course, we could picture jobs that have a variety of boring tasks such as screwing different-sized nuts onto different-colored bolts, but such jobs do not involve a number of different skills and talents.[42] **Identity** is the degree to which the job requires completing a whole, identifiable piece of work from beginning to end with a visible outcome.[43] When a job has high identity, employees can point to something and say, "There, I did that." The transformation from inputs to finished product is very visible, and the employee feels a distinct sense of beginning and closure.[44] **Significance** is the degree to which the job has a substantial impact on the lives of other people, particularly people in the world at large.[45] Virtually any job can be important if it helps put food on the table for a family, send kids to college, or make employees feel like they're doing their part for the working world. That said, significance as a core job characteristic captures something beyond that—the belief that this job *really matters*.

The other two core characteristics have a significant impact on the perceived responsibility for, and knowledge of, work outcomes. **Autonomy** is the degree to which the job provides freedom, independence, and discretion to the individual performing the work.[46] When your job provides autonomy, you view the outcomes of it as the product of your efforts rather than the result of careful instructions from your boss or a well-written manual of procedures.[47] Autonomy comes in multiple forms, including the freedom to control the timing, scheduling, and sequencing of work activities, as well as the procedures and methods used to complete work tasks.[48] To many of us, high levels of autonomy are the difference between "having a long leash" and being "micromanaged."

FIGURE 3-3 Job Characteristics Theory

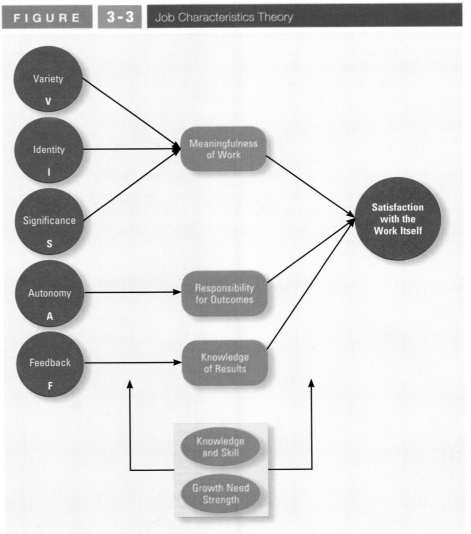

Feedback is the degree to which carrying out the activities required by the job provides the worker with clear information about how well he or she is performing.[49] A critical distinction must be noted: This core characteristic reflects feedback obtained *directly from the job* as opposed to feedback from coworkers or supervisors. Most employees receive formal performance appraisals from their bosses, but that feedback occurs once or maybe twice a year. When the job provides its own feedback, that feedback can be experienced almost every day.

How important are the core characteristics to satisfaction with the work itself? A meta-analysis of 75 different research studies showed that the five core job characteristics are moderately to strongly related to work satisfaction.[50] However, those results don't mean that *every* employee wants more variety, more autonomy, and so forth. The bottom of Figure 3-3 includes two other variables: *knowledge and skill* and *growth need strength* (which captures whether employees have strong needs for personal accomplishment or developing themselves beyond where they currently are).[51] In the jargon of theory diagrams, these variables are called "moderators." Rather than directly affecting other variables in the diagram, moderators influence the strength of the relationships between variables. If employees lack the required knowledge and skill or lack a desire for growth and development, more variety and autonomy should *not* increase their satisfaction very much.[52] However, when employees are very talented and feel a strong need for growth, the core job characteristics become even more powerful. A graphical depiction of this moderator effect appears in Figure 3-4, where you can see that the relationship between the core job characteristics and satisfaction becomes stronger when growth need strength increases.

Given how critical the five core job characteristics are to job satisfaction, many organizations have employed job characteristics theory to help improve satisfaction among their employees. The first step in this process is assessing the current level of the characteristics to arrive at a "satisfaction potential score." The organization, together with job design consultants, then attempts to redesign aspects of the job to increase the core job characteristic levels. Often this step results in job enrichment, such that the duties and responsibilities associated with a job are expanded to provide more variety, identity, autonomy, and so forth. Research suggests that such enrichment efforts can indeed boost job satisfaction levels.[53] Moreover, enrichment efforts can heighten work accuracy and customer satisfaction, though training and labor costs tend to rise as a result of such changes.[54]

Mood and Emotions

Let's say you're a satisfied employee, maybe because you get paid well and work for a good boss or because your work tasks provide you with variety and autonomy. Does this mean you'll definitely be satisfied at 11:00 a.m. next Tuesday? Or 2:30 p.m. the following Thursday? Obviously it doesn't. Each employee's satisfaction levels fluctuate over time, rising and falling like some sort of emotional stock market. This fluctuation might seem strange, given that people's pay, supervisors, coworkers, and work tasks don't change from one hour to the next. The key lies in remembering that job satisfaction reflects what you think and feel about your job. So part of it is rational, based on a careful appraisal of the job and the things it supplies. But another part of it is emotional, based on what you feel "in your gut" while you're at work or thinking about work. So a satisfied employee feels good about his or her job *on average*, but things happen during the course of the day to make him or her feel better at some times (and worse at others).

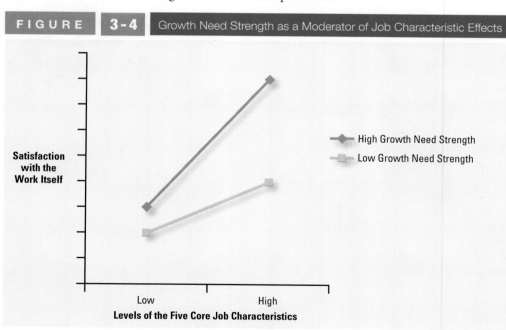

FIGURE 3-4 Growth Need Strength as a Moderator of Job Characteristic Effects

Satisfaction with the Work Itself

High Growth Need Strength
Low Growth Need Strength

Low   High
Levels of the Five Core Job Characteristics

Source: Adapted from B. T. Loher, R. A. Noe, N. L. Moeller, and M. P. Fitzgerald, "A Meta-Analysis of the Relation of Job Characteristics to Job Satisfaction," *Journal of Applied Psychology* 70 (1985), pp. 280–89.

"EACH EMPLOYEE'S SATISFACTION LEVELS FLUCTUATE OVER TIME, RISING AND FALLING LIKE SOME SORT OF EMOTIONAL STOCK MARKET."

● ● 3.5

Describe how job satisfaction is affected by day-to-day events.

Figure 3-5 illustrates the satisfaction levels for one employee during the course of a workday, from around 9:00 a.m. to 5:00 p.m. You can see that this employee did a number of different things during the day, from answering e-mails to eating lunch with friends to participating in a brainstorming meeting regarding a new project. You also can see that the employee came into the day feeling relatively satisfied, though satisfaction levels had several ebbs and flows during the next eight hours. What's responsible for those ebbs and flows in satisfaction levels? Two related concepts: mood and emotions.

● ● 3.6

Define mood and emotions and describe the specific forms they take.

What kind of mood are you in right now? Good? Bad? Somewhere in between? Why are you in that kind of mood?

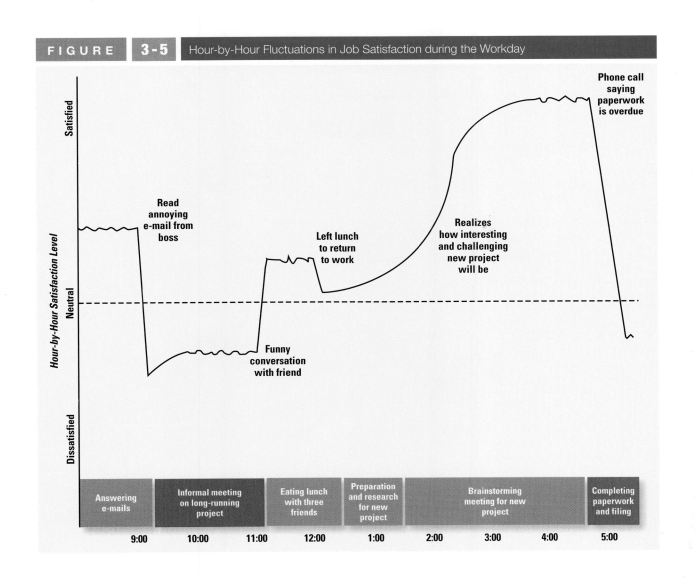

FIGURE 3-5 Hour-by-Hour Fluctuations in Job Satisfaction during the Workday

Hour-by-Hour Satisfaction Level

Satisfied — Neutral — Dissatisfied

Read annoying e-mail from boss

Funny conversation with friend

Left lunch to return to work

Realizes how interesting and challenging new project will be

Phone call saying paperwork is overdue

Answering e-mails | Informal meeting on long-running project | Eating lunch with three friends | Preparation and research for new project | Brainstorming meeting for new project | Completing paperwork and filing

9:00   10:00   11:00   12:00   1:00   2:00   3:00   4:00   5:00

● **MOODS** States of feeling that are often mild in intensity, last for an extended period of time, and are not explicitly directed at or caused by anything.

Do you really even know? (If it's a bad mood, we hope it has nothing to do with this book!) Moods are states of feeling that are often mild in intensity, last for an extended period of time, and are not explicitly directed at or caused by anything.[55] When people are in a good or bad mood, they don't always know who (or what) deserves the credit or blame; they just happen to be feeling that way for a stretch of their day. Of course, it would be oversimplifying things to call all moods either good or bad. Sometimes we're in a serene mood, and sometimes we're in an enthusiastic mood. Both are "good" but obviously feel quite different. Similarly, sometimes we're in a bored mood, and sometimes we're in a hostile mood. Both are "bad" but, again, feel quite different.

It turns out that there are a number of different moods that we might experience during the workday. Figure 3-6 summarizes the different moods in which people sometimes find themselves. The figure illustrates that moods can be categorized in two ways: *pleasantness* and *engagement*. First, the horizontal axis of the figure reflects whether you feel pleasant (in a "good mood") or unpleasant (in a "bad mood").[56] The figure uses green colors to illustrate pleasant moods and red to illustrate unpleasant moods. Second, the vertical axis of the figure reflects whether you feel engaged, activated, and aroused or disengaged, deactivated, and unaroused.[57] The figure uses darker colors to convey higher levels of engagement and lighter colors to convey lower levels. Note that some moods are neither good nor bad. For example, being surprised or astonished (high engagement) and quiet or still (low engagement) are neither pleasant nor unpleasant. As a result, those latter moods are left colorless in Figure 3-6.

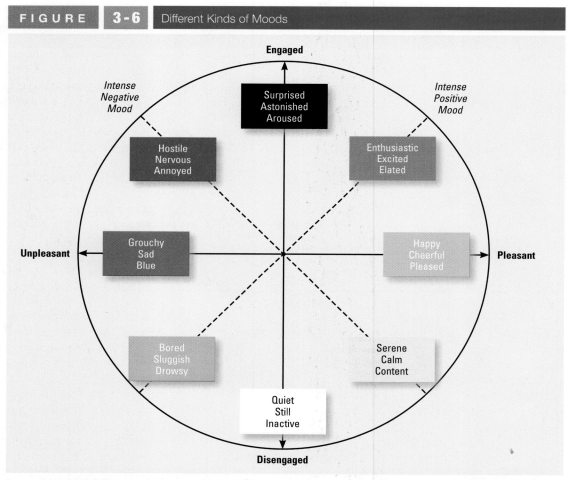

FIGURE 3-6 Different Kinds of Moods

Sources: Adapted from D. Watson and A. Tellegen, "Toward a Consensual Structure of Mood," *Psychological Bulletin* 98 (1985), pp. 219–35; J. A. Russell, "A Circumplex Model of Affect," *Journal of Personality and Social Psychology* 39 (1980), pp. 1161–78; R. J. Larsen and E. Diener, "Promises and Problems with the Circumplex Model of Emotion," in *Review of Personality and Social Psychology: Emotion,* Vol. 13, ed. M. S. Clark (Newbury Park, CA: Sage, 1992), pp. 25–59.

Figure 3-6 also illustrates that the most intense positive mood is characterized by feeling enthusiastic, excited, and elated. When employees feel this way, coworkers are likely to remark, "Wow, you're sure in a good mood!" In contrast, the most intense negative mood is characterized by feeling hostile, nervous, and annoyed. This kind of mood often triggers the question, "Wow, what's gotten you in such a bad mood?" If we return to our chart of hour-by-hour job satisfaction in Figure 3-5, what kind of mood do you think the employee was in while answering e-mails? Probably a happy, cheerful, and pleased mood. What kind of mood was the employee in during the informal meeting on the long-running project? Probably a grouchy, sad, and blue mood. Finally, what kind of mood do you think the employee was in during the brainstorming meeting for the new project? Clearly, an enthusiastic, excited, and elated mood. This employee would report especially high levels of job satisfaction at this point in time.

Some organizations take creative steps to foster positive moods among their employees. For example, the SAS Institute, the North Carolina–based maker of statistical software packages, has an on-site gym with a pool, billiards, volleyball courts, soccer fields, tennis courts, ping-pong tables, and a putting green.[58] Sometimes a good game of ping-pong is all it takes to make a grouchy mood turn cheerful! Griffin Hospital, based in Connecticut, offers its employees (and patients) family-style kitchens, strolling musicians, nonfluorescent lighting, and chair massages.[59] Such perks may not rival the importance of pay, promotions, supervision, coworkers, and the work itself as far as job satisfaction is concerned, but they can help boost employees' moods during a particular workday.

Let's return to our chart of hour-by-hour job satisfaction in Figure 3-5. Although it's fairly easy to see the different moods that occur during the day, it also is obvious that there are events that trigger sudden changes in mood. Why does this occur? Because specific events at work cause positive and negative emotions. Emotions are states of feeling that are often intense, last for only a few minutes, and are clearly directed at (and caused by) someone or some circumstance. The difference between moods and emotions becomes clear in the way we describe them to others. We describe moods by saying, "I'm feeling grouchy," but we describe emotions by saying, "I'm feeling angry *at my boss*."[60] Emotions are always *about something*.

People experience a variety of different emotions during their daily lives.[61] *Positive emotions* include joy, pride, relief, hope, love, and compassion. *Negative emotions* include anger, anxiety, fear, guilt, shame, sadness, envy, and disgust. What emotion do you think the employee experienced in Figure 3-5 when reading a disrespectful e-mail from the boss? Probably anger. What emotion do you think that same employee enjoyed during a funny conversation with a friend? Possibly joy, or maybe relief that lunch had arrived and a somewhat bad day was halfway over. Leaving lunch to return to work might have triggered either anxiety (because the bad day might resume) or sadness (because the fun time with friends had ended). Luckily, the employee's sense of joy at taking on a new project that was interesting and challenging was right around the corner. The day did end on a down note, however, as the phone call signaling overdue paperwork was likely met with some mix of anger, fear, guilt, or even disgust (no one likes paperwork!).

Of course, just because employees *feel* many different emotions during the workday doesn't mean they're supposed to *show* those emotions. Some jobs demand that employees live up to the adage "never let 'em see you sweat." In particular, service jobs in which employees make direct contact with customers often require those employees to hide any anger, anxiety, sadness, or disgust that they may feel. Such jobs are high in what is called emotional labor, or the need to manage emotions to complete job duties successfully.[62] Flight attendants are trained to "put on a happy face" in front of passengers, retail salespeople are trained to suppress any annoyance with customers, and restaurant servers are trained to act like they're having fun on their job even when they're not.

Is it a good idea to require emotional labor on the part of employees? Research on emotional contagion shows that one person can "catch" or "be infected by" the emotions of another person.[63] If a customer service representative is angry or sad, those negative emotions can be transferred to a customer (like a cold or disease). If that transfer occurs, it becomes less likely that customers will view the experience favorably and spend more money, which potentially harms the bottom line. From this perspective, emotional labor seems like a vital part of good customer service. Unfortunately, other evidence suggests that emotional labor places great strain on employees and that their "bottled up" emotions may end up bubbling over, sometimes resulting in angry outbursts against customers or emotional exhaustion

"Research on emotional contagion shows that one person can 'catch' or 'be infected by' the emotions of another person."

● EMOTIONS States of feeling that are often intense, last for only a few minutes, and are clearly directed at (and caused by) someone or some circumstance.

● EMOTIONAL LABOR The need to manage emotions to complete job duties successfully.

● EMOTIONAL CONTAGION A process whereby one person can "catch" or "be infected by" the emotions of another person.

and burnout on the part of employees.[64] For more on managing emotions, see our **OB on Screen** feature.

HOW IMPORTANT IS JOB SATISFACTION?

Several factors influence an employee's job satisfaction, from pay to coworkers to job tasks to day-to-day moods and emotions. Of course, the most obvious remaining question is, "Does job satisfaction really matter?" More precisely, does job satisfaction have a significant impact on job performance and organizational commitment—the two primary outcomes in our integrative model of OB? Figure 3-7 summarizes the research evidence linking job satisfaction to job performance and organizational commitment. This same sort of figure will appear in each of the remaining chapters of this book so that you can get a better feel for which of the concepts in our integrative model has the strongest impact on performance and commitment.

 3.7

Understand how job satisfaction affects job performance and organizational commitment, as well as how it affects life satisfaction.

Figure 3-7 reveals that job satisfaction does influence job performance. Why? One reason is that job satisfaction is moderately correlated with task performance. Satisfied employees do a better job of fulfilling the duties described in their job descriptions,[65] and evidence suggests that positive feelings improve creativity, problem solving, and decision making[66] and enhance memory and recall of certain kinds of information.[67] Positive feelings also improve general activity and energy levels.[68] Apart from these sorts of findings, the benefits of job satisfaction for task performance might be explained on an hour-by-hour basis. At any given moment, employees wage a war between paying attention to a given work task and attending to "off-task" things such as stray thoughts, distractions, interruptions, and so forth. Positive feelings when working on

OB on Screen

The Island

I wish that there was more . . . more than just waiting to go to the Island.

With those words, Lincoln Six Echo (Ewan McGregor) sums up his monotonous existence in *The Island* (Dir.: Michael Bay, Dream-Works, 2005). He gets up each morning, puts on his white jumpsuit, and goes through life within the boundaries of a sealed complex, designed to protect the survivors of "the contamination" from the pathogens that have destroyed the outside world. Life within the complex is dedicated to keeping its occupants alive and healthy over the long term, as the survivors slowly begin to repopulate the damaged planet.

Unfortunately for Lincoln, the complex seems dedicated to keeping its occupants in a relatively disengaged mood at all times: quiet, still, calm, and serene. Expressing annoyance at any little thing brings a visit from one of the security personnel. So does getting too cozy with any of the other occupants, as when Lincoln receives a "proximity warning" for touching the arm of Jordan Two Delta (Scarlett Johansson). The repeating message over the loudspeaker says it all: "Be polite, pleasant, and peaceful. A healthy person is a happy person."

Things aren't much better at Lincoln's job, where he monitors a set of thin tubes day in and day out, without even knowing where the tubes go or what's flowing through them. As he says to his friend, Jones Three Echo (Ethan Phillips), "Jones, do you ever get bored doing this . . . this boring job. . . . I mean, what are we doing here anyway?" His job is clearly low on every conceivable core job characteristic.

The only emotion that is encouraged in the complex is hope. Every day a lottery occurs in which one lucky soul wins a one-way ticket to "the island"—nature's last remaining pathogen-free zone. Each night, those who don't win the lottery are left to cling to this motto: "Your time will come." Unfortunately, things are not what they seem, and the island may not be the paradise it's made out to be. Suffice it to say that a trip to the island won't exactly result in feelings of serenity and contentment! ❖

FIGURE 3-7 Effects of Job Satisfaction on Performance and Commitment

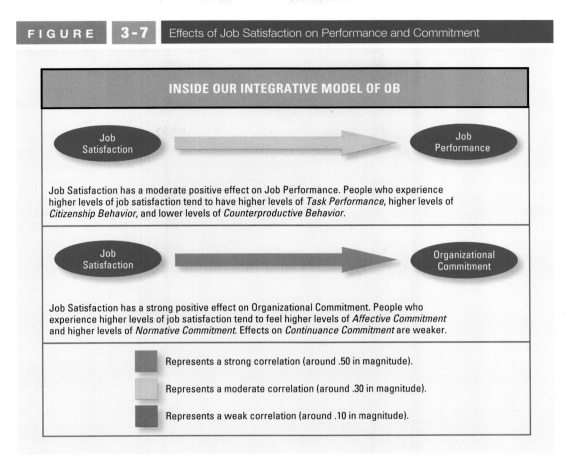

INSIDE OUR INTEGRATIVE MODEL OF OB

Job Satisfaction → Job Performance

Job Satisfaction has a moderate positive effect on Job Performance. People who experience higher levels of job satisfaction tend to have higher levels of *Task Performance*, higher levels of *Citizenship Behavior,* and lower levels of *Counterproductive Behavior.*

Job Satisfaction → Organizational Commitment

Job Satisfaction has a strong positive effect on Organizational Commitment. People who experience higher levels of job satisfaction tend to feel higher levels of *Affective Commitment* and higher levels of *Normative Commitment.* Effects on *Continuance Commitment* are weaker.

Represents a strong correlation (around .50 in magnitude).

Represents a moderate correlation (around .30 in magnitude).

Represents a weak correlation (around .10 in magnitude).

Sources: A. Cooper-Hakim and C. Viswesvaran, "The Construct of Work Commitment: Testing an Integrative Framework," *Psychological Bulletin* 131 (2005), pp. 241–59; R. S. Dalal, "A Meta-Analysis of the Relationship between Organizational Citizenship Behavior and Counterproductive Work Behavior," *Journal of Applied Psychology* 90 (2005), pp. 1241–55; D. A. Harrison, D. A. Newman, and P. L. Roth, "How Important Are Job Attitudes? Meta-Analytic Comparisons of Integrative Behavioral Outcomes and Time Sequences," *Academy of Management Journal* 49 (2006), pp. 305–25; T. A. Judge, C. J. Thoreson, J. E. Bono, and G. K. Patton, "The Job Satisfaction–Job Performance Relationship: A Qualitative and Quantitative Review," *Psychological Bulletin* 127 (2001), pp. 376–407; J. A. LePine, A. Erez, and D. E. Johnson, "The Nature and Dimensionality of Organizational Citizenship Behavior: A Critical Review and Meta-Analysis," *Journal of Applied Psychology* 87 (2002), pp. 52–65; J. P. Meyer, D. J. Stanley, L. Herscovitch, and L. Topolnytsky, "Affective, Continuance, and Normative Commitment to the Organization: A Meta-Analysis of Antecedents, Correlates, and Consequences," *Journal of Vocational Behavior* 61 (2002), pp. 20–52.

job tasks can pull attention away from those distractions and channel people's attention to task accomplishment.[69] When such concentration occurs, an employee is more focused on work at a given point in time. Of course, the relationship between satisfaction and task performance can work in reverse to some extent, such that people tend to enjoy jobs that they can perform more successfully.[70]

Job satisfaction also is correlated moderately with citizenship behavior. Satisfied employees engage in more frequent "extra mile" behaviors to help their coworkers and their organization.[71] Positive feelings increase their desire to interact with others and often result in spontaneous acts of helping because employees seek to behave in a manner that matches their current mood.[72] In addition, job satisfaction has a moderate negative correlation with counterproductive behavior. Satisfied employees engage

in fewer intentionally destructive actions that could harm their workplace.[73] Intense dissatisfaction is often the trigger that prompts an employee to "lash out" by engaging in rule breaking, theft, sabotage, or other retaliatory behaviors.[74] The more satisfied employees are, the less likely they will feel those sorts of temptations.

Figure 3-7 also reveals that job satisfaction influences organizational commitment. Why? Job satisfaction is strongly correlated with affective commitment, so satisfied employees are more likely to want to stay with the organization.[75] After all, why would employees want to leave a place where they're happy? Another reason is that job satisfaction is strongly correlated with normative commitment. Satisfied employees are more likely to feel an obligation to remain with their firm[76] and a need to "repay" the organization for whatever it is that makes them so satisfied, whether good pay, interesting job tasks, or effective supervision. However, job satisfaction is uncorrelated with continuance commitment because satisfaction does not create a cost-based need to remain with the organization. Still, when taken together, these commitment effects become more apparent when you consider the kinds of employees who withdraw from the organization. In many cases, dissatisfied employees are those who sit daydreaming at their desks, come in late, are frequently absent, and eventually decide to quit their jobs.

Stray thoughts and distractions interrupt an employee at any given moment. Positive feelings when working can pull attention away from these distractions.

Life Satisfaction

Of course, job satisfaction is important for other reasons as well—reasons that have little to do with job performance or organizational commitment. For example, job satisfaction is strongly related to life satisfaction, or the degree to which employees feel a sense of happiness with their lives. Research shows that job satisfaction is one of the strongest predictors of life satisfaction. Put simply, people feel better about their lives when they feel better about their jobs.[77] This link makes sense when you realize how much of our identity

OB Internationally

The "money can't buy happiness" adage can even be supported using national-level data. For example, survey data in the United States, Britain, and Japan show that people are no happier today than they were 50 years ago, even though average incomes have more than doubled during that span.[78] Another way of examining this issue explores the connection between national wealth and average happiness: Do wealthier nations have citizens with higher levels of life satisfaction? The figure to the right provides a representation of the relationship between average income per citizen for a nation and the percentage of respondents who describe themselves as happy, according to population surveys.[79]

Comparing countries reveals that nations above the poverty line are indeed happier than nations below the poverty line. However, for countries with an average income of $20,000 or more, additional income is not associated with higher levels of life satisfaction.[80] For example, the United States is the richest country on Earth, but it trails nations like the Netherlands and Ireland in life satisfaction. Understanding differences in life satisfaction across nations is important to organizations for two reasons. First, such differences may influence how receptive a

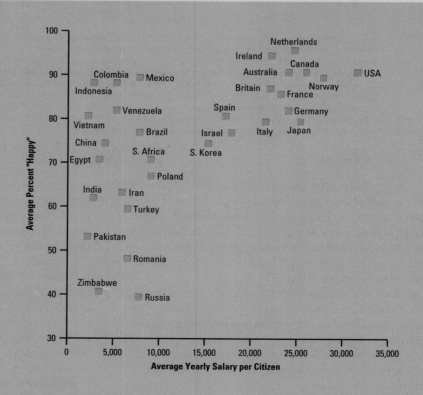

given nation is to the company's products. Second, such differences may affect the kinds of policies and practices an organization needs to use when employing individuals in that nation.

is wrapped up in our jobs. What's the first question that people ask one another after being introduced? That's right—"What do you do?" If you feel bad about your answer to that question, it's hard to feel good about your life.

As it turns out, increases in job satisfaction have a stronger impact on life satisfaction than do increases in salary or income. As the old adage goes, "money can't buy happiness." This finding may seem surprising, given that pay satisfaction is one facet of overall job satisfaction (see Figure 3-1). However, you might recall that pay satisfaction is a weaker driver of overall job satisfaction than other facets, such as the work itself, supervision, or coworkers (see Figure 3-2). We also should note that pay satisfaction depends less on absolute salary levels and more on relative salary levels (i.e., how your salary compares to your circle of peers). As the writer H. L. Mencken once remarked, "A wealthy man is one who earns $100 a year more than his wife's sister's husband."[81] For more on the relationship between money and happiness, see our **OB Internationally** feature. ■

CHECK OUT

www.mhhe.com/ColquittEss

for study materials including Interactive Exercises, Quizzes, iPod downloads, and video.

CASE: Patagonia

Whenever a company establishes a unique culture or a unique management style, the challenge becomes maintaining that uniqueness as time goes on. Yvon Chouinard has dealt with this challenge in two ways. First, he has limited Patagonia's growth to around 5 percent a year.[82] That growth rate allows the company to remain incredibly choosy about whom it hires while ensuring that new hires share the company's passions. Second, Chouinard has resisted the pressure to take Patagonia public, remaining the sole owner of the company. That choice prevents him from having to justify his "let my people surf" philosophy or his donations to grassroots environmental groups to shareholders who emphasize quarter-by-quarter profits. As Chouinard summarizes, "Everybody tells me it's an undervalued company . . . that we could grow this business like crazy and then go public, make a killing. But that would be the end of everything I've wanted to do."[83]

Patagonia is engaging in a new strategy that could prove challenging, however. Although Patagonia is most closely identified with cold-weather apparel or gear, Chouinard believes that climate change will allow for more growth in surfing products than skiing products.[84] The company has therefore partnered with three professional surfers to create a vision of what

Patagonia surf shops should look like. The surfers took pay cuts to go with Patagonia rather than the larger, more established surf chains, but they share Chouinard's vision and values. The plan is to focus on building more durable and long-lasting clothing and boards while using the shops as gathering places for surfers and environmentalists. Patagonia will open 10 surf stores within the next several years, with further openings contingent on store success. The challenge will be to replicate "the Patagonia experience" for employees at brand new locations and in an industry in which Patagonia is not the market expert.

3.1 If you were charged with the responsibility to open one of Patagonia's new surf shops, what would you emphasize about the company to applicants to convince them that Patagonia is a satisfying place to work?

3.2 What steps could you take to make sure that potential recruits would be passionate about the company and its causes? Are there any drawbacks to those sorts of steps?

3.3 What is it, exactly, about the "let my people surf" philosophy that would be so satisfying? If you were running one of the new surf shops, would anything concern you about that philosophy?

3.1 Job satisfaction is a pleasurable emotional state resulting from the appraisal of one's job or job experiences. It represents how you feel about your job and what you think about your job.

3.2 Values are things that people consciously or subconsciously want to seek or attain. According to value-percept theory, job satisfaction depends on whether you perceive that your job supplies those things that you value.

3.3 People often appraise their job satisfaction according to more specific facets of their job. These satisfaction facets include pay satisfaction, promotion satisfaction, supervision satisfaction, coworker satisfaction, and satisfaction with the work itself.

3.4 Job characteristics theory suggests that five "core characteristics"—variety, identity, significance, autonomy, and feedback—combine to result in particularly high levels of satisfaction with the work itself.

3.5 Apart from the influence of supervision, coworkers, pay, and the work itself, job satisfaction levels fluctuate during the course of the day. Rises and falls in job satisfaction are triggered by experiences of positive and negative events. Those events trigger changes in emotions that eventually give way to changes in mood.

3.6 Moods are states of feeling that are often mild in intensity, last for an extended period of time, and are not explicitly directed at anything. Intense positive moods include being enthusiastic, excited, and elated. Intense negative moods include being hostile, nervous, and annoyed. Emotions are states of feeling that are often intense, last only for a few minutes, and are clearly directed at someone or some circumstance. Positive emotions include joy, pride, relief, hope, love, and compassion. Negative emotions include anger, anxiety, fear, guilt, shame, sadness, envy, and disgust.

3.7 Job satisfaction has a moderately positive relationship with job performance and a strong positive relationship with organizational commitment. It also has a strong positive relationship with life satisfaction.

DISCUSSION QUESTIONS

3.1 Which of the values in Table 3-1 do you think are the most important to employees in general? Are there times when the values in the last three categories (altruism, status, and environment) become more important than the values in the first five categories (pay, promotions, supervision, coworkers, the work itself)?

3.2 What steps can organizations take to improve promotion satisfaction, supervision satisfaction, and coworker satisfaction?

3.3 Consider the five core job characteristics (variety, identity, significance, autonomy, and feedback). Do you think that any one of those characteristics is more important than the other four? Is it possible to have too much of some job characteristics?

3.4 We sometimes describe colleagues or friends as "moody." What do you think it means to be "moody" from the perspective of Figure 3-6?

ASSESSMENT: Core Job Characteristics

How satisfying are your work tasks? This assessment is designed to measure the five core job characteristics derived from job characteristics theory. Think of your current job or the last job that you held (even if it was a part-time or summer job). Answer each question using the response scale provided. Then subtract your answers to the bold-faced question from 8, with the difference being your new answer for that question. For example, if your original answer for Question V2 was "5," your new answer is "3" (8 – 5). Then use the formula to compute a satisfaction potential score (SPS). (For more assessments relevant to this chapter, please visit the Online Learning Center at www.mhhe.com/ColquittEss).

1	2	3	4	5	6	7
Very Inaccurate	**Mostly Inaccurate**	**Slightly Inaccurate**	**Uncertain**	**Slightly Accurate**	**Mostly Accurate**	**Very Accurate**

V1. The job requires me to use a number of complex or high-level skills. _____

V2. The job is quite simple and repetitive. _____

I1. The job is arranged so that I can do an entire piece of work from beginning to end. _____

I2. The job provides me the chance to completely finish the pieces of work I begin. _____

S1. This job is one where a lot of other people can be affected by how well the work gets done. _____

S2. The job itself is very significant and important in the broader scheme of things. _____

A1. The job gives me a chance to use my personal initiative and judgment in carrying out the work. _____

A2. The job gives me considerable opportunity for independence and freedom in how I do the work. _____

F1. Just doing the work required by the job provides many chances for me to figure out how well I am doing. _____

F2. After I finish a job, I know whether I performed well. _____

$$SPS = \left| \frac{V1+V2+I1+I2+S1+S2}{6} \right| \times \left| \frac{A1+A2}{2} \right| \times \left| \frac{F1+F2}{2} \right|$$

$$SPS = \left| \frac{}{6} \right| \times \left| \frac{}{2} \right| \times \left| \frac{}{2} \right|$$

$$SPS = \boxed{} \times \boxed{} \times \boxed{} = \boxed{}$$

Scoring

If your score is 150 or above, your work tasks tend to be satisfying and enjoyable. Therefore, you probably view your work as meaningful and feel that you are responsible for (and knowledgeable about) your work outcomes. If your score is less than 150, your work tasks may not be so satisfying and enjoyable. You might benefit from trying to "enrich" your job by asking your supervisor for more challenging assignments.

Sources: J. R. Hackman and G. R. Oldham, *The Job Diagnostic Survey: An Instrument for the Diagnosis of Jobs and the Evaluation of Job Redesign Projects* (New Haven, CT: Yale University, 1974); J. R. Idaszak and F. Drasgow, "A Revision of the Job Diagnostic Survey: Elimination of a Measurement Artifact," *Journal of Applied Psychology* 72 (1987), pp. 69–74.

EXERCISE: Job Satisfaction across Jobs

The purpose of this exercise is to examine satisfaction with the work itself across jobs. This exercise uses groups, so your instructor will either assign you to a group or ask you to create your own. The exercise has the following steps:

1. Use the Assessment for Chapter 3 to calculate the Satisfaction Potential Score (SPS) for the following four jobs:

   a. A lobster fisherman who runs his own boat with his son.

   b. A standup comedian.

   c. A computer programmer whose assignment is to replace "98" with "1998" in thousands of lines of computer code.

   d. A president of the United States.

2. Which job has the highest SPS? Which core job characteristics best explain why some jobs have high scores and other jobs have low scores? Write down the scores for the four jobs in an Excel file on the classroom computer or on the chalkboard.

3. Class discussion (whether in groups or as a class) should center on two questions. First, is the job that scored the highest really the one that would be the most enjoyable on a day-in, day-out basis? Second, does that mean it would be the job that you would pick if you could snap your fingers and magically attain one of the jobs on the list? Why or why not? What other job satisfaction theory is relevant to this issue?

END NOTES

1. Hamm, S. "A Passion for the Planet." *BusinessWeek,* August 21, 2006, pp. 92–94.

2. Ibid.

3. Casey, S. "Eminence Green." *Fortune*, April 2, 2007, pp. 62–69.

4. Hamm, "A Passion for the Planet."

5. Casey, "Eminence Green."

6. Hamm, "A Passion for the Planet."

7. Locke, E. A. "The Nature and Causes of Job Satisfaction." In *Handbook of Industrial and Organizational Psychology,* ed. M. Dunnette. Chicago, IL: Rand McNally, 1976, pp. 1297–350.

8. Koretz, G. "Hate Your Job? Join the Club." *BusinessWeek,* October 6, 2003, p. 40.

9. Locke, "The Nature and Causes."

10. Dawis, R. V. "Vocational Interests, Values, and Preferences." In *Handbook of Industrial and Organizational Psychology,* Vol. 2, ed. M. D. Dunnette and L. M. Hough. Palo Alto, CA: Consulting Psychologists Press, 1991, pp. 834–71.

11. Locke, "The Nature and Causes."

12. Judge, T. A., and A. H. Church. "Job Satisfaction: Research and Practice." In *Industrial and Organizational Psychology: Linking Theory with Practice,* ed. C. L. Cooper and E. A. Locke. Oxford, UK: Blackwell, 2000, pp. 166–98.

13. Locke, "The Nature and Causes."

14. Smith, P. C.; L. M. Kendall; and C. L. Hulin. *The Measurement of Satisfaction in Work and Retirement.* Chicago: Rand McNally, 1969.

15. Lawler, E. E. *Pay and Organizational Effectiveness: A Psychological View.* New York: McGraw-Hill, 1971.

16. Locke, "The Nature and Causes."

17. Levering, R., and M. Moskowitz. "The 100 Best Companies to Work For." *Fortune,* January 24, 2005, pp. 73–93.

18. Smith, Kendall, and Hulin, "The Measurement of Satisfaction."

19. Locke, "The Nature and Causes."

20. Levering and Moskowitz, "The 100 Best."

21. Smith, Kendall, and Hulin, "The Measurement of Satisfaction."

22. Locke, "The Nature and Causes."

23. Levering and Moskowitz, "The 100 Best."

24. Smith, Kendall, and Hulin, "The Measurement of Satisfaction."

25. Levering and Moskowitz, "The 100 Best."

26. Smith, Kendall, and Hulin, "The Measurement of Satisfaction."

27. Elfman, L. "Silky Smooth." *Hoop,* May 16, 2008, http://www.nba.com/hoop/Silky_Smooth_080516.html (accessed June 16, 2008).

28. Hollander, D. "Oh, Baby Leslie's Regained the Spark." *AOL,* May 19, 2008, http://sports.aol.com/voices/hollander/_a/oh-baby-leslies-regained-the-spark/2008051 4152509990001 (accessed June 16, 2008).

29. Collier, A. "Interview." *Ebony,* October 2001, http://findarticles.com/p/articles/mi_m1077/is_12_56/ai_78919280 (accessed June 16, 2008).

30. "Talk Today." *USA Today.com,* July 12, 2007, http://transcripts.usatoday.com/Chats/transcript.aspx?c=768 (accessed June 16, 2008).

31. Levering and Moskowitz, "The 100 Best."

32. Ironson, G. H.; P. C. Smith; M. T. Brannick; W. M. Gibson; and K. B. Paul, "Construction of a Job in General Scale: A Comparison of Global, Composite, and Specific Measures." *Journal of Applied Psychology* 74 (1989), pp. 193–200; Russell, S. S.; C. Spitzmuller; L. F. Lin; J. M. Stanton; P. C. Smith; and G. H. Ironson. "Shorter Can Also Be Better: The Abridged Job in General Scale." *Educational and Psychological Measurement* 64 (2004), pp. 878–93.

33. Taylor, F. W. *The Principles of Scientific Management.* New York: Wiley, 1911; Gilbreth, F. B. *Motion Study: A Method for Increasing the Efficiency of the Workman.* New York: Van Nostrand, 1911.

34. Hackman, J. R., and E. E. Lawler III. "Employee Reactions to Job Characteristics." *Journal of Applied Psychology* 55 (1971), pp. 259–86.

35. Hackman, J. R., and G. R. Oldham. *Work Redesign.* Reading, MA: Addison-Wesley, 1980.

36. Ibid.

37. Ibid.

38. Rode, J. C.; M. L. Arthaud-Day; C. H. Mooney; J. P. Near; T. T. Baldwin; W. H. Bommer; and R. S. Rubin. "Life Satisfaction and Student Performance." *Academy of Management Learning and Education* 4 (2005), pp. 421–33.

39. Hackman, J. R., and G. R. Oldham. "Motivation through the Design of Work: Test of a Theory." *Organizational Behavior and Human Decision Processes* 16 (1976), pp. 250–79.

40. Hackman and Oldham, *Work Redesign.*

41. Turner, A. N., and P. R. Lawrence. *Industrial Jobs and the Worker.* Boston: Harvard University Graduate School of Business Administration, 1965.

42. Hackman and Lawler, "Employee Reactions."

43. Hackman and Oldham, *Work Redesign.*

44. Turner and Lawrence, *Industrial Jobs.*

45. Hackman and Oldham, *Work Redesign.*

46. Ibid.

47. Turner and Lawrence, *Industrial Jobs.*

48. Breaugh, J. A. "The Measurement of Work Autonomy." *Human Relations* 38 (1985), pp. 551–70.

49. Hackman and Oldham, *Work Redesign.*

50. Fried, Y., and G. R. Ferris. "The Validity of the Job Characteristics Model: A Review and Meta-Analysis." *Personnel Psychology* 40 (1987), pp. 287–322.

51. Hackman and Oldham, *Work Redesign.*

52. Loher, B. T.; R. A. Noe; N. L. Moeller; and M. P. Fitzgerald. "A Meta-Analysis of the Relation of Job Characteristics to Job Satisfaction." *Journal of Applied Psychology* 70 (1985), pp. 280–89.

53. Campion, M. A., and C. L. McClelland. "Interdisciplinary Examination of the Costs and Benefits of Enlarged Jobs: A Job Design Quasi-Experiment." *Journal of Applied Psychology* 76 (1991), pp. 186–98.

54. Ibid.

55. Morris, W. N. *Mood: The Frame of Mind.* New York: Springer-Verlag, 1989.

56. Watson, D., and A. Tellegen. "Toward a Consensual Structure of Mood." *Psychological Bulletin* 98 (1985), pp. 219–35; Russell, J. A. "A Circumplex Model of Affect." *Journal of Personality and Social Psychology* 39 (1980), pp. 1161–78; Larsen, R. J., and E. Diener. "Promises and Problems with the Circumplex Model of Emotion." In *Review of Personality and Social Psychology: Emotion,* Vol. 13, ed. M. S. Clark. Newbury Park, CA: Sage, 1992, pp. 25–59.

57. Ibid.

58. Levering and Moskowitz, "The 100 Best."

59. Ibid.

60. Weiss, H. M., and K. E. Kurek. "Dispositional Influences on Affective Experiences at Work." In *Personality and Work: Reconsidering the Role of Personality in Organizations,* ed. M. R. Barrick and A. M. Ryan. San Francisco: Jossey-Bass, 2003, pp. 121–49.

61. Lazarus, R. S. *Emotion and Adaptation.* New York: Oxford University, 1991.

62. Hochschild, A. R. *The Managed Heart: Commercialization of Human Feeling.* Berkeley, CA: University of California Press, 1983; Rafaeli, A., and R. I. Sutton. "The Expression of Emotion in Organizational Life." *Research in Organizational Behavior* 11 (1989), pp. 1–42.

63. Hatfield, E.; J. T. Cacioppo; and R. L. Rapson. *Emotional Contagion.* New York: Cambridge University Press, 1994.

64. Ashkanasy, N. M.; C. E. J. Hartel; and C. S. Daus. "Diversity and Emotion: The New Frontiers in Organizational Behavior Research." *Journal of Management* 28 (2002), pp. 307–38.

65. Judge, T. A.; C. J. Thoreson; J. E. Bono; and G. K Patton. "The Job Satisfaction–Job Performance Relationship: A Qualitative and Quantitative Review." *Psychological Bulletin* 127 (2001), pp. 376–407.

66. Brief, A. P., and H. M. Weiss. "Organizational Behavior: Affect in the Workplace." *Annual Review of Psychology* 53 (2002), pp. 279–307.

67. Isen, A. M., and R. A. Baron. "Positive Affect as a Factor in Organizational Behavior." *Research in Organizational Behavior* 13 (1991), pp. 1–53.

68. Lucas, R. E., and E. Diener. "The Happy Worker: Hypotheses about the Role of Positive Affect in Worker Satisfaction." In *Personality and Work: Reconsidering the Role of Personality in Organizations,* ed. M. R. Barrick and A. M. Ryan. San Francisco: Jossey-Bass, 2003, pp. 30–59.

69. Beal, D. J.; H. M. Weiss; E. Barros; and S. M. MacDermid. "An Episodic Process Model of Affective Influences on Performance." *Journal of Applied Psychology* 90 (2005), pp. 1054–68.

70. Locke, "The Nature and Causes."

71. LePine, J. A.; A. Erez; and D. E. Johnson. "The Nature and Dimensionality of Organizational Citizenship Behavior: A Critical Review and Meta-Analysis." *Journal of Applied Psychology* 87 (2002), pp. 52–65.

72. George, J. M. "Trait and State Affect." In *Individual Differences and Behavior in Organizations,* ed. K. R. Murphy. San Francisco: Jossey-Bass, 1996, pp. 145–71.

73. Dalal, R. S. "A Meta-Analysis of the Relationship between Organizational Citizenship Behavior and Counterproductive Work Behavior." *Journal of Applied Psychology* 90 (2005), pp. 1241–55.

74. Sackett, P. R., and C. J. DeVore. "Counterproductive Behaviors at Work." In *Handbook of Industrial, Work, and Organizational Psychology,* Vol. 1, ed. N. Anderson, D. S. Ones, H. K. Sinangil, and C. Viswesvaran. Thousand Oaks, CA: Sage, 2001, pp. 145–51.

75. Cooper-Hakim, A., and C. Viswesvaran. "The Construct of Work Commitment: Testing an Integrative Framework." *Psychological Bulletin* 131 (2005), pp. 241–59; Harrison, D. A.; D. Newman; and P. L. Roth, "How Important Are Job Attitudes? Meta-Analytic Comparisons of Integrative Behavioral Outcomes and Time Sequences." *Academy of Management Journal* 49 (2006), pp. 305–25; Meyer, J. P.; D. J. Stanley; L. Herscovitch; and L. Topolnytsky. "Affective, Continuance, and Normative Commitment to the Organization: A Meta-Analysis of Antecedents, Correlates, and Consequences." *Journal of Vocational Behavior* 61 (2002), pp. 20–52.

76. Ibid.

77. Tait, M.; M. Y. Padgett; and T. T. Baldwin. "Job and Life Satisfaction: A Reexamination of the Strength of the Relationship and Gender Effects as a Function of the Date of the Study." *Journal of Applied Psychology* 74 (1989), pp. 502–507; Judge, T. A., and S. Watanabe, "Another Look at the Job Satisfaction–Life Satisfaction Relationship." *Journal of Applied Psychology* 78 (1993), pp. 939–48.

78. Layard, R. *Happiness.* New York: Penguin Press, 2005, p. 41.

79. R. Layard, quoted in E. Diener and E. Suh. "National Differences in Subjective Well-Being." In *Well-Being: The Foundations of Hedonic Psychology,* ed. D. Kahneman, E. Diener, and N. Schwarz. New York: Russell Sage Foundation, 1999.

80. Layard, *Happiness.*

81. Ibid.

82. Hamm, "A Passion for the Planet."

83. Casey, "Eminence Green."

84. Hamm, "A Passion for the Planet."

Stress

BEST BUY

Have you ever felt the stress of having to decide whether to go to work or call in sick to fulfill an important personal responsibility? Or think about the stress you felt in a situation in which you were pressured to stay at work when nothing much was going on, while at the same time you knew you were missing out on a family event or something else unrelated to work that you really wanted to do. Just imagine how great it would be if your employer gave you complete freedom to decide when and where you accomplished your work so you could manage these types of situations. You could choose to work when you're most productive and when it's convenient, if you wanted, on the way to the Bonaroo Music Festival. In fact, this description is how things run at Best Buy, the Minnesota-based electronics retailer, where most of the 4,000 employees at the corporate office work under a system called Results-Only Work Environment, or ROWE.[1]

Rather than having to spend regular hours at work in an office or cubicle, employees under ROWE can come and go as they please without permission, they can work where and when they want, and their job performance is judged on the basis of whether results are achieved.[2] The hope at Best Buy is that if employees are given control over how they balance their work and personal lives, they will be less affected by stress and burnout and, in turn, they will be more productive and committed.[3] How well has this hope been realized? Not only has job satisfaction increased among those employees who work under ROWE, but commitment and productivity are up as well.[4]

Because ROWE has worked well at corporate headquarters, Best Buy executives are making plans to use the system in their retail stores where stress and low commitment are major problems.[5] But can ROWE work in retail stores, which require employees to be responsive to customers? Think of the challenge managers will face in making sure that the sales floor and registers are covered when clerks and cashiers can come and go when they please. Other questions also come to mind when thinking about the long-term benefits of ROWE. For example, ROWE gives employees the freedom to work 24 hours a day, but this freedom may also make it difficult for some people to know exactly where to draw the line between their work and nonwork lives.[6] Given that ROWE is a fairly new practice, only time will tell if the system helps Best Buy thrive in a very competitive industry.

STRESS

Stress is an OB topic that is probably familiar to you. Even if you don't have a lot of work experience, consider how you feel toward the end of a semester when you have to cram for several final exams and finish a couple of term projects. At the same time, you might also be looking for a job or planning a trip with friends or family. Although some people might be able to deal with all of these demands without becoming too frazzled, most people would say that this type of situation causes them to feel "stressed-out." This stressed-out feeling might even be accompanied by headaches, stomach upsets, backaches, or sleeping difficulties. Although you might believe your stress will diminish once you graduate, high stress on the job is more prevalent than it has ever been before.[7] The Federal Government's National Institute for Occupational Safety and Health (NIOSH) summarized findings from several sources that indicated that up to 40 percent of U.S. workers feel their jobs are "very stressful" or "extremely stressful."[8] Unfortunately, managers are 21 percent more likely than the average worker to describe their jobs as stressful,[9] so stress is likely to be prevalent in the types of jobs most of you are likely to have after you graduate. Table 4-1 provides a listing of where several jobs rank on the list of least to most stressful.

●● 4.1
Define stress, stressors, and strains.

demands tax or exceed one's capacity or resources are called strains. This definition illustrates that stress depends on both the nature of the demand and the person who confronts it. People differ in terms of how they appraise stressors and the way they cope with them, and so they may experience different levels of stress even when confronted with the same demands.

How Do People Perceive and Appraise Stressful Demands?

To fully understand what it means to feel "stressed," it is necessary to describe how demands are perceived and appraised. When people first encounter demands, the process of primary appraisal is triggered whereby people evaluate the significance and the meaning of the demands they are confronting.[14] Here, people first consider whether a demand causes them to feel stressed, and if it does, they consider the implications of the stressor in terms of their personal goals and overall well-being. This process is illustrated in Figure 4-1.

● STRESS A psychological response to demands for which there is something at stake and where coping with those demands taxes or exceeds a person's capacity or resources.

● STRESSORS Demands that cause people to experience stress.

● STRAINS Negative consequences that occur when an individual's capacity or resources to cope are exceeded.

● PRIMARY APPRAISAL An evaluation of the significance and meaning of demands that are being confronted.

> **"Although you might believe your stress will diminish once you graduate, high stress on the job is more prevalent than it has ever been before."**

Of course, stress is also relevant from the organization's standpoint. Estimates are that between 60 and 90 percent of all doctor visits can be attributed to stress-related causes,[10] and the cost of providing health care to people who experience high levels of stress is approximately 50 percent higher than the cost for those who experience lower levels of stress.[11] Statistics from jobs in different industries indicate that the frequency of worker's compensation claims is dramatically higher when the level of stress on the job is high. As one example, the frequency of claims was more than 800 percent higher for a copy machine distributor when the level of stress at the job site was high.[12] Of course, as you will learn in this chapter, stress has other implications for management of organizational behavior. But first, it is important to develop a better understanding of what stress involves.

Stress is defined as a psychological response to demands for which there is something at stake and coping with those demands taxes or exceeds a person's capacity or resources.[13] The particular demands that cause people to experience stress are called stressors. The negative consequences that occur when

Looking for one of the least stressful jobs? Florists rank low in stress levels. Why do you think that is?

Least Stressful Jobs	Stress Level	Most Stressful Jobs	Stress Level
1. Musical instrument repairer	18.77	212. Registered nurse	62.14
2. Florist	18.80	220. Attorney	64.33
4. Actuary	20.18	223. Newspaper reporter	65.26
6. Appliance repairer	21.12	226. Architect	66.92
8. Librarian	21.40	228. Lumberjack	67.60
10. File clerk	21.71	229. Fisherman	69.82
11. Piano tuner	22.29	230. Stockbroker	71.65
12. Janitor	22.44	231. U.S. congressperson	72.05
16. Vending machine repairer	23.47	233. Real estate agent	73.06
18. Barber	23.62	234. Advertising account exec	74.55
24. Mathematician	24.67	238. Public relations exec	78.52
29. Cashier	25.11	240. Air traffic controller	83.13
30. Dishwasher	25.32	241. Airline pilot	85.35
32. Pharmacist	25.87	243. Police officer	93.89
40. Biologist	26.94	244. Astronaut	99.34
44. Computer programmer	27.00	245. Surgeon	99.46
50. Astronomer	28.06	246. Taxi driver	100.49
56. Historian	28.41	248. Senior corporate exec	108.62
67. Bank teller	30.12	249. Firefighter	110.93
78. Accountant	31.13	250. U.S. president	176.55

Source: Adapted from L. Krantz, *Jobs Rated Almanac*, 6th ed. (Fort Lee, NJ: Barricade Books, Inc., 2002).
The stress level score is calculated by summing points in 21 categories, including deadlines, competitiveness, environmental conditions, speed required, precision required, initiative required, physical demands, and hazards encountered.

Cashiers meet several demands in the course of their workday. How stressed do you think this cashier is? Why?

As an example of a primary appraisal, consider the job of a cashier at a well-run convenience store. In this store, cashiers engage in routine sales transactions with customers. Customers enter the store and select merchandise, and the cashier on duty rings up the sale and collects the money. Under normal day-to-day circumstances at this store, a well-trained cashier would not likely feel that these transactions are overly taxing or exceeding his or her capacity, so that cashier would not likely appraise these job demands as stressful. Job demands that tend not to be appraised as stressful are called *benign job demands*.

However, consider how convenience store cashiers would react in a different store in which the cash register and credit card machine break down often and without warning. The cashiers who work at this store would likely view their job as more

FIGURE **4-1** Stressors and Their Appraisal

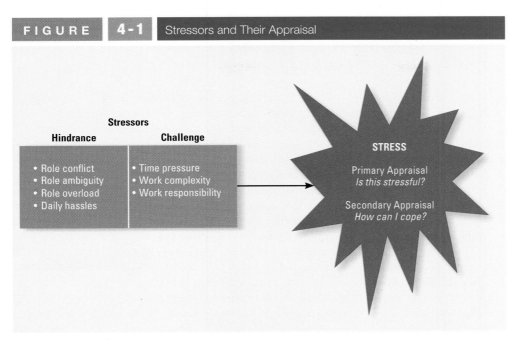

Stressors

Hindrance | **Challenge**

- Role conflict
- Role ambiguity
- Role overload
- Daily hassles

- Time pressure
- Work complexity
- Work responsibility

STRESS

Primary Appraisal
Is this stressful?

Secondary Appraisal
How can I cope?

● **HINDRANCE STRESS-ORS** Demands that most people perceive as hindering progress toward personal accomplishment or goal attainment.

● **CHALLENGE STRESS-ORS** Demands that most people perceive as opportunities for learning, growth, and achievement.

● **ROLE CONFLICT** Conflicting expectations that others have of us.

stressful because they would have to diagnose and fix problems with equipment while dealing with customers who are growing more and more impatient. Furthermore, the cashiers in this store might appraise the stressful situation as one that unnecessarily prevents them from achieving their goal of being viewed as an effective employee in the eyes of the customers and the store manager.

Finally, consider a third convenience store in which the cashier's workload is higher due to additional responsibilities that include receiving merchandise from vendors, taking physical inventory, and training new employees. In this store, the cashiers may appraise their jobs as stressful because of the higher workload and need to balance different priorities. However, in contrast to the cashiers in the previous example, cashiers in this store might appraise these demands as providing an opportunity to learn and demonstrate the type of competence that often is rewarded with satisfying promotions and pay raises.

Call center operators experience role conflict when they are expected to make high numbers of phone calls on their shift but also provide quality customer service to each of their customers.

In the previous two examples, the cashiers were confronted with demands that a primary appraisal would label as "stressful." However, research shows that the types of demands in the two examples have important differences.[15] Dealing with equipment breakdowns or unhappy customers has little to no benefit to the employee in the long term. These kinds of stressors are called **hindrance stressors**—stressful demands that most people perceive as hindering progress toward personal accomplishments or goal attainment. Hindrance stressors tend to trigger negative emotions such as anger and anxiety. In contrast, managing additional responsibilities or higher workloads has a long-term benefit in that it helps build the employee's skills. These kinds of stressors are called **challenge stressors**—stressful demands that most people perceive as opportunities for learning, growth, and achievement. Although challenge stressors can be exhausting, they often trigger positive emotions and enhance motivation. As shown in Figure 4-1, there are several specific types of hindrance and challenge stressors.

●●● **4.2**

Identify and describe the two main categories of stressors.

Hindrance Stressors. One type of hindrance stressor is **role conflict**, which refers to conflicting expectations that other people may have of us.[16] As an example of role

● **ROLE AMBIGUITY** Lack of information regarding what needs to be done in a role and unpredictability about consequences.

● **ROLE OVERLOAD** Number of demands is such that effective performance is impossible.

● **DAILY HASSLES** Minor day-to-day demands that add up to prevent accomplishment of more important tasks.

● **TIME PRESSURE** A perception that there may be too little time to accomplish a task.

conflict that occurs from incompatible demands within a single role that a person may hold, consider the job of a call center operator. People holding this job are generally expected to contact as many people as possible over a given time period, which means spending as little time as possible with each person who is contacted. At the same time, however, call center operators are also expected to be responsive to the questions and concerns raised by the people they contact. Because effectiveness in this aspect of the job may require a great deal of time, the call center operator is put in a position in which he or she simply cannot meet both types of expectations.

Role conflict also may come about when demands of a work role hinder the fulfillment of the demands in a family role (or vice versa).[17] For example, employees who have to deal with lots of hindrances at work may have trouble switching off the frustration after they get home, and, as a consequence, they may become irritable and impatient with family—this type of situation is called "work to family conflict" because work demands interfere with the effectiveness in the family role. However, this type of role conflict can occur in the other

Role overload occurs when the number of demanding roles a person holds is so high that the person simply cannot perform some or all of the roles very effectively. Role overload as a source of stress is becoming very prevalent for employees in many different industries. For example, the workload for executives and managers who work in investment banking, consulting, and law is so high that 80-hour workweeks are becoming the norm. Although this trend may not be surprising to some of you, people holding these jobs also indicate that they would not be able to complete most of  the work that is required of them even if they worked twice as many hours.[19] If employees actually put in enough time to meet those sorts of role demands, they might forget what life was like outside of their offices or cubicles!

One final type of hindrance stressor, daily hassles, reflects the relatively minor day-to-day demands that get in the way of accomplishing the things that we really want to accomplish.

> " . . . 40 percent of executives spend somewhere between a half day and a full day each week on communications that are not useful or necessary."

direction as well. That is, "family to work conflict" may occur when a salesperson who experiences the stress of marital conflict comes to work harboring negative feelings that make it difficult to interact with customers effectively.

Role ambiguity refers to the lack of information regarding what needs to be done in a role, as well as unpredictability regarding the consequences of performance in that role.[18] Employees are sometimes asked to work on projects for which they are given very few instructions or guidelines about how things are supposed to be done. In these cases, employees may not know how much money they can spend on the project, how long it's supposed to take, or what exactly the finished product is supposed to look like. Role ambiguity is often experienced among new employees who haven't been around long enough to receive instructions from supervisors or observe and model the role behaviors of more senior colleagues. Students sometimes experience role ambiguity when professors remain vague about particular course requirements or how grading is going to be performed. In such cases, the class becomes stressful because it's not quite clear what it takes to get a good grade.

Examples of hassles include having to deal with unnecessary paperwork, office equipment malfunctions, conflict with abrasive coworkers, and useless communications. Although these examples of daily hassles may seem relatively minor, taken together, they can be extremely time consuming and stressful. For example, according to one survey, 40 percent of executives spend somewhere between a half day and a full day each week on communications that are not useful or necessary.[20]

Challenge Stressors. One type of challenge stressor is time pressure—a strong sense that the amount of time you have to do a task is just not quite enough. Although most people appraise situations with high time pressure as rather stressful, they also tend to appraise these situations as more challenging than hindering. People tend to strive to meet time pressure demands because success in meeting such demands can be rewarding and intrinsically satisfying. As an example of this positive effect of high time pressure, consider Michael Jones, an architect at a top New York firm. His job involves overseeing multiple projects with tight deadlines, and, as a result, he has to work at a hectic pace. Although Jones readily acknowledges that his job is stressful, he also believes that the outcome of having all the stress is satisfying. Jones is able to see the product of his labor over the Manhattan skyline, which makes him feel like he is a part of something.[21]

Work complexity refers to the degree to which the requirements of the work, in terms of knowledge, skills, and abilities, tax or exceed the capabilities of the person who is responsible for performing the work. As an example of work complexity, consider the nature of employee development practices that organizations use to train future executives and organizational leaders. In many cases, these practices involve giving people jobs that require skills and knowledge that the people do not yet possess. A successful marketing manager who is being groomed for an executive-level position may, for example, be asked to manage a poorly performing production facility with poor labor relations in a country halfway around the world. Although these types of developmental experiences tend to be quite stressful, managers report that being stretched beyond their capacity is well worth the associated discomfort.[22]

Work responsibility refers to the nature of the obligations that a person has to others. Generally speaking, the level of responsibility in a job is higher when the number, scope, and importance of the obligations in that job are higher. As an example, consider the difference in responsibility levels of a grocery store manager compared with a grocery store bagger. Although the bagger is obligated to perform an important task—efficiently placing items in bags so as not to damage the items—the store manager is obligated to ensure that the store is profitable, the customers are satisfied, and the employees are happy and safe. As with people's reactions to time pressure and work complexity, people tend to evaluate demands associated with high responsibility as both stressful and potentially positive. For an example of exceptionally high work responsibility, see our **OB on Screen** feature.

Managing Stressors. One way that organizations try to manage stress is by managing the nature of the stressors that employees confront. The opening vignette illustrated how Best Buy accomplished this with the Results Only Work Environment. As another example of this approach to managing stress, 19 percent of organizations in one recent survey used job sharing to reduce role overload and foster work–life balance.[23] Job sharing does not mean splitting one job into two, but, rather, two people sharing the responsibilities of a single job as if the two people were a single performing unit. The assumption underlying the practice is that "although businesses are becoming 24/7, people don't."[24] You might be tempted to believe that job sharing would be most appropriate in lower-level jobs, where responsibilities and tasks are limited in number and relatively easy to divide.

- **WORK COMPLEXITY** The degree to which a task taxes an individual's knowledge, skills, or abilities.

- **WORK RESPONSIBILITY** The degree to which a job involves important obligations to others.

- **JOB SHARING** An approach to managing stress whereby a set of individuals share the responsibilities of a single job.

OB on Screen

Pushing Tin

This job can be a little bit STRESS-ful!

With those words, air traffic controllers in the movie *Pushing Tin* (Dir. Mike Newell, 20th Century Fox, 1999) describe what their job is like as they guide 7,000 aircraft a day around the Kennedy, LaGuardia, and Newark airports, the nation's most congested airspace.

From the action depicted in the opening scenes in the movie, you should be able to appreciate that one of the most obvious stressors in the job of an air traffic controller is the high workload. Controllers sit in a darkened room trying to keep track of hundreds of blips and other pieces of information on their radar scopes, all while talking to the pilots of several aircraft. In the opening scene, for example, Nick Falzone (John Cusack) says something along the lines of, "Continental 981,

8 miles from the outer marker, turn left heading 080, maintain 2,000, until intercepting localizer, cleared ILS runway 4 right approach." Although you might be able to bark this command in less than 6 seconds, like Nick did in this scene, consider that air traffic controllers are typically responsible for directing several aircraft at the same time, each moving in different directions at speeds of up to 300 miles per hour.

A second key stressor for air traffic controllers is the responsibility they have for tens of thousands of lives every day. Although errors that result in midair collisions are extremely rare, the possibility weighs heavily on the minds of controllers. As an example, a scene in the movie depicts the facility manager giving a tour to several elementary school children. He tells them, "Did you youngsters know that an air traffic controller is responsible for

more lives in a single shift than a surgeon is in his entire life?" A young boy responds by saying, "It looks like a computer game"—to which the manager responds, "This is no game, young man, I'll tell you that. If you make a mistake here, there's no reset button." ❖

In actuality, job sharing is being used even at the highest levels in organizations. At Boston-based Fleet Bank, for example, two women shared the position of vice president for global markets and foreign exchange for six years until their department was dissolved when Fleet was acquired by Bank of America. During this time, they had one desk, one chair, one computer, one telephone, one voice-mail account, one set of goals, and one performance review. They each worked 20–25 hours a week and performed the role effectively and seamlessly.[25]

● ● 4.3

Describe how individuals cope with stress

How Do People Cope with Stressors?

After people appraise a stressful demand, they ask themselves, "What *should* I do" and "What *can* I do" to deal with this situation? These questions, which reflect the second-ary appraisal shown in Figure 4-1, center on the issue of how people cope with the various stressors that they face.[26] Coping refers to the behaviors and thoughts that people use to manage both the stressful demands that they face and the emotions associated with those stressful demands.[27] As Table 4-2 illustrates, coping involves different types of activities that are grouped into four broad categories based on two dimensions.[28] The first dimension refers to the method of coping (behavioral versus cognitive), and the second dimension refers to the focus of coping (problem solving versus regulation of emotions).

First, coping activities can be categorized on the basis of whether they involve behaviors or cognitions. Behavioral coping involves the set of physical activities that are used to deal with a stressful situation. In one example of behavioral coping, a person who is confronted with a lot of time pressure at work might chose to cope by working faster. In another example of behavioral coping, an employee who has several daily hassles might cope by avoiding work—coming in late, leaving early, or even staying home.

In contrast to behavioral coping, cognitive coping refers to the thoughts that are involved in trying to deal with a stressful situation. For example, the person who is confronted with an increase in time pressure might cope by thinking of alternative ways of doing the work so that it can be accomplished more efficiently. As another example, the employee who is confronted with daily hassles might try to convince him- or herself that the hassles are not that bad after all.

Whereas the first part of our coping definition refers to the method of coping, the second part refers to the focus of coping—that is, does the coping attempt to address the stressful demand or the emotions triggered by the demand?[29] Prob-lem-focused coping refers to behaviors and cognitions intended to manage the stressful situation itself. To understand problem-focused coping, consider how the people in the previous two paragraphs coped with time pressure. In the first example, the person attempted to address the time pressure by working harder, whereas in the second example, the person tried to identify a way to accomplish the work more efficiently. Although the specific coping methods differed, both of these people focused effort on meeting the demand rather than trying to avoid it.

In contrast to problem-focused coping, emotion-focused coping refers to the various ways in which people manage their own emotional reactions to stressful demands. The reactions to the daily hassles that we described previously illustrated two types of emotion-focused coping. In the first example, the employee used avoidance and distancing behaviors to

> "The choice of a coping strategy has important implications for how effectively people can meet or adapt to the different stressors they face."

TABLE 4-2	Examples of Coping Strategies	
	Problem-Focused	**Emotion-Focused**
Behavioral Methods	Working harder Seeking assistance Acquiring additional resources	Engaging in alternative activities Seeking support Venting anger
Cognitive Methods	Strategizing Self-motivation Changing priorities	Avoiding, distancing, and ignoring Looking for the positive in the negative Reappraising

Source: Adapted from J. C. Latack and S. J. Havlovic, "Coping with Job Stress: A Conceptual Evaluation Framework for Coping Measures," *Journal of Organizational Behavior* 13 (1992), pp. 479–508.

FIGURE 4-2 General Adaptation Syndrome

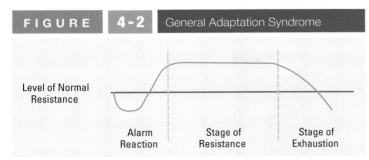

Level of Normal Resistance

Alarm Reaction   Stage of Resistance   Stage of Exhaustion

Source: Adapted from H. Seyle, *The Stress of Life*, revised ed. (New York: McGraw-Hill, 1976), p. 111.

● **GENERAL ADAPTATION SYNDROME** A theory that describes how the human body responds to stressors.

reduce the emotional distress caused by the stressful situation. In the second example, the employee reappraised the demand to make it seem less stressful and threatening. Although people may be successful at changing the way different situations are construed to avoid feeling unpleasant emotions, the demand or problem that initially triggered the appraisal process remains.

It might be obvious to you by now that the choice of a coping strategy has important implications for how effectively people can meet or adapt to the different stressors they face. In the work context, for example, a manager would most likely want subordinates to cope with the stress of a heavy workload by using a problem-focused strategy—working harder—rather than an emotion-focused strategy—drinking two saki bombs at lunch to create distance from the stressor. Of course, there are some situations in which emotion-focused coping may be functional. As an example, consider a person who repeatedly fails to make it through the auditions for *American Idol*, despite years of voice lessons and countless hours of practice. If this person did not cope emotionally—perhaps by lowering her aspirations, or at least ignoring Simon Cowell's sarcastic barbs—this person's self-concept could be damaged, which could translate into reduced effectiveness in other roles that she fills. See our **OB Internationally** box to learn about the organizational implications of how expatriates cope with the stress of international assignments.

The Experience of Strain

Earlier in this chapter, we defined strains as the negative consequences associated with stress. How exactly does stress cause strain? Medical researchers who study stress have spent years examining the body's response to different sorts of stressful demands.[30] Many of these findings have been summarized in a theory called the general adaptation syndrome (GAS), which is illustrated in Figure 4-2.[31] In a nutshell, GAS suggests that the body has a general set of responses that allow it to adapt and function effectively in the face of stressful demands. However, when stressful demands do not ramp down or demands occur too frequently, the body's adaptive responses become toxic, and this is what prompts strain.

Stages of the General Adaptation Syndrome.
The first stage of the GAS is the alarm reaction. Upon being confronted with a stressor, there is a relatively brief period of time in which resistance to the stressor is temporarily lowered. At this point the body and mind haven't reacted yet—in essence, the stressor simply "sinks in." Immediately thereafter, the body activates defense mechanisms to resist the stressor. The body begins to secrete chemical compounds that cause increases in heart rate and blood pressure,

OB Internationally

Due to the trend of increased globalization of business organizations, the number of employees who are sent abroad to work for their organization has increased. In one recent survey of global relocation data and trends, for example, 47 percent of the companies reported an increase in the number of expatriate assignments over the previous year, and 54 percent projected increases in these assignments in the following year. This survey also indicated that more than half of all employees sent abroad expected their assignment to last between one and three years.[32] Unfortunately, American expatriates often fail to perform their role as effectively as they could, and up to 40 percent return home early.[33] So what accounts for these problems?

One of the key drivers of expatriate effectiveness and retention is how they cope with the overwhelming stress of being abroad.[34] Expatriates experience a great deal of stress as a result of uncertainties regarding cultural differences in social and job-related activities, and because they are far away from colleagues and supervisors who have provided support and guidance, the stress tends to translate into frustration and dissatisfaction with the assignment and, in turn, behavioral coping in the form of returning home early.

Although cross-cultural training would seem like an obvious way to manage this problem, it isn't offered as frequently as you might think.[35] In fact, many U.S. companies offer no formal cross-cultural training at all, and even when training is offered, it tends not to emphasize cultural understanding and skills needed for effective cross-cultural interactions. Moreover, training tends to occur only on a pre-departure basis, with little follow-up once the employee is abroad. Clearly, it would seem that organizations in today's global economy would benefit from training that gave expatriates coping options beyond removing themselves from the situation. ❖

FIGURE 4-3 Examples of Strain

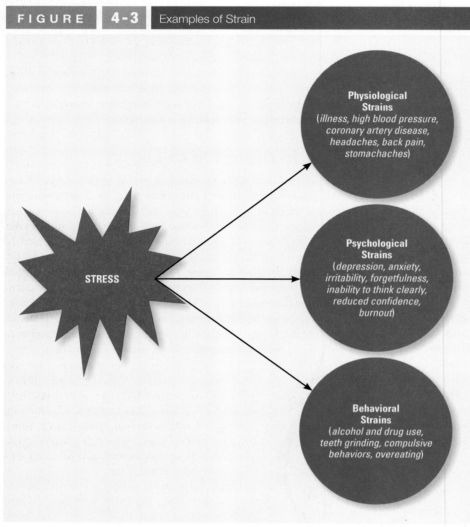

STRESS

Physiological Strains
(illness, high blood pressure, coronary artery disease, headaches, back pain, stomachaches)

Psychological Strains
(depression, anxiety, irritability, forgetfulness, inability to think clearly, reduced confidence, burnout)

Behavioral Strains
(alcohol and drug use, teeth grinding, compulsive behaviors, overeating)

Source: M. E. Burke, "2005 Benefits Survey Report," Society of Human Resource Management. Reprinted with permission.

extreme types of stressors—being chased through a jungle by a hungry tiger, for example—research suggests that most types of stressors evoke the same sequence of physiological events. As shown in Figure 4-3, those negative consequences of the stress process come in three varieties: physiological strains, psychological strains, and behavioral strains.[38]

Strains. Physiological strains that result from stressors occur in at least four systems of the human body. First, stressors can reduce the effectiveness of the body's immune system, which makes it more difficult for the body to ward off illness and infection. Second, stressors can harm the body's cardiovascular system, cause the heart to race, increase blood pressure, and create coronary artery disease. Third, stressors can cause problems in the body's musculoskeletal system. Tension headaches, tight shoulders, and back pain have all been linked to a variety of stressors. Fourth, stressors cause gastrointestinal system problems. Symptoms of this type of strain include stomachaches, indigestion, diarrhea, and constipation.[39]

Psychological strains that result from stressors include depression, anxiety, anger, hostility, reduced self-confidence, irritability, inability to think clearly, forgetfulness, lack of creativity, memory loss, and (not surprising, given the rest of this list) a loss of sense of humor.[40] These strains are likely to be a symptom of **burnout**, which refers to the emotional, mental, and physical exhaustion that results from having to cope with stressful demands on an ongoing basis.[41] Our **OB in Sports** box describes how even the toughest people are susceptible to burnout.

Relative to physiological and psychological strains, behavioral strains are the least connected to GAS. In fact, unhealthy behaviors such as grinding one's teeth at night, being overly critical and bossy, excessive smoking, compulsive gum chewing, overuse of alcohol, and compulsive eating[42] can be thought of as the behavioral symptoms of the other types of strains.

Managing Employee Strain. Because strains are a natural consequence of jobs filled with stress, some organizations have instituted practices to help reduce them.[43] One type of strain-reducing practice involves training in **relaxation techniques** such as progressive muscle relaxation, meditation, and miscellaneous calming activities like taking walks, writing in a journal, and deep breathing.[44] Although these relaxation

● **BURNOUT** The degree of emotional, mental, and physical exhaustion.

● **RELAXATION TECHNIQUES** Activities that counteract the effects of strains by reducing the heart rate, breathing rate, and blood pressure.

and blood is redirected away from organs such as the spleen to the brain and skeletal muscles.[36]

The changes that occur in the alarm stage prepare the mind and body for "fight or flight."[37] After this point, the person is in the second stage of the GAS, the stage of resistance. Here, the increased arousal of his or her mind and body caused by the secretion of chemicals helps the person respond and adapt to the demand. Unfortunately, if the chemicals in the blood remain elevated because of prolonged or repeated exposure to the stressor, the body begins to break down, and exhaustion and even death may occur. This last stage is the stage of exhaustion. Although the GAS might sound like a theory that describes reactions to

Some people find that jogging or other physical activities help reduce and even eliminate stress.

techniques differ, the basic idea is the same—they teach people how to counteract the effects of strain by engaging in activities that slow the heart rate, breathing rate, and blood pressure.[45] As an example of a relatively simple relaxation technique, consider the recommendation of Herbert Benson, a physician and president of the Mind/Body Medical Institute in Boston. He suggests that people under stress should repeat a word, sound, prayer, phrase, or motion for 10–20 minutes once or twice a day and, during that time, try to completely ignore other thoughts that may come to mind.[46]

A second category of strain-reducing practices involves training in cognitive–behavioral techniques. In general,

these techniques attempt to help people appraise and cope with stressors in a more rational manner.[47] To understand what these techniques involve, think of someone you know who not only exaggerates the level and importance of stressful demands but also predicts doom and disaster after quickly concluding that the demands simply cannot be met. If you know someone like this, you might recommend cognitive–behavioral training that involves "self-talk," a technique in which people learn to say things about stressful demands that reflect rationality and optimism. So, when confronted with a stressful demand, this person might be trained to say, "This demand isn't so tough; if I work hard I can accomplish it." In addition, cognitive–behavioral training typically involves instruction about tools that foster effective coping. So, in addition to the self-talk, the person might be trained on how to prioritize demands, manage time, communicate needs, and seek support.[48]

A third category of strain-reducing practices involves health and wellness programs. For example, almost three-quarters of the organizations in one survey reported having employee assistance programs intended to help people with personal problems such as alcoholism and other addictions. More than 60 percent of organizations in this survey provided employees with wellness programs and resources. The

OB in Sports

Brett Favre, former quarterback of the Green Bay Packers and one of the most successful and recognizable players in the National Football League, announced his retirement in March 2008 after playing 17 seasons.[49] Why did this three-time NFL Most Valuable Player and nine-time Pro Bowler retire? Was it because he was injured or otherwise physically incapable of playing effectively after so many seasons? No, Favre indicated that he was physically fine, and his final season was one of his best from a statistical standpoint.[50] Was it because of the frustration of being on a team that was incapable of competing against the better teams in the league? No, in his final season, he led the Packers to the NFC Championship game, and he believed the team had the potential to make it to the Super Bowl the following year.[51] It turns out that Favre decided to retire because of stress and burnout. But how could someone that Lance Armstrong once referred to as an "Ironman" get burned out from playing a game that he loved so much?[52]

A voice mail that Favre left for ESPN reporter Chris Mortensen provides the explanation: "I'm just tired, you know. Mentally I'm tired. Physically, I feel OK, you know. I can't complain. I just, stress. I mean studying every week, preparing, and the more we won, the more stressful it got, which you would think otherwise, but, you know, I was always trying to top what I had done the previous week." The ongoing pressure from the challenge of winning compelled Favre to spend an ever-increasing amount of time preparing, and over time, this pressure built up and resulted in exhaustion and a loss of commitment. In a press release, he commented that when he got home after games, he would sit at his computer to watch film of the next opponent rather than relaxing and enjoying the win with his wife Deanna, and that this inability to relax began to take a toll on him.[53] Although Favre initially dismissed the possibility that he would come back to the NFL, he later expressed a desire to play again, and was traded to the

Brett Favre has said, "the more we won, the more stressful it got, which you would think otherwise, but, you know, I was always trying to top what I had done the previous week."

New York Jets.[54] A change of heart like this is not unusual after a retirement from sports due to burnout. A break from the game not only gives an athlete a chance to rest and recharge his or her energies, but it also provides a lot of free time to think about the excitement and challenge of playing again. ❖

nature of these programs and their resources vary a great deal from organization to organization, but, in general, they are comprehensive efforts that include health screening (blood pressure, cholesterol levels, pulmonary functioning) and health-related courses and information. Other examples of health and wellness programs intended to reduce strain include smoking cessation programs, on-site fitness centers or fitness center memberships, and weight loss and nutrition programs.[55]

● ● 4.4

Describe how the Type A Behavior Pattern influences the stress process.

Accounting for Individuals in the Stress Process

So far in this chapter, we've discussed how the typical or average person reacts to different sorts of stressors. Of course, people differ in terms of how they typically react to stressful demands. One way that people differ in their reaction to stress depends on whether they exhibit the **Type A Behavior Pattern**. "Type A" people have a strong sense of time urgency and tend to be impatient, hard-driving, competitive, controlling, aggressive, and even hostile.[56] If you walk, talk, and eat at a quick pace, and if you find yourself constantly annoyed with people who do things too slowly, chances are that you're a Type A person.

The Type A Behavior Pattern is important because it can influence each variable in our general model of stress. First, the Type A Behavior Pattern may have a direct influence on the level of stressors that a person confronts. To understand why this connection might be true, consider that Type A persons tend to be hard-driving and have a strong desire to achieve. Because the behaviors that reflect these tendencies are valued by the organization, Type A individuals receive "rewards" in the form of increases in the amount and level of work required. Second, the Type A Behavior Pattern influences the appraisal process.[57] In essence, Type A individuals are simply more likely to appraise demands as being stressful rather than being benign. Third, and perhaps most important, the Type A Behavior Pattern has been directly linked to coronary heart disease[58] and other physiological, psychological, and behavioral strains.[59] The size of the relationship between the Type A Behavior Pattern and these strains is not so strong as to suggest that if you're a Type A person, you should immediately dial 911. However, the linkage is strong enough to suggest that the risk of these problems is significantly higher for Type A people.

● ● **"The Type A Behavior Pattern has been directly linked to coronary heart disease."**

● ● ● 4.5

Describe how social support influences the stress process.

Another individual factor that affects the way people manage stress is the degree of **social support** that they receive from supervisors, peers, friends, and family members.[60] Social support refers to the help that people receive when they are confronted with stressful demands, and there are at least two major types.[61] One type of social support is called instrumental support, which refers to the assistance people receive that can be used to address the stressful demand directly. For example, if a person is overloaded with work, a coworker could provide instrumental support by taking over some of the work or offering suggestions about how to do the work more efficiently. A second type of social support is called emotional support. This type of support refers to the help people receive in addressing the emotional distress that accompanies stressful demands. As an example, the supervisor of the individual who is overloaded with work might provide emotional support by showing interest in the employee's situation and appearing to be understanding and empathetic.

Most research on social support focuses on the ways that social support buffers the relationship between stressors and strains. According to this research, higher levels of social support provide a person with instrumental or emotional resources that are useful for coping with the stressor, which tends to reduce the harmful consequences of the stressor to that individual. With lower levels of social support, the person does not have extra coping resources available, so the stressor tends to have effects that are more harmful. Although not every research study has found support for the buffering effect of social support,[62] the majority of research evidence has been supportive.[63]

● ● 4.6

Describe the effects that stress has on job performance and organizational commitment?

HOW IMPORTANT IS STRESS?

At this point, you're probably curious about how stress impacts job performance and organizational commitment, the two outcomes in our integrative model of OB. However, describing the impact of stress is somewhat complicated because there are so many variables involved in the stress process. So, to simplify things a bit, we focus our discussion on effects that strains have. Figure 4-4 reveals that strains have a moderately negative effect on job performance.[64] A general explanation for this negative relationship between strains and job performance is that strains

FIGURE 4-4 Effects of Strains on Performance and Commitment

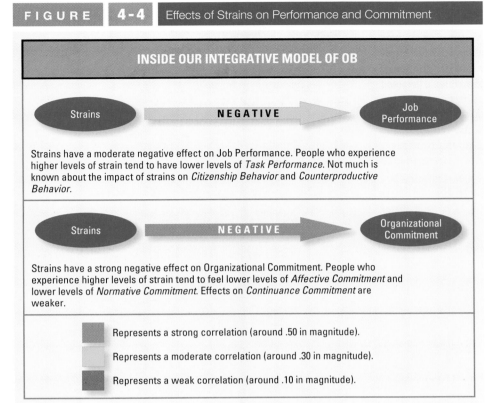

INSIDE OUR INTEGRATIVE MODEL OF OB

Strains → NEGATIVE → Job Performance

Strains have a moderate negative effect on Job Performance. People who experience higher levels of strain tend to have lower levels of *Task Performance*. Not much is known about the impact of strains on *Citizenship Behavior* and *Counterproductive Behavior*.

Strains → NEGATIVE → Organizational Commitment

Strains have a strong negative effect on Organizational Commitment. People who experience higher levels of strain tend to feel lower levels of *Affective Commitment* and lower levels of *Normative Commitment*. Effects on *Continuance Commitment* are weaker.

Represents a strong correlation (around .50 in magnitude).

Represents a moderate correlation (around .30 in magnitude).

Represents a weak correlation (around .10 in magnitude).

Sources: J. A. LePine, N. P. Podsakoff, and M. A. LePine, "A Meta-Analytic Test of the Challenge Stressor–Hindrance Stressor Framework: An Explanation for Inconsistent Relationships among Stressors and Performance," *Academy of Management Journal* 48 (2005), pp. 764–75; N. P. Podsakoff, J. A. LePine, and M. A. LePine, "Differential Challenge Stressor–Hindrance Stressor Relationships with Job Attitudes, Turnover Intentions, Turnover, and Withdrawal Behavior: A Meta-Analysis," *Journal of Applied Psychology* 92 (2007), pp. 438–54.

reduce the overall level of energy and attention that people could otherwise bring to their job duties.[65] Certainly, it is easy to appreciate that physiological, psychological, and behavioral strains in the form of illnesses, exhaustion, and drunkenness detract from employee effectiveness in almost any job context.

Figure 4-4 also reveals that strains have a strong negative effect on organizational commitment.[66] Why might this be? Well, strains are generally dissatisfying to people, and, as we discussed in the previous chapter, satisfaction has a strong impact on the degree to which people feel committed to their organization.[67] People who work at jobs that they know are causing them to feel constantly sick and exhausted will likely be dissatisfied with their jobs and feel less desire to stay with the organization and more desire to consider alternatives.

So in this discussion and Figure 4-4, we portray stress as something that has a negative impact on both job performance and organizational commitment. But this is not quite the whole story. In fact, though all types of stressors are positively associated with strains, certain types of stressors have positive relationships with performance

OB for Students

You might be wondering how the concepts and theories of stress apply in the context of your role as a student. Well, one recent study found that students face a number of hindrance stressors and challenge stressors in an academic context, and that these two types of stressors had different effects on their grades.[68]

Students who experienced higher levels of hindrance stressors, which included the amount of time spent on busywork for classes, the degree to which favoritism affected final grades in classes, and the amount of hassles students needed to go through to get projects/assignments done, tended to get lower grades. Coping with hindrance stressors was exhausting for students, and feeling exhausted made it difficult to put forth the energy to study. In addition, students who faced high levels of hindrance stressors tended not to believe that studying hard would result in good grades, and, accordingly, they did not put forth as

much effort as they could have.

Students who experienced higher levels of challenge stressors, which included the difficulty of the work required in classes, the volume of coursework required for classes, and the time pressures experienced for completing the work, tended to get higher grades. Although students felt that coping with challenge stressors was exhausting, the positive force of motivation from these types of stressors was significantly more powerful. In essence, challenge stressors motivated students to work hard in spite of feeling extremely tired.

So what can you do with this information? One option might be to take action to decrease the level of hindrance stressors you experience. Although this approach might be possible with some hindrances—asking professors to provide clarifying instruction for example—the approach may be more difficult with others—such as asking the professor to

What coping strategy do you use to keep track of all your assignments, exams, and deadlines for your classes?

reduce the amount of busywork. Of course, another option is to try to think of hindrances as challenges by keeping in mind that there may be real value in learning how to cope with these types of demands. ❖

and commitment.[69] But how can that be? To understand this somewhat counterintuitive pattern of relationships, recall from our previous discussions that challenge stressors such as time pressure and responsibility tend to evoke positive emotions, and that when people are confronted with challenge stressors, they tend to deal with them using problem-focused coping strategies. The net benefits of those positive emotions and coping strategies tend to outweigh the costs of the added strain, and the result is that challenge stressors tend to have positive relationships with performance and commitment. These positive effects of challenge stressors on performance and commitment have been demonstrated for executives,[70] employees in lower-level jobs,[71] and, as our **OB for Students** feature illustrates, students as well.[72] ■

CHECK OUT

www.mhhe.com/ColquittEss

for study materials including Interactive Exercises, Quizzes, iPod downloads, and video.

CASE: Best Buy

As we discussed in the opening vignette, the Results Only Work Environment (ROWE) at Best Buy gives employees the freedom to determine where and when they do their work. Although characteristics of the system would seem to reduce stress and burnout among employees, some people have expressed concerns about the system's potential drawbacks. For example, consider the case of Jane Kirshbaum, an attorney who works in the legal department, which has not transitioned to ROWE.[73] Kirshbaum recently had her second child and changed her work schedule to four days a week, and though she still struggles with balancing the demands of work and her family, she questions whether the transition to ROWE would improve her situation. She still has to deal with e-mails and voice mails on her "day off," and she believes that ROWE would further increase the pressure to work during what's supposed to be her downtime. She also realizes that sometimes things pop up at work that need immediate attention, and she believes that the associated work will get "dumped on" the people who are available or who are easiest to contact. Finally, the effectiveness of the legal department depends on how well it serves other departments, and, therefore, she believes her "results" are tied to her availability at the office when people need her.

Concerns such as those raised by Kirshbaum raise the question of whether ROWE has side effects that may result

in increases in employee stress and burnout rather than the intended decreases. Cali Ressler and Jody Thompson, the inventors of ROWE, explain that the likelihood of negative side effects such as those voiced by Kirshbaum are reduced because there are no longer incentives to work longer than absolutely necessary, and people are much more efficient doing work when they don't have to deal with hassles, politics, and other distractions at work.[74] Although results of some early research supports Ressler and Thompson's position, the effectiveness of ROWE has only been demonstrated in the context of employees at the corporate office, and there has not been any research on the long-term effects of the system.

4.1 Consider Best Buy's Results Only Work Environment. What are its key strengths? What are its key weaknesses?

4.2 Describe various ways in which ROWE is likely to affect the stress process. How might ROWE impact the degree to which employees experience the various types of challenge and hindrance stressors? How might ROWE impact social support, and what effect might this improvement have on the stress process?

4.3 Do you think that Best Buy's plan to implement ROWE in its retail stores will work? What could be done to address potential shortcomings of using ROWE in the retail store context?

TAKEAWAYS

4.1 Stress refers to the psychological response to demands when there is something at stake for the individual and when coping with these demands would tax or exceed the individual's capacity or resources. Stressors are the demands that cause the stress response, and strains are the negative consequences of the stress response.

4.2 Stressors come in two general forms: challenge stressors, which are perceived as opportunities for growth and achievement, and hindrance stressors, which are perceived as hurdles to goal achievement.

4.3 Coping with stress involves thoughts and behaviors that address one of two goals: addressing the stressful demand or decreasing the emotional discomfort associated with the demand.

4.4 Individual differences in the Type A Behavior Pattern affect the stress process in three ways. Type A people tend to experience more stressors, appraise more demands as stressful, and experience more strains.

4.5 Individual differences in social support influence the strength of the stress–strain relationship such that support acts as a buffer that prevents the onset of strain.

4.6 Although the body tries to adapt to different sorts of stressors along the lines of what is described by the general adaptation syndrome (GAS), over time, this adaptive response wears out the body, and exhaustion and collapse may occur. The resulting strain has a moderate negative relationship with job performance and a strong negative relationship with organizational commitment.

DISCUSSION QUESTIONS

4.1 Prior to reading this chapter, how did you define stress? Did your definition of stress reflect stressors, the stress process, strains, or some combination?

4.2 Describe your dream job and then provide a list of the types of stressors that you would expect to be present. Is the list dominated by challenge stressors or hindrance stressors? Why do you think this is?

4.3 Think about the dream job that you described in the previous question. How much of your salary, if any at all, would you give up to eliminate the most important hindrance stressors? Why?

4.4 If you had several job offers after graduating, to what degree would the level of challenge stressors in the different jobs influence your choice of which job to take? Why?

4.5 How would you assess your ability to handle stress? Given the information provided in this chapter, what could you do to improve your effectiveness in this area?

4.6 If you managed people in an organization in which there were lots of hindrance stressors, what actions would you take to help ensure that your employees coped with the stressors using a problem-focused as opposed to an emotion-focused coping strategy?

ASSESSMENT: The Type A Behavior Pattern

Do you think that you are especially sensitive to stress? This assessment is designed to measure the extent to which you're a Type A person—someone who typically engages in hard-driving, competitive, and aggressive behavior. (For more assessments relevant to this chapter, please visit the Online Learning Center at www.mhhe.com/ColquittEss.)

Answer each question using the response scale provided. Then subtract your answers to the bold-faced questions from 8, with the difference being your new answers for those questions. For example, if your original answer for Question 3 was "2," your new answer is "6" (8 – 2). Then sum your answers for the 12 questions.

1	2	3	4	5	6	7
Strongly Disagree	Disagree	Slightly Disagree	Neutral	Slightly Agree	Agree	Strongly Agree

1. Having work to complete "stirs me into action" more than other people. _____

2. When a person is talking and takes too long to come to the point, I frequently feel like hurrying the person along. _____

3. **Nowadays, I consider myself to be relaxed and easygoing.** _____

4. Typically, I get irritated extremely easily. _____

5. My best friends would rate my general activity level as very high. _____

6. I definitely tend to do most things in a hurry. _____

7. I take my work much more seriously than most. _____

8. **I seldom get angry.** _____

9. I often set deadlines for myself work-wise. _____

10. I feel very impatient when I have to wait in line. _____

11. I put much more effort into my work than other people do. _____

12. **Compared with others, I approach life much less seriously.** _____

Scoring

If your scores sum up to 53 or above, you would be considered a Type A person, which means that you may perceive higher stress levels in your life and be more sensitive to that stress. If your scores sum up to 52 or below, you would be considered a Type B person. This means that you sense less stress in your life and are less sensitive to the stress that is experienced.

Source: C. D. Jenkins, S. J. Zyzanski, and R. H. Rosenman, "Progress toward Validation of a Computer Scored Test for the Type A Coronary Prone Behavior Pattern," *Psychosomatic Medicine* 33 (1971), pp. 193–202. Reprinted with permission of Lippincott, Williams & Wilkins.

EXERCISE: Managing Stress

The purpose of this exercise is to explore ways of managing stress to reduce strain. This exercise uses groups, so your instructor will either assign you to a group or ask you to create your own groups. The exercise has the following steps:

1. One method of managing stress is finding a way to reduce the hindrance stressors encountered on the job. In your group, describe the hindrance stressors that you currently are experiencing. Each student should describe the two to three most important stressors. Other students should then offer strategies for reducing or alleviating the stressors.

Hindrance Stressors Experienced	Strategies for Managing Stressors
Role Conflict:	
Role Ambiguity:	
Role Overload:	
Daily Hassles:	

2. Another method of managing stress is to improve work–life balance. The circle below represents how "waking hours" are divided among five types of activities: school, work, personal relaxation, time with friends, and time with family. Draw two versions of your own circle: your waking hours as they currently are and your waking hours as you wish them

to be. Other students should then offer strategies for making the necessary life changes.

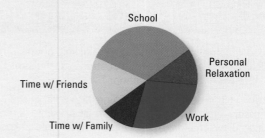

3. A third method of managing stress is improving *hardiness*—a sort of mental and physical health that can act as a buffer, preventing stress from resulting in strain. The table below lists a number of questions that can help diagnose your hardiness. Discuss your answers for each question, then, with the help of other students, brainstorm ways to increase that hardiness factor.

4. Class discussion (whether in groups or as a class) should center on two issues. First, many of the stress-managing factors, especially in Steps 2 and 3, take up precious time. Does this make them an ineffective strategy for managing stress? Why or why not? Second, consider your Type A score in the OB Assessments for this chapter. If you are high on Type A, does that make these strategies more or less important?

Hardiness Factor	Strategies for Improving Hardiness Factor
Relaxation: Do you spend enough time reading, listening to music, meditating, or pursuing your hobbies?	
Exercise: Do you spend enough time doing cardiovascular, strength, and flexibility sorts of exercises?	
Diet: Do you manage your diet adequately by eating healthily and avoiding foods high in fat?	

END NOTES

1. Kiger, P. "Throwing Out the Rules of Work." *Workforce Management,* September 26, 2006, www.workforce.com/section/09/feature/24/54/28 (accessed June 11, 2008).

2. Ressler, C., and J. Thompson. *Why Work Sucks and How to Fix It.* New York: Portfolio, 2008.

3. Conlin, M. "Smashing the Clock: No Schedules. No Mandatory Meetings. Inside Best Buy's Radical Reshaping of the Workplace." *BusinessWeek* online edition, December 11, 2006, www.businessweek.com/print/magazine/content/06_50/b4013001.htm (accessed June 6, 2008).

4. Ibid.

5. Barbaro, M. "Service in a Store Stocked with Stress." *Washington Post.com,* December 24, 2004, http://www.washingtonpost.com/wp-dyn/articles/A23383-2004Dec23.html (accessed June 11, 2008); Brandon, J. "Rethinking the Time Clock: Best Buy Is Getting Rid of Its Time Clocks—and Wants to Persuade You to Get Rid of Yours Too." *CNNMoney.com,* April 4, 2007, http://money.cnn.com/magazines/business2/business2_archive/2007/03/01/8401022/index.htm (accessed June 10, 2008).

6. Thottam, J. "Reworking Work." *Time* online edition, July 18, 2005, http://www.time.com/time/magazine/article/0,9171,1083900,00.html (accessed June 10, 2008).

7. Miller, J., and M. Miller. "Get a Life!" *Fortune* 152, no. 11 (November 28, 2005), pp. 109–24, available at www.ProQuest.com (accessed March 27, 2007).

8. Sauter, S.; L. Murphy; M. Colligan; N. Swanson; J. Hurrell Jr.; F. Scharf Jr.; R. Sinclair; P. Grubb; L. Goldenhar; T. Alterman; J. Johnston; A. Hamilton; and J. Tisdale. *Stress at Work.* DHHS (NIOSH) Publication No. 99-101. Cincinnati, OH: U.S. Department of Health and Human Services, Public Health Service, Centers for Disease Control and Prevention, National Institute for Occupational Safety and Health, 1999.

9. Johnson, S. R., and L. D. Eldridge. *Employee-Related Stress on the Job: Sources, Consequences, and What's Next.* Technical Report #003. Rochester, NY: Genesee Survey Services, Inc., 2004.

10. Perkins, A. "Medical Costs: Saving Money by Reducing Stress." *Harvard Business Review* 72, no. 6 (1994), p. 12.

11. Sauter, S.; L. Murphy; M. Colligan; N. Swanson; J. Hurrell Jr.; F. Scharf Jr.; R. Sinclair; P. Grubb; L. Goldenhar; T. Alterman; J. Johnston; A. Hamilton; and J. Tisdale. *Is Your Boss Making You Sick?* http://abcnews.go.com/GMA/Careers/story? id=1251346&gma=true (accessed October 27, 2005).

12. Defrank, R. S., and J. M. Ivancevich. "Stress on the Job: An Executive Update." *Academy of Management Executive* 12 (1998), pp. 55–66.

13. Lazarus, R. S., and S. Folkman. *Stress, Appraisal, and Coping.* New York: Springer Publishing Company, Inc., 1984.

14. Ibid.

15. LePine, J. A.; M. A. LePine; and C. L. Jackson. "Challenge and Hindrance Stress: Relationships with Exhaustion, Motivation to Learn, and Learning Performance." *Journal of Applied Psychology* 89 (2004), pp. 883–91; LePine, J. A.; N. P. Podsakoff; and M. A. LePine. "A Meta-Analytic Test of the Challenge Stressor–Hindrance Stressor Framework: An Explanation for Inconsistent Relationships among Stressors and Performance." *Academy of Management Journal* 48 (2005), pp. 764–75; Podsakoff, N. P.; J. A. LePine; and M. A. LePine. "Differential Challenge Stressor–Hindrance Stressor Relationships with Job Attitudes, Turnover Intentions, Turnover, and Withdrawal Behavior: A Meta-Analysis." *Journal of Applied Psychology* 92 (2007), pp. 438–54.

16. Kahn, R.; D. Wolfe; R. Quinn; J. Snoek; and R. A. Rosenthal. *Organizational Stress: Studies in Role Conflict and Ambiguity.* New York: John Wiley, 1964; Pearce, J. "Bringing Some Clarity to Role Ambiguity Research." *Academy of Management Review* 6 (1981), pp. 665–74.

17. LePine, J. A.; M. A. LePine; and J. R. Saul. "Relationships among Work and Non-work Challenge and Hindrance Stressors and Non-work and Work Criteria: A Theory of Cross-Domain Stressor Effects." In *Research in Occupational Stress and Well Being,* ed. P. L. Perrewé and D. C. Ganster. San Diego: JAI Press/Elsevier, 2006, pp. 35–72.

18. Kahn et al., "Organizational Stress."

19. Miller and Miller, "Get a Life!"

20. Mandel, M. "The Real Reasons You're Working So Hard . . . and What You Can Do about It." *BusinessWeek* 3953 (October 3, 2005), pp. 60–67, available at www.ProQuest.com (accessed March 27, 2007).

21. O'Connor, A. "Cracking under Pressure? It's Just the Opposite for Some; Sick of Work—Last of Three Articles: Thriving under Stress." *New York Times,* Section A, Column 5 (September 10, 2004), p. 1, available at www.ProQuest.com (accessed March 27, 2007).

22. McCall, M. W.; M. M. Lombardo; and A. M. Morrison. *The Lessons of Experience: How Successful Executives Develop on the Job.* Lexington, MA: Lexington Books, 1988.

23. Burke, M. E. "2005 Benefits Survey Report." Alexandria, VA: Society of Human Resource Management Research Department, 2005.

24. Miller and Miller, "Get a Life!"

25. Ibid.; Cunningham, C. R., and S. S. Murray. "Two Executives, One Career." *Harvard Business Review* 83, no. 2 (February 2005), pp. 125–31.

26. Lazarus and Folkman, *Stress, Appraisal, and Coping.*

27. Folkman, S.; R. S. Lazarus; C. Dunkel-Schetter; A. Delongis; and R. J. Gruen. "Dynamics of a Stressful Encounter: Cognitive Appraisal, Coping, and Encounter Outcomes." *Journal of Personality and Social Psychology* 50 (1986), pp. 992–1003.

28. Latack, J. C., and S. J. Havlovic. "Coping with Job Stress: A Conceptual Evaluation Framework for Coping Mea-

sures." *Journal of Organizational Behavior* 13 (1992), pp. 479–508.

29. Kahn et al., *Organizational Stress;* Lazarus and Folkman, *Stress, Appraisal, and Coping.*

30. Selye, H. *The Stress of Life.* New York: McGraw-Hill, 1976.

31. Ibid.

32. *Global Relocation Trends, 2005 Survey Report.* Woodridge, IL: GMAC Global Relocation Services, 2006, http://www.gmacglobalrelocation.com/insight_support/global _relocation.asp (accessed March 27, 2007).

33. Black, J. S.; M. Mendenhall; and G. Oddou. "Toward a Comprehensive Model of International Adjustment: An Integration of Multiple Theoretical Perspectives." *Academy of Management Review* 16 (1991), pp. 291–317.

34. Bhaskar-Shrinivas, P.; D. A. Harrison; M. A. Shaffer; and D. M. Luk. "Input-Based and Time-Based Models of International Adjustment: Meta-Analytic Evidence and Theoretical Extensions." *Academy of Management Journal* 48 (2005), pp. 257–81.

35. Mendenhall, M. E.; T. M. Kulmann; G. K. Stahl; and J. S. Osland. "Employee Development and Expatriate Assignments." In *Blackwell Handbook of Cross-Cultural Management,* ed. M. J. Gannon and K. L. Newman. Malden, MA: Blackwell, 2002, pp. 155–84.

36. Goldstein, D. L. *Stress, Catecholamines, & Cardiovascular Disease.* New York: Oxford University Press, 1995.

37. Cannon, W. B. "Stresses and Strains of Homeostasis." *American Journal of Medical Science* 189 (1935), pp. 1–14.

38. Kahn, R. L., and P. Byosiere. "Stress in Organizations." In *Handbook of Industrial and Organizational Psychology,* Vol. 4., ed. M. D. Dunette, J. M. R. Hough, and H. C. Triandis. Palo Alto, CA: Consulting Psychologists Press, 1992, pp. 517–650.

39. Defrank and Ivancevich, "Stress on the Job"; Haran, C. "Do You Know Your Early Warning Stress Signals?" 2005, http://abcnews.go.com/Health/Healthology/story?id=421825 (accessed October 27, 2005).

40. Ibid.

41. Pines, A., and D. Kafry. "Occupational Tedium in the Social Services." *Social Work* 23, no. 6 (1978), pp. 499–507.

42. Defrank and Ivancevich, "Stress on the Job."

43. Murphy, L. R. "Stress Management in Work Settings: A Critical Review of Health Effects." *American Journal of Health Promotion* 11 (1996), pp. 112–35.

44. Neufeld, S. *Work-Related Stress: What You Need to Know.* October 17, 2001, http://healthyplace.healthology.com/

focus_article.asp?f=mentalhealth&c=work_related_stress (accessed October 27, 2005).

45. Haran, "Do You Know."

46. Ibid.

47. Sonnentag, S., and M. Frese. "Stress in Organizations." In *Comprehensive Handbook of Psychology:* Vol. 12. *Industrial and Organizational Psychology,* ed. W. C. Borman, D. R. Ilgen, and R. J. Klimoski. New York: Wiley, 2003, pp. 453–91.

48. Neufeld, *Work-Related Stress.*

49. ESPN.com. "Mentally Tired Favre Tells Packers His Playing Career Is Over." March 4, 2008, http://sports.espn.go.com/nfl/news/story?id=3276034 (accessed June 5, 2008).

50. Ibid.

51. Packers.com. "Brett Favre Retirement Press Conference Transcript—March 6," March 6, 2008.

52. Scout.com. "Burnout Gets the Best of Favre." March 4, 2008, http://gnb.scout.com/2/734602.html (accessed June 5, 2008).

53. Packers.com, "Brett Favre Retirement Press Conference Transcript."

54. http://www.reuters.com/article/sportsNews/idUSL11424 09120080711?feedType=RSS&feedName=sportsNews (accessed, July 18, 2008).

55. Neufeld, *Work-Related Stress;* Burke, "2005 Benefits Survey Report."

56. Friedman, M., and R. H. Rosenman. *Type A Behavior and Your Heart.* New York: Knopf, 1974.

57. Ganster, D. C. "Type A Behavior and Occupational Stress. Job Stress: From Theory to Suggestion." *Journal of Organizational Behavior Management* 8 (Special issue, 1987), pp. 61–84.

58. Friedman and Rosenman, *Type A Behavior;* Yarnold, P. R., and F. B. Bryant. "A Note on Measurement Issues in Type A Research: Let's Not Throw Out the Baby with the Bath Water." *Journal of Personality Assessment* 52 (1988), pp. 410–19.

59. Abush, R., and E. J. Burkhead. "Job Stress in Midlife Working Women: Relationships among Personality Type, Job Characteristics, and Job Tension." *Journal of Counseling Psychology* 31 (1984), pp. 36–44; Dearborn, M. J., and J. E. Hastings. "Type A Personality as a Mediator of Stress and Strain in Employed Women." *Journal of Human Stress* 13 (1987), pp. 53–60; Howard, J. H.; D. A. Cunningham; and P. A. Rechnitzer. "Role Ambiguity, Type A Behavior, and Job Satisfaction: Moderating Effects on Cardiovascular and Biochemical Responses Associated with Coronary Risk." *Journal of Applied Psychology* 71 (1986), pp. 95–101.

60. Fusilier, M. R.; D. C. Ganster; and B. T. Mayes. "Effects of Social Support, Role Stress, and Locus of Control on Health." *Journal of Management* 13 (1987), pp. 517–28.

61. Cooper, C. L.; P. J. Dewe; and M. P. O'Driscoll. *Organizational Stress*. Thousand Oaks, CA: Sage Publications, 2001.

62. Jayaratne, S.; T. Tripodi; and W. A. Chess. "Perceptions of Emotional Support, Stress, and Strain by Male and Female Social Workers." *Social Work Research and Abstracts* 19 (1983), pp. 19–27; Kobasa, S. "Commitment and Coping in Stress among Lawyers." *Journal of Personality and Social Psychology* 42 (1982), pp. 707–17; LaRocco, J. M., and A. P. Jones. "Co-worker and Leader Support as Moderators of Stress–Strain Relationships in Work Situations." *Journal of Applied Psychology* 63 (1978), pp. 629–34.

63. Kahn and Byosiere, "Stress in Organizations."

64. LePine et al., "A Meta-Analytic Test."

65. Cohen, S. "After Effects of Stress on Human Performance and Social Behavior: A Review of Research and Theory." *Psychological Bulletin* 88 (1980), pp. 82–108.

66. Podsakoff et al., "Differential Challenge Stressor–Hindrance Stressor Relationships."

67. Bedeian, A. G., and A. Armenakis. "A Path-Analytic Study of the Consequences of Role Conflict and Ambiguity." *Academy of Management Journal* 24 (1981), pp. 417–24; Schaubroeck, J.; J. L. Cotton; and K. R. Jennings. "Antecedents and Consequences of Role Stress: A Covariance Structure Analysis." *Journal of Organizational Behavior* 10 (1989), pp. 35–58.

68. LePine et al., "Challenge and Hindrance Stress."

69. LePine et al., "A Meta-Analytic Test"; Podsakoff et al., "Differential Challenge Stressor–Hindrance Stressor Relationships."

70. Cavanaugh, M. A.; W. R. Boswell; M. V. Roehling; and J. W. Boudreau. "An Empirical Examination of Self-Reported Work Stress among U.S. Managers." *Journal of Applied Psychology* 85 (2000), pp. 65–74.

71. Boswell, W. R.; J. B. Olson-Buchanan; and M. A. LePine. "The Relationship between Work-Related Stress and Work Outcomes: The Role of Felt-Challenge and Psychological Strain." *Journal of Vocational Behavior* 64 (2004), pp. 165–81.

72. LePine et al., "Challenge and Hindrance Stress."

73. Thottam, "Reworking Work."

74. Ressler and Thompson, *Why Work Sucks and How to Fix It*.

MOTIVATION

NETFLIX

Want to know about someone's taste in movies? If they're a Netflix subscriber, just ask them what's in their "Netflix queue." Netflix, the California-based distributor of DVD movies, charges a monthly membership fee to its subscribers. Those subscribers go to the Netflix Web site, create a queue of preferred movies, then receive them in the mail, along with a return envelope. Best of all, there's no due date or late fee, with subscribers keeping the DVDs as long as they want before switching them out for the next movie in their queue. That flexibility is one of the reasons that Netflix has cut into the profits of popular "brick-and-mortar" stores like Blockbuster or Movie Gallery.[1] Another reason is that Netflix caters to customers who are interested in older movies or smaller-scale films, with only 30 percent of its rentals coming from new releases (versus 70 percent for Blockbuster).

Much of Netflix's success is credited to its 47-year-old founder, Reed Hastings.[2] Hastings, who previously founded a software company that eventually became too bureaucratic, is determined to avoid past mistakes. Noting that his prior company evolved into a dronish, when-does-the-day-end factory, Hastings has built Netflix around a "freedom and responsibility" philosophy.[3] The freedom part of the equation comes in the form of very few rules, as Netflix employees are free to structure their work the way they want. The hope is that such high autonomy will breed innovation and creativity. Netflix employees can also structure their compensation by choosing how much of their pay comes in the form of salary versus stock. In this way, employees can tailor their compensation to their own risk tolerance and their own career and life stage. The ultimate freedom, however, comes in the form of unlimited vacations. Employees are free to choose how long they take off and how frequently.

Now for the responsibility component. Hastings expects exceptional performance from his employees, believing that they should do the work of three to four people.[4] Heather McIlhany, a marketing manager, describes the company as a tough, fulfilling, fully formed adult culture, noting, "There's no place to hide at Netflix." Employees who only perform at an average level are shown the door. Netflix offers an exceptionally generous severance package to make managers feel less guilty about firing average employees. Employees who live up to expectations are handsomely rewarded, however. Whereas most companies go to great lengths to pay just enough to attract and retain talent, Netflix pays significantly more than the typical Silicon Valley rate. As Hastings deadpans, "We're unafraid to pay high." Pay increases are also tied to the job market rather than to performance evaluations. The company constantly gathers market compensation data, boosting salaries when needed to stay "ahead of the curve" on pay.

MOTIVATION

● ● **5.1**

Define motivation.

Few OB topics matter more to employees and managers than motivation. How many times have you wondered to yourself, "Why can't I get myself going today?" Or how many times have you looked at a friend or coworker and wondered, "Why are they working so slowly right now?" Both of these questions are asking about "motivation," which is a derivation of the Latin word for movement, *movere*.[5] Those Latin roots nicely capture the meaning of motivation, as motivated employees simply move faster and longer than unmotivated employees. More formally, motivation is defined as a set of energetic forces that originates both within and outside an employee, initiates work-related effort, and determines its direction, intensity, and persistence.[6] Motivation is a critical consideration because, in addition to the other variables in our integrative model, job performance is strongly related to motivation and ability (see Chapter 8's discussion of ability for more on such issues).[7]

The first part of the motivation definition illustrates that motivation is not one thing but rather a set of distinct forces. Some of those forces are internal to the employee, such as a sense of self-confidence, whereas others are external to the employee, such as the goals an employee is given. The next part of that definition illustrates that motivation determines a number of facets of an employee's work effort. These facets are summarized in Figure 5-1, which depicts a scenario in which your boss has given you an assignment to work on. Motivation determines *what* employees do at a given moment—the direction in which their effort is channeled. Every moment of the workday offers choices between task and citizenship sorts of actions or withdrawal and counterproductive sorts of actions. When it's 3:00 p.m. on a Thursday, do you keep working on the assignment your boss gave you, or do you launch Internet Explorer and start browsing for a while? Once the direction of effort has been decided, motivation goes on to determine *how hard* an employee works—the intensity of effort—and *for how long*—the persistence of effort. We all have friends or coworkers who work extremely hard for . . . say . . . 5 minutes. We also have friends or coworkers who work extremely long hours but always seem to be functioning at half-speed. Neither of those groups of people would be described as extremely motivated.

There are a number of theories and concepts that attempt to explain why some employees are more motivated than others. The sections that follow review those theories and concepts in some detail. Most of them are relevant to each of the three motivation components described in Figure 5-1. However, some of them are uniquely suited to explaining the direction of effort, whereas others do a better job of explaining the intensity and persistence of effort.

Expectancy Theory

What makes you decide to direct your effort to work assignments rather than taking a break or wasting time? Or what makes you decide to be a "good citizen" by helping out a colleague or attending some optional company function? Expectancy theory describes the cognitive process that employees go through to make choices among different voluntary responses.[8] Drawing on earlier models from psychology, expectancy theory argues that employee behavior is directed toward pleasure and away from pain or, more generally, toward certain outcomes and away from others.[9] How do employees make the choices that take them in the "right direction"? The theory suggests that our choices depend on three specific beliefs that are based in our past learning and experience: expectancy, instrumentality, and valence. These three beliefs are summarized in Figure 5-2, and we review each of them in turn.

● MOTIVATION A set of energetic forces that originate both within and outside an employee, initiate work-related effort, and determine its direction, intensity, and persistence.

● EXPECTANCY THEORY A theory that describes the cognitive process that employees go through to make choices among different voluntary responses.

FIGURE 5-1 Motivation and Effort

MOTIVATION DETERMINES THE . . .

DIRECTION of Effort:	INTENSITY of Effort:	PERSISTENCE of Effort:
What are you going to do right now?	*How hard are you going to work on it?*	*How long are you going to work on it?*
☑ The assignment your boss gave you yesterday	As hard as you can, or only at half-speed?	For five hours or five minutes?
☐ Send e-mails to your friends		
☐ Surf the Web for a while		

● ● 5.2

Describe expectancy theory and the three beliefs that help determine how work effort is directed.

Expectancy.

Expectancy represents the belief that exerting a high level of effort will result in the successful performance of some task. More technically, expectancy is a subjective probability, ranging from 0 (no chance!) to 1 (a mortal lock!) that a specific amount of effort will result in a specific level of performance (abbreviated E → P). Think of a task at which you're not particularly good, such as writing romantic poetry. You may not be very motivated to write romantic poetry because you don't believe that your effort, no matter how hard you try, will result in a poem that "moves" your significant other. As another example, you'll be more motivated to work on the assignment described in Figure 5-1 if you're confident that trying hard will allow you to complete it successfully.

● **EXPECTANCY** The belief that exerting a high level of effort will result in the successful performance of some task.

● **SELF-EFFICACY** The belief that a person has the capabilities needed to execute the behaviors required for task success.

● **INSTRUMENTALITY** The belief that successful performance will result in some outcome(s).

What factors shape our expectancy for a particular task? One of the most critical factors is **self-efficacy**, defined as the belief that a person has the capabilities needed to execute the behaviors required for task success.[10] Think of self-efficacy as a kind of self-confidence or a task-specific version of self-esteem.[11] Employees who feel more "efficacious" (that is, self-confident) for a particular task will tend to perceive higher levels of expectancy—and therefore be more likely to choose to exert high levels of effort. Why do some employees have higher self-efficacy for a given task than other employees? Figure 5-3 can help explain such differences.

When employees consider efficacy levels for a given task, they first consider their *past accomplishments*—the degree to which they have succeeded or failed on similar sorts of tasks in the past.[12] They also consider *vicarious experiences* by taking into account their observations and discussions with others who have performed such tasks.[13] Self-efficacy is also dictated by *verbal persuasion* because friends, coworkers, and leaders can persuade employees that they can "get the job done." Finally, efficacy is dictated by *emotional cues*, in that feelings of fear or anxiety can create doubts about task accomplishment, whereas pride and enthusiasm can bolster confidence levels.[14] Taken together, these efficacy sources shape analyses of how difficult the task requirements are and how adequate an employee's personal and situational resources will prove to be.[15] They also explain the content of most "halftime speeches" offered by coaches during sporting events. Such speeches commonly include references to past comebacks or victories (past accomplishments), pep talks about how good the team is (verbal persuasion), and cheers to rally the troops (emotional cues).

Instrumentality.

Instrumentality represents the belief that successful performance will result in some outcome(s).[16] More technically, instrumentality is a set of subjective probabilities, each ranging from 0 (no chance!) to 1 (a mortal lock!) that successful performance will bring a set of outcomes (abbreviated P→O). The term "instrumentality" makes sense when you consider the meaning of the adjective "instrumental." We say something is "instrumental" when it helps attain something else—for example, reading this chapter is instrumental for getting a good grade in an OB class (at least, we hope so!).[17] Unfortunately, evidence indicates that many employees don't perceive high levels of instrumentality in their workplace. One survey of more than 10,000 employees in 2005 revealed that 60 percent viewed seniority as the key determinant of their pay.[18] Those that viewed successful performance as the key driver: only 35 percent. For a discussion of instrumentality in the world of professional golf, see our **OB in Sports** feature.

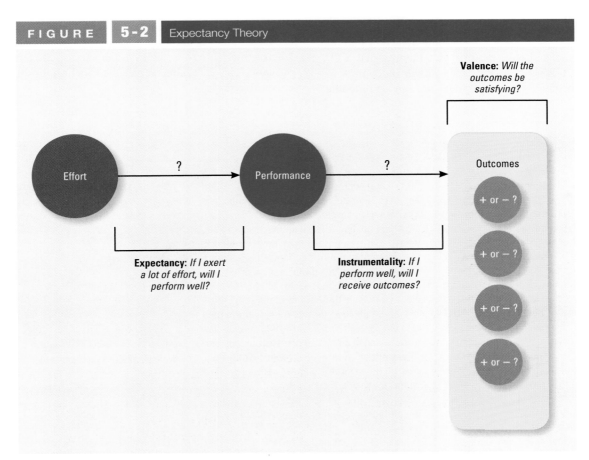

FIGURE 5-2 Expectancy Theory

Source: Adapted from V. H. Vroom, *Work and Motivation* (New York: Wiley, 1964).

FIGURE 5-3 Sources of Self-Efficacy

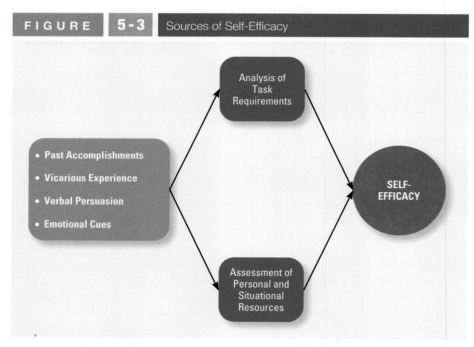

Sources: Adapted from A. Bandura, "Self-Efficacy: Toward a Unifying Theory of Behavioral Change," *Psychological Review* 84 (1977), pp. 191–215; M. E. Gist and T. R. Mitchell, "Self-Efficacy: A Theoretical Analysis of its Determinants and Malleability," *Academy of Management Review* 17 (1992), pp. 183–211.

Valence. Valence reflects the anticipated value of the outcomes associated with performance (abbreviated V).[19] Valences can be positive ("I would prefer *having* outcome X to not having it"), negative ("I would prefer *not having* outcome X to having it"), or zero ("I'm bored . . . are we still talking about outcome X?"). Salary increases, bonuses, and more informal rewards are typical examples of "positively valenced" outcomes, whereas disciplinary actions, demotions, and terminations are typical examples of "negatively valenced" outcomes.[20] In this way, employees are more motivated when successful performance helps them attain attractive outcomes such as bonuses, while helping them avoid unattractive outcomes such as termination.

What exactly makes some outcomes more "positively valenced" than others? In general, outcomes are deemed more attractive when they help satisfy needs. Needs can be defined as cognitive groupings or clusters of outcomes that are viewed as having critical psychological or physiological consequences.[21] Although scholars once suggested that certain needs are "universal" across people,[22] it is likely that different people have different "need hierarchies" that they use to evaluate potential outcomes. Table 5-1 describes many of the needs that are commonly studied in OB.[23] The terms and labels assigned to those needs often vary, so the table includes our labels as well as alternative labels that might sometimes be encountered.

OB in Sports

At six months old, he began imitating his father's swing.[24] At two years old, he putted against Bob Hope on national television.[25] At age three, he shot a 48 for nine holes at the Navy Golf Club in California. He, of course, is Eldrick Tont ("Tiger") Woods. After winning the U.S. Open in a playoff in 2008, Tiger had won 14 major championships, trailing only Jack Nicklaus on golf's all-time list.[26] Clearly Tiger's ability is a key factor in his dominance. That said, it is Tiger's motivation that often draws the most admiration. He is able to channel an intense amount of effort and concentration for a very long period of time. As one columnist wrote after his U.S. Open win, "As I've been trying to write this column, I've toggled over to check my email a few times. I've looked out the window. I've jotted down random thoughts for the paragraphs ahead. But Woods seems able to mute the chatter that normal people have in their heads and build a tunnel of focused attention."[27] That focused attention was especially vital during the U.S. Open because Tiger played on an injured knee that later required surgery.

Although Tiger's motivation is remarkable, what's just as interesting is how he affects the motivation of other golfers. One research study examined the performance of professional golfers from 1999 to 2006 in tournaments in which Tiger did (and did not) play.[28] The study showed that golfers' performance was almost one stroke worse when Tiger was also playing in that particular tournament. The "Tiger effect" was even stronger when Tiger was on a hot streak, whereas it was weaker when he was in a cooler period or when he struggled in the earlier rounds. Interestingly, the performance decrement occurred equally for players who played alongside Tiger and those who played earlier or later in the day, lessening the likelihood that fear or intimidation explains the effect. What might explain it? It may be that other players simply perceive

It is Tiger Woods's motivation that often draws the most admiration. He is able to channel an intense amount of effort and concentration for a very long period of time.

less instrumentality when playing in tournaments with Tiger. Even if they perform well by putting up a good score, they probably won't win the prize money because Tiger will just play better. ❖

● **VALENCE** The antici-
pated value of the out-
comes associated with
performance.

● **NEEDS** Cognitive groupings or clusters of outcomes
that are viewed as having
critical psychological or
physiological consequences.

● **EXTRINSIC MOTIVA-
TION** Motivation that is
controlled by some contingency that depends on task
performance.

● **INTRINSIC MOTIVA-
TION** Motivation that is felt
when task performance
serves as its own reward.

Table 5-2 lists some of the most commonly considered outcomes in studies of motivation. Outcomes that are deemed particularly attractive are likely to satisfy a number of different needs. For example, praise can signal that interpersonal bonds are strong (satisfying relatedness needs) while also signaling competence (satisfying esteem needs). Note also that some of the outcomes in Table 5-2 result from other people acknowledging successful performance, whereas others are self-generated, originating in task performance itself. The former set creates extrinsic motivation—motivation that is controlled by some contingency that depends on task performance.[29] The latter set creates intrinsic motivation—motivation that is felt when task performance serves as its own reward.[30] Extrinsic and intrinsic motivation together represent an employee's "total motivation" level. For more on the distinction between intrinsic and extrinsic motivation, see our **OB on Screen** feature.

You might wonder which of the outcomes in the table are most attractive to employees. That's a difficult question to answer, given that different employees emphasize different needs, but two things are clear. First, the attractiveness of outcomes varies across cultures. For example, good performance on a project in an American company might earn a "spot award" such as an expensive watch or a trip to Las Vegas. However, a moped would likely be deemed more attractive in congested areas like India or China, and trips to alcohol- and gambling-intensive areas are taboo in parts of Asia and the Middle East.[31]

Second, research suggests that employees underestimate how powerful a motivator pay is to them.[32] When employees rank the importance of outcomes like those in Table 5-2, they often put pay in fifth or sixth place. However, research studies show that financial incentives almost always have a stronger impact on motivation than other sorts of outcomes.[33]

Need a new moped? Employers in this town in Vietnam might be more inclined to give one as a "spot award" than those in North America, where vacations or expensive watches would be more valuable.

TABLE 5-1	Commonly Studied Needs in OB	
Need Label	**Alternative Labels**	**Description**
Existence	Physiological, Safety	The need for the food, shelter, safety, and protection required for human existence.
Relatedness	Love, Belongingness	The need to create and maintain lasting, positive, interpersonal relationships.
Control	Autonomy, Responsibility	The need to be able to predict and control one's future.
Esteem	Self-regard, Growth	The need to hold a high evaluation of oneself and to feel effective and respected by others.
Meaning	Self-actualization	The need to perform tasks that one cares about and that appeal to one's ideals and sense of purpose.

Sources: Adapted from A. H. Maslow, "A Theory of Human Motivation," *Psychological Review* 50 (1943), pp. 370–96; C. P. Alderfer, "An Empirical Test of a New Theory of Human Needs," *Organizational Behavior and Human Performance* 4 (1969), pp. 142–75; E. L. Deci and R. M Ryan, "The 'What' and 'Why' of Goal Pursuits: Human Needs and the Self-Determination of Behavior," *Psychological Inquiry* 11 (2000), pp. 227–68; R. Cropanzano, Z. S. Byrne, D. R. Bobocel, and D. R. Rupp, "Moral Virtues, Fairness Heuristics, Social Entities, and Other Denizens of Organizational Justice," *Journal of Vocational Behavior* 58 (2001), pp. 164–209; K. D. Williams, "Social Ostracism," in *Aversive Interpersonal Behaviors*, ed. R. M. Kowalski (New York: Plenum Press, 1997), pp. 133–70.

Why can pay and bonuses be so motivational? One reason is that money, like many of the outcomes in Table 5-2, is relevant to multiple needs. For example, money can help satisfy existence needs by helping employees buy food, afford a house, and save for retirement. However, money also conveys a sense of esteem by sending the signal that employees are competent and well-regarded.[34] In fact, research suggests that people differ in how they view the meaning of money—the degree to which they view money as having symbolic, not just economic, value.[35] The symbolic value of money can be summarized in at least three dimensions: achievement (i.e., money symbolizes success), respect (i.e., money brings respect in one's community), and freedom (i.e., money provides opportunity).[36]

Who is more likely to view money from these more symbolic perspectives? Some research suggests that men are more likely to view money as representing achievement, respect, and freedom than are women.[37] Research also suggests that employees with higher salaries are more likely to view money in achievement-related terms.[38] Younger employees are less likely to view money in a positive light, relative to older employees.[39] Differences in education do not appear to impact the meaning of money, however.[40]

Motivational Force.

According to expectancy theory, the direction of effort is dictated by three beliefs: expectancy ($E \rightarrow P$), instrumentality ($P \rightarrow O$), and valence (V). More specifically, the theory suggests that the total "motivational force" to perform a given action can be described using the following formula:[41]

$$\text{Motivational Force} = \boxed{E \rightarrow P} \times \boxed{\Sigma[(P \rightarrow O) \times V]}$$

The Σ symbol in the equation signifies that instrumentalities and valences are judged with various outcomes in mind, and motivation increases as successful performance is linked to more and more attractive outcomes. Note the significance of the multiplication signs in the formula: Motivational force equals zero if any one of the three beliefs is zero. In other words, it doesn't matter how confident you are if performance doesn't result in any outcomes. Similarly, it doesn't matter how well performance is evaluated and rewarded if you don't believe you can perform well.

Goal-Setting Theory

So, returning to the choice shown in Figure 5-1, let's say that you feel confident you can perform well on the assignment your boss gave you and that you also believe successful performance will bring valued outcomes. Now that you've chosen to direct your effort to that assignment, two critical questions remain: How hard will you work, and for how long? To shed some more light on these questions, you stop by your boss's office and ask her, "So, when exactly do you need this done?" After thinking about it for a while, she concludes, "Just do your best." After returning to your desk, you realize that you're still not sure how much to focus on the assignment, or how long you should work on it before turning to something else.

TABLE 5-2	Extrinsic and Intrinsic Outcomes
Extrinsic Outcomes	**Intrinsic Outcomes**
Pay	Enjoyment
Bonuses	Interestingness
Promotions	Accomplishment
Benefits and perks	Knowledge gain
Spot awards	Skill development
Praise	Personal expression
Job security	(Lack of) Boredom
Support	(Lack of) Anxiety
Free time	(Lack of) Frustration
(Lack of) Disciplinary actions	
(Lack of) Demotions	
(Lack of) Terminations	

Sources: Adapted from E. E. Lawler III and J. L. Suttle, "Expectancy Theory and Job Behavior," *Organizational Behavior and Human Performance* 9 (1973), pp. 482–503; J. Galbraith and L. L. Cummings, "An Empirical Investigation of the Motivational Determinants of Task Performance: Interactive Effects between Instrumentality–Valence and Motivation–Ability," *Organizational Behavior and Human Performance* 2 (1967), pp. 237–57; E. McAuley, S. Wraith, and T. E. Duncan, "Self-Efficacy, Perceptions of Success, and Intrinsic Motivation for Exercise," *Journal of Applied Social Psychology* 21 (1991), pp. 139–55; A. S. Waterman, S. J. Schwartz, E. Goldbacher, H. Green, C. Miller, and S. Philip, "Predicting the Subjective Experience of Intrinsic Motivation: The Roles of Self-Determination, the Balance of Challenges and Skills, and Self-Realization Values," *Personality and Social Psychology Bulletin* 29 (2003), pp. 1447–58.

● ● **5.3**

Understand the two qualities that make goals strong predictors of task performance, according to goal-setting theory.

Goal-setting theory views goals as the primary drivers of the intensity and persistence of effort.[42] Goals are defined as the objective or aim of an action and typically refer to attaining a specific standard of proficiency, often within a specified time limit.[43] More specifically, the theory argues that assigning employees *specific and difficult goals* will result in higher levels of performance than assigning no goals, easy goals, or "do-your-best" goals.[44] Why are specific and difficult goals more effective than do-your-best ones? After all, doesn't "your best" imply the highest possible levels of effort? The reason is that few people know what their "best" is (and even fewer managers can tell whether employees are truly doing their "best"). Assigning specific and difficult goals gives people a number to shoot for—a "measuring stick" that can

task effort is lower. As goals move from moderate to difficult, the intensity and persistence of effort become maximized. At some point, however, the limits of a person's ability get reached, and self-efficacy begins to diminish. At that point, goals move from difficult to impossible, and employees feel somewhat helpless when attempting to achieve them. At that point, effort and performance inevitably decline. So a difficult goal is one that stretches an employee to perform at his or her

"Assigning specific and difficult goals gives people a number to shoot for—a 'measuring stick' that can be used to tell them how hard they need to work and for how long."

be used to tell them how hard they need to work and for how long. So if your boss had said, "Have the assignment on my desk by 10:30 a.m. on Tuesday, with no more than two mistakes," you would have known exactly how hard to work and for how long.

Of course, a key question then becomes, "What's a difficult goal?" Figure 5-4 illustrates the predicted relationship between goal difficulty and task performance. When goals are easy, there's no reason to work your hardest or your longest, so

maximum level while still staying within the boundaries of his or her ability.

Why exactly do specific and difficult goals have positive effects? Figure 5-5 presents goal-setting theory in more detail to understand that question better.[45] First, the assignment of a specific and difficult goal shapes people's own *self-set goals*—the internalized goals that people use to monitor their own task progress.[46] In the absence of an assigned goal, employees may not even consider what their own goals are, or they may self-set

OB on Screen

Talladega Nights: The Ballad of Ricky Bobby

It's because it's what you love, Ricky. It is who you were born to be. And here you sit. Thinking. Well, Ricky Bobby is not a thinker. Ricky Bobby is a driver. He is a doer, and that's what you need to do. You don't need to think . . . you need to drive. . . . When the fear rises up in your belly, you use it. And you know that fear is powerful, because it has been there for billions of years. And it is good. And you use it . . . and then you win, Ricky. You WIN! And you don't win for anybody else. You win for you. . . .

With those words, Susan (Amy Adams) tries to motivate Ricky Bobby (Will Ferrell) to return to NASCAR in *Talladega Nights* (Dir. Adam

McKay, Sony Pictures, 2006). A few months earlier, no speech would have been needed, as Ricky Bobby was one of the most successful drivers around. At that point, Ricky Bobby's motivation was based on winning and the extrinsic rewards that came with it. He adopted his father's mantra: "If you ain't first, you're last!" He also opened every meal with a long list of the things for which he was thankful.

All that changed after a serious accident. Ricky Bobby lost his self-efficacy, his sponsor, his house, and his wife. To add insult to injury, his dad admitted that the "If you ain't first, you're last!" philosophy had been nonsense all along. Lacking any motivation to return to NASCAR, Ricky Bobby settled for delivering pizza on a bicycle. It took his former assistant, Susan, to awaken Ricky Bobby from his malaise. Her speech reminded him that he chose to become a driver in the first place for one

reason only: He wanted to go fast. Driving a race car used to be intrinsically motivating for him, providing him with enjoyment and personal expression rather than the boredom that his current life possessed. Without giving away the ending, Susan's words inspired Ricky to return to NASCAR, armed with a deeper sense of intrinsic motivation for driving fast. ❖

relatively easy goals that they're certain to meet. As a self-set goal becomes more difficult, the intensity of effort increases, and the persistence of effort gets extended. However, goals have another effect; they trigger the creation of *task strategies*, defined as learning plans and problem-solving approaches used to achieve successful performance.[47] In the absence of a goal, it's easy to rely on trial and error to figure out how best to do a task. Under the pressure of a measuring stick, however, it becomes more effective to plan out the next move.

Figure 5-5 also includes three variables that specify when assigned goals will have stronger or weaker effects on task performance. In the jargon of theory diagrams, these variables are called "moderators." Rather than directly affecting other variables in the diagram, moderators affect the strength of the relationships between variables. One moderator is *feedback*, which consists of updates on employee progress toward goal attainment.[48] Imagine being challenged to beat a friend's score on the

After receiving a goal to discover 12 new drug compounds every year, scientists at Wyeth increased their performance, earning a bonus in the process.

Halo 3 video game but then not being told what exactly your score was as you were playing. How would you know how hard to try? Another moderator is *task complexity*, which reflects how complicated the information and actions involved in a task are, as well as how much the task changes.[49] In general, the effects of specific and difficult goals are almost twice as strong on simple tasks as on complex tasks, though the effects of goals remain beneficial even in complex cases.[50] Goal setting at Wyeth, the New Jersey–based pharmaceuticals company, illustrates the value of goals for complex tasks (after all, what's more complicated than chemistry?).[51] When Robert Ruffolo was appointed the new chief of R&D six years ago, he was concerned about the low number of new drug compounds being generated by Wyeth's labs. His solution? He gave scientists a goal of discovering 12 new drug compounds every year, up from the 4 compounds they were previously averaging, with bonuses contingent on reaching the goals. Wyeth's scientists have reached the goal every year since, and the goal was upped to 15 compounds in 2006.

The final moderator shown in Figure 5-5 is goal commitment, defined as the degree to which a person accepts a goal and is determined to try to reach it.[52] When goal commitment is high, assigning specific and difficult goals will have significant benefits for task performance. However, when goal commitment is low, those effects become much weaker.[53] The importance of goal commitment raises the question of how best to foster commitment when assigning goals to employees. Research suggests that commitment can be fostered in a number of ways, including tying rewards to goal achievement, making goals public, providing supportive supervision, and allowing employees to participate in the goal-setting process.[54] For insights into how goal setting operates across cultures, see our **OB Internationally** feature.

Equity Theory

Returning to our running example in Figure 5-1, imagine that at this point, you've decided to work on the assignment your boss gave you, and you've been told that it is due by Tuesday at 10:30 a.m. and cannot have any more than two mistakes in it. That's a specific and difficult goal, so Internet Explorer hasn't

---

| FIGURE | 5-4 | Goal Difficulty and Task Performance |

Source: Adapted from E. A. Locke and G. P. Latham, *A Theory of Goal Setting and Task Performance* (Englewood Cliffs, NJ: Prentice Hall, 1990).

been launched in a while, and you haven't even thought about checking your e-mail. In short, you've been working very hard for a few hours, until the guy from across the hall pops his head in. You tell him what you're working on, and he nods sympathetically, saying, "Yeah, the boss gave me a similar assignment that sounds just as tough. I think she realized how tough it was though, because she said I could use the company's playoff tickets if I finish it on time." Playoff tickets? Playoff tickets?? Looks like it's time to check that e-mail after all. . . .

Unlike the first two theories, equity theory acknowledges that motivation doesn't just depend on your own beliefs and circumstances but also on what happens to *other people*.[55] More specifically, equity theory suggests that employees create a "mental ledger" of the outcomes (or rewards) they get from their job duties.[56] What outcomes might be part of your mental ledger? That's completely up to you and depends on what you find valuable, though pay, benefits, status symbols, perks, and satisfying supervision are typically critical. Equity theory further suggests that employees create a mental ledger of the inputs (or contributions and investments) they put into their job duties.[57] Again, the composition of your mental ledger is completely specific to you, but many employees focus on effort, performance, skills, education, experience, and seniority.

● ● **5.4**

Describe what it means to be equitably treated according to equity theory and how employees respond when they feel a sense of inequity.

So what exactly do you do with these mental tallies of outcomes and inputs? Equity theory argues that you compare your ratio of outcomes and inputs to the ratio of some *comparison other*—some person who seems to provide an intuitive frame of reference for judging equity.[58] There are three general possibilities that can result from this "cognitive calculus," as shown in Figure 5-6. The first possibility is that the ratio of outcomes to inputs is balanced between you and your comparison other. In this case, you feel a sense of equity, and you're likely to maintain the intensity and persistence of your effort. This situation would have occurred if you have been offered playoff tickets, just like your colleague.

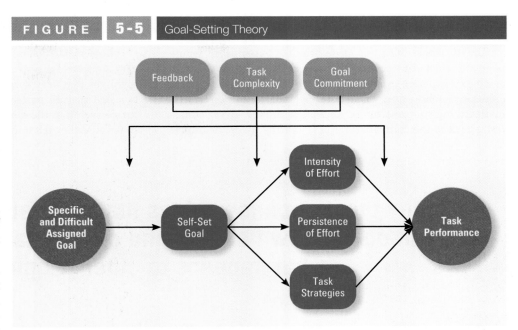

FIGURE 5-5 Goal-Setting Theory

Sources: Adapted from E. A. Locke and G. P. Latham, *A Theory of Goal Setting and Task Performance* (Englewood Cliffs, NJ: Prentice Hall, 1990); E. A. Locke and G. P. Latham, "Building a Practically Useful Theory of Goal Setting and Task Motivation: A 35-Year Odyssey," *American Psychologist* 57 (2002), pp. 705–17; G. P. Latham, "Motivate Employee Performance through Goal-Setting," in *Blackwell Handbook of Principles of Organizational Behavior*, ed. E. A. Locke (Malden, MA: Blackwell, 2000), pp. 107–19.

The second possibility is that your ratio of outcomes to inputs is less than your comparison other's ratio. According to equity theory, any imbalance in ratios triggers equity distress—an internal tension that can only be alleviated by restoring balance to the ratios.[59] In an underreward case, the equity distress likely takes the form of negative emotions such as anger or envy. One way to stop feeling those emotions is to try to restore the balance in some way; Figure 5-6 reveals two methods for doing so. You could be constructive and proactive by talking to your boss and explaining why you deserve better outcomes. Such actions would result in the growth of your outcomes, restoring balance to the ratio. Of course, anger often results in actions that are destructive rather than constructive, and research shows that feelings of underreward inequity are among the strongest predictors of counterproductive behaviors such as employee theft (see Chapter 6 on Trust, Justice, and Ethics for more on this issue).[60] More relevant to this chapter, another means of restoring balance is to shrink your inputs by lowering the intensity and persistence

● **GOAL COMMITMENT** The degree to which a person accepts a goal and is determined to try to reach it.

● **EQUITY THEORY** A theory that suggests that motivation and performance depend on how one's own ratio of outcomes to inputs compares to the ratio of a comparison other.

● **EQUITY DISTRESS** An internal tension that can only be alleviated by restoring balance to the outcome/input ratio.

of effort. Remember, it's not the total outcomes or inputs that matter in equity theory—it's only the ratio.

The third possibility is that your ratio of outcomes to inputs is greater than your comparison other's ratio. Equity distress again gets experienced, and the tension likely creates negative emotions such as guilt or anxiety. Balance could be restored by shrinking your outcomes (taking less money, giving something back to the comparison other), but the theory acknowl-

distortion allows you to restore balance mentally, without altering your behavior in any way.

These mechanisms make it clear that judging equity is a very subjective process. Recent data from a Salary.com report highlight that very subjectivity. A survey of 1,500 employees revealed that 65 percent of the respondents planned to look for a new job in the next three months, with 57 percent doing so because they felt underpaid. However, Salary.com estimated

> ## "Equity theory acknowledges that motivation doesn't just depend on your own beliefs and circumstances but also on what happens to other people."

edges that such actions are unlikely in most cases.[61] Instead, the more likely solution is to increase your inputs in some way. You could increase the intensity and persistence of your task effort or decide to engage in more "extra mile" citizenship behaviors. At some point though, there may not be enough hours in the day to increase your inputs any further. An alternative (and less labor-intensive) means of increasing your inputs is to simply rethink them—to reexamine your mental ledger to see if you may have "undersold" your true contributions. On second thought, maybe your education or seniority is more critical than you realized, or maybe your skills and abilities are more vital to the organization. This *cognitive*

that only 19 percent of those workers really were underpaid, taking into account their relevant inputs and the current market conditions. In fact, it was estimated that 17 percent were actually being overpaid by their companies! On the one hand, that subjectivity is likely to be frustrating to most managers in charge of compensation. On the other hand, it's important to realize that the intensity and persistence of employees' effort is driven by their own equity perceptions, not anyone else's. Some organizations grapple with concerns about equity by emphasizing pay secrecy. One survey indicated that 36 percent of companies explicitly discourage employees from discussing pay with their colleagues, and surveys also indicate that most

OB Internationally

Research in cross-cultural OB suggests that there are some "universals" when it comes to motivation. For example, interesting work, pay, achievement, and growth are billed as motivating forces whose importance does not vary across cultures.[62] Of course, some motivation principles do vary in their effectiveness across cultures, including some of the strategies for fostering goal commitment.

Types of Goals. Should goals be given on an individual or a groupwide basis? Employees in the United States usually prefer to be given individual goals. In contrast, employees in other countries, including China and Japan, prefer to receive team goals.[63] This difference likely reflects the stronger emphasis on collective responsibility and cooperation in those cultures.

Rewards. Rewards tend to increase goal commitment across cultures, but cultures vary in the types of rewards that they value. Employees in the United States prefer to have rewards allocated according to merit. In contrast, employees in other countries, including China, Japan, and Sweden, prefer that rewards be allocated equally across members of the work unit.[64] Employees in India prefer a third allocation strategy—doling out rewards according to need. These cultural differences show that nations differ in how they prioritize individual achievement, collective solidarity, and the welfare of others.

Participation. National culture also affects the importance of participation in setting goals. Research suggests that employees in the United States are likely to accept assigned goals because the culture emphasizes

hierarchical authority. In contrast, employees in Israel, which lacks a cultural emphasis on hierarchy, do not respond as well to assigned goals.[65] Instead, employees in Israel place a premium on participation in goal setting.

Feedback. Culture also influences how individuals respond when they receive feedback regarding goal progress. As with participation, research suggests that employees in the United States are more likely to accept feedback because they are comfortable with hierarchical authority relationships and have a strong desire to reduce uncertainty.[66] Other cultures, like England, place less value on reducing uncertainty, making feedback less critical to them. ❖

employees approve of pay secrecy.[67] What does the issue of secrecy have to do with you as a student? See our **OB for Students** feature for a discussion of grade secrecy.

Psychological Empowerment

Now we return, for one last time, to our running example in Figure 5-1. When last we checked in, your motivation levels had suffered because you learned your coworker was offered the company's playoff tickets for successfully completing a similar assignment. As you browse the Web in total "time-wasting mode," you begin thinking about all the reasons you hate working on this assignment. Even aside from the issue of goals and rewards, you keep coming back to this issue: You would never have taken on this project *by choice*. More specifically, the project itself doesn't seem very meaningful, and you doubt that it will have any real impact on the functioning of the organization.

● ● **5.5**

Describe psychological empowerment and the four beliefs that determine how empowered employees feel.

FIGURE 5-6 Three Possible Outcomes of Equity Theory Comparisons

COMPARISON RESULT: **WAYS TO RESTORE BALANCE:**

Equity

$$\frac{\text{Your Outcomes}}{\text{Your Inputs}} = \frac{\text{Other's Outcomes}}{\text{Other's Inputs}}$$

No actions needed.

Underreward Inequity

$$\frac{\text{Your Outcomes}}{\text{Your Inputs}} < \frac{\text{Other's Outcomes}}{\text{Other's Inputs}}$$

Grow your outcomes by talking to your boss or by stealing from the company.

Shrink your inputs by lowering the intensity or persistence of effort.

Overreward Inequity

$$\frac{\text{Your Outcomes}}{\text{Your Inputs}} > \frac{\text{Other's Outcomes}}{\text{Other's Inputs}}$$

Shrink your outcomes (yeah, right!... let's see what we can do about those inputs...)

Grow your inputs through more high quality work or through some "cognitive distortion."

Source: Adapted from J. S. Adams, "Inequity in Social Exchange," in *Advances in Experimental Social Psychology*, Vol. 2, ed. L. Berkowitz (New York: Academic Press, 1965), pp. 267–99.

Those sentiments signal a low level of **psychological empowerment**, which reflects an energy rooted in the belief that work tasks contribute to some larger purpose.[68] Psychological empowerment represents a form of intrinsic motivation, in that merely performing the work tasks serves as its own reward and supplies many of the intrinsic outcomes shown in Table 5-2. The concept of psychological empowerment has much in common with our discussion of "satisfaction with the work itself" in Chapter 3 on Job Satisfaction. That discussion illustrated that jobs with high levels of variety, significance, and autonomy can be intrinsically satisfying.[69] Models of psychological empowerment argue that a similar set of concepts can make work tasks intrinsically motivating. Four concepts are particularly important: meaningfulness, self-determination, competence, and impact.

Meaningfulness captures the value of a work goal or purpose relative to a person's own ideals and passions.[70] When a task is relevant to a meaningful purpose, it becomes easier to concentrate on the task and get excited about it. You might even find yourself cutting other

● **PSYCHOLOGICAL EMPOWERMENT** An energy rooted in the belief that work tasks contribute to some larger purpose.

● **MEANINGFULNESS** The value of a work goal or purpose relative to a person's own ideals and passions.

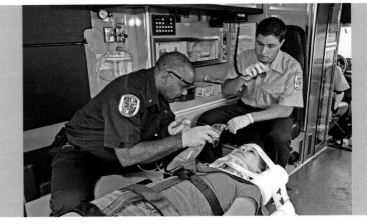

The belief that your work makes a difference or has impact is psychologically empowering.

tasks short so you can devote more time to the meaningful one or thinking about the task outside of work hours.[71] In contrast, working on tasks that are not meaningful brings with it a sense of emptiness and detachment. As a result, you might need to mentally force yourself to keep working on the task. Managers can instill a sense of meaningfulness by articulating an exciting vision and fostering a noncynical climate where employees are free to express passion without criticism.[72] For their part, employees can build their own sense of meaningfulness by identifying and clarifying their own passions. What exactly makes them excited and fulfilled at work, and how can they seek out more opportunities to feel that way?

Self-determination reflects a sense of choice in the initiation and continuation of work tasks. Employees with high levels of self-determination can choose what tasks to work on, how to structure those tasks, and how long to pursue those tasks. That sense of self-determination is a strong driver of intrinsic motivation because it allows employees to pursue activities that they themselves find meaningful and interesting.[73] Managers can instill a sense of self-determination in their employees by delegating work tasks, rather than micromanaging them, and by trusting employees to come up with their own approach to certain tasks.[74] For their part, employees can gain more self-determination by earning the trust of their bosses and negotiating for the latitude that comes with that increased trust.

> ● ● **"Phrases such as 'moving forward,' 'being on track,' and 'getting there' convey a sense of impact."**

Competence captures a person's belief in his or her capability to perform work tasks successfully.[75] Competence is identical to the self-efficacy concept reviewed previously in this chapter. Employees with a strong sense of competence (or self-efficacy) believe they can execute the particular behaviors needed to achieve success at work. Competence brings with it a sense of pride and mastery that is itself intrinsically motivating. Managers can instill a sense of competence in their employees by providing opportunities for training and knowledge gain, expressing positive feedback, and providing challenges that are an appropriate match for employees' skill levels.[76] Employees can build their own competence by engaging in self-directed learning, seeking out feedback from their managers, and managing their own workloads.

Impact reflects the sense that a person's actions "make a difference"—that progress is being made toward fulfilling some important purpose.[77] Phrases such as "moving forward," "being on track," and "getting there" convey a sense of impact.[78] The polar opposite of impact is "learned helplessness"—the sense that it doesn't matter what a person does, nothing will make a difference. Here, phrases such as "stuck in a rut," "at a standstill," or "going nowhere" become more relevant. Managers can instill a sense of impact by celebrating milestones along the journey to task accomplishment, particularly for tasks that span a long time frame.[79] Employees can attain a deeper sense of impact by building the collaborative relationships

OB for Students

Grades are one of the primary motivators for students, as more effort is needed to earn A's than C's in most classes. Think about your own motivation levels as a student—how much of that motivation is due to trying for a higher grade?

Now here's the question we want you to consider: What would happen to your motivation to learn if your grades *became secret*, or more specifically, if your school adopted a policy that prohibited you or your university from disclosing grades to recruiters? Four of the nation's top business schools, including Harvard University, Stanford University, and the University of Chicago, have implemented just such a policy.[80] Students at those schools are forbidden from sharing grades with recruiters, even if that means jeopardizing a potential job offer. The rationale for grade secrecy policies

is twofold. First, grade secrecy is believed to reduce competitiveness between students, fostering a more cohesive atmosphere within student cohorts. Second, grade secrecy is meant to allow students to take tougher, more challenging electives without worrying about their GPA.

So what would happen to your motivation levels if grade secrecy was instituted at your school? The more salient norm of secrecy might discourage you from sharing grades with your classmates, making it more difficult to judge the equity of your grades relative to those received by other students. Grade secrecy might also reduce the valence of the grades themselves, with an A losing some of its anticipated value relative to a B or C. If those effects occurred, then motivation to learn would decline under a grade secrecy system.

Faculty at the University of Pennsylvania's Wharton School believe that grade secrecy has had that sort of negative impact in their MBA program. As a result, they are pushing to relax their nondisclosure policy. At Wharton, undergraduates who are not affected by the grade secrecy policy are outperforming MBAs in the same courses. Meanwhile, student surveys reveal that the time spent on academics has fallen by 22 percent for MBA students over the past four years. For their part, recruiters have had to resort to testing applicants' quantitative skills because grades in technical classes are no longer available. Still, the MBA students at Wharton remain firmly in support of the grade secrecy policy. Which side would you take in this debate? ❖

needed to speed task progress and initiating their own celebrations of "small wins" along the way.

Designing Compensation Systems

Many of the concepts contained in expectancy theory, goal-setting theory, equity theory, and psychological empowerment can be used to describe effective (and ineffective) compensation systems. After all, compensation is one of an organization's most powerful tools for motivating its employees. Table 5-3 provides an overview of many of the elements used in typical compensation systems. We use the term "element" in the table to acknowledge that most organizations use a combination of multiple approaches to compensate their employees. Two points must be noted about Table 5-3. First, the descriptions of the elements are simplistic; the reality is that each of the elements can be implemented and executed in a variety of ways.[81] Second, the elements are designed to do more than just motivate. For example, plans that put pay "at risk" rather than creating increases in base salary are geared toward control of labor costs. As another example, plans that reward unit or organizational performance are designed to reinforce collaboration, information sharing, and monitoring among employees, regardless of their impact on motivation levels.

One way of judging the motivational impact of compensation plan elements is to consider whether the elements provide difficult and specific goals for channeling work effort. Merit pay and profit sharing offer little in the way of difficult and specific goals because both essentially challenge employees to make next year as good (or better) than this year. In contrast, lump-sum bonuses and gainsharing provide a forum for assigning difficult and specific goals; the former does so at the individual level and the latter at the unit level. Partly for this reason, both types of plans have been credited with improvements in employee productivity.[82]

Another way of judging the motivational impact of the compensation plan elements is to consider the correspondence between individual performance levels and individual monetary outcomes. After all, that correspondence influences perceptions

Piece-rate compensation plans are individual-focused and can create stronger performance in certain industries like textiles.

TABLE 5-3	Compensation Plan Elements
Element	**Description**
Individual-Focused	
Piece rate	A specified rate is paid for each unit produced, each unit sold, or each service provided.
Merit pay	An increase to base salary is made in accordance with performance evaluation ratings.
Lump-sum bonuses	A bonus is received for meeting individual goals, but no change is made to base salary. The potential bonus represents "at risk" pay that must be re-earned each year. Base salary may be lower in cases in which potential bonuses may be large.
Recognition awards	Tangible awards (gift cards, merchandise, trips, special events, time off, plaques) or intangible awards (praise) are given on an impromptu basis to recognize achievement.
Unit-Focused	
Gainsharing	A bonus is received for meeting unit goals (department goals, plant goals, business unit goals) for criteria controllable by employees (labor costs, use of materials, quality). No change is made to base salary. The potential bonus represents "at risk" pay that must be re-earned each year. Base salary may be lower in cases in which potential bonuses may be large.
Organization-Focused	
Profit sharing	A bonus is received when the publicly reported earnings of a company exceed some minimum level, with the magnitude of the bonus contingent on the magnitude of the profits. No change is made to base salary. The potential bonus represents "at risk" pay that must be re-earned each year. Base salary may be lower in cases in which potential bonuses may be large.

of both instrumentality and equity. Profit sharing, for example, is unlikely to have strong motivational consequences because an individual employee can do little to improve the profitability of the company, regardless of his or her job performance.[83] Instrumentality and equity are more achievable with gainsharing because the relevant unit is smaller, and the relevant outcomes are more controllable. Still, the highest instrumentality and equity levels will typically be achieved through individual-focused compensation elements. Piece-rate plans can create stronger performance–outcome contingencies but are difficult to apply outside of manufacturing, sales, and service contexts. Merit pay represents the most common element of organizational compensation plans, yet the pay increase for top performers (5.6 percent on average) is only modestly greater than the pay increase for poor performers (2.5 percent on average).[84] Why such a small difference? One reason is that many managers give lenient ratings to avoid upsetting employees. To combat such trends, Yahoo, the California-based Internet company, has instituted a "stacked ranking" system to determine compensation, in which managers rank all the employees within their unit from top to bottom.[85] Employees at the top end of those rankings then receive higher bonuses than employees at the bottom end. Although such practices raise concerns about employee morale and excessive competitiveness, research suggests that such forced distribution systems can boost the performance of a company's workforce, especially for the first few years after their implementation.[86]

HOW IMPORTANT IS MOTIVATION?

Does motivation have a significant impact on the two primary outcomes in our integrative model of OB—does it correlate with job performance and organizational commitment? Answering that question is somewhat complicated because motivation is not just one thing but rather a set of energetic forces. Figure 5-7 summarizes the research evidence linking motivation to job performance and organizational commitment. The figure expresses the likely combined impact of all those energetic forces on the two outcomes in our OB model.

●● 5.6

Understand how motivation affects job performance and organizational commitment.

Turning first to job performance, literally thousands of studies support the relationships between the various motivating forces and task performance. The motivating force with the strongest performance effect is self-efficacy/competence because people who feel a sense of internal self-confidence tend to outperform those who doubt their capabilities.[87] Difficult goals are the second most powerful motivating force; people who receive such goals outperform the recipients of easy goals.[88] The motivational force created by high levels of valence, instrumentality, and expectancy is the next most powerful motivational variable for task performance.[89] Finally, perceptions of equity have a somewhat weaker effect on task performance.[90]

Less attention has been devoted to the linkages between motivation variables and citizenship and counterproductive behavior. With respect to the former, employees who engage in more work-related effort would seem more likely to perform "extra-mile" sorts of actions because those actions themselves require extra effort. The best evidence in support of that claim comes from research on equity. Specifically, employees who feel a sense of equity on the job are more likely to engage in citizenship behaviors, particularly when those behaviors aid the organization.[91] The same employees are less likely to engage in counterproductive behaviors because such behaviors often serve as a retaliation against perceived inequities.[92]

As with citizenship behaviors, the relationship between motivation and organizational commitment seems straightforward. After all, the psychological and physical forms of withdrawal that characterize less-committed employees are themselves evidence of low levels of motivation. Clearly employees who are daydreaming, coming in late, and taking longer breaks are struggling to put forth consistently high levels of work effort. Research on equity and organizational commitment offers the clearest insights into the motivation–commitment relationship. Specifically, employees who feel a sense of equity are more emotionally attached to their firms and feel a stronger sense of obligation to remain.[93] ■

CHECK OUT

www.mhhe.com/ColquittEss

for study materials including Interactive Exercises, Quizzes, iPod downloads, and video.

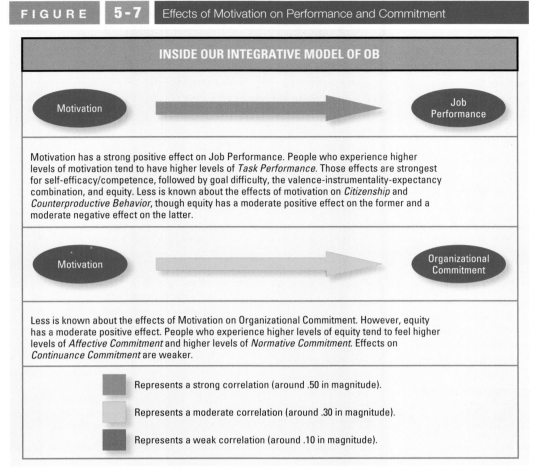

FIGURE 5-7 Effects of Motivation on Performance and Commitment

INSIDE OUR INTEGRATIVE MODEL OF OB

Motivation → Job Performance

Motivation has a strong positive effect on Job Performance. People who experience higher levels of motivation tend to have higher levels of *Task Performance*. Those effects are strongest for self-efficacy/competence, followed by goal difficulty, the valence-instrumentality-expectancy combination, and equity. Less is known about the effects of motivation on *Citizenship* and *Counterproductive Behavior*, though equity has a moderate positive effect on the former and a moderate negative effect on the latter.

Motivation → Organizational Commitment

Less is known about the effects of Motivation on Organizational Commitment. However, equity has a moderate positive effect. People who experience higher levels of equity tend to feel higher levels of *Affective Commitment* and higher levels of *Normative Commitment*. Effects on *Continuance Commitment* are weaker.

■ Represents a strong correlation (around .50 in magnitude).

□ Represents a moderate correlation (around .30 in magnitude).

■ Represents a weak correlation (around .10 in magnitude).

Sources: Y. Cohen-Charash and P. E. Spector, "The Role of Justice in Organizations: A Meta-Analysis," *Organizational Behavior and Human Decision Processes* 86 (2001), pp. 287–321; J. A. Colquitt, D. E. Conlon, M. J. Wesson, C. O. L. H. Porter, and K. Y. Ng, "Justice at the Millennium: A Meta-Analytic Review of 25 Years of Organizational Justice Research," *Journal of Applied Psychology* 86 (2001), pp. 425–45; J. P. Meyer, D. J. Stanley, L. Herscovitch, and L. Topolnytsky, "Affective, Continuance, and Normative Commitment to the Organization: A Meta-Analysis of Antecedents, Correlates, and Consequences," *Journal of Vocational Behavior* 61 (2002), pp. 20–52; A. D. Stajkovic and F. Luthans, "Self-Efficacy and Work-Related Performance: A Meta-Analysis," *Psychological Bulletin* 124 (1998), pp. 240–61; W. Van Eerde and H. Thierry, "Vroom's Expectancy Models and Work-Related Criteria: A Meta-Analysis," *Journal of Applied Psychology* 81 (1996), pp. 575–86; R. E. Wood, A. J. Mento, and E. A. Locke, "Task Complexity as a Moderator of Goal Effects: A Meta-Analysis," *Journal of Applied Psychology* 72 (1987), pp. 416–25.

CASE: Netflix

For all its success, Netflix faces a number of challenges in the coming months and years. For one, Blockbuster has entered the mail-to-home DVD market, launching its own competing service.[94] For another, Apple has begun renting downloadable movies through its iTunes store; customers can stream movies to an Apple TV box connected to their television.[95] Amazon also offers a service that lets users stream movies to their TiVo video recorder.[96] In response to these competitors, Netflix recently launched a streaming movie service.[97] Customers buy a box to attach to their television, then pay a monthly fee to watch as many streaming movies as they want. Of course, as with any new service, there are drawbacks. For example, Netflix is currently offering only about 8 percent of the 100,000 titles in its

DVD catalog. The service also demands a fast Internet connection, and the resulting movies are only of standard-definition TV quality.

Despite the drawbacks in the initial version of its streaming service, the new initiative is indicative of the kinds of efforts the company will need to survive and remain profitable in such a competitive industry. Reed Hastings believes the talent of his workforce will help Netflix fend off its rivals. After all, paying above-market salaries and being aggressive when hiring new employees should create a smart workforce, which is an asset in competitive times. Hastings also points out that Netflix has been able to withstand new rivals in the past, as when it survived Wal-Mart's brief foray into online movie rentals from

2002–2005.[98] Still, it may be challenging for Netflix to maintain its compensation practices and continue to offer unlimited vacations if the company begins to struggle. Yet eliminating those things would remove some of what makes Netflix such a unique company and employer.

5.1 From a motivation perspective, what are the benefits of tying salaries to job market levels rather than to performance evaluations? What are the drawbacks?

5.2 Although the unlimited vacations policy is a popular perk, might it create some challenges for Netflix managers in terms of motivating employees? How would you handle those challenges?

5.3 If Netflix's profits begin to drop as a result of competition from Blockbuster, Apple, or Amazon, should Netflix revisit these sorts of management practices, or should it remain steadfast in its commitment to them? Why?

TAKEAWAYS

5.1 Motivation is defined as a set of energetic forces that originates both within and outside an employee, initiates work-related effort, and determines its direction, intensity, and persistence.

5.2 Expectancy theory describes the cognitive process that employees go through to make choices among different voluntary behaviors. Effort is directed toward behaviors when effort is believed to result in performance (expectancy), performance is believed to result in outcomes (instrumentality), and those outcomes are anticipated to be valuable (valence).

5.3 Goal-setting theory describes the impact of assigned goals on the intensity and persistence of effort. Goals become strong drivers of motivation and performance when they are difficult and specific. Specific and difficult goals affect performance by increasing self-set goals and task strategies. Those effects occur more frequently when employees are given feedback, tasks are not too complex, and goal commitment is high.

5.4 Rewards are equitable when a person's ratio of outcomes to inputs matches those of some relevant comparison other. A sense of inequity triggers equity distress. Underreward inequity typically results in lower levels of motivation or higher levels of counterproductive behavior. Overreward inequity typically results in cognitive distortion, in which inputs are reevaluated in a more positive light.

5.5 Psychological empowerment reflects an energy rooted in the belief that tasks are contributing to some larger purpose. Psychological empowerment is fostered when work goals appeal to employees' passions (meaningfulness), employees have a sense of choice regarding work tasks (self-determination), employees feel capable of performing successfully (competence), and employees feel they are making progress toward fulfilling their purpose (impact).

5.6 Motivation has a strong positive relationship with job performance and a moderate positive relationship with organizational commitment. Of all the energetic forces subsumed by motivation, self-efficacy/competence has the strongest relationship with performance.

DISCUSSION QUESTIONS

5.1 Which of the outcomes in Table 5-2 are most appealing to you? Are you more attracted to extrinsic outcomes or intrinsic outcomes? Do you think that your preferences will change as you get older?

5.2 Assume that you were working on a group project and that one of your teammates was nervous about speaking in front of the class during the presentation. Drawing on Figure 5-3, what exactly could you do to make your classmate feel more confident?

5.3 How do you tend to respond when you experience overreward and underreward inequity? Why do you respond that way rather than with some other combination in Figure 5-6?

5.4 Think about a job that you've held in which you felt very low levels of psychological empowerment. What could the organization have done to increase empowerment levels?

6

TRUST, JUSTICE, and ETHICS

● ● learning **OBJECTIVES**

After reading this chapter, you should be able to:

6.1 Define trust, and describe how it relates to justice and ethics.

6.2 Understand the three sources in which trust can be rooted.

6.3 Describe the dimensions that can be used to describe how trustworthy an authority is.

6.4 Understand the four dimensions that can be used to evaluate the fairness of an authority's decision making.

6.5 Understand the four-component model of ethical decision making.

6.6 Understand how trust affects job performance and organizational commitment.

PEPSICO

Picture a company whose product line could be termed "morally controversial." Which company did you picture? A tobacco company? A weapons manufacturer? You probably didn't picture a company best known for its soda. Fortunately for PepsiCo, CEO Indra Nooyi is well aware of the moral and ethical issues facing her company.[1] PepsiCo, which grew out of a merger of Pepsi-Cola and Frito-Lay (maker of Doritos, Cheetos, and other snacks), has been one of the more profitable and admired members of the *Fortune* 500 for the past decade. Nooyi took over PepsiCo in 2006, creating the motto "Performance with Purpose." Those three words are meant to convey that the company is responsible for more than just shareholder returns. As Nooyi explains: "Companies today are bigger than many economies. We are little republics. . . . If companies don't do [responsible] things, who is going to?"[2]

So what areas require the focus of Nooyi's moral compass? For one, the impact of PepsiCo's products on the health of the world. Internally, the company groups its sugary beverages and salty snacks into three categories: "fun for you," "better for you," and "good for you."[3] More than 70 percent of its products are currently in the "fun for you" category, but that's something Nooyi is working to change. Her goal is to shift PepsiCo's product offerings gradually until the two healthier categories com-

prise 50 percent of the portfolio. If Mountain Dew and Frito's represent the old PepsiCo, Naked Juice Pomegranate Blueberry and Stacy's Simply Naked pita chips represent the new PepsiCo. In addition, with international growth occurring at triple the rate of domestic growth, Nooyi must monitor how PepsiCo's products are received overseas. Then there are emerging ethical issues as well. A few years back, who would have dreamed that Aquafina—one of PepsiCo's healthiest products—would draw fire for the environmental impact of plastic bottles?

Of course, there are sound business reasons to be an ethical company. For example, if job applicants and current employees view a company as trustworthy, they may be more likely to want to work there. For this reason, Nooyi is spearheading efforts to increase the diversity of PepsiCo's workforce so that a sense of fairness pervades the company.[4] As another example, heeding the concerns of the public lessens the likelihood of potential litigation or regulation and serves as good public relations. In this age of global communication and bloggers, even one misstep somewhere in the world can trigger boycotts in several different areas. But good deeds—and healthier ingredients—can be very expensive and challenging to maintain when the economy hits a downturn. Nooyi seems determined in the face of such costs. As she says of PepsiCo, "This is a company with a soul."[5]

●● 6.1

Define trust, and describe how it relates to justice and ethics.

TRUST, JUSTICE, AND ETHICS

Nooyi's efforts are, in part, an attempt to boost the perceived trustworthiness of PepsiCo, for consumers and employees alike. Consumers need to be able to trust that a product is as healthy as PepsiCo says it is. Employees need to be able to trust that PepsiCo will treat them fairly once they're hired. Trust is defined as the willingness to be vulnerable to an authority based on positive expectations about the authority's actions and intentions.[6] When we trust, we become willing to "put ourselves out there," even though that choice could be met with disappointment. This definition can be used to highlight the important distinction between "trust" and "risk." Actually making oneself vulnerable to an authority is a risk; trust reflects the willingness to

are in accordance with generally accepted moral norms.[9] When employees perceive high levels of ethics, they believe that things are being done the way they "should be" or "ought to be" done. Ethics concepts can be used to explain why authorities decide to act in a trustworthy or untrustworthy manner.

Think about a particular boss or instructor—one whom you've spent a significant amount of time around. Do you trust that person? Would you be willing to let that person have significant influence over your professional or educational future? For example, would you be willing to let that person serve as a reference for you or write you a letter of recommendation, even though you'd have no way of monitoring what he or she said about you? When you think about the level of trust you feel for that particular authority, what exactly makes you feel that way? This question speaks to the factors that drive trust—the factors that help inspire a willingness to be vulnerable.

> ## "When we trust, we become willing to 'put ourselves out there,' even though that choice could be met with disappointment."

take that risk. This definition also illustrates where trust comes from, as it is based on an assessment of how a given authority is likely to behave in a particular situation.

Who is the authority referenced in the trust definition? Sometimes that authority is person-based, as when a specific PepsiCo manager is trusted to be honest about a product's ingredients. Sometimes that authority is organization-based, as when you trust that PepsiCo, as a company, will treat your cousin fairly if he accepts a job. Because we don't usually have direct knowledge about the company as a whole, an organization-based version of trust depends largely on a company's reputation.

Issues of trust are intertwined with two related concepts. Justice reflects the perceived fairness of an authority's decision making.[7] When employees perceive high levels of justice, they believe that decision outcomes are fair and that decision-making processes are designed and implemented in a fair manner. Justice concepts can be used to explain why employees judge some authorities as more trustworthy than others.[8] Ethics reflects the degree to which the behaviors of an authority

●● 6.2

Understand the three sources in which trust can be rooted.

Trust

As shown in Figure 6-1, trust is rooted in different kinds of factors. Sometimes trust is disposition-based, meaning that your personality traits include a general propensity to trust others. Sometimes trust is cognition-based, meaning that it is rooted in a rational assessment of the authority's trustworthiness.[10] Sometimes trust is affect-based, meaning that it depends on feelings toward the authority that go beyond any rational assessment.[11] The sections that follow describe each of these trust forms in more detail.

> ## "IN FACT, TRUST PROPENSITY MAY BE ONE OF THE FIRST PERSONALITY TRAITS TO DEVELOP BECAUSE INFANTS MUST IMMEDIATELY LEARN TO TRUST THEIR PARENTS TO MEET THEIR NEEDS."

Disposition-Based Trust. Disposition-based trust has less to do with the authority and more to do with the trustor. Some trustors are high in **trust propensity**—a general expectation that the words, promises, and statements of individuals and groups can be relied upon.[12] Some have argued that trust propensity represents a sort of "faith in human nature," in that trusting people view others in more favorable terms than do suspicious people.[13] The importance of trust propensity is most obvious in interactions with strangers, in which any acceptance of vulnerability would amount to "blind trust."[14] On the one hand, people who are high in trust propensity may be fooled into trusting others who are not worthy of it.[15] On the other hand, those who are low in trust propensity may be fooled by not trusting someone who is actually deserving of it. Both situations can be damaging; as one scholar noted, "We are doomed if we trust all and equally doomed if we trust none."[16]

Where does our trust propensity come from? As with all traits, trust propensity is a product of both nature and nurture. If our parents are dispositionally suspicious, we may either inherit that tendency genetically or model it as we watch them exhibit distrust in their day-to-day lives. Research also suggests that trust propensity is shaped by early childhood experiences.[17] In fact, trust propensity may be one of the first personality traits to develop because infants must immediately learn to trust their parents to meet their needs. The more our needs are met as children, the more trusting we may become; the more we are disappointed as children, the less trusting we may become. Our propensities continue to be shaped later in life as we gain experiences with friends, schools, churches, local government authorities, and other relevant groups.[18]

The nation in which we live also affects our trust propensity. Research by the World Values Study Group examines differences between nations on various attitudes and perceptions. The study group collects interview data from 45 different societies with a total sample size of more than 90,000 participants. One of the questions asked by the study group measures trust propensity. Specifically, participants are asked, "Generally speaking, would you say that most people can be trusted or that you can't be too careful in dealing with people?" Figure 6-2 shows the percentage of participants who answered "Most people can be trusted" for this question, as opposed to "Can't be too careful," for several of the nations included in the study. The results reveal that trust propensity levels are actually relatively high in the United States, especially in relation to countries in Europe and South America.

● ● 6.3

Describe the dimensions that can be used to describe how trustworthy an authority is.

Children whose needs are generally met tend to grow into trusting adults.

Cognition-Based Trust. Disposition-based trust guides us in cases when we don't yet have data about a particular authority. However, eventually we gain enough knowledge to gauge the authority's **trustworthiness**, defined as the characteristics or attributes of a trustee that inspire trust.[19] At that point, our trust begins to be based on cognitions we've developed about the authority, as opposed to our own personality or disposition. In this way, cognition-based trust is driven by the authority's "track record."[20] If that track record has shown the authority to be trustworthy, then vulnerability to the authority can be accepted. If that track record is spotty, however, then trust may not be warranted. Research suggests that we gauge the track record of an authority along three dimensions: ability, integrity, and benevolence.[21]

The first dimension of trustworthiness is **ability**, defined as the skills, competencies, and areas of expertise that enable an authority to be successful in some specific area (see Chapter 8 on Personality, Cultural Values, and Ability for more discussion of ability).[22] Think about the decision-making process that you go through when choosing a doctor, lawyer, or mechanic. Clearly one of the first things you consider is ability because you're not going to trust them if they don't know a scalpel from a retractor, a tort from a writ, or a camshaft from a crankshaft. Of course, listing a specific area is a key component of the ability definition; you wouldn't trust a mechanic to perform surgery, nor would you trust a doctor to fix your car! The ability of business authorities may be considered on a number of levels. For example, a manager may be judged according to the functional expertise of a particular industry or vocation but also according to his or her leadership skills and general business sense.[23]

The only surgery this mechanic would be trusted to perform is car surgery. This form of trust, based on abilities, is cognition-based trust.

The second dimension of trustworthiness is *integrity*, defined as the perception that the authority adheres to a set of values and principles that the trustor finds acceptable.[24] When authorities are perceived to have integrity, it means that they have good character—that they have honest motives and intentions. Integrity also conveys an alignment between words and deeds—a sense that authorities keep their promises, "walk the talk," and "do what they say they will do."[25] Unfortunately, a recent survey indicated that only around 20 percent of American workers view senior managers as acting in accordance with their words.[26] The series of high-profile scandals at companies like Enron, WorldCom, and Tyco can be viewed as examples of the costs of low integrity. In those cases, top management hid debt, misstated earnings, and used profits for personal gain—all of which constituted dishonest actions that went against the espoused values and principles of those companies.

The third dimension of trustworthiness is **benevolence**, defined as the belief that the authority wants to do good for the trustor, apart from any selfish or profit-centered motives.[27] When authorities are perceived as benevolent, it means that they care for employees, are concerned about their well-being, and feel a sense of loyalty to them. The mentor–protégé relationship provides a good example of benevolence at work.[28] The best mentors would never do anything to hurt their protégés. They go out of their way to be helpful, even at the cost of their own personal productivity and in the absence of any financial reward. Clearly benevolence, along with ability and integrity, provides a set of good reasons to trust a particular authority.[29] For more on how these three trustworthiness facets can be used to gauge trust,[30] see our **OB on Screen** feature.

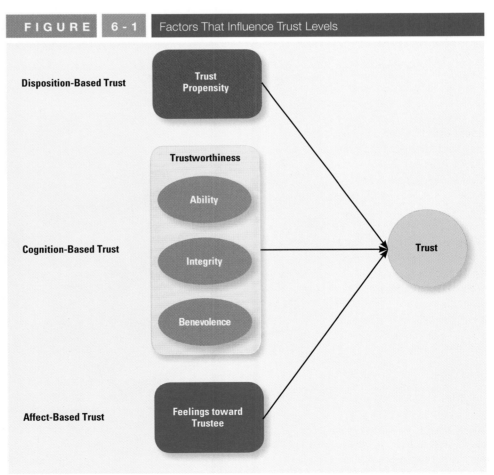

FIGURE 6-1 Factors That Influence Trust Levels

Disposition-Based Trust — Trust Propensity

Trustworthiness
- Ability
- Integrity
- Benevolence

Cognition-Based Trust

Affect-Based Trust — Feelings toward Trustee

Trust

Sources: Adapted from R. C. Mayer, J. H. Davis, and F. D. Schoorman, "An Integrative Model of Organizational Trust," *Academy of Management Review* 20 (1995), pp. 709–34; D. J. McAllister, "Affect- and Cognition-Based Trust as Foundations for Interpersonal Cooperation in Organizations," *Academy of Management Journal* 38 (1995), pp. 24–59.

FIGURE 6-2 Trust Propensities by Nation

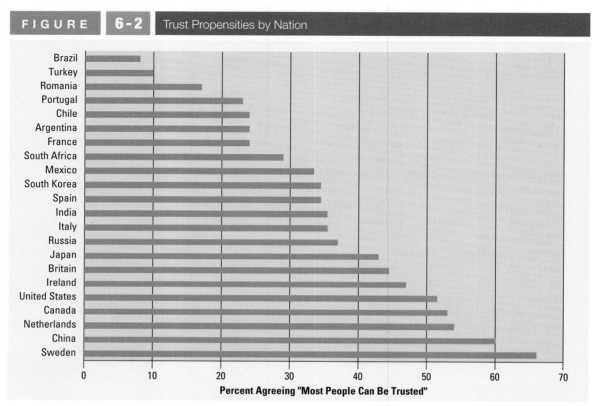

Percent Agreeing "Most People Can Be Trusted"

Source: Adapted from J. J. Johnson and J. B. Cullen, "Trust in Cross-Cultural Relationships," in *Blackwell Handbook of Cross-Cultural Management,* ed. M. J. Gannon and K. L. Newman (Malden, MA: Blackwell, 2002), pp. 335–60.

OB on Screen

Pirates of the Caribbean: The Curse of the Black Pearl

May I ask you something? Have I ever given you reason not to trust me?

With those words, Captain Jack Sparrow (Johnny Depp) poses a difficult question in *Pirates of the Caribbean: The Curse of the Black Pearl* (Dir. Gore Verbinski, Disney, 2003). There are a whole host of reasons not to trust Jack. The most obvious comes during a swordfight between Jack and young Will Turner (Orlando Bloom), when Jack breaks the rules of engagement by pulling his gun. "You cheated," Will pleads. "Pirate," Jack answers.

From an ability perspective, Jack actually does a lot to inspire trust. His skills at hatching a plan belie his crazy demeanor. He also happens to be a good swordsman and a remarkably good escape artist. Indeed, early in the film, after Jack steals a ship from Britain's Port Royal, one of the British soldiers remarks that Jack must be the best pirate he's ever seen. As with any pirate, however, Jack struggles with integrity.

In addition to the aforementioned gun incident, Jack lies, steals, and rarely does exactly what he says he'd do. Although he appears to hold firmly to the "pirate's code," that code includes such lofty sayings as, "Anyone who falls behind is left behind." From a benevolence perspective, Jack does seem to care sincerely for Will and Elizabeth (Keira Knightley), the British governor's daughter for whom Will is secretly carrying a torch. But does Jack care about them for profit-driven reasons?

Jack's nemesis, Captain Barbossa (Geoffrey Rush), sums up the uncertainty about Jack's trustworthiness, saying, "I must admit, Jack, I thought I had you figured, but it turns out you're a hard man to predict." Jack's reply: "Me? I'm dishonest, and a dishonest man you can always trust to be dishonest . . . honestly." That answer doesn't really clear things up, does it? As Elizabeth asks near the climax of the film, "Whose side is Jack on?" Will's answer: "At the moment?" ❖

Affect-Based Trust.

Although ability, integrity, and benevolence provide three good reasons to trust an authority, the third form of trust isn't really rooted in reason at all. Affect-based trust is more emotional than rational. With affect-based trust, we trust because we have feelings for the person in question; we really like them and have a fondness for them. Those feelings are what prompt us to accept vulnerability to another person. Put simply, we trust them because we like them.

Affect-based trust acts as a supplement to the types of trust discussed previously.[31] Figure 6-3 describes how the various forms of trust can build on one another over time. In new relationships, trust depends solely on our own trust propensity. In most relationships, that propensity eventually gets supplemented by knowledge about ability, integrity, or benevolence, at which point cognition-based trust develops. In a select few of those relationships, an emotional bond develops, and our feelings for the trustee further increase our willingness to accept vulnerability. These relationships are characterized by a mutual investment of time and energy, a sense of deep attachment, and the realization that both parties would feel a sense of loss if the relationship were dissolved.[32]

Relationships in which affect-based trust has been established develop over time and are characterized by investments of time and energy, a sense of deep attachment, and the realization that both parties will feel a loss if the relationship ends.

Summary.

Taken together, disposition-based trust, cognition-based trust, and affect-based trust provide three completely different sources of trust in a particular authority. In the case of disposition-based trust, our willingness to be vulnerable has little to do with the authority and more to do with our genes and our early life experiences. In the case of affect-based trust, our willingness to be vulnerable has little to do with a rational assessment of the authority's merits and more to do with our emotional fondness for the authority. Only in the case of cognition-based trust do we rationally evaluate the pluses and minuses of an authority, in terms of ability, integrity, and benevolence. But how exactly do we gauge those trustworthiness forms? One way is to consider whether authorities adhere to rules of justice.

●●6.4

Understand the four dimensions that can be used to evaluate the fairness of an authority's decision making.

Justice

It's often difficult to assess the ability, integrity, and benevolence of authorities accurately, particularly early in a working relationship. What employees need in such circumstances is some sort of observable behavioral evidence that an authority might be trustworthy. Justice provides that sort of behavioral evidence because authorities who treat employees more fairly are usually judged to be more trustworthy.[33] As shown in Table 6-1, employees can judge the fairness of an authority's decision making along four dimensions: distributive justice, procedural justice, interpersonal justice, and informational justice.

Distributive Justice.

Distributive justice reflects the perceived fairness of decision-making outcomes.[34] Employees gauge distributive justice by asking whether decision outcomes such as pay, rewards, evaluations, promotions, and work assignments are allocated using proper norms. In most business situations, the proper norm is equity, with more outcomes allocated to those who contribute more inputs (see Chapter 5 on Motivation for more discussion of equity). The equity norm is typically judged to be the fairest choice in situations in which the goal is to maximize the productivity of individual employees.[35]

● **DISTRIBUTIVE JUSTICE** The perceived fairness of decision-making outcomes.

However, other allocation norms become appropriate in situations in which other goals are critical. In team-based work, building harmony and solidarity in work groups can become

FIGURE 6-3 Types of Trust over Time

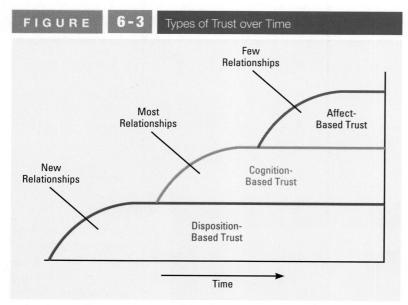

Sources: Adapted from R. J. Lewicki and B. B. Bunker, "Developing and Maintaining Trust in Work Relationships," in *Trust in Organizations: Frontiers of Theory and Research,* ed. R. M. Kramer and T. R. Tyler (Thousand Oaks, CA: Sage, 1996), pp. 114–39; R. C. Mayer, J. H. Davis, and F. D. Schoorman, "An Integrative Model of Organizational Trust," *Academy of Management Review* 20 (1995), pp. 709–34.

Did the person who put in the most work receive the most pay? Did all members of a winning work team receive the same reward? Did the salesperson who most needed a new workspace receive it? Such questions made by employees represent distributive justice.

just as important as individual productivity. In such cases, an equality norm may be judged more fair, such that all team members receive the same amount of relevant rewards.[36] The equality norm is typically used in student project groups, in which all group members receive exactly the same grade on a project, regardless of their individual productivity levels. In cases in which the welfare of a particular employee is the critical concern, a need norm may be judged more fair. For example, PricewaterhouseCoopers, the New York–based accounting firm, wired $4,000 to 43 employees who were affected by Hurricane Katrina.[37] The company also gave those employees food, lodging, and transportation for a three-month period.

Procedural Justice. In addition to judging the fairness of a decision outcome, employees may consider the process that led to that outcome. **Procedural justice** reflects the perceived fairness of decision-making processes.[38] Procedural justice is fostered when authorities adhere to rules of fair process. One of those rules is voice, which concerns giving employees a chance to express their opinions and views during the course of decision making.[39] A related rule is correctability, which provides employees with a chance to request an appeal when a

procedure seems to have worked ineffectively. Research suggests that voice improves employees' reactions to decisions,[40] largely because it gives employees a sense of ownership over the decisions that occur at work. In fact, employees value voice even when it doesn't always result in the outcomes they want or when their appeals don't always reverse the decisions that were made.[41] Why? Because employees like to be heard—the expression of opinions is a valued end, in and of itself, as long as employees feel those opinions were truly considered.

Aside from voice and correctability, procedural justice is fostered when authorities adhere to four rules that serve to create equal employment opportunity. The consistency, bias suppression, representativeness, and accuracy rules help ensure that procedures are neutral and objective, as opposed to biased and discriminatory. These sorts of procedural rules are relevant in many areas of working life. As one example, the rules can be used to make hiring practices more fair by ensuring that interview questions are unbiased and asked in the same manner across applications. As another example, the rules can be used to make compensation practices more fair by ensuring that accurate measures of job performance are used to provide input for merit raises. For a discussion of procedural justice in the world of college football, see our **OB in Sports** feature.

You might be wondering, "Does procedural justice really matter—don't people just care about the outcomes that they receive?" If an employee receives favorable pay, rewards, evaluations, promotions, and work assignments, does he or she really care about the process? Research suggests that distributive justice and procedural justice combine to influence employee reactions, as shown in Figure 6-4.[42] It's true that when outcomes are good, people don't spend as much time worrying about how fair the process was, as illustrated by the green line in the figure, which shows that procedural justice has little impact on reactions when distributive justice is high. However, when outcomes are bad, procedural justice becomes enormously important. Research shows that negative or unexpected events trigger a thorough examination of process issues, making adherence to rules like consistency, bias suppression, and accuracy much more vital.[43]

In fact, research shows that procedural justice tends to be a stronger driver of reactions to authorities than distributive justice. For example, a meta-analysis of 183 studies showed that procedural justice was a stronger predictor of satisfaction with supervision, overall job satisfaction, and organizational commitment than distributive justice.[44] Why does the decision-making process sometimes matter more than the decision-making outcome? Likely because employees understand that outcomes come and go—some may be in your favor while others may be a bit disappointing. Procedures, however, are more long-lasting and stay in place until the organization redesigns them or a new leader arrives to revise them.

Interpersonal Justice.

In addition to judging the fairness of decision outcomes and processes, employees might consider how authorities treat them as the procedures are implemented. Interpersonal justice reflects the perceived fairness of the treatment received by employees from authorities.[45] Interpersonal justice is fostered when authorities adhere to two particular rules. The respect rule pertains to whether authorities treat employees in a dignified and sincere manner, and the propriety rule reflects whether authorities refrain from making improper or offensive remarks. From this perspective, interpersonal *injustice* occurs when authorities bad-mouth employees; criticize, berate, embarrass, or humiliate them in public; or refer to them with racist or sexist labels.[46]

How common are instances of interpersonal injustice? A survey of nearly 5,000 employees found that 36 percent reported persistent hostility from authorities and coworkers, when persistent hostility was defined as experiencing one abusive act at least weekly for a period of one year.[47] How damaging are such acts? One study asked 41 employees to complete a survey on interactions with authorities and coworkers four times a day for 2 to 3 weeks using a palmtop computer.[48] Two kinds of interactions were coded—positive experiences and negative experiences—and participants also reported on their current mood (e.g., happy, pleased, sad, blue, unhappy). The results of the study showed that positive interactions were more common than negative interactions, but the effects of negative interactions on mood were five times stronger than the effects of positive interactions. Such findings suggest that violations of the respect and propriety rules loom much larger than adherence to such rules.[49] Indeed, research indicates that violations of interpersonal justice rules reduce employees' job satisfaction, life satisfaction, and organizational commitment while increasing feelings of depression, anxiety, and burnout.[50]

Informational Justice.

Finally, employees may consider the kind of information that authorities provide during the course of organizational decision making. Informational justice reflects the perceived fairness of the communications provided to employees from authorities.[51] Informational justice is fostered when authorities adhere to two particular rules. The justification rule mandates that authorities explain decision-making procedures and outcomes in a comprehensive and reasonable manner, and the truthfulness rule requires that those communications be honest and candid. Although it seems like common sense that

organizations would explain decisions in a comprehensive and adequate manner, that's often not the case. For example, RadioShack, the Texas-based home electronics retailer, was recently criticized for firing 400 employees via e-mail.[52]

RadioShack recently violated the norms of informational justice by laying off 400 employees in Fort Worth via a curt e-mail of 18 words.

TABLE 6-1 The Four Dimensions of Justice

Distributive Justice Rules	Description
Equity vs. equality vs. need	Are rewards allocated according to the proper norm?
Procedural Justice Rules	
Voice	Do employees get to provide input into procedures?
Correctability	Do procedures build in mechanisms for appeals?
Consistency	Are procedures consistent across people and time?
Bias suppression	Are procedures neutral and unbiased?
Representativeness	Do procedures consider the needs of all groups?
Accuracy	Are procedures based on accurate information?
Interpersonal Justice Rules	
Respect	Do authorities treat employees with sincerity?
Propriety	Do authorities refrain from improper remarks?
Informational Justice Rules	
Justification	Do authorities explain procedures thoroughly?
Truthfulness	Are those explanations honest?

Sources: J. S. Adams, "Inequity in Social Exchange," in *Advances in Experimental Social Psychology,* Vol. 2, ed. L. Berkowitz (New York: Academic Press, 1965), pp. 267–99; R. J. Bies and J. F. Moag, "Interactional Justice: Communication Criteria of Fairness," in *Research on Negotiations in Organizations,* Vol. 1, ed. R. J. Lewicki, B. H. Sheppard, and M. H. Bazerman (Greenwich, CT: JAI Press, 1986), pp. 43–55; G. S. Leventhal, "The Distribution of Rewards and Resources in Groups and Organizations," in *Advances in Experimental Social Psychology,* Vol. 9, ed. L. Berkowitz and W. Walster (New York: Academic Press, 1976), pp. 91–131; G. S. Leventhal, "What Should Be Done with Equity Theory? New Approaches to the Study of Fairness in Social Relationships," in *Social Exchange: Advances in Theory and Research,* ed. K. Gergen, M. Greenberg, and R. Willis (New York: Plenum Press, 1980), pp. 27–55; J. Thibaut and L. Walker, *Procedural Justice: A Psychological Analysis* (Hillsdale, NJ: Erlbaum, 1975).

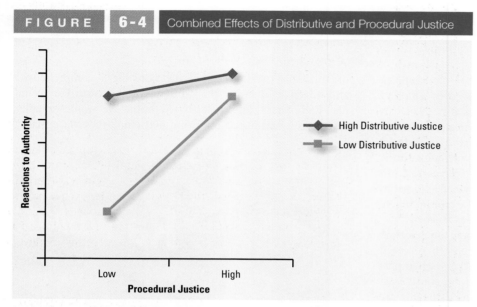

FIGURE 6-4 Combined Effects of Distributive and Procedural Justice

(Chart: Y-axis "Reactions to Authority"; X-axis "Procedural Justice" ranging from Low to High. Two lines — "High Distributive Justice" (diamond markers) and "Low Distributive Justice" (square markers).)

Source: Adapted from J. Brockner and B. M. Wiesenfeld, "An Integrative Framework for Explaining Reactions to Decisions: Interactive Effects of Outcomes and Procedures," *Psychological Bulletin* 120 (1996), pp. 189–208.

Employees at the Fort Worth headquarters received messages on a Tuesday morning saying: "The work force reduction notification is currently in progress. Unfortunately your position is one that has been eliminated." After receiving the 18-word message, employees had 30 minutes to make phone calls and say goodbye to fellow employees before packing up their belongings in boxes and plastic bags.

These sorts of informational injustices are all too common, for a variety of reasons. One reason is that sharing bad news is the worst part of the job for many managers, leading them to distance themselves when it's time to play messenger.[53] Another reason is that managers worry about triggering a lawsuit if they comprehensively and honestly explain the real reasons for a layoff, a poor evaluation, or a missed promotion. Ironically, that defense mechanism is typically counterproductive because research suggests that honest and adequate explanations are actually a powerful strategy for reducing retaliation responses against the organization.[54] In fact, low levels of informational justice can come back to haunt the organization if a wrongful termination claim is actually filed. How? Because the organization typically needs to provide performance evaluations for the terminated employee over the past few years to show that the employee was fired for poor performance.[55] If managers refrained from offering

OB in Sports

If you're a college football fan, you hear procedural justice issues discussed every Monday of the fall. That's because the Bowl Championship Series (BCS) standings are released on Mondays, starting a few weeks into the football season. Unlike other college sports, football does not have a season-ending playoff to crown its champion. Instead, a procedure ranks teams, week-in and week-out, with the top two teams in the season-ending rankings squaring off for the national championship. The BCS rankings are (more or less) an average of three types of rankings: (1) the *USA Today* College Coaches Poll, whose rankings depend on the opinions of 63 Division 1-A football coaches; (2) the Harris Interactive Poll, whose rankings come from 114 former coaches, players, and administrators, along with members of the media; and (3) computer polls, which determine rankings by averaging together six completely different sets of computer rankings.[56]

The Monday release of the BCS standings typically brings a wave of complaints to local sports talk radio programs. Why? Often because the process seems unfair. The bias suppression rule is violated because coaches are free to vote for their own team or teams in their conference, and the members of the Harris Interactive Poll also have conference affiliations that could color their voting. The accuracy rule is violated because it's a good bet that the East Coast coaches and Harris Poll members are in bed before the big Oregon versus Washington State game kicks off at 10:15 p.m. Eastern time. The correctability rule is violated because when things go wrong with the polls, they can't be "tweaked" until the next off-season. Finally, the representativeness rule is violated because schools from smaller conferences face an uphill climb, even when they keep winning their games. That's because the computer polls consider "strength of schedule" in their rankings, and smaller schools almost always have a weaker strength of schedule. Even if Fresno State wants to play Ohio State, it's a good bet the Buckeyes will only agree to play the game if it's in Columbus. Of course, most college football fans don't know all the ins and outs of the BCS process—they just know that it seems awfully unfair. ❖

Is the process for ranking college football teams fair? Many fans who know the procedure for ranking teams in the Bowl Championship Series (BCS) think not. The process violates many of the procedural justice rules discussed in this chapter.

candid and honest explanations on those evaluations, then the organization can't offer anything to justify the termination.

One study provides a particularly effective demonstration of the power of informational justice (and interpersonal justice). The study occurred in three plants of a Midwestern manufacturing company that specialized in small mechanical parts for the aerospace and automotive industries.[57] The company had recently lost two of its largest contracts and was forced to cut wages by 15 percent in two of the three plants. The company was planning to offer a short, impersonal explanation for the pay cut to both of the affected plants. However, as part of a research study, the company was convinced to offer a longer, more sincere explanation at one of the plants. Theft levels were then tracked before, during, and after the 10-week pay cut using the company's standard accounting formulas for inventory "shrinkage."

Ethics

Research on ethics seeks to explain why people behave in a manner consistent with generally accepted norms of morality, and why they sometimes violate those norms.[59] Some ethics studies focus on behaviors that exceed minimum standards of morality, such as charitable giving or whistle-blowing, which occurs when employees expose illegal actions by their employer. Other studies focus on behaviors that fall below minimum standards of morality, such as lying and cheating. Still other studies focus on behaviors that merely reach minimum standards of morality, such as obeying the law. Regardless of the particular area of focus, such research continues to be a critical area of OB because unethical acts are so common in organizations. For example, recent surveys suggest that 76 percent of employees

> A survey of nearly 5,000 employees found that 36 percent reported persistent hostility from authorities and coworkers, when persistent hostility was defined as experiencing one abusive act at least weekly for a period of one year."

The results of the study are shown in Figure 6-5. In the plant without the pay cut, no change in theft levels occurred over the 10-week period. In the plant with the short, impersonal explanation, theft rose dramatically during the pay cut, likely as a means of retaliating for perceived inequity, before falling to previous levels once the cut had passed. Importantly, in the plant with the long, sincere explanation, the rise in theft was much less significant during the pay cut, with theft levels again falling back to normal levels once the cut had ended. Clearly, the higher levels of informational and interpersonal justice were worth it from a cost-savings perspective. The difference in theft across the two plants is remarkable, given that the long, sincere explanation was only 143 words longer than the short, impersonal explanation. What's an extra 45 seconds if it can save a few thousand dollars?

Summary. Taken together, distributive, procedural, interpersonal, and informational justice can be used to describe how fairly employees are treated by authorities. When an authority adheres to the justice rules in Table 6-1, it provides behavioral data that the authority might be trustworthy. Studies show that all four justice forms have strong correlations with trust levels.[58] All else being equal, employees trust authorities who allocate outcomes fairly; make decisions in a consistent, unbiased, and accurate way; and communicate decision-making details in a respectful, comprehensive, and honest manner. Which authorities are most likely to adhere to these sorts of rules? Research on ethics can provide some answers.

have observed illegal or unethical conduct on the job within the past 12 months.[60] Those base rates may be even higher in some countries, as described in our **OB Internationally** feature.

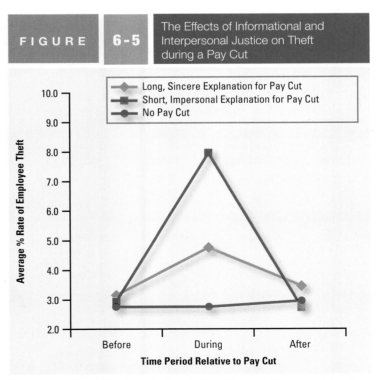

FIGURE 6-5 The Effects of Informational and Interpersonal Justice on Theft during a Pay Cut

Source: Adapted from J. Greenberg, "Employee Theft as a Reaction to Underpayment Inequity: The Hidden Cost of Paycuts," *Journal of Applied Psychology* 75 (1990), pp. 561–68.

How can we explain exactly why an authority would choose to act in an unethical manner? One set of answers can be derived from research in social psychology. As shown in Figure 6-6, the four-component model of ethical decision making argues that ethical behaviors result from a multistage sequence beginning with moral awareness, continuing on to moral judgment, and then moral intent and ethical behavior.[61] The sections that follow review the components of this model in more detail.

 6.5

Understand the four-component model of ethical decision making.

Moral Awareness. The first step needed to explain why an authority acts ethically is **moral awareness**, which occurs when an authority recognizes that a moral issue exists in a situation or that an ethical standard or principle is relevant to the circumstance.[62] Ethical issues rarely come equipped with "red flags" that mark them as morally sensitive—something is needed to make moral standards salient.[63] As an example, assume you worked for a videogame company whose most popular game involves assuming the role of a criminal in a big city and taking part in multiple storylines involving a variety of illegal activities, such as carjacking, bank robbery, assassination, and the killing of law enforcement personnel and innocent bystanders. A member of this game's development team has suggested embedding hidden sex scenes into the game, which is currently rated "mature" by the Entertainment Software Rating Board.

Is there an ethical issue at play here? On the one hand, you might be tempted to say that the game is already rated

OB Internationally

Unethical actions can be defined as behaviors that fall below minimum standards of morality. For multinational corporations, however, the relevant question becomes "Whose standards of morality?" Research on business ethics across cultures reveals that different countries have very different baseline levels of unethical actions. Transparency International is an organization that monitors unethical practices in countries around the world. Using data from business-people, risk analysts, investigative journalists, country experts, and public citizens, the organization rates countries on a scale of 1 (unethical) to 10 (ethical).[64] Here are some of the scores from the 1999 version of the rankings:

These rankings reveal the challenges involved for any multinational corporation that does business in areas at the top and bottom of the rankings. Should the company have the same ethical expectations for employees in all countries, regardless of ethical norms? For now, that seems to be the most common position. For example, the Coca-Cola Company's Code of Business Conduct "applies to all the Company's business worldwide and to all Company employees."[65] The code is given to all employees along with a letter from the CEO and covers topics such as conflicts of interest, dealing with government officials, customer and supplier interactions, and political contributions. The code also describes the disciplinary actions associated with any violations of the code. ❖

Score	Country	Score	Country	Score	Country	Score	Country
10.0	Denmark	6.6	France	3.8	South Korea	2.6	Ukraine
9.8	Finland	6.0	Japan	3.6	Philippines	2.6	Venezuela
9.4	Sweden	5.6	Taiwan	3.6	Turkey	2.6	Vietnam
9.2	Canada	5.3	Belgium	3.4	China	2.4	Russia
9.0	Netherlands	5.1	Costa Rica	3.4	Mexico	2.3	Kazakhstan
8.7	Australia	4.9	Greece	3.3	Egypt	2.2	Pakistan
8.6	Germany	4.7	Italy	3.3	Romania	2.0	Kenya
7.7	Hong Kong	4.6	Czech Republic	3.2	Thailand	1.6	Nigeria
7.7	Ireland	4.1	Brazil	3.0	Argentina	1.5	Cameroon
7.5	United States	3.8	Jamaica	2.9	Colombia		
6.8	Israel	3.8	Lithuania	2.9	India		

"mature" and that such hidden scenes are only extending the already less-than-wholesome nature of the game. Besides, "Easter eggs"—hidden objects in movies, DVDs, or computer and video games—have a long history in the entertainment industry. On the other hand, the hidden scenes constitute deception of the rating board, the customer, and potentially the customer's parents. And that deception issue stands apart from any moral issues raised by the actual content of the hidden scenes. If this story sounds familiar to you, it's because it actually happened with *Grand Theft Auto: San Andreas*, a game manufactured by a division of Take Two Interactive Software.[66] The hidden scenes, which began with the invitation, "How 'bout some coffee?" could be accessed using software available on the Internet. Take Two contends that the code for the scenes was put into early drafts of the game but was supposed to be removed before the game went to market.

Moral awareness depends in part on the characteristics of the authority involved. An authority's **ethical sensitivity** reflects the ability to recognize that a particular decision has ethical content.[67] Ethical sensitivity can be measured by giving people a business case to read that includes a number of somewhat subtle ethical issues, along with a number of other sorts of issues (work sequencing challenges, organizing challenges, specific technical issues). Participants describe the issues that are raised in the case in an open-ended fashion, with ethical sensitivity captured by the number of ethical issues spotted within the case. In the Take Two example, it may be that the employees in charge of the *Grand Theft Auto* game weren't sensitive enough to recognize that the hidden scenes represented an ethical issue. That premise makes some sense, given that Take Two has had other ethical struggles, including having to settle charges of fraudulent accounting with the Securities and Exchange Commission.

Moral awareness also depends on the characteristics of the issue itself. **Moral intensity** captures the degree to which the issue has ethical urgency.[68] Moral intensity is driven by six factors, summarized in Table 6-2. A particular issue is high in moral intensity if the magnitude of its consequences are high, there is strong social consensus about the act, the probability of the act occurring and having the predicted consequences is high, those consequences will occur soon, the decision makers are close to those who will be affected, and the consequences are not concentrated on a select few. In the case of the *Grand Theft Auto* hidden scenes, it may be that Take Two felt that the

The programmers of Grand Theft Auto *appeared to lack moral awareness when it was discovered that a hidden portion of the popular computer game, which could be easily accessed with free software, contained sex scenes.*

| FIGURE | 6-6 | The Four Component Model of Ethical Decision Making |

Moral Awareness → Moral Judgment → Moral Intent → Ethical Behavior

Source: Adapted from J. R. Rest, *Moral Development: Advances in Research and Theory* (New York: Praeger, 1986).

TABLE 6-2 The Six Facets of Moral Intensity

Facet	Description
Magnitude of consequences	How much harm (or benefit) would be done to other people?
Social consensus	How much agreement is there that the proposed act would be evil (or good)?
Probability of effect	How likely is it that the act will actually occur and that the assumed consequences will match predictions?
Temporal immediacy	How much time will pass between the act and the onset of its consequences?
Proximity	How near (in a psychological or physical sense) is the authority to those who will be affected?
Concentration of effect	Will the consequences be concentrated on a limited set of people, or will they be more far reaching?

Source: Adapted from T. M. Jones, "Ethical Decision Making by Individuals in Organizations: An Issue-Contingent Model," *Academy of Management Review* 16 (1991), pp. 366–95.

consequences of the act would be minor, the scenes might not be discovered, or the people who would be adversely affected are very different in a psychological sense.

Moral Judgment.
Assuming an authority recognizes that a moral issue exists in a situation, the next step is moral judgment, which is when the authority accurately identifies the morally "right" course of action.[69] What factors affect moral judgment? One factor is moral development, as described by Kohlberg's theory of cognitive moral development.[70] This theory argues that as people age and mature, they move through several stages of moral development—each more mature and sophisticated than the prior one. These stages are shown in Figure 6-7. Research suggests that most children are at the precon-

ventional level, so their actions are motivated by the avoidance of punishment (Stage 1) and the maintenance of "You scratch my back, I'll scratch yours" sorts of relationships (Stage 2). Most adults, in contrast, are at the conventional level, with their ethical thinking influenced by the opinions of relevant authorities (Stage 3), along with more formal rules and standards (Stage 4).[71] That positioning is relevant for organizations because it suggests that the ethical decisions of employees can be influenced by organizational norms, practices, and reward systems.

Research suggests that fewer than 20 percent of Americans reach the principled (sometimes called "postconventional") level.[72] The principles those individuals utilize during ethical decision making are called ethical ideologies.[73] Those in Stage 5 may be more likely to adopt a *relativism* ideology and reject the notion of universal moral rules.[74] Relativists agree with statements like, "Whether a lie is judged to be moral or immoral depends upon the circumstances surrounding the decision."[75] Such people also may be more likely to adopt a *utilitarianism* ideology in which ethical actions are defined as those that achieve the most valuable ends.[76] When asked to describe the character traits that are most important to them, utilitarians prioritize traits such as "resourceful," "effective," "productive," and "winner."[77] In contrast, those in Stage 6 should be more likely to adopt an *idealism* ideology and embrace the notion of universal moral rules.[78] Idealists agree with statements like, "The existence of potential harm to others is always wrong, irrespective of the benefits to be gained."[79] Such people also may be more likely to adopt a *formalism* ideology that defines ethical actions using a set of guiding principles.[80] When asked to describe the character traits that are most important to them, formalists prioritize traits like "trustworthy," "honest," "principled," and "dependable."[81]

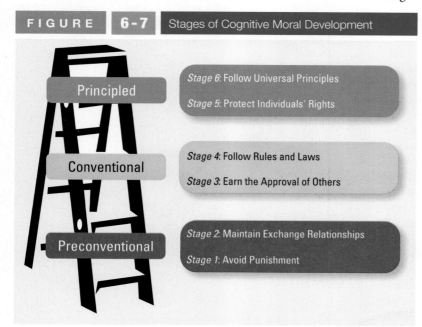

FIGURE 6-7 Stages of Cognitive Moral Development

Principled

Stage 6: Follow Universal Principles

Stage 5: Protect Individuals' Rights

Conventional

Stage 4: Follow Rules and Laws

Stage 3: Earn the Approval of Others

Preconventional

Stage 2: Maintain Exchange Relationships

Stage 1: Avoid Punishment

Moral Intent. Assuming that an authority recognizes that a moral issue exists in a situation and possesses the cognitive moral development to choose the right course of action, one step remains: The authority has to *want* to act ethically. **Moral intent** reflects an authority's degree of commitment to the moral course of action.[82] The distinction among awareness, judgment, and intent is important because many unethical people know and understand that what they do is wrong—they just don't really care. One driver of moral intent is *moral identity*—the degree to which a person sees him- or herself as a "moral person."[83] Having a strong moral identity increases ethical behaviors because failing to act morally will trigger a strong sense of guilt or shame. However, moral intent also is driven by a number of situational factors, including the existence of on-the-job pressures, role conflict, and rewards and incentives that can be more easily attained by unethical

> **Many unethical people know and understand that what they do is wrong—they just don't really care.**

means.[84] See our **OB for Students** feature for more on these issues.

● ● **6.6**
Understand how trust affects job performance and organizational commitment.

OB for Students

The most relevant form of unethical behavior for students is cheating on exams and assignments. How common is cheating? One survey of almost 50,000 students at 69 schools found that 26 percent of undergraduate business majors admitted to serious cheating on exams, with 54 percent admitting to cheating on written assignments (including plagiarism or using a friend's homework).[85] And the problem is not confined to undergraduate business students. In April 2007, the dean of the Duke Business School announced that almost 10 percent of the MBA class of 2008 had been caught cheating on a take-home final exam.[86]

Why do students cheat? One likely reason is that grade pressures reduce moral intent—even when students recognize that cheating is a moral issue and that the right decision is not to cheat, they do it anyway. Some support for this notion comes from a recent study of cheating among 5,331 students at 54 colleges.[87] The students filled out anonymous surveys measuring 13 different cheating behaviors, along with four potential predictors of cheating: (1) understanding of academic integrity policies, (2) likelihood of being reported by a peer if caught cheating, (3) perceived severity of cheating penalties, and (4) how often they had observed another student cheating. Of those four potential predictors, which do you think had the strongest effect? That's right—observing another student cheating. In fact, none of the other three factors had any statistical relationship with cheating behaviors. It may be that seeing others cheat creates a sort of peer pressure to "keep up with one's classmates," particularly when classes are graded on a curve.

Another possible reason for cheating is that students' moral judgments about the act have changed. In reflecting on the Duke incident, observers noted that the cheaters were all of the "cut and paste" or "Napster" generation, many of whom had worked in technology jobs in which open source code was championed and technological collaboration was vital to job success.[88] From this perspective, cheating may simply be viewed as an extension of that sort of collaboration. Regardless, schools need to gain a much deeper understanding of why students cheat if such unethical behaviors are to be curbed. ❖

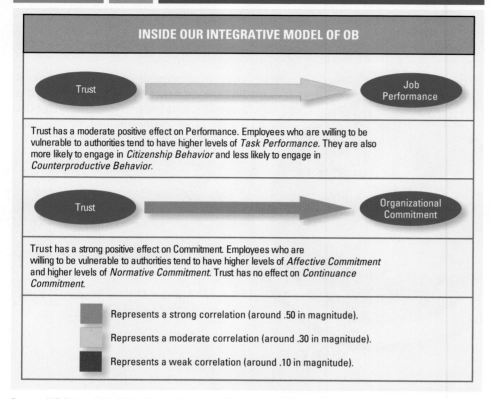

FIGURE 6-8 | Effects of Trust on Performance and Commitment

INSIDE OUR INTEGRATIVE MODEL OF OB

Trust ⟶ Job Performance

Trust has a moderate positive effect on Performance. Employees who are willing to be vulnerable to authorities tend to have higher levels of *Task Performance*. They are also more likely to engage in *Citizenship Behavior* and less likely to engage in *Counterproductive Behavior*.

Trust ⟶ Organizational Commitment

Trust has a strong positive effect on Commitment. Employees who are willing to be vulnerable to authorities tend to have higher levels of *Affective Commitment* and higher levels of *Normative Commitment*. Trust has no effect on *Continuance Commitment*.

Represents a strong correlation (around .50 in magnitude).

Represents a moderate correlation (around .30 in magnitude).

Represents a weak correlation (around .10 in magnitude).

Sources: K. T. Dirks and D. L. Ferrin, "Trust in Leadership: Meta-Analytic Findings and Implications for Research and Practice," *Journal of Applied Psychology* 87 (2002), pp. 611–28; J. A. Colquitt, B. A. Scott, and J. A. LePine, "Trust, Trustworthiness, and Trust Propensity: A Meta-Analytic Test of their Unique Relationships with Risk Taking and Job Performance," *Journal of Applied Psychology* 92 (2007), pp. 909–27.

HOW IMPORTANT IS TRUST?

Does trust have a significant impact on the two primary outcomes in our integrative model of OB—does it correlate with job performance and organizational commitment? Figure 6-8 summarizes the research evidence linking trust to job performance and organizational commitment. The figure reveals that trust does affect job performance. Why? One reason is that trust is moderately correlated with task performance. A study of employees in eight plants of a tool manufacturing company sheds some light on why trust benefits task performance.[89] The study gave employees survey measures of their trust in two different authorities: their plant's manager and the company's top management team. Both trust measures were significant predictors of employees' *ability to focus*, which reflects the degree to which employees can devote their attention to work, as opposed to "covering their backside," "playing politics," and "keeping an eye on the boss." The ability to focus is clearly vital to task performance in many jobs, particularly when job duties become more complex. Trust also influences citizenship

behavior and counterproductive behavior. Why? One reason is that the willingness to accept vulnerability changes the nature of the employee–employer relationship. Employees become more likely to do "extra things" to help out the organization because they trust that relevant authorities will have their best interests in mind and repay their efforts over the long term.

Figure 6-8 also reveals that trust affects organizational commitment. Why? One reason is that trusting an authority increases the likelihood that an emotional bond will develop,[90] particularly if that trust is rooted in positive feelings for the authority. Trusting an authority also makes it more likely that a sense of obligation will develop because employees feel more confident that the authority deserves that obligation. When negative events occur, employees who trust the authority are willing to accept the vulnerability that comes with continued employment,[91] remaining confident in their belief that the situation will eventually improve. ■

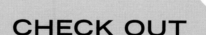

CHECK OUT

www.mhhe.com/ColquittEss

for study materials including Interactive Exercises, Quizzes, iPod downloads, and video.

CASE: PepsiCo

PepsiCo's international business grew 22 percent in 2007, to the point that it now contributes 40 percent of the company's total revenue.[92] That growth puts more pressure on PepsiCo's management of trust issues in emerging markets. In 2003, activists in India leveled two controversial claims against the company.[93] First, they suggested that the company was using too much groundwater in parched Indian communities, wasting a valued resource that has spiritual significance to Indians. Second, they suggested that PepsiCo's (and Coca-Cola's) soda products contained unacceptable levels of chemicals and pesticides. Pepsi and Coke were forced to hold a rare joint press conference in New Delhi to defend the safety of their products. Similar claims were leveled in 2006, though the Indian government has yet to set firm standards for the chemicals that can be used in bottled drinks (the chemical levels in soda are much lower than the chemical levels in milk, for example).

This controversy has damaged the trust that Indians feel toward PepsiCo. Although Nooyi was not yet CEO when the charges were leveled from her native country, she still regrets not moving faster, noting, "but I was the face of India. I should have hopped on a plane right away and said, 'Guys, I assure you, these products are the safest.' . . . At that point it didn't occur to me. That's the thing I regret. Now if it happened—man, I would be there in an instant."[94] The company has taken steps to reverse its trust problem. For example, one plant near New Delhi has reduced its water usage from 35 liters per two dozen bottles down to 8.6.[95] The company also paid to construct a well, pipes, and taps to bring water to 50 homes in a village where access to water was a three-hour walk away. Unfortunately, the village's local governing council refused to pay for the electricity to run the pumps, limiting them to once-a-day use. When Pepsi managers visited recently, one villager asked if the company could cover the extra utility costs. These sorts of events illustrate the difficulty of acting ethically on a global scale.

6.1 Consider the efforts that PepsiCo has taken to restore its trustworthiness in India. Do those efforts align with PepsiCo's responsibility to its shareholders, or do they conflict with that responsibility? Explain.

6.2 If a similar event occurs in another PepsiCo market, how should the company handle it?

6.3 Does a multinational company have an obligation to treat consumers and employees more ethically than the native companies in that region do? Why or why not?

TAKEAWAYS

6.1 Trust is the willingness to be vulnerable to an authority based on positive expectations about the authority's actions and intentions. Justice reflects the perceived fairness of an authority's decision making and can be used to explain why employees judge some authorities as more trustworthy than others. Ethics reflects the degree to which the behaviors of an authority are in accordance with generally accepted moral norms and can be used to explain why authorities choose to act in a trustworthy manner.

6.2 Trust can be disposition-based, meaning that one's personality includes a general propensity to trust others. Trust also can be cognition-based, meaning that it's rooted in a rational assessment of the authority's trustworthiness. Finally, trust can be affect-based, meaning that it is rooted in feelings toward the authority that go beyond any rational assessment of trustworthiness.

6.3 Trustworthiness is judged along three dimensions: ability, integrity, and benevolence. Ability reflects the skills and competencies of an authority. Integrity reflects whether the authority adheres to a set of acceptable values and principles. Benevolence reflects the belief that the authority wants to "do good" for the trustor.

6.4 The fairness of an authority's decision making can be judged along four dimensions. Distributive justice reflects the perceived fairness of decision-making outcomes. Procedural justice reflects the perceived fairness of decision-making processes. Interpersonal justice reflects the perceived fairness of the treatment received by employees from authorities. Informational justice reflects the perceived fairness of the communications provided to employees from authorities.

6.5 The four-component model of ethical decision making argues that ethical behavior depends on three concepts. Moral awareness reflects whether an authority recognizes that a moral issue exists in a situation. Moral judgment reflects whether the authority can accurately identify the "right" course of action. Moral intent reflects an authority's degree of commitment to the moral course of action.

6.6 Trust has a moderate positive relationship with job performance and a strong positive relationship with organizational commitment.

DISCUSSION QUESTIONS

6.1 Consider the three dimensions of trustworthiness (ability, integrity, and benevolence). Which of those dimensions would be most important when deciding whether to trust your boss? What about when deciding whether to trust a friend? If your two answers differ, why do they?

6.2 Putting yourself in the shoes of a manager, which of the four justice dimensions (distributive, procedural, interpersonal, informational) would you find most difficult to maximize? Which would be the easiest to maximize?

6.3 Which component of ethical decision making do you believe best explains student cheating: moral awareness, moral judgment, or moral intent? Why do you feel that way?

6.4 Assume you were applying for a job at a company known for its fair and ethical practices. How important would that information be to you when deciding whether to accept a job offer?

ASSESSMENT: Trust Propensity

Are you a trusting person or a suspicious person by nature? This assessment is designed to measure trust propensity—a dispositional willingness to trust other people. Answer each question using the response scale provided. Then subtract your answers to the bold-faced questions from 6, with the difference being your new answers for those questions. For example, if your original answer for question 4 was "4," your new answer is "2" (6 – 4). Then sum up your answers for the eight questions. (For more assessments relevant to this chapter, please visit the Online Learning Center at www.mhhe.com/ColquittEss.)

1	2	3	4	5
Strongly Disagree	Disagree	Neutral	Agree	Strongly Agree

1. **One should be very cautious with strangers.** _____
2. Most experts tell the truth about the limits of their knowledge. _____
3. Most people can be counted on to do what they say they will do. _____
4. **These days, you must be alert or someone is likely to take advantage of you.** _____
5. Most salespeople are honest in describing their products. _____
6. Most repair people will not overcharge people who are ignorant of their specialty. _____
7. Most people answer public opinion polls honestly. _____
8. Most adults are competent at their jobs. _____

Scoring

If your scores sum up to 21 or above, you tend to be trusting of other people, which means you are often willing to accept some vulnerability to others under conditions of risk. If your scores sum up to 20 or below, you tend to be suspicious of other people, which means you are rarely willing to accept some vulnerability to others under conditions of risk.

Sources: R. C. Mayer and J. H. Davis, "The Effect of the Performance Appraisal System on Trust for Management: A Field Quasi-Experiment," *Journal of Applied Psychology* 84 (1999), pp. 123–36. Copyright © 1999 by the American Psychological Association. Adapted with permission. No further reproduction or distribution is permitted without written permission from the American Psychological Association. See also F. D. Schoorman, R. C. Mayer, C. Roger, and J. H. Davis, "Empowerment in Veterinary Clinics: The Role of Trust in Delegation," Symposium on Trust, 11th Annual Conference, Society for Industrial and Organizational Psychology (SIOP), April 1996, San Diego, CA.

EXERCISE: Trustworthiness and Trust

The purpose of this exercise is to explore the factors that lead one person to trust another. This exercise uses groups, so your instructor will either assign you to a group or ask you to create your own group. The exercise has the following steps:

1. Individually, read the following paragraphs that describe three people *who might work for you*. For each, how comfortable would you be turning over to him or her a project that was very important to you if you could not monitor what he or she did? (1 = *petrified*; 10 = *completely comfortable*).

J.B. was promoted to his/her current position shortly before you were transferred in as head of the department. On paper, J.B. is qualified, but you have some serious doubts about his/her skills. J.B. has an MBA from a well-respected university and has been in the current position for over a year. During that time, you have found some very surprising mistakes and oversights in J.B.'s work. J.B. doesn't seem to have a grasp of how the company operates and what his/her role is supposed to be. When you have tried to explain these things, J.B. claims to understand. However, J.B.'s work doesn't seem to show it. J.B. really likes you and bends over backward to help you out whenever possible. All of J.B.'s peers seem to like him/her, and J.B. has gained a bit of a reputation among them and the customers for being very fair.

Sandy has been with your company for a long time and has worked for you for about a year. Inasmuch as Sandy's job is fairly technical, Sandy has continued to attend seminars and read technical journals to keep up to date. Sandy's work is always careful and complete. Sandy has on a number of occasions shown great loyalty to you, the boss. For example, just last month, Sandy blocked information from getting to your boss that would have made you look bad. On several occasions, Sandy has misled people in other departments to keep them from taking resources away from your department.

Pat recently transferred to your division from the company's East Coast division. Pat wanted to get back closer to family. Pat's former department head had tried unsuccessfully to block Pat's leaving, arguing that Pat was "just too important" to let him/her go. The quality of Pat's work appears to justify the former manager's reluctance to let Pat leave. Pat does not seem to have trouble making friends and is quite popular but has refused all of your attempts to get to know him/her. When you have gone to lunch together, Pat mostly listened to what you had to say and didn't say much. Pat often seems to have his/her guard up when talking with you. In dealings with other employees and with customers, Pat is fair and honest.

Based on your ratings, whom would you trust the most? In your groups, explain your ratings. What factors were most critical to your trust assessments?

2. Individually, read the following paragraphs that describe three people for *whom you might work.* For each, how comfortable would you be turning over to this manager control over *your destiny in the company* if you could not monitor what he or she did? (1 = petrified; 10 = completely comfortable).

In dealing with you, Terry is a no-nonsense kind of manager. Terry has always acted on the up-and-up from everything you've seen and heard. Terry always gets things done well and is respected by all. Your attempts to go to lunch, socialize, and build a relationship have always been politely refused. Terry has a number of friends at work, but you do not seem to be one of them.

You've worked for Taylor for several years. Taylor has always been honest with you and shown a genuine concern for others, as well as for the profitability of the business. Taylor has been particularly good to you, and it's clear that Taylor likes and respects you. Taylor frequently has problems getting the bills paid and customers served on time and does not seem to manage the company's finances very well. Taylor does not seem to have clear objectives about what things are important for the operation of the business.

You have always found your manager, Jesse, to have strong skills. Jesse is on the phone with another manager. You hear Jesse commit to getting a report done by Friday. Once off the phone, Jesse makes a snappy remark about hell freezing over and continues your performance review. You can recall a number of other occasions when Jesse told someone one thing and turned around and told you something entirely different. Jesse has always been nice to you and seems to like you. Jesse tells you you're meeting all your goals and should expect a promotion and pay increase within the next six months to a year.

Based on your ratings, whom would you trust most? In your groups, explain your ratings. What factors were most critical to your trust assessments?

3. Class discussion, whether in groups or as a class, should center on this question: What factors caused you to trust one person more than the others in the two sets of scenarios? Do the relevant factors vary when trust refers to a subordinate compared with when trust refers to a supervisor? How?

Source: Adapted from R. C. Mayer and P. M. Norman, "Exploring Attributes of Trustworthiness: A Classroom Exercise," *Journal of Management Education* 28 (2004), pp. 224–49.

END NOTES

1. Morris, B. "The Pepsi Challenge." *Fortune,* March 3, 2008, pp. 54–66.

2. Ibid.

3. Ibid.

4. Brady, D. "Pepsi: Repairing a Poisoned Reputation in India." *BusinessWeek,* June 11, 2007, pp. 46–54.

5. Ibid.

6. Mayer, R. C.; J. H. Davis; and F. D. Schoorman. "An Integrative Model of Organizational Trust." *Academy of Management Review* 20 (1995), pp. 709–34; Rousseau, D. M.; S. B. Sitkin; R. S. Burt; and C. Camerer. "Not So Different After All: A Cross-Discipline View of Trust." *Academy of Management Review* 23 (1998), pp. 393–404.

7. Greenberg, J. "A Taxonomy of Organizational Justice Theories." *Academy of Management Review* 12 (1987), pp. 9–22.

8. Lind, E. A. "Fairness Heuristic Theory: Justice Judgments as Pivotal Cognitions in Organizational Relations." In *Advances in Organizational Justice,* ed. J. Greenberg and R. Cropanzano. Stanford, CA: Stanford University Press, 2001, pp. 56–88; Van den Bos, K. "Fairness Heuristic Theory: Assessing the Information to Which People Are Reacting Has a Pivotal Role in Understanding Organizational Justice." In *Theoretical and Cultural Perspectives on Organizational Justice,* ed. S. Gilliland, D. Steiner, and D. Skarlicki. Greenwich, CT: Information Age Publishing, 2001, pp. 63–84; Van den Bos, K.; E. A. Lind; and H. A. M. Wilke. "The Psychology of Procedural and Distributive Justice Viewed from the Perspective of Fairness Heuristic Theory." In *Justice in the Workplace,* Vol. 2, ed. R. Cropanzano. Mahwah, NJ: Erlbaum, 2001, pp. 49–66.

9. Trevino, L. K.; G. R. Weaver; and S. J. Reynolds. "Behavioral Ethics in Organizations: A Review." *Journal of Management* 32 (2006), pp. 951–90.

10. McAllister, D. J. "Affect- and Cognition-Based Trust as Foundations for Interpersonal Cooperation in Organizations." *Academy of Management Journal* 38 (1995), pp. 24–59.

11. Ibid.

12. Mayer et al., "An Integrative Model"; Rotter, J. B. "A New Scale for the Measurement of Interpersonal Trust." *Journal of Personality* 35 (1967), pp. 651–65; Rotter, J. B. "Generalized Expectancies for Interpersonal Trust." *American Psychologist* 26 (1971), pp. 443–52; Rotter, J. B. "Interpersonal Trust, Trustworthiness, and Gullibility." *American Psychologist* 35 (1980), pp. 1–7.

13. Rosenberg, M. "Misanthropy and Political Ideology." *American Sociological Review* 21 (1956), pp. 690–95; Wrightsman, L. S., Jr. "Measurement of Philosophies of Human Nature." *Psychological Reports* 14 (1964), pp. 743–51.

14. Mayer et al., "An Integrative Model."

15. Jones, W. H.; L. L. Couch; and S. Scott. "Trust and Betrayal: The Psychology of Getting Along and Getting Ahead." In *Handbook of Personality Psychology,* ed. R. Hogan, J. S. Johnson, and S. R. Briggs. San Diego, CA: Academic Press, 1997, pp. 465–82.

16. Stack, L. C. "Trust." In *Dimensionality of Personality,* ed. H. London and J. E. Exner Jr. New York: Wiley, 1978, pp. 561–99.

17. Webb, W. M., and P. Worchel. "Trust and Distrust." In *Psychology of Intergroup Relations,* ed. S. Worchel and W. G. Austin. Chicago: Nelson-Hall, 1986, pp. 213–28; Erickson, E. H. *Childhood and Society.* 2nd ed. New York: Norton, 1963.

18. Stack, "Trust."

19. Mayer et al., "An Integrative Model."

20. McAllister, "Affect- and Cognition-Based Trust"; Lewicki, R. J., and B. B. Bunker. "Developing and Maintaining Trust in Work Relationships." In *Trust in Organizations: Frontiers of Theory and Research,* ed. R. M. Kramer and T. R. Tyler. Thousand Oaks, CA: Sage, 1996, pp. 114–39.

21. Mayer et al., "An Integrative Model."

22. Ibid.; Gabarro, J. J. "The Development of Trust, Influence, and Expectations." In *Interpersonal Behavior: Communication and Understanding in Relationships,* ed. G. Athos and J. J. Gabarro. Englewood Cliffs, NJ: Prentice Hall, 1978, pp. 290–303.

23. Gabarro, "The Development."

24. Mayer et al., "An Integrative Model"; Gabarro, "The Development."

25. Mayer et al., "An Integrative Model"; Simons, T. "Behavioral Integrity: The Perceived Alignment between Managers' Words and Deeds as a Research Focus." *Organization Science* 13 (2002), pp. 18–35; Dineen, B. R.; R. J. Lewicki; and E. C. Tomlinson. "Supervisory Guidance and Behavioral Integrity: Relationships with Employee Citizenship and Deviant Behavior." *Journal of Applied Psychology* 91 (2006), pp. 622–35.

26. Dineen et al. "Supervisory Guidance"; Bates, S. "Poll: Employees Skeptical about Management Actions." *HR Magazine,* June 2002, p. 12.

27. Mayer et al., "An Integrative Model."

28. Ibid.

29. Lewis, J. D., and A. Weigert. "Trust as a Social Reality." *Social Forces* 63 (1985), pp. 967–85.

30. Becker, L. C. "Trust as Noncognitive Security about Motives." *Ethics* 107 (1996), pp. 43–61.

31. McAllister, "Affect- and Cognition-Based Trust"; Lewicki and Bunker, "Developing and Maintaining Trust"; Lewis and Weigert, "Trust as Noncognitive Security."

32. McAllister, "Affect- and Cognition-Based Trust."

33. Lind, "Fairness Heuristic Theory: Assessing"; Van den Bos, "Fairness Heuristic Theory: Justice"; Van den Bos et al., "The Psychology of Procedural and Distributive Justice."

34. Adams, J. S. "Inequity in Social Exchange." In *Advances in Experimental Social Psychology,* Vol. 2, ed. L. Berkowitz. New York: Academic Press, 1965, pp. 267–99; Leventhal, G. S. "The Distribution of Rewards and Resources in Groups and Organizations." In *Advances in Experimental Social Psychology,* Vol. 9, ed. L. Berkowitz and W. Walster. New York: Academic Press, 1976, pp. 91–131.

35. Leventhal, "The Distribution of Rewards."

36. Ibid.

37. Levering, R., and M. Moskowitz. "In Good Company." *Fortune,* January 22, 2007, pp. 94–114.

38. Leventhal, G. S. "What Should Be Done with Equity Theory? New Approaches to the Study of Fairness in Social Relationships." In *Social Exchange: Advances in Theory*

Relationships." In *Social Exchange: Advances in Theory and Research,* ed. K. Gergen, M. Greenberg, and R. Willis. New York: Plenum Press, 1980, pp. 27–55; Thibaut, J., and L. Walker. *Procedural Justice: A Psychological Analysis.* Hillsdale, NJ: Erlbaum, 1975.

39. Folger, R. "Distributive and Procedural Justice: Combined Impact of 'Voice' and Improvement on Experienced Inequity." *Journal of Personality and Social Psychology* 35 (1977), pp. 108–19.

40. Colquitt, J. A.; D. E. Conlon; M. J. Wesson; C. O. L. H. Porter; and K. Y. Ng. "Justice at the Millennium: A Meta-Analytic Review of 25 Years of Organizational Justice Research." *Journal of Applied Psychology* 86 (2001), pp. 425–45.

41. Tyler, T. R.; K. A. Rasinski; and N. Spodick. "Influence of Voice on Satisfaction with Leaders: Exploring the Meaning of Process Control." *Journal of Personality and Social Psychology* 48 (1985), pp. 72–81; Earley, P. C.; and E. A. Lind. "Procedural Justice and Participation in Task Selection: The Role of Control in Mediating Justice Judgments." *Journal of Personality and Social Psychology* 52 (1987), pp. 1148–60; Lind, E. A.; R. Kanfer; and P. C. Earley. "Voice, Control, and Procedural Justice: Instrumental and Noninstrumental Concerns in Fairness Judgments." *Journal of Personality and Social Psychology* 59 (1990), pp. 952–59; Korsgaard, M. A., and L. Roberson. "Procedural Justice in Performance Evaluation: The Role of Instrumental and Non-instrumental Voice in Performance Appraisal Discussions." *Journal of Management* 21 (1995), pp. 657–69.

42. Brockner, J., and B. M. Wiesenfeld. "An Integrative Framework for Explaining Reactions to Decisions: Interactive Effects of Outcomes and Procedures." *Psychological Bulletin* 120 (1996), pp. 189–208.

43. Ibid.

44. Colquitt et al., "Justice at the Millennium"; Cohen-Charash, Y., and P. E. Spector. "The Role of Justice in Organizations: A Meta-Analysis." *Organizational Behavior and Human Decision Processes* 86 (2001), pp. 278–321.

45. Bies, R. J., and J. F. Moag. "Interactional Justice: Communication Criteria of Fairness." In *Research on Negotiations in Organizations,* Vol. 1, ed. R. J. Lewicki, B. H. Sheppard, and M. H. Bazerman. Greenwich, CT: JAI Press, 1986, pp. 43–55; Greenberg, J. "The Social Side of Fairness: Interpersonal and Informational Classes of Organizational Justice." In *Justice in the Workplace: Approaching Fairness in Human Resource Management,* ed. R. Cropanzano. Hillsdale, NJ: Erlbaum, 1993, pp. 79–103.

46. Bies, R. J. "Interactional (In)justice: The Sacred and the Profane." In *Advances in Organizational Justice,* ed. J. Greenberg and R. Cropanzano. Stanford, CA: Stanford University Press, 2001, pp. 85–108.

47. Sutton, R. I. *The No Asshole Rule.* New York: Warner Business Books, 2007.

48. Miner, A. G.; T. M. Glomb; and C. Hulin. "Experience Sampling Mode and Its Correlates at Work." *Journal of Occupational and Organizational Psychology* 78 (2005), pp. 171–93.

49. Gilliland, S. W.; L. Benson; and D. H. Schepers. "A Rejection Threshold in Justice Evaluations: Effects on Judgment and Decision-Making." *Organizational Behavior and Human Decision Processes* 76 (1998), pp. 113–31.

50. Tepper, B. J. "Consequences of Abusive Supervision." *Academy of Management Journal* 43 (2000), pp. 178–90.

51. Bies and Moag, "Interactional Justice"; Greenberg, "The Social Side of Fairness."

52. "RadioShack Fires 400 Employees by Email." http://abc-news.go.com/Technology/wireStory?id52374917&CMPOTC-RSSFeeds0312 (accessed May 28, 2007).

53. Folger, R., and D. P. Skarlicki. "Fairness as a Dependent Variable: Why Tough Times Can Lead to Bad Management." In *Justice in the Workplace: From Theory to Practice,* ed. R. Cropanzano. Mahwah, NJ: Erlbaum, 2001, pp. 97–118.

54. Shaw, J. C.; R. E. Wild; and J. A. Colquitt. "To Justify or Excuse?: A Meta-Analysis of the Effects of Explanations." *Journal of Applied Psychology* 88 (2003), pp. 444–58.

55. Orey, M. "Fear of Firing." *BusinessWeek,* April 23, 2007, pp. 52–62.

56. BCS Standings. http://www.bcsfootball.org/bcsfb/standings (accessed May 27, 2007).

57. Greenberg, J. "Employee Theft as a Reaction to Underpayment Inequity: The Hidden Cost of Paycuts." *Journal of Applied Psychology* 75 (1990), pp. 561–68.

58. Colquitt et al., "Justice at the Millennium"; Cohen-Charash and Spector, "The Role of Justice."

59. Trevino et al., "Behavioral Ethics."

60. Covey, S. M. R. *The Speed of Trust: The One Thing That Changes Everything.* New York: Free Press, 2006.

61. Trevino et al., "Behavioral Ethics"; Rest, J. R. *Moral Development: Advances in Research and Theory.* New York: Praeger, 2006; Butterfield, K. D.; L. K. Trevino; and G. R. Weaver. "Moral Awareness in Business Organizations: Influences of Issue-Related and Social Context Factors." *Human Relations* 53 (2000), pp. 981–1018.

62. Trevino et al., "Behavioral Ethics"; Rest, *Moral Development.*

63. Butterfield et al., "Moral Awareness."

64. Robertson, D. C. "Business Ethics across Cultures." In *The Blackwell Handbook of Cross-Cultural Management,* ed. M. J. Gannon and K. L. Newman. Malden, MA: Blackwell, 2002, pp. 361–92.

65. Ibid.

66. McLean, B. "Sex, Lies, and Videogames." *Fortune,* August 22, 2005, pp. 66–70.

67. Sparks, J. R., and S. D. Hunt. "Marketing Research Ethical Sensitivity: Conceptualization, Measurement, and Exploratory Investigation." *Journal of Marketing* 62 (1998), pp. 92–109.

68. Jones, T. M. "Ethical Decision Making by Individuals in Organizations: An Issue-Contingent Model." *Academy of Management Review* 16 (1991), pp. 366–95; Butterfield et al., "Moral Awareness."

69. Trevino et al., "Behavioral Ethics"; Rest, *Moral Development.*

70. Kohlberg, L. "Stage and Sequence: The Cognitive Developmental Approach to Socialization." In *Handbook of Socialization Theory,* ed. D. A. Goslin. Chicago: Rand McNally, 1969, pp. 347–480; Kohlberg, L. "The Claim to Moral Adequacy of a Highest Stage of Moral Judgment." *Journal of Philosophy* 70 (1973), pp. 630–46.

71. Trevino et al., "Behavioral Ethics."

72. Ibid.; Rest, J.; D. Narvaez; M. J. Bebeau; and S. J. Thoma. *Postconventional Moral Thinking: A Neo-Kohlbergian Approach.* Mahwah, NJ: Lawrence Erlbaum, 1999.

73. Forsyth, D. R. "A Taxonomy of Ethical Ideologies." *Journal of Personality and Social Psychology* 39 (1980), pp. 175–84.

74. Ibid.

75. Ibid.

76. Schminke, M.; M. L. Ambrose; and T. W. Noel. "The Effect of Ethical Frameworks on Perceptions of Organizational Justice." *Academy of Management Journal* 40 (1997), pp. 1190–1207; Brady, F. N., and G. E. Wheeler. "An Empirical Study of Ethical Predispositions." *Journal of Business Ethics* 15 (1996), pp. 927–40.

77. Ibid.

78. Forsyth, "A Taxonomy of Ethical Ideologies."

79. Ibid.

80. Schminke et al., "The Effect of Ethical Frameworks"; Brady and Wheeler, "An Empirical Study of Ethical Predispositions."

81. Ibid.

82. Trevino et al., "Behavioral Ethics"; Rest, *Moral Development.*

83. Bergman, R. "Identity as Motivation: Toward a Theory of the Moral Self." In *Moral Development, Self and Identity,* ed. D. K. Lapsley and D. Narvaez. Mahwah, NJ: Lawrence Erlbaum, 2004, pp. 21–46.

84. Trevino et al., "Behavioral Ethics"; Schweitzer, M. E.; L. Ordonez; and B. Douma. "Goal Setting as a Motivator of Unethical Behavior." *Academy of Management Journal* 47 (2004), pp. 422–32.

85. Oh, H. "Biz Majors Get an F for Honesty." *BusinessWeek,* February 6, 2006, p. 14.

86. Conlin, M. "Cheating—or Postmodern Learning?" *BusinessWeek,* May 14, 2007, p. 42.

87. McCabe, D. L. "Academic Dishonesty in Graduate Business Programs: Prevalence, Causes, and Proposed Action." *Academy of Management Learning and Education* 5 (2006), pp. 294–305.

88. Conlin, "Cheating—or Postmodern Learning?"

89. Mayer, R. C., and M. B. Gavin. "Trust in Management and Performance: Who Minds the Shop While the Employees Watch the Boss?" *Academy of Management Journal* 48 (2005), pp. 874–88.

90. Dirks, K. T., and D. L. Ferrin. "Trust in Leadership: Meta-Analytic Findings and Implications for Research and Practice." *Journal of Applied Psychology* 87 (2002), pp. 611–28.

91. Ibid.

92. Morris, "The Pepsi Challenge."

93. Brady, "Pepsi: Repairing a Poisoned Reputation in India."

94. Morris, "The Pepsi Challenge."

95. Brady, "Pepsi: Repairing a Poisoned Reputation in India."

LEARNING and DECISION MAKING

● ● learning **OBJECTIVES**

After reading this chapter, you should be able to:

7.1 Define learning and decision making.

7.2 Describe the types of knowledge that employees can gain as they learn and build expertise.

7.3 Explain the methods by which employees learn in organizations.

7.4 Describe what steps organizations take to foster learning.

7.5 Describe the two methods that employees use to make decisions.

7.6 Understand the decision-making problems that can prevent employees from translating their learning into accurate decisions.

7.7 Understand how learning affects job performance and organizational commitment.

CATERPILLAR

There is perhaps no more familiar sight on a construction site than to see the large, bright-yellow trucks, engines, and tools produced by Caterpillar, the world's leading manufacturer of construction and mining equipment, diesel and natural gas engines, and industrial gas turbines, based in Peoria, Illinois. What you likely don't know though is that this *Fortune* 100 company has one of the largest and most effective systems of knowledge sharing in the world. This ability to share and harness knowledge has played a large role in its ability to double in size during the past three years.[1] As Caterpillar CEO Jim Owens recently said, "Learning is essential to our aspiration to be a great company."[2]

One reason learning is so important to Caterpillar is the fact that intellectual capital accounts for almost 85 percent of its value (as opposed to only 30 percent 30 years ago).[3] To feed this intellectual capital, in 2000, the company formed "Caterpillar University," using a learning model that Jim Owens says is based on three important elements: "a culture that supports learning, comprehensive knowledge sharing throughout the company and with our value chain partners, and the development of leadership that is very supportive of learning."[4] Some of this capital is acquired by employees at Caterpillar University through traditional training opportunities and more than 3,000 online courses in various languages dealing with job tasks, business-unit opportunities, and discretionary learning. Every employee at Caterpillar has an individual learning plan he or she is expected to follow. Caterpillar spends more than $100 million a year on employee education.[5]

However, the real heart of what makes Caterpillar different than most companies is its "Knowledge Network." You might ask yourself how 100,000 employees spread out over 300 manufacturing operations in 40 countries share knowledge and learn to make better decisions. The answer is an extensive intranet-based social network organized around "communities of practice."[6] Employees within the organization that work with related jobs, related processes, or related customers can come together through a bulletin-board/e-mail system to share knowledge. More than 3,000 groups, ranging from small teams to hundreds of employees from multiple countries, come together to gather information, examine best practices, post information, and ask questions.[7] This process of knowledge sharing, which is driven primarily by employees (no top-down oversight), has achieved a record-setting return on investment for Caterpillar and sets it apart from its competitors and most other companies when it comes to learning.

LEARNING AND DECISION MAKING

●● 7.1

Define learning and decision making.

Caterpillar is extremely concerned about knowledge transfer because learning and decision making are so important in organizations. Learning reflects relatively permanent changes in an employee's knowledge or skill that result from experience.[8] The more employees learn, the more they bring to the table when they come to work. Why is learning so important? Because it has a significant impact on decision making, which refers to the process of generating and choosing from a set of alternatives to solve a problem. The more knowledge and skills employees possess, the more likely they are to make accurate and sound decisions. The risk, at Caterpillar and other organizations, is that less experienced employees will lack the knowledge base needed to make the right decisions when stepping into new roles.

One reason inexperience can be so problematic is that learning is not necessarily easy. Have you ever watched "experts" perform their jobs? How is it that someone becomes an expert? It takes a significant amount of time to become proficient at most complex jobs. It takes most employees anywhere from three months to a year to perform at a satisfactory level.[9] To develop high levels of expertise takes significantly longer. This difficulty makes it even more important for companies to find a way to improve learning and decision making by their employees.

WHY DO SOME EMPLOYEES LEARN TO MAKE DECISIONS BETTER THAN OTHERS?

Bill Buford, a journalist interested in becoming a chef, was hired by Mario Batali's world-renowned restaurant Babbo in New York. At some point early in his tenure in the kitchen, he realized he was in over his head while he stood and watched other, more experienced cooks work at an unbelievably frantic pace. He knew right then that he had a decision to make:

I was at a go-forward-or-backward moment. If I went backward, I'd be saying, "Thanks for the visit, very interesting, that's sure not me." But how to go forward? There was no place for me. These people were at a higher level of labor. They didn't think. Their skills were so deeply inculcated they were available to them as instincts. I didn't have skills of that kind and couldn't imagine how you'd learn them. I was aware of being poised on the verge of something: a long, arduous, confidence-bashing, profoundly humiliating experience.[10]

In this situation, Buford realized that his coworkers had more expertise than he did. Expertise refers to the knowledge and skills that distinguish experts from novices and less-experienced people.[11] Research shows that the differences between experts and novices is almost always a function of learning as opposed to the more popular view that intelligence or other innate differences make the difference.[12] Although learning cannot be directly seen or observed, we can tell when people have learned by observing their behaviors. It is those behaviors that can be used to tell experts from novices, and it is changes in those behaviors that can be used to show that learners are gaining knowledge. Although it's sometimes easy for employees to mimic a behavior once or twice, or get lucky with a few key decisions, true learning only occurs when changes in behavior become relatively permanent and are repeated over time. Understanding why some employees prove better at this than others requires understanding what exactly employees learn and how they do it.

- ● **LEARNING** A relatively permanent change in an employee's knowledge or skill that results from experience.

- ● **DECISION MAKING** The process of generating and choosing from a set of alternatives to solve a problem.

- ● **EXPERTISE** The knowledge and skills that distinguish experts from novices.

Expertise is the accumulation of superior knowledge and skills in a field that separates experts from everyone else.

7.2

Describe the types of knowledge that employees can gain as they learn and build expertise.

Types of Knowledge

Employees learn two basic types of knowledge, both of which have important implications for organizations. **Explicit knowledge** is the kind of information you are likely to think about when you picture someone sitting down at a desk to learn. It's information that is relatively easily communicated and a large part of what companies teach during training sessions. Although such information is necessary to perform well, it winds up being a relatively minor portion of all that you need to know.

> ● **EXPLICIT KNOWLEDGE** Knowledge that is easily communicated and available to everyone.

who" acquired solely through experience.[16] Table 7-1 lists the qualities that help explain the differences between explicit and tacit knowledge. Some would go as far as to say that explicit knowledge is what everyone can find and use, but tacit knowledge is what separates experts from common people.[17]

7.3

Explain the methods by which employees learn in organizations.

Methods of Learning

Tacit and explicit knowledge are extremely important to employees and organizations. As an employee, it's hard to build a high level of tacit knowledge without some level of explicit knowledge to build off of. From an organization's perspective, the tacit knowledge its employees accumulate may be the single most important strategic asset a company possesses.[18] The question then becomes: How do employees learn these

> ## "Research shows that the differences between experts and novices is almost always a function of learning as opposed to the more popular view that intelligence or other innate differences make the difference."

Tacit knowledge, in contrast, is what employees can typically learn only through experience.[13] It's not easily communicated but could very well be the most important aspect of what we learn in organizations.[14] In fact, it's been argued that up to 90 percent of the knowledge contained in organizations occurs in tacit form.[15] Did you ever get to be so good at something that you had the ability to do it but couldn't really explain it to someone else? That's a common way to explain tacit knowledge. It's been described as the "know-how," "know-what," and "know

types of knowledge? The short answer is that we learn through reinforcement (rewards and punishments), observation, and experience.

Reinforcement. We've known for a long time that managers use various methods of reinforcement to induce desirable or reduce undesirable behaviors by their employees. Originally known as operant conditioning, B. F. Skinner was the first to pioneer the notion that we learn by observing the

TABLE 7-1	Characteristics of Explicit and Tacit Knowledge
Explicit Knowledge	**Tacit Knowledge**
Easily transferred through written or verbal communication	Very difficult, if not impossible, to articulate to others
Readily available to most	Highly personal in nature
Can be learned through books	Based on experience
Always conscious and accessible information	Sometimes holders don't even recognize that they possess it
General information	Typically job- and/or situation-specific

Source: Adapted from R. McAdam, B. Mason, and J. McCrory, "Exploring the Dichotomies within the Tacit Knowledge Literature: Towards a Process of Tacit Knowing in Organizations," *Journal of Knowledge Management* 11 (2007), pp. 43–59.

● **TACIT KNOWL-EDGE** Knowledge that employees can only learn through experience.

● **POSITIVE REINFORCE-MENT** When a positive outcome follows a desired behavior.

● **NEGATIVE REINFORCE-MENT** An unwanted outcome is removed following a desired behavior.

● **PUNISHMENT** When an unwanted outcome follows an unwanted behavior.

● **EXTINCTION** The removal of a positive outcome following an unwanted behavior.

link between our voluntary behavior and the consequences that follow it. Research has continually demonstrated that people will exhibit specific behaviors if they are rewarded for doing so. Not surprisingly, we have a tendency to repeat behaviors that result in consequences that we like and to not exhibit behaviors that result in consequences we don't like. Figure 7-1 shows this operant conditioning process.

In that model, you can see that there are antecedents or events that precede or signal certain behaviors, which are then followed by consequences. Antecedents in organizations are typically goals, rules, instructions, or other types of information that help show employees what is expected of them. Although antecedents are useful for motivational reasons, it is primarily the consequences of actions that drive behavior. This entire process of reinforcement is a continuous cycle, and the repetition of behaviors is strengthened to the degree that reinforcement continues to occur. There are four specific consequences typically used by organizations to modify employee behavior, known as the contingencies of reinforcement.[19] Figure 7-2 summarizes these contingencies. It's important to separate these contingencies into what they are designed to do, namely, increase desired behaviors or decrease unwanted behaviors.

Two contingencies of reinforcement are used to increase desired behaviors. **Positive reinforcement** occurs when a positive outcome follows a desired behavior. It is perhaps the most common type of reinforcement and the type we think of when an employee receives some type of "reward." Increased pay, promotions, praise from a manager or coworkers, and public recognition would all be considered positive reinforcement when given as a result of an employee exhibiting wanted behaviors. **Negative reinforcement** occurs when an unwanted outcome is removed following a desired behavior. Have you ever performed a task for the specific reason of not getting yelled

"From an organization's perspective, the tacit knowledge its employees accumulate may be the single most important strategic asset a company possesses."

Positive reinforcement, like public recognition, both encourages employees and helps ensure that desirable behaviors will be imitated and repeated.

at? If so, you learned to perform certain behaviors through the use of negative reinforcement. It is important to remember that even though the word "negative" has a sour connotation to it, it is designed to *increase* desired behaviors.

The next two contingencies of reinforcement are designed to decrease undesired behaviors. **Punishment** occurs when an unwanted outcome follows an unwanted behavior. Punishment is exactly what it sounds like. In other words, the employee is given something he or she doesn't like as a result of performing a behavior that the organization doesn't like. Suspending an employee for showing up to work late, assigning job tasks generally seen as demeaning for not following safety procedures, or even firing an employee for gross misconduct are all examples of punishment. **Extinction** occurs when there is the removal of a consequence following an unwanted behavior. The use of extinction to reinforce behavior can be purposeful or accidental. Perhaps an employee receives attention from coworkers when he or she acts in ways that are somewhat childish at work. Finding a way to remove the attention would be a purposeful act of extinction. Similarly though, perhaps an employee works late every now and then to finish up job tasks when work gets busy, but his or her manager stops acknowledging that hard work. Desired behavior that is not reinforced will diminish over time. In this way, a manager who does nothing to reinforce good behavior is actually decreasing the odds that it will be repeated!

In general, positive reinforcement and extinction should be the most common forms of reinforcement used by managers to create learning among their employees. Positive reinforcement doesn't have to be in the form of material rewards to be effective. There are many ways for managers to encourage wanted behaviors. Offering praise, providing feedback, public recognition, and small celebrations are all ways to

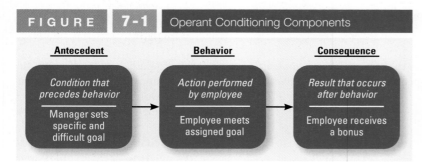

FIGURE 7-1 Operant Conditioning Components

Antecedent	Behavior	Consequence
Condition that precedes behavior — Manager sets specific and difficult goal	*Action performed by employee* — Employee meets assigned goal	*Result that occurs after behavior* — Employee receives a bonus

encourage employees and increase the chances they will continue to exhibit desired behaviors. At the same time, extinction is an effective way to stop unwanted behaviors. Both of these contingencies deliver their intended results, but perhaps more important, they do so without creating feelings of animosity and conflict. Although punishment and negative reinforcement will work, they tend to bring other, detrimental consequences along with them.

Observation. In addition to learning through reinforcement, social learning theory argues that people in organizations have the ability to learn through the observation of others.[20] In fact, many would argue that social learning is the primary way by which employees gain knowledge in organizations.[21] Think about where you are most likely to get your cues while working in an organization. When possible, chances are good you'll look around at other employees to figure out the appropriate behaviors on your job. Not only do employees have the ability to see the link between their own behaviors and their consequences, they also can observe the behaviors and consequences of others.[22] When employees observe the actions of others, learn from what they observe, and then repeat the observed behavior, they are engaging in behavioral modeling.

In fact, because tacit knowledge is so difficult to communicate, modeling might be the single best way to acquire it. For that reason, modeling is a continual process that is used at all levels of many organizations. Kellogg's, the Michigan-based cereal company, groomed current CEO David Mackay for two years by allowing him to observe and model an interim, experienced CEO prior to taking over the helm. Mackay shadowed the CEO and observed boardroom proceedings to gain the insider experience that the Kellogg's board felt he was lacking.[23] Needless to say, choosing a good model is important, and not all models are good ones. Salomon Brothers, the New York–based investment bank, learned this lesson the hard way when employees began to model the unethical behaviors of their managers and leaders.[24]

David Mackay was provided an unusual opportunity to learn by observation and behavioral modeling before becoming CEO of Kellogg's. He "shadowed" his predecessor for two years to gain insider experience before taking the helm.

●●7.4
Describe what steps organizations take to foster learning.

How can organizations proactively take advantage of these methods of learning in an effort to boost employee expertise and, ultimately, improve decision making? One approach is to rely on training, which represents a systematic effort by organizations to facilitate the learning of job-related knowledge and behavior. Organizations spent over $55.8 billion and approximately $1,273 per learner on formal training and development costs in 2006.[25] Estimates suggest that organizations spend three to six times that amount on informal, observational, and on-the-job training.[26] A full discussion of all the types of training companies offer is beyond the scope of this section, but suffice it to say that companies are using many different methods to help their employees acquire explicit and tacit

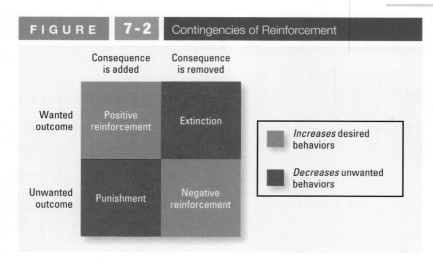

FIGURE 7-2 Contingencies of Reinforcement

	Consequence is added	Consequence is removed
Wanted outcome	Positive reinforcement	Extinction
Unwanted outcome	Punishment	Negative reinforcement

Increases desired behaviors

Decreases unwanted behaviors

knowledge. Technological changes are altering the way those methods are delivered, as instructor-led classroom training has declined while online self-study programs have increased.[27] As described in our **OB for Students** section, these technological changes are occurring on university campuses as well. Indeed, some of you may be working in a virtual classroom right now!

As evidenced in our opening example, another form of knowledge transfer that's being used by companies more frequently is communities of practice. **Communities of practice** are groups of employees who work together and learn from one another by collaborating over an extended period of time.[28] A large number of companies are utilizing this newer form of informal social learning. Communities of practice introduce their own unique complications, but the potential of their ability to transfer knowledge through employees is significant.[29]

Goal Orientation.

Before we leave this section, it's important to recognize that people learn somewhat differently according to their predispositions or attitudes toward learning and performance. These differences are reflected in an individual's **goal orientation**, which captures the kinds of activities and goals that they prioritize. Some people have what is known as a learning orientation, according to which building competence is deemed more important than demonstrating competence. "Learning-oriented" persons enjoy working on new kinds of tasks, even if they fail during their early experiences. Such people view failure in positive terms—as a means of increasing knowledge and skills in the long run.[30] For others, the demonstration of competence is deemed a more important goal than the building of competence. That demonstration of competence can be motivated by two different thought processes. Those with a performance-prove orientation focus on demonstrating their competence so that others think favorably of them. Those with a performance-avoid orientation focus on demonstrating their competence so that others will not think poorly of them. In either case, "performance-oriented" people tend to work mainly on tasks at which they're already good, preventing them from failing in front of others. Such individuals view failure in negative terms—as an indictment of their ability and competence.

OB for Students

What does learning and training have to do with you as a student? We hope this is a reasonably clear question for you already! However, there are some changes on the way in terms of how you might get taught in the future by both companies and universities. Technology and the changing marketplace (that includes you!) are forcing universities to incorporate online education as part of their ongoing strategies.[31] Online courses are growing by leaps and bounds across campuses all over the United States and internationally. If you're not already experiencing virtual content in some form, chances are good many of you will have the opportunity to receive it in the not-too-distant future. Overall, higher education enrollment in the United States is relatively stable, but enrollment in online courses is increasing exponentially.[32] For example, going into the 2007 academic school year, Penn State University had 5,691 students participating in online classes, and the University of Massachusetts had almost double that number.[33]

One of the reasons universities have been slow to incorporate online education is the belief by many faculty members that the same level of knowledge cannot be transmitted online. However, a recent meta-analysis suggests that this belief is unfounded! Research shows no difference between online and regular classroom instruction in terms of the measured learning of explicit knowledge. Interestingly enough though, the study found that the highest levels of learning occurred when the two methods were mixed (part of the class online, part in the classroom).[34] It may be that two different learning strategies are used under such scenarios, which allows different kinds of learners to take advantage of what suits them best.[35] At the moment, companies are well ahead of the curve at delivering effective online classes. Intuit, the maker of personal and small-business software including Quicken and TurboTax, has been using the mixed method of training for quite a while. It employs face-to-face training to establish relationships prior to moving into

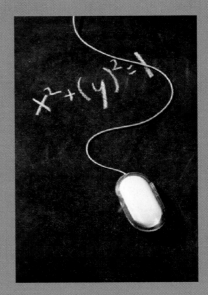

a virtual classroom.[36] Such corporate efforts will likely help establish a blueprint for universities to follow as they expand their online offerings. ❖

Research has shown that a learning goal orientation improves self-confidence, feedback-seeking behavior, learning strategy development, and learning performance.[37] Research on the two performance orientations is more mixed. Although it would seem that focusing on performance should improve performance-based outcomes, research shows that isn't necessarily the case. On the whole, a performance-prove orientation tends to be a mixed bag, producing varying levels of performance and outcomes. What kind of orientation do you tend to exhibit? See our **Assessments** feature at the end of the chapter to find out.

To experts, this kind of decision making sometimes comes across as intuition or a "gut feeling." Intuition can be described as emotionally charged judgments that arise through quick, nonconscious, and holistic associations.[38] Because of their tacit knowledge, experts sometimes cannot put into words why they know that a problem exists, why a solution will work, or how they accomplished a task. They just "know." Of course, the difficulty arises in knowing when to trust that "gut instinct" and when not to.[39] As a general rule of thumb, you should probably ask yourself how much expertise you have in that on which you

> ❝**Because of their tacit knowledge, experts sometimes cannot put into words why they know that a problem exists, why a solution will work, or how they accomplished a task. They just 'know.'**❞

7.5

Describe the two methods that employees use to make decisions.

Methods of Decision Making

How do employees take explicit and tacit knowledge, however it's gained, and turn that knowledge into effective decision making? Sometimes that process is very straightforward. Programmed decisions are decisions that become somewhat automatic because a person's knowledge allows him or her to recognize and identify a situation and the course of action that needs to be taken. As shown in Figure 7-3, experts often respond to an identified problem by realizing that they've dealt with it before. That realization triggers a programmed decision that is implemented and then evaluated according to its ability to deliver the expected outcome. For experts who possess high levels of explicit and tacit knowledge, many decisions they face are of this programmed variety. That's not to say that the decisions are necessarily easy. It simply means that their experience and knowledge allow them to see the problems more easily and recognize and implement solutions more quickly.

 **"As employees move up the corporate ladder, a larger percentage of their decisions become less and less programmed."**

are making a judgment. In other words, don't go laying down your life savings on a spin of the roulette wheel in Vegas because your intuition tells you "red"! Effective intuition results when people have a certain amount of tacit knowledge.

When a situation arises that is new, complex, and not recognized, it calls for a nonprogrammed decision on the part of the employee. Organizations are complex and changing environments, and many workers are faced with uncertainty on a daily basis. In these instances, employees have to make sense of their environment, understand the problems they are faced with, and come up with solutions to overcome them. As a general rule of thumb, as employees move up the corporate ladder, a larger percentage of their decisions become less and less programmed. How should decision making proceed in such contexts? The rational decision-making model presented on the right side of Figure 7-3 offers a step-by-step approach to making decisions that maximize outcomes by examining all available alternatives. Also shown in Figure 7-3, this model only becomes relevant when people don't recognize a problem as one they have dealt with before.

The rational decision-making model assumes that people are, of course, perfectly rational. However, problems immediately

FIGURE 7-3 Programmed and Nonprogrammed Decisions

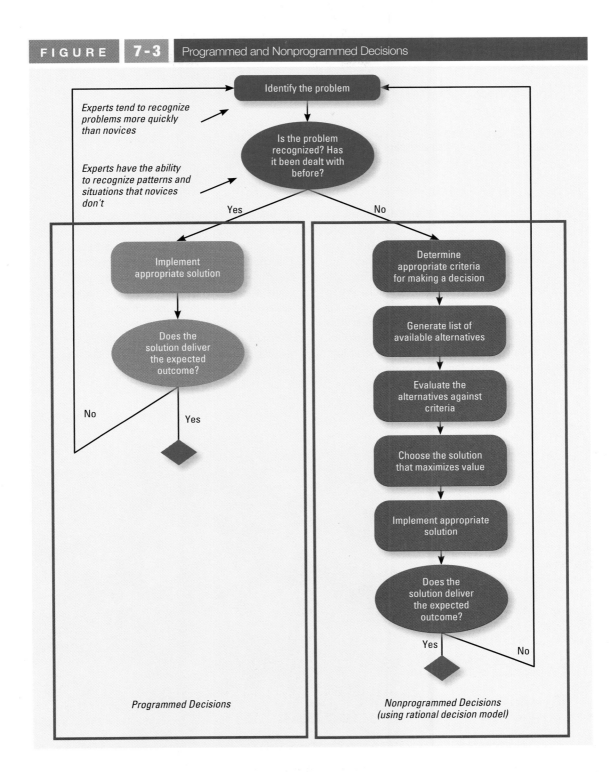

Programmed Decisions

Nonprogrammed Decisions
(using rational decision model)

arise when we start to examine some of the assumptions the model makes about human decision makers.[40] The model assumes there is a clear and definite problem to solve and that people have the ability to identify what that exact problem is. It also assumes that decision makers have perfect information—that they know and are able to identify the available alternatives

and the outcomes that would be associated with those alternatives. The model further assumes that time and money are generally not issues when it comes to making a decision, that decision makers always choose the solution that maximizes value, and that they will act in the best interests of the organization. Given all these assumptions, perhaps we shouldn't label the model as "rational" after all! For an example of one decision maker who can follow the tenets of the rational decision-making model, see our **OB on Screen** feature.

●● 7.6

Understand the decision-making problems that can prevent employees from translating their learning into accurate decisions.

Decision-Making Problems

Because employees don't always make rational decisions, it's easy to second-guess decisions after the fact. Many decisions made inside organizations look good at the time and were made with perfectly good justifications to support them but turn out to have what are perceived as "bad results." The reality, however, is that it's a lot easier to question decisions in hindsight. As Warren Buffet, CEO of Berkshire Hathaway, is often quoted as saying, "In the business world, the rearview mirror is always clearer than the windshield."[41] Our responsibility here is not to rehash all the poor decisions employees and managers have made (and there are many of them!)

but rather to detail some of the most common reasons for bad decision making—in other words, when are people most likely to falter in terms of the rational decision-making model and why?

Limited Information. Although most employees perceive themselves as rational decision makers, the reality is that they are all subject to bounded rationality. Bounded rationality is the notion that decision makers simply do not have the ability or resources to process all available information and alternatives to make an optimal decision.[42] A comparison of bounded rationality and rational decision making is presented in Table 7-2. This limit results in two major problems for making decisions. First, people have to filter and simplify information to make sense of their complex environment and the myriad of potential choices they face.[43] This simplification leads them to miss information when perceiving problems, generating and evaluating alternatives, or judging the results. Second, because people cannot possibly consider every single alternative when making a decision, they satisfice. Satisficing results when decision makers select the first acceptable alternative considered.[44]

OB on Screen

Star Trek: First Contact

> Data: Captain, I believe I am feeling . . . anxiety. It is an intriguing sensation. A most distracting—
>
> Picard: (Interrupting) Data, I am sure it is a fascinating experience, but perhaps you should deactivate your emotion chip for now.
>
> Data: Good idea sir. (click) Done.
>
> Picard: Data, there are times when I envy you.

With these words, Captain Jean-Luc Picard (Patrick Stewart) tells Data (Brent Spiner) that he wished he had Data's ability to do what all of us would like to be able to do from time to time: make perfectly rational decisions. You see, Data is an android (a robot made to resemble a human) who serves as the chief operations officer aboard the *USS Enterprise* in *Star Trek: First Contact* (Dir. Jonathan Frakes, Paramount Pictures, 1996). Data, with his extremely advanced computer for a brain, is able to make close to perfect decisions by calculating probabilities with all possible available information. Wouldn't we all like to have that ability?

Throughout the newer generation of *Star Trek* episodes and movies, Data exhibits an overwhelming desire to become more "human" in order to understand his shipmates. As an android with no emotions, he lacks the ability to understand why humans make the irrational mistakes they sometimes do. In a prior *Star Trek* movie, Data receives an "emotion chip" that allows him to be distracted by

the emotions and feelings that we're faced with every day. In the scene shown, Data and Captain Picard are about to enter what is an extremely dangerous, life-and-death situation. Needless to say, Captain Picard prefers that Data enter the situation with the enviable ability to turn off his emotions and make rational decisions. ❖

● **BOUNDED RATION-
ALITY** The notion that
people do not have the ability or resources to process
all available information and
alternatives when making a
decision.

● **SATISFICING** When a
decision maker chooses the
first acceptable alternative
considered.

● **SELECTIVE PERCEP-
TION** The tendency for
people to see their environment only as it affects them
and as it is consistent with
their expectations.

● **SOCIAL IDENTITY
THEORY** A theory that
people identify themselves
based on the various groups
to which they belong and
judge others based on the
groups they associate with.

In addition to choosing the first acceptable alternative, decision makers tend to come up with alternatives that are straightforward, familiar, and not that different from what they're
already doing. When you and another person are deciding
where to go out for dinner tonight, will you sit down and list
every restaurant available to you within a certain mile limit? Of
course not. You'll start listing off alternatives, generally starting
with the closest and most familiar, until both parties arrive at
a restaurant that is acceptable to them. Making decisions this
way is no big deal when it comes to deciding where to go for
dinner because the consequences of a poor decision are mini-
mal. However, many managers make decisions that have critical
consequences for their employees and their customers. In those
cases, making a decision without thoroughly looking into the
alternatives becomes a problem!

Faulty Perceptions. As decision makers, employees are forced to rely on their perceptions to make decisions.
Perception is the process of selecting, organizing, storing, and
retrieving information about the environment. Although perceptions can be very useful because they help us make sense of
the environment around us, they can often become distorted
versions of reality. Perceptions can be dangerous in decision
making because we tend to make assumptions or evaluations
on the basis of them. Selective perception is the tendency
for people to see their environment only as it affects them and
as it is consistent with their expectations. Has someone ever
told you, "You only see what you want to see"? If a relative,

spouse, or significant other said that to you, chances are good
it probably wasn't the best experience. That person was likely
upset that you did not perceive the environment (or what was
important to them) the same way he or she did. Selective perception affects our ability to identify problems, generate and
evaluate alternatives, and judge outcomes. In other words, we
take "shortcuts" when we process information. In the following
paragraphs, we'll discuss some of the ways in which we take
perceptual shortcuts when dealing with people and situations.

Another example of faulty perceptions is caused by the way
we cognitively organize people into groups. Social identity
theory holds that people identify themselves by the groups to
which they belong and perceive and judge others by their group
memberships.[45] There is a substantial amount of research that
shows that we like to categorize people on the basis of the
groups to which they belong.[46] These groups could be based on
demographic information (gender, race, religion, hair color),
occupational information (scientists, engineers, accountants),
where they work (GE, Halliburton, Microsoft), what country
they are from (Americans, French, Chinese), or any other sub-
group that makes sense to the perceiver. You might categorize
students on campus by whether they are a member of a fraternity or sorority. Those inside the Greek system categorize people by which fraternity or sorority they belong to. And people
within a certain fraternity might group their own members on
the basis of whom they hang out with the most. There is practically no end to the number of subgroups that people can come
up with.

TABLE 7-2 Rational Decision Making vs. Bounded Rationality	
To be rational decision makers, we should . . .	**Bounded rationality says we are likely to . . .**
Identify the problem by thoroughly examining the situation and considering all interested parties.	Boil the problem down to something that is easily understood.
Develop an exhaustive list of alternatives to consider as solutions.	Come up with a few solutions that tend to be straightforward, familiar, and similar to what is currently being done.
Evaluate all the alternatives simultaneously.	Evaluate each alternative as soon as we think of it.
Use accurate information to evaluate alternatives.	Use distorted and inaccurate information during the evaluation process.
Pick the alternative that maximizes value.	Pick the first acceptable alternative (satisfice).

Sources: Adapted from H. A. Simon, "Rational Decision Making in Organizations," *American Economic Review* 69 (1979), pp. 493–513; D. Kahneman, "Maps of Bounded Rationality: Psychology for Behavioral Economics," *The American Economic Review* 93 (2003), pp. 1449–75; S. W. Williams, *Making Better Business Decisions* (Thousand Oaks, CA: Sage Publications, 2002).

When confronted with situations of uncertainty that require a decision on our part, we often use heuristics—simple, efficient rules of thumb that allow us to make decisions more easily. In general, heuristics are not bad. In fact, they lead to correct decisions more often than not.[47] However, heuristics can also bias us toward inaccurate decisions at times. Consider this example from one of the earliest studies on decision-making heuristics: "Consider the letter R. Is R more likely to appear in the first position of a word or the third position of a word?"[48] If your answer was the first position of a word, you answered incorrectly and fell victim to one of the most frequently talked about heuristics. The availability bias is the tendency for people to base their judgments on information that is easier to recall. It is significantly easier for almost everyone to remember words in which R is the first letter as opposed to the third. The availability bias is why more people are afraid to fly than statistics would support. Every single plane crash is plastered all over the news, making plane crashes more available in memory than successful plane landings. Aside from the availability bias, there are many other biases that affect the way we make decisions. Regardless of how often we fall victim to the biases, being aware of potential decision errors can help us make them less frequently.

Far more planes land safely in a year than not. However, safe plane landings are reported in the news and discussed in public far less often than are crashes, creating a tendency for people to base their judgment of how safe planes are on the number of crashes they hear about.

Faulty Attributions.
Another category of decision-making problems centers on how we explain the actions and events that occur around us. Research on attributions suggests that when people witness a behavior or outcome, they make a judgment about whether it was internally or externally caused. For example, when a coworker of yours named Joe shows up late to work and misses an important group presentation, you'll almost certainly make a judgment about why that happened. You might attribute Joe's outcome to internal factors—for example, suggesting that he is lazy or has a poor work ethic. Or you might attribute Joe's outcome to external factors—for example, suggesting that there was unusually bad traffic that day or that other factors prevented him from arriving on time.

The fundamental attribution error argues that people have a tendency to judge others' behaviors as due to internal factors.[49] This error suggests that you would likely judge

OB Internationally

Any time a major accident or ethical breach occurs in a company, the company is expected to respond accordingly. One natural reaction of employees, customers, and other observers is to attribute the cause of the negative event to someone. Who this blame gets placed on might be very different, depending on the part of the world in which the company is operating. A culture such as the United States tends to blame the particular individuals most responsible for the event, whereas East Asian (China, Korea, Japan) cultures tend to blame the organization itself.[50] For example, when scandals within organizations occur (e.g., "rogue trading" in an investment bank), newspapers in the United States often publish the name of the employee and discuss the individual worker involved, whereas East Asian newspapers refer to the organization itself.[51]

These biases place different responsibilities on the leaders of organizations in these countries. In East Asian cultures, it's typical for the leader of an organization to take the blame for accidents, regardless of whether he or she had direct responsibility for them.[52] For example, in 2002, the director of a hospital in Tokyo was forced to resign when the cover-up of a medical accident was discovered, even though the director didn't start his job until after the cover-up took place! In the United States, in contrast, CEOs rarely take the same level of blame. When Joseph Hazelwood crashed the Exxon *Valdez* into the Alaskan coastline, there were no calls for the Exxon CEO to resign.

Much of the reasoning for such differences has to do with the way the cultures view individuals and groups. East Asian cultures tend to treat groups as entities and not as individuals, whereas the culture in the United States tends to see individuals acting of their own accord.[53] This difference means that organizational leaders should be very cognizant of how to handle crises, depending on the country in which the negative event occurs. An apology offered by a senior leader is likely to be seen by East Asians as the company taking responsibility, whereas in the United States, it's more likely to be taken as an admission of personal guilt.[54] ❖

● HEURISTICS Simple and efficient rules of thumb that allow one to make decisions more easily.

● AVAILABILITY BIAS The tendency for people to base their judgments on information that is easier to recall.

● FUNDAMENTAL ATTRIBUTION ERROR The tendency for people to judge others' behaviors as being due to internal factors such as ability, motivation, or attitudes.

● SELF-SERVING BIAS When one attributes one's own failures to external factors and success to internal factors.

● ESCALATION OF COMMITMENT A common decision-making error in which the decision maker continues to follow a failing course of action.

Joe as having low motivation, poor organizational skills, or some other negative internal attribute. What if you yourself had showed up late? It turns out that we're less harsh when judging ourselves. The self-serving bias occurs when we attribute our own failures to external factors and our own successes to internal factors. Interestingly, evidence suggests that attributions across cultures don't always work the same way; see our **OB Internationally** feature for more discussion of this issue.

One model of attribution processes suggests that when people have a level of familiarity with the person being judged, they'll use a more detailed decision framework. This model is illustrated in Figure 7-4.[55] To return to our previous example, if we want to explore why Joe arrived late to work, we can ask three kinds of questions:

arrived late), high distinctiveness (Joe is responsible with other commitments), and low consistency (Joe has never come late to work before).

Escalation of Commitment.

Our last category of decision-making problems centers on what happens as a decision begins to go wrong. Escalation of commitment refers to the decision to continue to follow a failing course of action.[56] The expression "throwing good money after bad" captures this common decision-making error. An enormous amount of research shows that people have a tendency, when presented with a series of decisions, to escalate their commitment to previous decisions, even in the face of obvious failures.[57] Why do decision makers fall victim to this sort of error? They may feel an obligation to stick with their decision

> "An enormous amount of research shows that people have a tendency, when presented with a series of decisions, to escalate their commitment to previous decisions, even in the face of obvious failures."

Consensus: Did others act the same way under similar situations? In other words, did others arrive late on the same day?

Distinctiveness: Does this person tend to act differently in other circumstances? In other words, is Joe responsible when it comes to personal appointments, not just work appointments?

Consistency: Does this person always do this when performing this task? In other words, has Joe arrived late for work before?

The way in which these questions are answered will determine if an internal or external attribution is made. An internal attribution such as laziness or low motivation for Joe will occur if there is low consensus (others arrived on time), low distinctiveness (Joe is irresponsible with other commitments as well), and high consistency (Joe has arrived late before). An external attribution such as bad traffic or a power outage will occur if there is high consensus (others

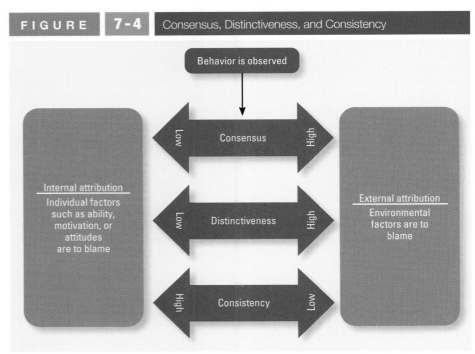

FIGURE 7-4 Consensus, Distinctiveness, and Consistency

Behavior is observed

Consensus — Low / High

Distinctiveness — Low / High

Consistency — High / Low

Internal attribution
Individual factors such as ability, motivation, or attitudes are to blame

External attribution
Environmental factors are to blame

to avoid looking incompetent. They also may want to avoid admitting that they made a mistake. Those escalation tendencies become particularly strong when decision makers have invested a lot of money into the decision and when the project in question seems quite close to completion.[58] One example of escalation of commitment can be found in this chapter's **OB in Sports** feature.

One recent example of escalation of commitment is United Airlines' abandonment of the automated baggage-handling system at the Denver International Airport. When it opened in 1995 (after a two-year delay), the baggage-handling system with 26 miles of track designed to haul baggage across three terminals was supposed to be the single most advanced baggage-handling system in the world. However, though it was originally scheduled to cost $186 million, a series of delays and technological problems caused the cost of the system to skyrocket by $1 million per day. Because of a series of technological issues, the system never really worked very well. In fact, United was the only airline in the airport willing to use it. It took 10 years and many mangled and lost suitcases before United finally "cut its losses" in 2005, saving itself $1 million a month in maintenance fees.[59]

 7.7

Understand how learning affects job performance and organizational commitment.

HOW IMPORTANT IS LEARNING?

Does learning have a significant impact on the two primary outcomes in our integrative model of OB—does it correlate with job performance and organizational commitment? Figure 7-5 summarizes the research evidence linking learning to job performance and organizational commitment.[60] The figure reveals that learning does influence job performance. Why? The primary reason is that learning is moderately correlated with task performance. It's difficult to fulfill job duties if the employee doesn't possess adequate levels of job knowledge. In fact, there are reasons to suggest that the moderate correlation depicted in the figure is actually an underestimate of learning's importance.

OB in Sports

Under most circumstances, you would think that a coach or a team would put the best team on the court—a team that maximizes the team's chances of winning. One National Basketball Association vice president thus claimed that "coaches play their best players and don't care what the person costs. Wins and losses are all that matters." Of course, that assertion assumes that these decision makers are rational in the way in which they go about making decisions. The fact is, they aren't. Both NBA general managers and coaches are fallible to the same kinds of decision-making errors that we all are. One notorious (and continuing) example is the escalation of commitment to high draft choices in the NBA.

Every year, the NBA draft allows teams to select the most promising and talented non-league players to join their teams (mostly from the college ranks, though some have come straight out of high school). An enormous amount of effort and thought goes into selecting the best player available for each team. Top draft choices get large contracts and are expected to contribute to their teams almost immediately. Unfortunately, sometimes a bad choice is made. Michael Olowokandi, Kwame Brown, Darko Milicic, and Sam Bowie are but a few names of very high draft choices (#1 or #2) that never played anywhere near their billing. Escalation of commitment rears its ugly head when general managers and coaches are not willing to cut their losses when a choice doesn't work out. One study clearly shows that high draft choices are given more minutes of playing time, are less likely to be traded, and stay around longer in the league than their performance warrants.[61] Why does this happen? Perhaps general managers and coaches don't want to look like they have made a poor decision, or perhaps they aren't willing to admit they made a bad mistake. ❖

In the 1998 draft, Michael Olowokandi was chosen first by the Los Angeles Clippers. For five years, he struggled with the team, never showing the skills he should have as a number 1 draft pick, before he was finally let go.

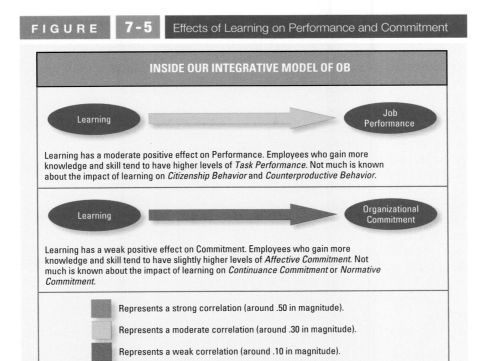

FIGURE 7-5 Effects of Learning on Performance and Commitment

INSIDE OUR INTEGRATIVE MODEL OF OB

Learning → Job Performance

Learning has a moderate positive effect on Performance. Employees who gain more knowledge and skill tend to have higher levels of *Task Performance*. Not much is known about the impact of learning on *Citizenship Behavior* and *Counterproductive Behavior*.

Learning → Organizational Commitment

Learning has a weak positive effect on Commitment. Employees who gain more knowledge and skill tend to have slightly higher levels of *Affective Commitment*. Not much is known about the impact of learning on *Continuance Commitment* or *Normative Commitment*.

Represents a strong correlation (around .50 in magnitude).

Represents a moderate correlation (around .30 in magnitude).

Represents a weak correlation (around .10 in magnitude).

Sources: G. M. Alliger, S. I. Tannenbaum, W. Bennett Jr., H. Traver, and A. Shotland, "A Meta-Analysis of the Relations among Training Criteria," *Personnel Psychology* 50 (1997), pp. 341–58; J. A. Colquitt, J. A. Lepine, and R. A. Noe, "Toward an Integrative Theory of Training Motivation: A Meta-Analytic Path Analysis of 20 Years of Research," *Journal of Applied Psychology* 85 (2000), pp. 678–707; J. P. Meyer, D. J. Stanley, L. Herscovitch, and L. Topolnytsky, "Affective, Continuance, and Normative Commitment to the Organization: A Meta-Analysis of Antecedents, Correlates, and Consequences," *Journal of Vocational Behavior* 61 (2002), pp. 20–52.

That's because most of the research linking learning to task performance focuses on explicit learning, which is more practical to measure. It's difficult to measure tacit knowledge because of its unspoken nature, but clearly such knowledge is relevant to task performance. Learning seems less relevant to citizenship behavior and counterproductive behavior however, given that those behaviors are often less dependent on knowledge and expertise.

Figure 7-5 also reveals that learning is only weakly related to organizational commitment. In general, having higher levels of job knowledge is associated with slight increases in emotional attachment to the firm. It is true that companies that have a reputation as organizations that value learning tend to receive higher-quality applicants for jobs.[62] However, there is an important distinction between organizations that offer learning opportunities and employees who take advantage of those opportunities to actually gain knowledge. Moreover, it may be that employees with higher levels of expertise become more highly valued commodities on the job market, thereby reducing their levels of continuance commitment. ■

CHECK OUT

www.mhhe.com/ColquittEss

for study materials including Interactive Exercises, Quizzes, iPod downloads, and video.

CASE: Caterpillar

Current demographic trends hold that many companies have a large number of older workers in comparison to a relatively smaller number of younger employees. Caterpillar is no exception. This situation is known to companies as the impending "brain drain." The strong worry is that when older workers retire, they will be taking a huge amount of knowledge and experience with them that cannot be easily replaced or passed on. Less than 25 percent of companies are considering how to transfer knowledge from aging, soon-to-retire employees to younger workers,[63] which means Caterpillar has accomplished something few other companies have. At least it is doing something to manage knowledge sharing within its organization. However, it are far from being finished.

Although much of the information within Caterpillar is explicit in nature, the reality is that there is a huge amount of tacit knowledge that is difficult to transfer from one employee to the next. Ideally, this information would get passed through Caterpillar's Knowledge Management System; however, many of the employees that know it might not even recognize their specialized knowledge. Even if they did, these experienced employees might not be able to express it in written form.

7.1 Can tacit knowledge be transferred to new Caterpillar employees through its Knowledge Management System? Explain.

7.2 How can Caterpillar go about identifying who holds this kind of knowledge and which aspects of the knowledge are most important?

7.3 How else might Caterpillar transfer knowledge in a way that might get at some of the tacit knowledge its older workers have? Should this method be a replacement for or an addition to its current knowledge transfer system?

TAKEAWAYS

7.1 Learning is a relatively permanent change in an employee's knowledge or skill that results from experience. Decision making refers to the process of generating and choosing from a set of alternatives to solve a problem.

7.2 Employees gain both explicit and tacit knowledge as they build expertise. Explicit knowledge is easily communicated and available to everyone. Tacit knowledge, however, is something employees can only learn through experience.

7.3 Employees learn new knowledge through reinforcement and observation of others. That learning also depends on whether the employees are learning-oriented or performance-oriented.

7.4 Through various forms of training, companies can give employees more knowledge and a wider array of experiences that they can use to make decisions.

7.5 Programmed decisions are decisions that become somewhat automatic because a person's knowledge allows him or her to recognize and identify a situation and the course of action that needs to be taken. Many task-related decisions made by experts are programmed decisions. Nonprogrammed decisions are made when a problem is new, complex, or not recognized. Ideally, such decisions are made by following the steps in the rational decision-making model.

7.6 Employees are less able to translate their learning into accurate decisions when they struggle with limited information, faulty perceptions, faulty attributions, and escalation of commitment.

7.7 Learning has a moderate positive relationship with job performance and a weak positive relationship with organizational commitment.

DISCUSSION QUESTIONS

7.1 In your current or past workplaces, what types of tacit knowledge did experienced workers possess? What did this knowledge allow them to do?

7.2 Given your occupational choice, how do you expect to learn what you need to know when you start working? Do you expect the company to provide you with these opportunities, or will you have to seek them out on your own?

7.3 Do you consider yourself a "rational" decision maker? For what types of decisions are you determined to be the most rational? What types of decisions are likely to cause you to behave irrationally?

7.4 Given your background, which of the decision-making biases listed in the chapter do you most struggle with? What could you do to overcome those biases to make more accurate decisions?

ASSESSMENT: Goal Orientation

What does your goal orientation look like? This assessment is designed to measure all three dimensions of goal orientation. Please write a number next to each statement that indicates the extent to which it accurately describes your attitude toward work while you are on the job. Answer each question using the response scale provided. Then sum up your answers for each of the three dimensions. (For more assessments relevant to this chapter, please visit the Online Learning Center at www.mhhe.com/ColquittEss.)

1	2	3	4	5
Strongly Disagree	**Disagree**	**Neutral**	**Agree**	**Strongly Agree**

1. I am willing to select challenging assignments that I can learn a lot from. _____
2. I often look for opportunities to develop new skills and knowledge. _____
3. I enjoy challenging and difficult tasks where I'll learn new skills. _____
4. For me, development of my ability is important enough to take risks. _____
5. I prefer to work in situations that require a high level of ability and talent. _____
6. I like to show that I can perform better than my coworkers. _____
7. I try to figure out what it takes to prove my ability to others at work. _____
8. I enjoy it when others at work are aware of how well I am doing. _____
9. I prefer to work on projects where I can prove my ability to others. _____
10. I would avoid taking on a new task if there was a chance that I would appear incompetent to others. _____
11. Avoiding a show of low ability is more important to me than learning a new skill. _____
12. I'm concerned about taking on a task at work if my performance would reveal that I had low ability. _____
13. I prefer to avoid situations at work where I might perform poorly.

Scoring

Learning Orientation: Sum up items 1–5.
Performance-Prove Orientation: Sum up items 6–9.
Performance-Avoid Orientation: Sum up items 10–13.

Interpretation

For learning orientation, scores of 20 or more are above average, and scores of 19 or less are below average. For the two performance orientations, scores of 15 or more are above average, and scores of 14 or less are below average.

Source: Adapted from J. F. Brett and D. VandeWalle, "Goal Orientation and Goal Content as Predictors of Performance in a Training Program," *Journal of Applied Psychology* 84 (1999), pp. 863–73.

EXERCISE: Decision-Making Bias

The purpose of this exercise is to illustrate how decision making can be influenced by decision heuristics, availability bias, and escalation of commitment. This exercise uses groups, so your instructor will either assign you to a group or ask you to create your own group. The exercise has the following steps:

1. Answer each of the problems below.

   A. A certain town is served by two hospitals. In the larger hospital, about 45 babies are born each day, and in the smaller hospital, about 15 babies are born each day. Although the overall proportion of boys is about 50 percent, the actual proportion at either hospital may be greater or less than 50 percent on any given day. At the end of a year, which hospital will have the greater number of days on which more than 60 percent of the babies born were boys?

   a. The large hospital.

   b. The small hospital.

   c. Neither—the number of days will be about the same (within 5 percent of each other).

   B. Linda is 31, single, outspoken, and very bright. She majored in philosophy in college. As a student, she was deeply concerned with discrimination and other social issues and participated in antinuclear demonstrations. Which statement is more likely:

   a. Linda is a bank teller.

   b. Linda is a bank teller and active in the feminist movement.

   C. A cab was involved in a hit-and-run accident. Two cab companies serve the city: the Green, which operates

85 percent of the cabs, and the Blue, which operates the remaining 15 percent. A witness identifies the hit-and-run cab as Blue. When the court tests the reliability of the witness under circumstances similar to those on the night of the accident, he correctly identifies the color of the cab 80 percent of the time and misidentifies it the other 20 percent. What's the probability that the cab involved in the accident was Blue, as the witness stated?

D. Imagine that you face this pair of concurrent decisions. Examine these decisions, then indicate which choices you prefer.

Decision I: Choose between:

   a. a sure gain of $240 and

   b. a 25 percent chance of winning $1,000 and a 75 percent chance of winning nothing.

Decision II: Choose between:

   a. a sure loss of $750 and

   b. a 75 percent chance of losing $1,000 and a 25 percent chance of losing nothing.

Decision III: Choose between:

   a. a sure loss of $3,000 and

   b. an 80 percent chance of losing $4,000 and a 20 percent chance of losing nothing.

E. a. You've decided to see a Broadway play and have bought a $40 ticket. As you enter the theater, you realize you've lost your ticket. You can't remember the seat number, so you can't prove to the management that you bought a ticket. Would you spend $40 for a new ticket?

   b. You've reserved a seat for a Broadway play, for which the ticket price is $40. As you enter the theater to buy your ticket, you discover you've lost $40 from your pocket. Would you still buy the ticket? (Assume you have enough cash left to do so.)

F. Imagine you have operable lung cancer and must choose between two treatments: surgery and radiation. Of 100 people having surgery, 10 die during the operation, 32 (including those original 10) are dead after one year, and 66 are dead after five years. Of 100 people having radiation therapy, none dies during treatment, 23 are dead after one year, and 78 after five years. Which treatment would you prefer?

2. Your instructor will give you the correct answer to each problem.

3. Class discussion, whether in groups or as a class, should focus on the following questions: How accurate were the decisions you reached? What decision-making problems were evident in the decisions you reached? Consider especially where decision heuristics, availability, and escalation of commitment may have influenced your decisions. How could you improve your decision making to make it more accurate?

This exercise originally appeared in *Organizational Behavior and Management* (7th ed.) by J. M. Ivancevich, R. Konopaske, and M. T. Matteson (New York: McGraw-Hill, 2005); used with permission. Original exercises are based on (1) A. Tversky and D. Kahneman, "Rational Choice and the Framing of Decisions," *Journal of Business* 59 (1986), pp. 251–78; (2) A. Tversky and D. Kahneman, "The Framing of Decisions and the Psychology of Choice," *Science* 211 (1981), pp. 453–58; (3) A. Tversky and D. Kahneman, "Extensional vs. Intuitive Reasoning: The Conjunction Fallacy in Probability Judgment," *Psychological Review* 90 (1983), pp. 293–315; and (4) K. McKean, "Decisions, Decisions," *Discovery Magazine*, June 1985.

END NOTES

1. Bingham, T., and P. Galagan. "Learning Is a Powerful Tool." *T + D* 62 (2008), pp. 31–37.

2. Ibid.

3. Powers, V. "Virtual Communities at Caterpillar Foster Knowledge Sharing." *T + D* 58 (2004), pp. 40–45.

4. Bingham, "Learning Is a Powerful Tool."

5. Ibid.

6. "Caterpillar Nurtures Knowledge-Sharing Environment." *LXBriefing*, 2007, http://www.astd.org (accessed June 16, 2008).

7. Powers, "Virtual Communities."

8. Weiss, H. M. "Learning Theory and Industrial and Organizational Psychology." In *Handbook of Industrial and Organizational Psychology,* ed. M. D. Dunnette and L. M. Hough. Palo Alto, CA: Consulting Psychologists Press, 1990, pp. 75–169.

9. Tai, B., and N. R. Lockwood. "Organizational Entry: Onboarding, Orientation, and Socialization." *SHRM Research Paper,* http://www.shrm.org (accessed June 4, 2007).

10. Buford, B. *Heat.* New York: Knopf, 2006, pp. 49–50.

11. Ericsson, K. A. "An Introduction to *Cambridge Handbook of Expertise and Expert Performance*: Its Development, Organization, and Content." In *The Cambridge Handbook of Expertise and Expert Performance,* ed. K. A. Ericsson, N. Charness, P. J. Feltovich, and R. R. Hoffman. New York: Cambridge University Press, 2006, pp. 3–19.

12. Ericsson, K. A., and A. C. Lehmann. "Experts and Exceptional Performance: Evidence of Maximal Adaptation to

Task Constraints." *Annual Review of Psychology* 47 (1996), pp. 273–305.

13. Brockmann, E. N., and W. P. Anthony. "Tacit Knowledge and Strategic Decision Making." *Group & Organizational Management* 27 (December 2002), pp. 436–55.

14. Wagner, R. K., and R. J. Sternberg. "Practical Intelligence in Real-World Pursuits: The Role of Tacit Knowledge." *Journal of Personality and Social Psychology* 4 (1985), pp. 436–58.

15. Wah, L. "Making Knowledge Stick." *Management Review* 88 (1999), pp. 24–33.

16. Eucker, T. R. "Understanding the Impact of Tacit Knowledge Loss." *Knowledge Management Review*, March 2007, pp. 10–13.

17. Lawson, C., and E. Lorenzi. "Collective Learning, Tacit Knowledge, and Regional Innovative Capacity." *Regional Studies* 21 (1999), pp. 487–513.

18. Nonaka, I. "The Knowledge-Creating Company." *Harvard Business Review* 69 (1991), pp. 96–104; Nonaka, I. "A Dynamic Theory of Organizational Knowledge Creation." *Organizational Science* 5 (1994), pp. 14–37.

19. Luthans, F., and R. Kreitner. *Organizational Behavior Modification and Beyond.* Glenview, IL: Scott, Foresman, 1985.

20. Bandura, A. *Social Foundations of Thought and Action: A Social Cognitive Theory.* Englewood Cliffs, NJ: Prentice Hall, 1986.

21. Weiss, "Learning Theory."

22. Pescuric, A., and W. C. Byham. "The New Look of Behavior Modeling." *Training & Development* 50 (July 1996), pp. 24–30.

23. Weber, J. "The Accidental CEO." *BusinessWeek*, April 23, 2007, pp. 64–72.

24. Sims, R. R., and J. Brinkmann. "Leaders as Moral Role Models: The Case of John Gutfreund at Salomon Brothers." *Journal of Business Ethics* 35 (2002), pp. 327–40.

25. "Spending on Learning and Training is Increasing: ASTD Report." *HR Focus* 83 (2006), p. 9; "$56 Billion Budgeted for Formal Training." *Training* 43, 2006, pp. 20–32.

26. Carnevale, A. P. "The Learning Enterprise." *Training and Development Journal*, February 1989, pp. 26–37.

27. "$56 Billion Budgeted for Formal Training."

28. Sauve, E. "Informal Knowledge Transfer." *T + D* 61 (2007), pp. 22–24.

29. Noe, R. A. *Employee Training and Development.* Burr Ridge, IL: Irwin/McGraw-Hill, 1999.

30. VandeWalle, D. "Development and Validation of a Work Domain Goal Orientation Instrument." *Educational and Psychological Measurement* 8 (1997), pp. 995–1015.

31. Folkers, D. "Competing in the Marketspace: Incorporating Online Education into Higher Education—An Organizational Perspective." *Information Resources Management Journal* 18 (2005), pp. 61–77.

32. Golden, D. "Degrees@StateU; Online University Enrollment Soars as Quality Improves; Tuition Funds Other Projects." *The Wall Street Journal*, May 9, 2006, p. B1.

33. Ibid.

34. Sitzman, T.; K. Kraiger; D. Stewart; and R. Wisher. "The Comparative Effectiveness of Web-Based and Classroom Instruction: A Meta-Analysis." *Personnel Psychology* 59 (2006), pp. 623–64. See also Zhao, Y.; J. Lei; B. Y. C. Lai; and H. S. Tan. "What Makes the Difference? A Practical Analysis of Research on the Effectiveness of Distance Education." *Teachers College Record* 107 (2005), pp. 1836–84.

35. Arbaugh, J. B. "Is There an Optimal Design for On-Line MBA Courses?" *Academy of Management Learning and Education* 4 (2005), pp. 135–49.

36. Clark, R. C. "Harnessing the Virtual Classroom." *T + D* 59 (2005), pp. 40–45.

37. Payne, S. C.; S. Youngcourt; and J. M. Beaubien. "A Meta-Analytic Examination of the Goal Orientation Nomological Net." *Journal of Applied Psychology* 92 (2007), pp. 128–50.

38. Dane, E., and M. G. Pratt. "Exploring Intuition and Its Role in Managerial Decision Making." *Academy of Management Review* 32 (2007), pp. 33–54.

39. Hayashi, A. M. "When to Trust Your Gut." *Harvard Business Review*, February 2001, pp. 59–65.

40. March, J. G. *A Primer on Decision Making.* New York: Free Press, 1994.

41. http://www.quotationspage.com/quote/25953.html (accessed April 2007).

42. Simon, H. A. "A Behavioral Model of Rational Choice." *Quarterly Journal of Economics* 69 (1955), pp. 99–118.

43. Simon, H. A. "Rational Decision Making in Organizations." *American Economic Review* 69 (1979), pp. 493–513.

44. March, J. G., and H. A. Simon. *Organizations.* New York: Wiley, 1958.

45. Hogg, M. A., and D. J. Terry. "Social Identity and Self-Categorization Process in Organizational Contexts." *Academy of Management Review* 25 (January 2000), pp. 121–40; Judd, C. M., and B. Park. "Definition and Assessment of Accuracy in Social Stereotypes." *Psychological Review* 100 (January 1993), pp. 109–28.

46. Ashforth, B. E., and F. Mael. "Social Identity Theory and the Organization." *Academy of Management Review* 14 (1989), pp. 20–39; Howard, J. A. "Social Psychology of Identities." *Annual Review of Sociology* 26 (2000), pp. 367–93.

47. Kahneman, D.; P. Slovic; and A. Tversky, eds. *Judgment under Uncertainty: Heuristics and Biases.* Cambridge, UK: Cambridge University Press, 1982.

48. Kahneman, D., and A. Tversky. "On the Psychology of Prediction." *Psychological Review* 80 (1973), pp. 237–51.

49. Ross, L. "The Intuitive Psychologist and His Shortcomings: Distortions in the Attribution Process." In *Advances in Experimental Social Psychology*, ed. L. Berkowitz. New York: Academic Press, 1977, pp. 173–220. See also Jones, E. E., and V. A. Harris. "The Attribution of Attitudes." *Journal of Experimental Social Psychology* 3 (1967), pp. 1–24.

50. Zemba, Y.; M. I. Young; and M. W. Morris. "Blaming Leaders for Organizational Accidents: Proxy Logic in Collective versus Individual-Agency Cultures." *Organizational Behavior and Human Decision Processes* 101 (2006), pp. 36–51.

51. Menon, T.; M. W. Morris; C. Chiu; and Y. Hong. "Culture and the Construal of Agency: Attribution to Individual versus Group Dispositions." *Journal of Personality and Social Psychology* 76 (1999), pp. 701–17.

52. Zemba et al., "Blaming Leaders."

53. Chiu, C.; M. W. Morris; Y. Hong; and T. Menon. "Motivated Cultural Cognition: The Impact of Implicit Cultural Theories on Dispositional Attribution Varies as a Function of Need for Closure." *Journal of Personality and Social Psychology* 78 (2000), pp. 247–59.

54. Zemba et al., "Blaming Leaders."

55. Kelley, H. H. "The Processes of Casual Attribution." *American Psychologist* 28 (1973), pp. 107–28; Kelley, H. H. "Attribution in Social Interaction." In *Attribution: Perceiving the Causes of Behavior*, ed. E. Jones. Morristown, NJ: General Learning Press, 1972.

56. Staw, B. M., and J. Ross. "Behavior in Escalation Situations: Antecedents, Prototypes, and Solutions." In *Research in Organizational Behavior*, Vol. 9, ed. L. L. Cummings and B. M. Staw. Greenwich, CT: JAI Press, 1987, pp. 39–78; Staw, B. M. "Knee-Deep in the Big Muddy: A Study of Escalating Commitment to a Chosen Course of Action." *Organizational Behavior and Human Performance* 16 (1976), pp. 27–44.

57. Brockner, J. "The Escalation of Commitment to a Failing Course of Action: Toward Theoretical Progress." *Academy of Management Review* 17 (1992), pp. 39–61; Staw, B. M. "The Escalation of Commitment: An Update and Appraisal." In *Organizational Decision Making,* ed. Z. Shapira. New York: Cambridge University Press, 1997.

58. Conlon, D. E., and H. Garland. "The Role of Project Completion Information in Resource Allocation Decisions." *Academy of Management Journal* 36 (1993), pp. 402–13; Moon, H. "Looking Forward and Looking Back: Integrating Completion and Sunk-Cost Effects within an Escalation of Commitment Progress Decision." *Journal of Applied Psychology* 86 (2001), pp. 104–13.

59. Johnson, K. "Denver Airport to Mangle Last Bag." *New York Times*, August 27, 2005.

60. Alliger, G. M.; S. I. Tannenbaum; W. Bennett Jr.; H. Traver; and A. Shotland. "A Meta-Analysis of the Relations among Training Criteria." *Personnel Psychology* 50 (1997), pp. 341–58; Colquitt, J. A.; J. A. Lepine; and R. A. Noe. "Toward an Integrative Theory of Training Motivation: A Meta-Analytic Path Analysis of 20 Years of Research." *Journal of Applied Psychology* 85 (2000), pp. 678–707; Meyer, J. P.; D. J. Stanley; L. Herscovitch, and L. Topolnytsky. "Affective, Continuance, and Normative Commitment to the Organization: A Meta-Analysis of Antecedents, Correlates, and Consequences." *Journal of Vocational Behavior* 61 (2002), pp. 20–52.

61. Staw, B. M., and H. Hoang. "Sunk Costs in the NBA: Why Draft Order Affects Playing Time and Survival in Professional Basketball." *Administrative Science Quarterly* 40 (1995), pp. 474–94.

62. Averbrook, J. "Connecting CLO's with the Recruiting Process." *Chief Learning Officer* 4 (2005), pp. 24–27.

63. Leonard, B. "Small Firms Prepare for Aging Workforce." *HRMagazine* 53 (2008), p. 32.

PERSONALITY, CULTURAL VALUES *and* ABILITY

● ● learning **OBJECTIVES**

After reading this chapter, you should be able to:

8.1 Define personality, cultural values, and ability.

8.2 Understand the "Big Five" dimensions of personality.

8.3 Understand Hofstede's dimensions of cultural values.

8.4 Describe the dimensions of cognitive ability.

8.5 Describe the dimensions of emotional ability.

8.6 Understand how ability and personality affect job performance and organizational commitment.

FOUR SEASONS

"If there's a heaven, I hope it's run by Four Seasons."[1] Those words, uttered by a guest at the hotel's Maui location, illustrate how much affection its customers have for the Canada-based luxury hotel and resorts company. Isadore Sharp opened the first Four Seasons in Toronto in 1961, envisioning a hotel that was large enough to offer an extensive array of amenities but small enough to create a sense of intimacy and personalized attention.[2] Four Seasons pioneered many of the amenities that are now taken for granted at upscale hotels, including complimentary shampoo, 24-hour room service, bathrobes, a two-line phone, and a pillow-top bed. The number of Four Seasons hotels has grown to 73 in 31 countries, with 18 of those ranked in Condé Nast Traveler's Top 100 hotels in the world (that's more than three times the next-most-cited chain).[3] Sharp explains that sort of success by contrasting Four Season's philosophy with the traditional view of upscale hotels: "Luxury, at that time, was seen chiefly as architecture and décor. . . . We decided to redefine luxury as service—a support system to fill in for the one left at home and the office."

Differentiating its hotels based on the quality of their service obviously puts a great deal of pressure on Four Seasons employees. Fortunately, the chain goes to great lengths to find the right employees. Every applicant—from prospective laundry folders to potential yoga trainers—is put through at least four interviews.[4] After all, the company isn't just looking for experience, which can be seen on a resume; it's looking for the right personality. Thomas Steinhauer, the vice president of the hotel's Hawaiian locations, describes that personality this way: "In this business, you have to have an adventurous streak. . . . You need to take pride in what you do, and you have to have a sense of compassion. And if you're judgmental, you're dead." For his part, Sharp emphasizes that the interviews look for people who have a positive outlook and who are comfortable with a "do unto others" philosophy, noting, "I can teach anyone to be a waiter. . . . But you can't change an ingrained poor attitude." The company is also looking for a specific set of abilities and talents. Because Four Seasons wants its employees to do their jobs in their own unique way,[5] employees have to demonstrate an ability to think on their feet, read and anticipate the needs of guests, be original and instinctive, and improvise.[6]

Of course, all the interviews in the world can't deliver the right mix of personality, values, and ability if there are only 20 applicants for 20 openings. Four Seasons doesn't have to worry about that sort of ratio, however, as it's taken a number of steps to become the "employer of choice" in the hotel industry. Salaries are in the 75th to 90th percentile of the industry, and any employee with six months of tenure can stay three nights free at any Four Seasons hotel.[7] For applicants on the managerial track, Four Seasons offers an aggressive policy of promoting from within while giving trainees the chance to see the world by working at different hotels in different cultures. As a result of such policies, Four Seasons received 25,000 applications for the 600 openings in its new hotel in Doha, Qatar. Moreover, its 18 percent turnover rate stands at just half the industry average. As Sharp summarizes, "Personal service is not something you can dictate as a policy. . . . How you treat your employees is how you expect them to treat the customer."

PERSONALITY, CULTURAL VALUES, AND ABILITY

It seems clear from the opening example that Four Seasons looks for a particular set of characteristics in its employees. Of course, employees can be described, evaluated, and differentiated in a variety of ways, on a number of dimensions. For example, employees can be described on the basis of their personality. **Personality** refers to the structures, propensities, and traits inside a person that explain his or her characteristic patterns of thought, emotion, and behavior.[8] Personality creates a person's social reputation—the way he or she is perceived by friends, family, coworkers, and supervisors.[9] Employees also can be described on the basis of their cultural values. **Cultural values** reflect the shared beliefs about desirable end states or modes of conduct in a given culture.[10] These shared values influence the traits, thoughts, feelings, and behaviors of the individuals who grow up in, or experience, a given culture. Finally, employees can be described on the basis of their ability. **Ability** refers to the relatively stable capabilities employees possess that allow them to perform a particular range of related activities.[11] In contrast to skills, which can be improved over time with training and experience, ability is relatively stable.

What people are like, what people can do, and where people are from make up a set of individual differences that are important to address and understand.

 8.1

Define personality, cultural values, and ability.

Taken together, these sorts of "individual differences" can tell us a lot about people, with personality capturing *what people are like*, ability capturing *what people can do*, and cultural values capturing *where people are from* (in a cultural sense). Indeed, we rely on these individual differences whenever we try to describe one person to another. For example, think about the last time a new coworker joined your work unit. Perhaps you described that coworker as organized, polite, and somewhat shy. Each of those adjectives is an aspect of personality. Or maybe you described him or her as smart and quick, both of which reflect aspects of ability. After spending more time around your new coworker, you might notice that he or she is especially attentive to group norms and feels uncomfortable questioning the opinions of "higher-ups." Both tendencies may be expressions of key cultural values that have shaped the employee's thoughts, feelings, and behaviors. The sections to follow review personality, cultural values, and ability in more detail.

Personality

Even though we sometimes describe people as having "a good personality," personality is actually a collection of multiple specific traits. **Traits** are defined as recurring regularities or trends in people's responses to their environment.[12] When we described your coworker as organized, polite, and shy, we used three specific personality traits. Of course, it takes more than three traits to describe a person's personality, and we can typically offer a laundry list of adjectives to describe friends, coworkers, and family members. How long could that list potentially be? Well, personality researchers note that the third edition of *Webster's Unabridged Dictionary* contains 1,710 adjectives that can be used to describe someone's traits![13] Fortunately, it turns out that most adjectives are variations of five broad "factors" or "dimensions" that can be used to summarize our personalities.[14] Those five personality dimensions include *conscientiousness*, *agreeableness*, *neuroticism*, *openness to experience*, and *extraversion*. Collectively, these dimensions have been dubbed the **Big Five**.[15] Figure 8-1 lists the traits that can be found within each of the Big Five dimensions. We acknowledge that it can be hard to remember the particular labels for the Big Five dimensions, and we only wish there was some acronym that could make the process easier. . . .

FIGURE 8-1 Trait Adjectives Associated with the Big Five

C	A	N	O	E
Conscientiousness	Agreeableness	Neuroticism	Openness	Extraversion
• Dependable • Organized • Reliable • Ambitious • Hardworking • Persevering	• Kind • Cooperative • Sympathetic • Helpful • Courteous • Warm	• Nervous • Moody • Emotional • Insecure • Jealous • Unstable	• Curious • Imaginative • Creative • Complex • Refined • Sophisticated	• Talkative • Sociable • Passionate • Assertive • Bold • Dominant
NOT	NOT	NOT	NOT	NOT
• Careless • Sloppy • Inefficient • Negligent • Lazy • Irresponsible	• Critical • Antagonistic • Callous • Selfish • Rude • Cold	• Calm • Steady • Relaxed • At ease • Secure • Contented	• Uninquisitive • Conventional • Conforming • Simple • Unartistic • Traditional	• Quiet • Shy • Inhibited • Bashful • Reserved • Submissive

Sources: G. Saucier, "Mini-Markers: A Brief Version of Goldberg's Unipolar Big-Five Markers," *Journal of Personality Assessment* 63 (1994), pp. 506–16; L. R. Goldberg, "The Development of Markers for the Big-Five Factor Structure," *Psychological Assessment* 4 (1992), pp. 26–42; R. R. McCrae and P. T. Costa Jr., "Validation of the Five-Factor Model of Personality across Instruments and Observers," *Journal of Personality and Social Psychology* 52 (1987), pp. 81–90.

8.2

Understand the "Big Five" dimensions of personality.

Conscientiousness. As shown in Figure 8-1, conscientious people are dependable, organized, reliable, ambitious, hardworking, and persevering.[16] It's difficult, if not impossible, to envision a job in which those traits will not be beneficial.[17] That's not a claim we make about all of the Big Five because some jobs require high levels of agreeableness, extraversion, or openness, while others demand low levels of those same traits. We don't want to spoil the "how important is personality?" discussion that concludes this chapter, but suffice it to say that conscientiousness has the biggest influence on job performance of any of the Big Five. Of course, the key question therefore becomes: Why is conscientiousness so valuable?

Conscientious salespeople set higher goals for themselves and are more committed to meeting those goals.

One reason can be found in the general goals that people prioritize in their working life. Conscientious employees prioritize **accomplishment striving**, which reflects a strong desire to accomplish task-related goals as a means of expressing personality.[18] People who are "accomplishment strivers" have a built-in desire to finish work tasks, channel a high proportion of their efforts toward those tasks, and work harder and longer on task assignments. As evidence of their accomplishment-striving nature, one research study showed that conscientious salespeople set higher sales goals for themselves than unconscientious salespeople and were more committed to meeting those goals.[19] Another study of salespeople showed that conscientious salespeople's organizational skills were particularly valuable during their first year of employment, and their ambitious nature became more critical as they gained tenure and experience.[20]

A third research study provides particularly compelling evidence regarding the benefits of conscientiousness.[21] The study used data from the University of California, Berkeley's Intergenerational Studies, which collected data about a set of children in the late 1920s and early 1930s. Those researchers gathered personality data using interviews and assessments of the children by trained psychologists. Follow-up studies collected data on the same sample as they reached early adulthood, middle age, and late adulthood. This last time period included assessments of career success, which included ratings of annual income and occupational prestige. The results of the study showed that childhood conscientiousness was strongly correlated with ratings of career success five decades later! In fact, those conscientiousness effects were roughly twice as strong as the effects of the other Big Five dimensions. For more insights into the benefits of conscientiousness, see our **OB on Screen** feature.

Agreeableness. Agreeable people are warm, kind, cooperative, sympathetic, helpful, and courteous. Agreeable people prioritize **communion striving**, which reflects a strong desire to obtain acceptance in personal relationships as a means of expressing personality.[22] Put differently, agreeable people focus on "getting along," not necessarily "getting ahead."[23] Unlike conscientiousness, agreeableness is not related to performance across all jobs or occupations.[24] Why not? The biggest reason is that communion striving is beneficial in some positions but detrimental in others. For example, managers often need to prioritize the effectiveness of the unit over a desire to gain acceptance. In such cases, effective job performance may demand being disagreeable in the face of unreasonable requests or demands.

Of course, there are some jobs in which agreeableness can be beneficial. The most obvious example is service jobs—jobs in which the employee has direct, face-to-face, or verbal contact with a customer. How many times have you encountered a customer service person who is cold, rude, or antagonistic? Did you tend to buy the company's product after such experiences? Research suggests that agreeable employees have stronger customer service skills.[25] One reason for their effectiveness in customer service environments is that they are reluctant to react to conflict with criticism, threats, or manipulation.[26] Instead, they tend to react to conflict by walking away, adopting a "wait-and-see" attitude, or giving in to the other person.

Extraversion. Extraverted people are talkative, sociable, passionate, assertive, bold, and dominant (in contrast to introverts, who are quiet, shy, and reserved). Like agreeableness, extraversion is not necessarily related to performance across all jobs or occupations. However, extraverted people prioritize status striving, which reflects a strong desire to obtain power and influence within a social structure as a means of expressing personality.[27] Extraverts care a lot about being successful and influential and direct their work efforts toward "moving up" and developing a strong reputation. Indeed, research suggests that extraverts are more likely to emerge as leaders in social and task-related

● **ACCOMPLISHMENT STRIVING** A strong desire to accomplish task-related goals as a means of expressing personality.

● **COMMUNION STRIVING** A strong desire to obtain acceptance in personal relationships as a means of expressing personality.

● **STATUS STRIVING** A strong desire to obtain power and influence within a social structure as a means of expressing personality.

OB on Screen

The Break-Up

Brooke: You know what, Gary? I asked you to do one thing today, one very simple thing—to bring me 12 lemons—and you brought me 3.

Gary: If I knew that it was gonna be this much trouble, I would've brought home 24 lemons, even 100 lemons. You know what I wish? I wish everyone that was at that table had their own little private bag of lemons!

Brooke: It's not about the lemons. . . . I'm just saying it'd be nice if you did things that I asked. It would be even nicer if you did things without me having to ask you!

With those words, Gary (Vince Vaughn) and Brooke (Jennifer Aniston) reveal one of the biggest stumbling blocks in their relationship in *The Break-Up* (Dir.: Adam McKay, Sony Pictures, 2006). From Brooke's perspective, Gary isn't very conscientious. She put together a dinner party for their families and gave Gary one assignment: Bring home 12 lemons for a centerpiece. He brought 3. After the party was over, she had one additional request—to help her do the dishes. Gary wanted to play a video game instead, noting that they could do the dishes in the morning. That lack of conscientiousness extends to Gary's job, where he's fallen three months behind on his paperwork.

If Brooke and Gary decide to break up, what could Brooke do to find a more conscientious boyfriend the next time around? One approach might be to turn to dating Web sites that use personality tests to assess conscientiousness. For example, eHarmony requires members to spend 45 minutes filling out a 436-question personality test that assesses 29 different personality dimensions.[28] Two of those dimensions—"industry" and "ambition"—clearly represent conscientiousness.[29] ❖

groups.[30] They also tend to be rated as more effective in a leadership role by the people who are following them.[31] One potential reason for these findings is that people tend to view extraverts, who are more energetic and outgoing, as more "leaderlike" than introverts.

In addition to being related to leadership emergence and effectiveness, research suggests that extraverts tend to be happier with their jobs. You may recall from Chapter 3 on Job Satisfaction that people's day-to-day moods can be categorized along two dimensions: pleasantness and engagement. As illustrated in Figure 8-2, extraverted employees tend to be high in what's called positive affectivity—a dispositional tendency to experience pleasant, engaging moods such as enthusiasm, excitement, and elation.[32] That tendency to experience positive moods across situations explains why extraverts tend to be more satisfied with their jobs.[33] Research now acknowledges that employees' genes have a significant impact on their job satisfaction and that

"Research now acknowledges that employees' genes have a significant impact on their job satisfaction."

much of that genetic influence is due to extraversion (and neuroticism, as discussed next). For example, one study of identical twins reared apart showed that twins' job satisfaction levels were significantly correlated, even when the twins held jobs that were quite different in terms of their duties, their complexity, and their working conditions.[34] In fact, this study suggested that around 30 percent of the variation in job satisfaction is due to genetic factors such as personality.

Other research suggests that extraverts have more to be happy about than just their jobs. One study asked students to complete a "life event checklist" by indicating whether various events had happened to them in the preceding four years.[35] The results showed that extraversion was associated with more positive events such as joining a club or athletic team, going on vacation with friends, getting a raise at work, receiving an award for nonacademic reasons, and getting married or engaged. Other studies have linked extraversion to the number of same-sex peers, number

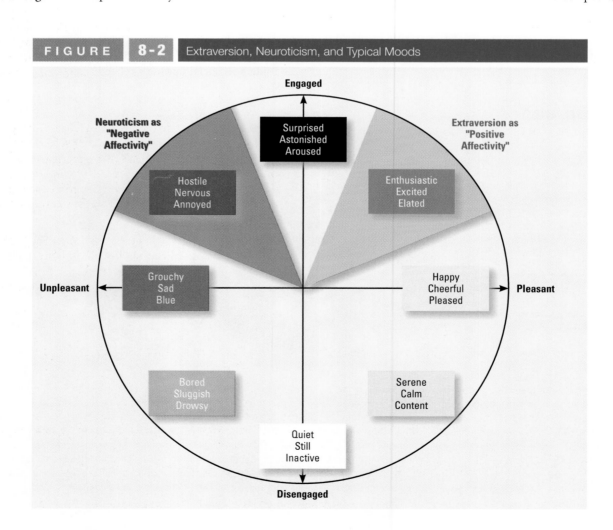

FIGURE 8-2 | Extraversion, Neuroticism, and Typical Moods

Engaged

Neuroticism as "Negative Affectivity"

Extraversion as "Positive Affectivity"

Surprised Astonished Aroused

Hostile Nervous Annoyed

Enthusiastic Excited Elated

Unpleasant

Grouchy Sad Blue

Happy Cheerful Pleased

Pleasant

Bored Sluggish Drowsy

Serene Calm Content

Quiet Still Inactive

Disengaged

● POSITIVE AFFECTIVI-
TY A dispositional tendency
to experience pleasant,
engaging moods such as
enthusiasm, excitement,
and elation.

● NEGATIVE AFFEC-
TIVITY A dispositional
tendency to experience
unpleasant moods such as
hostility, nervousness, and
annoyance.

● LOCUS OF CON-
TROL Whether people attribute the causes of events
to themselves or to the
external environment.

of dating partners, frequency of alcohol consumption, and frequency of attending parties.[36] However, extraverts spend so much time doing those things that they wind up having less frequent interactions with their family.[37] Even parents of extraverts enjoy a phone call home now and again!

Neuroticism.
Neurotic people are nervous, moody, emotional, insecure, and jealous. Occasionally you may see this Big Five dimension called by its flip side: "Emotional Stability" or "Emotional Adjustment." If conscientiousness is the most important of the Big Five from the perspective of job performance, neuroticism is the second most important.[38] There are few jobs for which the traits associated with neuroticism are beneficial to on-the-job behaviors. Instead, most jobs benefit from employees who are calm, steady, and secure.

Whereas extraversion is synonymous with positive affectivity, neuroticism is synonymous with negative affectivity—a dispositional tendency to experience unpleasant moods such as hostility, nervousness, and annoyance (see Figure 8-2).[39] That tendency to experience negative moods explains why neurotic employees often experience lower levels of job satisfaction than their less neurotic counterparts.[40] Along with extraversion, neuroticism explains much of the impact of genetic factors on job satisfaction. Research suggests that the negative affectivity associated with neuroticism even influences more general life satisfaction, such that neurotic people tend to be less happy with their lives in general.[41]

Neuroticism is also strongly related to locus of control, which reflects whether people attribute the causes of events to themselves or to the external environment.[42] Neurotic people tend to hold an *external* locus of control, meaning that they often believe that the events that occur around them are driven by luck, chance, or fate. Less neurotic people tend to hold an *internal* locus of control, meaning that they believe that their own behavior dictates events. Table 8-1 provides more detail about the external versus internal distinction. The table includes a number of beliefs that are representative of an external or internal viewpoint, including beliefs about life in general, work, school, politics, and relationships. If you tend to agree more strongly with the beliefs in the left column, then you have a more external locus of control. If you tend to agree more with the right column, your locus is more internal.

How important is locus of control? One meta-analysis of 135 different research studies showed that an internal locus of control was associated with higher levels of job satisfaction and job performance.[43] A second meta-analysis of 222 different research studies showed that people with an internal locus of control enjoyed better health, including higher self-reported mental well-being, fewer self-reported physical symptoms, lower blood pressure, and lower stress hormone secretion.[44] Internals also enjoyed more social support at work than externals and sensed that they had a stronger relationship with their supervisors. They viewed their jobs as having more beneficial characteristics such as autonomy and significance and fewer negative characteristics such as conflict and ambiguity. In addition, those with an internal locus of control earned a higher salary than those with an external locus.

Openness to Experience.
The final dimension of the Big Five is openness to experience. Open people are curious, imaginative, creative, complex, refined, and sophisticated. Of all the Big Five, openness to experience has the most alternative labels. Sometimes it's called "Inquisitiveness" or "Intellectualness" or even "Culture" (not in the national culture sense—rather, in the "high culture" sense of knowing fine wine,

TABLE 8-1	External and Internal Locus of Control
People with an External Locus of Control Tend to Believe:	**People with an Internal Locus of Control Tend to Believe:**
Many of the unhappy things in people's lives are partly due to bad luck.	People's misfortunes result from the mistakes they make.
Getting a good job depends mainly on being in the right place at the right time.	Becoming a success is a matter of hard work; luck has little or nothing to do with it.
Many times exam questions tend to be so unrelated to course work that studying is really useless.	In the case of the well-prepared student, there is rarely if ever such a thing as an unfair test.
This world is run by the few people in power, and there is not much the little guy can do about it.	The average citizen can have an influence in government decisions.
There's not much use in trying too hard to please people; if they like you, they like you.	People are lonely because they don't try to be friendly.

Source: Adapted from J. B. Rotter, "Generalized Expectancies for Internal versus External Control of Reinforcement," *Psychological Monographs* 80 (1966), pp. 1–28.

- **CREATIVITY** The capacity to generate novel and useful ideas and solutions.

- **INDIVIDUALISM–COLLECTIVISM** The degree to which a culture has a loosely knit social framework (individualism) or a tight social framework (collectivism).

- **POWER DISTANCE** The degree to which a culture prefers equal power distribution (low power distance) or an unequal power distribution (high power distance).

- **UNCERTAINTY AVOIDANCE** The degree to which a culture tolerates ambiguous situations (low uncertainty avoidance) or feels threatened by them (high uncertainty avoidance).

- **MASCULINITY–FEMININITY** The degree to which a culture values stereotypically male traits (masculinity) or stereotypically female traits (femininity).

art, and classical music). Much like agreeableness and extraversion, the traits associated with openness are beneficial in some jobs but not others. As a result, openness is not related to job performance across all occupations.

What jobs benefit from high levels of openness? Generally speaking, jobs that are very fluid and dynamic, with rapid changes in job demands. Research shows that open employees excel in learning and training environments because their curiosity gives them a built-in desire to learn new things.[45] They also tend to be more adaptable and quick to identify when the "old way of doing things" is no longer effective, excelling at the search for a new and better approach.[46] In fact, conscientious employees are sometimes less effective than open employees in such environments because their persevering nature sometimes prevents them from abandoning "tried-and-true" task strategies.

Openness to experience is also more likely to be valuable in jobs that require high levels of creativity, defined as the capacity to generate novel and useful ideas and solutions.[47] The relationship between openness and creativity can be seen in Figure 8-3. Together with cognitive ability (discussed later in this chapter), openness to experience is a key driver of creative thought, as smart and open people excel at the style of thinking demanded by creativity. Creative thought then results in creative behavior when people

> **"To some extent, cultural values provide countries with their own distinct personalities."**

come up with new ideas, create fresh approaches to problems, or suggest new innovations that can help improve the workplace.[48] The creativity benefits of openness likely explain why highly open individuals are more likely to migrate into artistic and scientific fields, in which novel and original products are so critical.[49]

Cultural Values

Now that we've described a number of personality traits, we turn our attention to the cultural values that can affect the expression of those traits. To some extent, cultural values provide countries with their own distinct personalities. For example, we can say that Australian people, on average, value the traits associated with extraversion more than Chinese people.[50] We also can say that Swiss people, on average, value the traits associated with openness more than Irish people. Such statements are based on research that reveals consistent between-nation differences on various personality traits. Of course, that doesn't mean that all Australian, Chinese, Swiss, and Irish citizens have exactly the same personality—merely that certain cultures tend to have higher levels of certain traits.

● ● 8.3

Understand Hofstede's dimensions of cultural values.

- **SHORT-TERM VS. LONG-TERM ORIENTATION** The degree to which a culture stresses values that are past- and present-oriented (short-term orientation) or future-oriented (long-term orientation).

Although it's possible to describe nations on values relevant to the Big Five, as we just did, there are other values that are more commonly used to categorize nations. Many of those values are derived from a landmark study in the late 1960s and early 1970s by Geert Hofstede, who analyzed data about 88,000 IBM employees from 72 countries in 20 languages.[51] His research showed that employees working in different countries tended to prioritize different values, and those values clustered into several distinct dimensions. Those dimensions are summarized in Table 8-2 and include individualism–collectivism, power distance, uncertainty avoidance, masculinity–femininity, and short-term vs. long-term orientation. The table also includes cultures that tend to be high on a given dimension.

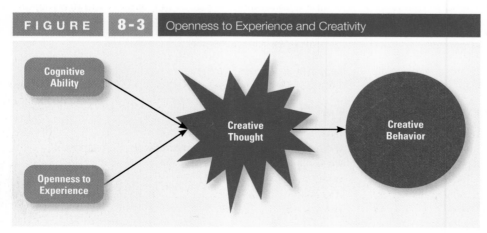

FIGURE 8-3 Openness to Experience and Creativity

Cognitive Ability → Creative Thought → Creative Behavior
Openness to Experience →

TABLE 8-2 Hofstede's Dimensions of Cultural Values

Individualism-Collectivism

INDIVIDUALISM	COLLECTIVISM
The culture is a loosely knit social framework in which people take care of themselves and their immediate family.	The culture is a tight social framework in which people take care of the members of a broader ingroup and act loyal to it.
United States, the Netherlands, France	*Indonesia, China, West Africa*

Power Distance

LOW	HIGH
The culture prefers that power be distributed uniformly where possible, in a more egalitarian fashion.	The culture accepts the fact that power is usually distributed unequally within organizations.
United States, Germany, the Netherlands	*Russia, China, Indonesia*

Uncertainty Avoidance

LOW	HIGH
The culture tolerates uncertain and ambiguous situations and values unusual ideas and behaviors.	The culture feels threatened by uncertain and ambiguous situations and relies on formal rules to create stability.
United States, Indonesia, the Netherlands	*Japan, Russia, France*

Masculinity-Femininity

MASCULINITY	FEMININITY
The culture values stereotypically male traits such as assertiveness and the acquisition of money and things.	The culture values stereotypically female traits such as caring for others and caring about quality of life.
United States, Japan, Germany	*The Netherlands, Russia, France*

Short-Term vs. Long-Term Orientation

SHORT TERM	LONG TERM
The culture stresses values that are more past- and present-oriented such as respect for tradition and fulfilling obligations.	The culture stresses values that are more future-oriented such as persistence, prudence, and thrift.
United States, Russia, West Africa	*China, Japan, the Netherlands*

Sources: G. Hofstede, *Culture's Consequences: International Differences in Work Related Values* (Beverly Hills, CA: Sage, 1980); G. Hofstede, "Cultural Constraints in Management Theories," *Academy of Management Executive* 7 (1993), pp. 81–94; G. Hofstede and M. H. Bond, "The Confucius Connection: From Cultural Roots to Economic Growth," *Organizational Dynamics* 16 (1988), pp. 5–21; B. L. Kirkman, K. B. Lowe, and C. B. Gibson, "A Quarter Century of *Culture's Consequences*: A Review of Empirical Research Incorporating Hofstede's Cultural Values Framework," *Journal of International Business Studies* 37 (2006), pp. 285–320.

The table reveals that citizens of the United States tend to be high on individualism, low on power distance, low on uncertainty avoidance, high on masculinity, and high on short-term orientation. Why is this description important to know? Because it illustrates the adjustments that American employees and American businesses may need to make when doing business in other cultures. Differences in cultural values can create differences in reactions to change, conflict management styles, negotiation approaches, and reward preferences.[52] Failing to understand those differences can compromise the effectiveness of multinational groups and organizations. Such problems are particularly likely if employees are high in ethnocentrism, defined as a propensity to view one's own cultural values as "right" and those of other cultures as "wrong."[53] For more discussion of this issue, see our **OB Internationally** feature.

● **ETHNOCENTRISM** A propensity to view one's own cultural values as "right" and those of other cultures as "wrong."

Of Hofstede's five dimensions, individualism–collectivism has received the most research attention, by a wide margin.[54] Much of this research has focused on the individualism–collectivism of individual people rather than nations, sometimes referred to as "psychological individualism" or "psychological collectivism."[55] This focus on individuals rather than nations is understandable, given that some experts estimate that only 60 percent of the citizens in a collective culture actually hold collective cultural values themselves.[56] Studies of psychological collectivism have revealed that collective employees identify deeply with relevant ingroups such as family members, close friends, or work teams. They prefer to interact with those ingroups, care for the members of those ingroups, and accept and prioritize ingroup norms and goals.[57]

American businesses and employees have to make a number of adjustments when doing business in other cultures.

levels of strength, stamina, and coordination. Other employees are especially good at cognitive tasks, with an aptitude for reading, mathematics, or logic and reasoning sorts of activities. Still other employees have emotional talents, being able to read the emotions of others while controlling the expression of their own emotions. Of course, training and practice can increase an employee's performance at these sorts of tasks. Still, employees who are genetically gifted in a given ability will always have a "higher ceiling" when it comes to performing particular tasks at an exceptionally high level. The sections to follow discuss cognitive ability and emotional ability in more detail. (We'll leave out a full discussion of physical abilities, given that cognitive and emotional aptitudes are more critical in most of the jobs that you'll hold.)

Ability

Besides personality and cultural values, employees can be characterized according to what they're innately good at. Some employees excel at physical tasks, possessing exceptionally high

Cognitive Ability.
Cognitive abilities are capabilities related to the acquisition and application of knowledge in problem solving.[58] Cognitive abilities are very relevant in jobs involving the use of information to make decisions and

OB Internationally

Research suggests that ethnocentrism hinders the effectiveness of expatriates, who are employees working full-time in other countries. Ethnocentrism makes expatriates less likely to adjust to a new culture, less likely to fulfill the duties required of their international assignment, and more likely to withdraw from that assignment. So how can organizations identify employees with the right personalities to serve as expatriates?

One potentially useful tool is the *multicultural personality questionnaire*, which assesses five personality dimensions that can maximize the satisfaction, commitment, and performance of expatriates.[59] Those dimensions are listed below, along with some sample items for each.

Cultural Empathy. A tendency to empathize with the feelings, thoughts, and behaviors of individuals with different cultural values.

- I understand other people's feelings.
- I take other people's habits into consideration.

Open-mindedness. A tendency to have an open and unprejudiced attitude toward other cultural values and norms.

- I get involved in other cultures.
- I find other religions interesting.

Emotional Stability. A tendency to remain calm in the kinds of stressful situations that can be encountered in foreign environments.

- I can put setbacks in perspective.
- I take it for granted that things will turn out right.

Social Initiative. A tendency to be proactive when approaching social situations, which aids in building connections.

- I easily approach other people.

- I am often the driving force behind things.

Flexibility. A tendency to regard new situations as a challenge and to adjust behaviors to meet that challenge.

- I could start a new life easily.
- I feel comfortable in different cultures.

Research has linked these five personality traits to a number of expatriate success factors. For example, individuals with a "multicultural personality" are more likely to aspire to international positions, more likely to gain international experience, more likely to adjust to new assignments, and more likely to be happy with their lives during those assignments.[60] In fact, research even suggests that expatriates who fit this profile are actually healthier, both physically and mentally. ❖

solve problems. Chances are good that your cognitive abilities have been tested several times throughout your life. For example, almost all children in the United States take standard-

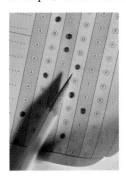

ized tests of intelligence at some point during elementary school. Although you might not remember taking one of these, you probably do remember taking the Scholastic Assessment Test (SAT). And though you probably only thought about the SAT as a test that would have a major impact on where you could and could not go to college, the SAT is actually a test of cognitive ability. See our **OB for Students** feature for more discussion of the SAT.

You might also remember that the SAT included a variety of different questions; some tested your ability to do math problems, whereas other questions assessed your ability to complete sentences and make analogies. The different types of questions reflect the several specific types of cognitive ability that contribute to effectiveness on intellectual tasks. Table 8-3 lists many of these cognitive ability types, along with their specific facets and some jobs in which they are thought to be important.

●● **8.4**

Describe the dimensions of cognitive ability.

Verbal ability refers to various capabilities associated with understanding and expressing oral and written communication. *Oral comprehension* is the ability to understand spoken words and sentences, and *written comprehension* is the ability to understand written words and sentences. Although these two aspects of verbal ability would seem highly related—that

is, people who have high oral comprehension would tend to have high written comprehensive, and vice versa—it's not difficult to think of people who might be high on one ability but low on the other. As an example, it has been reported that as a result of his dyslexia, Tom Cruise has poor written comprehension and can only learn his lines after listening to them on tape.[61]

Because of his dyslexia, Tom Cruise struggles with written comprehension. He learns the lines for his movies by listening to them on tape.

OB for Students

Generally speaking, the SAT includes sections that assess verbal and quantitative abilities, and when considered together, the scores indicate overall cognitive ability.[62] The latest version of the test, the SAT II, consists of 22 one-hour tests that measure knowledge in specific subject areas such as English, history, mathematics, science, and foreign languages.[63] Although the intent of the SAT II is to assess academic achievement rather than cognitive ability, scores on the tests correlate very strongly to performance on earlier versions of the SAT. Moreover, there is not much evidence that the SAT II is much more useful than the earlier versions in helping schools make decisions about which students to admit.[64]

But does the SAT really relate to how well someone does in college? Many of you are likely to be skeptical because you probably know someone who did extremely well on the SAT but performed poorly as a college student. Similarly, you probably know someone who didn't do that well on the SAT but who performed well as a college student. As it turns out, the SAT is actually fairly good at predicting college performance. Students with higher SAT scores tend to perform much better in their first year of college, end up with a higher cumulative grade point average, and have a higher likelihood of graduating.[65]

Another question you may have is whether information about the SAT is useful beyond information about high school grade point average. After all, it's reasonable that a student who was effective in high school would

also be effective in college. In fact, research shows that, although high school grade point average does predict college performance, SAT scores add significantly to the prediction.[66] Consider for a moment the results from a study that examined the college graduation rate for students with different levels of high school grade point averages and SAT scores.[67] For "A" students in high school, the rate of college graduation was 28 percent for students who scored less than 700 on their SAT and 80 percent for students who scored more than 1300. Interestingly, however, the SAT was not as useful in predicting the graduation rates for students who performed poorly in high school. For C+ students, for example, the rate of college graduation ranged from 17 to 28 percent across the full spectrum of SAT scores. ❖

TABLE 8-3 Types and Facets of Cognitive Ability

Type	More Specific Facet	Jobs Where Relevant
Verbal	**Oral and Written Comprehension:** Understanding written and spoken words and sentences **Oral and Written Expression:** Communicating ideas by speaking or writing so that others can understand	Business executives; police, fire, and ambulance dispatchers; clinical psychologists
Quantitative	**Number Facility:** Performing basic math operations quickly and correctly **Mathematical Reasoning:** Selecting the right method or formula to solve a problem	Treasurers; financial managers; mathematical technicians; statisticians
Reasoning	**Problem Sensitivity:** Understanding when there is a problem or when something may go wrong **Deductive Reasoning:** Applying general rules to specific problems **Inductive Reasoning:** Combining specific information to form general conclusions **Originality:** Developing new ideas	Anesthesiologists; surgeons; business executives; fire inspectors; judges; police detectives; forensic scientists; cartoonists; designers
Spatial	**Spatial Orientation:** Knowing where one is relative to objects in the environment **Visualization:** Imagining how something will look after it has been rearranged	Pilots; drivers; boat captains; photographers; set designers; sketch artists
Perceptual	**Speed and Flexibility of Closure:** Making sense of information and finding patterns **Perceptual Speed:** Comparing information or objects with remembered information or objects	Musicians; fire fighters; police officers; pilots; mail clerks; inspectors

Source: Adapted from E. A. Fleishman, D. P. Costanza, and J. Marshall-Mies, "Abilities," in *An Occupational Information System for the 21st Century: The Development of O*NET*, ed. N. G. Peterson, M. D. Mumford, W. C. Borman, P. R. Jeanneret, and E. A. Fleishman (Washington, DC: American Psychological Association, 1999), pp. 175–95.

Two other verbal abilities are *oral expression*, which refers to the ability to communicate ideas by speaking, and *written expression*, which refers to the ability to communicate ideas in writing. Again, though it might seem that these abilities should be highly related, they are not necessarily. You may have taken a class with a professor who has published several well-regarded books and articles but had a very difficult time expressing concepts and theories to students effectively. Although there could be many reasons, one possible explanation is that the professor had high ability in terms of written expression but low ability in terms of oral expression.

Generally speaking, verbal abilities are most important in jobs in which effectiveness depends on understanding and communicating ideas and information to others. The effectiveness of business executives depends on their ability to consider information from reports and other executives and staff, as well as their ability to articulate a vision and strategy that promotes employee understanding. As another example, consider how important the verbal abilities of a 9-1-1 dispatcher might be if a loved one suddenly became ill and stopped breathing one evening.

Quantitative ability refers to two types of mathematical capabilities. The first is *number facility*, which is the capability to do simple math operations (adding, subtracting, multiplying, and dividing). The second is *mathematical reasoning*, which refers to the ability to choose and apply formulas to solve problems that involve numbers. If you think back to the SAT, you can probably remember problems such as the following: "There were two trains 800 miles apart, and they were traveling toward each other on the same track. The first train began traveling at noon and averaged 45 miles per hour. The second train started off two hours later. At what speed did the second train average if the two trains smashed into each other at 10:00 p.m. of the same day?"

Although number facility may be necessary to solve this problem, mathematical reasoning is crucial because the test

Counting out change quickly and correctly is an important quantitative ability for cashiers.

● **QUANTITATIVE ABIL-ITY** Various capabilities associated with doing math operations and choosing and applying formulas to solve problems.

● **REASONING ABILITY** A diverse set of abilities associated with sensing and solving problems using insight, rules, and logic.

● **SPATIAL ABILITY** Various capabilities associated with understanding one's environment and imagining changes to that environment.

● **PERCEPTUAL ABILITIES** Being able to perceive, understand, and recall patterns of information.

● **GENERAL COGNITIVE ABILITY** An overall level of mental ability that drives more specific cognitive capabilities (often abbreviated *g*).

taker needs to know which formulas to apply. Although most of us wish that problems like this would be limited to test-taking contexts (especially this particular problem), there are countless situations in which quantitative abilities are important. For example, consider the importance of quantitative ability in jobs involving statistics, accounting, and engineering. Quantitative abilities may be important in less complex, lower-level jobs as well. Have you ever been at a fast-food restaurant or convenience store when the cash register wasn't working and the clerk couldn't manage to count out change correctly or quickly? If you have, you witnessed a very good example of low quantitative ability, and perhaps some very annoyed customers.

Reasoning ability is a diverse set of abilities associated with sensing and solving problems using insight, rules, and logic. The first reasoning ability, *problem sensitivity*, is the ability to sense that there's a problem right now or likely to be one in the near future. Anesthesiology is a great example of a job for which problem sensitivity is crucial. Before surgeries, anesthesiologists give drugs to patients so that surgical procedures can take place without the patients experiencing pain. However, during the surgery, patients can have negative reactions to the drugs that might result in the loss of life. So the ability of the anesthesiologist to sense when something is wrong even before the problem is fully apparent can be a life-or-death matter.

The second type of reasoning ability is called *deductive reasoning*. This ability, which refers to the use of general rules to solve problems, is important in any job in which people are presented with a set of facts that need to be applied to make effective decisions. The job of a judge requires deductive reasoning because it centers on making decisions by applying the rules of law to make verdicts. In contrast, *inductive reasoning* refers to the ability to consider several specific pieces of information and then reach a more general conclusion regarding how those pieces are related. Every episode of the CBS show *CSI* is filled with inductive reasoning. Crime scene investigators, like Gil Grissom, are experts at considering things like the blood-splatter patterns, bruises, abrasions, DNA, fibers, and fingerprints to reach conclusions about causes of death and possible perpetrators.

Finally, *originality* refers to the ability to develop clever and novel ways to solve problems. Larry Page and Sergey Brin, the two founders of Google, provide good examples of originality. They not only developed the search software that gave Google a competitive advantage, but they also created the first completely new advertising medium in nearly half a century. They also refuse to follow conventional wisdom when it comes to managerial practices and business decisions.[68] Clearly, originality is important in a wide variety of occupations, but in some jobs, originality is the most critical ability. For example, a cartoonist, designer, writer, or advertising executive without originality would find it difficult to be successful.

There are two main types of **spatial abilities**. The first is called *spatial orientation*, which refers to having a good understanding of where one is relative to other things in the environment. A tourist with high spatial organization would have no trouble finding her way back to her hotel on foot after a long day of sightseeing, even without a map or help from anyone on the street. The second spatial ability is called *visualization*, which is the ability to imagine how separate things will look if they were put together in a particular way. If you're good at imagining how a room would look if it were rearranged, or if your friends are impressed that you can buy things that go together well, chances are that you would score high on visualization.

Perceptual abilities generally refer to being able to perceive, understand, and recall patterns of information. More specifically, *speed and flexibility of closure* refers to being able to pick out a pattern of information quickly in the presence of distracting information, even without all the information present. This ability is easy to understand if you've ever seen the CBS show *Numbers*. In the show, Charlie Eppes helps the FBI solve crimes by using his genius to discover patterns in data and information. In the series premiere, for example, Charlie used the metaphor of a sprinkler to describe his unique ability, noting, "Say I couldn't see the sprinkler; from the pattern of the drops, I could calculate its precise location." Related to this ability is *perceptual speed*, which refers to being able to examine and compare numbers, letters, and objects quickly. If you can go into the produce section of a supermarket and choose the best tomatoes faster than the people around you, chances are you have high perceptual speed. Effectiveness in jobs in which people need to proofread documents, sort things, or categorize objects depends a lot on perceptual speed.

If you've read the preceding sections thoughtfully, you probably considered where you stand on the different types of cognitive abilities. In doing so, you also may have reached the conclusion that you are higher on some of these abilities and lower on others. Maybe you think of yourself as being smart in verbal abilities but not as smart in quantitative abilities. In fact, most people score more similarly across their cognitive abilities than they realize. People who are high on verbal abilities also tend to be high on reasoning, quantitative, spatial, and perceptual abilities, and people who are low on verbal abilities tend to be low on the other abilities. Although this consistency might not apply to everyone, it applies often enough that researchers have been trying to understand why this occurs for well over 100 years.[69]

The most popular explanation for the similarity in the levels of different cognitive abilities within people is that there is a **general cognitive ability**—sometimes called *g* or the *g factor*—that underlies or causes all of the more specific cognitive abilities we have discussed so far.[70] To understand

"...THERE IS A GENERAL COGNITIVE ABILITY—SOMETIMES CALLED *g* OR THE *g FACTOR*—THAT UNDERLIES OR CAUSES ALL OF THE MORE SPECIFIC COGNITIVE ABILITIES WE HAVE DISCUSSED SO FAR."

● **EMOTIONAL INTELLIGENCE** A set of abilities related to the understanding and use of emotions that affect social functioning.

● **SELF-AWARENESS** The appraisal and expression of emotions within oneself.

● **OTHER AWARENESS** The appraisal and recognition of emotion in others.

what this ability means more clearly, consider the diagram in Figure 8-4, which depicts general mental ability as the area in common across the more specific cognitive abilities that we have discussed. This overlap exists because each of the specific abilities depends somewhat on the brain's ability to process information effectively. So, because some brains are capable of processing information more effectively than others, some people tend to score higher across the specific abilities, whereas others tend to score lower. For a description of how the National Football League pays attention to general cognitive ability, see our **OB in Sports** feature.

Emotional Ability. Most of us know someone who is very smart from a cognitive ability standpoint, but at the same time, the person just can't manage to be effective in real-world situations that involve other people. Sometimes such individuals are held back by their personality, as it may be that extreme introversion or neuroticism is hindering them in certain social situations. However, research has begun to examine whether there is a type of ability that influences the degree to which people tend to be effective in social situations.[71] Although there has been some debate among these researchers,[72] many believe that there is indeed an ability that affects social functioning, called **emotional intelligence**.[73] Emotional intelligence is defined in terms of four different but related abilities.[74]

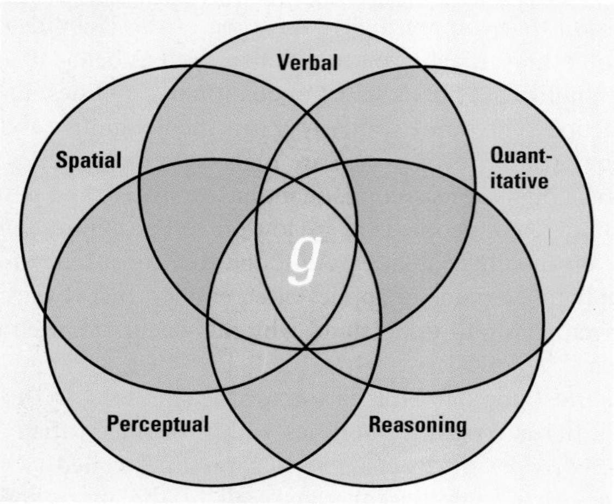

●● 8.5

Describe the dimensions of emotional ability.

The first type of emotional intelligence is **self-awareness**, or the appraisal and expression of emotions within oneself. This facet refers to a person' ability to understand the types of emotions he or she is experiencing, the willingness to acknowledge them, and the capability to express them naturally.[75] As an example, someone who is low in this aspect of emotional intelligence might not admit to himself or show to anyone else that he is feeling somewhat anxious during the first few days of a new job. These types of emotions are perfectly natural in this job context, and ignoring them might increase the stress of the situation. Ignoring those emotions also might send the wrong signal to new colleagues, who might wonder, "Why isn't the new hire more excited about his new job?"

The second facet of emotional intelligence is called **other awareness**, or the appraisal and recognition of emotion in others.[76] As the name of this facet implies, it refers to a person's ability to recognize and understand the emotions that other people are feeling. People who are high in this aspect of emotional intelligence not only are sensitive to the feelings of others but also can anticipate the emotions that people will experience in different situations. In contrast, people who are low in this aspect of emotional intelligence do not effectively sense the emotions that others are experiencing, and if the emotions are negative, this inability could result in the person doing something that worsens the situation. As a specific example, have you ever had a professor who could not sense that students in class did not understand the material being presented in a lecture? When that professor continued to press on with the overheads, oblivious to the fact that the students were becoming even more confused, it was poor other awareness in action.

The third facet of emotional intelligence, **emotion regulation**, refers to being able to recover quickly from emotional experiences.[77] As an example of this aspect of emotional

FIGURE 8-4 The *g* Factor

intelligence, consider the possible responses of someone who is listening to NPR while driving his brand new Saturn to work and is cut off by an aggressive driver who, as she passes by, throws a beer can and shouts an obscenity. If this person is able to regulate his emotions effectively, he would be able to recover quickly from the initial anger and shock of the encounter. He would be able to get back to whatever he was listening to on the radio, and by the time he got to work, the incident would likely be all but forgotten. However, if this person was not able to regulate his emotions effectively, he might lose his temper, tailgate the aggressive driver, and then ram into her rusted-out 1968 Ford pickup at the next stoplight. We hope it is obvious to you that the former response is much

OB in Sports

Aside from the SAT, the most famous test of cognitive ability is the *Wonderlic Personnel Test*, a 12-minute test of general cognitive ability that consists of 50 questions. You'll hear about the Wonderlic every March and April because NFL football teams take Wonderlic scores into account when drafting college players. The test has actually been in use for several decades now and has been given to more than 120 million people by thousands of organizations.[78] From the example items that appear below, you should be able to see how the items correspond with many of the cognitive abilities that we described previously.

One question that people always debate when the NFL draft occurs is whether scores on a test of cognitive ability are relevant to a football player's performance on the field. Although supporters of the Wonderlic's use in the NFL argue that cognitive ability is necessary to remember plays and learn complex offensive and defensive systems, many people wonder how the ability to answer questions like those below relates to a player's ability to complete a pass, run for a touchdown, tackle an opponent, or kick a field goal. Moreover, detractors of the Wonderlic wonder why a poor score should overshadow a record of superior accomplishments on the playing field. ❖

The draft process for the NFL goes beyond simple physical ability. Athletes have to take a 12-minute test called the Wonderlic Personnel Test to determine their cognitive ability as well.

1. Which of the following is the earliest date?
   A) Jan. 16, 1898   B) Feb. 21, 1889   C) Feb. 2, 1898
   D) Jan. 7, 1898   E) Jan. 30, 1889

2. LOW is to HIGH as EASY is to ___?___ .
   A) SUCCESSFUL   B) PURE   C) TALL   D) INTERESTING   E) DIFFICULT

3. A featured product from an Internet retailer generated 27, 99, 80, 115, and 213 orders over a 5-hour period. Which graph below best represents this trend?

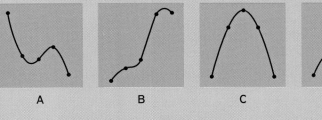

   A   B   C   D   E

4. What is the next number in the series?   29   41   53   65   77   ___?___
   A) 75   B) 88   C) 89   D) 98   E) 99

5. One word below appears in color. What is the OPPOSITE of that word?
   She gave a complex answer to the question and we all agreed with her.
   A) long   B) better   C) simple   D) wrong   E) kind

Source: Wonderlic WPT = R Sample Questions. Reprinted with permission of Wonderlic, Inc. Copyright 2007 Wonderlic, Inc.

more appropriate than the latter, which could prove quite costly to the individual. Although this example highlights the importance of regulating negative emotions, we should also point out that this aspect of emotional intelligence applies to positive emotions. Consider the response of someone who is told that she is about to receive a significant pay raise. If this person is unable to regulate her own emotions effectively, she might feel joyous and giddy the rest of the day and, as a consequence, not be able to accomplish any more work.

The fourth aspect of emotional intelligence is the use of emotions.[79] This capability reflects the degree to which people can harness emotions and employ them to improve their chances of being successful in whatever they are seeking to do. To understand this facet of emotional intelligence, consider a writer who is struggling to finish a book but is under a serious time crunch because of the contract with the publisher. If the writer was high in this aspect of emotional intelligence, she would likely psych herself up for the challenge and encourage herself to work hard through any bouts of writer's block. In contrast, if the writer is low in this aspect of emotional intelligence, she might begin to doubt her competence as a writer and think about different things she could do with her life. Because these behaviors will slow progress on the book even further, the number and intensity of self-defeating thoughts might increase, and ultimately, the writer might withdraw from the task entirely.

Although you may appreciate how emotional intelligence can be relevant to effectiveness in a variety of interpersonal situations, you might be wondering whether knowledge of emotional intelligence can be useful to managers in their quest to make their organizations more effective. It turns out there is growing evidence that the answer to this questions is "yes."[80] In fact, the U.S. Air Force studied recruiters and found that those recruiters who were high in some aspects of emotional intelligence were three times more likely to meet recruiting quotas than recruiters who scored lower in the same aspects of emotional intelligence.[81] Recruiters with high emotional intelligence were more effective because

Driving a car requires a good deal of emotion regulation, especially when other drivers on the road aren't driving well. Being able to recover quickly from an emotionally charged experience in the car reflects an ability to regulate emotions.

they projected positive emotions and could quickly sense and appropriately respond to recruits' concerns. Because these capabilities made recruiting easier, there was less pressure to meet performance quotas, which translated into fewer hours at the office, higher satisfaction, and ultimately higher retention. In fact, after the Air Force began requiring new recruiters to pass an emotional intelligence test, turnover among new recruiters dropped from 25 percent to 2 percent. Given that, on average, it costs about $30,000 to train a new recruiter, this lower turnover translated into about $2.75 million in savings a year. Figure 8-5 provides sample questions from one popular emotional intelligence test.

HOW IMPORTANT ARE PERSONALITY, CULTURAL VALUES, AND ABILITY?

Now that we've described all the personality traits, cultural values, and ability facets that can be used to describe and differentiate employees, the key question becomes: "Which of them are most strongly related to performance and commitment?" Well, it should come as no surprise, based on our earlier discussion, that two individual characteristics stand apart from the rest when it comes to relationships with performance and commitment: general cognitive ability and conscientiousness. In fact, a good rule of thumb to emphasize in virtually any hiring situation is to look at "*g* and *c*" (where g stands for general cognitive ability and *c* stands for conscientiousness).

● ● **8.6**

Understand how ability and personality affect job performance and organizational commitment.

Figure 8-6 reveals that cognitive ability is a strong predictor of job performance—in particular, the task performance aspect.[82] Across all jobs, smarter employees fulfill the requirements of their job descriptions more effectively than do less

1. Indicate how much of each emotion is expressed by this face:

	None				Very Much
a) Happiness	1	2	3	4	5
b) Anger	1	2	3	4	5
c) Fear	1	2	3	4	5
d) Excitement	1	2	3	4	5
e) Surprise	1	2	3	4	5

2. What mood(s) might be helpful to feel when meeting in-laws for the very first time?

	Not Useful				Useful
a) Slight tension	1	2	3	4	5
b) Surprise	1	2	3	4	5
c) Joy	1	2	3	4	5

3. Tom felt anxious, and became a bit stressed when he thought about all the work he needed to do. When his supervisor brought him an additional project, he felt _____. (Select the best choice.)

a) Overwhelmed

b) Depressed

c) Ashamed

d) Self-conscious

e) Jittery

4. Debbie just came back from vacation. She was feeling peaceful and content. How well would each action preserve her mood?

Action 1: She started to make a list of things at home that she needed to do.

Very Ineffective   1........2........3........4........5   Very Effective

Action 2: She began thinking about where and when she would go on her next vacation.

Very Ineffective   1........2........3........4........5   Very Effective

Action 3: She decided it was best to ignore the feeling since it wouldn't last anyway.

Very Ineffective   1........2........3........4........5   Very Effective

Source: Copyright © 2006 J. Mayer, P. Salovey, and D. Caruso. Reprinted with permission.

Note that the photo in item 1 does not appear in the test published by Multi-Health Systems.

smart employees. In fact, of all the variables discussed in this book, none has a stronger correlation with task performance than general cognitive ability. Thousands of organizations, and many that are quite well known, assess cognitive ability in an effort to select the best candidates available for specific jobs.[83] The use of cognitive ability tests for this purpose appears to be reasonable, given that scores on such tests have a strong positive correlation with measures of performance across different types of jobs.[84]

So what explains why general cognitive ability relates to task performance? People who have higher general cognitive ability tend to be better at *learning and decision making*. They are able to gain more knowledge from their experiences at a faster rate, and, as a result, they develop a bigger pool of knowledge regarding how to do their jobs effectively.[85] There are, however, three important caveats that we should mention. First, cognitive ability tends to be more strongly correlated with task performance than citizenship behavior or counterproductive behavior.[86] An increased amount of job knowledge helps an employee complete job tasks, but it does not necessarily affect the choice to help a coworker or refrain from breaking an important rule. Second, the positive correlation between cognitive ability and performance is even stronger in jobs that are complex or situations that demand adaptability.[87] Third, people may do poorly on a test of general cognitive ability for reasons other than a lack of cognitive ability. As an example, people who come from economically disadvantaged back-

grounds may do poorly on such tests, not because they lack the underlying cognitive ability but because they may not have had the learning opportunities needed to provide the appropriate responses.

In contrast to relationships with job performance, research has not supported a significant linkage between cognitive ability and organizational commitment.[88] On the one hand, we might expect a positive relationship with commitment because people with higher cognitive ability tend to perform more effectively,

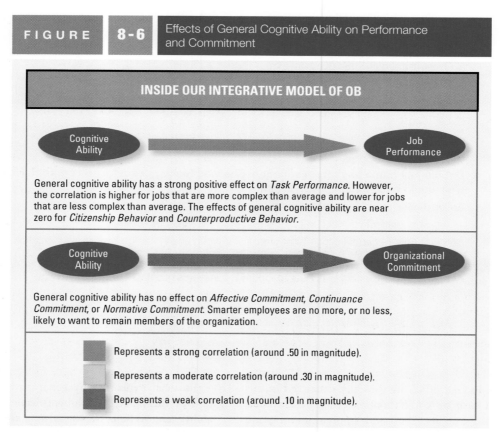

FIGURE 8-6 Effects of General Cognitive Ability on Performance and Commitment

INSIDE OUR INTEGRATIVE MODEL OF OB

Cognitive Ability → Job Performance

General cognitive ability has a strong positive effect on *Task Performance*. However, the correlation is higher for jobs that are more complex than average and lower for jobs that are less complex than average. The effects of general cognitive ability are near zero for *Citizenship Behavior* and *Counterproductive Behavior*.

Cognitive Ability → Organizational Commitment

General cognitive ability has no effect on *Affective Commitment*, *Continuance Commitment*, or *Normative Commitment*. Smarter employees are no more, or no less, likely to want to remain members of the organization.

▇ Represents a strong correlation (around .50 in magnitude).

▢ Represents a moderate correlation (around .30 in magnitude).

▨ Represents a weak correlation (around .10 in magnitude).

Sources: J. W. Boudreau, W. R. Boswell, T. A. Judge, and R. D Bretz, "Personality and Cognitive Ability as Predictors of Job Search among Employed Managers," *Personnel Psychology* 54 (2001), pp. 25–50; S. M. Colarelli, R. A. Dean, and C. Konstans, "Comparative Effects of Personal and Situational Influences on Job Outcomes of New Professionals," *Journal of Applied Psychology* 72 (1987), pp. 558–66; D. N. Dickter, M. Roznowski, and D. A. Harrison, "Temporal Tempering: An Event History Analysis of the Process of Voluntary Turnover," *Journal of Applied Psychology* 81 (1996), pp. 705–16; F. L. Schmidt and J. Hunter, "General Mental Ability in the World of Work: Occupational Attainment and Job Performance," *Journal of Personality and Social Psychology* 86 (2004), pp. 162–73.

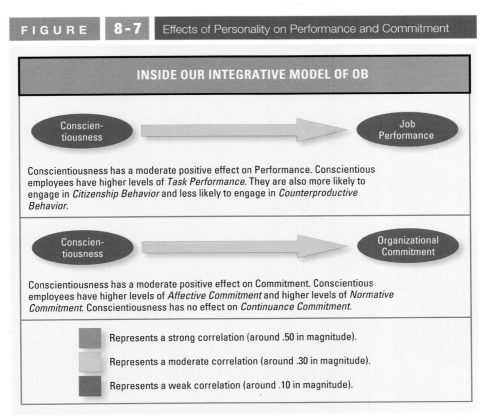

FIGURE 8-7   Effects of Personality on Performance and Commitment

INSIDE OUR INTEGRATIVE MODEL OF OB

Conscien-tiousness → Job Performance

Conscientiousness has a moderate positive effect on Performance. Conscientious employees have higher levels of *Task Performance*. They are also more likely to engage in *Citizenship Behavior* and less likely to engage in *Counterproductive Behavior*.

Conscien-tiousness → Organizational Commitment

Conscientiousness has a moderate positive effect on Commitment. Conscientious employees have higher levels of *Affective Commitment* and higher levels of *Normative Commitment*. Conscientiousness has no effect on *Continuance Commitment*.

▇ Represents a strong correlation (around .50 in magnitude).

▨ Represents a moderate correlation (around .30 in magnitude).

▨ Represents a weak correlation (around .10 in magnitude).

Sources: M. R. Barrick, M. K. Mount, and T. A. Judge, "Personality and Performance at the Beginning of the New Millennium: What Do We Know and Where Do We Go Next?" *International Journal of Selection and Assessment* 9 (2001), pp. 9–30; C. M. Berry, D. S. Ones, and P. R. Sackett, "Interpersonal Deviance, Organizational Deviance, and Their Common Correlates: A Review and Meta-Analysis," *Journal of Applied Psychology* 92 (2007), pp. 410–24; A. Cooper-Hakim and C. Viswesvaran, "The Construct of Work Commitment: Testing an Integrative Framework," *Psychological Bulletin* 131 (2005), pp. 241–59; L. M. Hough and A. Furnham, "Use of Personality Variables in Work Settings," in *Handbook of Psychology*, Vol. 12, ed. W. C. Borman, D. R. Ilgen, and R. J. Klimoski (Hoboken, NJ: Wiley, 2003), pp. 131–69; J. E. Mathieu and D. M. Zajac, "A Review and Meta-Analysis of the Antecedents, Correlates, and Consequences of Organizational Commitment," *Psychological Bulletin* 108 (1990), pp. 171–94; J. F. Salgado, "The Big Five Personality Dimensions and Counterproductive Behaviors," *International Journal of Selection and Assessment* 10 (2002), pp. 117–25.

and therefore, they might feel they fit well with their job. On the other hand, we might expect to see a negative relationship with commitment because people with higher cognitive ability possess more job knowledge, which increases their value on the job market and in turn the likelihood that they would leave for another job.[89] In the end, knowing how smart an employee is tells us very little about the likelihood that he or she will remain a member of the organization.

Figure 8-7 reveals that conscientiousness has a moderate relationship with task performance,[90] partly because conscientious employees have higher levels of *motivation* than other employees.[91] They are more self-confident, perceive a clearer linkage between their effort and their performance, and are more likely to set goals and commit to them. For these reasons, conscientiousness is a key driver of what's referred to as *typical performance*, reflecting performance in the routine conditions that surround daily job tasks.[92] General cognitive ability,

in contrast, is the stronger driver of *maximum performance*, reflecting performance in brief, special circumstances that demand a person's best effort.

Conscientious employees are also more likely to engage in citizenship behaviors.[93] Why? One reason is that conscientious employees are so punctual and have such good work attendance that they are simply more available to offer "extra mile" sorts of contributions. Another reason is that they engage in so much more work-related effort that they have more energy to devote to citizenship behaviors.[94] Finally, conscientious employees are less likely to engage in counterproductive behaviors,[95] for two major reasons. First, they tend to have higher levels of *job satisfaction*,[96] making it less likely that they'll feel a need to retaliate against their organization. Second, even if they do perceive some slight or injustice, their dependable and reliable nature should prevent them from violating organizational norms by engaging in negative actions.[97]

Figure 8-7 also reveals that conscientious employees tend to be more committed to their organization.[98] They are less likely to engage in day-to-day psychological and physical withdrawal behaviors because such actions go against their work habits. They are also significantly less likely to voluntarily leave the organization.[99] Why? One reason is that the persevering nature of conscientious employees prompts them to persist in a given course of action for long periods of time. That persistence can be seen in their daily work effort, but it extends to a sense of commitment to the organization as well.[100] Another reason is that conscientious employees are better at managing *stress*, perceiving lower levels of key stressors, and being less affected by them at work.[101] ∎

Conscientious employees are better at managing stress than their less organized colleagues.

CHECK OUT

www.mhhe.com/ColquittEss

for study materials including Interactive Exercises, Quizzes, iPod downloads, and video.

CASE: Four Seasons

The 2006 calendar year signaled a big change for Four Seasons, as the chain was purchased by Microsoft Chairman Bill Gates and Saudi Prince Al-Waleed bin Talal for $3.7 billion.[102] The move allows Isadore Sharp to grow his chain aggressively without worrying about the company's stock price. Sharp's plan is to double the number of Four Seasons locations within the next 10 years, with seven new locations (Bora Bora, Florence, Istanbul, Macau, Mauritius, Mumbai, and St. Louis) opening in 2008 alone. That expansion poses an important challenge for the chain, as it will need to hire 35,000 employees to staff its new locations.

For his part, Prince Al-Waleed appreciates the nature of that challenge, recognizing that maintaining service quality will be critical as the new locations open. The chain's four-interview hiring philosophy should be able to deliver the right mix of personalities and talents. The company's recruitment strategies also will likely prove helpful. Specifically, Four Seasons recruits from top hospitality programs like Cornell University or University of Nevada–Las Vegas in an effort to find the most

able employees. Of course, the chain may also need to tailor its approaches somewhat as it expands to countries that differ widely in their cultural values. Ultimately, the goal will be to recreate the same "Four Seasons experience" for customers in all of those diverse locales. After all, "The strength of Four Seasons," Prince Al-Waleed notes, "is consistency."

8.1 If you were in charge of Four Season's hiring strategies, which of the Big Five would you prioritize in the interviews? Are some Big Five dimensions easier to assess in an interview context than others?

8.2 If you consider the profile of the ideal Four Seasons employee, as described in the chapter, is that profile consistent with some of Hofstede's cultural values? Is it inconsistent with any of them? What challenges are created by hiring for hotels in a variety of different cultures?

8.3 What cognitive and emotional abilities are likely to be critical to Four Seasons employees? How easily can those be gauged in an interview? Can new hires be trained to overcome any deficiencies in those abilities?

8.1 Personality refers to the traits and propensities inside a person that explain his or her characteristic patterns of thought, emotion, and behavior. It also refers to a person's social reputation—the way he or she is perceived by others. Cultural values are shared beliefs about desirable end states or modes of conduct in a given culture that influence the expression of traits. Ability refers to the relatively stable capabilities of people to perform a particular range of related activities.

8.2 The "Big Five" include conscientiousness (e.g., dependable, organized, reliable), agreeableness (e.g., warm, kind, cooperative), neuroticism (e.g., nervous, moody, emotional), openness to experience (e.g., curious, imaginative, creative), and extraversion (e.g., talkative, sociable, passionate).

8.3 Hofstede's dimensions of cultural values include individualism–collectivism, power distance, uncertainty avoidance, masculinity–femininity, and short-term vs. long-term orientation.

8.4 Cognitive abilities include verbal ability, quantitative ability, reasoning ability, spatial ability, and perceptual ability. General mental ability, or g, underlies all of these more specific cognitive abilities.

8.5 Emotional intelligence includes four specific kinds of emotional skills: self-awareness, other awareness, emotion regulation, and use of emotions.

8.6 General cognitive ability has a strong positive relationship with job performance, due primarily to its effects on task performance. In contrast, general cognitive ability is not related to organizational commitment. Conscientiousness has a moderate positive relationship with job performance and a moderate positive relationship with organizational commitment. It has stronger effects on these outcomes than the rest of the Big Five.

DISCUSSION QUESTIONS

8.1 Consider the duties that you perform in your current job, or the last job that you held. Rank in order the Big Five dimensions from most important to least important in terms of their ability to help you succeed in that environment. Why did you rank them that way?

8.2 Consider the profile of the United States on Hofstede's cultural values, as shown in Table 8-2. Do you personally feel like you fit the United States profile, or do your values differ in some respects? If you served as an expatriate, meaning you were working in another country, which cultural value differences would be most difficult for you to deal with?

8.3 Think of a job that requires very high levels of certain cognitive abilities. Can you think of a way to redesign that job so that people who lack those abilities could still perform the job effectively?

8.4 Think of experiences you've had with people who demonstrated unusually high or low levels of emotional intelligence. Then consider how you would rate them in terms of their cognitive abilities. Do you think that emotional intelligence "bleeds over" to affect people's perceptions of cognitive ability?

ASSESSMENT: The Big Five

What does your personality profile look like? This assessment is designed to measure the five major dimensions of personality: conscientiousness (C), agreeableness (A), neuroticism (N), openness to experience (O), and extraversion (E). Listed below are phrases describing people's behaviors. Please write a number next to each statement that indicates the extent to which it accurately describes you. Answer each question using the response scale provided. Then subtract your answers to the bold-faced questions from 6, with the difference being your new answer for those questions. For example, if your original answer for question 6 was "2," your new answer is "4" (6 − 2). (For more assessments relevant to this chapter, please visit the Online Learning Center at www.mhhe.com/ColquittEss.)

1	2	3	4	5
Very Inaccurate	**Moderately Inaccurate**	**Neither Inaccurate Nor Accurate**	**Moderately Accurate**	**Very Accurate**

1. I am the life of the party. _____
2. I sympathize with others' feelings. _____
3. I get chores done right away. _____
4. I have frequent mood swings. _____
5. I have a vivid imagination. _____
6. **I don't talk a lot.** _____
7. **I am not interested in other people's problems.** _____
8. **I often forget to put things back in their proper place.** _____
9. **I am relaxed most of the time.** _____
10. **I am not interested in abstract ideas.** _____
11. I talk to a lot of different people at parties. _____
12. I feel others' emotions. _____
13. I like order. _____
14. I get upset easily. _____
15. **I have difficulty understanding abstract ideas.** _____
16. **I keep in the background.** _____
17. **I am not really interested in others.** _____
18. **I make a mess of things.** _____
19. **I seldom feel blue.** _____
20. **I do not have a good imagination.** _____

Scoring and Interpretation:

Conscientiousness: Sum up items 3, 8, 13, and 18.
Agreeableness: Sum up items 2, 7, 12, and 17.
Neuroticism: Sum up items 4, 9, 14, and 19.
Openness to Experience: Sum up items 5, 10, 15, and 20.
Extraversion: Sum up items 1, 6, 11, and 16.

Now chart your scores in the figure to the right to see whether you are above or below the norm for each dimension.

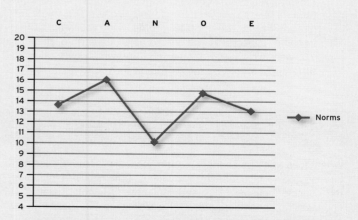

Source: M. B. Donnellan, F. L. Oswald, B. M. Baird, and R. E. Lucas, "The Mini-IPIP Scales: Tiny-Yet-Effective Measures of the Big Five Factors of Personality," *Psychological Assessment* 18 (2006), pp. 192–203. Copyright © 2006 by the American Psychological Association. Adopted with permission. No further reproduction or distribution is permitted without written permission from the American Psychological Association.

EXERCISE: Emotional Intelligence

The purpose of this exercise is to help you become more aware of your emotions and the emotions of others, as well as to see how emotions can be regulated and used in your daily life. This exercise uses groups, so your instructor will either assign you to a group or ask you to create your own group. The exercise has the following steps:

1. Think about situations in which you've experienced each of the following four emotions:

    • Joy

    • Anxiety

    • Sadness

    • Indignation

2. In writing or in group discussion, answer the following questions about each situation:

    a. What, exactly, triggered your emotion in this situation?

    b. What impact did your emotions have on the outcome of the situation? Consider how your emotions affected you, others, and the general outcome of the situation. (Was it positive or negative?)

    c. What strategies did you use to deal with the emotion?

    d. What other strategies could you have used to deal with the emotion?

    For example, one student noted: "I always get anxious when I take tests. Last week, I was supposed to have a midterm in Accounting, and, sure enough, the upcoming test triggered my anxiety. Because I was anxious, I put off studying, and I tried to get some friends to go out to a club with me. We all had a good time that night, but the next day I got a D on my Accounting test, and two of my friends failed their Management midterms. I was using procrastination and avoidance as strategies for dealing with my anxiety. Another strategy I could have used was to face the anxiety head on by talking to my professor to get a better understanding of the material that was going to be on the test, or by getting a group of my friends together to form a study group for Accounting."

3. Compare your responses with the responses of your fellow group members. As a group, answer the following questions:

    a. What emotional triggers do you share? In what ways are your emotional triggers different?

    b. Are there some strategies for dealing with emotions that seem especially helpful? Unhelpful?

    c. According to the stories told by the group, are there times when emotions actually help get a task done or a goal accomplished? How might you harness your emotions to help you achieve specific outcomes in the future?

Source: Adapted from material in M. A. Brackett and N. A. Katulak, "Emotional Intelligence in the Classroom: Skill-Based Training for Teachers and Students," in *Improving Emotional Intelligence: A Practitioner's Guide*, ed. J. Ciarrochi and J. D. Mayer (New York: Psychology Press/Taylor & Francis, 2006), pp. 1–27.

END NOTES

1. O'Brien, J. M. "Why We're Fixated on Four Seasons." *Fortune*, February 4, 2008, pp. 63–66.

2. Martin, R. L. "Creating the Four Seasons Difference." *BusinessWeek*, January 23, 2008, http://www.businessweek.com/innovate/content/jan2008/id20080122_671354.htm (accessed August 5, 2008).

3. Ibid.

4. O'Brien, "Why We're Fixated on Four Seasons."

5. Roth, D. "Trading Places." *Fortune*, January 23, 2006, pp. 121–28.

6. O'Brien, "Why We're Fixated on Four Seasons."

7. Ibid.

8. Funder, D. C. "Personality." *Annual Review of Psychology* 52 (2001), pp. 197–221; Hogan, R. T. "Personality and Personality Measurement." In *Handbook of Industrial and Organizational Psychology*, Vol. 2, ed. M. D. Dunnette and L. M. Hough. Palo Alto, CA: Consulting Psychologists Press, 1991, pp. 873–919.

9. Hogan, "Personality and Personality Measurement."

10. Rokeach, M. *The Nature of Human Values.* New York: Free Press, 1973; Steers, R. M., and C. J. Sanchez-Runde. "Culture, Motivation, and Work Behavior." In *Blackwell Handbook of Cross-Cultural Management*, ed. M. J. Gannon and K. L. Newman. Malden, MA: Blackwell, 2002, pp. 190–213.

11. Fleishman, E. A.; D. P. Costanza; and J. Marshall-Mies. "Abilities." In *An Occupational Information System for the 21st Century: The Development of O*NET*, ed. N. G. Peterson, M. D. Mumford, W. C. Borman, P. R. Jeanneret, and E. A. Fleishman. Washington, DC: American Psychological Association, 1999, pp. 175–95.

12. Hogan, "Personality and Personality Measurement."

13. Goldberg, L. R. "From Ace to Zombie: Some Explorations in the Language of Personality." In *Advances in Personality Assessment*, Vol. 1, ed. C. D. Spielberger and J. N. Butcher. Hillsdale, NJ: Erlbaum, 1982, pp. 203–34; see also Allport, G. W., and H. S. Odbert. "Trait-Names: A Psycho-Lexical Study." *Psychological Monographs* 47, no. 1 (1936), Whole No. 211; Norman, W. T. *2800 Personality Trait Descriptors: Normative Operating Characteristics*

for a University Population. Ann Arbor, MI: University of Michigan Department of Psychology, 1967.

14. Tupes, E. C., and R. E. Christal. *Recurrent Personality Factors Based on Trait Ratings.* USAF ASD Technical Report No. 61–97, Lackland Air Force Base, TX: U.S. Air Force, 1961, reprinted in *Journal of Personality* 60, pp. 225–51; Norman, W. T. "Toward an Adequate Taxonomy of Personality Attributes: Replicated Factor Structure in Peer Nomination Personality Ratings." *Journal of Abnormal and Social Psychology* 66 (1963), pp. 574–83; Digman, J. M., and N. K. Takemoto-Chock. "Factors in the Natural Language of Personality: Re-Analysis, Comparison, and Interpretation of Six Major Studies." *Multivariate Behavioral Research* 16 (1981), pp. 149–70; McCrae, R. R., and P. T. Costa Jr. "Updating Norman's 'Adequate Taxonomy': Intelligence and Personality Dimensions in Natural Language and in Questionnaires." *Journal of Personality and Social Psychology* 49 (1985), pp. 710–21; Goldberg, L. R. "An Alternative 'Description of Personality': The Big-Five Factor Structure." *Journal of Personality and Social Psychology* 59 (1990), pp. 1216–29.

15. Goldberg, L. R. "Language and Individual Differences: The Search for Universals in Personality Lexicons." In *Review of Personality and Social Psychology*, Vol. 2, ed. L. Wheeler. Beverly Hills, CA: Sage, 1981, pp. 141–65.

16. Saucier, G. "Mini-Markers: A Brief Version of Goldberg's Unipolar Big-Five Markers." *Journal of Personality Assessment* 63 (1994), pp. 506–16; Goldberg, L. R. "The Development of Markers for the Big-Five Factor Structure." *Psychological Assessment* 4 (1992), pp. 26–42; McCrae, R. R., and P. T. Costa Jr. "Validation of the Five-Factor Model of Personality across Instruments and Observers." *Journal of Personality and Social Psychology* 52 (1987), pp. 81–90.

17. Barrick, M. R., and M. K. Mount. "The Big Five Personality Dimensions and Job Performance: A Meta-Analysis." *Personnel Psychology* 44 (1991), pp. 1–26.

18. Barrick, M. R.; G. L. Stewart; and M. Piotrowski. "Personality and Job Performance: Test of the Mediating Effects of Motivation among Sales Representatives." *Journal of Applied Psychology* 87 (2002), pp. 43–51.

19. Barrick, M. R.; M. K. Mount; and J. P. Strauss. "Conscientiousness and Performance of Sales Representatives: Test of the Mediating Effects of Goal Setting." *Journal of Applied Psychology* 78 (1993), pp. 715–22.

20. Stewart, G. L. "Trait Bandwidth and Stages of Job Performance: Assessing Differential Effects for Conscientiousness and Its Subtraits." *Journal of Applied Psychology* 84 (1999), pp. 959–68.

21. Judge, T. A.; C. A. Higgins; C. J. Thoreson; and M. R. Barrick. "The Big Five Personality Traits, General Mental Ability, and Career Success across the Life Span." *Personnel Psychology* 52 (1999), pp. 621–52.

22. Barrick, Stewart, and Piotrowski, "Personality and Job Performance."

23. Hogan, J., and B. Holland. "Using Theory to Evaluate Personality and Job-Performance Relations: A Socioanalytic Perspective." *Journal of Applied Psychology* 88 (2003), pp. 100–12.

24. Barrick and Mount, "The Big Five Personality Dimensions."

25. Frei, R. L., and M. A. McDaniel. "Validity of Customer Service Measures in Personnel Selection: A Review of Criterion and Construct Evidence." *Human Performance* 11 (1998), pp. 1–27.

26. Graziano, W. G.; L. A. Jensen-Campbell; and E. C. Hair. "Perceiving Interpersonal Conflict and Reacting to It: The Case for Agreeableness." *Journal of Personality and Social Psychology* 70 (1996), pp. 820–35.

27. Barrick, Stewart, and Piotrowski, "Personality and Job Performance."

28. Palmeri, D. "Dr. Warren's Lonely Hearts Club." *BusinessWeek*, February 20, 2006, pp. 82–84.

29. "What Are the 29 Dimensions?" http://www.eharmony.com/singles/servlet/about/dimensions (accessed January 6, 2007).

30. Judge, T. A.; J. E. Bono; R. Ilies; and M. W. Gerhardt. "Personality and Leadership: A Qualitative and Quantitative Review." *Journal of Applied Psychology* 87 (2002), pp. 765–80.

31. Ibid.

32. Thoreson, C. J.; S. A. Kaplan; A. P. Barsky; C. R. Warren; and K. de Chermont. "The Affective Underpinnings of Job Perceptions and Attitudes: A Meta-Analytic Review and Integration." *Psychological Bulletin* 129 (2003), pp. 914–45.

33. Ibid; Judge, T. A.; D. Heller; and M. K. Mount. "Five-Factor Model of Personality and Job Satisfaction: A Meta-Analysis." *Journal of Applied Psychology* 87 (2003), pp. 530–41.

34. Arvey, R. D.; T. J. Bouchard; N. L. Segal; and L. M. Abraham. "Job Satisfaction: Environmental and Genetic Components." *Journal of Applied Psychology* 74 (1989), pp. 187–92.

35. Magnus, K.; E. Diener; F. Fujita; and W. Pavot. "Extraversion and Neuroticism as Predictors of Objective Life Events: A Longitudinal Analysis." *Journal of Personality and Social Psychology* 65 (1992), pp. 1046–53.

36. Paunonen, S. V. "Big Five Predictors of Personality and Replicated Predictions of Behavior." *Journal of Personality and Social Psychology* 84 (2003), pp. 411–24; Asendorpf, J. B., and S. Wilpers. "Personality Effects on Social Relationships." *Journal of Personality and Social Psychology* 74 (1998), pp. 1531–44.

37. Asendorpf and Wilpers, "Personality Effects on Social Relationships."

38. Barrick, M. R., and M. K. Mount. "Select on Conscientiousness and Emotional Stability." In *Blackwell Handbook of Principles of Organizational Behavior,* ed. E. A. Locke. Malden, MA: Blackwell, 2000, pp. 15–28.

39. Thoreson et al., "The Affective Underpinnings."

40. Ibid.

41. DeNeve, K. M., and H. Cooper. "The Happy Personality: A Meta-Analysis of 137 Personality Traits and Subjective Well-Being." *Psychological Bulletin* 124 (1998), pp. 197–229.

42. Rotter, J. B. "Generalized Expectancies for Internal versus External Control of Reinforcement." *Psychological Monographs* 80 (1966), pp. 1–28.

43. Judge, T. A., and J. E. Bono. "Relationship of Core Self-Evaluation Traits—Self-Esteem, Generalized Self-Efficacy, Locus of Control, and Emotional Stability—with Job Satisfaction and Job Performance: A Meta-Analysis." *Journal of Applied Psychology* 86 (2001), pp. 80–92.

44. Ng, T. W. H.; K. L. Sorensen; and L. T. Eby. "Locus of Control at Work: A Meta-Analysis." *Journal of Organizational Behavior* 27 (2006), pp. 1057–87.

45. Barrick and Mount, "The Big Five Personality Dimensions"; Cellar, D. F.; M. L. Miller; D. D. Doverspike; and J. D. Klawsky. "Comparison of Factor Structures and Criterion-Related Validity Coefficients for Two Measures of Personality Based on the Five Factor Model." *Journal of Applied Psychology* 81 (1996), pp. 694–704.

46. LePine, J. A.; J. A. Colquitt; and A. Erez. "Adaptability to Changing Task Contexts: Effects of General Cognitive Ability, Conscientiousness, and Openness to Experience." *Personnel Psychology* 53 (2000), pp. 563–93; Thoreson, C. J.; J. C. Bradley; P. D. Bliese; and J. D. Thoreson. "The Big Five Personality Traits and Individual Job Performance Growth Trajectories in Maintenance and Transitional Job Stages." *Journal of Applied Psychology* 89 (2004), pp. 835–53.

47. Shalley, C. E.; J. Zhou; and G. R. Oldham. "The Effects of Personal and Contextual Characteristics on Creativity: Where Should We Go from Here?" *Journal of Management* 30 (2004), pp. 933–58.

48. Zhou, J., and J. M. George. "When Job Dissatisfaction Leads to Creativity: Encouraging the Expression of Voice." *Academy of Management Journal* 44 (2001), pp. 682–96.

49. Feist, G. J. "A Meta-Analysis of Personality in Scientific and Artistic Creativity." *Personality and Social Psychology Review* 2 (1998), pp. 290–309.

50. McCrae, R. R.; A. Terracciano; et al. "Personality Profiles of Cultures: Aggregate Personality Traits." *Journal of Personality and Social Psychology* 89 (2005), pp. 407–25.

51. Hofstede, G. *Culture's Consequences: International Differences in Work Related Values.* Beverly Hills, CA: Sage, 1980; Kirkman, B. L.; K. B. Lowe; and C. B. Gibson. "A Quarter Century of *Culture's Consequences*: A Review of Empirical Research Incorporating Hofstede's Cultural Values Framework." *Journal of International Business Studies* 37 (2006), pp. 285–320.

52. Kirkman, Lowe, and Gibson, "A Quarter Century."

53. Black, J. S. "The Relationship of Personal Characteristics with the Adjustment of Japanese Expatriate Managers." *Management International Review* 30 (1990), pp. 119–34.

54. Oyserman, D.; H. M. Coon; and M. Kemmelmeier. "Rethinking Individualism and Collectivism: Evaluation of Theoretical Assumptions and Meta-Analyses." *Psychological Bulletin* 128 (2002), pp. 3–72.

55. Jackson, C. L.; J. A. Colquitt; M. J. Wesson; and C. P. Zapata-Phelan. "Psychological Collectivism: A Measurement Validation and Linkage to Group Member Performance." *Journal of Applied Psychology* 91 (2006), pp. 884–99.

56. Triandis, H. C., and E. M. Suh. "Cultural Influences on Personality." *Annual Review of Psychology* 53 (2002), pp. 133–60.

57. Jackson et al., "Psychological Collectivism."

58. O*Net Online. http://online.onetcenter.org/find/descriptor/browse/Abilities/#cur (accessed June 5, 2006).

59. Van der Zee, K. I., and J. P. Van Oudenhoven. "The Multicultural Personality Questionnaire: Reliability and Validity of Self- and Other Ratings of Multicultural Effectiveness." *Journal of Research in Personality* 35 (2001), pp. 278–88.

60. Van der Zee, K. I., and U. Brinkmann. "Construct Validity Evidence for the Intercultural Readiness Check against the Multicultural Personality Questionnaire." *International Journal of Selection and Assessment* 12 (2004), pp. 285–90; Van Oudenhoven, J. P., and K. I. Van der Zee. "Predicting Multicultural Effectiveness of International Students: The Multicultural Personality Questionnaire." *International Journal of Intercultural Relations* 26 (2002), pp. 679–94; Van Oudenhoven, J. P.; S. Mol; and K. I. Van der Zee. "Study of the Adjustment of Western Expatriates in Taiwan ROC with the Multicultural Personality Questionnaire." *Asian Journal of Social Psychology* 6 (2003), pp. 159–70.

61. *Disability Fact Sheet Handbook.* University of California, Irvine. http://www.disability.uci.edu/disability_handbook/famous_people.htm (accessed June 9, 2006).

62. Frey, M. C., and D. K. Detterman. "Scholastic Assessment of *g*? The Relationship between the Scholastic Assessment Test and General Cognitive Ability." *Psychological Science* 15 (2004), pp. 373–78.

63. Korbin, J. L.; W. J. Camara; and G. B. Milewski. "The Utility of the SAT I and SAT II for Admissions Decisions in California and the Nation." *The College Board, Research Report No. 2002-6.* New York: College Entrance Examination Board, 2002.

64. Ibid.

65. Ibid.

66. Camara, W. J., and G. Echternacht. "The SAT I and High School Grades: Utility in Predicting Success in College." *The College Board, Research Note RN-10.* New York: The College Entrance Examination Board, July 2000.

67. Austin, A.; L. Tsui; and J. Avalos. *Degree Attainment at American Colleges and Universities: Effect of Race, Gender, and Institutional Type.* Washington, DC: American Council on Education, 1996.

68. Vogelstein, F. "Google @ $165: Are These Guys for Real?" *Fortune* 150, no. 12 (December 13, 2004), p. 98. ProQuest database (May 14, 2007).

69. Carroll, J. B. *Human Cognitive Abilities: A Survey of Factor-Analytic Studies.* New York: Cambridge University Press, 1993; Cattell, R. B. "The Measurement of Adult Intelligence. *Psychological Bulletin* 40 (1943), pp. 153–93; Galton, F. *Inquire into Human Faculty and Its Development.* London: Macmillan, 1883; Spearman, C. "General Intelligence, Objectively Determined and Measured." *American Journal of Psychology* 15 (1904), pp. 201–93; Thurstone, L. L. "Primary Mental Abilities." *Psychometric Monographs* (Whole No. 1, 1938); Vernon, P. E. *The Structure of Human Abilities.* London: Methuen, 1950.

70. Spearman, "General Intelligence"; Spearman, C. *The Abilities of Man: Their Nature and Measurement.* New York: MacMillan, 1927.

71. Bar-On, R. *Development of the Bar-On EQ-i: A Measure of Emotional Intelligence and Social Intelligence.* Toronto: Multi-Health Systems, 1997; Gardner, H. *The Shattered Mind.* New York: Knopf, 1975; Goleman, D. *Emotional Intelligence: Why It Can Matter More Than IQ.* New York: Bantam Books, 1995; Thorndike, R. K. "Intelligence and Its Uses." *Harper's Magazine* 140 (1920), pp. 227–335.

72. Matthews, G.; A. K. Emo; R. D. Roberts; and M. Zeidner. "What Is This Thing Called Emotional Intelligence?" In *A Critique of Emotional Intelligence: What Are the Problems and How Can They Be Fixed?* ed. K. R. Murphy. Mahwah, NJ: Lawrence Erlbaum Associates, 2006, pp. 3–36.

73. Salovey, P., and J. D. Mayer. "Emotional Intelligence." *Imagination, Cognition, and Personality* 9 (1990), pp. 185–211.

74. Davies, M.; L. Stankov; and R. D. Roberts. "Emotional Intelligence: In Search of an Elusive Construct." *Journal of Personality and Social Psychology* 75 (1998), pp. 989–1015.

75. Ibid.; Law, K. S.; C. S. Wong; and L. J. Song. "The Construct and Criterion Validity of Emotional Intelligence and Its Potential Utility for Management Studies." *Journal of Applied Psychology* 89 (2004), pp. 483–96.

76. Ibid.

77. Ibid.

78. Wonderlic Web site. http://www.wonderlic.com/Products/product.asp?prod_id=4 (accessed July 12, 2006).

79. Davies et al., "Emotional Intelligence.".

80. Cherniss, C. "The Business Case for Emotional Intelligence." *Consortium for Research on Emotional Intelligence in Organizations.* 2004. http://www.eiconsortium.org/research/business_case_for_ei.htm (accessed July 7, 2006); Cote, S., and C. T. H. Miners. "Emotional Intelligence, Cognitive Intelligence, and Job Performance." *Administrative Science Quarterly* 51 (2006), pp. 1–28; Fisher, A. "Success Secret: A High Emotional IQ." *Fortune* 138, no. 8 (October 26, 1998), p. 293. ProQuest database (May 14, 2007); Kendell, J. "Can't We All Just Get Along?; 'Emotional Intelligence,' or EI, May Sound Like a Squishy Management Concept—But It Gets Results." *BusinessWeek* 3702 (October 9, 2000), p. F18. ProQuest database (May 14, 2007); Schwartz, T. "How Do You Feel?" *Fast Company* 35 (June 2000), p. 296. http://pf.fastcompany.com/magazine/35/emotion.html (accessed June 28, 2006).

81. Cherniss, "The Business Case"; Schwartz, "How Do You Feel?"

82. Lubinski, D. "Introduction to the Special Section on Cognitive Abilities: 100 Years after Spearman's (1904) 'General Intelligence,' 'Objectively Determined and Measured.'" *Journal of Personality and Social Psychology* 86 (2004), pp. 96–111.

83. Seligman, D. "Brains in the Office." *Fortune* 135, no. 1 (January 13, 1997), p. 38. ProQuest database (May 14, 2007).

84. Schmidt, F. L., and J. E. Hunter. "Select on Intelligence." In *Blackwell Handbook of Principles of Organizational Behavior*, ed. E. A. Locke. Malden, MA: Blackwell Publishers, Inc., 2000, pp. 3–14.

85. Hunter, J. E., and F. L. Schmidt. "Intelligence and Job Performance: Economic and Social Implications." *Psychology, Public Policy, and Law* 2 (1996), pp. 447–72; Schmidt, F. L.; J. E. Hunter; A. N. Outerbridge; and S. Goff. "The Joint Relations of Experience and Ability with Job Performance: A Test of Three Hypotheses." *Journal of Applied Psychology* 73 (1988), pp. 46–57.

86. Motowidlo, S. J.; W. S. Borman; and M. J. Schmit. "A Theory of Individual Differences in Task and Contextual Performance." *Human Performance* 10 (1997), pp. 71–83.

87. LePine, Colquitt, and Erez, "Adaptability to Changing Task Contexts"; Schmidt and Hunter, "Select on Intelligence."

88. Boudreau, J. W.; W. R. Boswell; T. A. Judge; and R. D. Bretz. "Personality and Cognitive Ability as Predictors of Job Search among Employed Managers." *Personnel Psychology* 54 (2001), pp. 25–50; Colarelli, S. M.; R. A. Dean; and C. Konstans. "Comparative Effects of Personal and Situational Influences on Job Outcomes of New Professionals." *Journal of Applied Psychology* 72 (1987), pp. 558–66; Dickter, D. N.; M. Roznowski; and D. A. Harrison. "Temporal Tempering: An Event History Analysis of the Process of Voluntary Turnover." *Journal of Applied Psychology* 81 (1996), pp. 705–16.

89. Boudreau et al., "Personality and Cognitive Ability."

90. Barrick, M. R.; M. K. Mount; and T. A. Judge. "Personality and Performance at the Beginning of the New Millennium: What Do We Know and Where Do We Go Next?" *International Journal of Selection and Assessment* 9 (2001),

pp. 9–30; Hough, L. M., and A. Furnham. "Use of Personality Variables in Work Settings." In *Handbook of Psychology,* Vol. 12, ed. W. C. Borman, D. R. Ilgen, and R. J. Klimoski. Hoboken, NJ: Wiley, 2003, pp. 131–69.

91. Judge, T. A., and Ilies, R. "Relationship of Personality to Performance Motivation: A Meta-Analysis." *Journal of Applied Psychology* 87 (2002), pp. 797–807.

92. Sackett, P. R.; S. Zedeck; and L. Fogli. "Relations between Measures of Typical and Maximum Job Performance." *Journal of Applied Psychology* 73 (1988), pp. 482–86.

93. Hough and Furnham, "Use of Personality Variables in Work Settings."

94. Mount, M. K., and Barrick, M. R. "The Big Five Personality Dimensions: Implications for Research and Practice in Human Resources Management." In *Research in Personnel and Human Resource Management*, ed. G. R. Ferris. Greenwich, CT: JAI Press, 1995, pp. 153–200.

95. Salgado, J. F. "The Big Five Personality Dimensions and Counterproductive Behaviors." *International Journal of Selection and Assessment* 10 (2002), pp. 117–25.

96. Judge, Heller, and Mount, "Five Factor Model."

97. Cullen, M. J., and P. Sackett. "Personality and Counterproductive Work Behavior." In *Personality and Work*, ed. M. A. Barrick and A. M. Ryan. San Francisco: Jossey-Bass, 2003, pp. 150–82.

98. Cooper-Hakim, A., and C. Viswesvaran. "The Construct of Work Commitment: Testing an Integrative Framework." *Psychological Bulletin* 131 (2005), pp. 241–59; Mathieu, J. E., and D. M. Zajac. "A Review and Meta-Analysis of the Antecedents, Correlates, and Consequences of Organizational Commitment." *Psychological Bulletin* 108 (1990), pp. 171–94.

99. Salgado, "The Big Five Personality Dimensions."

100. Cooper-Hakim and Viswesvaran, "The Construct of Work Commitment."

101. Grant, S., and J. Langan-Fox. "Personality and Occupational Stressor–Strain Relationships: The Role of the Big Five." *Journal of Occupational Health Psychology* 12 (2007), pp. 20–33.

102. O'Brien, "Why We're Fixated on Four Seasons."

TEAMS

LOGITECH

When's the last time you used a computer mouse or keyboard? What about a universal remote for your home entertainment system, external speakers for your iPod, or a controller or racing wheel for your PlayStation 3? If you've used any of these things recently, chances are good that it was designed and manufactured by Logitech, a Swiss company known for highly innovative and reasonably priced "personal peripherals." Founded in 1981, the company earns revenues of about $2 billion per year and ships about 150 million products to customers in approximately 100 countries across the globe.[1] At a general level, Logitech's success can be attributed to its ability to bring a large number of highly innovative products to market. In a recent year, for example, Logitech introduced 130 new products, and many of these products were honored with industry awards for superior innovation and design.[2]

So what gives Logitech the ability to offer such a large number of innovative products? In a nutshell, Logitech uses teams with highly specialized members who are dispersed throughout the globe, then manages the teams' processes in such a way that work can be accomplished continuously. Consider, for example, the team that developed and manufactured Logitech's flagship mouse, the Revolution. Product design and mechanical engineering took place in Ireland, electrical engineering took place in Switzerland, tooling took place in Taiwan, manufacturing took place in China, and software engineering and quality assurance took place in California.[3] Although you might be inclined to believe that time zone differences would be a hindrance to this sort of team, Logitech turned it into a competitive advantage by letting the work *follow the sun.*[4] Specifically, work was accomplished continuously because members of a team who finished their workday in one country handed off the work to team members in another country who had just arrived at the office. Because hand-offs occurred continuously, product development and other work needed to bring the mouse to market were completed much more quickly.

Although "follow-the-sun" practices are gaining attention in many companies that operate globally, there are some issues that need to be considered.[5] As one example, language and cultural differences among team members can create misunderstandings that prevent work from being accomplished effectively after it has been handed off. Moreover, beyond obvious language issues, just imagine how difficult it must be for members of this sort of dispersed team to find convenient times to communicate with one another. If a team member in California needed to meet virtually with the team on Friday at noon (Pacific Standard Time), it would be 8:00 p.m. Friday evening in Ireland and 4:00 a.m. Saturday morning in Taiwan.

TEAMS

Granted, you probably have not been a member of a team such as the one we described in the opening vignette; however, it is likely that you have had first-hand experiences that will help you relate to the material in this chapter. For example, most of you have participated in a team sport at some point in your life. As another example, many of you have worked in a team with classmates to complete assignments. Finally, some of you may have been a member of an organizational team responsible for making a product, providing a service, or generating recommendations for solving company problems. These teams are obviously different from one another; however, there are some striking similarities as well. In fact, teams are simply groups that possess a set of defining characteristics. Specifically, a **team** is a group of two or more people who work interdependently over some time period to accomplish common goals related to some task-oriented purpose.[6]

●● 9.1

Define teams and identify their characteristics.

Today, teams are used in the majority of organizations in the United States, regardless of whether the organization is large or small.[7] In fact, some researchers have suggested that almost all major U.S. companies are currently using teams or planning to implement them and that up to 50 percent of all employees in the United States work in a team as part of their job.[8] Thus, whereas the use of teams was limited to pioneers such as Procter & Gamble in the 1960s, teams are currently used in all types of industries to accomplish all the types of work necessary to make organizations run effectively.[9] Why have teams become widespread? The most obvious reason is that the nature of the work today requires them. As work has become more complex, interaction among individuals has become more vital because it facilitates the pooling and synthesis of complementary knowledge and skill.

Procter & Gamble was one of the first large companies to implement teamwork as part of the regular job function in the 1960s.

The concepts and theories we will be discussing in this chapter can be grouped into two broad categories, as shown in Figure 9-1. We will begin by discussing team characteristics, or the various qualities of teams and team members. Team characteristics can be taken into account when designing teams, and this is very important because team characteristics impact team processes and team performance. We then overview team processes, which can be defined as the characteristic behaviors and attitudes that emerge in a team after members work with one another for some time. Understanding the various categories of team processes is important because effective processes can result in synergies that translate into improved team performance.

● "Almost all major U.S. companies are currently using teams or planning to implement them."

TEAM CHARACTERISTICS

Although teams can be described by referring to many different characteristics, it is helpful to organize them into three general categories: team types, team interdependence, and team composition.

Team Types

One way to describe teams is to refer to taxonomies that organize teams into various types. One such taxonomy is illustrated in Table 9-1. This table shows that there are five general types of teams, and that each is associated with a number of defining characteristics.[10] The most notable characteristics include the team's purpose, the life span of a team's existence, and the amount of time involvement the team requires of its individual members.

●● 9.2

Identify and describe the five general team types.

Work Teams. Work teams are designed to be relatively permanent. Their purpose is to produce goods or provide services, and they generally require a full-time commitment from their members. Although all work teams have these defining characteristics, they can vary a great deal across organizations in other important ways. One way that work teams vary is in the degree to which members have autonomy in defining their roles and decision making. In traditional work teams, members have very specific sets of job duties, and their decision making is confined to the activities required by those duties. Members of self-managed work teams, in contrast, are not locked into specific jobs. Instead, they jointly decide how to organize themselves and carry out the team's work.

Management Teams. Management teams are similar to work teams in that they are designed to be relatively permanent; however, they are also distinct in a number of important ways. Whereas work teams focus on the accomplishment of core operational-level production and service tasks, management teams participate in managerial tasks that affect the entire organization. Specifically, management teams are responsible

FIGURE **9-1** Team Characteristics and Processes

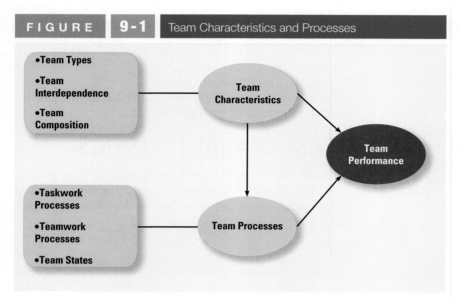

- •Team Types
- •Team Interdependence
- •Team Composition

Team Characteristics

- •Taskwork Processes
- •Teamwork Processes
- •Team States

Team Processes

Team Performance

Parallel Teams. Parallel teams are composed of members from various jobs who provide recommendations to managers about important issues that run "parallel" to the organization's production process.[11] Parallel teams require only part-time commitment from members, and they can be permanent or temporary, depending on their aim. Quality circles, for example, consist of individuals who perform their own jobs but also meet as a team regularly to identify problems and opportunities for improvements in production. As an example of a more temporary parallel team, a committee might form to deal with an issue that arises only periodically.

Project Teams. Project teams are formed to take on "one-time" tasks that are generally complex and require a lot of input from members with different types of training and expertise.[12] Although project teams only exist as long as it takes to finish a project, some projects are quite complex and can take years to complete. Some project teams require full-time commitment, whereas others demand only part-time commitment. A planning team comprised of engineers, architects, designers, and builders, charged with designing a suburban town center, might work together full-time for a year or more. In contrast, the engineers and artists who constitute a team responsible for designing a toothbrush might work together for a month on the project while also serving on other project teams.

for coordinating the activities of organizational subunits—typically departments or functional areas—to help the organization achieve its long-term goals. Top management teams, for example, consist of senior-level executives who meet to make decisions about the strategic direction of the organization. It also may be worth mentioning that because members of management teams are typically heads of departments, their commitment to the management team is offset somewhat by the responsibilities they have in leading their own unit.

TABLE **9-1** Types of Teams

Type of Team	Purpose and Activities	Life Span	Member Involvement	Specific Examples
Work team	Produce goods or provide services.	Long	High	Self-managed work team Production team Maintenance team Sales team
Management team	Integrate activities of subunits across business functions.	Long	Moderate	Top management team
Parallel team	Provide recommendations and resolve issues.	Varies	Low	Quality circle Advisory council Committee
Project team	Produce a one-time output (product, service, plan, design, etc.).	Varies	Varies	Product design team Research group Planning team
Action team	Perform complex tasks that vary in duration and take place in highly visible or challenging circumstances.	Varies	Varies	Surgical team Musical group Expedition team Sports team

Sources: S. G. Cohen and D. E. Bailey, "What Makes Teams Work: Group Effectiveness Research from the Shop Floor to the Executive Suite," *Journal of Management* 27 (1997), pp. 239–90; E. Sundstrom, K. P. De Meuse, and D. Futrell, "Work Teams: Applications and Effectiveness." *American Psychologist* 45 (1990), pp. 120–33.

Action Teams. Action teams perform tasks that are normally limited in duration. However, those tasks are quite complex and take place in contexts that are either highly visible to an audience or of a highly challenging nature.[13] Some types of action teams work together for an extended period of time. For example, sport teams typically remain together for a season, and musical groups like the Rolling Stones may stick together for decades. Other types of action teams stay together only as long as the task takes to complete. A surgical team or an aircraft flight crew may only work together as a unit for a single two-hour surgery or flight.

Variations within Teams: Virtuality. Even knowing whether a team is a project team, an action team, or some other type of team doesn't tell you the whole story. Often there are important variations within those categories that determine a team's functioning. For example, virtual teams are teams in which the members are geographically dispersed, and interdependent activity occurs through electronic communications such as e-mail, instant messaging, and Web conferencing. Although communications and group networking software is far from perfect, it has advanced to the point that it is possible for almost all types of teams to function virtually. In other words, there are exam-

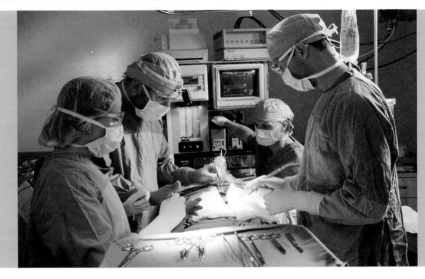

An action team like a surgical team often performs tasks that are complex in execution but of limited duration.

forming, members orient themselves by trying to understand the boundaries in the team. Members try to get a feel for what is expected of them, what types of behaviors are out of bounds,

> ## "Although communications and group networking software is far from perfect, it has advanced to the point that it is possible for almost all types of teams to function virtually."

ples of teams in every category of Table 9-1 that could function either face-to-face or virtually with the right technology. As we described in the opening vignette, virtual teams are not just an efficient way to accomplish work when members are geographically separated. They also may be used to make continuous progress on work tasks without members having to work 24/7.

Variations within Teams: Phase of Team Development. In addition to varying in their "virtuality," teams of any type can differ in the amount of experience they have working together. One way to understand this point is to consider what occurs in teams as they progress from a newly formed group of individuals to a well-established team. According to the Four Stage Theory of team development, teams go through a progression of four stages shown in the top panel of Figure 9-2.[14] In the first stage, called

and who's in charge. In the next stage, called *storming*, members remain committed to ideas they bring with them to the team. This initial unwillingness to accommodate others' ideas triggers conflict that negatively affects some interpersonal relationships and harms the team's progress. During the next stage, *norming*, members realize that they need to work together to accomplish team goals, and, consequently, they begin to cooperate with one another. Feelings of solidarity develop as members work toward team goals. Over time, norms and expectations develop regarding what different members are responsible for doing. In the final stage of team development, which is called *performing*, members are comfortable working within their roles, and the team makes progress toward goals.

A theory of team development that may be more applicable to certain types of project teams is called punctuated equilibrium.[15] The sequence of team development described by

FIGURE 9-2 Two Models of Team Development

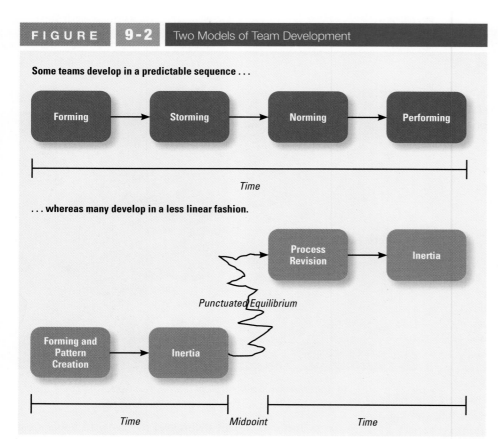

Some teams develop in a predictable sequence . . .

Forming → Storming → Norming → Performing

Time

. . . whereas many develop in a less linear fashion.

Forming and Pattern Creation → Inertia

Punctuated Equilibrium

Process Revision → Inertia

Time — Midpoint — Time

behavior as it settles into a sort of inertia. At the midway point of the project—and this is true regardless of the length of the project—something remarkable happens. Members realize that they have to change their task paradigm fundamentally to complete it on time. Teams that take this opportunity to plan a new approach during this transition tend to do well, and the new framework dominates their behavior until task completion. However, teams that do not take the opportunity to change their approach tend to persist with their original pattern and may "go down with a sinking ship."

Team Interdependence

In addition to taxonomies of team types, we can describe teams by talking about the interdependence that governs connections among team members. In a general sense, you can think of interdependence as the way in which the members of a team are linked to one another.

this theory appears in the bottom panel of Figure 9-2. At the initial team meeting, members make assumptions and establish a pattern of behavior that lasts for the first half of its life. That pattern of behavior continues to dominate the team's

● ● **9.3**

Describe the three general types of team interdependence.

Task Interdependence. Task interdependence refers to the degree to which team members interact with and rely on other team members for the information, materials, and resources needed to accomplish work for the team.[16] As Figure 9-3 illustrates, there are four primary types of task interdependence, and each requires a different degree of interaction and coordination.[17]

The type of task interdependence with the lowest degree of required coordination is *pooled interdependence*.[18] With this type of interdependence, group members complete their work independently, and then this work is "piled up" to represent the group's output. Consider what pooled interdependence would be like on a fishing boat. Each fisherman would bait his or her own pole, drop the baited line into the water, reel the fish in, remove the fish from the hook, and, finally, throw the fish into a tank filled with ice and other fish. At the end of the day, the boat's production would be the weight of the total fish that were caught.

The next type of task interdependence is called *sequential interdependence*.[19] With this type of interdependence, different tasks are done in a prescribed order, and the group is structured such that the members specialize in these tasks. Although members in groups with sequential interdependence interact to carry

The members of this group interact as they clean the beach, but rely primarily on pooled interdependence to do their work. Each member picks up trash and puts it in a bag, and at the end of the day, the group's output can be judged by how many bags are filled, and, of course, how clean the beach looks.

FIGURE 9-3 Task Interdependence and Coordination Requirement

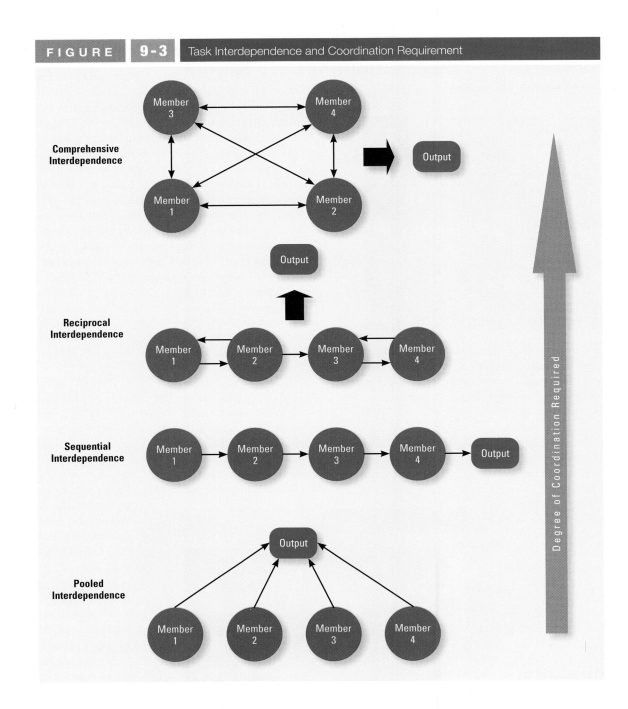

out their work, the interaction only occurs between members who perform tasks that are next to each other in the sequence. Moreover, the member performing the task in the latter part of the sequence depends on the member performing the task in the earlier part of the sequence, but not the other way around. The classic assembly line in manufacturing contexts provides an excellent example of this type of interdependence. In this context, an employee attaches a part to the unit being built, and once this is accomplished, the unit moves on to another employee who adds another part. The process typically ends with the unit being inspected and then packaged for shipping.

Reciprocal interdependence is the next type of task interdependence.[20] Similar to sequential interdependence, members are specialized to perform specific tasks. However, instead of a strict sequence of activities, members interact with a subset of other members to complete the team's work. To understand reciprocal interdependence, consider a team of people who are involved in a business that designs custom homes for wealthy

● **TASK INTERDEPEN-DENCE** The degree to which team members rely on other team members as the team carries out its work.

clients. After meeting with a client, the salesperson would provide general criteria, structural and aesthetic details, and some rough sketches to

IDEO designed the "ultimate cubicle" for the comic strip Dilbert, shown here with the creator of the comic strip, Scott Adams. IDEO relies on the power of comprehensive interdependence to generate new and improved offerings for hundreds of clients, Dilbert included.

an architect who would work up some initial plans and elevations. The architect then would submit the initial plans to the salesperson, who would review the plans with the customer. Typically, the plans need to be revised by the architect several times, and during this process, customers have questions and requests that require the architect to consult with other members of the team. For example, the architect and structural engineer may have to interact to decide where to locate support beams and load-bearing walls. The architect and construction supervisor also might have to meet to discuss revisions to a design feature that turns out to be too costly. As a final example, the salesperson might have to interact with the designers to assist the customer in the selection of additional features, materials, and colors, which would then need to be included in a revision of the plan by the architect.

Finally, *comprehensive interdependence* requires the highest level of interaction and coordination among members as they try to accomplish work.[21] With comprehensive

interdependence, each member has a great deal of discretion in terms of what he or she does and with whom he or she interacts in the course of the collaboration involved in accomplishing the team's work. Teams at IDEO, arguably the world's most successful product design firm, function with comprehensive interdependence. These teams are composed of individuals from very diverse backgrounds, and they meet as a team quite often to share knowledge and ideas to solve problems related to their design projects.[22]

There is no one right way to design teams with respect to task interdependence. However, it is important to recognize the trade-offs associated with the different types. On the one hand, as the level of task interdependence increases, members must spend increasing amounts of time communicating and coordinating with other members to complete tasks. These additional demands decrease productivity, which is the ratio of work completed per the amount of time worked. On the other hand, increases in task interdependence increase the ability of the team to adapt to new situations. The more members interact and communicate with one another, the more likely it is that the team will be able to devise solutions to novel problems it faces.

Goal Interdependence.

In addition to being linked to one another by task activities, members may be linked by their goals.[23] A high degree of goal interdependence exists when team members have a shared vision of the team's goal and align their individual goals with that vision as a result.[24] To understand the power of goal interdependence, visualize a row boat with several people on board, each with a paddle.[25] If each person on the boat wants to go to the exact same place on

What happens when one of these team members wants to head in a different direction?

the other side of a lake, they will all row in the same direction, and the boat will arrive at the desired location. If, however, each person believes the boat should go someplace different, each person will row in a different direction, and the boat will have major problems getting anywhere.

So how do you create high levels of goal interdependence? One thing to do would be to ensure that the team has a formalized mission statement. Mission statements can take a variety of forms, but good ones clearly describe what the team is trying to accomplish in a way that creates a sense of commitment and urgency among team members.[26] Mission statements can come directly from the organization or team leaders, but in many circumstances, it makes sense for teams to go through the process of developing their own mission statements. This process helps members better understand what the team needs to do, and it increases feelings of ownership toward the mission itself.

Outcome Interdependence.

The final type of interdependence relates to how members are linked to one another in terms of the feedback and outcomes they receive as a consequence of working in the team.[27] A high degree of outcome interdependence exists when team members share in the rewards that the team earns, with reward examples including pay, bonuses, formal feedback and recognition, pats on the back, extra time off, and continued team survival. Of course, because team achievement depends on the performance of each team member, high outcome interdependence also implies that team members depend on the performance of other team members for the rewards that they receive.

react if you scored enough points for an A on your final exam, but your professor averaged everyone's grades together and gave all students a C. Chances are you wouldn't be happy with either scenario.

Team Composition

You probably already agree that team effectiveness hinges on team composition—or the mix of people who make up the team in terms of the five characteristics shown in Figure 9-4. For example, if you've been a member of a particularly effective team, you may have noticed that the team members were not only capable of performing their

> "In many circumstances, it makes sense for teams to go through the process of developing their own mission statements. This process helps members better understand what the team needs to do, and it increases feelings of ownership toward the mission itself."

In contrast, low outcome interdependence exists in teams in which individual members receive rewards and punishments on the basis of their own performance, without regard to the performance of the team.

Outcome interdependence presents managers with a tough dilemma when it's considered in team design. High outcome interdependence promotes higher levels of cooperation because members understand that they share the same fate—if the team wins, everyone wins, and if the team fails, everyone fails.[28] However, at the same time, high outcome interdependence may result in reduced motivation, especially among higher performing members. The reason is that high performers may perceive that they are not paid in proportion to what they contributed to the team and that their teammates are taking advantage of this inequity for their own benefit.[29]

One solution to this dilemma has been to implement a level of outcome interdependence that matches the level of task interdependence. Members tend to be more productive in high task interdependence situations when there is also high outcome interdependence. Similarly, members prefer low task interdependent situations when there is low outcome interdependence.[30] To understand the power of aligning task and outcome interdependence, consider scenarios in which there is not a good match. For example, how would you react if you worked very closely with your teammates on a project in one of your classes, and though your professor said the team's project was outstanding, she awarded an A to one of your team members, a B to another, and a C to you? Similarly, consider how you would

role responsibilities effectively, but they also were reliable and cooperative. Our **OB in Sports** box provides another example of the importance of team composition in determining team effectiveness.

● ● 9.4

Describe factors involved in team composition.

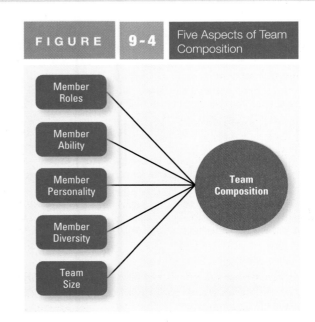

| FIGURE | 9-4 | Five Aspects of Team Composition |

> "HIGH OUTCOME INTERDEPENDENCE PROMOTES HIGHER LEVELS OF COOPERATION BECAUSE MEMBERS UNDERSTAND THAT THEY SHARE THE SAME FATE—IF THE TEAM WINS, EVERYONE WINS, AND IF THE TEAM FAILS, EVERYONE FAILS."

The first aspect of team composition is the mix of member roles, where a role refers to the set of behaviors a person is expected to display in a given context. In a team setting, there are three broad categories of roles that members can take or develop, and depending on the specific situation, the presence or absence of members who possess these roles may have a strong impact on team effectiveness.[31]

Team task roles refer to behaviors that directly facilitate the accomplishment of team tasks. Examples include the orienter who establishes the direction for the team, the devil's advocate who offers constructive challenges to the team's status quo, and the energizer who motivates team members to work harder toward team goals. As you may have realized, the importance of specific task-oriented roles depends on the nature of the work in which the team is involved. The orienter role may be particularly important in teams involved in work for which the team has autonomy about how to accomplish the work. The devil's advocate role may be particularly important in team contexts in which

● ROLE A set of behaviors a person is expected to display in a given context.

decisions are "high stakes" in nature and in situations where teams reach consensus on decisions before considering a reasonable range of alternatives. Finally, the energizer role may be most important in team contexts in which the work is important but not intrinsically motivating.

In contrast to task-oriented roles, *team-building roles* refer to behaviors that influence the quality of the team's social climate. Examples of team-building roles include the harmonizer who steps in to resolve differences among teammates, the encourager who praises the work of teammates, and the compromiser who helps the team see alternative solutions that teammates can accept. As you might have gathered, the presence of members who take on team-building roles helps teams manage conflicts that could hinder team effectiveness.

Finally, whereas task roles and team-building roles focus on activities that benefit the team, *individualistic roles* reflect behaviors that benefit the individual members at the expense of the team. For example, the *aggressor* "puts down" or deflates fellow teammates. The *recognition seeker* takes credit for team successes. The *dominator* manipulates teammates to acquire control and power. If you've ever been on a team in which members took on individualistic roles, you realize just how

OB in Sports

If you were the general manager of one of the worst teams in the National Basketball Association (NBA), what could you do to turn the team around and win the NBA title the next year? One obvious answer is to get better players. In fact, year after year, struggling teams try to draft rookies with star potential and make trades for star veterans. But if that's all there were to it, great turnarounds in the NBA would be routine. Rather, it isn't just getting great players that make turnarounds possible; it's finding the right mix of great players. Boston Celtics' General Manager Danny Ainge used this approach in guiding his team to a record one-year turnaround and the 2007–2008 NBA Championship. So how did Ainge do it?

First, he made trades for Ray Allen and Kevin Garnett. Although adding two perennial All-Stars to a roster might seem like a no-brainer, star players are often concerned about their own statistics and marketability, and, as a result, this strategy is not always successful in helping a team win. Sharing the spotlight was even more of a concern because the Celtics already had a proven All-Star in Paul Pierce.

It turns out, however, that the "Big 3" (Allen, Garnett, and Pierce) had personalities that meshed, and they shared similar goals and values—each had a strong desire to win and a willingness to sacrifice personal statistics to achieve this end.[32] Second, after adding Allen and Garnett, Ainge brought in several veteran players who were willing to play roles that were secondary to the Big 3. In the end, though several teams in the NBA had rosters with players that compared favorably to the Celtics with respect to pure basketball talent, the specific combination of

Ray Allen, Kevin Garnett, and Paul Pierce, dubbed the "Big 3," helped lead the Boston Celtics to an NBA Championship in 2008. It isn't simply a combination of skilled players that make up a team but rather finding the right mix of great players with a combination of skills and shared goals and values, as these three represent.

players on the Celtics proved to be superior to that of any other team in the league. ❖

damaging they can be. Having teammates who take on individualistic roles is not only dissatisfying, but trying to cope with the associated problems also requires a great deal of time and effort.

Abilities. A second aspect of team composition refers to member abilities, and in the context of managerial work, cognitive abilities may be particularly important to consider when designing teams (see Chapter 8 for a discussion of cognitive ability). In general, teams with members who possess higher levels of cognitive ability perform better because teamwork tends to be quite complex.[33] Team members not only have to be involved in several different aspects of the team's task, but they

son, it would be difficult for your team to perform as effectively as other teams in which all members are more interpersonally responsible and engaged in the team's work.

The *agreeableness* of team members is also an important consideration. In general, research has shown that in team settings, the overall level of members' agreeableness may be even more important than conscientiousness.[39] Why? Because agreeable people tend to be more cooperative and trusting, tendencies that promote positive attitudes about the team and smooth interpersonal interactions. Moreover, because agreeable people may be more concerned about their team's interests than their own, they should work hard on behalf of the team.[40] There is a caveat regarding agreeableness in teams, however. Because

> ## "Having teammates who take on individualistic roles is not only dissatisfying, but trying to cope with the associated problems also requires a great deal of time and effort."

also have to learn how best to combine their individual efforts to accomplish team goals.[34] In fact, the more that this type of learning is required, the more important team member cognitive ability becomes. Research has shown that cognitive ability is more important to teams when team members have to learn from one another to adapt to changes, compared with contexts in which team members perform their assigned tasks in a routine fashion.[35]

Personality. A third aspect of team composition refers to *member personality traits* (see Chapter 8 for a discussion of personality), which affect how teams function and perform. For example, team composition in terms of members' *conscientiousness* is important to teams.[36] After all, almost any team would benefit from having members who tend to be dependable and work hard to achieve team goals. What might be less obvious to you is the strong negative effect on the team of having even one member who is particularly low on conscientiousness.[37] To understand why this is true, consider how you would react to a team member who was not dependable and did not appear to be motivated to work hard toward team goals. If you're like most people, you would find the situation dissatisfying, and you would consider different ways of dealing with it. Some people might try to motivate the person to be more responsible and work harder; others might try to get the person ejected from the team.[38] The problem is that these natural reactions to a low-conscientiousness team member not only divert attention away from accomplishing work responsibilities, but they also can result in some very uncomfortable and time-consuming interpersonal conflicts. Moreover, even if you and the other members of the team work harder to compensate for this person,

agreeable people tend to prefer harmony and cooperation over conflict and competition, they may be less apt to speak up and offer constructive criticisms that might help the team improve.[41] Thus, when composed of highly agreeable members, there is a chance that the team will behave in a way that enhances harmony at the expense of task accomplishment.[42]

People who are *extraverted* tend to perform more effectively in interpersonal contexts and are more positive and optimistic in general.[43] Therefore, it shouldn't surprise you to hear that having extraverted team members is generally beneficial to the social climate of the group, as well as to team effectiveness in the eyes of supervisors.[44] At the same time, however, research has shown that having too many members who are very high on extraversion can hurt the team. The reason for this can be attributed to extraverts' tendency to be assertive and dominant. As you would expect when there are too many members with these types of tendencies, power struggles and unproductive conflict occur with greater frequency.[45]

Diversity. Another aspect of team composition refers to the degree to which members are different from one another in terms of any attribute that might be used by someone as a basis of categorizing people. We refer to those differences as *team diversity*.[46] Trying to understand the effects of team diversity is somewhat difficult because there are so many different characteristics that may be used to categorize people. There are also several reasons diversity might influence team functioning and effectiveness, and some of these reasons seem contradictory.

The predominant theory that has been used to explain why diversity has positive effects is called the *value in diversity problem-solving approach*.[47] From this perspective, diversity in teams is beneficial because it provides for a larger pool of knowledge and perspectives from which a team can draw as it carries out its work. Teams that engage in work that is relatively complex and requires creativity benefit most from diversity, and research on teams that are diverse in terms of many different characteristics related to knowledge and perspectives—ethnicity, expertise, personality, attitudes—supports this idea.[48]

A theory that has been used widely to explain why diversity may have detrimental effects on teams is called the *similarity-attraction approach*.[49] According to this perspective, people tend to be more attracted to others who are perceived as more similar. People also tend to avoid interacting with those who are perceived to be dissimilar to reduce the likelihood of having uncomfortable disagreements. Consistent with this perspective, research has shown that diversity on attributes such as cultural background, race, and attitudes is associated with communication problems and ultimately poor team effectiveness.[50]

So it appears that there are two different theories about diversity effects that are relevant to teams, and each has been supported in research. Which perspective is correct? As it turns out, one key to understanding the impact of team diversity requires that you consider both the general type of diversity and the length of time the team has been in existence.[51] Surface-level diversity refers to diversity regarding observable attributes such as race, ethnicity, sex, and age.[52] Although this type of diversity may have a negative impact on teams early in their existence because of similarity-attraction issues, those negative effects tend to disappear as members become more knowledgeable about one another. In essence, the stereotypes that members have about one another based on surface differences are replaced with knowledge regarding underlying characteristics that are more relevant to social and task interactions.[53]

Deep-level diversity, in contrast, refers to diversity with respect to attributes that are less easy to observe initially but that can be inferred after more direct experience. Differences in attitudes, values, and personality are good examples of deep-level diversity.[54] In contrast to the effects of surface-level diversity, time appears to increase the negative effects of deep-level diversity on team functioning and effectiveness.[55] Over time, as team members learn about one another, differences that relate to underlying values and goals become increasingly apparent. Those differences can therefore create problems among team members that ultimately result in reduced effectiveness.

Team Size. In addressing team size, two adages are relevant: "the more the merrier" and "too many cooks spoil the broth." But which statement do you believe is true in terms of how many members to include on a team? The answer, according to research, is that having a greater number of members is beneficial for management and project teams but not for teams engaged in production tasks.[56] Management and project teams engage in work that is complex and knowledge intensive, and these teams therefore benefit from the additional resources and expertise contributed by additional members.[57] In contrast, production teams tend to engage in routine tasks that are less complex. Having additional members beyond what is necessary to accomplish the work tends to result in unnecessary coordination and communication problems. Additional members may therefore be less productive because there is more socializing and they feel less accountable for team outcomes.[58] Although making a claim about the absolute best team size is impossible, research with student teams concluded that team members tend to be most satisfied with their team when the number of members is between 4 and 5 (4.6 to be exact).[59] Of course, there are other rules of thumb you can use to keep team size optimal. Jeff Bezos, the CEO of Amazon.com, uses the two-pizza rule: "If a team can't be fed by two pizzas, it's too large."[60]

> ●● **"If a team can't be fed by two pizzas, it's too large."**

Jeff Bezos of Amazon.com has said a team is too large if it can't be fed by two pizzas. Do you agree?

TEAM PROCESSES

Team process is a term that refers to the different types of activities and interactions that occur within teams that contribute to their ultimate end goals.[61] Some of the team processes we describe in this chapter are observable by the naked eye. For example, it would be possible to see team members gathering information, building on one another's ideas, and collaborating to solve some problem. Other team processes, in contrast, are less visible. As an example, an outside observer wouldn't be able to directly see the emotional bonds between members of a highly cohesive team. Thus, team processes include interactions among members that occur behaviorally, as well as the hard-to-see feelings and thoughts that coalesce as a consequence of member interactions.

● **SURFACE-LEVEL DIVERSITY** Diversity regarding observable characteristics.

DEEP-LEVEL DIVERSITY Diversity regarding characteristics that are less directly observable.

● **TEAM PROCESS** Activities and interactions that occur within teams that contribute to their ultimate end goals.

● **COORDINATION LOSS** Extra effort expended in order to accomplish and integrate work in a team context.

● **MOTIVATIONAL LOSS** The reduction in motivation an individual experiences in a team setting.

"PROCESS GAIN IS IMPORTANT BECAUSE IT RESULTS IN USEFUL RESOURCES AND CAPABILITIES THAT DID NOT EXIST BEFORE THE TEAM CREATED THEM."

⬤⬤ 9.5

Define team process and discuss how team process can result in process gain or process loss.

Why are processes important to learn about? One reason is that effective team processes allow teams to benefit from *process gain*, or getting more from the team than you would expect according to the capabilities of its individual members. Process gain is synonymous with *synergy* and is most critical in situations in which the complexity of the work is high or tasks require combinations of members' knowledge, skills, and efforts to solve problems. In essence, process gain is important because it results in useful resources and capabilities that did not exist before the team created them.[62] Our **OB on Screen** feature illustrates vividly how a team that achieves process gain develops capabilities that help it achieve much more than what most people would rationally expect.

Of course, *process loss*, or getting less from the team than you would expect based on the capabilities of its individual members, is also possible. What factors conspire to create process loss? One factor is that in teams, members have to work to not only accomplish their own tasks but also coordinate their activities with the activities of their teammates.[63] Although this extra effort focused on integrating work is a necessary aspect of the team experience, it is called **coordination loss** because it consumes time and energy that could otherwise be devoted to task activity.[64] Such coordination losses are often driven by *production blocking*, which occurs when members have to wait on one another before they can do their part of the team task.[65] If you've ever worked in a team in which you felt like you couldn't get any of your own work done because of all the time spent in meetings, following up requests for information from other team members, and waiting on team members to do their part of the team task, you already understand how frustrating production blocking (and coordination loss) can be.

The second force that fosters process loss in team contexts is **motivational loss**, or the loss in team productivity that occurs when team members do not work as hard as they could.[66] Why does motivation loss occur in team contexts? One explanation is that it's often quite difficult to gauge exactly how much each team member contributes to the team. Members of teams can work together on projects over an extended period of time, and, as a consequence, it's difficult to keep an accurate accounting of who does what. Similarly, members contribute to their team in many different ways, and contributions of some members may be less obvious than others. Finally, members of teams do not always work together at the same time as a unit. Regardless of the reasons for it, uncertainty regarding "who contributes what" results in team members feeling less accountable for team outcomes. Those feelings of reduced accountability, in turn, cause members to exert less effort when working on team tasks than they would if they worked alone on those same tasks. This phenomenon is called *social loafing*,[67] and it can significantly hinder a team's effectiveness.[68]

Taskwork Processes

Having described process gains and process losses, it's time to describe the particular team processes that can help teams increase their synergy while reducing their inefficiency. One relevant category of team processes is **taskwork processes**, which are the activities of team members that relate directly to the accomplishment of team tasks. In a general sense, taskwork occurs any time that team members interact with the tools or technologies that are used to complete their work. In this regard, taskwork is similar to the concept of task performance described in Chapter 2. However, in the context of teams, especially those that engage in knowledge work, the two types of taskwork shown in Figure 9-5 are crucially important: creative behavior and decision making.

> ⬤ **TASKWORK PROCESSES** Activities of team members that relate directly to the accomplishment of team tasks.

⬤⬤ 9.6

Define taskwork, and describe examples of team activities that fit into this process category.

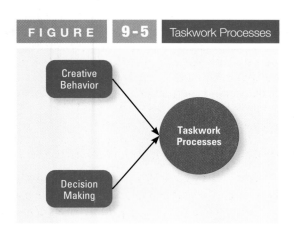

FIGURE 9-5 Taskwork Processes

Creative Behavior → Taskwork Processes ← Decision Making

Creative Behavior. Creative behavior involves team members engaging in activities focused on generating novel and useful ideas and solutions.[69] In Chapter 8 on Personality, Cultural Values, and Ability, we noted that creative behavior is driven in part by the creativity of individual employees because some employees are simply more original and imaginative than others. However, the team environment is also uniquely suited to fostering creative outcomes because with teams, the unique knowledge and skills of members can be combined in a manner that results in novel and useful ideas. However, achieving such outcomes depends on much more than just putting a diverse mix of people together and letting them go at it. In fact, creative behavior in teams can be fostered when members participate in a specific set of taskwork activities.

Brainstorming may be the most well-known activity for generating creative ideas, but research suggests that social loafing, potentially harmful criticism of ideas, and production blocking behavior actually make this activity not as useful as one would believe.

Perhaps the best-known activity that teams use to foster creative behavior is **brainstorming**. Generally speaking, brainstorming involves a face-to-face meeting of team members in which each offers as many ideas as possible about some focal problem or issue.[70] Most brainstorming sessions center around the following rules: (1) Express all ideas that come to mind (no matter how strange), (2) go for quantity of ideas rather than quality, (3) don't criticize or evaluate the ideas of others, and (4) build on the ideas of others. The theory is that if a team follows these rules, it will develop a large pool of ideas that it can use to address the issue at hand.[71] This concept sounds good in theory, so it may surprise you to learn then that traditional brainstorming sessions rarely work as well as intended. In fact, research

OB on Screen

300

The world will know that free men stood against a tyrant, that few stood against many, and before this battle was over, that even a god-king can bleed.

With those words, King Leonidis (Gerard Butler) announces that his band of 300 Spartan soldiers is capable of pulling off a truly remarkable feat—standing against the Persian army led by Xerxes (Rodrigo Santoro) in *300* (Dir. Zack Snyder, Warner Brothers, 2006). Why would that feat be so remarkable? Because the Persian army includes well over 100,000 soldiers (and a few mutated elephants and rhinos).

The movie centers on the battle of Thermopylae, during which a small band of Spartans employs strategies and tactics that give them the fighting capabilities of a much larger force. Those tactics result in process gain because the army is able to achieve more than you'd expect if you simply added up the capabilities of the individual soldiers.

For example, when the Persian army "darkens the sky" by launching tens of thou-

sands of arrows simultaneously, the Spartans immediately get into a tight formation, lift their shields, and then link them together in a manner that creates a collective shield over the entire formation (think of a giant turtle shell, and you get the picture).

Although the movie vividly illustrates the power of process gain, it also alludes to its fragility. For example, as long as each and every soldier executes his part of the process of creating the collective shield, the tactic is effective, and the Spartans can withstand repeated onslaughts of countless arrows. However, if just one Spartan soldier fails to raise his shield on time, it creates a breach in the formation that will only widen as the soldier is struck down (thereby exposing the soldier next to him). Thus, a single soldier's failure in the team process could lead to the destruction of the entire army. ❖

suggests that team members would be better off coming up with ideas on their own, as individuals, before pooling those ideas and evaluating them to arrive at a solution.[72]

Why doesn't brainstorming work as well as individual idea generation? There appear to be at least three reasons.[73] First, there may be a tendency for people to social loaf in group brainstorming contexts. That is, members may not work as hard to think up ideas as they would have if they had to turn in an individually generated list with their name on it. Second, though the brainstorming rules explicitly forbid criticizing others' ideas, members may be hesitant to express ideas that seem silly or not well thought-out. Third, brainstorming results in production blocking because members have to wait their turn to express their ideas. This waiting around consumes time that could otherwise be used by individuals to generate new ideas.

Given the problems associated with brainstorming, why do organizations continue to use it? One reason is that the general idea of brainstorming is well-known, and common sense leads people to believe that it works as advertised. Another reason is that there are benefits of brainstorming beyond just generating ideas. For example, brainstorming builds morale and results in the sharing of knowledge that might otherwise be locked inside the minds of the individual team members.[74] Although this knowledge may not be useful for the particular problem that's being debated, it might be useful for issues that arise in the future.

One offshoot of brainstorming that addresses some of its limitations is the nominal group technique.[75] Similar to a traditional brainstorming session, this process starts off by bringing the team together and outlining the purpose of the meeting. The next step takes place on an individual level, however, as members have a set period of time to write down their own ideas on a piece of paper. The subsequent step goes back into the team setting, as members share their ideas with the team in a round-robin fashion. After the ideas are recorded, members have a discussion intended to clarify the ideas and build on the ideas of others. After this, it's back to an individual environment; members rank order ideas on a card that they submit to a facilitator. A facilitator then tabulates the scores to determine the winning idea. From this description, you probably can guess how the nominal group technique addresses the problems with brainstorming. By making people write down ideas on their own, it decreases social loafing and production blocking. In addition, ranking items as individuals makes people less apprehensive about voicing support for an unpopular idea.

Decision Making. In Chapter 7 on Learning and Decision Making, we described how people use information and intuition to make specific decisions. In team contexts, however, decision making is somewhat more complex because it involves multiple members gathering and considering information that is relevant to their area of specialization, and then making recommendations to a team leader who is ultimately responsible for the final decision.[76] If you ever watched the TV show *The Apprentice*, you should be able to understand this process quite clearly. The show typically begins with Donald Trump assigning two teams a fairly complex task. A member from each team then volunteers to be project leader, and this person assigns to the other team members roles like marketing, logistics, and sales. Throughout the project, members make suggestions and recommendations to the leader, who ultimately is responsible for making the decisions that determine the success of the project. Of course, project success is important because someone from the losing team—most often the project leader—gets to hear Trump say those famous words: "You're fired."

What factors account for a team's ability to make effective decisions in this type of context? At least three factors appear to be involved.[77] The first factor is *decision informity*, which reflects whether members possess adequate information about their own task responsibilities. Project teams on *The Apprentice* often fail, for example, because the team member in charge of marketing does not gather information necessary to help the team understand the desires and needs of the client. The second factor is *staff validity*, which is the degree to which members

> "The team environment is also uniquely suited to fostering creative outcomes."

● BRAINSTORMING A face-to-face group meeting in which team members offer as many ideas as possible.

● NOMINAL GROUP TECHNIQUE An approach to generating ideas and solutions that involves both individual work and work in team meetings.

Like many teams in the real world, the teams on the popular television show The Apprentice *often struggle to make good decisions.*

make good recommendations to the leader. Team members can possess all the information needed to make a valid recommendation but then fail to do so because of a lack of ability, insight, or good judgment. The third factor is *hierarchical sensitivity*, which is the degree to which the leader effectively weighs the members' recommendations. Whom does the leader listen to, and whom does the leader ignore? Teams that make good decisions tend to have leaders that do a good job giving recommendations the weight they deserve. So how can knowledge of these three factors be used to improve team decision making?

Research shows that more experienced teams tend to make better decisions. Over time members develop an understanding of the information that's needed and how to use it, and leaders develop an understanding of which members provide the best recommendations.[78] Thus, because experience is so

posed of members from different countries have unique challenges in decision making; however, there are some things they can do to manage these issues.

Teamwork Processes

The second major category of team processes is **teamwork processes**, which refer to the interpersonal activities that facilitate the accomplishment of the team's work but do not directly involve task accomplishment itself.[81] You can think of teamwork processes as the behaviors that create the setting or context in which taskwork processes can be carried out. So what types of behaviors do teamwork processes involve? Figure 9-6 summarizes research that has identified several teamwork processes, and we describe these in detail below.[82]

> ["Teams that make good decisions tend to have leaders that do a good job giving recommendations the weight they deserve."]

important, it may be important to give decision-making teams a chance to work together before they are assigned to critical team responsibilities. As another example, team decision making may be improved by giving members feedback about the three variables involved in the decision-making process.[79] For example, a team can improve its decision making if the members are told that they have to share and consider additional pieces of information before making recommendations to the leader. Although this recommendation may seem obvious, all too often teams only receive feedback about their final decision. There also may be a benefit to separating the process of sharing information from the process of making recommendations and final decisions, at least in terms of how information is communicated among members.[80] Whereas teams tend to share more information when they meet face to face, leaders do a better job considering recommendations and making final decisions when they're away from the members. Once they're separated, they don't have to deal with pressure from members who may be more assertive or better at articulating and defending their positions. As our **OB Internationally** box reveals, teams com-

●● 9.7

Define teamwork, and describe examples of team activities that fit into this process category.

Transition Processes. *Transition processes* are teamwork activities that focus on preparation for future work. For example, *mission analysis* involves an analysis of the team's task, the challenges that face the team, and the resources available for completing the team's work. *Strategy formulation* refers to the development of courses of action and contingency plans, and then adapting those plans in light of changes that occur in the team's environment. Finally, *goal specification* involves the development and prioritization of goals related to the team's mission and strategy. Each of these transition processes is relevant before the team actually begins to conduct the core aspects of its work. However, these transition processes also may be important between periods of work activity. For example, think about the adjustments made by a design team that is falling behind schedule. The team could consider how much work needs to be done to finish on time, and then devise a new strategy to ensure timely completion of the project in order to satisfy the customer.

Action Processes. Whereas transition processes are important before and between periods of taskwork, *action processes* are important as the taskwork is being accomplished. One type of action process involves monitoring progress toward goals. Teams that pay attention to goal-related information—perhaps by charting the team's performance relative to team

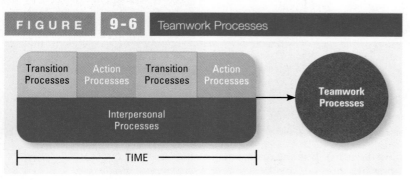

FIGURE 9-6 Teamwork Processes

Transition Processes | Action Processes | Transition Processes | Action Processes

Interpersonal Processes

TIME

Teamwork Processes

goals—are typically in a good position to realize when they are "off-track" and need to make changes. *Systems monitoring* involves keeping track of things that the team needs to accomplish its work. A team that does not engage in systems monitoring may fail because it runs out of inventory, time, or other necessary resources. *Helping behavior* involves members going out of their way to help or back up other team members. Team members can provide indirect help to their teammates in the form of feedback or coaching, as well as direct help in the form of assistance with members' tasks and responsibilities. *Coordination* refers to synchronizing team members' activities in a way that makes them mesh effectively and seamlessly. Poor coordination results in team members constantly having to wait on others for information or other resources necessary to do their part of the team's work.[83]

Interpersonal Processes.

The third category of teamwork processes is called *interpersonal processes*. The processes in this category are important before, during, or in between periods of taskwork, and each relates to the manner in which team members manage their relationships. The first type of interpersonal process is *motivating* and *confidence building*, which refers to things team members do or say that affect the degree to which members are motivated to work hard on the team's task. Expressions that create a sense of urgency and optimism are examples of communications that would fit in this category. Similarly, *affect management* involves activities that foster a sense of emotional balance and unity. If you've ever worked in a team in which members got short tempered when facing pressure or blamed one another when there were problems, you have first-hand experience with poor affect management. Another interpersonal process is *conflict management*, which involves the activities that the team uses to manage conflicts that arise in the course of its work. Conflict tends to

have a negative impact on a team, but the nature of this effect depends on the focus of the conflict as well as the manner in which the conflict is managed.[84]

Relationship conflict refers to disagreements among team members in terms of interpersonal relationships or incompatibilities with respect to personal values or preferences. This type of conflict centers on issues that are not directly connected to the team's task. Relationship conflict is not only dissatisfying to most people, it also tends to result in reduced team performance. *Task conflict*, in contrast, refers to disagreements among members about the team's task. In theory, this type of conflict can be beneficial to teams if it stimulates conversations that result in the development and expression of new ideas.[85] Research findings, however, indicate that task conflict tends to result in reduced team effectiveness unless certain conditions are present.[86] Members need to trust one another and be confident that they can express their opinions openly without fear of reprisals, and they also need to engage in effective conflict management processes. Our **OB for Students** feature provides an example of how conflict management can have a significant impact on the effectiveness of student teams.

Team States

The third category of team process is less visible to the naked eye. Team states such as those summarized in Figure 9-7 refer to specific feelings and thoughts that coalesce in the minds of team members as a consequence of their experience working together.

● **TEAMWORK PROCESSES** Interpersonal activities that facilitate the accomplishment of the team's work but do not directly involve task accomplishment itself.

● **TEAM STATES** Feelings and thoughts that coalesce in the minds of team members as a consequence of their experience working together.

OB Internationally

Organizations have become increasingly reliant on multinational teams, or teams composed of individuals who do not share the same national identification.[87] Because multinational teams have a diverse set of experiences and perspectives from which to draw in the decision-making process, decisions can be more innovative.[88] Along with this benefit, there are costs in terms of potential problems with team processes. The most obvious problem is language barriers that prevent team members from communicating effectively with one another. Beyond simple misunderstandings, communication barriers may hinder members from receiving or understanding the information they need to make

good recommendations and decisions.[89] So what can multinational teams do to address this issue?

One solution is to implement *group decision support systems*, which involve the use of computer technology to help the team structure its decision-making process.[90] As an example, members of a multinational team might meet in rooms where each member sits at a networked laptop. At different points during the meeting, members are directed to provide their ideas and recommendations into the computer. These inputs are then summarized and shared visually with the entire team on their computer screens. Advantages of this approach are that the system keeps the meet-

ing focused squarely on the task and information can be presented in a logical sequence at a pace that makes it easier to digest. Moreover, no single member can dominate the meeting. As a consequence of these advantages, team members may participate more uniformly in the meeting and develop a more consistent understanding of the information that was exchanged. Another advantage is that the technique can be modified and used when members are geographically dispersed. The downside of group decision support systems, especially if the meetings are held virtually, is that the process is depersonalized, and members may leave the meetings feeling less connected to the team and its decisions. ❖

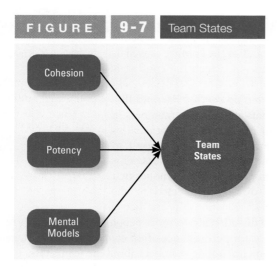

FIGURE **9-7** Team States

with feelings of overconfidence about the team's capabilities.[93] In the end, groupthink has been blamed for decision-making fiascos in politics as well as in business. Some famous examples include John F. Kennedy's decision to go forward with the Bay of Pigs invasion of Cuba,[94] NASA's decision to launch the space shuttle *Challenger* in unusually cold weather,[95] and Enron's board of directors' decisions to ignore illegal accounting practices.[96]

So how do you leverage the benefits of cohesion without taking on the potential costs? One way is to acknowledge that cohesion can potentially have detrimental consequences. A good first step in this regard would be to measure the team's cohesion using an assessment such as the one included at the end of this chapter. A high score on cohesion may indicate potential vulnerability to groupthink. A second step in preventing problems associated with cohesion would be to formally institute the role of devil's advocate. The person filling this role would be responsible for evaluating and challenging prevailing points of view in a constructive manner and also bringing in fresh perspectives and ideas to the team. Although the devil's advocate role could be filled by an existing team member, it's also possible that the team could bring in an outsider to fill that role.

9.8

Define team states, and describe concepts that fit into this process category.

Cohesion. For a number of different reasons, members of teams can develop strong emotional bonds to other members of their team and to the team itself. This emotional attachment, which is called **cohesion**,[91] tends to foster high levels of motivation and commitment to the team, and, as a consequence, cohesiveness tends to promote higher levels of team performance.[92] But is a cohesive team necessarily a good team? According to researchers, the answer to this question is no. In highly cohesive teams, members may try to maintain harmony by striving toward consensus on issues without ever offering, seeking, or seriously considering alternative viewpoints and perspectives. This drive toward conformity at the expense of other team priorities is called *groupthink* and is thought to be associated

● **COHESION** Emotional attachment that tends to foster high levels of motivation and commitment to the team.

Potency. The second team state, *potency*, refers to the degree to which members believe that the team can be effective across a variety of situations and tasks.[97] When a team has high potency, members are confident that their team can perform well, and, as a consequence, they focus more of their energy on achieving team goals. When a team has low potency, members are not as confident about their team, and so they begin to question the team's goals and one another. Ultimately, this reaction can result in members focusing their energies on activities that don't benefit the team. As a result, research studies have shown that potency has a strong positive impact on team performance.[98] So how does high potency develop in teams? Team members' confidence in their own capabilities, their trust in other members' capabilities, and feedback about past performance are all likely to play a role. Specifically, team potency is promoted in teams in which members are confident in themselves and their teammates and when the team has found success in the past.

OB for Students

If you have experience working in student teams in your courses, you know that conflict can have some really negative consequences—not the least of which is the discomfort it provokes and the huge waste of time that can ensue. To avoid this dissatisfying experience, many students try to avoid conflict in their team altogether. But is there a better way to manage conflict?

One study of teams of undergraduate business students investigated the role that task conflict had on two important team outcomes: the grade on a semester-long team project and members' satisfaction with the team experience.[99] The results of the study indicated that the effects of task conflict on these two outcomes depended a lot on the way the team managed its conflict. First, higher levels of task conflict tended to result in higher scores on team projects, but only for teams that approached the conflict proactively. Members of these teams openly discussed points of disagreement and tried to resolve their disagreements collaboratively. In contrast, teams tended to perform less well on team projects when the members managed high levels of task conflict in a more passive way. Members of these teams tended to avoid openly expressing disagreements or ended potential disagreement prematurely by being overly accommodating of other members' positions.

Second, higher levels of task conflict resulted in higher levels of satisfaction with the team experience, but only for teams that managed conflict in an agreeable manner. When members expressed their positions harshly or in a more emotional way, higher levels of task conflict tended to reduce member satisfaction. ❖

Mental Models.   *Mental models* refer to the level of common understanding among team members with regard to important aspects of the team and its task.[100] A team may have shared mental models with respect to the capabilities that members bring to the team as well as the processes the team needs to use to be effective.[101] How can these two types of mental models foster team effectiveness? When team members share in their understanding of one another's capabilities, they're more likely to know where to go for the help they might need to complete their work. In addition, they should be able to anticipate when another member needs help to do his or her work. When members have a shared understanding of which processes are necessary to help the team be effective, they can carry out these processes efficiently and smoothly. To help you understand why this is true, consider what would happen in a team of students who had different understandings about how the team should manage conflict. Few disagreements would get resolved if some of the members believed that direct confrontation was best, whereas others believed that avoidance was best.

HOW IMPORTANT ARE TEAM PROCESSES?

How much do team processes affect performance and commitment? Answering this question is somewhat complicated because when we say "performance and commitment," we are not referring to the performance of individuals or their attachment to the organization. Instead, we are referring to the performance of teams and the degree to which team members are

> Confidence, trust, and feedback about past performance play a role in developing high potency in teams.

collectively committed to the team. In the jargon of research on teams, we are concerned with team performance and cohesion. Additionally, as have we described throughout this chapter, there are several different types of team processes that we could consider in our summary. In Figure 9-8,

| FIGURE | 9-8 | Effects of Teamwork Process on Performance and Commitment |

INSIDE OUR INTEGRATIVE MODEL OF OB

Teamwork Processes → Team Performance

Teamwork processes have a moderate positive effect on *Team Performance*. That aspect of team process has a stronger effect on performance for teams involved in more complex knowledge work rather than less complex work.

Teamwork Processes → Team Commitment

Teamwork processes have a strong positive effect on *Team Commitment*. That aspect of team process has a stronger effect on commitment for teams involved in more complex knowledge work rather than less complex work.

Represents a strong correlation (around .50 in magnitude).

Represents a moderate correlation (around .30 in magnitude).

Represents a weak correlation (around .10 in magnitude).

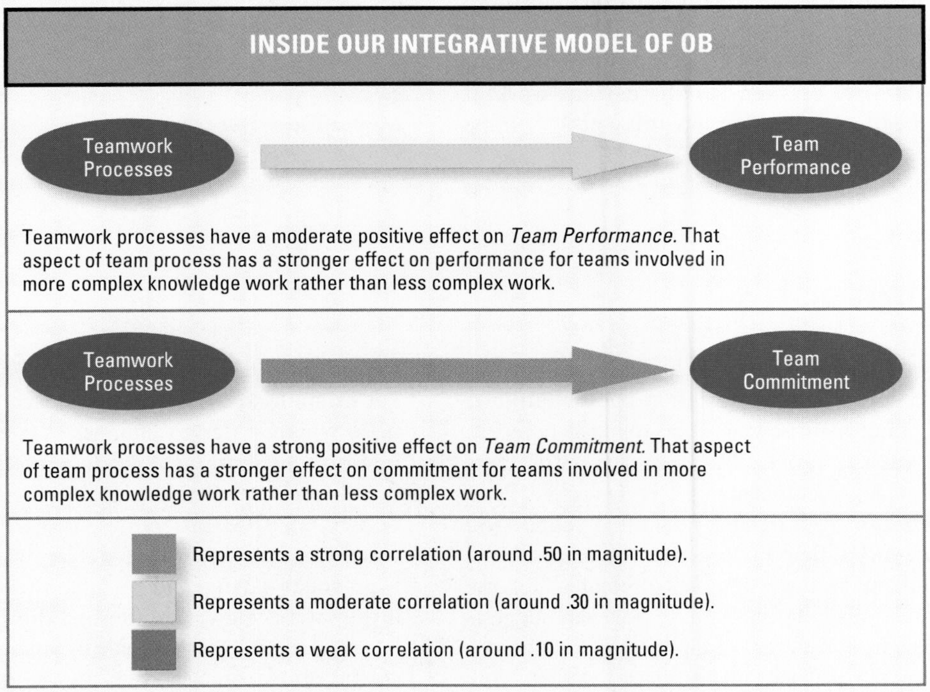

Source: J. A. LePine, R. F. Piccolo, C. L. Jackson, J. E. Mathieu, and J. R. Saul, "A Meta-Analysis of Teamwork Processes: Tests of a Multidimensional Model and Relationships with Team Effectiveness Criteria," *Personnel Psychology* 61 (2008), pp. 273–307.

we characterize the relationship between teamwork processes and performance and commitment by focusing specifically on research involving teamwork processes. The figure therefore represents a summary of existing research on transition processes, action processes, and interpersonal processes.

 9.9

Describe how team processes affect team performance and team commitment.

Research conducted in a wide variety of team settings has shown that teamwork processes have a moderate positive relationship with team performance.[102] This same moderate positive relationship appears to hold true, regardless of whether the research examines transition processes, action processes, or interpersonal processes. Apparently, effectiveness with respect to a wide variety of teamwork processes is needed to help teams achieve process gain and, in turn, perform effectively. Activities that prepare teams for work appear to be just as important as those that help members integrate their work and those that build team confidence and a positive team climate.

Research also indicates that teamwork processes have a strong positive relationship with team commitment.[103] In other words, teams that engage in effective teamwork processes tend to have members who are psychologically connected to one another and a desire for the team to remain intact. Why should teamwork and team commitment be so strongly related? One reason is that people tend to be satisfied in teams in which there are effective interpersonal interactions, and, as a consequence, they go out of their way to do things that they believe will help the team stick together. Think about a team situation that you've been in when everyone shared the same goals for the team, work was coordinated smoothly, and everyone was positive, pleasant to be around, and willing to do their fair share of the work. If you've ever actually been in a situation like this—and we hope that you have—chances are that you did your best to make sure the team could continue on together. It's likely that you worked extra hard to make sure that the team achieved its goals. It's also likely that you expressed positive sentiments about the team and your desire for the team to remain together. ■

CHECK OUT

www.mhhe.com/ColquittEss

for study materials including Interactive Exercises, Quizzes, iPod downloads, and video.

CASE: Logitech

The opening vignette described how Logitech uses geographically diverse "virtual teams" and a "follow-the-sun" process of product development to bring innovative new products to market quickly. Although the follow-the-sun process has been successful, there are some significant management challenges. For example, Peter Sheehan, a creative director from Ireland, noted that people tend to approach the work very differently based on their functional areas, and this is a problem because members of Logitech follow-the-sun teams are functionally specialized.[104] Sheehan suggests that it helps if members from different disciplines get together for face time to develop more familiarity and establish relationships.

Other companies in the electronics industry that use the follow-the-sun approach are struggling with similar problems. For example, IBM uses the approach in their chip design business, whereby design changes that are made during the day in North America are sent to India later in the day for additional work and physical implementation.[105] As noted by Mike Gruver, an IBM program manager, it's often difficult to tell whether someone from a different culture really understands what you're saying, and it's uncomfortable to keep asking them if they want you to restate something that you said.[106] Gruver has tried to address this issue by encouraging his people to open conversations on nonwork topics so that they become more familiar and comfortable with virtual teammates. As another example, Kathleen Gillam, a manager from Intel, noted that despite the positives from the use of globally distributed virtual teams, there are very simple things, such as having different holidays and working days, that make the process difficult.[107] In the end, the follow-the-sun approach to accomplishing project work appears to be catching on in the electronics industry. Accordingly, companies that learn to manage the shortcomings of the approach may gain a competitive edge.

9.1 Identify specific examples of process losses for which follow-the-sun teams are particularly susceptible.

9.2 If you were a manager of a follow-the-sun team at Logitech, how would you design your team to help ensure that it avoided some of these process losses and achieved synergy?

9.3 Which team processes are most important for virtual teams that use a follow-the-sun approach, and what practices would you recommend that could help improve these processes?

TAKEAWAYS

9.1 Teams are groups comprised of two or more people who work interdependently over some time period to accomplish common goals related to some task-oriented purpose.

9.2 There are several different types of teams: work teams, management teams, parallel teams, project teams, and parallel teams.

9.3 Teams can be interdependent in terms of the team task, goals, and outcomes. Each type of interdependence has important implications for team functioning and effectiveness.

9.4 Team composition refers to the characteristics of the members who work in the team. These characteristics include roles, ability, personality, and member diversity, as well as the number of team members.

9.5 Team process reflects the different types of activities and interactions that occur within teams that contribute to their ultimate end goals.

9.6 Taskwork processes are the activities of team members that relate directly to the accomplishment of team tasks. Taskwork processes include creative behavior and decision making.

9.7 Teamwork processes refer to the interpersonal activities that facilitate the accomplishment of the team's work but do not directly involve task accomplishment itself. Teamwork processes include transition processes, action processes, and interpersonal processes.

9.8 Team states refer to specific types of feelings and thoughts that coalesce in the minds of team members as a consequence of their experience working together. Team states include cohesion, potency, and mental models.

9.9 Teamwork processes have a moderate positive relationship with team performance and a strong positive relationship with team commitment.

DISCUSSION QUESTIONS

9.1 In which types of teams have you worked? Were these teams consistent with the team types discussed in this chapter, or were they a combination of types?

9.2 Think about your student teams. Which aspects of both models of team development apply the most and least to teams in this context?

9.3 Think about a highly successful team with which you are familiar. What types of task, goal, and outcome interdependence does this team have? Describe how changes in task, goal, and outcome interdependence might have a negative impact on this team.

9.4 What type of roles do you normally take on in a team setting? Are there task or social roles that you simply don't perform well? If so, why do you think this is?

9.5 What is the most important team composition factor in your student teams? If a student team has limitations in its composition, what can it do to improve?

9.6 Think of a team in which you worked that performed poorly. Were any of the causes of the poor performance related to the forces that tend to create process loss? If so, which force was most particularly problematic? What steps, if any, did your team take to deal with the problem?

9.7 Think of a team in which you worked that performed exceptionally well. What type of taskwork process did the team engage in? Which teamwork processes did the team seem to depend on most to produce the exceptional results?

9.8 Which types of teamwork training would your student team benefit most from? What exactly would this training cover? What specific benefits would you expect? What would prevent a team from training itself on this material?

ASSESSMENT: Cohesion

How cohesive is your team? This assessment is designed to measure cohesion—the strength of the emotional bonds that develop among members of a team. Think of your current student project team or an important team that you belong to in your job. Answer each question using the response scale provided. Then subtract your answers to the boldfaced questions from 8, with the difference being your new answers for those questions. For example, if your original answer for question 6 was "5," your new answer is "3" (8 − 5). Then sum up your answers for the eight questions. For more assessments relevant to this chapter, please see the Online Learning Center at www.mhhe.com/ColquittEss.

1	2	3	4	5	6	7
Strongly Disagree	Disagree	Slightly Disagree	Neutral	Slightly Disagree	Agree	Strongly Agree

1. If given a chance, I would choose to leave my team to join another. _____

2. The members of my team get along well together. _____

3. The members of my team will readily defend each other from criticism. _____

4. I feel that I am really a part of my team. _____

5. I look forward to being with the members of my team every day. _____

6. I find that I generally do not get along with other members of my team. _____

7. I enjoy belonging to this team because I am friends with many members. _____

8. The team to which I belong is a close one. _____

Scoring

If your scores sum up to 48 or above, you feel a strong bond to your team, suggesting that your team is cohesive. If your scores sum up to less than 48, you feel a weaker bond to your team, suggesting that your team is not as cohesive.

Source: G. H. Dobbins and S. J. Zacarro, "The Effects of Group Cohesion and Leader Behavior on Subordinate Satisfaction," *Group and Organization Management* 11 (1986), pp. 203–19. Copyright © 1986 Sage Publications Inc. Reproduced via permission from Copyright Clearance Center.

EXERCISE: Wilderness Survival

The purpose of this exercise is to experience team processes during a decision-making task. This exercise uses groups of participants, so your instructor will either assign you to a group or ask you to create your own group. The exercise has the following steps:

1. Working individually, read the following scenario:

    You have gone on a Boundary Waters canoe trip with five friends to upper Minnesota and southern Ontario in the Quetico Provincial Park. Your group has been traveling Saganagons Lake to Kawnipi Lake, following through Canyon Falls and Kennebas Falls and Kenny Lake. Fifteen to eighteen miles away is the closest road, which is arrived at by paddling through lakes and rivers and usually portaging (taking the land path) around numerous falls. Saganagons Lake is impossible to cross in bad weather, generally because of heavy rain. The nearest town is Grand Marais, Minnesota, 60 miles away. That town has plenty of camping outfitters but limited medical help, so residents rely on hospitals farther to the south. The terrain is about 70 percent land and 30 percent water, with small patches of land here and there in between the lakes and rivers. Bears are not uncommon in this region. It is now mid-May, when the (daytime) temperature ranges from about 25° to 70°, often

in the same day. Nighttime temperatures can be in the 20s. Rain is frequent during the day (nights, too) and can be life threatening if the temperature is cold. It is unusual for the weather to stay the same for more than a day or two. Generally, it will rain one day and be warm and clear the next, with a third day windy—and it is not easy to predict what type of weather will come next. In fact, it may be clear and warm, rainy and windy, all in the same day. Your group of six was in two canoes going down the river and came to some rapids. Rather than taking the portage route on land, the group foolishly decided to shoot the rapids by canoe. Unfortunately, everyone fell out of the canoes, and some were banged against the rocks. Luckily no one was killed, but one person suffered a broken leg, and several others had cuts and bruises. Both canoes were damaged severely. Both were bent in half, one with an open tear of 18 inches, while the other suffered two tears of 12 and 15 inches long. Both have broken gunwales (the upper edges on both sides). You lost the packs that held the tent; most clothing; nearly all the food, cooking equipment, and fuel; the first aid kit; and the flashlight. Your combined possessions include the items shown in the table on the opposite page. You had permits to take this trip, but no one knows for sure where you are, and the closest phone is in Grand

Marais. You were scheduled back four days from now, so it is likely a search party would be sent out in about five days (because you could have been delayed a day or so in getting back). Just now it has started to drizzle, and it looks like rain will follow. Your task is to figure out how to survive in these unpredictable and possibly harsh conditions until you can get help.

2. Working individually, consider how important each of the items in the table would be to you in this situation. Begin with the most important item, giving it a rank of "1," and wind up with the least important item, giving it a rank of "14." Put your rankings in Column B.

3. In your groups, come to a consensus about the ranking of the items. Put those consensus rankings in Column C. Group members should not merely vote or average rankings together. Instead, try to get everyone to more or less agree on the rankings. When someone disagrees, try to listen carefully. When someone feels strongly, that person should attempt to use persuasive techniques to create a consensus.

4. The instructor will post the correct answers and provide the reasons for those rankings, according to two experts (Jeff Stemmerman and Ken Gieske of REI Outfitters, both of whom act as guides for many canoe trips in the Boundary Waters region). Put those expert rankings in Column D. At this point, the Individual Error scores in Column A can be computed by taking the absolute difference between Column B and Column D. The Group Error scores in Column E can also be computed by taking the absolute difference between Column C and Column D. Finally, the Persuasion scores can be computed by taking the absolute difference between Column B and Column C. Remember that all of the differences are absolute differences—there should not be any negative numbers in the table. After completing all these computations, fill in the three scores below the table: the Individual Score (total of Column A), the Group Score (total of Column E), and the Persuasion Score (total of Column F). The Persuasion score measures how much you are able to influence other group members to match your thinking.

	A Individual Error (B – D)	B Your Ranking	C Group Ranking	D Expert Ranking	E Group Error (C – D)	F Persuasion Score (B – C)
Fanny pack of food (cheese, salami, etc.)						
Plastic-covered map of the region						
Six personal flotation devices						
Two fishing poles (broken)						
Set of clothes for three (wet)						
One yellow Frisbee						
Water purification tablets						
Duct tape (one 30′ roll)						
Whiskey (one pint, 180 proof)						
Insect repellant (one bottle)						
Matches (30, dry)						
Parachute cord (35′)						
Compass						
Six sleeping bags (synthetic)						

Individual Score (Total all numbers in Column A): _____

Group Score (Total all numbers in Column E): _____

Persuasion Score (Total all numbers in Column F): _____

5. The instructor will create a table similar to the one that follows in an Excel file in the classroom or on the chalkboard. All groups should provide the instructor with their Average Member Score (the average of all of the Individual Scores for the group), the Group Score, their Best Member Score (the lowest of all the Individual Scores for the group), and that member's Persuasion Score (the Persuasion Score for the member who had the lowest Individual Score).

Groups	1	2	3	4	5	6	7	8
Average Member Score								
Group Score								
Best Member Score								
Best Member's Persuasion								
Process Gain? (Yes or No)								

6. Fill in a "Yes" for the Process Gain row if the Group Score was lower than the Average Member Score. This score would reflect a circumstance in which the group discussion actually resulted in more accurate decisions—when "the whole" seemed to be more effective than "the sum of its parts." Fill in a "No" for the Process Gain row if the Group Score was higher than the Average Member Score. In this circumstance, the group discussion actually resulted in less accurate decisions—and the group would have been better off if no talking had occurred.

7. Class discussion (whether in groups or as a class) should center on the following questions: Did most groups tend to achieve process gain in terms of group scores that were better than the average individual scores? Were the group scores usually better than the best member's score? Why not; where did the groups that lacked synergy tend to go wrong? In other words, what behaviors led to process loss rather than process gain? What role does the best member's persuasion score play in all of this? Did groups that tended to listen more to the best member (as reflected in lower persuasion numbers) have more frequent instances of process gain?

Source: D. Marcic, J. Seltzer, and P. Vail. *Organizational Behavior: Experiences and Cases* (Cincinnati, OH: South-Western, 2001).

END NOTES

1. Logitech corporate Web site. http://www.logitech.com/index.cfm/175/481&cl=us,en (accessed June 23, 2008).

2. Ibid.

3. Schiff, D. "Global Teams Rock around the Clock." *Electronic Engineering Times* 1435 (August 7, 2006), pp. 12, 20.

4. Godinez, V. "Sunshine 24/7: As EDS' Work Stops in One Time Zone, It Picks Up in Another." *Knight Ridder Tribune Business News*, January 2, 2007. ProQuest database (February 12, 2007); Schiff, "Global Teams Rock"; Treinen, J. J., and S. L. Miller-Frost, "Following the Sun: Case Studies in Global Software Development." *IBM Systems Journal* 45 (2006), pp. 773–83.

5. Treinen and Miller-Frost, "Following the Sun."

6. Ilgen, D. R.; D. A. Major; J. R. Hollenbeck; and D. J. Sego. "Team Research in the 1990s." In *Leadership Theory and Research: Perspectives and Directions*, ed. M. M. Chemers and R. Ayman. New York: Academic Press, Inc., 1993, pp. 245–70.

7. Devine, D. J.; L. D. Clayton; J. L. Philips; B. B. Dunford; and S. B. Melner. "Teams in Organizations: Prevalence, Characteristics, and Effectiveness." *Small Group Research* 30 (1999), pp. 678–711; Gordan, J. "Work Teams: How Far Have They Come?" *Training* 29 (1992), pp. 59–65; Lawler, E. E., III; S. A. Mohrman, and G. E. Ledford Jr. *Creating High Performance Organizations: Practices and Results of Employee Involvement and Total Quality Management in* Fortune *1000 Companies.* San Francisco: Jossey-Bass, 1995.

8. Stewart, G. L.; C. C. Manz; and H. P. Sims Jr. *Team Work and Group Dynamics.* New York: John Wiley & Sons, 1999.

9. Ibid.

10. Cohen, S. G., and D. E. Bailey. "What Makes Teams Work: Group Effectiveness Research from the Shop Floor to the Executive Suite." *Journal of Management* 23 (1997), pp. 239–90.

11. Ibid.

12. Ibid.

13. Sundstrom, E.; M. McIntyre; T. Halfhill; and H. Richards. "Work Groups: From the Hawthorne Studies to Work Teams of the 1990s and Beyond." *Group Dynamics, Theory, Research, and Practice* 4 (2000), pp. 44–67.

14. Tuckman, B. W. "Developmental Sequence in Small Groups." *Psychological Bulletin* 63 (1965), pp. 384–99.

15. Gersick, C. J. G. "Time and Transition in Work Teams: Toward a New Model of Group Development." *Academy of Management Journal* 33 (1988), pp. 9–41; Gersick, C. J. G. "Marking Time: Predictable Transitions in Task

Groups." *Academy of Management Journal* 32 (1989), pp. 274–309.

16. Thompson, J. D. *Organizations in Action*. New York: McGraw-Hill, 1967; Van de Ven, A. H.; A. L. Delbeccq; and R. Koenig. "Determinants of Coordination Modes within Organizations." *American Sociological Review* 41 (1976), pp. 322–38.

17. Ibid.

18. Thompson, *Organizations in Action*.

19. Ibid.

20. Ibid.

21. Van de Ven et al., "Determinants of Coordination Modes."

22. Kelley, T. *The Art of Innovation*. New York: Doubleday, 2001.

23. Saavedra, R.; P. C. Earley; and L. Van Dyne. "Complex Interdependence in Task Performing Groups." *Journal of Applied Psychology* 78 (1993), pp. 61–72.

24. Deutsch, M. *The Resolution of Conflict*. New Haven, CT: Yale University Press, 1973; Wong, A.; D. Tjosvold; and Zi-you Yu. "Organizational Partnerships in China: Self-Interest, Goal Interdependence, and Opportunism." *Journal of Applied Psychology* 90 (2005), pp. 782–91.

25. MacMillan, P. S. *The Performance Factor: Unlocking the Secrets of Teamwork*. Nashville, TN: Broadman & Holman Publishers, 2001.

26. Ibid.

27. Shea, G. P., and R. A. Guzzo. "Groups as Human Resources." In *Research in Personnel and Human Resources Management*, Vol. 5, ed. K. M. Rowland and G. R. Ferris. Greenwich CT: JAI Press, 1987, pp. 323–56.

28. Deutsch, M. A. "A Theory of Cooperation and Competition." *Human Relations* 2 (1949), pp. 199–231.

29. Williams, K.; S. G. Harkins; and B. Latane. "Identifiability as a Deterrent to Social Loafing: Two Cheering Experiments." *Journal of Personality and Social Psychology* 40 (1981), pp. 303–11.

30. Johnson, D. W.; G. Maruyama; R. Johnson; D. Nelson; and L. Skon. "Effects of Cooperative, Competitive, and Individualistic Goal Structures on Achievement: A Meta-Analysis." *Psychological Bulletin* 89 (1981), pp. 47–62; Miller, L. K., and R. L. Hamblin. "Interdependence, Differential Rewarding and Productivity." *American Sociological Review* 28 (1963), pp. 768–78; Rosenbaum, M. E. "Cooperation and Competition." In *Psychology of Group Influence*, ed. P. B. Paulus. Hillsdale, NJ: Lawrence Erlbaum, 1980.

31. Benne, K., and P. Sheats. "Functional Roles of Group Members." *Journal of Social Issues* 4 (1948), pp. 41–49.

32. Golen, J. "NBA Finals: Boston Celtics Big 3 Sacrificed Stats for Wins." June 5, 2008, *The Seattle Times*, Internet edition, http://seattletimes.nwsource.com/html/sonics/2004458469_nbafinals05.html (accessed June 5, 2008).

33. Devine, D. J., and J. L. Philips. "Do Smarter Teams Do Better: A Meta-Analysis of Cognitive Ability and Team Performance." *Small Group Research* 32 (2001), pp. 507–32; Stewart, G. L. "A Meta-Analytic Review of Relationships between Team Design Features and Team Performance." *Journal of Management* 32 (2006), pp. 29–54.

34. LePine, J. A.; J. R. Hollenbeck; D. R. Ilgen; and J. Hedlund. "Effects of Individual Differences on the Performance of Hierarchical Decision-Making Teams: Much More Than *g*." *Journal of Applied Psychology* 82 (1997), pp. 803–11.

35. LePine, J. A. "Team Adaptation and Postchange Performance: Effects of Team Composition in Terms of Members' Cognitive Ability and Personality." *Journal of Applied Psychology* 88 (2003), pp. 27–39; LePine, J. A. "Adaptation of Teams in Response to Unforeseen Change: Effects of Goal Difficulty and Team Composition in Terms of Cognitive Ability and Goal Orientation." *Journal of Applied Psychology* 90 (2005), pp. 1153–67.

36. Peeters, M. A. G.; Tuijl, H. F. J. M. van; Rutte, C. G.; and Reymen, I. M. M. J. "Personality and Team Performance: A Meta-Analysis." *European Journal of Personality* 20 (2006), pp. 377–96.

37. Barrick, M. R.; G. L. Stewart; M. J. Neubert; and M. K. Mount. "Relating Member Ability and Personality to Work-Team Processes and Team Effectiveness." *Journal of Applied Psychology* 83 (1998), pp. 377–91; LePine et al., "Effects of Individual Differences"; Neuman, G. A., and J. Wright. "Team Effectiveness: Beyond Skills and Cognitive Ability." *Journal of Applied Psychology* 84 (1999), pp. 376–89.

38. LePine, J. A., and L. Van Dyne. "An Attributional Model of Helping in the Context of Work Groups." *Academy of Management Review* 26 (2001), pp. 67–84.

39. Peeters et al., "Personality and Team Performance."

40. Comer, D. R. "A Model of Social Loafing in Real Work Groups." *Human Relations* 48 (1995), pp. 647–67; Wagner, J. A., III. "Studies of Individualism–Collectivism: Effects on Cooperation in Groups." *Academy of Management Journal* 38 (1995), pp. 152–72.

41. LePine, J. A., and L. Van Dyne. "Voice and Cooperative Behavior as Contrasting Forms of Contextual Performance: Evidence of Differential Relationships with Personality Characteristics and Cognitive Ability." *Journal of Applied Psychology* 86 (2001), pp. 326–36.

42. McGrath, J. E. "The Influence of Positive Interpersonal Relations on Adjustment and Interpersonal Relations in Rifle Teams." *Journal of Abnormal and Social Psychology* 65 (1962), pp. 365–75.

43. Barrick, M. R., and M. K. Mount. "The Big Five Personality Dimensions and Job Performance: A Meta-Analysis." *Personnel Psychology* 44 (1991), pp. 1–26.

44. Barrick et al., "Relating Member Ability and Personality."

45. Barry, B., and G. L. Stewart. "Composition, Process, and Performance in Self-Managed Groups: The Role of Personality." *Journal of Applied Psychology* 82 (1997), pp. 62–78.

46. Williams, K., and C. O'Reilly. "The Complexity of Diversity: A Review of Forty Years of Research." In *Research in Organizational Behavior*, Vol. 21, ed. B. Staw and R. Sutton. Greenwich, CT: JAI Press, 1998, pp. 77–140.

47. Cox, T.; S. Lobel; and P. McLeod. "Effects of Ethnic Group Cultural Differences on Cooperative and Competitive Behavior on a Group Task." *Academy of Management Journal* 34 (1991), pp. 827–47; Mannix, E., and M. A. Neal. "What Differences Make a Difference? The Promise and Reality of Diverse Teams in Organizations." *Psychological Science in the Public Interest* 6 (2005), pp. 31–55.

48. Gruenfeld, D. H.; E. A. Mannix; K. Y. Williams; and M. A. Neale. "Group Composition and Decision Making: How Member Familiarity and Information Distribution Affect Processes and Performance." *Organizational Behavior and Human Decision Processes* 67 (1996), pp. 1–15; Hoffman, L. "Homogeneity and Member Personality and Its Effect on Group Problem Solving." *Journal of Abnormal and Social Psychology* 58 (1959), pp. 27–32; Hoffman, L., and N. Maier. "Quality and Acceptance of Problem Solutions by Members of Homogeneous and Heterogeneous Groups." *Journal of Abnormal and Social Psychology* 62 (1961), pp. 401–407; Nemeth, C. J. "Differential Contributions of Majority and Minority Influence." *Psychological Review* 93 (1986), pp. 22–32; Stasster, G.; D. Steward; and G. Wittenbaum. "Expert Roles and Information Exchange during Discussion: The Importance of Knowing Who Knows What." *Journal of Experimental Social Psychology* 57 (1995), pp. 244–65; Triandis, H.; E. Hall; and R. Ewen. "Member Heterogeneity and Dyadic Creativity." *Human Relations* 18 (1965), pp. 33–55; Watson, W.; K. Kuman; and I. Michaelsen. "Cultural Diversity's Impact on Interaction Process and Performance: Comparing Homogeneous and Diverse Task Groups." *Academy of Management Journal* 36 (1993), pp. 590–602.

49. Byrne, D. *The Attraction Paradigm.* New York: Academic Press, 1971; Newcomb, T. M. *The Acquaintance Process.* New York: Holt, Rinehart, and Winston, 1961.

50. Byrne, D.; G. Clore; and P. Worchel. "The Effect of Economic Similarity-Dissimilarity as Determinants of Attraction." *Journal of Personality and Social Psychology* 4 (1996), pp. 220–24; Lincoln, J., and J. Miller. "Work and Friendship Ties in Organizations: A Comparative Analysis of Relational Networks." *Administrative Science Quarterly* 24 (1979), pp. 181–99; Triandis, H. "Cognitive Similarity and Interpersonal Communication in Industry." *Journal of Applied Psychology* 43 (1959), pp. 321–26; Triandis, H. "Cognitive Similarity and Communication in a Dyad." *Human Relations* 13 (1960), pp. 279–87.

51. Jackson, S. E.; K. E. May; and K. Whitney. "Understanding the Dynamics of Diversity in Decision-Making Teams." In *Team Decision-Making Effectiveness in Organizations*, ed. R. A. Guzzo and E. Salas. San Francisco: Jossey-Bass, 1995, pp. 204–61; Milliken, F. J., and L. L. Martins. "Searching for Common Threads: Understanding the Multiple Effects of Diversity in Organizational Groups." *Academy of Management Review* 21 (1996), pp. 402–33.

52. Harrison, D. A.; K. H. Price; and M. P. Bell. "Beyond Relational Demography: Time and the Effects of Surface- and Deep-Level Diversity on Work Group Cohesion." *Academy of Management Journal* 41 (1998), pp. 96–107; Harrison, D. A.; K. H. Price; J. H. Gavin; and A. T. Florey. "Time, Teams, and Task Performance: Changing Effects of Surface- and Deep-Level Diversity on Group Functioning." *Academy of Management Journal* 45 (2002), pp. 1029–45.

53. Ibid.

54. Ibid.

55. Ibid.

56. Stewart, "A Meta-Analytic Review."

57. Kozlowski, S. W. J., and B. S. Bell. "Work Groups and Teams in Organization." In *Comprehensive Handbook of Psychology: Industrial and Organizational Psychology*, Vol. 12, ed. W. C. Borman, D. R. Ilgen, and R. J. Klimoski. New York: John Wiley & Sons, 2003, pp. 333–75.

58. Gooding, R. Z., and J. A. Wagner III. "A Meta-Analytic Review of the Relationship between Size and Performance: The Productivity and Efficiency of Organizations and Their Subunits." *Administrative Science Quarterly* 30 (1985), pp. 462–81; Markham, S. E.; F. Dansereau; and J. A. Alutto. "Group Size and Absenteeism Rates: A Longitudinal Analysis." *Academy of Management Journal* 25 (1982), pp. 921–27.

59. Hackman, J. R., and N. J. Vidmar. "Effects of Size and Task Type on Group Performance and Member Reactions." *Sociometry* 33 (1970), pp. 37–54.

60. Yank, J. L. "The Power of Number 4.6." *Fortune* 153, no. 11 (June 12, 2006), p. 122. ProQuest database (May 28, 2007).

61. "Process." *Merriam-Webster* online dictionary, http://www.merriam-webster.com/dictionary/process (accessed May 27, 2007).

62. Hackman, J. R. "The Design of Work Teams." In *Handbook of Organizational Behavior*, ed. J. W. Lorsch. Englewood Cliffs, NJ: Prentice Hall, 1987, pp. 315–42.

63. Steiner, I. D. *Group Processes and Productivity.* New York: Academic Press, 1972.

64. Hackman, "The Design of Work Teams."

65. Lamm, H., and G. Trommsdorff. "Group versus Individual Performance on Tasks Requiring Ideational Proficiency (Brainstorming)." *European Journal of Social Psychology* 3 (1973), pp. 361–87.

66. Hackman, "The Design of Work Teams."

67. Latane, B.; K. Williams; and S. Harkins. "Many Hands Make Light the Work: The Causes and Consequences of Social Loafing." *Journal of Personality and Social Psychology* 37 (1979), pp. 822–32.

68. Ibid.; Jackson, C. L., and J. A. LePine. "Peer Responses to a Team's Weakest Link: A Test and Extension of LePine and Van Dyne's Model." *Journal of Applied Psychology* 88 (2003), pp. 459–75; Sheppard, A. "Productivity Loss in

Performance Groups: A Motivation Analysis." *Psychological Bulletin* 113 (1993), pp. 67–81.

69. Shalley, C. E.; J. Zhou; and G. R. Oldham. "The Effects of Personal and Contextual Characteristics on Creativity: Where Should We Go from Here?" *Journal of Management* 30 (2004), pp. 933–58.

70. Osborn, A. F. *Applied Imagination.* Revised ed. New York: Scribner, 1957.

71. Ibid.

72. Diehl, M., and W. Stroebe. "Productivity Loss in Brainstorming Groups: Toward a Solution of a Riddle." *Journal of Personality and Social Psychology* 53 (1987), pp. 497–509; Mullen, B.; C. Johnson; and E. Salas. "Productivity Loss in Brainstorming Groups: A Meta-Analytic Investigation." *Basic and Applied Social Psychology* 12 (1991), pp. 3–23.

73. Diehl and Stroebe, "Productivity Loss."

74. Sutton, R. I., and A. Hargadon. "Brainstorming Groups in Context: Effectiveness in a Product Design Firm." *Administrative Science Quarterly* 41 (1996), pp. 685–718.

75. Delbecq, A. L., and A. H. Van de Ven. "A Group Process Model for Identification and Program Planning." *Journal of Applied Behavioral Sciences* 7 (1971), pp. 466–92; Geschka, H.; G. R. Schaude; and H. Schlicksupp. "Modern Techniques for Solving Problems." *Chemical Engineering*, August 1973, pp. 91–97.

76. Brehmer, B., and R. Hagafors. "Use of Experts in Complex Decision Making: A Paradigm for the Study of Staff Work." *Organizational Behavior and Human Decision Processes* 38 (1986), pp. 181–95; Ilgen, D. R.; D. Major; J. R. Hollenbeck; and D. Sego. "Raising an Individual Decision Making Model to the Team Level: A New Research Model and Paradigm." In *Team Effectiveness and Decision Making in Organizations*, ed. R. Guzzo and E. Salas. San Francisco: Jossey-Bass, 1995, pp. 113–48.

77. Hollenbeck, J. R.; J. A. Colquitt; D. R. Ilgen; J. A. LePine; and J. Hedlund. "Accuracy Decomposition and Team Decision Making: Testing Theoretical Boundary Conditions." *Journal of Applied Psychology* 83 (1998), pp. 494–500; Hollenbeck, J. R.; D. R. Ilgen; D. J. Sego; J. Hedlund; D. A. Major; and J. Phillips. "Multilevel Theory of Team Decision Making; Decision Performance in Teams Incorporating Distributed Expertise." *Journal of Applied Psychology* 80 (1995), pp. 292–316.

78. Hollenbeck et al., "Multilevel Theory of Team Decision Making"; Hollenbeck, J. R.; D. R. Ilgen; J. A. LePine; J. A. Colquitt; and J. Hedlund. "Extending the Multilevel Theory of Team Decision Making. Effects of Feedback and Experience in Hierarchical Teams." *Academy of Management Journal* 41 (1998), pp. 269–82.

79. Hollenbeck et al., "Extending the Multilevel Theory."

80. Hedlund, J.; D. R. Ilgen; and J. R. Hollenbeck. "Decision Accuracy in Computer-Mediated vs. Face-to-Face Decision Making Teams." *Organizational Behavior and Human Decision Processes* 76 (1998), pp. 30–47.

81. LePine, J. A.; R. F. Piccolo; C. L. Jackson; J. E. Mathieu; and J. R. Saul. "A Meta-Analysis of Teamwork Processes: Tests of a Multidimensional Model and Relationships with Team Effectiveness Criteria." *Personnel Psychology* 61 (2008), pp. 273–307; Marks, M. A.; J. E. Mathieu; and S. J. Zaccaro. "A Temporally Based Framework and Taxonomy of Team Processes." *Academy of Management Review* 26 (2001), pp. 356–76.

82. Marks et al., "A Temporally Based Framework." This entire section on teamwork processes is largely based on this body of work.

83. Kozlowski, S. W. J., and B. S. Bell. "Work Groups and Teams in Organizations." In *Handbook of Psychology*, Vol. 12: *Industrial and Organizational Psychology*, ed. W. C. Borman, D. R. Ilgen, and R. J. Klimoski. Hoboken, NJ: John Wiley & Sons, 2003, pp. 333–75.

84. De Dreu, C. K. W., and L. R. Weingart. "Task versus Relationship Conflict, Team Performance, and Team Member Satisfaction: A Meta-Analysis." *Journal of Applied Psychology* 88 (2003), pp. 741–49.

85. Jehn, K. "A Multimethod Examination of the Benefits and Detriments of Intergroup Conflict." *Administrative Science Quarterly* 40 (1995), pp. 256–82.

86. De Dreu and Weingart, "Task versus Relationship Conflict."

87. Dwyer, P.; P. Engardio; S. Schiller; and S. Reed. "The New Model: Tearing up Today's Organization Chart." *BusinessWeek*, November 18, 1994, pp. 80–90.

88. Ilgen, D. R.; J. A. LePine; and J. R. Hollenbeck. "Effective Decision Making in Multinational Teams." In *New Perspectives on International Industrial/Organizational Psychology*, ed. P. C. Earley and M. Erez. San Francisco: New Lexington Press, 1997, pp. 377–409.

89. Prieto Zamora, J. M., and R. Martinez Arias. "Those Things Yonder Are Not Giants, but Decision Makers in International Teams." In *New Perspectives on International Industrial/Organizational Psychology*, ed. P. C. Earley and M. Erez. San Francisco: New Lexington Press, 1997, pp. 410–45.

90. Ibid.; Hollenbeck et al., "Accuracy Decomposition."

91. Beal, D. J.; R. R. Cohen; M. J. Burke; and C. L. McLendon. "Cohesion and Performance in Groups: A Meta-Analytic Clarification of Construct Relations." *Journal of Applied Psychology* 88 (2003), pp. 989–1004.

92. Mullen, B., and C. Copper. "The Relation between Group Cohesiveness and Performance: An Integration." *Psychological Bulletin* 115 (1994), pp. 210–27.

93. Janis, I. L. *Victims of Groupthink: A Psychological Study of Foreign Policy Decisions and Fiascos.* Boston, MA: Houghton Mifflin, 1972.

94. Ibid.

95. Hirokawa, R.; D. Gouran; and A. Martz. "Understanding the Sources of Faulty Group Decision Making: A Lesson from the *Challenger* Disaster." *Small Group Behavior*

19 (1988), pp. 411–33; Esser, J., and J. Linoerfer. "Group-think and the Space Shuttle *Challenger* Accident: Toward a Quantitative Case Analysis." *Journal of Behavioral Decision Making* 2 (1989), pp. 167–77; Moorhead, G.; R. Ference; and C. Neck. "Group Decision Fiascoes Continue: Space Shuttle *Challenger* and a Revised Groupthink Framework." *Human Relations* 44 (1991), pp. 539–50.

96. Stephens, J., and P. Behr. "Enron Culture Fed Its Demise." *Washington Post*, June 27, 2002, pp. A1–2.

97. Shea, G. P., and R. A. Guzzo. "Groups as Human Resources." In *Research in Personnel and Human Resource Management*, Vol. 5, ed. K. M. Rowland and G. R. Ferris. Greenwich, CT: JAI Press, 1987, pp. 323–56.

98. Gully, S. M.; K. A. Incalcaterra; A. Joshi; and J. M. Beubien. "A Meta-Analysis of Team-Efficacy, Potency, and Performance: Interdependence and Level of Analysis as Moderators of Observed Relationships." *Journal of Applied Psychology* 87 (2002), pp. 819–32.

99. De Church, L. A., and M. A. Marks. "Maximizing the Benefits of Task Conflict: The Role of Conflict Management." *International Journal of Conflict Management* 12 (2001), pp. 4–22; Festinger, L. "Informal Social Communication." *Psychological Review* 57 (1950), pp. 271–82.

100. Klimoski, R. J., and S. Mohammed. "Team Mental Model: Construct or Metaphor?" *Journal of Management* 20 (1994), pp. 403–37.

101. Cannon-Bowers, J. A.; E. Salas; and S. A. Converse. "Shared Mental Models in Expert Team Decision Making." *Individual and Group Decision Making*, ed. N. J. Castellan. Hillsdale, NJ: Erlbaum, 1993, pp. 221–46.

102. LePine et al., "A Meta-Analysis of Teamwork Processes."

103. Ibid.

104. Schiff, "Global Teams Rock around the Clock."

105. Ibid.

106. Ibid.

107. Ibid.

10

LEADERSHIP

● ● learning **OBJECTIVES**

After reading this chapter, you should be able to:

10.1 Define leadership. Define power. Explain what role power plays in leadership.

10.2 Describe the different types of power that leaders possess and when they can use those types most effectively.

10.3 Explain what behaviors leaders exhibit when trying to influence others. Understand which of these behaviors is most effective.

10.4 Explain how leaders use their power and influence to resolve conflicts in the workplace.

10.5 Describe what it means for a leader to be "effective."

10.6 Explain the four styles leaders can use to make decisions. Describe which factors combine to make some styles more effective in a given situation.

10.7 Describe the two dimensions that capture most of the day-to-day leadership behaviors that leaders engage in.

10.8 Understand how transformational leadership differs from transactional leadership. Describe which kinds of behaviors underlie transformational leadership.

10.9 Explain how leadership affects job performance and organizational commitment.

XEROX

"Somebody needs to Xerox that for me." Few companies end up with their name actually being included in the dictionary as a verb, but this is something that Xerox has the privilege (or some would say bears the burden) of. Today's Xerox is not the company it was 20 or even just 10 years ago. For instance, if you wanted to simply go out and buy a stand-alone Xerox machine to make copies with, you couldn't do it. The company now operates only as a business-to-business enterprise, forming "partnering" relationships with clients to help solve their document needs. When Anne Mulcahy took over the reins at Xerox in 2001, the company took a $273 million loss, and its stock price had dived from $60 to $5. Under her leadership, Xerox made a highly questioned push in R&D that is now paying huge dividends. Xerox is expected to make $1.2 billion in profit on $18 billion in revenue in 2008. Mulcahy was dubbed "The Accidental CEO" by *Fortune* in 2003 because of her unlikely rise to the top of the organization.[1] Under similar circumstances, most CEOs brought in to turn around a failing company come from outside the organization. In Mulcahy's case, she had worked at Xerox for 24 years, had no CEO experience, and did not have a seat on the company's board of directors. "I never expected to be CEO of Xerox. I was never groomed to be CEO of Xerox. It was a total surprise to everyone, including myself," says Mulcahy.[2]

It is pretty clear to everyone now though that Mulcahy was the perfect choice. Recently named CEO of the year by her peers, she is known as being a "customer-oriented leader," the "model turnaround leader," and a leader with great vision and tenacity.[3] Ursula Burns, recently named Mulcahy's successor to CEO at Xerox, says that "She is a superb motivator who can push people to step up their game without demoralizing them in the process." As a leader, it appears that Mulcahy has the ability to change styles depending on the situation; she is known by coworkers as being compassionate and tough at the same time.[4] She has a knack for leading by exhibiting transformational leadership behaviors such as setting a vision and helping others to get there. "Our employees needed clear directions. Good people aligned around a common goal can do anything," writes Mulcahy.[5]

Now that Xerox has turned itself around, Mulcahy faces different kinds of leadership issues, including how to sustain the growth the company has created. Developing more than 100 new products in the past three years and leading the world in color digital technology is a good start. However, Mulcahy is struggling in the process of sharing power with Burns, her newly appointed successor. Having already appointed Mulcahy's successor puts Xerox in a great position to be ready for the future, but in the meantime, it presents difficulties associated with sharing power between two very different types of leaders.

LEADERSHIP

As evidenced by the turnaround at Xerox, leaders within organizations can make a huge difference to the success of an organization or group. There is perhaps no subject written about more in business circles than the topic of leadership. A quick search on Amazon.com of the topic "leadership" will generate a list of more than 200,000 books! That number doesn't even count the myriad of videos, calendars, cassette tapes, and other items, all designed to help people become better leaders. Given all the interest in this topic, a natural question becomes, "What exactly is a leader?" We define leadership as the use of power and influence to direct the activities of followers toward goal achievement.[6] That direction can affect followers' interpretation of events, the organization of their work activities, their commitment to key goals, their relationships with other followers, and their access to cooperation and support from other work units.[7] This chapter focuses on how leaders *get* the power and influence they use to direct others and how they actually *use* their power and influence to help followers achieve their goals.

● ● **10.1**

Define leadership. Define power. Explain what role power plays in leadership.

POWER AND INFLUENCE

What exactly comes to mind when you think of the term "power"? Does it raise a positive or negative image for you? Certainly it's easy to think of leaders who have used power for what we would consider good purposes, but it's just as easy to think of leaders who have used power for unethical or immoral purposes. For now, try not to focus on how leaders use power but instead on how they acquire that power. Power can be defined as the ability to influence the behavior of others and resist unwanted influence in return.[8] Note that this definition gives us a couple of key points to think about. First, just because a person has the ability to influence others does not mean he or she will actually choose to do so. In fact, many times in organizations, the most powerful employees don't even realize how influential they could be! Second, in addition to influencing others, power can be seen as the ability to resist the influence attempts of others.[9] This resistance could come in the form of the simple voicing of a dissenting opinion, the refusal to perform a specific behavior, or the organization of an opposing group of coworkers.[10] Sometimes leaders need to resist the influence of other leaders or higher-ups to do what's best for their own unit. Other times leaders need to resist the influence of their own employees to avoid being a "pushover" when employees try to go their own way.

Acquiring Power

Think about the people you currently work with or have worked with in the past, or think of students that are involved in many of the same activities you are. Do any of those people seem to have especially high levels of power, meaning that they had the ability to influence your behavior? What is it that gives them that power? In some cases, their power may come from some formal position (e.g., supervisor, team leader, teaching assistant, resident advisor). However, sometimes the most powerful people we know lack any sort of formal authority. It turns out that power in organizations can come from a number of different sources. Specifically, there are five major types of power that can be grouped along two dimensions: organizational power and personal power.[11] These types of power are illustrated in Figure 10-1.

● ● **10.2**

Describe the different types of power that leaders possess and when they can use those types most effectively.

Organizational Power. The three types of organizational power derive primarily from a person's position within the organization. These types of power are considered to be more formal in nature.[12] Legitimate power is derived from a position of authority inside the organization and is sometimes referred to as "formal authority." People with legitimate power have some title—some term on an organizational chart or on their door that says, "Look, I'm supposed to have influence over you." Those with legitimate power have the understood right to ask others to do things that are considered within the scope of their authority. When a manager asks an employee to stay late to work on a project, work on one task instead of another, or work faster, he or she is exercising legitimate power. The higher up in an organization a person is, the more legitimate power he or she generally possesses. *Fortune* magazine provides rankings of the most powerful women in business. As shown in Table 10-1, all of those women possess legitimate power in that they hold a title that affords them the ability to influence others.

Legitimate power does have its limits, however. It doesn't generally give a person the right to ask employees to do something outside the scope of their jobs or roles within the organization.

> ● ● "A quick search on Amazon .com of the topic 'leadership' will generate a list of more than 200,000 books!"

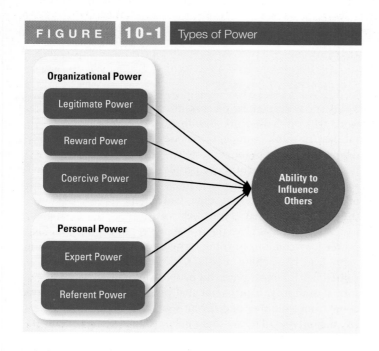

FIGURE 10-1 Types of Power

Organizational Power
- Legitimate Power
- Reward Power
- Coercive Power

Personal Power
- Expert Power
- Referent Power

→ Ability to Influence Others

Reward power exists when someone has control over the resources or rewards another person wants. For example, managers generally have control over raises, performance evaluations, awards, more desirable job assignments, and the resources an employee might require to perform a job effectively. Those with reward power have the ability to influence others if those being influenced believe they will get the rewards by behaving in a certain way. **Coercive power** exists when a person has control over punishments in an organization. Coercive power operates primarily on the principle of fear. It exists when one person believes that another has the ability to punish him or her and is willing to use that power. For example, a manager might have the right to fire, demote, suspend, or lower the pay of an employee. Sometimes the limitations of a manager to impose punishments are formally spelled out in an organization. However, in many instances, managers have a considerable amount of leeway in this regard. Coercive power is generally regarded as a poor form of power to use regularly because it tends to result in negative feelings toward those who wield it.

Personal Power. Of course, the women in Table 10-1 do not appear on that list just because they have some formal title that affords them the ability to reward and punish others. There's something else about them as people that provides them additional capabilities to influence others. Personal forms of power capture that "something else." **Expert power** is derived from a person's expertise, skill, or knowledge on which others depend. When people have a track record of high performance, the ability to solve problems, or specific knowledge that is necessary to accomplish tasks, they are more likely to be able to influence other people who need that expertise. Consider a

For example, if a manager asked an employee to wash her car or mow his lawn, it would likely be seen as an inappropriate request. As we'll see later in this chapter, there is a big difference between having legitimate power and using it effectively.

The next two forms of organizational power are somewhat intertwined with legitimate power.

● **REWARD POWER** A form of organizational power based on the control of resources or benefits.

TABLE 10-1 *Fortune's* 10 Most Powerful Women in Business in 2006

	Name	Company	Position	Age
1	Indra Nooyi	PepsiCo	CEO	50
2	Anne Mulcahy	Xerox	Chairperson and CEO	53
3	Meg Whitman	eBay	CEO and President	50
4	Pat Woertz	Archer Daniels Midland	CEO and President	53
5	Irene Rosenfeld	Kraft Foods	CEO	53
6	Brenda Barnes	Sara Lee	Chairperson and CEO	52
7	Andrea Jung	Avon	Chairperson and CEO	48
8	Oprah Winfrey	Harpo, Inc.	Chairperson	52
9	Sally Krawcheck	Citigroup	CFO, Head of Strategy	41
10	Susan Arnold	Procter & Gamble	Vice Chair, Beauty and Health	52

Source: E. Levenson, C. Tkaczyk, and J. L. Yang, "Indra Rising, 50 Most Powerful Women in Business," *Fortune* (October 16, 2006), p. 145. Copyright © 2006 Time Inc. All rights reserved.

lone programmer who knows how to operate a piece of antiquated software, a machinist who was recently trained to operate a new piece of equipment, or the only engineer who has experience working on a specific type of project. All of these individuals will have a degree of expert power because of what they individually bring to the organization. Pat Woertz, the CEO of Archer Daniels Midland (ADM), the Illinois-based agricultural firm, appears on Table 10-1 largely because of her expert power. ADM hired Woertz as CEO because it felt that her time at Chevron would provide energy expertise that could help the firm in its push for renewable fuels.[13] There is perhaps no place where expert power comes into play more than in Silicon Valley, where it is widely perceived that the best leaders are those with significant technological experience and expertise. Jerry Yang, one of the cofounders of Yahoo!, returned as CEO in the summer of 2007, only to step down in November of 2008. During his brief tenure, Yang's expert power gave him immediate levels of authority that the prior CEO never had.[14]

"Personal forms of power capture that 'something else.'"

Referent power exists when others have a desire to identify and be associated with a person. This desire is generally derived from an affection, admiration, or loyalty toward a specific individual.[15] Although our focus is on individuals within organizations, there are many examples of political leaders, celebrities, and sports figures who seem to possess high levels of referent power. Bill Clinton, Angelina Jolie, and Peyton Manning all possess referent power to some degree because others want to emulate them. The same could be said of leaders in organizations who possess a good reputation, attractive personal qualities, or a certain level of charisma. Oprah Winfrey, the chairperson of Harpo, Inc., clearly wields an incredible amount of referent power. The people who watch Oprah on TV or listen to her on satellite radio admire her views and often seek to emulate her actions.

Of course, it's possible for a person to possess all of the forms of power at the same time. In fact, the most powerful leaders—like those in Table 10-1—have bases of power that include all five dimensions. From an employee's perspective, it's sometimes difficult to gauge what form of power is most important. Why exactly do you do what your boss asks you to do? Is it because the boss has the formal right to provide direction, because the boss controls your evaluations, or because you admire and like the boss? Many times, we don't know exactly what type of power leaders possess until they attempt to use it. Generally speaking, the personal forms of power are more strongly related to organizational commitment and job performance than are the organizational forms. If you think about the authorities for whom you worked the hardest, they probably possessed some form of expertise and charisma, rather than just an ability to reward and punish. Such is the case in this chapter's **OB in Sports** feature.

Contingency Factors. Power contingency factors are certain situations in organizations that are likely to

increase or decrease the degree to which leaders can use their power to influence others. Most of these situations revolve around the idea that the more other employees depend on a person, the more powerful that person becomes. A person can have high levels of expert and referent power, but if he or she works alone and performs tasks that nobody sees, the ability to influence others is greatly reduced. That being said, there are four factors that have an effect on the strength of a person's ability to use power to influence others.[16] These factors are summarized in Table 10-2. Substitutability is the degree to which people have alternatives in accessing resources. Leaders that control resources to which no one else has access can use their power to gain greater influence. Discretion is the degree to which managers have the

Jerry Yang, former CEO of Yahoo!, meets with the founders of Google, Larry Page and Sergey Brin.

right to make decisions on their own. If managers are forced to follow organizational policies and rules, their ability to influence others is reduced. Centrality represents how important a person's job is and how many people depend on that person to accomplish their tasks. Leaders who perform critical tasks and interact with others regularly have a greater ability to use their power to influence others. Visibility is how aware others are of a leader's power and position. If everyone knows that a leader has a certain level of power, the ability to use that power to influence others is likely to be high.

| TABLE | 10-2 | The Contingencies of Power |

Contingency	Leader's ability to influence others increases when . . .
Substitutability	There are no substitutes for the rewards or resources the leader controls.
Centrality	The leader's role is important and interdependent with others in the organization.
Discretion	The leader has the freedom to make his or her own decisions without being restrained by organizational rules.
Visibility	Others know about the leader and the resources he or she can provide.

Ken Loughridge, an information technology manager working for MWH Global—an environmental and engineering consulting firm based

> Social network maps are one method that executives such as Ken Loughridge are using to better understand how employees are connected to one another and how information is relayed throughout an organization.

in England—took these ideas to heart when he changed jobs within the organization. He used a survey the company had done to map out the "social network" within his organization. He used that network map to tell where his employees went for information, who possessed certain types of expertise, and who offered the most help to his employees. He then went to each of the most well-connected individuals so that he could meet them face-to-face. In a sense, he was seeking out and networking with the individuals in his organization who were likely to have the most power.[17] Companies are increasingly using such networking maps to understand the power structures in their organizations.

OB in Sports

How would you like to coach a basketball team with 12 of the best basketball players in the world? U.S. coach Mike Krzyzewski had the opportunity to do just that during the United States' drive to win the gold medal in the 2008 summer Olympics. Affectionately known as "Coach K," he has coached three national championship teams and has 800 victories at Duke University. However, Coach K had a tough road to walk going into the 2008 Olympics; the United States had not won a world championship in more than six years and had failed to win the gold in the 2004 Olympics or the world championships in 2002 and 2006.

Hiring Krzyzewski was considered a highly risky move; only NBA coaches had coached the team since the addition of pro players in 1992. Coach Krzyzewski had to use a different set of power bases and leadership styles than he is accustomed to at Duke to lead his team effectively, especially with 12 superstars who are used to being the center of attention. As coach, he clearly had a degree of legitimate power once he was selected, but his reward and coercive power were substantially lower than what he holds over his Duke team. The NBA players were playing on a purely voluntary basis. As a collegiate coach with no NBA experience, Krzyzewski's expert power might have been questioned at times, but it was also clear that the NBA players perceived him favorably in that regard. Carlos Boozer, who played for Coach K at Duke, stated, "He's a winner. Any time you're playing for a winner, the respect is given before he even comes into the gym. His winning precedes him."[18] Coach Krzyzewski also holds quite a bit of referent power to help him: This power is so strong that NBA superstar Kobe Bryant still keeps a letter that Krzyzewski wrote Bryant while he was in high school.[19] ❖

One of Coach Mike Krzyzewski's former players has said about him, "He's a winner. Any time you're playing for a winner, the respect is given before he even comes into the gym. His winning precedes him."

Using Influence

Until now, we have discussed the types of power leaders possess and when their opportunities to use that power will grow or diminish. Now we turn to the specific strategies that leaders use to translate that power into actual influence. Recall that having power increases our *ability* to influence behavior. It does not mean that we will use or exert that power. **Influence** is the use of an actual behavior that causes behavioral or attitudinal changes in others.[20] There are two important aspects of influence to keep in mind. First, influence can be seen as directional. It most frequently occurs downward (managers influencing employees) but can also be lateral (peers influencing peers) or upward (employees influencing managers). Second, influence is all relative. The absolute power of the "influencer" and "influencee" isn't as important as the disparity between them.[21]

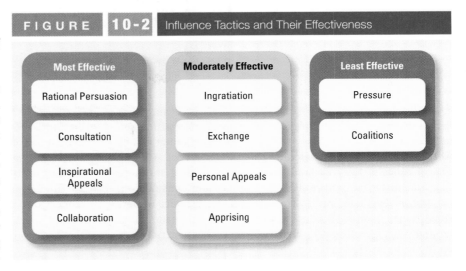

FIGURE 10-2 Influence Tactics and Their Effectiveness

Most Effective
- Rational Persuasion
- Consultation
- Inspirational Appeals
- Collaboration

Moderately Effective
- Ingratiation
- Exchange
- Personal Appeals
- Apprising

Least Effective
- Pressure
- Coalitions

●● 10.3

Explain what behaviors leaders exhibit when trying to influence others. Understand which of these behaviors is most effective.

Influence Tactics. Leaders depend on a number of tactics to cause behavioral or attitudinal changes in others. In fact, there are 10 types of tactics that leaders can use to try to influence others.[22] These tactics and their general levels of effectiveness are illustrated in Figure 10-2. The four most effective tactics have been shown to be rational persuasion, inspirational appeals, consultation, and collaboration. Rational persuasion is the use of logical arguments and hard facts to show the target that the request is a worthwhile one. Research shows that rational persuasion is most effective when it helps show that the proposal is important and feasible.[23] Rational persuasion is particularly important because it's the only tactic that is consistently successful in the case of upward influence.[24] An inspirational appeal is a tactic designed to appeal to the target's values and ideals, thereby creating an emotional or attitudinal reaction. To use this tactic effectively, leaders must have insight into what kinds of things are important to the target. Consultation occurs when the target is allowed to participate in deciding how to carry out or implement a request. This tactic increases commitment from the target, who now has a stake in seeing that his or her opinions were right. A leader uses collaboration by attempting to make it easier for the target to complete the request. Collaboration could involve the leader helping complete the task, providing required resources, or removing obstacles that make task completion difficult.[25]

Four other influence tactics are sometimes effective and sometimes not. Ingratiation is the use of favors, compliments, or friendly behavior to make the target feel better about the influencer. You might more commonly hear this referred to this as "sucking up," especially when used in an upward-influence sense. Ingratiation has been shown to be more effective when used as a long-term strategy and not nearly as effective when used immediately prior to making an influence attempt.[26] Personal appeals are when the requestor asks for something based on personal friendship or loyalty. The stronger the friendship, the more successful the attempt is likely to be. An exchange tactic is used when the requestor offers a reward or resource to the target in return for performing a request. This type of request requires that the requestor have something of value to offer.[27] Finally, apprising occurs when the requestor clearly explains why performing the request will benefit the target personally. It differs from rational persuasion in that it focuses solely on the benefit to the target as opposed to simple logic or benefits to the group or organization. It differs from exchange in that the benefit is not necessarily something that the requestor gives to the target but rather something that results from the action.[28]

The two tactics that have been shown to be least effective and could result in resistance from the target are pressure and coalitions. Of course this does not mean that they aren't used or can't be effective at times. Pressure is the use of coercive power through threats and demands. As we have discussed previously, coercion is a poor way to influence others and may only bring benefits over the short term. The last tactic is the formation of coalitions. Coalitions occur when the influencer enlists other people to help influence the target. These people could be peers, subordinates, or one of the target's superiors. Coalitions are generally used in combination with one of the other tactics. For instance, if rational persuasion is not strong enough, the influencer might bring in another person to show that that person agrees with the logic of the argument.

> ● **INFLUENCE** The use of behaviors to cause behavioral or attitudinal changes in others.

● **ENGAGEMENT** When targets of influence agree with and become committed to an influencer's request.

● **COMPLIANCE** When targets of influence are willing to do what the leader asks but do it with a degree of ambivalence.

● **RESISTANCE** When a target refuses to perform a request and puts forth an effort to avoid having to do it.

● **COMPETING** A conflict resolution style by which one party attempts to get his or her own goals met without concern for the other party's results.

● **AVOIDING** A conflict resolution style by which one party wants to remain neutral, stay away from conflict, or postpone the conflict to gather information or let things cool down.

Two points should be noted about leaders' use of influence tactics. First, influence tactics tend to be most successful when used in combination.[29] Many tactics have some limitations or weaknesses that can be overcome using other tactics. Second, the influence tactics that tend to be most successful are those that are "softer" in nature. Rational persuasion, consultation, inspirational appeals, and collaboration take advantage of personal rather than organizational forms of power. Leaders that are the most effective at influencing others will generally rely on the softer tactics, make appropriate requests, and ensure the tactics they use match the types of power they have.

Responses to Influence Tactics. As illustrated in Figure 10-3, there are three possible responses people have to influence tactics.[30] **Engagement** occurs when the target of influence agrees with and becomes committed to the influence request.[31] For a leader, this is the best outcome because it results in employees putting forth the greatest level of effort in accomplishing what they are asked to do. Engagement reflects a shift in both the behaviors and the attitudes of employees. **Compliance** occurs when targets of influence are willing to do what the leader asks, but they do it with a degree of ambivalence. Compliance reflects a shift in the behaviors of employees but not their attitudes. This behavior is the most common response to influence attempts in organizations because anyone with some degree of power who makes a reasonable request is likely to achieve compliance. That response allows leaders to accomplish their purpose, but it doesn't bring about the highest levels of employee effort and dedication. Still, it's clearly preferable to

resistance, which occurs when the target refuses to perform the influence request and puts forth an effort to avoid having to do it. Employee resistance could come in the form of making excuses, trying to influence the requestor in return, or simply refusing to carry out the request. Resistance is most likely when the influencer's power is low relative to the target or when the request itself is inappropriate or unreasonable.[32]

10.4

Explain how leaders use their power and influence to resolve conflicts in the workplace.

Conflict Resolution. One highly important area in which leaders can use their influence is in the context of conflict resolution. Conflict arises when two or more individuals perceive that their goals are in opposition. When conflict arises in organizations, leaders have the ability to use their power and influence to resolve it. As illustrated in Figure 10-4, there are five different styles a leader can use when handling conflict, each of which is appropriate in different circumstances.[33] The five styles can be viewed as combinations of two separate factors: how *assertive* leaders want to be in pursuing their own goals and how *cooperative* they are with regard to the concerns of others.

Competing (high assertiveness, low cooperation) occurs when one party attempts to get his or her own goals met without concern for the other party's results. It could be considered a win–lose approach to conflict management. Competing occurs most often when one party has high levels of organizational power and can use legitimate or coercive power to settle the conflict. It also generally involves the hard forms of influence such as pressure or coalitions. Although this strategy for resolving conflict might get the result initially, it won't win a leader many friends, given the negative reactions that tend to accompany such tactics. It's best used in situations in which the leader knows he or she is right and a quick decision needs to be made.

Avoiding (low assertiveness, low cooperation) occurs when one party wants to remain neutral, stay away from conflict, or postpone the conflict to gather information or let things cool down. Avoiding usually results in an unfavorable result for everyone, including the organization, and may result in negative feelings toward the leader. Most important, avoiding never really resolves the conflict. **Accommodating** (low assertiveness, high cooperation) occurs when one party gives in to the other and acts in a completely unselfish way. Leaders will typically use an accommodating strategy when the issue is really not that important to them but is very important to the

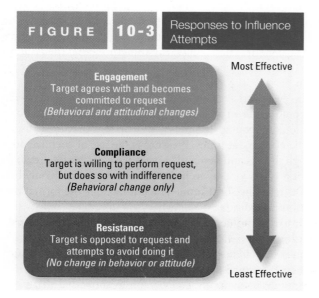

FIGURE 10-3 Responses to Influence Attempts

Most Effective

Engagement
Target agrees with and becomes committed to request
(Behavioral and attitudinal changes)

Compliance
Target is willing to perform request, but does so with indifference
(Behavioral change only)

Resistance
Target is opposed to request and attempts to avoid doing it
(No change in behavior or attitude)

Least Effective

FIGURE 10-4 Styles of Conflict Resolution

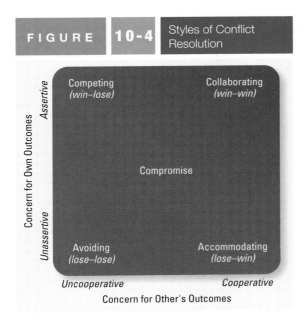

One recent and unique example of conflict resolution is occurring through the One Laptop per Child project. Nicolas Negroponte is the founder and chairperson of this nonprofit organization whose mission is to make millions of $100 laptops for undereducated children in the world's poorest nations. Needless to say, manufacturing a $100 laptop (named the XO) is no small feat. Negroponte is leading a network of vastly different individuals, all working on their own time or on loan from other organizations, through a painstaking collaboration process of design and manufacturing. The process hasn't always been easy. There have been times when Negroponte has had to adopt a competing style of conflict resolution to make a custom wireless system for the laptop function. This competitive response upset a faction of volunteers who subsequently quit the project. However, other times Negroponte has facilitated collaboration among very disparate groups. As a leader with varying degrees of power, Negroponte constantly has to

other party. It's also an important strategy to think about when the leader has less power than the other party. If leaders know they are going to lose the conflict due to their lack of power anyway, it might be a better long-term strategy to give in to the demands from the other party.

Collaboration (high assertiveness, high cooperation) occurs when both parties work together to maximize outcomes. Collaboration is seen as a win–win form of conflict resolution. Collaboration is generally regarded as the most effective form of conflict resolution, especially in reference to task-oriented rather than personal conflicts.[34] However, it's also the most difficult to come by because it requires full sharing of information by both parties, a full discussion of concerns, relatively equal power between parties, and a lot of time investment to arrive at a resolution. However, this style also results in the best outcomes and reactions from both parties. **Compromise** (moderate assertiveness, moderate cooperation) occurs when conflict is resolved through give-and-take concessions. Compromise is perhaps the most common form of conflict resolution, whereby each party's losses are offset by gains and vice versa. It is seen as an easy form of resolution, maintains relations between parties, and generally results in favorable evaluations for the leader.[35]

The One Laptop per Child project intends to provide millions of $100 laptops for the world's poorest children. Founder and director Nicolas Negroponte has put together a large team of volunteers, "borrowed" workers from many different organizations, and worked to establish an effective collaboration among them by adopting a wide variety of conflict resolution strategies, even the competing style.

● **NEGOTIATION** A process in which two or more interdependent individuals discuss and attempt to come to an agreement about their different preferences.

● **LEADER EFFECTIVENESS** The degree to which the leader's actions result in the achievement of the unit's goals, the continued commitment of the unit's employees, and the development of mutual trust, respect, and obligation with followers.

balance the needs of the project with the needs of individuals and attempt to resolve conflict effectively.[36]

There is perhaps no better place for leaders to use their power, influence, and conflict resolution skills than when conducting negotiations. Negotiation is a process in which two or more interdependent individuals discuss and attempt to come to an agreement about their different preferences.[37] Negotiations can take place inside the organization or when dealing with organizational outsiders. Negotiations can involve settling a contract dispute between labor and management, determining a purchasing price for products, haggling over a performance review rating, or determining the starting salary for a new employee. Clearly, negotiations are a critical part of organizational life, for both leaders and employees. For an example of a negotiation that might interest you, see this chapter's **OB for Students** feature.

 10.5

Describe what it means for a leader to be "effective."

LEADER STYLES AND BEHAVIORS

The first half of this chapter described how leaders *get* the power and the types of influence needed to direct others. The rest of the chapter describes how leaders actually *use*

their power and influence in an effective way. Of course, most leaders can't judge their performance by pointing to changes in stock price. Although organizations gauge leader effectiveness in a number of ways, for our purposes, leader effectiveness will be defined as the degree to which the leader's actions result in the achievement of the unit's goals, the continued commitment of the unit's employees, and the development of mutual trust, respect, and obligation with followers.

Leader Decision-Making Styles

One of the most important things leaders do is make decisions. Think about the job you currently hold or the last job you had. Now picture your boss. How many decisions did he or she have to make in a given week? How did he or she go about making those decisions? A leader's decision-making style reflects the process the leader uses to generate and choose from a set of alternatives to solve a problem (see Chapter 7 on Learning and Decision Making for more on such issues). Decision-making styles capture *how* a leader decides as opposed to *what* a leader decides.

The most important element of a leader's decision-making style is this: Does the leader decide most things for him- or herself, or does the leader involve others in the process? We've probably all had bosses (or professors, or even parents) who made virtually all decisions by themselves, stopping by to announce what had happened once the call had been made. We've probably also had other bosses (or professors, or parents) who tended to do the opposite—involving us, asking our opinions, or seeking our vote even when we didn't even care about what was being discussed. It turns out that this issue of leader versus follower control can be used to define some specific decision-making styles. Figure 10-5 shows those styles,

OB for Students

Nine out of ten recruiters say that their initial compensation offer to a job candidate is lower than they are prepared to pay.[38] Many of you are in the midst of or starting to consider a job search as you graduate. Research has plenty to say about your ability to negotiate and secure an acceptable salary. One major issue is that the majority of us never attempt to negotiate the offered salary.[39] A second major issue is that those who do negotiate do a pretty poor job of it. Although the conventional wisdom that men negotiate more often than women is false, a study of MBA students showed that men do perhaps negotiate more effectively than their female counterparts and that these differences could account for a lot of money over time.[40]

Regardless, here are some suggestions for negotiating your salary:[41]

1. Know your worth going in. You should know the approximate salaries for others within your major or functional area. You can ask your career center for this information in many cases.

2. You need to know your "BATNA," or your best alternative to a negotiated agreement. What is the lowest possible offer that you would be willing to accept? At what point would you be willing to walk away? Negotiators with a clear BATNA generally walk away with higher results.

3. What is your goal for a salary? Do not be afraid to put this number on the table.

Avoid vague responses such as, "I want more money," which does nothing to help further the negotiation process.

4. You need to be prepared to sell yourself. What value do you bring to the table that they might not know about? If you want to convince the company that raising your offer is a win–win result, you need to be able to convince the company that your value is more significant than it thought it was.

5. Last but not least: Don't threaten to leave the table unless you really are prepared to do it. Do you indeed have a worthwhile backup plan? ❖

arranged on a continuum from high follower control to high leader control.

●● 10.6

Explain the four styles leaders can use to make decisions. Describe which factors combine to make some styles more effective in a given situation.

Defining the Styles. With an autocratic style, the leader makes the decision alone without asking for the opinions or suggestions of the employees in the work unit.[42] The employees may provide information that the leader needs but are not asked to generate or evaluate potential solutions. In fact, they may not even be told about the decision that needs to be made, knowing only that the leader wants information for some reason. This decision-making style seems to be a favorite of Mike Jeffries, the quirky CEO of Abercrombie & Fitch, the Ohio-based clothing retailer best known for its racy catalog and preppy but edgy styles.[43] Even as CEO, Jeffries interviews every model used in the company's catalog, approves all merchandise in the stores, and describes how clothes should be folded on store tables.

The next two styles in Figure 10-5 offer more employee involvement. With a consultative style, the leader presents the problem to individual employees or a group of employees, asking for their opinions and suggestions before ultimately making the decision him- or herself.[44] With this style, employees do "have a say" in the process, but the ultimate authority still rests with the leader. That ultimate authority changes with a facilitative style, in which the leader presents the problem to a group of employees and seeks consensus on a solution, making sure that his or her own opinion receives no more weight than anyone else's.[45] With this style, the leader is more facilitator than decision maker. Disney CEO Bob Iger seems to embrace a combination of consultative and facilitative styles.[46] Since taking over for Michael Eisner, Iger has made meetings with his division heads less autocratic. Whereas Eisner held court, Iger encourages a conversation. Iger describes his style this way: "You put good people in jobs and give them

Mike Jeffries (on the left), CEO of Abercrombie & Fitch, is regarded as having an autocratic leadership style.

room to run. . . . You involve yourself in a responsible way, but not to the point where you are usurping their authority. I don't have the time or concentration—and you could argue maybe even the talent—to do that."[47]

With a delegative style, the leader gives an individual employee or a group of employees the responsibility for making the decision within some set of specified boundary conditions.[48] The leader plays no role in the deliberations unless asked, though he or she may offer encouragement and provide necessary resources behind the scenes. Phil Knight, the chairman of Nike, the Oregon-based athletic apparel company, often embraces a delegative style.[49] A quiet and enigmatic figure, Knight has been described as the ultimate delegator, with executives interpreting his silences and nods as the freedom to make their own decisions, even when those decisions take the company in different directions. The management style that has defined Knight's approach over the past 40 years is straightforward: Find people who care about the product and let them handle the details. Given his delegative style, it's ironic that Knight has

> **"Of course, most leaders can't judge their performance by pointing to changes in stock price."**

FIGURE 10-5 Leader Decision-Making Styles

| Delegative Style | Facilitative Style | Consultative Style | Autocratic Style |

High Follower Control ← → High Leader Control

● TIME-DRIVEN MODEL OF LEADERSHIP A model that suggests that seven factors, including the importance of the decision, the expertise of the leader, and the competence of the followers, combine to make some decision-making styles more effective than others in a given situation.

● INITIATING STRUCTURE A pattern of behavior where the leader defines and structures the roles of employees in pursuit of goal attainment.

had trouble ceding the CEO position to others during his tenure at Nike.[50]

When Are the Styles Most Effective?

Which decision-making style is best? As you may have guessed, there is no one decision-making style that's effective across all situations, and all styles have their pluses and minuses. There are many factors to consider when leaders choose a decision-making style.[51] The most obvious consideration is the quality of the resulting decision because making the correct decision is the ultimate means of judging the leader. However, leaders also have to consider whether employees will accept and commit to their decision. Research studies have repeatedly shown that allowing employees to participate in decision making increases their job satisfaction.[52] Such participation also helps develop employees' own decision-making skills.[53]

Of course, such participation has a downside for employees because it takes up time. Many employees view meetings as an interruption of their work. One recent study found that employees spend, on average, six hours a week in scheduled meetings, and that time spent in meetings was negatively related to job satisfaction when employees didn't depend on others in their jobs, were focused on their own task accomplishment, and felt that meetings were run ineffectively.[54] Consider the case of Paul Pressler, whose five-year term as CEO of The Gap Inc., the California-based apparel company, ended in 2007.[55] Pressler had been hired from Disney to use his expertise to bring discipline to the struggling company. His tenure was criticized for its increase in meetings, with employees asked to explain incredibly specific details to The Gap Inc.'s new chief financial officer. One former employee describes the demands as "the antithesis of being creative and nimble. It was talking about the work vs. doing the work." Criticisms about decision-making style were also leveled at Cynthia Harriss, whom Pressler had hired to lead the Gap brand. "She made no decisions," says one employee. "She defaulted to Paul, who made no decisions."

How can leaders effectively manage their choice of decision-making styles? The **time-driven model of leadership** offers one potential guide.[56] The model suggests that the focus should shift away from autocratic, consultative, facilitative, and delegative *leaders* to autocratic, consultative, facilitative, and delegative *situations*. More specifically, the model suggests that seven factors combine to make some decision-making styles more effective in a given situation and other styles less effective. Those seven factors include

- *Decision significance*: Is the decision significant to the success of the project or the organization?
- *Importance of commitment*: Is it important that employees "buy in" to the decision?

- *Leader expertise*: Does the leader have significant knowledge or expertise regarding the problem?
- *Likelihood of commitment*: How likely is it that employees will trust the leader's decision and commit to it?
- *Shared objectives*: Do employees share and support the same objectives, or do they have an agenda of their own?
- *Employee expertise*: Do the employees have significant knowledge or expertise regarding the problem?
- *Teamwork skills*: Do the employees have the ability to work together to solve the problem, or will they struggle with conflicts or inefficiencies?

Figure 10-6 illustrates how these seven factors can be used to illustrate the most effective decision-making style in a given situation. The figure asks whether levels of each of the seven factors are "high" (H) or "low" (L). The figure functions like a funnel moving from left to right, with each answer bringing you closer to the eventual recommended style (dashes mean that a given factor can be skipped with that combination). Although the model seems complex on first look, the principles within it are straightforward. Autocratic styles are reserved for decisions that are insignificant or decisions for which employee commitment is unimportant. The only exception is when the leader's expertise is high and the leader is trusted. Going with the autocratic style in these situations should result in an accurate decision that makes the most efficient use of employees' time. Delegative styles are reserved for circumstances in which employees have strong teamwork skills and aren't likely to just commit to whatever decision the leader provides. Deciding between the remaining two styles—consultative and facilitative—is more nuanced and requires a more complete consideration of all seven factors.

Research has tended to support many of the time-driven model's propositions, particularly when the research uses practicing managers as participants.[57] For example, one study asked managers to recall past decisions, the context surrounding those decisions, and the eventual successes (or failures) of their decisions.[58] When managers used the decision-making styles recommended by the model, those decisions were rated as successful 68 percent of the time. When managers went against the model's prescriptions, their decisions were only rated as successful 22 percent of the time. It's also interesting to note that studies suggest that managers tend to choose the style recommended by the model only around 40 percent of the time and exhibit less variation in styles than the model suggests they should.[59] In particular, managers seem to overuse the consultative style and underutilize autocratic and facilitative styles. For a more informal test (and "test drive") of the model, see our **OB on Screen** feature.

 10.7

Describe the two dimensions that capture most of the day-to-day leadership behaviors that leaders engage in.

Day-to-Day Leadership Behaviors

Leaving aside how they go about making decisions, what do leaders *do* on a day-to-day basis? When you think about bosses that you've had, what behaviors do they tend to perform as part of their daily leadership responsibilities? A series of studies at Ohio State in the 1950s attempted to answer that question. Working under grants from the Office of Naval Research and the International Harvester Company, the studies began by generating a list of all the behaviors leaders engage in—around 1,800 in all.[60] Those behaviors were trimmed down to 150 specific examples, then grouped into several categories, as shown in Table 10-3.[61] The table reveals that many leaders spend their time engaging in a mix of initiating, organizing, producing, socializing, integrating, communicating, recognizing, and representing behaviors. Although eight categories are easier to remember than 1,800 behaviors,

---

FIGURE 10-6 The Time-Driven Model of Leadership

START HERE → (columns) ← END HERE

Decision Significance	Importance of Commitment	Leader Expertise	Likelihood of Commitment	Shared Objectives	Employee Expertise	Teamwork Skills	
H	H	H	H	—	—	—	Autocratic
			L	H	H	H	Delegative
						L	Consultative
					L	—	Consultative
				L	—	—	Consultative
		L	H	H	H	H	Facilitative
						L	Consultative
					L	—	Consultative
				L	—	—	Consultative
			L	H	H	H	Facilitative
						L	Consultative
					L	—	Consultative
				L	—	—	Consultative
	L	H	—	—	—	—	Autocratic
		L		H	H	H	Facilitative
						L	Consultative
					L	—	Consultative
				L	—	—	Consultative
L	H	—	H	—	—	—	Autocratic
			L	—	—	H	Delegative
						L	Facilitative
	L		L	—	—	—	Autocratic

Source: Adapted from V. H. Vroom, "Leadership and the Decision-Making Process," *Organizational Dynamics* 28 (2000), pp. 82–94.

TABLE 10-3 Day-to-Day Behaviors Performed by Leaders

Behavior	Description
Initiating Structure	
Initiation	Originating, facilitating, and sometimes resisting new ideas and practices
Organization	Defining and structuring work, clarifying leader versus member roles, coordinating employee tasks
Production	Setting goals and providing incentives for the effort and productivity of employees
Consideration	
Membership	Mixing with employees, stressing informal interactions, and exchanging personal services
Integration	Encouraging a pleasant atmosphere, reducing conflict, promoting individual adjustment to the group
Communication	Providing information to employees, seeking information from them, showing an awareness of matters that affect them
Recognition	Expressing approval or disapproval of the behaviors of employees
Representation	Acting on behalf of the group, defending the group, and advancing the interests of the group

Source: J. K. Hemphill and A. E. Coons, "Development of the Leader Behavior Description Questionnaire," in *Leader Behavior: Its Description and Measurement,* ed. R. M. Stogdill and A. E. Coons (Columbus, OH: Bureau of Business Research, Ohio State University, 1957), pp. 6–38.

further analyses suggested that the categories in Table 10-3 really boil down to just two dimensions: initiating structure and consideration.[62]

Initiating structure reflects the extent to which the leader defines and structures the roles of employees in pursuit of goal attainment.[63] Leaders who are high on initiating structure play a more active role in directing group activities and prioritize planning, scheduling, and trying out new ideas. They might emphasize the importance of meeting deadlines, describe explicit standards of performance, ask employees to follow formalized procedures, and criticize poor work when necessary.[64] **Consideration** reflects the extent to which leaders create job relationships characterized by mutual trust, respect for employee ideas, and consideration of employee feelings.[65] Leaders who are high on consideration create a climate of good rapport and strong, two-way communication and exhibit a deep concern for the welfare of employees. They might do personal favors for employees, take time to listen to their problems, "go to bat" for them when needed, and treat them as equals.[66]

The Ohio State studies argued that initiating structure and consideration were (more or less) independent concepts, meaning that leaders could be high on both, low on both, or high on one and low on the other. That view differed from a series of studies conducted at the University of Michigan during the same time period. Those studies identified concepts similar to initiating structure and consideration, calling them production-centered (or task-oriented) and employee-centered (or relations-oriented) behaviors.[67] However, the Michigan studies framed their task-oriented and relations-oriented concepts as two ends of one continuum, implying that leaders couldn't be high on both dimensions.[68] In fact, a recent meta-analysis of 78 studies showed that initiating structure and consideration are only weakly related—knowing whether a leader engages in one brand of behavior says little about whether he or she engages in the other brand.[69] To see how much initiating structure and consideration you engage in during leadership roles, see the assessment at the end of the chapter.

After an initial wave of research on initiating structure and consideration, leadership experts began to doubt the usefulness of the two dimensions for predicting leadership effectiveness.[70] More recent research has painted a more encouraging picture, however. A meta-analysis of 103 studies showed that initiating structure and consideration both had beneficial relationships with a number of outcomes.[71] For example, consideration had a strong positive relationship with perceived leader effectiveness, employee motivation, and employee job satisfaction. It also had a moderate positive relationship with overall unit performance. For its part, initiating structure had a strong positive relationship with employee motivation and moderate positive relationships with perceived leader effectiveness, employee job satisfaction, and overall unit performance.

OB on Screen

Thirteen Days

There's something immoral about abandoning your own judgment.

With those words, President John F. Kennedy (Bruce Greenwood) foreshadows the decision-making style he's going to use during the Cuban missile crisis, as depicted in *Thirteen Days* (Dir. Roger Donaldson, New Line, 2001). During a conversation with his brother, Robert Kennedy (Steven Culp), and his chief of staff, Kenny O'Donnell (Kevin Costner), Kennedy expresses concern over dealing with a new crisis: the installation of Soviet missiles in Cuba. Kennedy assembles the best team of advisors he can to deal with the crisis, but the question remains: What decision-making style should he use?

If we work our way through Figure 10-6, it seems clear that the decision is significant (the missiles can reach every major city in the United States, except for Seattle). O'Donnell himself notes how important it is for U.S. generals to commit to the decision, and it's clear that Kennedy doesn't have the expertise needed to drive the discussions. Unfortunately for Kennedy, the movie's depiction of the events shows that his generals don't trust him, resulting in a low likelihood of commitment. To make matters worse, the generals appear to have their own objectives. If you're scoring at home, our journey through Figure 10-6 results in H-H-L-L-L, suggesting that the most effective decision-making style for Kennedy is consultative.

Did Kennedy use that style? In the end, Kennedy's advisors present him with two feasible options. Once those options are delivered, Kennedy doesn't call for a show of hands and makes no attempt to bring the room to consensus. He asks his speechwriters to get time on

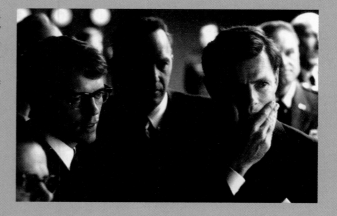

the network news the next day and write up speeches for invasion and for blockade. Then he tells the room he'll give them *his decision* in the morning. Thus, Kennedy did exactly what the time-driven model of leadership suggests he should have done: Gather the opinions and suggestions of others but maintain the ultimate authority for himself. ❖

Transformational Leadership Behaviors

By describing decision-making styles and day-to-day leader behaviors, we've covered a broad spectrum of what it is that leaders do. Still, something is missing. Take a small piece of scrap paper and jot down five people who are famous for their effective leadership. They can come from inside or outside the business world and can be either living people or historical figures. All that's important is that their name be practically synonymous with great leadership. Once you've compiled your list, take a look at the names. Do they appear on your list because they tend to use the right decision-making styles in the right situations and engage in effective levels of consideration and initiating structure? What about the case of Anne Mulcahy? Do decision-making styles and day-to-day leadership behaviors explain her importance to the fortunes of Xerox?

The missing piece of this leadership puzzle is what leaders do to motivate their employees to perform beyond expectations. Transformational leadership involves inspiring followers to commit to a shared vision that provides meaning to their work while also serving as role models who help followers develop their own potential and view problems from new perspectives.[72] Transformational leaders heighten followers' awareness of the importance of certain outcomes while increasing their confidence that those outcomes can be achieved.[73] What gets "transformed" is the way followers view their work, causing them to focus on the collective good more than just their own short-term self-interests and to perform beyond expectations as a result.[74] Former President Dwight D. Eisenhower once noted, "Leadership is the ability to decide what is to be done, and then to get others to want to do it."[75] Former President Harry S Truman similarly observed, "A leader is a man who has the ability to get other people to do what they don't want to do, and like it."[76] Both quotes capture a transformation in the way followers view their work and what motivates them on the job.

Transformational leadership is viewed as a more motivational approach to leadership than other managerial approaches. Figure 10-7 contrasts various approaches to leadership according to how active or passive they are and, ultimately, how effective they prove to be. The colored cubes in the figure represent five distinct approaches to motivating employees, and the depth of the cubes represents how much a leader prioritizes each of the approaches. The figure therefore represents an optimal leadership approach that prioritizes more effective and more active behaviors. That optimal approach includes low levels of laissez-faire (i.e., hands-off) leadership, represented by the red cube, which is the avoidance of leadership altogether.[77] Important actions are delayed, responsibility is ignored, and power and influence go unutilized. One common measure of leadership reflects laissez-faire styles with this statement: "The leader avoids getting involved when important issues arise."[78]

The three yellow cubes represent transactional leadership, which occurs when the leader rewards or disciplines the follower depending on the adequacy of the follower's performance.[79] With passive management-by-exception, the leader waits around for mistakes and errors, then takes corrective action as necessary.[80] After all, "if it ain't broke, don't fix it!"[81] This approach is represented by statements like: "The leader takes no action until complaints are received."[82] With active management-by-exception, the leader arranges to monitor mistakes and errors actively and again takes corrective action when required.[83] This approach is represented by statements like: "The leader directs attention toward failures to meet standards."[84] Contingent reward represents a more active and effective brand of transactional leadership, in which the leader attains follower agreement on what needs to be done using promised or actual rewards in exchange for adequate performance.[85] Statements like "The leader makes clear what one can expect to receive when performance goals are achieved" exemplify contingent reward leadership.[86]

Transactional leadership represents the "carrot-and-stick" approach to leadership, with management-by-exception providing the "sticks" and contingent reward supplying the "carrots." Of course, transactional leadership represents the dominant approach to motivating employees in most organizations, and research suggests that it can be effective. A meta-analysis of

"Leadership is the ability to decide what is to be done, and then to get others to want to do it."

—Dwight D. Eisenhower

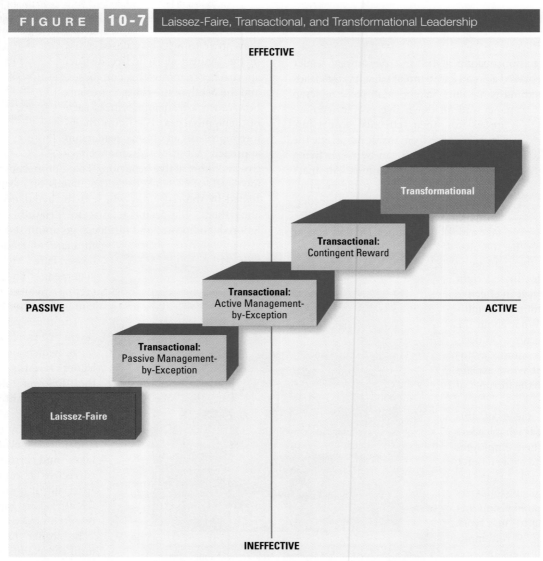

EFFECTIVE

Transformational

Transactional:
Contingent Reward

Transactional:
Active Management-
by-Exception

PASSIVE   ACTIVE

Transactional:
Passive Management-
by-Exception

Laissez-Faire

INEFFECTIVE

Source: Adapted from B. M. Bass and R. E. Riggio, *Transformational Leadership*, 2nd ed. (Mahwah, NJ: Lawrence Erlbaum Associates, 2006).

87 studies showed that contingent reward was strongly related to follower motivation and perceived leader effectiveness[87] (see Chapter 5 on Motivation for more discussion of contingent reward issues). Active management-by-exception was only weakly related to follower motivation and perceived leader effectiveness, however, and passive management-by-exception seems to actually harm those outcomes.[88] Such results support the progression shown in Figure 10-7, with contingent reward standing as the most effective approach under the transactional leadership umbrella.

●● 10.8

Understand how transformational leadership differs from transactional leadership. Describe which kinds of behaviors underlie transformational leadership.

Finally, the green cube represents transformational leadership—the most active and effective approach in Figure 10-7. How effective is transformational leadership? Well, we'll save that discussion for the "How Important Is Leadership" section that concludes this chapter, but suffice it to say that transformational leadership has the strongest and most beneficial effects of any of the leadership variables described in this chapter. It's also the leadership approach that is most universally endorsed across cultures, as described in our **OB Internationally** feature. In addition, it probably captures the key qualities of the famous leaders we asked you to list a few paragraphs back. To understand why it's so powerful, we need to dig deeper into the specific kinds of actions and behaviors that leaders can utilize to become more transformational. We'll also take a look at the transformational behaviors of a well-known transformational leader: Steve Jobs, the CEO of Apple. It turns out that the full spectrum of transformational leadership can be summarized using four dimensions: idealized influence, inspirational motivation, intellectual stimulation, and individualized consideration. Collectively, these four dimensions of transformational leadership are often called "the Four I's."[89]

Idealized influence involves behaving in ways that earn the admiration, trust, and respect of followers, causing followers to want to identify with and emulate the leader.[90] Idealized influence is represented by statements like "The leader instills pride in me for being associated with him/her."[91] Idealized influence is synonymous with *charisma*—a Greek word that means "divinely inspired gift"—which reflects a sense among followers that the leader possesses extraordinary qualities.[92] Charisma is a word often associated with Steve Jobs. One observer noted that even though Jobs could be very difficult to work with, his remarkable charisma created a mysterious attraction that drew people to him, keeping them loyal to his collective sense of mission.[93]

Inspirational motivation involves behaving in ways that foster an enthusiasm for and commitment to a shared vision of the future.[94] That vision is transmitted through a sort of "meaning-making" process in which the negative features of

the status quo are emphasized while highlighting the positive features of the potential future.[95] Inspirational motivation is represented by statements like "The leader articulates a compelling vision of the future."[96] At Apple, Steve Jobs is renowned for spinning a "reality distortion field" that reshapes employees' views of the current work environment.[97] One Apple employee explained, "Steve has this power of vision that is almost frightening. When Steve believes in something, the power of that vision can literally sweep aside any objections, problems, or whatever. They just cease to exist."[98]

Intellectual stimulation involves behaving in ways that challenge followers to be innovative and creative by questioning assumptions and reframing old situations in new ways.[99]

OB Internationally

Does the effectiveness of leader styles and behaviors vary across cultures? Answering that question is one of the objectives of *Project GLOBE* (Global Leadership and Organizational Behavior Effectiveness), a collection of 170 researchers from 62 cultures who have studied leadership with 17,300 managers in 951 organizations since 1991.[100] In part, Project GLOBE represents a test of *culturally endorsed implicit leadership theory*, which argues that effective leadership is "in the eye of the beholder" and that cultural variables can alter how people define such leadership.[101] To test that theory, the GLOBE researchers asked participants to rate a number of leader styles and behaviors using a 1–7 scale, where 1 represents the perception that the style or behavior inhibits a person from being an outstanding leader and 7 represents the perception that the style or behavior contributes greatly to a person being an outstanding leader. The figure to the right shows how three of the styles and behaviors described in this chapter were rated across 10 different regions (note that the term "Anglo" represents people of English ethnicity, including the United States, Great Britain, and Australia).

It turns out that transformational leadership is the most universally accepted approach to leadership of any of the concepts studied by Project GLOBE,[102] receiving an average rating near 6 among the citizens

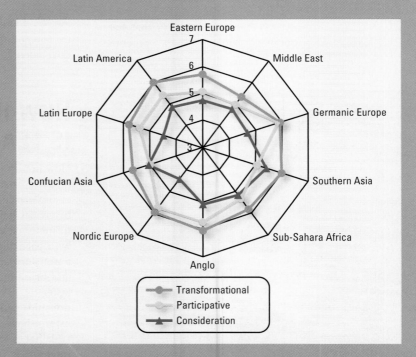

of every region except the Middle East. That universal appeal is likely explained by the fact that transformational leaders appeal to values like idealism and virtue that are accepted and endorsed in almost all countries.[103] The figure also shows that participative styles and consideration behaviors are favorably viewed in most countries, though substan-

tially more variation is evident. These results suggest that participative styles and consideration behaviors appeal to cultural values that differ across regions. Understanding these kinds of results can help organizations select, counsel, and train managers who will better fit the profile of an effective leader in a given region. ❖

"WHEN STEVE BELIEVES IN SOMETHING, THE POWER OF THAT VISION CAN LITERALLY SWEEP ASIDE ANY OBJECTIONS, PROBLEMS, OR WHATEVER. THEY JUST CEASE TO EXIST."

● **INTELLECTUAL STIMULATION** When the leader behaves in ways that challenge followers to be innovative and creative by questioning assumptions and reframing old situations in new ways.

● **INDIVIDUALIZED CONSIDERATION** When the leader behaves in ways that help followers achieve their potential through coaching, development, and mentoring.

Intellectual stimulation is represented by statements like "The leader gets others to look at problems from many different angles."[104] Intellectual stimulation has been a staple of Jobs's tenure at Apple. He pushed for a different power supply on the Apple II so that the fan could be removed, preventing it from humming and churning like other computers of the time. Years later, he insisted on removing the floppy drive from the iMac because it seemed silly to transfer data one megabyte at a time, a decision that drew merciless criticism when the iMac debuted.

Individualized consideration involves behaving in ways that help followers achieve their potential

through coaching, development, and mentoring.[105] Not to be confused with the consideration behavior derived from the Ohio State studies, individualized consideration represents treating employees as unique individuals with specific needs, abilities, and aspirations that need to be tied into the unit's mission. Individualized consideration is represented by statements like "The leader spends time teaching and coaching."[106] Of the four facets of transformational leadership, Steve Jobs seems lowest on individualized consideration. Employees who are not regarded as his equals are given a relatively short leash and sometimes face an uncertain future in the company. In fact, some Apple employees resist riding the elevator for fear of ending up trapped with Jobs for the ride between floors. As one observer describes it, by the time the doors open, you might have had your confidence undermined for weeks.[107]

● ● **10.9**

Explain how leadership affects job performance and organizational commitment.

Apple's CEO Steve Jobs has the leadership ability to articulate a compelling vision of the future.

HOW IMPORTANT IS LEADERSHIP?

How important is leadership? As with some other topics in organizational behavior, that's a complicated question because "leadership" isn't just one thing. Instead, all of the leadership styles and behaviors have their own unique importance. However, transformational leadership stands apart from the rest to some extent, with particularly strong effects in organizations. Groups led by a transformational leader tend to be more financially successful and bring higher-quality products and services to market at a faster rate.[108] Transformational leaders also tend to foster relationships with their followers that are of higher quality, marked by especially strong levels of mutual respect and obligation.[109]

What if we focus specifically on the two outcomes in our integrative model of OB: performance and commitment? Figure 10-8 summarizes the research evidence linking transformational leadership to those two outcomes. The figure reveals that transformational leadership indeed affects the job performance of the employees who report to the leader. Employees with transformational leaders tend to have higher levels of task performance and engage in higher levels of citizenship behaviors.[110] Why? One reason is that employees with transformational leaders have higher levels of *motivation* than other employees.[111] They feel a stronger sense of psychological empowerment, feel more self-confident, and set more demanding work goals for themselves.[112] They also *trust* the leader more, making them willing to exert extra effort even when that effort might not be immediately rewarded.[113]

Figure 10-8 also reveals that employees with transformational leaders tend to be more committed to their organization.[114] They feel a stronger emotional bond with their organization and a stronger sense of obligation to remain present and engaged in their work. Why? One reason is that employees with transformational leaders have higher levels of *job satisfaction* than other employees.[115] One study showed that transformational leaders can make employees feel that their jobs have more variety and significance, enhancing intrinsic satisfaction with the work itself.[116] Other studies have shown that charismatic leaders express positive emotions more frequently and that those emotions are "caught" by employees through a sort of "emotional contagion" process.[117] For example, followers of trans-

formational leaders tend to feel more optimism and less frustration during their workday, which makes it a bit easier to stay committed to work.

Although leadership is very important to unit effectiveness and the performance and commitment of employees, there is evidence that there are contexts in which the importance of the leader can be reduced. The substitutes for leadership model suggests that certain characteristics of the situation can constrain the influence of the leader, making it more difficult for the leader to influence employee performance.[118] Those situational characteristics come in two varieties, as shown in Table 10-4. Substitutes reduce the importance of the leader while simultaneously providing a direct benefit to employee performance. For example, a cohesive work group can provide

● SUBSTITUTES FOR LEADERSHIP MODEL A model that suggests that characteristics of the situation can constrain the influence of the leader, which makes it more difficult for the leader to influence employee performance.

● SUBSTITUTES Situational characteristics that reduce the importance of the leader while simultaneously providing a direct benefit to employee performance.

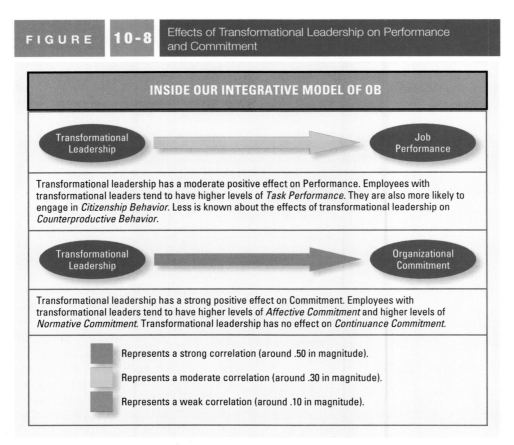

FIGURE 10-8 Effects of Transformational Leadership on Performance and Commitment

INSIDE OUR INTEGRATIVE MODEL OF OB

Transformational Leadership → Job Performance

Transformational leadership has a moderate positive effect on Performance. Employees with transformational leaders tend to have higher levels of *Task Performance*. They are also more likely to engage in *Citizenship Behavior*. Less is known about the effects of transformational leadership on *Counterproductive Behavior*.

Transformational Leadership → Organizational Commitment

Transformational leadership has a strong positive effect on Commitment. Employees with transformational leaders tend to have higher levels of *Affective Commitment* and higher levels of *Normative Commitment*. Transformational leadership has no effect on *Continuance Commitment*.

Represents a strong correlation (around .50 in magnitude).

Represents a moderate correlation (around .30 in magnitude).

Represents a weak correlation (around .10 in magnitude).

Sources: T. A. Judge and R. F. Piccolo, "Transformational and Transactional Leadership: A Meta-Analytic Test of Their Relative Validity," *Journal of Applied Psychology* 89 (2004), pp. 755–68; J. P. Meyer, D. J. Stanley, L. Herscovitch, and L. Topolnytsky, "Affective, Continuance, and Normative Commitment to the Organization: A Meta-Analysis of Antecedents, Correlates, and Consequences," *Journal of Vocational Behavior* 61 (2002), pp. 20–52; P. M. Podsakoff, S. B. MacKenzie, J. B. Paine, and D. G. Bachrach, "Organizational Citizenship Behaviors: A Critical Review of the Theoretical and Empirical Literature and Suggestions for Future Research," *Journal of Management* 26 (2000), pp. 513–63.

● **NEUTRALIZERS** Situational characteristics that reduce the importance of the leader and do not improve employee performance in any way.

its own sort of governing behaviors, making the leader less relevant, while providing its own source of motivation and job satisfaction. **Neutralizers**, in contrast, only reduce the importance of the leader—they themselves have no beneficial impact on performance.[119] For example, spatial distance lessens the impact of a leader's behaviors and styles, but distance itself has no direct benefit for employee job performance. ■

CHECK OUT
www.mhhe.com/ColquittEss

for study materials including Interactive Exercises, Quizzes, iPod downloads, and video.

Substitutes such as group cohesion reduce the importance of the leader while simultaneously providing a direct benefit to employee performance.

TABLE 10-4	Leader Substitutes and Neutralizers
Substitutes	**Description**
• Task feedback	Receiving feedback on performance from the task itself
• Training and experience	Gaining the knowledge to act independently of the leader
• Professionalism	Having a professional specialty that offers guidance
• Staff support	Receiving information and assistance from outside staff
• Group cohesion	Working in a close-knit and interdependent work group
• Intrinsic satisfaction	Deriving personal satisfaction from one's work
Neutralizers	
• Task stability	Having tasks with a clear, unchanging sequence of steps
• Formalization	Having written policies and procedures that govern one's job
• Inflexibility	Working in an organization that prioritizes rule adherence
• Spatial distance	Being separated from one's leader by physical space

Source: Adapted from S. Kerr and J. M. Jermier, "Substitutes for Leadership: Their Meaning and Measurement," *Organizational Behavior and Human Performance* 22 (1978), pp. 375–403.

CASE: Xerox

For the past eight years, Anne Mulcahy (CEO) and Ursula Burns (now president and COO) have worked closely together in the historic turnaround of Xerox. Mulcahy has been known as the charismatic leader, whereas Burns has been known as the "fearless problem solver."[120] Together, they have been quite a force for change within the organization. Their relationship is extremely close but at the same time complex, as the two don't always agree on the best course of action. Mulcahy believes this disagreement is a result of both being passionate and "equally stubborn."[121] Mulcahy was Burns's role model as she moved up the organization, and now Burns has been slotted by Xerox's board of directors to take her place when she retires. The big problem is that though the thought has crossed her mind numerous times, Mulcahy has no definite plans to retire anytime soon. Nor would Xerox want her to.

Traditionally, during periods of succession, the roles for each party are spelled out by the board of directors. In this case though, Mulcahy wanted to work things out directly with Burns. It proved to be substantially more difficult than Mulcahy originally thought it would be. When they initially sat down to discuss how to split job duties, they could not come to an agreement. Burns's initial proposal was that everyone report to her and that she report to Mulcahy. Mulcahy's response was, "Well, what the heck will I do?"[122] At the request of both women, CFO Larry Zimmerman finally stepped in and told them not to worry about the organizational chart but instead consider what was best for Xerox. Since then, the two leaders have attempted to split their duties according to their strengths and based on what Burns needs to learn to take over one day.

10.1 What are the advantages and disadvantages to having two apparent leaders of a group or organization? Is it possible for two well-known leaders to share power effectively?

10.2 Do you think that this kind of an arrangement can last a long time? If you were on the management team at Xerox, to whom would you be more inclined to listen? Why?

10.3 Should all companies have a succession plan such as the one at Xerox? Why do you think companies don't do this more often?

TAKEAWAYS

10.1 Leadership is the use of power and influence to direct the activities of followers toward goal achievement. Power is the ability to influence the behavior of others and resist unwanted influence in return. Power is necessary, in that it gives leaders the ability to influence others.

10.2 Leaders have five major types of power. There are three organizational forms of power: Legitimate power is based on authority or position, reward power is based on the distribution of resources or benefits, and coercive power is based on the handing out of punishments. There are two personal forms of power: Expert power is derived from expertise and knowledge, whereas referent power is based on the attractiveness and charisma of the leader. These types of power can be used most effectively when leaders are central to the work process, are highly visible, have discretion, and are the sole controllers of resources and information.

10.3 Leaders can use 10 different influence tactics to achieve their objectives. The most effective are rational persuasion, consultation, inspirational appeals, and collaboration. The least effective are pressure and the forming of coalitions. Tactics with moderate levels of effectiveness are ingratiation, exchange, personal appeals, and apprising.

10.4 Leaders use power and influence to resolve conflicts through five conflict resolution styles: avoidance, competing, accommodating, collaborating, and compromising. The most effective and also most difficult tactic is collaboration.

10.5 A leader is "effective" to the degree to which the leader's actions result in the achievement of the unit's goals, the continued commitment of the unit's employees, and the development of mutual trust, respect, and obligation with followers.

10.6 Leaders can use a number of styles to make decisions. Beginning with high leader control and moving to high follower control, they include autocratic, consultative, facilitative, and delegative styles. According to the time-driven model of leadership, the appropriateness of these styles depends on decision significance, the importance of commitment, leader expertise, the likelihood of commitment, shared objectives, employee expertise, and teamwork skills.

10.7 Most of the day-to-day leadership behaviors that leaders engage in are examples of either initiating structure or consideration. Initiating structure behaviors include initiation, organization, and production sorts of duties. Consideration behaviors include membership, integration, communication, recognition, and representation sorts of duties.

10.8 Transactional leadership emphasizes "carrot-and-stick" approaches to motivating employees, whereas transformational leadership fundamentally changes the way employees view their work. More specifically, transformational leadership inspires them to commit to a shared vision or goal that provides meaning and challenge to their work. The specific behaviors that underlie transformational leadership include the "Four I's": idealized influence, inspirational motivation, intellectual stimulation, and individualized consideration.

10.9 Transformational leadership has a moderate positive relationship with job performance and a strong positive relationship with organizational commitment. It has stronger effects on these outcomes than other leadership behaviors.

10.1 Can a leader influence others without power? How exactly would that influence take place?

10.2 Which forms of power do you consider to be the strongest? Which types of power do you currently have? How could you go about obtaining higher levels of the forms that you're lacking?

10.3 Who is the most influential leader you have come in contact with personally? What forms of power did he or she have, and which types of influence did he or she use to accomplish objectives?

10.4 The time-sensitive model of leadership argues that leaders aren't just concerned about the accuracy of their decisions when deciding among autocratic, consultative, facilitative, and delegative styles; they're also concerned about the efficient use of time. What other considerations could influence a leader's use of the four decision-making styles?

10.5 Consider the four dimensions of transformational leadership: idealized influence, inspirational motivation, intellectual stimulation, and individualized consideration. Which of those dimensions would you respond to most favorably? Why?

10.6 Can you think of any potential "dark sides" to transformational leadership? What would they be?

ASSESSMENT: Initiating Structure and Consideration

How do you act when you're in a leadership role? This assessment is designed to measure the two dimensions of leaders' day-to-day behaviors: initiating structure and consideration. Please write a number next to each statement that reflects how frequently you engage in the behavior described. Answer each question using the response scale provided. Then subtract your answers to the boldfaced questions from 6, with the difference being your new answer for that question. For example, if your original answer for question 16 was "4," your new answer is "2" (6 – 4). Then sum up your answers for each of the dimensions. (For more assessments relevant to this chapter, please visit the Online Learning Center at www.mhhe.com/ColquittEss.)

1	2	3	4	5
Never	**Seldom**	**Occasionally**	**Often**	**Strongly Agree**

1. I let group members know what is expected of them. _____
2. I encourage the use of uniform procedures. _____
3. I try out my ideas in the group. _____
4. I make my attitudes clear to the group. _____
5. I decide what shall be done and how it shall be done. _____
6. I assign group members to particular tasks. _____
7. I make sure that my part in the group is understood by the group members. _____
8. I schedule the work to be done. _____
9. I maintain definite standards of performance. _____
10. I ask group members to follow standard rules and regulations. _____
11. I am friendly and approachable. _____
12. I do little things to make it pleasant to be a member of the group. _____
13. I put suggestions made by the group into operation. _____
14. I treat all group members as equals. _____
15. I give advance notice of changes. _____
16. **I keep to myself.** _____
17. I look out for the personal welfare of group members. _____
18. I am willing to make changes. _____
19. **I refuse to explain my actions.** _____
20. **I act without consulting the group.** _____

Scoring and Interpretation:

Initiating Structure: Sum up items 1–10.

Consideration: Sum up items 11–20.

For initiating structure, scores of 38 or more are above average, and scores of 37 or less are below average. For consideration, scores of 40 or more are above average, and scores of 39 or less are below average.

Source: R. M. Stogdill, *Manual for the Leader Behavior Description Questionnaire—Form XII* (Columbus, OH: Bureau of Business Research, The Ohio State University, 1963).

EXERCISE: Employee Involvement

The purpose of this exercise is to use the Time-Driven Model of Leadership (shown in Figure 10-6) to determine whether or not to involve employees in various decisions. This exercise uses groups, so your instructor will either assign you to a group or ask you to create your own group. The exercise has the following steps:

1. Review the two cases below, then answer the discussion questions that appear in Step 2 by yourself.

CASE 1: THE SUGAR SUBSTITUTE RESEARCH DECISION

You are the head of research and development (R&D) for a major beer company. While working on a new beer product, one of the scientists in your unit seems to have tentatively identified a new chemical compound that has few calories but tastes more like sugar than current sugar substitutes. The company has no foreseeable need for this product, but it could be patented and licensed to manufacturers in the food industry.

The sugar substitute discovery is in its preliminary stages, and considerable time and resources would be required before it would be commercially viable. Therefore, some resources would be taken away from other projects in the lab. The sugar substitute project is beyond your technical expertise, but some of the R&D lab researchers are familiar with that field of chemistry. As with most forms of research, the amount of research required to identify and perfect the sugar substitute is difficult to determine. You do not know how much demand is expected for this product. Your department has a decision process for funding projects that are behind schedule, but there are no rules or precedents about funding projects that would be licensed but not used by the organization.

The company's R&D budget is limited, and other scientists in your work group have recently complained that they require more resources and financial support to get their projects completed. Some of these other R&D projects hold promise for future beer sales. You believe that most researchers in the R&D unit are committed to ensuring that the company's interests are achieved.

CASE 2: COAST GUARD CUTTER DECISION PROBLEM

You are the captain of a 200-foot Coast Guard cutter, with a crew of 16, including officers. Your mission is general search and rescue at sea. At 2:00 this morning, while en route to your home port after a routine 28-day patrol, you received word from the nearest Coast Guard station that a small plane had crashed 60 miles offshore. You obtained all the available information about the location of the crash, informed your crew of the mission, and set a new course at maximum speed for the scene to commence a search for survivors and wreckage.

You have now been searching for 20 hours. Your search operation has been increasingly impaired by rough seas, and there is evidence of a severe storm building. The atmospherics associated with the deteriorating weather have made communications with the Coast Guard station impossible. A decision must be made shortly about whether to abandon the search and place your vessel on a course that would ride out the storm (thereby protecting the vessel and your crew but relegating any possible survivors to almost certain death from exposure) or continue a potentially futile search and the risks it would entail.

Before losing communications, you received an updated weather advisory about the severity and duration of the storm. Although your crew members are extremely conscientious about their responsibilities, you believe they would be divided on the decision of leaving or staying.

2. Come to a group consensus on the following questions:

   a. To what extent should your subordinates be involved in making this decision? Select one of the following levels of involvement:

   - *No involvement*: You make the decision alone without any participation from subordinates.

   - *Low involvement*: You ask one or more subordinates for information relating to the problem, but you don't ask for their recommendations and might not mention the problem to them.

   - *Medium involvement*: You describe the problem to one or more subordinates (alone or in a meeting) and ask for any relevant information as well as their recommendations on the issue. However, you make the final decision, which might or might not reflect their advice.

   - *High involvement*: You describe the problem to subordinates. They discuss the matter, identify a solution without your involvement (unless they invite your ideas), and implement that solution. You have agreed to support their decision.

   b. What factors led you to choose this level of employee involvement rather than the others?

3. Class discussion (whether in groups or as a class) should focus on this question: What problems might occur if less or more involvement was granted in these cases?

Sources: S. L. McShane and M. A. Von Glinow, *Organizational Behavior*, 3rd ed. (New York: McGraw-Hill, 2005). Used with permission. Case 1 prepared by Steven L. McShane © 2002; Case 2 adapted from *The New Leadership: Managing Participation in Organizations*, by V. H. Vroom and A. G. Jago, 1987.

END NOTES

1. Morris, B. "The Accidental CEO." *Fortune* 147, no. 13 (2003), p. 58.

2. Ibid.

3. Donlon, J. P. "The X-Factor." *Chief Executive*, June 2008, pp. 26–31.

4. Morris, "The Accidental CEO."

5. Mulcahy, A. "Anne Mulcahy on Customers." *Leadership Excellence*, June (2005), p. 15.

6. Yukl, G. *Leadership in Organizations.* 4th ed. Englewood Cliffs, NJ: Prentice Hall, 1998.

7. Ibid.

8. McMurray, V. V. "Some Unanswered Questions on Organizational Conflict." *Organization and Administrative Sciences* 6 (1975), pp. 35–53; Pfeffer, J. *Managing with Power.* Boston: Harvard Business School Press, 1992.

9. Cotton, J. L. "Measurement of Power-Balancing Styles and Some of Their Correlates." *Administrative Science Quarterly* 21 (1976), pp. 307–19; Emerson, R. M. "Power-Dependence Relationships." *American Sociological Review* 27 (1962), pp. 29–41.

10. Ashforth, B. E., and F. A. Mael. "The Power of Resistance." In *Power and Influence in Organizations*, ed. R. M. Kramer and M. E. Neal. Thousand Oaks, CA: Sage, 1998, pp. 89–120.

11. French, Jr., J. R. P., and B. Raven. "The Bases of Social Power." In *Studies in Social Power*, ed. D. Cartwright. Ann Arbor: University of Michigan, Institute for Social Research, 1959, pp. 150–67; Yukl, G., and C. M. Falbe. "The Importance of Different Power Sources in Downward and Lateral Relations." *Journal of Applied Psychology* 76 (1991), pp. 416–23.

12. Yukl, G. "Use Power Effectively." In *Handbook of Principles of Organizational Behavior*, ed. E. A. Locke. Madden, MA: Blackwell, 2004, pp. 242–47.

13. Levenson, E.; C. Tkaczyk; and J. L. Yang, "Indra Rising," *Fortune* 154, no. 8 (2006), p. 145.

14. Hof, R. D. "Back to the Future at Yahoo!." *BusinessWeek*, July 2, 2007, pp. 35–36.

15. French and Raven, "The Bases of Social Power."

16. Hickson, D. J.; C. R. Hinings; C. A. Lee; R. E. Schneck; and J. M. Pennings. "A Strategic Contingencies Theory of Intraorganizational Power." *Administrative Science Quarterly* 16 (1971), pp. 216–27; Hinings, C. R.; D. J. Hickson; J. M. Pennings; and R. E. Schneck. "Structural Conditions of Intraorganizational Power." *Administrative Science Quarterly* 19 (1974), pp. 22–44; Salancik, G. R., and J. Pfeffer. "Who Gets Power and How They Hold on to It: A Strategic Contingency Model of Power." *Organizational Dynamics* 5 (1977), pp. 3–21.

17. McGregor, J. "The Office Chart That Really Counts." *BusinessWeek*, February 27, 2006, pp. 48–49.

18. Abrams, J. "Mike Krzyzewski Sets Pace for Team USA." *L.A. Times*, June 29, 2008.

19. Associated Press. "Krzyzewski and U.S. Have Gold as Only Aim." *New York Times*, July 6, 2008.

20. Somech, A., and A. Drach-Zahavy. "Relative Power and Influence Strategy: The Effects of Agent/Target Organizational Power on Superiors' Choices of Influence Strategies." *Journal of Organizational Behavior* 23 (2002), pp. 167–79; Stahelski, A. J., and C. F. Paynton. "The Effects of Status Cues on Choices of Social Power and Influence Strategies." *Journal of Social Psychology* 135 (1995), pp. 553–60.

21. Yukl, *Leadership in Organizations.*

22. Ibid.; Yukl, G.; C. Chavez; and C. F. Seifert. "Assessing the Construct Validity and Utility of Two New Influence Tactics." *Journal of Organizational Behavior* 26 (2005), pp. 705–25.

23. Yukl, G.; H. Kim; and C. Chavez. "Task Importance, Feasibility, and Agent Influence Behavior as Determinants of Target Commitment." *Journal of Applied Psychology* 84 (1999), pp. 137–43.

24. Yukl, *Leadership in Organizations.*

25. Yukl et al., "Task Importance."

26. Wayne, S. J., and G. R. Ferris. "Influence Tactics, Affect, and Exchange Quality in Supervisor–Subordinate Interactions: A Laboratory Experiment and Field Study." *Journal of Applied Psychology* 75 (1990), pp. 487–99.

27. Kelman, H. C. "Compliance, Identification, and Internalization: Three Processes of Attitude Change." *Journal of Conflict Resolution* 2 (1958), pp. 51–56.

28. Yukl et al., "Assessing the Construct Validity."

29. Falbe, C. M., and G. Yukl. "Consequences for Managers of Using Single Influence Tactics and Combinations of Tactics." *Academy of Management Journal*, August 1992, pp. 638–52.

30. Yukl, *Leadership in Organizations.*

31. Engagement is more commonly referred to as "commitment" in this context. We have changed the original term to avoid any confusion with organizational commitment.

32. Somech and Drach-Zahavy, "Relative Power and Influence Strategy"; Yukl, *Leadership in Organizations*; Yukl, "Use Power Effectively."

33. Lewicki, R. J., and J. A. Litterer. *Negotiations.* Homewood, IL: Irwin, 1985; Thomas, K. W. "Conflict and Negotiation Processes in Organizations." In *Handbook of Industrial and Organizational Psychology*, 2nd ed., Vol. 3, ed. M. D. Dunnette and L. M. Hough. Palo Alto, CA: Consulting Psychologists Press, pp. 651–717.

34. Weingart, L., and K. A. Jehn. "Manage Intra-team Conflict through Collaboration." *Handbook of Principles of Organizational Behavior*, ed. E. A. Locke. Madden, MA: Blackwell, 2004, pp. 226–38.

35. Thomas, K. W. "Toward Multi-dimensional Values in Teaching: The Example of Conflict Behaviors." *Academy of Management Review* 2 (1977), pp. 484–90; de Dreu, C. K. W.; A. Evers; B. Beersma; E. S. Kluwer; and A. Nauta. "A

Theory-Based Measure of Conflict Management Strategies in the Workplace." *Journal of Organizational Behavior* 22 (2001), pp. 645–68.

36. Fahey, J. "The Soul of a Laptop." *Forbes*, May 7, 2007, pp. 100–104.

37. Adapted from Neale, M. A., and M. H. Bazerman. "Negotiating Rationally: The Power and Impact of the Negotiator's Frame." *Academy of Management Executive* 2 (1992), pp. 42–51.

38. Donkin, R. "So What Do You Think You're Worth? The Evidence Seems to Support a New Book's Contention That If You Want a Good Salary, You Had Better Negotiate for It. But Recognize That It Takes Practice." *Financial Times*, November 18, 2004, p. 11.

39. Pinkley, R. L., and G. B. Northcraft. *Get Paid What You're Worth: The Expert Negotiators' Guide to Salary and Compensation.* New York: St. Martin's Griffin, 2003.

40. Gerhart, B., and S. Rynes. "Determinants and Consequences of Salary Negotiations by Male and Female MBA Graduates." *Journal of Applied Psychology* 76 (1991), pp. 256–62.

41. Adapted from Thompson, L. L. *The Mind and Heart of the Negotiator.* 3rd ed. Upper Saddle River, NJ: Prentice Hall, 2005; Pinkley and Northcraft, *Get Paid.*

42. Vroom, V. H. "Leadership and the Decision-Making Process." *Organizational Dynamics* 28 (2000), pp. 82–94; Yukl, *Leadership in Organizations.*

43. Berner, R. "Flip-Flops, Torn Jeans—and Control." *BusinessWeek*, May 30, 2005, pp. 68–70.

44. Vroom, "Leadership and the Decision-Making Process"; Yukl, *Leadership in Organizations.*

45. Ibid.

46. Grover, R. "How Bob Iger Unchained Disney." *BusinessWeek*, February 5, 2007, pp. 74–79.

47. Ibid.

48. Vroom, "Leadership and the Decision-Making Process"; Yukl, *Leadership in Organizations.*

49. Roth, D. "Can Nike Still Do It without Phil Knight?" *Fortune*, April 4, 2005, pp. 59–68.

50. Holmes, S. "Inside the Coup at Nike." *BusinessWeek*, February 6, 2006, pp. 34–37.

51. Vroom, "Leadership and the Decision-Making Process."

52. Miller, K. I., and P. R. Monge. "Participation, Satisfaction, and Productivity: A Meta-Analytic Review." *Academy of Management Journal* 29 (1986), pp. 727–53; Wagner, J. A., III. "Participation's Effects on Performance and Satisfaction: A Reconsideration of Research Evidence." *Academy of Management Review* 19 (1994), pp. 312–30.

53. Vroom, "Leadership and the Decision-Making Process."

54. Rogelberg, S. G.; D. J. Leach; P. B. Warr; and J. L. Burnfield. "'Not Another Meeting!' Are Meeting Time Demands Related to Employee Well-Being?" *Journal of Applied Psychology* 91 (2006), pp. 86–96.

55. Lee, L. "Paul Pressler's Fall from The Gap." *BusinessWeek*, February 26, 2007, pp. 80–84.

56. Vroom, "Leadership and the Decision-Making Process"; Vroom, V. H., and A. G. Jago. *The New Leadership: Managing Participation in Organizations.* Englewood Cliffs, NJ: Prentice Hall, 1988; Vroom, V. H., and A. G. Jago. "Decision Making as a Social Process: Normative and Descriptive Models of Leader Behavior." *Decision Sciences* 5 (1974), pp. 743–69; Vroom, V. H., and P. W. Yetton. *Leadership and Decision-Making.* Pittsburgh, PA: University of Pittsburgh Press, 1973.

57. Aditya, R. N.; R. J. House; and S. Kerr. "Theory and Practice of Leadership: Into the New Millennium." In *Industrial and Organizational Psychology: Linking Theory with Practice*, ed. C. L. Cooper and E. A. Locke. Malden, MA: Blackwell, 2000, pp. 130–65; House, R. J., and R. N. Aditya. "The Social Scientific Study of Leadership: Quo Vadis?" *Journal of Management* 23 (1997), pp. 409–73; Yukl, *Leadership in Organizations.*

58. Vroom, V. H., and A. G. Jago. "On the Validity of the Vroom-Yetton Model." *Journal of Applied Psychology* 63 (1978), pp. 151–62. See also Vroom and Yetton, *Leadership and Decision Making*; Vroom and Jago, *The New Leadership*; Field, R. H. G. "A Test of the Vroom-Yetton Normative Model of Leadership." *Journal of Applied Psychology* 67 (1982), pp. 523–32.

59. Vroom and Yetton, *Leadership and Decision-Making.*

60. Hemphill, J. K. *Leader Behavior Description.* Columbus, OH: Ohio State University, 1950. Cited in Fleishman, E. A.; E. F. Harris; and H. E. Burtt. *Leadership and Supervision in Industry: An Evaluation of a Supervisory Training Program.* Columbus, OH: Bureau of Educational Research, Ohio State University, 1955.

61. Hemphill, J. K., and A. E. Coons. "Development of the Leader Behavior Description Questionnaire." In *Leader Behavior: Its Description and Measurement*, ed. R. M. Stogdill and A. E. Coons. Columbus, OH: Bureau of Business Research, Ohio State University, 1957, pp. 6–38.

62. Fleishman, E. A. "The Description of Supervisory Behavior." *Journal of Applied Psychology* 37 (1953), pp. 1–6; Fleishman et al., *Leadership and Supervision in Industry*; Hemphill and Coons, "Development of the Leader Behavior Description Questionnaire"; Halpin, A. W., and B. J. Winer. *Studies in Aircrew Composition: The Leadership Behavior of the Airplane Commander* (Technical Report No. 3). Columbus, OH: Personnel Research Board, Ohio State University, 1952. Cited in Fleishman et al., *Leadership and Supervision.*

63. Fleishman, "The Description of Supervisory Behavior"; Fleishman et al., *Leadership and Supervision*; Fleishman, E. A., and D. R. Peters. "Interpersonal Values, Leadership Attitudes, and Managerial 'Success.'" *Personnel Psychology* 15 (1962), pp. 127–43.

64. Yukl, *Leadership in Organizations.*

65. Fleishman, "The Description of Supervisory Behavior"; Fleishman et al., *Leadership and Supervision*; Fleishman and Peters, "Interpersonal Values."

66. Yukl, *Leadership in Organizations*.

67. Katz, D.; N. Maccoby; and N. Morse. *Productivity, Supervision, and Morale in an Office Situation.* Ann Arbor, MI: Institute for Social Research, University of Michigan, 1950; Katz, D.; N. Maccoby; G. Gurin; and L. Floor. *Productivity, Supervision, and Morale among Railroad Workers.* Ann Arbor, MI: Survey Research Center, University of Michigan, 1951; Katz, D., and R. L. Kahn. "Some Recent Findings in Human-Relations Research in Industry." In *Readings in Social Psychology*, ed. E. Swanson, T. Newcomb, and E. Hartley. New York: Holt, pp. 650–65; Likert, R. *New Patterns of Management.* New York: McGraw-Hill, 1961; Likert, R. *The Human Organization.* New York: McGraw-Hill, 1967.

68. Fleishman, E. A. "Twenty Years of Consideration and Structure." In *Current Developments in the Study of Leadership*, ed. E. A. Fleishman and J. G. Hunt. Carbondale, IL: Southern Illinois Press, 1973, pp. 1–37.

69. Judge, T. A.; R. F. Piccolo; and R. Ilies. "The Forgotten Ones? The Validity of Consideration and Initiating Structure in Leadership Research." *Journal of Applied Psychology* 89 (2004), pp. 36–51.

70. Aditya et al., "Theory and Practice of Leadership"; Den Hartog and Koopman, "Leadership in Organizations"; House and Aditya, "The Social Scientific Study of Leadership"; Korman, A. K. "'Consideration,' 'Initiating Structure,' and Organizational Criteria—A Review." *Personnel Psychology* 19 (1966), pp. 349–61; Yukl, *Leadership in Organizations*; Yukl, G., and D. D. Van Fleet. "Theory and Research on Leadership in Organizations." In *Handbook of Industrial and Organizational Psychology*, Vol. 3, ed. M. D. Dunnette and L. M. Hough. Palo Alto, CA: Consulting Psychologists Press, 1992, pp. 147–97.

71. Judge et al., "The Forgotten Ones?"

72. Bass, B. M., and R. E. Riggio. *Transformational Leadership.* 2nd ed. Mahwah, NJ: Lawrence Erlbaum Associates, 2006; Bass, B. M. *Leadership and Performance beyond Expectations.* New York: Free Press, 1985; Burns, L. M. *Leadership.* New York: Harper & Row, 1978.

73. Bass, *Leadership and Performance beyond Expectations*.

74. Ibid.

75. Larson, A. *The President Nobody Knew.* New York: Popular Library, 1968, p. 68. Cited in ibid.

76. Truman, H. S. *Memoirs.* New York: Doubleday, 1958. Cited in Bass, *Leadership and Performance beyond Expectations*.

77. Bass and Riggio, *Transformational Leadership*.

78. Ibid.; Bass, B. M., and B. J. Avolio. *MLQ: Multifactor Leadership Questionnaire.* Redwood City, CA: Mind Garden, 2000.

79. Bass and Riggio, *Transformational Leadership*; Bass, *Leadership and Performance beyond Expectations*; Burns, *Leadership*.

80. Bass and Riggio, *Transformational Leadership*.

81. Bass, *Leadership and Performance beyond Expectations*.

82. Bass and Riggio, *Transformational Leadership*; Bass and Avolio, *MLQ*.

83. Bass and Riggio, *Transformational Leadership*.

84. Ibid.; Bass and Avolio, *MLQ*.

85. Bass and Riggio, *Transformational Leadership*.

86. Ibid.; Bass and Avolio, *MLQ*.

87. Judge, T. A., and R. F. Piccolo. "Transformational and Transactional Leadership: A Meta-Analytic Test of Their Relative Validity." *Journal of Applied Psychology* 89 (2004), pp. 755–68.

88. Ibid.

89. Bass and Riggio, *Transformational Leadership*.

90. Ibid.

91. Ibid.; Bass and Avolio, *MLQ*.

92. Conger, J. A. "Charismatic and Transformational Leadership in Organizations: An Insider's Perspective on these Developing Research Streams." *Leadership Quarterly* 10 (1999), pp. 145–79.

93. Young, J. S., and W. L. Simon. *iCon: Steve Jobs—The Greatest Second Act in the History of Business.* Hoboken, NJ: Wiley, 2005.

94. Bass and Riggio, *Transformational Leadership*.

95. Conger, "Charismatic and Transformational Leadership in Organizations."

96. Bass and Riggio, *Transformational Leadership*; Bass and Avolio, *MLQ*.

97. Young and Simon, *iCon*.

98. Ibid.

99. Bass and Riggio, *Transformational Leadership*.

100. House, R. J.; P. J. Hanges; M. Javidan; P. W. Dorfman; and V. Gupta. *Culture, Leadership, and Organizations.* Thousand Oaks, CA: Sage, 2004.

101. Dorfman, P. W.; P. J. Hanges; and F. C. Brodbeck. "Leadership and Cultural Variation: The Identification of Culturally Endorsed Leadership Profiles." In *Culture, Leadership, and Organizations*, ed. R. J. House, P. J. Hanges, M. Javidan, P. W. Dorfman, and V. Gupta. Thousand Oaks, CA: Sage, 2004, pp. 669–720.

102. Javidan, M.; R. J. House; and P. W. Dorfman. "A Nontechnical Summary of GLOBE Findings." In *Culture, Leadership, and Organizations*, ed. R. J. House, P. J. Hanges, M. Javidan, P. W. Dorfman, and V. Gupta. Thousand Oaks, CA: Sage, 2004, pp. 29–48.

103. Dorfman et al., "Leadership and Cultural Variation."

104. Bass and Riggio, *Transformational Leadership*; Bass and Avolio, *MLQ*.

105. Bass and Riggio, *Transformational Leadership*.

106. Ibid.; Bass and Avolio, *MLQ*.

107. Young and Simon, *iCon*.

108. Howell, J. M., and B. J. Avolio. "Transformational Leadership, Transactional Leadership, Locus of Control, and Support for Innovation: Key Predictors of Consolidated-Business-Unit Performance." *Journal of Applied Psychology* 78 (1993), pp. 891–902; Howell, J. M.; D. J. Neufeld; and B. J. Avolio. "Examining the Relationship of Leadership and Physical Distance with Business Unit Performance." *Leadership Quarterly* 16 (2005), pp. 273–85; Keller, R. T. "Transformational Leadership, Initiating Structure, and Substitutes for Leadership: A Longitudinal Study of Research and Development Project Team Performance." *Journal of Applied Psychology* 91 (2006), pp. 202–10; Waldman, D. A.; G. G. Ramirez; R. J. House; and P. Puranam. "Does Leadership Matter? CEO Leadership Attributes and Profitability under Conditions of Perceived Environmental Uncertainty." *Academy of Management Journal* 44 (2001), pp. 134–43.

109. Howell, J. M., and K. E. Hall-Merenda. "The Ties That Bind: The Impact of Leader-Member Exchange, Transformational and Transactional Leadership, and Distance on Predicting Follower Performance." *Journal of Applied Psychology* 84 (1999), pp. 680–94; Piccolo, R. F., and J. A. Colquitt. "Transformational Leadership and Job Behaviors: The Mediating Role of Core Job Characteristics." *Academy of Management Journal* 49 (2006), pp. 327–40; Wang, H.; K. S. Law; R. D. Hackett; D. Wang; and Z. X. Chen. "Leader-Member Exchange as a Mediator of the Relationship between Transformational Leadership and Followers' Performance and Organizational Citizenship Behavior." *Academy of Management Journal* 48 (2005), pp. 420–32.

110. Judge and Piccolo, "Transformational and Transactional Leadership"; Podsakoff, P. M.; S. B. MacKenzie; J. B. Paine; and D. G. Bachrach. "Organizational Citizenship Behaviors: A Critical Review of the Theoretical and Empirical Literature and Suggestions for Future Research." *Journal of Management* 26 (2000), pp. 513–63.

111. Judge and Piccolo, "Transformational and Transactional Leadership."

112. Avolio, B. J.; W. Zhu; W. Koh; and P. Bhatia. "Transformational Leadership and Organizational Commitment: Mediating Role of Psychological Empowerment and Moderating Role of Structural Distance." *Journal of Organizational Behavior* 25 (2004), pp. 951–68; Kirkpatrick, S. A., and E. A. Locke. "Direct and Indirect Effects of Three Core Charismatic Leadership Components on Performance and Attitudes." *Journal of Applied Psychology* 81 (1996), pp. 36–51; Shamir, B.; E. Zakay; E. Breinin; and M. Popper. "Correlates of Charismatic Leader Behaviors in Military Units: Subordinates' Attitudes, Unit Characteristics, and Superiors' Appraisals of Leader Performance." *Academy of Management Journal* 41 (1998), pp. 387–409.

113. Podsakoff, P. M.; S. B. MacKenzie; and W. H. Bommer. "Transformational Leader Behaviors and Substitutes for Leadership as Determinants of Employee Satisfaction, Commitment, Trust, and Organizational Citizenship Behaviors." *Journal of Management* 22 (1996), pp. 259–98; Podsakoff, P. M.; S. B. MacKenzie; R. H. Moorman; and R. Fetter. "Transformational Leader Behaviors and Their Effects on Followers' Trust in Leader, Satisfaction, and Organizational Citizenship Behaviors." *Leadership Quarterly* 1 (1990), pp. 107–42; Shamir et al., "Correlates of Charismatic Leader Behaviors."

114. Meyer, J. P.; D. J. Stanley; L. Herscovitch; and L. Topolnytsky. "Affective, Continuance, and Normative Commitment to the Organization: A Meta-Analysis of Antecedents, Correlates, and Consequences." *Journal of Vocational Behavior* 61 (2002), pp. 20–52.

115. Judge and Piccolo, "Transformational and Transactional Leadership."

116. Piccolo and Colquitt, "Transformational Leadership and Job Behaviors." See also Bono, J. E., and T. A. Judge. "Self-Concordance at Work: Toward Understanding the Motivational Effects of Transformational Leaders." *Academy of Management Journal* 46 (2003), pp. 554–71; Shin, S. J., and J. Zhou. "Transformational Leadership, Conservation, and Creativity: Evidence from Korea." *Academy of Management Journal* 46 (2003), pp. 703–14.

117. Bono, J. E., and R. Ilies. "Charisma, Positive Emotions, and Mood Contagion." *Leadership Quarterly* 17 (2006), pp. 317–34; McColl-Kennedy, J. R., and R. D. Anderson. "Impact of Leadership Style and Emotions on Subordinate Performance." *Leadership Quarterly* 13 (2002), pp. 545–59.

118. Kerr, S., and J. M. Jermier. "Substitutes for Leadership: Their Meaning and Measurement." *Organizational Behavior and Human Performance* 22 (1978), pp. 375–403.

119. Howell, J. P.; P. W. Dorfman; and S. Kerr. "Moderator Variables in Leadership Research." *Academy of Management Review* 11 (1986), pp. 88–102.

120. Morris, B. "Dynamic Duo." *Fortune* 156, no. 8 (2007), p. 78.

121. Ibid.

122. Ibid.

11

ORGANIZATIONAL STRUCTURE

● ● learning OBJECTIVES

After reading this chapter, you should be able to answer the following questions:

11.1 Define organizational structure and understand what it consists of.

11.2 Describe the major elements of an organizational structure.

11.3 Understand what organizational design is and what the organizational design process depends on.

11.4 Describe some of the more common organizational forms that an organization might adopt for its structure.

11.5 Describe the steps organizations can take to reduce the negative effects of restructuring.

11.6 Understand how restructuring affects job performance and organizational commitment.

IBM

Willy Chiu, in charge of IBM's worldwide network of elite labs, received an instant message one night informing him that a major competitor was moving in on a $100 million project developing a new IT system for a Korean bank. What happened after that could only happen in today's technologically advanced world—BlackBerry texts, cell phone conversations, and 18 Internet chat windows all operating at the same time, across four continents.[1] Today's organizations are faced with trying to find a way to organize themselves as efficiently as possible using technology that allows them to do things they never could before. When you hear that the world is growing flatter for companies, don't doubt it for a second.

Traditionally, IBM has structured its 200,000-employee organization along geographic lines. In fact, some might argue that IBM was the company that pioneered the first multinational geographic structure by setting up mini-IBMs in countries around the globe. Each country in which IBM operated had its own workforce and management team that reacted to the clients for which it provided services in each country.[2] It was a structure that made perfect sense in a world where consultants needed to be on location with their clients when those customers were having software or computer issues. However, IBM's environmental factors are changing rapidly. Competitors such as those out of India are providing many of the same services for significantly less money.

To change with its competitors and the "flattening world," IBM is reorganizing its workforce by creating and utilizing what it calls "competency centers." These centers group employees from around the world on the basis of the specific skill sets that they have to offer clients. Some workers will be grouped into one location that can service clients all over the world through the use of technology. In Boulder, Colorado, IBM employs 6,200 professionals as part of a call center that monitors clients' computing functions worldwide. If something goes wrong in one of IBM's 426 data centers, employees in Boulder will more than likely be the ones to handle it or send it to someone who can. Other IBM workers will be grouped by broader geographic locations so that they can still be in relatively close proximity to their customers. When these employees are needed by a client, IBM has a computer database that allows it to put together teams of highly specialized consultants by examining the skill sets listed on 70,000 IBM resumes. As the world becomes flatter through technology, clients expect the best talent from around the world, not just the best talent that happens to be sitting in their city. These structural changes will allow IBM to give clients just that. For IBM, these are the necessary changes that come with being a global company. According to IBM Senior Vice President Robert W. Moffat Jr.: "Our customers need us to put the right skills in the right place at the right time."[3]

ORGANIZATIONAL STRUCTURE

As the preceding example illustrates, an organization's structure can have a significant impact on its financial performance and ability to manage its employees. The decisions that IBM makes regarding its organizational structure will have an impact on how employees communicate and cooperate with one another, how power is distributed, and how individuals view their work environment. In fact, an organization's structure dictates more than you might think. We've spent a great deal of time in this book talking about how employee attitudes and behaviors are shaped by individual characteristics such as personality and ability and group mechanisms such as teams and leaders. In this and the following chapter, we discuss how the organization as a whole affects employee attitudes and behavior.

Think about some of the jobs you've held in the past (or perhaps the job you hope to have after graduation). What types of

WHY DO SOME ORGANIZATIONS HAVE DIFFERENT STRUCTURES THAN OTHERS?

One way of getting a feel for an organization's structure is by looking at an organizational chart. An **organizational chart** is a drawing that represents every job in the organization and the formal reporting relationships between those jobs. It helps organizational members and outsiders understand and comprehend how work is structured within the company. Figure 11-1 illustrates two sample organizational charts. In a real chart, the boxes would generally be filled with actual names

> ## "Organizational structures can be relatively simple when a company only has 5–20 employees but grow incredibly complex in the case of IBM's 375,000 employees who provide hundreds of products and services."

employees did you interact with on a daily basis? Were they employees who performed the same tasks that you performed? Or maybe they didn't do exactly what you did, but did they serve the same customer? How many employees did your manager supervise? Was every decision you made scrutinized by your supervisor, or were you given a "long leash"? The answers to all of these questions are influenced by organizational structure. An **organizational structure** formally dictates how jobs and tasks are divided and coordinated between individuals and groups within the company. Organizational structures can be relatively simple when a company only has 5–20 employees but grow incredibly complex in the case of IBM's 375,000 employees who provide hundreds of products and services.

and job titles. As you can imagine, as companies grow larger, their organizational charts get more complex. Can you imagine drawing an organizational chart that included every one of IBM's employees? Not

> Organizational charts are one way of getting a feel for an organization's structure.

only would that require a lot of boxes and a lot of paper, it would probably take a couple of years to put together (plus, as soon as someone left the organization, it would be time to update the chart!).

Elements of Organizational Structure

The organizational charts described in this chapter are relatively simple and designed to illustrate specific points (if you want to see how complex some of these charts can get, do a search on

●●● **11.1**

Define organizational structure and understand what it consists of.

FIGURE 11-1 Two Sample Organizational Structures

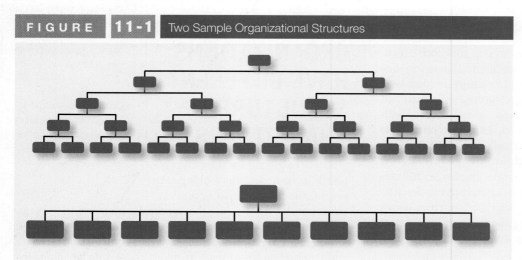

the Internet for "organizational chart," and you'll begin to see how varied organizations can be in the way they design their company). Specifically, charts like those in Figure 11-1 can illustrate the five key elements of an organization's structure. Those five key elements, summarized in Table 11-1, describe how work tasks, authority relationships, and decision-making responsibilities are organized within the company. These elements will be discussed in the next several sections.

●● 11.2

Describe the major elements of an organizational structure.

Work specialization. Work specialization is the way in which tasks in an organization are divided into separate jobs. In some organizations, this categorization is referred to as a company's division of labor. How many tasks does any one employee perform? To some degree, work specialization is a never-ending trade-off among productivity, flexibility, and worker motivation. Take an assembly-line worker at Ford as an example. Henry Ford was perhaps the earliest (and clearly most well-known) believer in high degrees of work specialization. He

divided tasks among his manufacturing employees to such a degree that each employee might only perform one single task, over and over again, all day long. Having only one task to perform allowed those employees to be extremely productive at doing that one thing. It also meant that training new workers was much easier when replacements were needed.

However, there are trade-offs when organizations make jobs highly specialized. Organizations may struggle with employee job satisfaction when they make jobs highly specialized. If you recall Chapter 3 on Job Satisfaction, we discussed five core characteristics of jobs that significantly affect satisfaction. One of those characteristics was variety, or the degree to which the job requires a number of different activities involving a number of different skills and talents.[4] Employees tend to be more satisfied with jobs that require them to perform a number of different kinds of activities. Even though you might be very efficient and productive performing a job with only one task, how happy would you be to perform that job on a daily basis?

Chain of command. The chain of command within an organization essentially answers the question "Who reports to whom?" Every employee in a traditional organizational structure has one person to whom he or she reports. That person then reports to someone else, and on and on, until the buck stops with the CEO (though, in a public company, even the CEO is responsible to the board of directors). The chain of command can be seen as the specific flow of authority down through the levels of an organization's structure. Organizations depend on this flow of authority to attain order, control, and predictable performance.[5] Some newer organizational structures make this chain of command a bit more complex. It has

TABLE 11-1 Elements of Organizational Structure

Organizational Structure Dimension	Definition
Work specialization	The degree to which tasks in an organization are divided into separate jobs.
Chain of command	Answers the question of "who reports to whom?" and signifies formal authority relationships.
Span of control	Represents how many employees each manager in the organization has responsibility for.
Centralization	Refers to where decisions are formally made in organizations.
Formalization	The degree to which rules and procedures are used to standardize behaviors and decisions in an organization.

● **WORK SPECIALIZA-TION** The degree to which tasks in an organization are divided into separate jobs.

● **CHAIN OF COM-MAND** Answers the question "who reports to whom?" and signifies formal authority relationships.

● **SPAN OF CON-TROL** Represents how many employees each manager in the organization has responsibility for.

● **CENTRALIZATION** Refers to where decisions are made in organizations.

● **FORMALIZATION** The degree to which rules and procedures are used to standardize behaviors and decisions in an organization.

become common to have positions that report to two or more different managers.

Span of control.

A manager's span of control represents how many employees he or she is responsible for in the organization. The organizational charts in Figure 11-1 provide an illustration of the differences in span of control. In the top chart, each manager is responsible for leading two subordinates. In most instances, this level would be considered a narrow span of control. In the bottom chart, the manager is responsible for 10 employees. Typically, this number would be considered a wide span of control. Of course, the key question in many organizations is how many employees one manager can supervise effectively. Answering that question requires a better understanding of the benefits of narrow and wide spans of control.

Narrow spans of control allow managers to be much more hands-on with employees, giving them the opportunity to use directive leadership styles while developing close mentoring relationships with employees. A narrow span of control is especially important if the manager has substantially more skill or expertise than the subordinates. Early writings on management assumed that the narrower the span of control, the more productive employees would become.[6] However, a narrow span of control requires organizations to hire many managers, which can significantly increase labor costs. Moreover, if the span of control becomes too narrow, employees can become resentful of their close supervision and long for more latitude in their day-to-day decision making. In fact, current research suggests that a moderate span of control is best for an organization's productivity.[7] This relationship is illustrated in Figure 11-2. Note that organizational performance increases as span of control increases, but only up to the point that managers no longer have the ability to coordinate and supervise the large numbers of employees underneath them. Most organizations work hard to try to find the right balance, and this balance differs for every organization, depending on its unique circumstances. However, there is no question that spans of control in organizations have increased significantly in recent years.[8] Organizations such as Coca-Cola have vice presidents with up to 90 employees reporting to them![9]

Centralization.

Centralization reflects where decisions are formally made in organizations. If only the top managers within a company have the authority to make final decisions, we would say that the organization has a highly

Span of control has increased significantly in recent years. As an example, organizations such as Coca-Cola have vice presidents with up to 90 employees reporting to them!

"centralized" structure. In contrast, if decision-making authority is pushed down to lower-level employees and these employees feel empowered to make decisions on their own, an organization has a "decentralized" structure. Decentralization becomes necessary as a company grows larger. Sooner or later, the top management of an organization cannot make every single decision within the organization. Centralized organizational structures tend to concentrate power and authority within a relatively tight group of individuals in the firm because they are the ones who have formal authority over important decisions. This point is illustrated at a cosmic level in our **OB on Screen** feature. Have the organizations where you have worked been largely centralized or decentralized? See our end-of-chapter **Assessments** feature to find out.

Formalization.

A company is high in formalization when there are many specific rules and procedures used to standardize behaviors and decisions. Although not something you can necessarily see on an organizational chart, the impact of formalization is felt throughout the organization. Rules and procedures are a necessary mechanism for control in every organization. Although the word "formalization" has a somewhat negative connotation, think about your reaction if every McDonald's made its French fries in different ways at each location. Or think about this: Would it bother you if every time you called Dell for

> ● ● **"Employees tend to be more satisfied with jobs that require them to perform a number of different kinds of activities."**

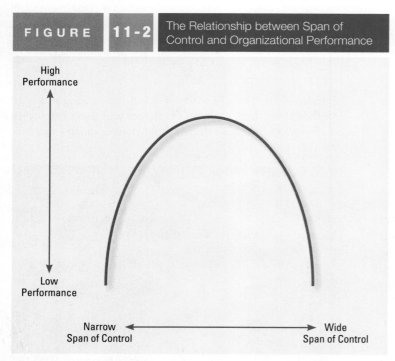

FIGURE 11-2 The Relationship between Span of Control and Organizational Performance

High
Performance

Low
Performance

Narrow ←——————————→ Wide
Span of Control   Span of Control

Source: Adapted from N. A. Theobald and S. Nicholson-Crotty, "The Many Faces of Span of Control: Organizational Structure across Multiple Goals," *Administration and Society* 36 (2005), pp. 648–60.

technical support, you got an operator who treated you differently and gave you conflicting answers? Formalization is a necessary coordination mechanism that organizations rely on to get a standardized product or deliver a standardized service.

Alcoa's Michigan Casting Center, a leading automotive part supplier, was plagued by the fact that it could have two machine operators running the same machine on two different shifts and get up to a 50 percent performance difference in output and quality between the workers. The company conducted a study to identify the best practices for each machine in its plant. These best practices became standard operating procedures for each worker, and that formalization allowed the company to get a more predictable level of output.[10] Companies such as W.L. Gore, the manufacturer of Gore-Tex and hundreds of other products, fall at

Formalization at McDonald's means that French fries and other products are made the same every time in every restaurant. It is an important mechanism that organizations rely on to achieve a standardized product.

the other extreme when it comes to formalization. Whereas most companies have titles for their jobs and job descriptions that specify the tasks each job is responsible for, Bill Gore (company founder) felt that such formalization stifles communication and creativity. After one of his employees mentioned that she needed to put some kind of job title on a business card to hand out at an outside conference, Gore replied that she could put "supreme commander" on the card for all he cared. She liked the title so much that she followed through on his suggestion, and it became a running joke throughout the company.[11]

Elements in combination. You might have noticed that some elements of an organization's structure seem to go hand-in-hand with other elements. For example, wide spans of control tend to be associated with decentralization in decision making. A high level of work specialization tends to bring about a high level of formalization. Moreover, if you take a closer look at the elements, you might notice that many of the elements capture the struggle between efficiency and flexibility. **Mechanistic organizations** are efficient, rigid, predictable, and standardized organizations that thrive in stable environments. Mechanistic organizations are typified by a structure that relies on high levels of formalization, a rigid and hierarchical chain of command, high degrees of work specialization, centralization of decision making, and narrow spans of control. In contrast, **organic organizations** are flexible, adaptive, outward-focused organizations that thrive in dynamic environments. Organic organizations are typified by a structure that relies on low levels of formalization, weak or multiple chains of command, low levels of work specialization, and wide spans of control.

If you think about the differences between the two types, it probably wouldn't be too difficult to come up with a few companies that fall more toward one end of the continuum or the other. However, it is important to remember that few organizations are perfect examples of either of these extremes. Most fall somewhere near the middle, with certain areas within the organization having mechanistic qualities and others being more organic in nature. Although it is tempting to label mechanistic as "bad" and organic as "good," this perception is not necessarily true. Being mechanistic is the only way for many organizations to survive, and it can be a highly appropriate and fruitful way to structure work functions. To find out why that's the case, we need to explore why organizations develop the kinds of structures they do.

● ● ● 11.3

Understand what organizational design is and what the organizational design process depends on.

Organizational Design

Organizational design is the process of creating, selecting, or changing the structure of an organization. Ideally, organizations don't just "let" a structure develop on its own; they proactively design it to match their specific circumstances

organizations may then be forced to change their structure to become more effective. A number of factors influence the process of organizational design. Those factors include the environment in which the organization does business, its strategy and technology, and the size of the firm.

An organization's business environment consists of its customers, competitors, suppliers, distributors, and other factors external to the firm, all of which have an impact on organizational design. One of the biggest factors in an environment's effect on structure is whether the outside environment is stable

> "After one of his employees mentioned that she needed to put some kind of job title on a business card to hand out at an outside conference, Gore replied that she could put "supreme commander" on the card for all he cared."

and needs. However, some organizations aren't that proactive and find themselves with a structure that has unintentionally developed on its own, without any careful planning. Those

or dynamic. Stable environments do not change frequently, and any changes that do occur happen very slowly. Stable environments allow organizations to focus on efficiency and require

OB on Screen

Star Wars II: Attack of the Clones

It is with great reluctance that I have agreed to this calling. I love democracy. . . . I love the Republic. But I am mild by nature, and I do not desire to see the destruction of democracy. The power you give me I will lay down when this crisis has abated, I promise you. And as my first act with this new authority, I will create a grand army of the Republic to counter the increasing threats of the separatists.

With those words, Supreme Chancellor Palpatine (Ian McDiarmid) takes control of the Republic in *Star Wars II: Attack of the Clones* (Dir. George Lucas, 20th Century Fox, 2002). Even in distant worlds, organizations are a way of life. Although the six *Star Wars* movies during the past 30 years have included a lot of space battles, they also have witnessed the formation, transformation, and ruling of a galaxy

through the use of organizational structure.

One of the main plot lines in Episodes I through III of the *Star Wars* saga revolves around Chancellor Palpatine. He is the elected leader of the Galactic Senate, which serves as the governing body for the Galactic Republic (a group of hundreds of planets whose members agreed to form an organization for mutual protection and economic alliance). Unfortunately for Palpatine, his powers as chancellor are extremely limited because all his decisions require a vote from all participating senators.

Unbeknownst to those around him, Chancellor Palpatine is really an evil menace (named Darth Sidious) that secretly controls a group known as the Trade Federation, which he uses to attack and threaten members of the Republic. Episodes II and III of the *Star Wars* saga show Palpatine using this threat to have the Republic grant him centralized decision-making authority. That centralized authority gives him the power and authority needed to create a grand army of the Republic.

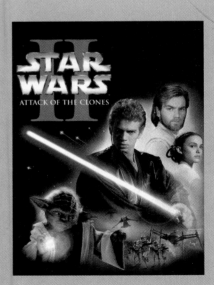

That centralized authority (and army) helps Palpatine rule the galaxy—until one Luke Skywalker comes along . . . . ❖

little change over time. In contrast, dynamic environments change on a frequent basis and require organizations to have structures that are more adaptive.[12] A company strategy describes an organization's objectives and goals and how it tries to capitalize on its assets to make money. Although the myriad of organizational strategies is too cumbersome to discuss here, two common strategies revolve around being either a low-cost producer or a differentiator.[13] Companies that focus on a low-cost producer strategy rely on selling products at the lowest possible cost. To do this well, they have to focus on being as efficient as they can be. Such companies are more likely to take a mechanistic approach to organizational design. Other companies might follow a differentiation strategy. Rather than focusing on supplying a product or service at the lowest cost, these companies believe that people will pay more for a product that is unique in some way. It could be that their product has a higher level of quality or offers features that a low-cost product doesn't. A differentiation strategy often hinges on adjusting to changing environments quickly, which often makes an organic structure more appropriate.

Very early on in the study of organizations, it was assumed that technology was the major determinant of an organization's structure.[14] Since then, the picture has become less clear regarding the appropriate relationship between technology and structure.[15] Although not completely conclusive, research suggests that the more routine a technology is, the more mechanistic a structure should be. In many ways, this suggestion makes perfect sense: If a company makes the exact same thing over and over, it should focus on creating that one thing as efficiently as possible by having high levels of specialization, formalization, and centralization. However, if technologies need to be changed or altered to suit the needs of various

consumers, it follows that decisions would be more decentralized and the rules and procedures the organization relies on would need to be more flexible. There is no question that there is a significant relationship between company size, or total number of employees, and structure.[16] As organizations become larger, they need to rely on some combination of specialization, formalization, and centralization to control their activities and thus become more mechanistic in nature. When it comes to organizational performance, however, there is no definite answer to "how big is too big."[17] As many organizations get bigger, they attempt to create smaller units within the firm to create a "feeling of smallness." W.L. Gore did just that by attempting to prevent any one location in the company from having more than 150 employees. Top management was convinced that a size of 150 would still allow all the employees to talk to one another in the hallways. However, even W.L. Gore hasn't been able to keep that goal as it has grown to encompass 7,300 employees in 45 locations.[18]

W.L. Gore and Associates, Inc., best known for Gore-Tex fabric, has tried to create a "feeling of smallness" in the organization by keeping locations in the company under 150 employees. Since this goal has been unreachable due to company growth, what are some other ways it could promote a "feeling of smallness"?

Common Organizational Forms

Our discussion of organizational design describes how an organization's business environment, strategy, technology, and size conspire to make some organizational structures more effective than others. Now we turn our attention to a logical next question: What structures do most organizations utilize? The sections that follow describe some of the most common organizational forms. As you read their descriptions, think about whether these forms would fall on the mechanistic or organic side of the structure continuum. You might also consider what kinds of design factors would lead an organization to choose that particular form.

11.4

Describe some of the more common organizational forms that an organization might adopt for its structure.

Simple structures. Simple structures are perhaps the most common form of organizational design, primarily because there are more small organizations than large ones. In fact, more than 80 percent of employing organizations have fewer than 19 employees.[19] Small accounting and law firms, family-owned grocery stores, individual-owned retail outlets, independent churches, and landscaping services are all organizations that are likely to use

"More than 80 percent of employing organizations have fewer than 19 employees."

a simple structure. Figure 11-3 shows a simple structure for a manager-owned restaurant. The figure reveals that simple structures are just that: simple. Simple structures are generally used by extremely small organizations in which the manager, president, and owner are all the same person. A simple structure is a flat organization with one person as the central decision-making figure; it is not large enough to have a high degree of formalization and will only have very basic differences in work specialization. For an example of how aspects of a simple structure can exist in a seemingly very large company, see this chapter's **OB in Sports** feature.

● **SIMPLE STRUC-TURES** An organizational form that features one person as the central decision-making figure.

OB in Sports

NASCAR (National Association for Stock Car Auto Racing), a multibillion-dollar industry, is perhaps one of sport's most lucrative operations. In 2007, the organization began a $4.5 billion TV contract with ABC/ESPN, Fox, FX, and TNT.[20] It is the second most-watched spectator sport behind the NFL, claims one-third of all American adults as followers, and has corporate sponsorship revenue of $1.5 billion (light-years ahead of the NFL's $445 million and Major League Baseball's $340 million).[21] How exactly does the company do it? Mainly by being smart and agile and having the ability to make quick decisions. You see, NASCAR is a private, family-controlled, for-profit business with Brian France, a third-generation chairman and CEO, at the helm.

When Brian France took over in 2004, he made some massive changes—namely, moving the company toward creating a package television deal (as opposed to tracks negotiating with networks on their own) and creating the Chase for the Championship "playoff" format that determines each year's winning race team.[22] These changes all came from the top, though France did have advisors below him. The France-owned business has been called over the years a "benevolent dictatorship" because of its relatively simple centralized decision-making structure. There are many that question whether this type of structure is actually what is best for NASCAR and advocate a joint owner–player, profit-sharing format; however, it is tough to question the success of NASCAR over the past

The structure at NASCAR has grown more bureaucratic because of the size of its business. But at its core, it is a private, family-controlled, for-profit business.

decade. The fact is that most family-owned businesses are and remain simple structures, especially when it comes to decision-making authority. In the case of NASCAR, its structure has necessarily grown more bureaucratic because of the size of its business. Don't ever doubt who is really in charge though. ❖

FIGURE **11-3** An Organizational Structure for a Small Restaurant

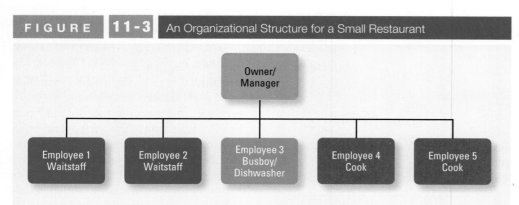

Bureaucratic structures.

When you think of the word "bureaucracy," what thoughts come to mind? Stuffy, boring, restrictive, formal, hard to change, and needlessly complex are some of the terms that have a tendency to be associated with bureaucracies. Those unflattering adjectives aside, chances are very good that you either currently work in a bureaucracy or will after you graduate. A **bureaucratic structure** is an organizational form that exhibits many of the facets of the mechanistic organization. Bureaucracies are designed for efficiency and rely on high levels of work specialization,

● **BUREAUCRATIC STRUCTURE** An organizational form that exhibits many of the facets of a mechanistic organization.

● **FUNCTIONAL STRUCTURE** An organizational form in which employees are grouped by the functions they serve.

formalization, centralization of authority, rigid and well-defined chains of command, and relatively narrow spans of control. As mentioned previously, as an organization's size increases, it is incredibly difficult not to develop some form of bureaucracy. How attractive might bureaucratic structures be to you? See our **OB for Students** feature to find out.

There are numerous types of bureaucratic structures on which we might focus. The most basic of these is the **functional structure**. As shown in Figure 11-4, a functional structure groups employees by the functions they perform for the organization. For example, employees with marketing expertise are grouped together, those with finance duties are grouped together, and so on. The success of the functional structure is based on the efficiency advantages that come with having a high degree of work specialization that is centrally coordinated.[23] Many small companies naturally evolve into functionally based structures as they grow larger.

Functional structures are extremely efficient when the organization as a whole has a relatively narrow focus, fewer product lines or services, and a stable environment. The biggest weaknesses of a functional structure tend to revolve around the fact that individuals within each function get so wrapped up in their own goals and viewpoints that they lose sight of

OB for Students

Whether it's obvious to you or not, structure has a significant effect on you as a student. What organizations are you a part of? Fraternities, sororities, professional associations, student government, and other campus organizations all have structures that influence how decisions are made, where the power lies, and how involved members are in the day-to-day goings on. Indeed, even your university as a whole affects you by the way it is structured.

As you begin to search for jobs, there is some evidence that you will be attracted to certain organizations on the basis of their organizational structure. On the whole, college-level job seekers tend to find centralization in organizations an unattractive company characteristic. It's not hard to picture why. Most job seekers like the idea of being

able to work in an organization in which they will be able to make decisions on their own without someone else's approval.

Does anyone find centralization attractive? Not usually, but there is evidence that some job seekers are less affected by centralization than others. For example, research has shown that job seekers with high self-esteem are less bothered by centralization.[24] That is, the negative effect of centralization on organizational attractiveness is weaker for them. Perhaps they feel confident that they can "fight the bureaucracy" if they need to!

Regardless, when you begin your search for a job, some good questions to ask in an interview might revolve around the

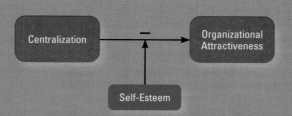

organizational structure of the company. How many people will be working for your immediate supervisor? Will you be working for one direct supervisor or have reporting responsibilities to a number of managers? You are likely to find that questions like these will impress your interviewer. Understanding these aspects of organizational structure also might help you make a decision between multiple job offers. ❖

the bigger organizational picture. In other words, employees don't communicate as well across functions as they do within functions.

Multidivisional structures. In contrast to functional structures, multidivisional structures are bureaucratic organizational forms in which employees are grouped into divisions around products, geographic regions, or clients (see

Figure 11-4). Each of these divisions operates relatively autonomously from the others and has its own functional groups. Multidivisional structures generally develop from companies with functional structures whose interests and goals become too diverse for that structure to handle. For example, if a company with a functional structure begins to add customers that require localized versions of its product, the company might adopt a geographic structure to handle the product variations. Which

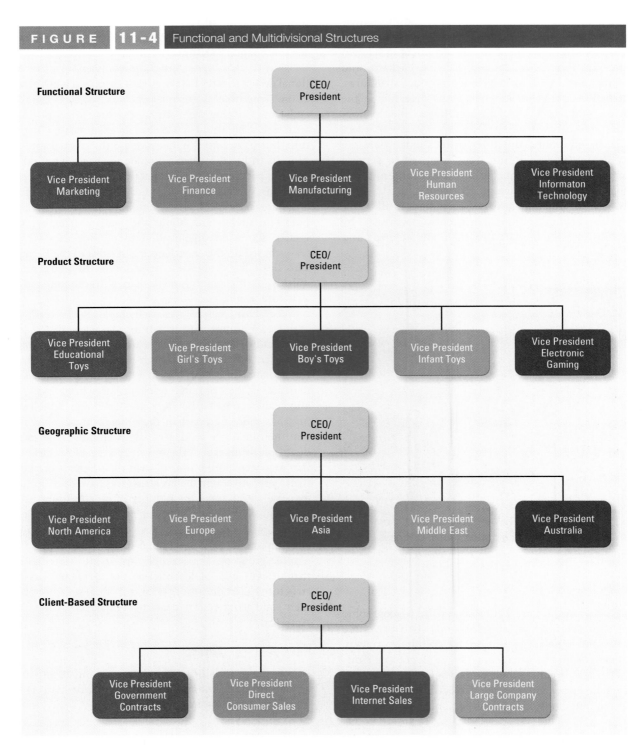

FIGURE 11-4 Functional and Multidivisional Structures

Functional Structure

CEO/President

- Vice President Marketing
- Vice President Finance
- Vice President Manufacturing
- Vice President Human Resources
- Vice President Informaton Technology

Product Structure

CEO/President

- Vice President Educational Toys
- Vice President Girl's Toys
- Vice President Boy's Toys
- Vice President Infant Toys
- Vice President Electronic Gaming

Geographic Structure

CEO/President

- Vice President North America
- Vice President Europe
- Vice President Asia
- Vice President Middle East
- Vice President Australia

Client-Based Structure

CEO/President

- Vice President Government Contracts
- Vice President Direct Consumer Sales
- Vice President Internet Sales
- Vice President Large Company Contracts

● **PRODUCT STRUC-TURES** An organizational form in which employees are grouped around different products that the company produces.

● **GEOGRAPHIC STRUC-TURES** An organizational form in which employees are grouped around the different locations where the company does business.

● **CLIENT STRUCTURE** An organizational form in which employees are organized around the customers they serve.

● **MATRIX STRUC-TURES** A complex form of organizational structure that combines a functional and multidivisional grouping.

● **RESTRUCTURING** The process of changing an organization's structure.

form a company chooses will likely depend on where the diversity in its business lies.

Product structures group business units around different products that the company produces. Each of those divisions becomes responsible for manufacturing, marketing, and doing research and development for the products in its own division. Boeing, Procter & Gamble, Hewlett-Packard, and Sony are companies that have developed product structures. Product structures make sense when firms diversify to the point that the products they sell are so different that managing them becomes overwhelming. Geographic structures are generally based around the different locations where the company does business. The functions required to serve a business are placed under a manager who is in charge of a specific location. Reasons for developing a geographic structure revolve around the different tastes of customers in different regions, the size of the locations that need to be covered by different salespeople, or the fact that the manufacturing and

Small banks traditionally organize themselves into a client structure with divisions such as personal, small business, banking, and lending.

distribution of a product are better served by a geographic breakdown. One last form of multidivisional structure is the client structure. When organizations have a number of very large customers or groups of customers that all act in a similar way, they might organize their businesses around serving those customers. For example, small banks traditionally organize themselves into divisions such as personal banking, small

business banking, personal lending, and commercial lending. Similarly, consulting firms often organize themselves into divisions that are responsible for small business clients, large business clients, and federal clients. For an example of how a merger affected two multinational firms and their structures, see this chapter's **OB Internationally** feature.

Matrix structures are more complex forms of organizational design that try to take advantage of two types of structures at the same time. Companies such as Xerox, General Electric, and Dow Corning were among the first to adopt this type of structure.[25] Figure 11-5 provides an example of a matrix structure. In this example, employees are distributed into teams or projects within the organization on the basis of both their functional expertise and the product that they happen to be working on. Thus, the matrix represents a combination of a functional structure and a product structure. There are two important points to understand about the matrix structure. First, the matrix allows an organization to put together very flexible teams based on the experiences and skills of their employees.[26] This flexibility enables the organization to adjust much more quickly to the environment than a traditional bureaucratic structure would.

Second, the matrix gives each employee two chains of command, two groups with which to interact, and two sources of information to consider. This doubling of traditional structural elements can create high stress levels for employees if the demands of their functional grouping are at odds with the demands of their product- or client-based grouping.[27] The situation can become particularly stressful if one of the two groupings has more power than the other. For example, it may be that the functional manager assigns employees to teams, conducts performance evaluations, and decides raises—making that manager more powerful than the product- or client-based manager.[28] Although matrix structures have been around for an extremely long time, the number of organizations using them is growing as teams become a more common form of organizing work. They also have become more common in global companies, with the functional grouping balanced by a geographic grouping. For example, Areva NP, a French company that designs and builds nuclear power plants, has a matrix structure based on products (plants, fuel, services, and equipment) and geographical locations (France, Germany, and North America).[29]

Restructuring

As you have read through our discussion of organizational structure, you may have noticed how important it is for organizations to adapt to their environment. The first step in

FIGURE 11-5 Matrix Structure

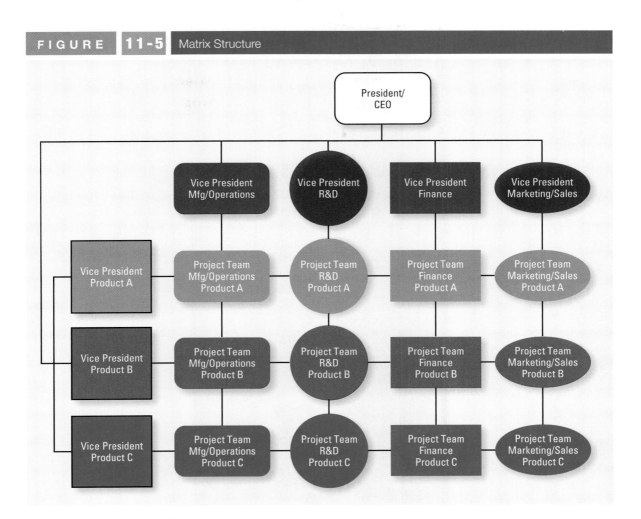

adapting is recognizing the need to change. The second (and sometimes much more problematic) step is actually doing it by restructuring. The process of changing an organization's structure is called restructuring. Organizations attempt to restructure all the time—in fact, it's difficult to pick up a copy of *BusinessWeek* or *Fortune* without reading about some organization's restructuring initiatives. General Motors has undertaken a massive restructuring effort no less than six times over

OB Internationally

As a company, if you want to set up offices in geographically dispersed locations, one of your major concerns has to be where to put them. You might not necessarily think right away about needing a physical location to put employees, but the fact is that they have to sit somewhere! Or perhaps you simply need office space on an irregular basis to meet clients in locations where you don't have a physical presence. The Regus Group is a company that will help you meet those needs. Regus operates over 950 business centers across 400 cities in 70 countries. Products and services include fully furnished, equipped, and staffed offices; world-class business support services; meeting, conference, and training facilities; and the largest network of public videoconference rooms, all serving more than 200,000 clients daily.[30] Rather than establishing a full-time location with facilities, you can call Regus, which will give your company a phone number, mailing address, and someone answering the phone in that location's native language.[31]

While Regus can help organizations with some of their structural needs, it also faces some of their own. Not long ago, the Regus Group (a U.K.-based company) merged with HQ Global Workplaces (a U.S.-based company). When they merged, HQ and Regus had substantially different structures. Given its necessarily geographic-based type of business (i.e., the distances between facilities and the range of their customers), the new Regus group is structured by geographic region.[32] Many global companies are also organized by geographic location. As illustrated in the chapter's opening example, IBM was one of the first to do so—but that might be changing. ❖

the past 20 years![33] Indeed, most of the examples we put into this chapter center on organizations that were restructuring.

● ● 11.5

Describe the steps organizations can take to reduce the negative effects of restructuring.

When employees get a sense that their company might be getting ready to restructure, it causes a great deal of stress because they become worried that they will be one of those to lose their jobs (due to a possible "flattening" of the organization). When Hewlett-Packard recently decided to restructure, it caused widespread fear and panic among employees. For the 60 days prior to the actual restructuring announcement, work came to a standstill at the company—tales of high stress, low motivation, political battles, and power struggles abounded.[34] It is estimated that Hewlett-Packard as a company lost an entire quarter's worth of productivity.[35]

One of the ways in which managers can do their best to help a restructuring succeed is to help manage layoff survivors (employees that remain with the company following a layoff).

Homeowners have to comply with the structure of the house that the builder decided upon, just as employees and managers must comply with the structure of the organization.

Many layoff survivors are known to experience a great deal of guilt and remorse following an organization's decision to remove some employees from the company.[36] Researchers and practitioners recently have been trying to understand layoff survivors better, as well as how to help them adjust more quickly. One

of the major problems for layoff survivors is the increased job demands placed on them. After all, that coworker or boss the employee had was doing *something*. Layoff survivors are generally burdened with having to pick up the leftover tasks that used to be done by somebody else.[37] This burden creates a sense of uncertainty and stress. Recent research suggests that one of the best ways to help layoff survivors adjust is to do things that give them a stronger sense of control.[38] Allowing survivors to have a voice in how to move forward or help set the plans about how to accomplish future goals are two ways managers can help employees feel more in control. In addition, honest and frequent communication with layoff survivors greatly helps reduce their feelings of uncertainty and stress.[39]

HOW IMPORTANT IS STRUCTURE?

To some degree, an organization's structure provides the foundation for almost everything in organizational behavior. Think about some of the things that organizational structure affects: communication patterns between employees, the tasks an employee performs, the types of groups an organization uses, the freedom employees have to innovate and try new things, how power and influence are divided up in the company . . . we could go on and on. Picture the walls of a house. The occupants within those walls can decorate or personalize the structure as best they can. They can make it more attractive according to their individual preferences by adding and taking away furniture, but at the end of the day, they are still stuck with that structure. They have to work within the confines that the builder envisioned (unless they are willing to tear down walls or build new ones at considerable time, effort, and expense!). Organizational structures operate in much the same way for employees and their managers. A given manager can do many things to try to motivate, inspire, and set up an effective work environment so that employees have high levels of performance and commitment; however, at the end of the day, a manager must work within the structure created by the organization.

●● 11.6

Understand how organizational restructuring affects job performance and organizational commitment.

Given how many organizational forms there are, it is almost impossible to give an accurate representation of the impact of organizational structure on job performance. In fact, we might

even say that an organization's structure determines what job performance is supposed to look like! In addition, the elements of structure are not necessarily good or bad for performance. For example, a narrow span of control is not necessarily better than a broad one; rather, the organization must find the optimal "middle ground." One thing we can say, as illustrated in Figure 11-6, is that changes to an organization's structure can have negative effects on the employees who work for the company, at least in the short term. Research suggests that restructuring has a small negative effect on task performance, likely because changes in specialization, centralization, or formalization may lead to confusion about how exactly employees are supposed to do their jobs, which hinders *learning* and *decision making*. Restructuring has a more significant negative effect on organizational commitment, however. Restructuring efforts can increase *stress* and jeopardize employees' *trust* in the organization. There is some evidence that the end result is a lower level of affective commitment on the part of employees because they feel less emotionally attached to the firm. ■

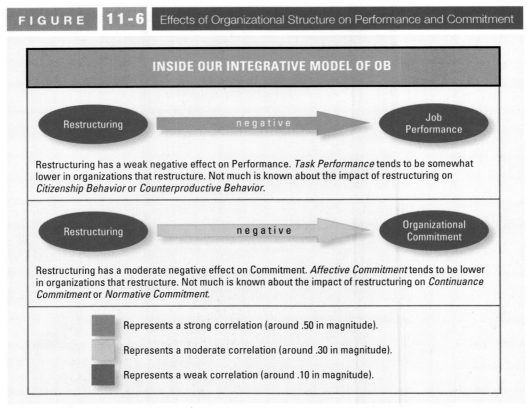

FIGURE 11-6 Effects of Organizational Structure on Performance and Commitment

INSIDE OUR INTEGRATIVE MODEL OF OB

Restructuring → negative → Job Performance

Restructuring has a weak negative effect on Performance. *Task Performance* tends to be somewhat lower in organizations that restructure. Not much is known about the impact of restructuring on *Citizenship Behavior* or *Counterproductive Behavior.*

Restructuring → negative → Organizational Commitment

Restructuring has a moderate negative effect on Commitment. *Affective Commitment* tends to be lower in organizations that restructure. Not much is known about the impact of restructuring on *Continuance Commitment* or *Normative Commitment.*

Represents a strong correlation (around .50 in magnitude).

Represents a moderate correlation (around .30 in magnitude).

Represents a weak correlation (around .10 in magnitude).

Sources: C. Gopinath and T. E. Becker, "Communication, Procedural Justice, and Employee Attitudes: Relationships under Conditions of Divestiture," *Journal of Management* 26 (2000), pp. 63–83; J. Brockner, G. Spreitzer, A. Mishra, W. Hockwarter, L. Pepper, and J. Weinberg, "Perceived Control as an Antidote to the Negative Effects of Layoffs on Survivors' Organizational Commitment and Job Performance," *Administrative Science Quarterly* 49 (2004), pp. 76–100.

Restructuring efforts can increase stress and jeopardize employees' trust in the organization.

CHECK OUT

www.mhhe.com/ColquittEss

for study materials including Interactive Exercises, Quizzes, iPod downloads, and video.

CASE: IBM

Although the massive restructuring effort detailed in the chapter's example is probably the smart move long-term for IBM, it doesn't mean that it comes without costs. As with any restructuring effort, there are those that remain skeptical. IBM's Senior Vice President Robert W. Moffat Jr. found that out the hard way when 10 percent of the 450 managers he invited to a three-day organizing meeting surrounding the globalization effort stood him up.[40] Many managers within IBM are skeptical, having suffered through numerous restructurings, and they didn't really feel that previous changes had produced much change in terms of day-to-day operations.

Those who aren't on board had better get on board quickly though, according to Moffat. In the past three years, IBM has hired 90,000 new employees in low-cost countries, bringing its total organizational size to 375,000 people on six continents.[41] No better example of this globalization effort is an IBM facility in Hortolandia, Brazil. What was once a mainframe manufacturing facility now houses hundreds of Brazilians sitting in rows of cubicles that span more than a football field in length.

These workers provide information about various services such as software programming and financial accounting to over 100 clients across 40 countries.[42] Yet even there the transition was difficult, as Brazilian employees tended to favor local customers. American Robert Payne, who runs part of the tech services organization in Brazil, told them that the rule of thumb was to "think as if you're the president of IBM. What's best for the company long-term?"

11.1 If you had to classify the types of organizational restructuring that IBM is trying to accomplish, what would it be?

11.2 What are the potential drawbacks of moving the organization in this direction? How might IBM combat these difficulties as they arise?

11.3 How is technology allowing IBM to organize itself differently than it has been in the past? Although this technology might allow the organization to become more efficient, what effect do you think it will have on workers and the teams in which they operate?

11.1 An organization's structure formally dictates how jobs and tasks are divided and coordinated between individuals and groups within the organization. This structure, partially illustrated through the use of organizational charts, provides the foundation for organizing jobs, controlling employee behavior, shaping communication channels, and providing a lens through which employees view their work environment.

11.2 There are five major elements to an organization's structure: work specialization, chain of command, span of control, centralization of decision making, and formalization. These elements can be organized in such a way as to make an organization more mechanistic in nature, which allows it to be highly efficient in stable environments, or more organic in nature, which allows it to be flexible and adaptive in changing environments.

11.3 Organizational design is the process of creating, selecting, or changing the structure of an organization. Factors to be considered in organizational design include a company's business environment, its strategy, its technology, and its size.

11.4 There are literally thousands of organizational forms. The most common is the simple structure, which is used by most small companies. Larger companies adopt a more bureaucratic structure. This structure may be functional in nature, such that employees are grouped by job tasks, or multidivisional, such that employees are grouped by product, geography, or client. Organizations also may adopt a matrix structure that combines functional and multidivisional grouping.

11.5 To reduce the negative effects of restructuring, organizations should focus on managing the stress levels of the employees who remain after the restructuring. Providing employees with a sense of control can help them learn to navigate their new work environment.

11.6 Organizational restructuring efforts have a weak negative effect on job performance. They have a more significant negative effect on organizational commitment because employees tend to feel less emotional attachment to organizations that are restructuring.

DISCUSSION QUESTIONS

11.1 Is it possible to be a great leader of employees in a highly mechanistic organization? What special talents or abilities might be required?

11.2 Why do the elements of structure such as work specialization, formalization, span of control, chain of command, and centralization have a tendency to change together? Which of the five do you feel is the most important?

11.3 Which is more important for an organization: the ability to be efficient or the ability to adapt to its environment?

What does this say about how an organization's structure should be set up?

11.4 Which of the organizational forms described in this chapter do you think leads to the highest levels of motivation among workers? Why?

11.5 If you worked in a matrix organization, what would be some of the career development challenges that you might face? Does the idea of working in a matrix structure appeal to you? Why or why not?

ASSESSMENT: Centralization

Have you experienced life inside an organization with a highly centralized structure? This assessment is designed to measure two facets of what would be considered a centralized organizational structure. Those two facets are hierarchy of authority, which reflects the degree to which managers are needed to approve decisions, and participation in decision making, which reflects how involved rank-and-file employees are in day-to-

day deliberations. Think about the last job you held (even if it was a part-time or summer job). Alternatively, think about a student group of yours that seems to have a definite "leader." Then answer each question using the response scale provided. (For more assessments relevant to this chapter, please visit the Online Learning Center at www.mhhe.com/ColquittEss.)

1	2	3	4	5
Strongly Disagree	**Disagree**	**Uncertain**	**Agree**	**Strongly Agree**

1. There can be little action here until a supervisor approves a decision.   _____

2. A person who wants to make his own decisions would be quickly discouraged.   _____

3. Even small matters have to be referred to someone higher up for a final answer.   _____

4. I have to ask my boss before I do almost anything.   _____

5. Any decision I make has to have my boss's approval.   _____

6. I participate frequently in the decision to adopt new programs.   _____

7. I participate frequently in the decision to adopt new policies and rules.   _____

8. I usually participate in the decision to hire or adopt new group members.   _____

9. I often participate in decisions that affect my working environment.   _____

Scoring

Hierarchy of Authority: Sum up items 1–5.

Participation in Decision Making: Sum up items 6–9.

Interpretation

A centralized structure would be one in which Hierarchy of Authority is high and Participation in Decision Making is low. If your score is above 20 for Hierarchy of Authority and below 8 for Participation in Decision Making, your organization (or student group) has a highly centralized structure. Think about the implications that this structure has on your view toward work and your interactions with your coworkers or boss.

Source: Adapted from M. Schminke, R. Cropanzano, and D. E. Rupp, "Organization Structure and Fairness Perceptions: The Moderating Effects of Organizational Level," *Organizational Behavior and Human Decision Processes* 89 (2002), pp. 881–905.

EXERCISE: Creative Cards, Inc.

The purpose of this exercise is to demonstrate the effects of structure on organizational efficiency. Creative Cards, Inc., is a small but growing company, started 10 years ago by Angela Naom, a graphic designer. The company has added many employees over the years but without a master plan. Now Angela wants to reorganize the company. The current structure of Creative Cards, Inc., looks like this:

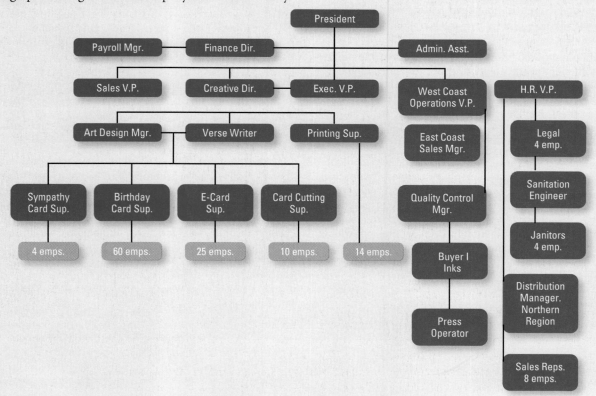

This exercise uses groups, so your instructor will either assign you to a group or ask you to create your own group. The exercise has the following steps:

1. Review the organizational chart and identify at least 10 problems with the design of Creative Cards, Inc. Be sure to consider work specialization, chain of command, span of control, centralization, and formalization in developing your answer.

2. Create a new organizational design that you think would help the company operate more efficiently and effectively.

END NOTES

1. Engardio, P. "A Guide for Multinationals; One of the Great Challenges for a Multinational Is Learning How to Build a Productive Team." *BusinessWeek*, August 20, 2007, pp. 48–51.

2. Hamm, S. "Big Blue Shift." *BusinessWeek*, June 5, 2006, pp. 108–10.

3. Ibid.

4. Hackman, J. R., and G. R. Oldham. *Work Redesign.* Reading, MA: Addison-Wesley, 1980.

5. Simon, H. *Administrative Behavior.* New York: Macmillan, 1947.

6. Meier, K. J., and J. Bohte. "Ode to Luther Gulick: Span of Control and Organizational Performance." *Administration and Society* 32 (2000), pp. 115–37.

7. Theobald, N. A., and S. Nicholson-Crotty. "The Many Faces of Span of Control: Organizational Structure across Multiple Goals." *Administration and Society* 36 (2005), pp. 648–60.

8. Child, J., and M. McGrath. "Organizations Unfettered: Organizational Forms in an Information-Intensive Economy." *Academy of Management Journal* 44 (2001), pp. 1135–48.

9. Hymowitz, C. "Today's Bosses Find Mentoring Isn't Worth the Time and Risks." *The Wall Street Journal*, March 13, 2006, p. B1.

10. Groszkiewicz, D., and B. Warren. "Alcoa's Michigan Casting Center Runs the Business from the Bottom Up." *Journal of Organizational Excellence*, Spring 2006, pp. 13–23.

11. Kiger, P. "Power of the Individual." *Workforce Management*, February 27, 2006, p. 1, 22–27.

12. Scott, W. R., and G. F. Davis. *Organizations and Organizing: Rational, Natural, and Open System Perspectives.* New Jersey: Pearson Prentice Hall, 2007.

13. Porter, M. *Competitive Strategy.* New York: Free Press, 1980.

14. Woodward, J. *Industrial Organization: Theory and Practice.* London: Oxford University Press, 1965.

15. Miller, C. C.; W. H. Glick; Y. Wang; and G. P. Huber. "Understanding Technology–Structure Relationships: Theory Development and Meta-Analytic Theory Testing." *Academy of Management Journal* 34 (1991), pp. 370–99.

16. Gooding, J. Z., and J. A. Wagner III. "A Meta-Analytic Review of the Relationship between Size and Performance: The Productivity and Efficiency of Organizations and Their Subunits."

Administrative Science Quarterly 30 (1985), pp. 462–81; see also Bluedorn, A. C. "Pilgrim's Progress: Trends and Convergence in Research on Organizational Size and Environments." *Journal of Management* 21 (1993), pp. 163–92.

17. Lawler, E. E., III. "Rethinking Organizational Size." *Organizational Dynamics* 26 (1997), pp. 24–35.

18. Kiger, "Power of the Individual."

19. Scott and Davis, *Organizations and Organizing.*

20. Edelstein, R. "Brian France." *Broadcasting & Cable*, October 22, 2007, p. 24.

21. O'Keefe, B., and J. Schlosser. "America's Fastest Growing Sport." *Fortune*, September 5, 2005, pp. 48–59.

22. Ibid.

23. Miles, R. E., and C. C. Snow. *Organizational Strategy, Structure, and Process.* New York: McGraw Hill, 1978.

24. Turban, D. B., and T. L. Keon. "Organizational Attractiveness: An Interactionist Perspective." *Journal of Applied Psychology* 78 (1993), pp. 184–93.

25. Burns, L. R., and D. R. Wholey. "Adoption and Abandonment of Matrix Management Programs: Effects of Organizational Characteristics and Interorganizational Programs." *Academy of Management Journal* 36 (1993), pp. 106–38.

26. Hackman, J. R. "The Design of Work Teams." In *Handbook of Organizational Behavior*, ed. J. W. Lorsch. New Jersey: Prentice Hall, 1987, pp. 315–42.

27. Larson, E. W., and D. H. Gobeli. "Matrix Management: Contradictions and Insight." *California Management Review* 29 (1987), pp. 126–38.

28. Rees, D. W., and C. Porter. "Matrix Structures and the Training Implications." *Industrial and Commercial Training* 36 (2004), pp. 189–93.

29. http://www.areva-np.com (accessed April 26, 2007).

30. http://www.regus.com (accessed June 2, 2008).

31. Bounds, G. "Small Business; Here, There and Everywhere." *The Wall Street Journal*, April 30, 2007, p. R5.

32. Hosford, C. "Behind the Regus–HQ Merger: A Clash of Cultures That Wasn't." *Sales and Marketing Management*, March 2006, pp. 47–48.

33. Taylor, A., III. "GM Gets Its Act Together. Finally." *Fortune*, April 5, 2004, pp. 136–46.

34. Gopinath, C. "Businesses in a Merger Need to Make Sense Together." *Businessline*, June 26, 2006, p. 1.

35. Hamm, J. "The Five Messages Leaders Must Manage." *Harvard Business Review*, May 2006, pp. 114–23.

36. Noer, D. M. *Healing the Wounds.* San Francisco: Jossey-Bass, 1993; Mishra, K.; G. M. Spreitzer; and A. Mishra. "Preserving Employee Morale during Downsizing." *Sloan Management Review* 39 (1998), pp. 83–95.

37. Conlin, M. "The Big Squeeze on Workers; Is There a Risk to Wringing More from a Smaller Staff?" *BusinessWeek*, May 13, 2002, p. 96.

38. Brockner, J.; G. Spreitzer; A. Mishra; W. Hockwarter; L. Pepper; and J. Weinberg. "Perceived Control as an Antidote to the Negative Effects of Layoffs on Survivors' Organizational Commitment and Job Performance." *Administrative Science Quarterly* 49 (2004), pp. 76–100.

39. Brockner, J. "The Effects of Work Layoffs on Survivors: Research, Theory and Practice." In *Research in Organizational Behavior*, Vol. 10, ed. B. M. Staw and L. L. Cummings. Berkeley: University of California Press, 1988, pp. 213–55.

40. Hamm, "Big Blue Shift."

41. Hamm, S., and J. Schneyer. "International Isn't Just IBM's First Name." *BusinessWeek*, January 28, 2008, p. 36.

42. Ibid.

ORGANIZATIONAL CULTURE

● ● learning OBJECTIVES

After reading this chapter, you should be able to:

12.1 Define organizational culture and describe its components.

12.2 Describe general and specific types of organizational cultures.

12.3 Describe a strong culture and what makes a culture strong. Explain why a strong culture is not necessarily good or bad.

12.4 Explain how organizations maintain their culture. Describe how companies change their culture.

12.5 Describe two steps organizations can take to make sure that newcomers will fit with their culture.

12.6 Explain person–organization fit. Describe how fitting with an organization's culture affects job performance and organizational commitment.

EBAY, PAYPAL, AND SKYPE

Can't find the present you want to give because all the stores are sold out? Getting ready to throw an item away, but then wonder to yourself if someone might be willing to pay you money for it? Where do you go? As many of us know, what used to be an impossibility is now a very quick click over to ebay.com, which allows you to reach millions of registered users trying to buy and sell new and used merchandise. Chances are good many of you have actually purchased an item from eBay. If you did, chances are also good you used PayPal to finance the transaction. eBay and PayPal—two company names seemingly intertwined in a symbiotic relationship, such that neither can survive as effectively without the other. During the late 1990s and early 2000s, PayPal became the de facto bank for most transactions between parties on eBay (arguably the largest ongoing garage sale on the planet). They were so intertwined that eBay finally decided in 2002 to purchase PayPal for $1.5 billion after a failed attempt to start its own company to achieve the same objectives (RIP Billpoint...). However, though the technology was a perfect strategic fit, the merger of the two companies did not go well.[1] Many (if not most) of the key employees at PayPal were gone almost immediately (some by choice, some not by choice). Those that didn't leave initially didn't stay long. As it turns out, many of those PayPal employees have gone on to great things, some through investing in and others by founding new successful companies (e.g., Facebook, Slide, Yelp, Digg, YouTube).[2] You would think that eBay would have done whatever it could to keep employees like this around, but the merger between these two companies was almost doomed from the start. Why? The clash between their respective organizational cultures.

PayPal's founders (Peter Theil and Max Levchin) credit much of their success to hiring exceptionally talented and entrepreneurial individuals (mostly math geeks), but one definite prerequisite was that they were NOT MBAs, consultants, frat boys, or jocks.[3] PayPal was the ultimate "flat" organization with an anti-establishment mentality. eBay, in contrast, is a company made up almost primarily of the types of individuals that PayPal wouldn't hire. Then-CEO Meg Whitman, a Harvard Business School grad with training at some of the most prestigious marketing organizations (Disney, Procter & Gamble) and a stint with Bain Consulting, was the epitome of everything that PayPal was not.[4] eBay might look like a traditional dot-com company to those on the outside, but inside, the company is as corporate as it gets, with a focus solely on profit margins and business metrics.[5] The two companies, though they looked similar from a business standpoint, could not have been more opposite in terms of the cultures they had created and the employees they hired.

Organizational culture must remain a core consideration in eBay's future, as eBay recently bought the Internet phone company Skype for $2.5 billion. Former CEO Meg Whitman said at the time, "Now the key decision will be how to let the Skype people feel that they are still running an entrepreneurial entity within our $4.5B company. There's such art to orchestrating that. We learned from buying PayPal that you don't want to overwhelm a young division with corporate prophecies and structures."[6]

ORGANIZATIONAL CULTURE

In almost every chapter up to this point, we have simply given you definitions of important topics. However, in this case, it is important for you to understand that there are just about as many definitions of organizational culture as there are people who study it. In fact, research on organizational culture has produced well over 50 different definitions![7] It seems that the term "culture" means a great many things to a great many people. Definitions of culture have ranged from as broad as, "The way we do things around here"[8] to as specific as . . . well, let's just suffice it to say that they can get complicated. Not surprisingly, the various definitions of organizational culture stem from how people have studied it. Sociologists study culture using a broad lens and anthropological research methods, like those applied to study tribes and civilizations. Psychologists tend to study culture and its effects on people using survey methods. In fact, many psychologists actually prefer the term "climate," but for our purposes, we'll use the two terms interchangeably. In this chapter, we define organizational culture as the shared social knowledge within an organization regarding the rules, norms, and values that shape the attitudes and behaviors of its employees.[9]

This definition helps highlight a number of facets of organizational culture. First, culture is social knowledge among members of the organization. Employees learn about most important aspects of culture through other employees. This transfer of knowledge might be through explicit communication, simple observation, or other, less obvious methods. In addition, culture is shared knowledge, which means that members of the organization understand and have a degree of consensus regarding what the culture is. Second, culture tells employees what the rules, norms, and values are within the organization. What are the most important work outcomes to focus on? What behaviors are appropriate or inappropriate at work? How should a person act or dress while at work? Indeed, some cultures even go so far as to say how employees should act when they aren't at work. Third, organizational culture shapes and reinforces certain employee attitudes and behaviors by creating a system of control over employees.[10] There is evidence that your individual goals and values will grow over time to match those of the organization for which you work.[11] This development really isn't that hard to imagine, given how much time employees spend working inside an organization.

 12.1

Define organizational culture and describe its components.

> "The term 'culture' means a great many things to a great many people."

WHY DO SOME ORGANIZATIONS HAVE DIFFERENT CULTURES THAN OTHERS?

One of the most common questions people ask when you tell them where you are employed is, "So, tell me . . . what's it like there?" The description you use in your response is likely to have a lot to do with what the organization's culture is all about. In calculating your response to the question, you might consider describing the kinds of people who work at your company. More than likely, you will do your best to describe the work atmosphere on a regular day. Perhaps you will painstakingly describe the facilities you work in or how you feel the employees are treated. You might even go as far as to describe what it is that defines "success" at your company. All of those answers give clues that help organizational outsiders understand what a company is actually like. To give you a feel for the full range of potential answers to the "what's it like there?" question, it's necessary to review the facets of culture in more detail.

> ● **ORGANIZATIONAL CULTURE** The shared social knowledge within an organization regarding the rules, norms, and values that shape the attitudes and behaviors of its employees.

Culture Components

There are three major components to any organization's culture: observable artifacts, espoused values, and basic underlying assumptions. You can understand the differences among these three components if you view culture like an onion, as in Figure 12-1. Some components of an organization's culture are readily apparent and observable, like the skin of an onion. However, other components are less observable to organizational outsiders or newcomers. Such outsiders can observe, interpret, and make conclusions based on what they see on the surface, but the inside remains a mystery until they can peel back the outside layers to gauge the values and assumptions that lie beneath. The sections that follow review the culture components in more detail.

Observable Artifacts. Observable artifacts are the manifestations of an organization's culture that employees can easily see or talk about. They supply the signals that employees interpret to gauge how they should act

- **OBSERVABLE ARTIFACTS** Aspects of an organization's culture that employees and outsiders can easily talk about.

- **SYMBOLS** The images an organization uses, which generally convey messages.

- **PHYSICAL STRUCTURES** The organization's buildings and internal office designs.

- **LANGUAGE** The jargon, slang, and slogans used within an organization.

- **STORIES** Anecdotes, accounts, legends, and myths passed down from cohort to cohort within an organization.

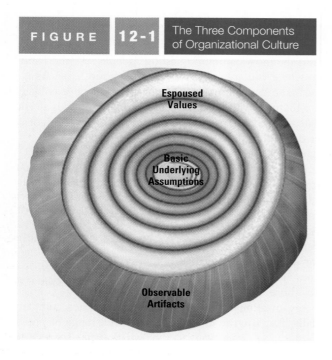

FIGURE 12-1 The Three Components of Organizational Culture

during the workday. Artifacts supply the primary means of transmitting an organization's culture to its workforce. It is difficult to overestimate the importance of artifacts because they help show not only current employees but also potential employees, customers, shareholders, and investors what the organization is all about. There are six major types of artifacts:

The Apple Computer logo conveys the importance of innovation within their culture, conjuring images of Isaac Newton's discovery of gravity under the apple tree.

symbols, physical structures, language, stories, rituals, and ceremonies.[12]

Symbols can be found throughout an organization, from its corporate logo to the images it places on its Web site to the uniforms its employees wear. Think about what Nike's "swoosh" represents: speed, movement, velocity. What might that symbol convey about Nike's culture? Or consider Apple Computer's "apple" logo. That symbol brings to mind Newton's discovery of gravity under the apple tree, conveying the importance of innovation within Apple's culture. **Physical structures** also say a lot about a culture. Is the workplace open? Does top management work in a separate section of the building? Is the setting devoid of anything unique, or can employees express their personalities? Bloomberg, an information services, news, and media company based in New York, built its new headquarters in Manhattan primarily out of steel and glass, resembling what workers call a "beehive." It has no private offices and no cubicles, and even the conference rooms have glass walls. CEO Lex Fenwick sits on the third floor, surrounded by his sales and customer service staff. He believes this setup leads to instantaneous communication among employees.[13] IDEO, a creative think tank, also has an open office environment, though IDEO lets employees set up their offices however they like. When you walk around their work areas, you'll be walking underneath bicycles hanging over your head and crazy objects and toys in every direction.[14]

Language reflects the jargon, slang, and slogans used within the walls of an organization. Do you know what a CTR, CPC, or Crawler is? Chances are you don't. If you worked for Yahoo!, however, those terms would be second nature to you: CTR stands for click-through rate, CPC stands for cost-per-click, and a Crawler is a computer program that gathers information from other Web sites. Yum Brands Inc., which owns Pizza Hut, Taco Bell, KFC, and other fast-food restaurants, expects employees to be "customer maniacs"[15]—language that conveys its culture for customer interaction. **Stories** consist of anecdotes, accounts, legends, and myths that are passed down from cohort to cohort within an organization. When the London-based, global conglomerate Unilever purchased Ben & Jerry's Homemade Inc. in 2001, the Unilever chairman first walked into the Vermont-based company to a sight he didn't often see: All the employees were wearing togas![16] This story captures some of the cultural differences between Unilever and Ben & Jerry's and will likely be told over and over again within the organization.

Rituals are the daily or weekly planned routines that occur in an organization. Employees at New Belgium Brewing in Colorado, home of Fat Tire Ale, receive a case of beer a week after a year on the job, conveying the importance of both employees and the company's product.[17] At UPS, every driver and package handler attends a mandatory "three-minute meeting" with their managers to help with communication. The 180-second time limit helps enforce the importance of punctuality in the UPS culture. The Men's Wearhouse pays managers quarterly bonuses when theft (referred to as "shrink") is kept low. That ritual sends a message that "when workers steal from you, they are stealing from themselves and their colleagues."[18] **Ceremonies** are formal events, generally performed in front of an audience of organizational members. In the process of turning around the company, Continental Airlines held a ceremony to burn an employee-despised 800-page policy manual. Gordon Bethune, then-CEO of Continental, put together a task force that came up with a new 80-page manual.[19]

Espoused Values.

Espoused values are the beliefs, philosophies, and norms that an organization explicitly states. Espoused values can range from published documents such as a company's vision or mission statement to verbal statements made to employees by executives and managers. Examples of some of UPS's outward representations of espoused values can be found in Table 12-1. What do each of these statements tell you about UPS and what it cares about?

It is certainly important to draw a distinction between espoused values and enacted values. It is one thing for a company to outwardly say something is important; it is another thing for employees to consistently act in ways that support those espoused values. When a company holds to its espoused values over time and regardless of the situations it operates in, the values become more believable to both employees and outsiders. However, in times of economic downturns, staying true

The ability to set up your own work space, as at the think tank IDEO, is a hallmark of an open corporate culture. Would this environment suit your working style?

to espoused values is not always easy. One group that seemingly enacts their espoused values even in the face of adversity can be found in this chapter's **OB in Sports** feature.

Basic Underlying Assumptions.

Basic underlying assumptions are taken-for-granted beliefs and philosophies that are so ingrained that employees simply act on them rather than questioning the validity of their behavior in a given situation.[20] These assumptions represent the deepest and least observable part of a culture and may not be consciously apparent, even to organizational veterans. Edgar Schein, one of the preeminent scholars on the topic of organizational culture, uses the example of safety in an engineering firm. He states, "In an occupation such as engineering, it would be inconceivable to deliberately design something that is unsafe; it is a taken-for-granted assumption that things should be safe."[21] Whatever a company's underlying assumptions are, its hidden beliefs are those that are the most likely to dictate employee behavior and affect employee attitudes. They are also the aspects of an

| TABLE | 12-1 | The Espoused Values of UPS |

Below is a sample of some of the 37 values that spell out UPS's vision for managing its workforce. These values are spelled out in a "policy book" that is handed out to the company's management team.

1. We build our organization around people.
2. We place great value on diversity.
3. We treat our people fairly and without favoritism.
4. We insist upon integrity in our people.
5. We promote from within.
6. We promote an open-door approach to managing people.
7. We keep our buildings and equipment clean.
8. We expect our people to be neat in appearance.

Source: "UPS's 37 Principles for Managing People," *Workforce Management Online*, May 2005, http://www.workforce.com (accessed February 24, 2007). Reprinted with permission. Copyright © 2005 Crain Communications Inc.

● **RITUALS** The daily or weekly planned routines that occur in an organization.

● **CEREMONIES** Formal events, generally performed in front of an audience of organizational members.

● **ESPOUSED VALUES** The beliefs, philosophies, and norms that a company explicitly states.

● **BASIC UNDERLYING ASSUMPTIONS** The ingrained beliefs and philosophies of employees.

organizational culture that are the most long-lasting and difficult to change.[22]

General Culture Types

If we can consider the combination of an organization's observable artifacts, espoused values, and underlying assumptions, we can begin to classify its culture along various dimensions. Of course, there are many different types of organizational cultures, just like there are many different types of personalities. Many researchers have tried to create general typologies that can be used to describe the culture of any organization. For instance, one popular general typology divides organizational culture along two dimensions: solidarity and sociability. Solidarity is the degree to which group members think and act alike, and sociability represents how friendly employees are to one another.[23] Figure 12-2 shows how we might describe organizations that are either high or low on these dimensions. Organizations that are low on both dimensions have a fragmented culture in which employees are distant and disconnected from one another. Organizations that have cultures in which employees think alike but aren't friendly to one another can be considered mercenary cultures. These types of organizations are likely to be very political, "what's in it for me" environments. Cultures in which all employees are friendly to one another, but everyone thinks differently and does his or her own thing, are communal cultures. Many highly creative organizations have a communal culture. Organizations with friendly employees who all think alike are networked cultures.

 12.2

Describe general and specific types of organizational cultures.

UPS has a "policy book" that contains a number of its espoused values, including values supporting clean equipment and employees who are neat in appearance.

Specific Culture Types

The typology shown in Figure 12-2 is general enough to be applied to almost any organization. However, there are obviously other ways to classify an organization's culture. In fact, many organizations attempt to manipulate observable artifacts and espoused values to create specific cultures that help them achieve their organizational goals. Some of these specific cultures are more relevant in some industries than in others. Although the number of specific cultures an organization might strive for are virtually endless, we focus on three examples: customer service cultures, diversity cultures, and creativity cultures.

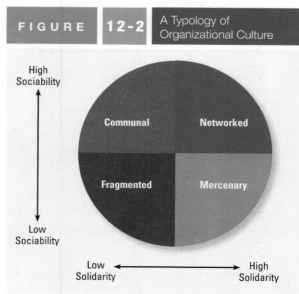

FIGURE 12-2 A Typology of Organizational Culture

Source: Adapted from R. Goffee and G. Jones, *The Character of a Corporation* (New York: Harper Business, 1998).

Many organizations try to create a **customer service culture** focused on service quality. After all, 65 percent of the gross domestic product in the United States is generated by service-based organizations.[24] Organizations that have successfully created a service culture have been shown to change employee attitudes and behaviors toward customers.[25] These changes in attitudes and behaviors then manifest themselves in higher levels of customer satisfaction and sales.[26] Figure 12-3 illustrates the process of creating a service culture and the effects it has on company results. Numerous companies claim that the sole reason for their continued existence is their ability to create a service culture in their organization when it wasn't originally present.[27] Other companies, such as Circuit City, have tried to reinvigorate customer service by recreating a service culture within their stores. After falling way behind rival Best Buy, the retailer has been inching its way back to respectability by making changes such as shifting its mostly commission-based workforce to an hourly pay rate.

There are a number of reasons why an organization might want to foster a **diversity culture**. What images come to mind when you think of Denny's? Do you think of the nation's largest family-style, full-service restaurant chain in the country and the Grand Slam breakfast, or do you think of race discrimination? Although the lawsuits that charged company discrimination against African Americans were settled back in 1994, the stigma of Denny's discrimination complaints still lingers. Since 1994, Denny's has maintained a position within the company of chief diversity officer whose sole responsibility is to help create a culture of diversity. Denny's has since become a prime example of how to aggressively lead a charge toward a diversity culture. Denny's has tried to transform itself by hiring a large number of new minority managers and franchise owners, replacing half of the all-male board of directors with women, conducting diversity sensitivity training sessions, and performing other symbolic actions. Many of the techniques used by Denny's are now recognized as key elements in successful corporate diversity initiatives.[28]

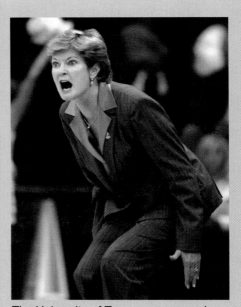

● **CUSTOMER SERVICE CULTURE** A specific culture type focused on customer service quality.

● **DIVERSITY CULTURE** A specific culture type focused on fostering or taking advantage of a diverse group of employees.

OB in Sports

There is perhaps no sports group known more for success than the University of Tennessee Lady Volunteers basketball team. One of the first things that comes to mind when thinking of the Lady Vol basketball program is the unmistakable scowl and menacing looks of its head coach. Tennessee Coach Pat Summit and the Lady Vols have eight national championships (after beating Stanford in the finals this past year) and have been to the NCAA Women's Final Four a record 18 times.[29] Even though there is a constant rotation of players over numerous years, somehow the Lady Volunteers still manage to put out the best teams in the country. Part of it is the culture that Coach Summit has created that permeates the program regardless of who comes in. When Coach Summit gives speaking engagements or writes books, she constantly credits her "Definite Dozen" as part of the reason for the program's success.[30] The Definite Dozen, listed in this box, is a list of the program's espoused values. If a player doesn't live by these values, she is asked to leave the program. If Coach Summit doesn't believe a player can follow the values, she is never offered a scholarship. Taking a look at these espoused values helps show the kind of culture that Coach Summit believes in, one of the reasons for the program's continued success.

1. Respect yourself and others.
2. Take full responsibility.
3. Develop and demonstrate loyalty.
4. Learn to be a great communicator.
5. Discipline yourself so no one else has to.
6. Make hard work your passion.
7. Don't just work hard; work smart.
8. Put the team before yourself.
9. Make winning an attitude.
10. Be a competitor.
11. Change is a must.
12. Handle success like you handle failure. ❖

The University of Tennessee women's basketball coach Pat Summit has led the team to a record number of NCAA Women's Final Four championships and credits her list of a dozen espoused values, the "Definite Dozen," that she expects her players to embrace as part of the reason behind their success.

Denny's has worked hard to recover from lawsuits charging that it discriminated against minorities. In the process, it developed techniques to encourage diversity that other firms have now adopted.

vation at the organization.[32] In part to foster a culture of creativity, Pfizer Canada has banned all e-mails and voice mails on weekends and after 6:00 p.m. on weekdays to keep their employees fresh while they are on the job. The company feels this 12-hour break has led to a higher-quality flow of ideas and provided a morale boost to go along with it.[33] To see whether you've spent time working in a creativity culture, see the **Assessment** feature at the end of the chapter.

Culture Strength

Although most organizations seem to strive for one, not all companies have a culture that creates a sense of definite norms and appropriate behaviors for their employees. If you've worked for a company and can't identify whether it has a strong culture or not, it probably doesn't. A high level of culture strength exists when employees definitively agree about the way things are supposed to happen within the organization (high consensus) and when their subsequent behaviors are consistent with those expectations (high intensity).[34] As shown in Figure 12-4, a strong culture serves to unite and direct employees. Weak cultures exist when employees

> ## "Numerous companies claim that the sole reason for their continued existence is their ability to create a service culture in their organization when it wasn't originally present."

● **CREATIVITY CULTURE** A specific culture type focused on fostering a creative atmosphere.

● **CULTURE STRENGTH** The degree to which employees agree about how things should happen within the organization and behave accordingly.

Given the importance of new ideas and innovation in many industries, it is understandable that some organizations focus on fostering a creativity culture. Creativity cultures have been shown to affect both the quantity and quality of creative ideas within an organization.[31] Google recently put policies in place that will allow its engineers to spend 20 percent of their working time pursuing projects that they feel passionate about to foster inno-

disagree about the way things are supposed to be or what is expected of them, meaning that there is nothing to unite or direct their attitudes and actions.

● ● **12.3**

Describe a strong culture, and what makes a culture strong. Explain why a strong culture is not necessarily good or bad.

Strong cultures take a long time to develop and are very difficult to change. Individuals working within strong cultures are typically very aware of it. However, this discussion brings us to an important point: "Strong" cultures are not always "good"

| FIGURE | 12-3 | The Service Culture Process |

Service-Oriented Leadership Behavior → Service Culture → Service-Oriented Employee Behaviors → Customer Satisfaction → Unit Sales

Source: Adapted from B. Schneider, M. G. Ehrhart, D. M. Mayer, J. L. Saltz, and K. Niles-Jolly, "Understanding Organization–Customer Links in Service Settings," *Academy of Management Journal* 48 (2005), pp. 1017–32.

cultures. Strong cultures guide employee attitudes and behaviors, but that doesn't always mean that they guide them toward the most successful organizational outcomes. As such, it is useful to recognize some of the positive and negative aspects of having a strong organizational culture. Table 12-2 lists some of the advantages and disadvantages.[35] You might have noticed that all of the advantages in the left-hand column of Table 12-2 allow the organization to become more efficient at whatever aspect of culture is strong within the organization. The right-hand column's disadvantages all lead toward an organization's inability to adapt.

In some cases, the culture of an organization is not really strong or weak. Instead, there might be **subcultures** that unite a smaller subset of the organization's employees. These subgroups may be created because there is a strong leader in one area of the company that engenders different norms and values or because different divisions in a company act independently and create their own cultures. As shown in Figure 12-4, subcultures exist when the overall organizational culture is supplemented by another culture governing a more specific set of employees. Subcultures are more likely to exist in large organizations than they are in small companies.[36] Most organizations don't mind having subcultures, to the degree that they do not interfere with the values of the overall culture. In fact, subcultures can be very useful for organizations if there are certain areas of the organization that have different demands and needs for their employees.[37] However, when their values don't match those of the larger organization, we call subcultures **countercultures**. Countercultures can sometimes serve a useful purpose by challenging the values of the overall organization or signifying the need for change.[38] In extreme cases, however, countercultures can split the organization's culture right down the middle, resulting in the differentiated culture in Figure 12-4.

 12.4

Explain how organizations maintain their culture. Describe how companies change their culture.

FIGURE **12-4** Culture Strength and Subcultures

Strong Culture

Weak Culture

Organizational Subcultures

Differentiated Culture

Maintaining an Organizational Culture

Clearly an organization's culture can be described in many ways, from espoused values and underlying assumptions, to general dimensions such as solidarity or sociability, to more specific types such as service cultures or creativity cultures. No matter how we describe an organization's culture, however, that culture will be put to the test when an organization's founders and original employees begin to recruit and hire

● **SUBCULTURES** A culture created within a small subset of the organization's employees.

● **COUNTERCULTURES** When a subculture's values do not match those of the organization.

TABLE **12-2** Pros and Cons of a Strong Culture	
Advantages of a Strong Culture	**Disadvantages of a Strong Culture**
Differentiates the organization from others	Makes merging with another organization more difficult
Allows employees to identify themselves with the organization	Attracts and retains similar kinds of employees, thereby limiting diversity of thought
Facilitates desired behaviors among employees	Can be "too much of a good thing" if it creates extreme behaviors among employees
Creates stability within the organization	Makes adapting to the environment more difficult

new members. If those new members do not fit the culture, then the culture may become weakened or differentiated. However, two processes can conspire to help keep cultures strong: attraction–selection–attrition and socialization.

Attraction–Selection–Attrition (ASA).

The **ASA framework** holds that potential employees will be attracted to organizations whose cultures match their own personality, meaning that some potential job applicants won't apply due to a perceived lack of fit.[39] In addition, organizations will select candidates based on whether their personalities fit the culture, further weeding out potential "misfits." Finally, those people who still don't fit will either be unhappy or ineffective when working in the organization, which leads to attrition (i.e., voluntary or involuntary turnover).

Several companies can provide an example of ASA in action. FedEx has worked hard to create a culture of ethics. The executives at FedEx believe that a strong ethical culture will attract ethical employees who will strengthen moral behavior at FedEx.[40] The Cheesecake Factory believes that selection is where maintaining a culture begins. Management suggests that its heavily service-oriented culture calls for certain types of employees. They believe that teaching people how to perform regular restaurant duties is possible, but teaching people to have the right personality and attitudes is not. As a company, it consistently tries to identify the traits that allow employees to thrive in a Cheesecake Factory environment.[41] Of course, attraction and selection processes do not always align employees' personalities with organizational culture—one reason voluntary and involuntary turnover occur in every organization.

Socialization.

In addition to taking advantage of attraction–

The Cheesecake Factory isn't simply looking for waiters and host staff who can perform regular restaurant duties; it is also looking for the right personalities and attitudes that will allow staff members to thrive within the culture at the restaurant.

● **ASA FRAMEWORK** A theory (attraction–selection–attrition) that states that employees will be drawn to organizations with cultures that match their personality, organizations will select employees that match, and employees will leave or be forced out when they are not a good fit.

● **SOCIALIZATION** The primary process by which employees learn the social knowledge that enables them to understand and adapt to the organization's culture.

selection–attrition, organizations also maintain an organizational culture by shaping and molding new employees. Starting a new job with a company is a stressful, complex, and challenging undertaking for both employees and organizations.[42] In reality, no outsider can fully grasp or understand the culture of an organization simply by looking at artifacts visible from outside the company. A complete understanding of organizational culture is a process that happens over time. **Socialization** is the primary process by which employees learn the social knowledge that enables them to understand and adapt to the organization's culture. It is a process that begins before an employee starts work and doesn't end until an employee leaves the organization.[43] What is it that an employee needs to learn and adapt to in order to be socialized into his or her new role within an organization? Most of the important information can be grouped into six dimensions, highlighted in Figure 12-5.[44] Research shows that each of these six dimensions is an important area in the process of socialization. Each has unique contributions to job performance, organizational commitment, and person–organization fit.[45]

 12.5

Describe two steps organizations can take to make sure that newcomers will fit with their culture.

One of the most inexpensive and effective ways of socializing employees and thus reducing early turnover is the use of **realistic job previews**.[46] Realistic job previews (RJPs) occur before an employee even starts working for the company! These RJPs involve making sure a potential employee has an accurate picture of what working for an organization is going to be like by providing both the positive *and* the negative aspects of the job.[47] Kal Tire, a leading Canadian automotive retail outlet, allows job candidates to spend an entire day inside the company becoming familiar with the organization and the job they are applying for. By allowing applicants to see what the organization's idea of customer service is and the job demands of road tire repairs, Kal Tire is effectively reducing the likelihood of employees being surprised by what they find when they start work and shortening the time it takes for employees to socialize.[48]

Another way organizations try to speed up the socialization process is through mentoring. **Mentoring** is a process by which a junior-level employee (protégé) develops a deep and long-lasting relationship with a more senior-level employee (mentor) within the organization. The mentor can provide social knowledge, resources, and psychological support to the protégé both at the beginning of employment and as the protégé continues his or her career with the company. Mentoring has always existed in companies on an informal basis. However, as organizations continue to learn about the strong benefits of these relationships, they are more frequently instituting mentoring programs that formally match newcomers with mentors.[49] This process has worked well for Budco, a marketing services and distribution firm that works with GM and Disney, which pairs four protégés with two mentors and has them meet twice a month. Group mentoring at the 850-employee company has significantly reduced turnover among new hires.[50] Mentoring does not just occur in business organizations, however. See our **OB for Students** feature for a discussion of mentoring for university students.

Changing an Organizational Culture

Given all the effort it takes to create and maintain a culture, changing a culture once one has been established is perhaps even more difficult. In fact, estimates put the rate of successful major culture change at less than 20 percent.[51] Mark Fields, head of Ford Motor Company's North and South American auto operations, knows how difficult it can be to change the culture at an organization. Prior CEOs at Ford have tried, unsuccessfully, to change a culture that current employees call "toxic," "cautious," "hierarchical," and "cliquish." To instigate a change, Fields took drastic measures, including purposefully creating a sense of stress and crisis among employees. Ford is calling its new attempt at major culture change the "Way Forward." In the "Way Forward" war room (where Fields and colleagues map out the drastic changes the company needs to make), big sheets of white paper hang on the wall reading, "Culture eats strategy for breakfast," and "Culture is unspoken, but powerful. It develops over time—difficult to change." Fields has gone to many extremes to create a climate for change among those responsible for helping him with the plans to overhaul Ford's culture. He has banned PowerPoint presentations, uses phrases such as "change or die" in meetings, and makes employees wear blue wristbands with "Red, White and Bold" inscribed on them, signifying a new Ford.[52] In practice, there are two primary ways to change a culture: changes in leadership and mergers or acquisitions.

Changes in Leadership.
There is perhaps no bigger driver of culture than the leaders and top executives of organizations. Just as the founders and originators of organizations set the tone and develop the culture

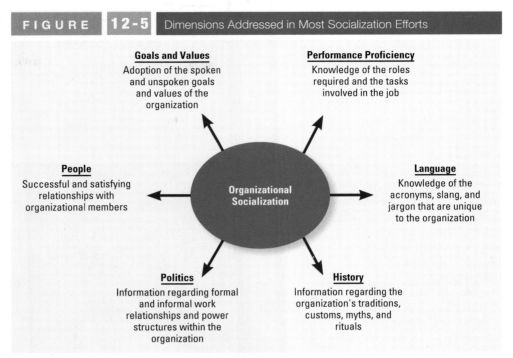

FIGURE **12-5** Dimensions Addressed in Most Socialization Efforts

Goals and Values
Adoption of the spoken and unspoken goals and values of the organization

Performance Proficiency
Knowledge of the roles required and the tasks involved in the job

People
Successful and satisfying relationships with organizational members

Organizational Socialization

Language
Knowledge of the acronyms, slang, and jargon that are unique to the organization

Politics
Information regarding formal and informal work relationships and power structures within the organization

History
Information regarding the organization's traditions, customs, myths, and rituals

Source: G. T. Chao, A. M. O'Leary-Kelly, S. Wolf, H. J. Klein, and P. D. Gardner, "Organizational Socialization: Its Content and Consequences," *Journal of Applied Psychology* 79 (1994), pp. 730–43. Copyright © 1994 by the American Psychological Association. Adapted with permission. No further reproduction or distribution is permitted without written permission from the American Psychological Association.

⦿ ⦿ **"Socialization isaprocessthatbegins before an employee starts work and doesn't end until an employee leaves the organization."**

of a new company, subsequent CEOs and presidents leave their mark on the culture. Many times, leaders are expected simply to sustain the culture that has already been created.[53] At other times, leaders have to be the driving force for change as the environment around the organization shifts. This expectation is one of the biggest reasons organizations change their top leadership. For example, Nortel Networks recently hired two former Cisco executives into the roles of chief operating officer and chief technology officer. It is Nortel's hope that these executives will help bring some of Cisco's culture of aggressiveness to Nortel and thus allow it to compete more effectively in the high-technology industry environment.[54]

Mergers and Acquisitions.
Merging two companies with two distinct cultures is a surefire way to change the culture in an organization. The problem is that there is just no way to know what the culture will look like after the merger takes place. What the new culture will resemble is a function of both

⦿ **REALISTIC JOB PREVIEWS** The process of ensuring that a potential employee understands both the positive and negative aspects of the potential job.

⦿ **MENTORING** The process by which a junior-level employee develops a deep and long-lasting relationship with a more senior-level employee within the organization.

> # "ONE OF THE MOST INEXPENSIVE AND EFFECTIVE WAYS OF SOCIALIZING EMPLOYEES AND THUS REDUCING EARLY TURNOVER IS THE USE OF REALISTIC JOB PREVIEWS."

the strength of the two cultures involved in the merger and how similar they are to each other.[55] Ideally, a new culture would be created out of a compromise in which the best of both companies is represented by the new culture. There are many stories that have arisen from the mergers of companies with very different cultures: AOL/Time Warner, Exxon/Mobil, HP/Compaq, and RJR/Nabisco, to name a few. Unfortunately, very few of these stories are good ones. Mergers rarely result in the strong culture that managers hope will appear when they make the decision to merge. In fact, most merged companies operate under a differentiated culture for an extended period of time. Some of them never

Working at the corner liquor store wouldn't be the right person–organization fit for someone who believes that alcohol and tobacco are harmful to others.

really adopt a new identity, and when they do, many of them are seen as failures by the outside world. This perception is especially true in global mergers, in which each of the companies not only has a different organizational culture but is from a different country as well. See our **OB Internationally** box for more details.

Merging two different cultures has major effects on the attitudes and behaviors of organizational employees. Companies merge for many different strategic reasons, and though many managers and executives may realize its importance, whether the cultures will match is rarely the deciding criterion.[56] Slightly less troublesome but still a

OB for Students

What does culture mean for you as a student? Think back on all the things you had to learn and all the ambiguity you faced during your first semester in college. Just as organizational newcomers experience reality shock when they enter an organization, so do freshmen when they initially enter the university culture. Just as organizations have a culture that affects employees, universities have a culture that affects students. One recent study at a university investigated whether it was worthwhile to help socialize students in much the same way that organizations socialize new employees. The university set up a mentoring program to help facilitate the transition toward being a successful student.

As shown in the diagram to the right, whether a freshman was provided a mentor

Source: Adapted from R. J. Sanchez, T. N. Bauer, and M. E. Paronto, "Peer-Mentoring Freshmen: Implications for Satisfaction, Commitment, and Retention to Graduation," *Academy of Management Learning and Education* 5 (2006), pp. 25–37.

and the quality of the relationship he or she had with that mentor positively affected both satisfaction with and commitment to the university. In turn, levels of satisfaction with and

commitment to the university had positive effects on the student's intention to graduate. Of course, many of you are now wondering why your university didn't do this for you!

major hurdle to overcome are acquisitions. In most instances, and as evidenced by the chapter's opening example, the company doing the acquiring has a dominant culture to which the other is expected to adapt. We've noted how difficult it is just to get one person to adapt to an established culture through the socialization process. Can you imagine how difficult it is to change an entire organization at the same time? See our **OB on Screen** feature for one potential answer.

HOW IMPORTANT IS ORGANIZATIONAL CULTURE?

Normally, this section is where we summarize the importance of organizational culture by describing how it affects job performance and organizational commitment—the two outcomes in our integrative model of OB. However (similar to organizational structure in Chapter 11), it's difficult to summarize the importance of culture in this way because there are so many different types and dimensions of the concept. High solidarity cultures, high sociability cultures, diversity cultures, creativity cultures, and so forth all have different effects on performance and commitment—effects that likely vary across different types of organizations and industries.

 12.6

Explain person–organization fit. Describe how fitting with an organization's culture affects job performance and organizational commitment.

Regardless of the type of culture we're talking about, however, one concept remains important for any employee in any business: fit. Think for a moment about working for an organization whose culture doesn't match your own values. Maybe you work for an organization that produces a product that you don't believe in or that might be harmful to others, such as Phillip Morris, Budweiser, or Harrah's casinos. Maybe your employer is an organization that expects you to perform questionable behaviors from an ethical standpoint or produces a product that is of poor quality. **Person–organization fit** is the degree to which a person's personality and values match the culture of an organization. Employees judge fit by thinking about the values they prioritize the most, then judging whether the organization shares those values. Which values would you say are the most important to you?

A recent meta-analysis illustrates the importance of person–organization fit to employees.[57] When employees feel that their values and personality match those of the organization, they experience higher levels of *job satisfaction* and feel less *stress* about their day-to-day tasks. They also feel higher levels of *trust* toward their managers. Taken together, those results

Ford Motor Company's new CEO has called his new attempt at major culture change the "Way Forward."

OB Internationally

As mentioned previously, there is perhaps no more perilous journey for a company to take than merging with or acquiring another large firm. These problems are exacerbated when the two companies are from different countries. As few as 30 percent of international mergers and acquisitions create shareholder value.[58] Nevertheless, 2006 set a record pace for global mergers and acquisitions.[59] Why is this the case? Hopefully, we've illustrated the inherent difficulties of simply trying to merge two different cultures when the organizations are in the same country. These cultural differences can be magnified when international culture plays a role as well. People who come from different countries tend to view the world

differently and have different sets of values as well. For instance, DaimlerChrysler bought a controlling stake in Mitsubishi Motors, thinking that a strong alliance between the two would result in high levels of value for both companies. Unfortunately, this merger was recently broken up for reasons that have been attributed to international culture differences between the two firms (Japan vs. United States and Germany).[60] Japanese managers had a tendency to avoid "unpleasant truths" and stay away from major change efforts—a tendency that DaimlerChrysler never confronted.

There are many stories of failed international mergers, and one of the greatest

reasons for them is that corporations do not recognize the impact that national culture differences (in addition to organizational culture differences) have on their ability to be successful. One such merger that doesn't intend to fall victim to this issue is the creation of a joint venture between telecommunication giants Nokia (Finland) and Siemens (Germany). The CEOs of the two companies (Siemens's Klaus Kleinfeld and Nokia's Olli-Pekka Kallasvuo) are determined not to let differences in national or organizational cultures cause the merger fatal problems. Toward this end, cultural integration has been in the forefront of their minds.[61] ❖

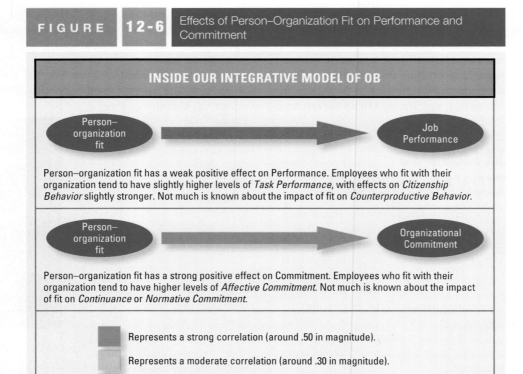

INSIDE OUR INTEGRATIVE MODEL OF OB

Person–organization fit → Job Performance

Person–organization fit has a weak positive effect on Performance. Employees who fit with their organization tend to have slightly higher levels of *Task Performance*, with effects on *Citizenship Behavior* slightly stronger. Not much is known about the impact of fit on *Counterproductive Behavior*.

Person–organization fit → Organizational Commitment

Person–organization fit has a strong positive effect on Commitment. Employees who fit with their organization tend to have higher levels of *Affective Commitment*. Not much is known about the impact of fit on *Continuance* or *Normative Commitment*.

Represents a strong correlation (around .50 in magnitude).

Represents a moderate correlation (around .30 in magnitude).

Represents a weak correlation (around .10 in magnitude).

Source: A. L. Kristof-Brown, R. D. Zimmerman, and E. C. Johnson, "Consequences of Individuals' Fit at Work: A Meta-Analysis of Person–Job, Person–Organization, Person–Group, and Person–Supervisor Fit," *Personnel Psychology* 58 (2005), pp. 281–342. Reprinted with permission of Blackwell Publishing.

OB on Screen

In Good Company

I'm not sure I understand what you are talking about. . . . What I mean is, what do computers have to do with sports? Are you literally saying that there should be a section in the magazine about computers? Who's going to want to read that?

By interjecting those words, Dan Forman (Dennis Quaid) interrupts Globecom CEO Teddy K (Malcom McDowell) in the middle of a division-wide speech during *In Good Company* (Dir. Paul Wietz, Universal, 2005). Globecom purchased *Sports America* magazine in a hostile takeover, hoping that the company would be a cash cow. However, problems arise when the two cultures of the companies don't mesh. Dan's words at the meeting speak volumes about what every *Sports America* employee is thinking but does not say out of fear for his or her job: "We simply don't fit the Globecom culture!"

Teddy K's Globecom is a no-holds-barred, dog-eat-dog, profit-means-everything type of firm whose employees use language like "synergy" to describe what leads to success. In fact, it very much resembles a mercenary culture. One telling example of the culture emerges when Globecom appoints an inexperienced, 26-year-old Carter Duryea (Topher Grace) to take 51-year-old Dan Forman's place because the CEO remembered that Carter had done "something with cell phones." Carter soon finds that *Sports America* is a more traditional, family-oriented company that values employees and relationships with customers. His fast-talking, smooth-moving ways don't exactly go over well with his new subordinates. And it really doesn't help when he starts dating Dan's daughter (Scarlett

Johansson). The lack of fit between Globecom and *Sports America* isn't unlike many acquisitions that take place in corporate America: Two very different cultures that value different things are thrown together for the sake of "potential." You'll have to rent the movie to find out what happens to Dan and Carter. ❖

illustrate why person–organization fit is so highly correlated with organizational commitment, one of the two outcomes in our integrative model of OB (see Figure 12-6). When employees feel they fit with their organization's culture, they are much more likely to develop an emotional attachment to the company. The effects of fit on job performance are weaker, however. In general, person–organization fit is more related to citizenship behaviors than task performance. Employees who sense a good fit are therefore more likely to help their colleagues and "go the extra mile" to benefit the company. ■

Employees who sense a good fit with the company they work for will be more likely to go the extra mile to help their colleagues.

CHECK OUT

www.mhhe.com/ColquittEss

for study materials including Interactive Exercises, Quizzes, iPod downloads, and video.

CASE: eBay, PayPal, and Skype

Newly named CEO John Donahoe faces numerous issues as he takes over eBay.[62] One of these issues is how to best find a way to take advantage of newly acquired Skype. Skype is a company that was founded around a software program that allows users to make telephone calls over the Internet. These calls (to anywhere in the world) are free to other computers also equipped with Skype software. Skype users also can call landlines and cell phones, but only if they pay a fee. eBay hopes, of course, that users will select PayPal to pay those fees. Indeed, new versions of Skype software have a "send money" feature that allows Skype users to transfer money to one another using PayPal. While the decision to purchase Skype (at an expensive $2.5 billion) is controversial in numerous circles,[63] there is no question that one of the major keys to making the merger work is finding a way to allow the two distinct corporate cultures to merge.

eBay values Skype for its entrepreneurial, dot-com type of spirit—much like it did PayPal. However, whereas PayPal might be considered by some to be a business success (there were

some who thought that eBay bought the company more for its technology and brand than it did for its people), there is no doubting that in this newest merger, eBay needs the employees of Skype to merge with its culture. How it goes about accomplishing that, while allowing Skype to maintain its own unique culture, will be the key.

12.1 If you were the CEO of eBay, what types of things might you consider doing to facilitate the Skype acquisition while allowing Skype to maintain its own subculture?

12.2 Do you think that Skype will be overwhelmed and affected by the demands of eBay's culture for profits and results? How might eBay's corporate culture have a detrimental effect on Skype as an entity?

12.3 Do you think that eBay learned from its acquisition of PayPal? How might having gone through that experience help eBay have a more successful time merging with Skype?

TAKEAWAYS

12.1 Organizational culture is the shared social knowledge within an organization regarding the rules, norms, and values that shape the attitudes and behaviors of its employees. There are three components of organizational culture: observable artifacts, espoused values, and basic underlying assumptions. Observable artifacts include symbols, physical structures, language, stories, rituals, and ceremonies.

12.2 An organization's culture can be described on dimensions such as solidarity and sociability to create four general culture types: networked, communal, fragmented, and mercenary. Organizations often strive to create a more specific cultural emphasis, as in customer service cultures, diversity cultures, and creativity cultures.

12.3 Strong cultures have the ability to influence employee behaviors and attitudes. Strong cultures exist when employees agree on the way things are supposed to happen and their behaviors are consistent with those expectations.

Strong cultures are not necessarily good or bad. Generally, a culture's effectiveness depends on how well it matches the company's outside environment. To this degree, adaptive cultures can be very useful.

12.4 Organizations maintain their cultures through attraction, selection, and attrition processes and socialization practices. Organizations change their cultures by changing their leadership or through mergers and acquisitions.

12.5 There are a number of practices organizations can utilize to improve the socialization of new employees, including realistic job previews and mentoring.

12.6 Person–organization fit is the degree to which a person's values and personality match the culture of the organization. Person–organization fit has a weak positive effect on job performance and a strong positive effect on organizational commitment.

DISCUSSION QUESTIONS

12.1 Have you or a family member worked for an organization that you would consider to have a strong culture? If so, what made the culture strong? Did you or they enjoy working there? What do you think led to that conclusion?

12.2 Is it possible for an employee to have personal values that are inconsistent with the values of the organization? If so, how is this inconsistency likely to affect the employee's behavior and attitudes while at work?

12.3 If you had to describe the culture of your university, what would it be like? What observable artifacts are present to be perceived by students? Are there any underlying assumptions that guide your behavior at your university?

12.4 How can two companies with very different cultures that operate in the same industry both be successful? Shouldn't

one company's culture automatically be a better fit for the environment?

12.5 If an organization wanted to foster a diversity culture, what steps might management take to ensure that employees will support the new culture? What observable artifacts might a company change to instill this culture?

12.6 When you think of the U.S. Postal Service's culture, what kinds of words come to mind? Where do these impressions come from? Do you think your impressions are accurate? What has the potential to make them inaccurate?

12.7 Think about the last job you started. What are some unique things that companies might do to reduce the amount of reality shock that new employees encounter? Are these methods likely to be expensive?

ASSESSMENT: Creativity Culture

Have you experienced a creativity culture? This assessment is designed to measure two facets of that type of culture. Think of your current job, or the last job that you held (even if it was a part-time or summer job). If you haven't worked, think of a current or former student group that developed strong norms for how tasks should be done. Answer each question using the response

scale provided. Then subtract your answers to the boldfaced questions from 6, with the difference being your new answer for that question. For example, if your original answer for question 7 was "4," your new answer is "2" (6−4). Then sum up your scores for the two facets.

1	2	3	4	5
Strongly Disagree	**Disagree**	**Uncertain**	**Agree**	**Strongly Agree**

1. New ideas are readily accepted here. _____
2. This company is quick to respond when changes need to be made. _____
3. Management here is quick to spot the need to do things differently. _____
4. This organization is very flexible; it can quickly change procedures to meet new conditions and solve problems as they arise. _____
5. People in this organization are always searching for new ways of looking at problems. _____
6. It is considered extremely important here to follow the rules. _____
7. **People can ignore formal procedures and rules if it helps to get the job done.** _____
8. Everything has to be done by the book. _____
9. **It is not necessary to follow procedures to the letter around here.** _____
10. **Nobody gets too upset if people break the rules around here.** _____

Scoring

Innovation: Sum up items 1–5.

Formalization: Sum up items 6–10.

Interpretation

If your score is 22 or above for either facet, your organization or workgroup is high on that particular dimension. Creative cultures tend to be high on innovation and low on formalization. So if your score was 22 or above for innovation and 21 or below for formalization, then chances are you've experienced a strong creativity culture.

Source: M. G. Patterson, M. A. West, V. J. Shackleton, J. F. Dawson, R. Lawthom, S. Maitlis, D. L. Robinson, and A. M. Wallace, "Validating the Organizational Climate Measure: Links to Managerial Practices, Productivity and Innovation," *Journal of Organizational Behavior* 26 (2005), pp. 379–408. Copyright © 2005 John Wiley & Sons Limited. Reproduced with permission.

EXERCISE: University Culture

The purpose of this exercise is to explore how organizational culture is transmitted through observable artifacts. This exercise uses groups, so your instructor will either assign you to a group or ask you to create your own group. The exercise has the following steps:

Symbols	Think about the logo and images associated with your university. What message do they convey about the university's culture?
Physical structures	Think about the most visible physical structures on campus. What do those structures say about your university's culture?
Language	Think about the jargon, slang, slogans, and sayings associated with your university. What insights do they offer into the university's culture?
Stories	What anecdotes, accounts, legends, and myths are associated with your university? What messages do they convey about your university's culture?
Rituals	What are the daily or weekly routines that occur at your university, and what do they say about the culture?
Ceremonies	What are the formal events and celebrations that occur at your university, and what cultural signals do they convey?

1. Consider the observable artifacts that transmit the organizational culture of your university.

2. If you consider the symbols, physical structures, language, stories, rituals, and ceremonies identified in Step 1, what core values seem to summarize your university's culture? Using a transparency, laptop, or chalkboard, list the one value that seems to be most central to your university's culture. Then list the three cultural artifacts that are most

responsible for transmitting that core value. Present your results to the class.

3. Discuss (in groups or as a class) two main questions. First, do you like how your university's culture is viewed, as rep-

resented in the group presentations? Why or why not? Second, if you wanted to change the university's culture to represent other sorts of values, what process would you use to change the culture?

END NOTES

1. O'Brien, J. M. "The PayPal Mafia." *Fortune*, November 14, 2007, pp. 96–106.

2. Ibid.

3. Ibid.

4. Sellers, P. "eBay's Secret." *Fortune*, October 18, 2004, pp. 160–68.

5. Brown, E. "How Can a Dot-Com Be This Hot?" *Fortune*, January 21, 2002, pp. 78–83.

6. Sellers, P. "Knowing It's Time to Buy." *Fortune*, November 14, 2005, p. 147.

7. Verbeke, W.; M. Volgering; and M. Hessels. "Exploring the Conceptual Expansion within the Field of Organizational Behavior: Organizational Climate and Organizational Culture." *Journal of Management Studies* 35 (1998), pp. 303–29.

8. Deal, T. E., and A. A. Kennedy. *Corporate Cultures: The Rites and Rituals of Corporate Life.* Reading, MA: Addison-Wesley, 1982.

9. Adapted from O'Reilly, C. A., III; J. Chatman; and D. L. Caldwell. "People and Organizational Culture: A Profile Comparison Approach to Assessing Person–Organization Fit." *Academy of Management Journal* 34 (1991), pp. 487–516; Tsui, A. S.; Z. Zhang; W. Hui; K. R. Xin, and J. B. Wu. "Unpacking the Relationship between CEO Leadership Behavior and Organizational Culture." *The Leadership Quarterly* 17 (2006), pp. 113–37.

10. O'Reilly, C. A., and J. A. Chatman. "Culture as Social Control: Corporations, Cults, and Commitment." In *Research in Organizational Behavior*, Vol. 18, ed. B. M. Staw and L. L. Cummings. Stamford, CT: JAI Press, 1996, pp. 157–200.

11. Chatman, J. A. "Matching People and Organizations: Selection and Socialization in Public Accounting Firms." *Administrative Science Quarterly* 36 (1991), pp. 459–84.

12. Trice, H. M., and J. M. Beyer. *The Cultures of Work Organizations.* Englewood Cliffs, NJ: Prentice Hall, 1993.

13. Kaihla, P. "Best-Kept Secrets of the World's Best Companies." *Business 2.0* 7 (2006), pp. 82–87.

14. Stibbe, M. "Mothers of Invention." *Director* 55 (2002), pp. 64–68.

15. Shuit, D. P. "Yum Does a 360." *Workforce Management*, April 2005, pp. 59–60.

16. Kiger, P. J. "Corporate Crunch." *Workforce Management*, April 2005, pp. 32–38.

17. Jacobson, D. "Extreme Extras." *Money Magazine*, April 7, 2006, p. 99.

18. Kaihla, "Best-Kept Secrets."

19. Higgins, J. M., and C. McAllaster. "If You Want Strategic Change, Don't Forget to Change Your Cultural Artifacts." *Journal of Change Management* 4 (2004), pp. 63–74.

20. Schein, E. H. "Organizational Culture." *American Psychologist* 45 (1990), pp. 109–19.

21. Schein, E. H. *Organization Culture and Leadership.* San Francisco, CA: Jossey-Bass, 2004.

22. Schein, E. H. "What Is Culture?" In *Reframing Organizational Culture*, ed. P. J. Frost, L. F. Moore, M. R. Louis, C. C. Lundberg, and J. Martin. Beverly Hills, CA: Sage, 1991, pp. 243–53.

23. Goffee, R., and G. Jones. *The Character of a Corporation.* New York: Harper Business, 1998.

24. Lum, S., and B. C. Moyer. "Gross Product by Industry, 1995–1997." *Survey of Current Business*, November 1998, pp. 20–40.

25. Schneider, B.; D. E. Bowen; M. G. Ehrhart; and K. M. Holcombe. "The Climate for Service: Evolution of a Construct." In *Handbook of Organizational Culture and Climate*, ed. N. M. Ashkanasy, C. Wilderom, and M. F. Peterson. Thousand Oaks, CA: Sage, 2000.

26. Schneider, B.; M. G. Ehrhart; D. M. Mayer; J. L. Saltz; and K. Niles-Jolly. "Understanding Organization–Customer Links in Service Settings." *Academy of Management Journal* 48 (2005), pp. 1017–32.

27. du Gay, P., and G. Salaman. "The Cult(ure) of the Customer." In *Strategic Human Resource Management*, ed. C. Mabey, G. Salaman, and J. Storey. London: Sage, 1998, pp. 58–67.

28. Speizer, I. "Diversity on the Menu." *Workforce Management*, November 2004, pp. 41–45.

29. Voepel, M. "Summit's Drive Has Served Lady Vols Well." April 9, 2008, http://sports.espn.go.com/ncw/ncaatourney08/columns/story?columnist=voepel_mechelle&id=3336694 (accessed June 6, 2008).

30. Summit, P. *Raise the Roof.* New York: Broadway, 1999; see also Summit, P. *Reach the Summit.* New York: Broadway, 1999.

31. McLean, L. D. "Organizational Culture's Influence on Creativity and Innovation: A Review of the Literature and Implications for Human Resource Development." *Advances in Developing Human Resources* 7 (2005), pp. 226–46.

32. Frauenheim, E. "On the Clock but Off on Their Own: Pet-Project Programs Set to Gain Wider Acceptance." *Workforce Management*, April 24, 2006, pp. 40–41.

33. Poulton, T. "Got a Creative Creative Process? Fostering Creativity in an ROI-Focused Cubicle-Ridden Environment Ain't Easy. Here's How to Get Your Team's Juices Flowing." *Strategy*, April 2006, p. 11.

34. O'Reilly, C. A. "Corporations, Culture, and Commitment: Motivation and Social Control in Organizations." *California Management Review* 31 (1989), pp. 9–25.

35. O'Reilly et al., "People and Organizational Culture."

36. Schein, E. H. "Three Cultures of Management: The Key to Organizational Learning." *Sloan Management Review* 38 (1996), pp. 9–20.

37. Boisner, A., and J. Chatman. "The Role of Subcultures in Agile Organizations." In *Leading and Managing People in Dynamic Organizations*, ed. R. Petersen and E. Mannix. Mahwah, NJ: Lawrence Erlbaum Associates, 2003.

38. See Howard-Grenville, J. A. "Inside the 'BLACK BOX': How Organizational Culture and Subcultures Inform Interpretations and Actions on Environmental Issues." *Organization & Environment* 19 (2006) , pp. 46–73; Jermier, J.; J. Slocum; L. Fry; and J. Gaines. "Organizational Subcultures in a Soft Bureaucracy: Resistance behind the Myth and Façade of an Official Culture." *Organizational Science* 2 (1991), pp. 170–94.

39. Schneider, B.; H. W. Goldstein; and D. B. Smith. "The ASA Framework: An Update." *Personnel Psychology* 48 (1995), pp. 747–73.

40. Graf, A. B. "Building Corporate Cultures." *Chief Executive*, March 2005, p. 18.

41. Ruiz, G "Tall Order." *Workforce Management*, April 2006, pp. 22–29.

42. For good summaries of socialization, see Fisher, C. D. "Organizational Socialization: An Integrative View." *Research in Personnel and Human Resource Management* 4 (1986), pp. 101–45; Bauer, T. N.; E. W. Morrison; and R. R. Callister. "Organizational Socialization: A Review and Directions for Future Research." In *Research in Personnel and Human Resource Management*, Vol. 16, ed. G. R. Ferris. Greenwich, CT: JAI Press, 1998, pp. 149–214.

43. Cable, D. M.; L. Aiman-Smith; P. W. Mulvey; and J. R. Edwards. "The Sources and Accuracy of Job Applicants' Beliefs about Organizational Culture." *Academy of Management Journal* 43 (2000), pp. 1076–85; Louis, M. R. "Surprise and Sense-Making: What Newcomers Experience in Entering Unfamiliar Organizational Settings." *Administrative Science Quarterly* 25 (1980), pp. 226–51.

44. Chao, G. T.; A. O'Leary-Kelly; S. Wolf; H. J. Klein; and P. D. Gardner. "Organizational Socialization: Its Content and Consequences." *Journal of Applied Psychology* 79 (1994), pp. 450–63.

45. Ibid.; Klein, H., and N. Weaver. "The Effectiveness of an Organizational-Level Orientation Training Program in the Socialization of New Hires." *Personnel Psychology*, Spring 2000, pp. 47–66; Wesson, M. J., and C. I. Gogus. "Shaking Hands with a Computer: An Examination of Two Methods of Organizational Newcomer Orientation." *Journal of Applied Psychology* 90 (2005), pp. 1018–26.

46. Barber, A. E. *Recruiting Employees: Individual and Organizational Perspectives.* Thousand Oaks, CA: Sage, 1998.

47. Wanous, J. P. *Organizational Entry: Recruitment, Selection, Orientation and Socialization of Newcomers.* Reading, MA: Addison-Wesley, 1992.

48. Gravelle, M. "The Five Most Common Hiring Mistakes and How to Avoid Them." *The Canadian Manager* 29 (2004), pp. 11–13.

49. Allen, T. D.; L. T. Eby; M. L. Poteet; E. Lentz; and L. Lima. "Outcomes Associated with Mentoring Protégés: A Meta-Analysis." *Journal of Applied Psychology* 89 (2004), pp. 127–36.

50. Ibid.

51. Mourier, P., and M. Smith. *Conquering Organizational Change: How to Succeed Where Most Companies Fail.* Atlanta: CEP Press, 2001.

52. McCracken, J. "'Way Forward' Requires Culture Shift at Ford." *The Wall Street Journal*, January 23, 2006, p. B1.

53. Schein, *Organization Culture and Leadership.*

54. Gubbins, E. "Nortel's New Execs Bring Cisco Experience." *Telephony*, April 11, 2005. pp. 14–15.

55. Weber, Y. "Measuring Cultural Fit in Mergers and Acquisitions." In *Handbook of Organizational Culture and Climate*, ed. N. M. Ashkanasy, C. Wilderom, and M. F. Peterson. Thousand Oaks, CA: Sage, 2000, pp. 309–20.

56. Stahl, G. K., and M. E. Mendenhall. *Mergers and Acquisitions: Managing Culture and Human Resources.* Stanford, CA: Stanford University Press, 2005.

57. Kristof-Brown, A. L.; R. D. Zimmerman; and E. C. Johnson, "Consequences of Individuals' Fit at Work: A Meta-Analysis of Person–Job, Person–Organization, Person–Group, and Person–Supervisor Fit," *Personnel Psychology* 58 (2005), pp. 281–342.

58. Brahy, S. "Six Solution Pillars for Successful Cultural Integration of International M&As." *Journal of Organizational Excellence*, Autumn 2006, pp. 53–63.

59. Platt, G. "Global Merger Activity Sets Record Pace." *Global Finance* 20 (2006), p. 60.

60. Edmondson, G. "Auf Wiedersehen, Mitsubishi." *BusinessWeek*, November 11, 2005, http://www.businessweek.com (accessed February 9, 2007); Bremmer, B. "A Tale of Two Auto Mergers." *BusinessWeek*, April 29, 2004, http://www.businessweek.com (accessed February 9, 2007).

61. Ewing, J. "Nokia and Siemens: Exciting the Market." *BusinessWeek*, June 19, 2006.

62. Holahan, C. "eBay's New Tough Love CEO." *BusinessWeek*, February 4, 2008, p. 58.

63. Lashinsky, A. "Building eBay 2.0." *Fortune*, October 16, 2006, pp. 160–64.

PHOTO CREDITS

Chapter 10

Chapter 11

Chapter 12

NAME INDEX

Page numbers followed by n refer to notes.

A

Bommer, W. H., 72n, 249n
Bond, M. H., 173
Bono, J. E., 67, 73n, 188n, 189n, 249n
Boozer, Carlos, 228
Borman, W. C., 46n, 47n, 92n, 176, 183, 187n, 191n, 218n, 219n
Borman, W. S., 190n
Boswell, W. R., 93n, 182, 190n
Bouchard, T. J., 188n
Boudreau, J. W., 93n, 182, 190n
Bounds, G., 269n
Bowen, D. E., 290n
Bowie, Sam, 156
Boyle, M., 114n
Brackett, M. A., 187
Bradley, J. C., 189n
Brady, D., 137n
Brady, F. N., 140n
Brahy, S., 291n
Brandon, J., 91n
Brannick, M. T., 59, 72n
Breaugh, J. A., 72n
Brehmer, B., 219n
Breinin, E., 249n
Bremmer, B., 291n
Brett, J. F., 159
Bretz, R. D., 182, 190n
Brief, A. P., 73n
Briggs, S. R., 138n
Brin, Sergey, 17, 177
Brinkmann, J., 161n, 189n
Brockmann, E. N., 161n
Brockner, J., 114n, 129, 139n, 162n, 265, 270n
Brodbeck, F. C., 248n
Brooks, D., 114n
Brown, E., 290n
Brown, J., 115n
Brown, K. G., 115n
Brown, Kwame, 156
Bryant, F. B., 92n
Bryant, Kobe, 228
Buffet, Warren, 153
Buford, B., 160n
Buford, Bill, 145
Bunker, B. B., 126, 138n
Burke, M. E., 84, 91n
Burke, M. J., 219n
Burkhead, E. J., 92n
Burnfield, J. L., 247n
Burns, L. R., 269n
Burns, Ursula, 224, 243
Burt, R. S., 137n
Burtt, H. E., 247n
Buss, A. H., 19
Butcher, J. N., 187n
Butler, Gerard, 206
Butterfield, K. D., 139n
Byham, W. C., 161n
Byosiere, P., 92n, 93n
Byrne, D., 218n
Byrne, Z. S., 101, 114n

C

Cable, D. M., 291n
Cacioppo, J. T., 73n

Caldwell, D. L., 290n
Callister, R. R., 291n
Camara, W. J., 189n
Camerer, C., 137n
Campbell, D. T., 21n
Campbell, J. P., 20n, 46n
Campion, M. A., 49n, 73n
Cannon, W. B., 92n
Cannon-Bowers, J. A., 220n
Carnevale, A. P., 161n
Carroll, J. B., 190n
Caruso, D., 181
Casey, S., 72n
Castellan, N. J., 220n
Catania, A., 50n
Cattell, R. B., 190n
Cavanaugh, M. A., 93n
Cellar, D. F., 189n
Cellitti, D. R., 47n
Chao, G. T., 283, 291n
Charness, N., 160n
Chatman, J., 290n, 291n
Chavez, C., 246n
Chemers, M. M., 216n
Chen, Z. X., 249n
Cherniss, C., 190n
Cherrington, D., 49n
Chess, W. A., 93n
Child, J., 269n
Chiu, C., 162n
Chiu, Willy, 252
Chouinard, Yvon, 54, 69
Christal, R. E., 188n
Church, A. H., 72n
Ciarrochi, J., 187
Clark, M. S., 64
Clark, R. C., 161n
Clarke, L., 49n
Clayton, L. D., 216n
Clinton, Bill, 227
Clore, G., 218n
Cohen, J., 21n
Cohen, P., 21n
Cohen, R. R., 219n
Cohen, S., 93n
Cohen, S. G., 196, 216n
Cohen-Charash, Y., 111, 116n, 139n
Colarelli, S. M., 182, 190n
Colbert, A. E., 115n
Colella, A., 116n
Coleman, V. I., 47n
Collier, A., 72n
Colligan, M., 91n
Colquitt, J. A., 46n, 111, 116n, 134, 139n, 157, 189n, 219n, 249n
Comer, D. R., 217n
Conger, J. A., 248n
Conlin, M., 91n, 114n, 140n, 270n
Conlon, D. E., 111, 116n, 139n, 162n
Converse, S. A., 220n
Cook, T. D., 21n
Coon, H. M., 189n
Coons, A. E., 235, 247n
Cooper, C., 219n
Cooper, C. L., 72n, 93n, 247n
Cooper, H., 189n
Cooper, Michael, 58

Fetter, R., 47n, 249n
Fichman, M., 49n
Field, R. H. G., 247n
Fields, Mark, 283
Fisher, A., 49n, 190n
Fisher, C. D., 291n
Fitzgerald, M. P., 62, 73n
Fleishman, E. A., 176, 187n, 247n, 248n
Floor, L., 248n
Florey, A. T., 218n
Fogli, L., 191n
Folger, R., 139n
Folkers, D., 161n
Folkman, S., 91n, 92n
Foltz, J., 49n
Ford, Henry, 254
Forsyth, D. R., 140n
Frakes, Jonathan, 152
France, Brian, 259
Frantz, C., 114n
Frauenheim, E., 291n
Frei, R. L., 188n
Freidberg, J., 47n
Freidberg, K., 47n
French, J. R. P., Jr., 246n
Frese, 92n
Frey, M. C., 189n
Fried, Y., 72n
Friedman, M., 92n
Friedman, Thomas T., 9, 20n
Frost, P. J., 290n
Fry, L., 291n
Fujita, F., 188n
Fulmer, I. S., 20n
Funder, D. C., 187n
Furnham, A., 183, 190n, 191n
Fusilier, M. R., 92n
Futrell, D., 196

G

Gabarro, J. J., 138n
Gaertner, S., 39, 49n, 50n
Gaines, J., 291n
Galagan, P., 160n
Galbraith, J., 102
Galton, F., 190n
Gannon, M. J., 92n, 116n, 124, 139n, 187n
Ganster, D. C., 91n, 92n
Gardner, H., 190n
Gardner, P. D., 283, 291n
Garland, H., 162n
Garnett, Kevin, 202
Gates, Bill, 38, 184
Gavin, J. H., 218n
Gavin, M. B., 140n
George, J. M., 73n, 189n
Gergen, K., 127, 138n
Gerhardt, M. W., 188n
Gerhart, B., 20n, 115n, 116n, 247n
Gersick, C. J. G., 216n
Geschka, H., 219n
Gibbons, Peter, 13
Gibson, C. B., 116n, 173, 189n
Gibson, W. M., 59, 72n

Gieske, Ken, 215
Gilbreth, F. B., 72n
Gillam, Kathleen, 213
Gilliland, S., 138n
Gilliland, S. W., 139n
Gist, M. E., 100, 114n
Glick, W. H., 269n
Gloeckler, G., 116n
Glomb, T. M., 139n
Gobeli, D. H., 269n
Godinez, V., 216n
Goff, S., 190n
Goffee, R., 278, 290n
Gogus, C. I., 291n
Goldbacher, E., 102
Goldberg, L. R., 168, 187n, 188n
Golden, D., 161n
Goldenhar, L., 91n
Goldstein, D. L., 92n
Goldstein, H. W., 291n
Goleman, D., 190n
Golen, J., 217n
Gooding, J. Z., 269n
Gooding, R. Z., 218n
Goodman, P. S., 50n
Gopinath, C., 265, 269n
Gordan, J., 216n
Gore, Bill, 256
Goslin, D. A., 140n
Gouran, D., 219n
Grace, Topher, 286
Graf, A. B., 291n
Grant, S., 191n
Gravelle, 291n
Graziano, W. G., 188n
Green, H., 102
Greenberg, J., 20n, 115n, 129, 138n, 139n
Greenberg, M., 127, 138n
Greenwood, Bruce, 237
Griffeth, R. W., 39, 49n, 50n
Grissom, Gil, 177
Groszkiewicz, D., 269n
Grover, R., 247n
Grow, B., 46n, 48n
Grubb, P., 91n
Gruen, R. J., 91n
Gruenfeld, D. H., 218n
Gruver, Mike, 212
Gubbins, E., 291n
Gully, S. M., 220n
Gupta, V., 248n
Gurin, G., 248n
Guzzo, R., 219n, 220n
Guzzo, R. A., 217n, 218n

H

Hachiya, D., 49n
Hackett, R. D., 249n
Hackman, J. R., 71, 72n, 116n, 218n, 269n
Hagafors, R., 219n
Hair, E. C., 188n
Halfhill, T., 216n
Hall, E., 218n
Hall-Merenda, K. E., 249n

Moag, J. F., 127, 139n
Mobley, W., 49n
Moeller, N. L., 62, 73n
Moffat, Robert W., Jr., 252, 266
Mohammed, S., 220n
Mohrman, S. A., 216n
Mokoto, R., 20n
Mol, S., 189n
Monge, P. R., 247n
Moon, H., 162n
Mooney, C. H., 72n
Moore, L. F., 290n
Moorhead, G., 220n
Moorman, R. H., 249n
Morris, B., 137n, 246n, 249n
Morris, M. W., 162n
Morris, W. N., 73n
Morrison, A. M., 91n
Morrison, E. W., 47n, 291n
Morrison, M., 114n
Morse, N., 248n
Mortensen, Chris, 85
Moskowitz, M., 12, 20n, 48n, 72n, 73n, 138n
Motowidlo, S. J., 46n, 47n, 190n
Mount, M. K., 183, 188n–191n, 217n
Mourier, P., 291n
Mowday, R. T., 46n, 48n, 114n
Moyer, B. C., 290n
Muchinsky, P. M., 49n
Mulcahy, Anne, 224, 226, 237, 243, 246n
Mullaney, T. J., 114n
Mullen, B., 219n
Mulvey, P. W., 291n
Mumford, M. D., 176, 187n
Murphy, K. R., 73n, 190n
Murphy, L., 91n
Murphy, L. R., 92n
Murray, S. S., 91n

N

Nardelli, Bob, 24, 43
Narvaez, D., 140n
Nauta, A., 246n
Naylor, J. C., 114n
Neal, M. A., 218n
Neal, M. E., 246n
Neale, M. A., 218n, 247n
Near, J. P., 72n
Neck, C., 220n
Negroponte, Nicolas, 231–232
Neihoff, B. P., 47n
Nelson, D., 217n
Nemeth, C. J., 218n
Neubert, M. J., 217n
Neufeld, D. J., 92n, 249n
Neuman, G. A., 217n
Newcomb, T. M., 218n, 248n
Newman, D. A., 67, 73n
Newman, K. L., 92n, 116n, 124, 139n, 187n
Newton, Isaac, 276
Ng, K. Y., 111, 116n, 139n
Ng, T. W. H., 189n
Nicholson, N., 49n
Nicholson-Crotty, S., 256, 269n

Nicklaus, Jack, 100
Niles-Jolly, K., 280, 290n
Noe, R. A., 62, 73n, 157, 161n
Noel, T. W., 140n
Noer, D. M., 270n
Nonaka, I., 161n
Nooyi, Indra, 120, 121, 135, 226
Norman, P. M., 137
Norman, W. T., 187n, 188n
Northcraft, G. B., 247n

O

O'Brien, J. M., 187n, 191n, 290n
O'Connor, A., 91n
Odbert, H. S., 187n
Oddou, G., 92n
O'Donnell, Kenny, 237
O'Driscoll, M. P., 93n
Oh, H., 140n
O'Keefe, B., 269n
Oldham, G. R., 71, 72n, 116n, 189n, 219n, 269n
O'Leary-Kelly, A. M., 283, 291n
Olowokandi, Michael, 156
Olsen, R. N., 116n
Olson-Buchanan, J. B., 93n
Ones, D. S., 48n, 73n, 183
Ordonez, L., 140n
O'Reilly, C. A., III, 28, 46n, 218n, 290n, 291n
Orey, M., 139n
Organ, D. W., 47n
Osborn, A. F., 219n
Osland, J. S., 92n
Oswald, F. L., 186
Outerbridge, A. N., 190n
Owens, Jim, 144
Oyserman, D., 189n

P

Padgett, M. Y., 73n
Paetzold, R. L., 116n
Page, Lawrence, 17, 177
Paine, J. B., 47n, 241, 249n
Palmeri, D., 188n
Park, B., 161n
Park, O. S., 47n
Parker, Candace, 58
Patterson, M. G., 289
Patton, G. K., 67, 73n
Paul, K. B., 59, 72n
Paulus, P. B., 217n
Paunonen, S. V., 188n
Pavot, W., 188n
Payne, Robert, 266
Payne, S. C., 161n
Paynton, C. F., 246n
Pearce, J., 91n
Pearson, C. M., 48n
Peeters, M. A. G., 217n
Pennings, J. M., 246n
Pepper, L., 265, 270n
Perkins, A., 91n
Perrewé, P. L., 91n
Pescuric, A., 161n

SUBJECT INDEX

Commitment. *See also* Organizational commitment
    affective, 34–36, 39, 45
    cognitive abilities and, 182
    continuance, 34–37
    escalation of, 155–156
    focus of, 35
    leadership and, 240–241
    motivation and, 110, 111
    normative, 34–35, 37–39
    organizational structure and, 265
    person-organization fit and, 286, 287
    strains and, 87
    teamwork processes and, 211–212
    trust and, 134
Communion striving, 168, 169
Communities of practice, 149
Compensation plans, 109–110
Compensatory forms model of withdrawal, 43
Competence, 108
Competing, 230
Compliance, 230
Compliments, 229
Comprehensive interdependence, 200
Compromise, 231–232
Conflict
    relationship, 209
    role, 79–80
    task, 209
Conflict management, 209, 210
Conflict resolution
    explanation of, 230
    styles used in, 230–232
Conscientiousness
    as dimension of personality, 168
    job performance and, 183–184
    of team members, 203
Consideration, 235, 236
Consistency, 126
Consultation, 229
Consultative leadership style, 233
Continuance commitment
    explanation of, 34, 35
    function of, 36–37
Coordination loss, 204, 205
Coping, 82–83
Correctability, 126
Correlation, 15, 16
Countercultures, 281
Counterproductive behavior
    explanation of, 31
    motivation and, 110
    types of, 31–33
Courtesy, 29
Coworkers, 5
Coworker satisfaction, 57–58
Creativity
    explanation of, 172
    on teams, 206–207
Creativity culture, 280, 288–289
Cross-cultural organizational behavior, 9
Cross-cultural training, 83
Cultural diversity. *See also* Diversity; Globalization
    attributions and, 154, 155
    citizenship behavior and, 31
    ethical standards and, 130

expatriate effectiveness and, 83
leadership styles and, 238, 239
life satisfaction and, 68
money-happiness connection and, 68
motivation and, 106
multinational teams and, 209
trust propensities and, 124
values and, 172–174
Cultural values
    dimensions of, 172–174
    explanation of, 167
    function of, 8
Culture. *See* Organizational culture
Culture strength, 280–281
Customer service culture, 279, 280
Cyberloafing, 40

D

Daily hassles, 80
Daydreaming, 40, 68
Decision informity, 207
Decision making
    bias in, 154
    cognitive ability and, 181
    ethical, 130
    explanation of, 145
    by leaders, 232–234
    learning and, 145–146
    methods of, 150–152
    problems related to, 152–156
    on teams, 207–209
Decisions
    escalation of commitment and, 155–156
    faulty attributions and, 154–155
    faulty perceptions and, 153–154
    limited information and, 152–153
    nonprogrammed, 150, 151
    programmed, 150, 151
Deductive reasoning, 177
Deep-level diversity, 204
Delegative leadership style, 233–234
Demands, 77–82
Deviance, 31–32
Discretion, 227, 228
Disposition-based trust, 121, 122
Distributive justice, 125–126, 129
Diversity. *See also* Cultural diversity
    management of, 9
    in teams, 203–204
Diversity culture, 279

E

Education, online, 149
Emotional ability
    dimensions of, 179–180
    explanation of, 178–179
Emotional contagion, 65
Emotional cues, 98
Emotional intelligence
    awareness of, 187
    explanation of, 178
    types of, 178–180
Emotional regulation, 178–179

Emotion-focused coping, 82–83
Emotions
    explanation of, 65
    types of, 65–66
    use of, 180
Employees
    managing strain in, 84–86
    types of, 39–40
    withdrawal behavior by, 33, 38–41, 43
Empowerment, psychological, 107–109
Engagement
    explanation of, 64, 170
    influence and, 230
Equity distress, 105
Equity theory, 105–107
Erosion model, 36
Escalation of commitment, 155–156
Espoused values, 277
Ethical decision making
    components of, 130, 131
    moral awareness and, 130–132
    moral intent and, 133
    moral judgment and, 132
    principles utilized during, 132
Ethical ideologies, 132, 133
Ethical sensitivity, 130, 131
Ethics
    explanation of, 121, 129–130
    in multinational corporations, 130
    research on, 132
    for students, 133
Ethnocentrism, 173, 174
Exchange tactics, 229
Exit, 38
Exit-voice-loyalty-neglect framework, 38–39
Expatriates. *See also* Cultural diversity; Globalization; Multinational
    corporations
    adjustment of, 174
    effectiveness of, 83
    factors affecting, 9
Expectancy, 98–99
Expectancy theory
    expectancy and, 98–99
    explanation of, 97
    instrumentality and, 99
    motivational force and, 102
    valence and, 100–102
Expertise, 145
Expert power, 226–227
Explicit knowledge, 146, 150, 156
Extinction, 147–148
Extrinsic motivation, 101
Extroversion
    explanation of, 169–171
    leadership and, 170
    personality and, 169–171
    in team members, 203

F

Facilitative leadership style, 233
Faulty attributions, 154–155
Feedback
    cultural differences in responses to, 106
    explanation of, 62
    on goal attainment, 104

Focus, ability to, 134
Focus of commitment, 35
Formalism, 132
Formalization, 255–256
Forming, 197
Four Stage Theory of team development, 197
Friendly behavior, 229
Functional structures, 260–261
Fundamental attribution error, 154–155

G

Gainsharing, 109
Gender. *See* Women
General adaptation syndrome (GAS), 83–84
General cognitive ability, 177–178
Geographic structures, 262, 263
g-factor, 177–178
Globalization. *See also* Cultural diversity; Multinational corporations
    expatriate assignments and, 83
    mergers and acquisitions and, 285
    organizational behavior and, 9
Goal commitment, 104, 105
Goal interdependence, 200–201
Goal orientation, 149, 159
Goals
    cultural differences in, 106
    self-set, 103–104
    specific and difficult, 102–103
Goal-setting theory, 102–105
Gossip, 32
Grand Theft Auto: San Andreas, 131
Groupthink, 210
Growth need strength, 62

H

Happiness, money and, 68
Harrah's, 285
Health and wellness programs, 85–86
Heuristics, 154
Hierarchical sensitivity, 208
Hindrance stressors
    explanation of, 79
    on students, 87
    types of, 79–80
History, 10
Hurricane Katrina, 126
Hypotheses, 14–15

I

Idealism, 132
Idealized influence, 239
Identity, 61
Impact, 108–109
Incivility, 32
Independent forms model of withdrawal, 43
Individualism-collectivism, 172–174
Individualistic roles, 202
Individualized consideration, 240
Influence
    conflict resolution and, 230–232
    explanation of, 229
    idealized, 239
    leadership and, 225

job performance and, 86–88
management of, 84–86, 90
neuroticism and, 170, 171
strain resulting from, 83–84
on students, 87
variations in reactions to, 86
Stressors
challenge, 80–81, 87
explanation of, 77
hindrance, 79–80, 87
management of, 82
methods to cope with, 82–83
perception and appraisal of, 77–82
Subcultures, 281
Substance abuse, 32
Substitutability, 227, 228
Substitutes, leader, 241–242
Substitutes for leadership model, 241–242
Supervision satisfaction, 57
Surface-level diversity, 204
Symbols, 276
Synergy, 205

T

Tacit knowledge, 146, 148
Talladega Nights, 103
Tardiness, 40–41
Task complexity, 104
Task conflict, 209
Task interdependence, 198–200
Task performance
adaptive, 26–27
cognitive ability and, 181–182
explanation of, 25–26
identifying behaviors associated with, 27–28
job satisfaction and, 66–67
routine, 26
Taskwork processes
creative behavior and, 206–207
decision making and, 207–208
explanation of, 205
Team-building roles, 202
Team members
abilities of, 203
diversity of, 203–204
mental models and, 211
personality traits of, 203
roles of, 202–203
Team process
explanation of, 204–205
importance of, 211–212
taskwork processes and, 205–208
team states and, 209–211
teamwork processes and, 208–209
Teams
characteristics of, 195, 196
cohesion in, 210, 214
composition of, 201–204
development of, 197–198
explanation of, 195
interdependence in, 198–201
potency in, 210
size of, 204

types of, 195–197
variations within, 197–198
Team states, 209–211
Team task roles, 202
Teamwork processes, 208–209
Technological advances
organizational structure and, 258
training methods and, 149
virtual teams and, 197
Theft, 32
Theory, 14–17
Theory of cognitive moral development, 132, 133
Thirteen, 236
300, 206
Time-driven model of leadership, 234, 235
Time pressure, 80
Training
cross-cultural, 83
explanation of, 148, 149
methods for, 148–149
technological advances in, 149
Traits, 167
Transactional leadership, 237–238
Transformational leadership
dimensions of, 239–240
explanation of, 237–238
job performance and, 240–241
of presidents, 237
Transition processes, 208
Trust
affect-based, 121, 125
cognition-based, 121–123, 125
disposition-based, 121, 122, 125
explanation of, 121
importance of, 7, 134
Trust propensity
assessment of, 136
explanation of, 122, 123
by nation, 124
Trustworthiness, 123
Type A behavior pattern, 86, 89
Typical performance, 183

U

Uncertainty avoidance, 172, 173
Use of emotions, 180
Utilitarianism, 132

V

Valence, 100–102
Value in diversity problem-solving approach, 203–204
Value-percept theory, 55–59
Values
cultural, 167, 172–174
explanation of, 55
job satisfaction and, 55–56
work, 56
Variety, 61
Verbal ability, 175–176
Vicarious experiences, 98
Virtual classrooms, 149

Virtual teams, 197
Visibility, 227, 228
Visualization, 177
Voice, 29

W